A Nation under God

 (Rebuilding America with Biblical Principles)

Learn what the Bible says about God's view of:

Welfare Reform
Health Care Reform
Gun Control
Homosexuals in the Military
Freedom of Speech
Fixing Our Schools
Preventing Broken Homes
Tax Reform
Prison Reform
Fixing the Injustice in America's Courtrooms
and
How adopting God's principles of civil law could make America more healthy, peaceful, and prosperous, and save America hundreds of billions of dollars in taxes each year as well!

by David King, M.D.

Prescott Press, Inc

Copyright © 2000 David King, M.D.
All rights reserved. No part of this book may be reproduced without permission from the publisher, except by a reviewer who may quote brief passages in a review; nor may any part of this book be reproduced, stored in a retrieval system or copied by mechanical photocopying, recording or other means, without permission from the publisher.

Prescott Press, Inc.
P.O. Box 53788
Lafayette, Louisiana 70505

Library of Congress Card Catalog Number 00-100673
ISBN 0-933451-47-4

Dedication

This book is dedicated to Jesus Christ—the Lord of Lawmakers and architect of the biblical blueprint for perfect self-government. I was inspired by God to write this book to exalt our Lord and Savior for revealing to me how God designed His principles of Law and Grace to act in harmony—with Grace providing salvation for individuals and the Law providing God's divine plan for perfect self-government.

I hope this book will reveal to the Church and to the world just how God's principles of civil law were designed to solve all the social and political problems for all generations of all nations, so that the modern Church can also give praise, honor, and glory to Christ for giving the world His divine instructions concerning how to build better government with biblical principles.

Contents

Preface	VII
Acknowledgments	IX
A Message to All Readers	X
Some Mosaic Food for Thought	XI
Introduction	13
1. Jesus Christ—The Lord of Lawmakers	17
2. How the United States Became an Anti-God Nation	21
3. The Natural and Supernatural Blessings of Becoming a "Nation under God's Authority"	38
4. Why God's Promise to Bless Ancient Israel Can Also Apply to Modern America	46
5. God's View of Government Reform and God's Cure for Government Corruption, Scandals, and Gridlock	52
6. God's View of Censorship Versus The First Amendment Freedom of Speech	70
7. God's View of Sexual Immorality versus The Fourth Amendment Right of Privacy	75
8. God's View of Mercy for Crimes "Requiring" Execution	80
9. God's View of Court Reform versus The Fifth Amendment Right Not to Confess Your Sins	92
10. God's View of Prison Reform and How to Stop Crime in America without Prisons	119
11. God's View of Gun Control versus the Second Amendment Right to Bear Arms	132

12. How God's Rules for Execution Maximize the Deterrence of Capital Crime	137
13. God's View of Witchcraft & the Salem Witch Trials	149
14. God's View of Unrestrained Homosexuality and Its Political and Military Consequences	155
15. God's View of Abortion & The Civil War against Our Unborn Citizens	166
16. God's View of the First Commandment (which Outlaws Idolatry) versus The First Amendment (which Legalizes Idolatry)	174
17. God's View of Reintroducing the Blue Laws to Outlaw Work on Sunday	196
18. God's View of Pro-Family Legislation	222
19. How God's View of Welfare Reform Can Save America Hundreds of Billions of Dollars in Taxes	262
20. How God's View of Health Care Reform Can Save America Hundreds of Billions of Dollars in Taxers	306
21. God's View of Economic Reform, Nationwide Prosperity, and the Creation of a Nearly Poverty-Free Society	340
22. God's View of Military Policies which Can Give America A Stronger Defense and Dramatically Reduce America's Military Budget	382
23. God's View of Foreign Policy & Immigration Reform	417
24. God's View of Education Reform	442
25. Conclusion—A Mosaic Picture of a True Nation under God	469
26. Implementation—How to Create a Nation under God by Rebuilding America with Biblical Principles	502
Biography	550

❦ Preface ❦

Why is God refusing to "heal our land," even though multitudes of Christians are praying fervently for God to bless America?

Because God's goal for American government is different from our Christian leaders' goal for American government! God will not "heal our land" unless we aim for His target and play by His rules!

For, according to the biblical principles of government administration, God's goal for America would be to transform our government from an atheistic, secular democracy (where God's principles can be removed from legislation simply by majority vote) back into a Christian republic similar to what the Founders created (where, in theory, God's laws would form the foundation for all our legislation and can never be repealed, even by majority vote)!

Our Christian leaders, however, are content to merely add a few Christian restrictions to our atheistic, secular democracy and generally have no interest in making God's principles of civil law become the foundation for all our legislation once again, as the Founders did and as God commands!

God will not lead us to national victory just to be a silent partner in our government! As long as our Christian leaders are content with "Christian politics as usual" and wish to leave the atheistic philosophy of our secular democracy untouched, then God will never "heal our land" from the sickness of atheistic, secular democracy (where God's influence in government is silenced) to the health of a Christian republic (where God's word can be seen to influence all kinds of legislation)!

So, for God to lead us to victory and heal our land we must be willing to make the principles underlying God's civil laws become the foundation for America's legislation once again! To do this, we must thoroughly understand these principles.

The purpose of this book is to give praise, honor, and glory to Jesus Christ, the Lord of Lawmakers and architect of the biblical blueprint for perfect self-government! For it was Jesus Christ himself (in the form of the pre-incarnate Jehovah) who gave these principles of civil law to Moses in the first place. In this book, God's principles of civil law will come alive with meaning and purpose as you discover the hidden blessings God intended each law to have for the administration of sound and virtuous government. Furthermore, you will see evidence that the principles underlying God's civil laws are not only still valid today, but are superior to our current civil laws.

Also, by adopting God's principles of civil law into our legislation once again, our government can be placed back onto the shoulders of the Prince of Peace. For then, America will finally have a government. . . .
- of the people of God,
- by the principles of God,
- for the glory of God,

which shall not perish from the earth!

This is how to create a true nation under God! If we do our part as God commands, then He will hear our prayers and will heal our land! In this process of healing our land, God will also bring national revival to America once again!

May God bless America, and may God bless you!

Acknowledgments

First of all, I want to thank my parents for loving me, for raising me in a wonderful Christian home, for teaching me about Christ and the Bible, and for helping me find a saving faith in Christ as a spiritual and moral foundation for my life.

I am also most grateful to my wife, Hamiyet King, for her inspiration, her encouragement, her patience, her prayers, and her wise counsel over the last five years during the writing of this book. She is my best friend and I love her dearly. Several ideas in this book came through God's revelation to her dear heart first, before they came to me. I thank God very much for giving her to me as my wife.

Thirdly, I want to thank Sue Denton, the insurance clerk at my office, for her encouragement, her advice, and for the story about her sister and her as children, which she has graciously allowed me to record in chapter six. I also want to thank her for the many hours she spent listening to me as I reviewed with her many of the concepts in the book.

Fourthly, I want to thank Ruth Joyner, Becky Vester, and Diane Buaiz (my nurse, my receptionist, and office manager respectively) for the many hours which they too spent listening to me as I attempted to refine and express these biblical ideas into a simple framework so they could be easily presented in the book.

I want to thank Billie Frady for her library research on government spending.

I am also grateful for Steve Lane, David Childers, Debbie Bell, and Vaughn Benner for their encouragement, their advice, and their many hours of listening to me talk about the book.

I also want to thank Keith Shearon for his extremely valuable service in figuring out how to download the entire manuscript from my Canon StarWriter 70 to a usable format for my publisher, and for his many other ideas.

I want to thank my publisher, for being willing to take a chance on publishing a book as controversial as this one is.

Finally, I want to thank my entire Sunday School class for praying for me while writing this book, and I want to thank all the others who have either listened to me, encouraged me, or prayed for me over the last five years.

A Message to All Readers

Before reading this book, I ask that you please pray the following prayer with all seriousness so that together we may all have the same attitude as David (a "man after God's own heart") and yearn to understand the practical applications of God's civil laws for the administration of sound, virtuous, and Godly government:

O Lord . . .

"Open my eyes that I may see wonderful things in your law." (Ps. 119:18 NIV)

> For it's in Jesus name I pray.
> Amen

❧ Some Mosaic Food for Thought ❧

God did not make any unnecessary laws for nature. So why do we believe that God made some unnecessary laws for people?

For who among us believes that the universe could function properly if we left out some of God's laws of physics? Yet most Christians believe that society can function properly if we leave out some of God's laws for people!

Is not the architect of perfect natural law and perfect moral law also the architect of perfect civil law?

Surely the King of Kings is also the *Lord of Lawmakers;* and so all his civil laws should *still* have practical application today! Therefore, although we need God's *love* in our hearts, we need God's *laws* in our government.

❧ Introduction ❧

True Christians know that our salvation comes only by grace through faith in Christ and not by works of the law. Because of this wonderful truth however, the Church has quite naturally concluded that God's civil laws have no practical value for Christians or for Christian government. In fact, studying God's civil laws in any depth has fallen into such disfavor that anyone who dares to present God's civil laws in a favorable light is frequently called a legalist by his Christian brethren. This disparaging remark is used to declare that their brother may have mistakenly begun to believe in salvation by works of the law instead of by grace through faith.

Unfortunately, as a result of the Church's bias against God's civil laws, these biblical civil principles have never been systematically evaluated simply to see whether they might have any practical application for the administration of sound and virtuous government. Fortunately, the Christian founders of America did not suffer from this modern bias against God's civil laws, for they exalted the practical advantages of some of God's civil laws while still believing in salvation by grace! In fact, our founders not only based America's form of government upon biblical principles, but they also adopted nine of God's wonderful principles of civil law directly into our early legislation. For example:

- only godly Christian elders were eligible to serve in many state governments (to prevent government corruption, scandal, and gridlock)
- work on Sunday was illegal (to encourage everyone to go to church)
- all public schools had to be Christian schools (to train all America's youth in Christian doctrine and morality)
- divorce was illegal (unless your spouse committed a sin which was also a crime, such as adultery)
- drunkenness was illegal (to prevent violence, crime, and liver disease)
- fornication, adultery, and homosexuality were also illegal (to prevent the growth of sexual immorality, venereal disease, and unwed mothers, and to prevent having to raise taxes to pay for the welfare and health care costs of these sins).

These are just some of the wonderful biblical principles of civil law, which our founders adopted into our government. Unfortunately, all these biblical principles have been either ignored or repealed over the last several generations, and with disastrous consequences!

If the adoption of just nine biblical principles of civil law have such a wonderful effect upon our nation, what would happen if America adopted even more of God's civil principles? For instance, what if America adopted God's principles concerning how to have smaller, more decentralized government, with minimal (if any) taxes? Or, what if America adopted the five biblical principles of civil punishment, which were designed by God as a tax-free alternative to an expensive prison system, so we could stop crime in America without prisons, eliminate the problems associated with prisons, have the greatest deterrent to crime which could ever be devised, and save hundreds of billions of dollars in taxes at the same time? Or, what if America adopted God's principles concerning welfare—principles that were designed by God to provide a tax-free system of welfare support for all those who are truly in need, while at the same time discouraging welfare dependency? Or, what if America adopted God's principles concerning national health care, which could eliminate the eleven sins which cause more than half of America's health care costs; and eliminate the three other sources of skyrocketing health care costs in America as well? Or, what if America adopted God's principles of pro-family legislation—principles which could practically guarantee premarital virginity and marital fidelity, and practically ensure that there would no longer be any more drunkenness, wife abuse, child abuse, child molesting, rape, murder, disrespect for parental authority, separation or divorce? Or, what if America adopted God's principles of military policy—principles which could give us a stronger military defense while saving America hundreds of billions of dollars in taxes at the same time? Or, what if America adopted God's principles on foreign policy—principles which could generate an international fearful reverence of Jesus Christ and exalt America's reputation as a true nation under God, which would encourage all other nations to abandon their pagan idolatry and worship Christ—the God of America?

You see, we can be saved by grace and live under America's tens of thousands of federal, state, and local laws, regulations, ordinances, and codes (which not only create a tremendous burden and intrusion into our lives, but also encourage sexual immorality, drunkenness, and crime), or, we can be saved by grace and instead adopt God's principles of civil law into our national legislation—laws which will stop nearly all our crime, violence, immorality, drunkenness, drug abuse, divorce, disease, big government and high taxes! Now which would you prefer?

Well, this book will help you make up your mind. For in this book, you will begin to see all the wonderful practical applications of God's principles of civil law. I guarantee that you will begin to appreciate Jesus Christ in a whole new way, for you will learn to see him not only as Lord of Lords, but also as Lord of Lawmakers, and architect of the biblical blueprint for perfect self-government!

And guess what? After you learn all the wonderful advantages that God's principles of civil law can have for American government, you will find that you are still saved only by grace!

Chapter One

JESUS CHRIST—THE LORD OF LAWMAKERS

The purpose of this book is to give praise, honor, and glory to Jesus Christ—the Lord of Lawmakers!

You see, about thirty-four hundred years ago, Jesus Christ (in the form of the pre-incarnate Jehovah) personally gave to Moses a biblical blueprint for perfect self-government. Furthermore, the Holy Scriptures reveal that Jehovah continued to give the Israelites more and more biblical principles for the administration of sound and virtuous self-government until they finally had a complete set of instructions on how to create a nation under God!

Then, thousands of years later, Jehovah did something even more wonderful. He returned to earth to become our Messiah, Savior, and Lord—Jesus Christ, to die on the cross as an atoning sacrifice for our sins so we could be saved by grace through faith in Him—a faith which inspires obedient surrender to His Will!

This book celebrates Christ's work as Jehovah before He returned to earth and became our Messiah. For when Christ walked the earth as Jehovah, He was Lord of Lawmakers and architect of the biblical blueprint for perfect self-government!

In this book I have arranged most of Christ's principles of civil law into an understandable framework so our leaders can know how to create a nation under God's authority, so we can rebuild America with biblical principles.

You see, most all God's principles of civil law can be grouped into categories about justice, punishment, economics, government, healthcare, welfare, etc. Additionally, such grouping highlights the hidden wisdom of God's viewpoint concerning every major political issue which America faces today. So, in this book I have classified nearly all of God's principles into various groups, which I have entitled:

God's View of. . . .
- Government Reform,
- Court Reform,

- Justice Reform,
- Prison Reform,
- Pro-Family Legislation,
- Health Care Reform,
- Welfare Reform,
- Economic Reform,
- Education Reform,
- Military Policy, and
- Foreign Policy!

In other words, the Mosaic principles of civil law are like "Mosaic tiles," which, when assembled together, create a "Mosaic picture" of God's view of government reform, or, a "Mosaic picture" of God's view of court reform! And, if you stand back far enough and view all these "Mosaic pictures" together as a group, they will form a Mosaic mural of what a true nation under God's authority should look like!

Unfortunately, one of the greatest tragedies in the history of the world is that the Israelites themselves never fully adopted all these wonderful principles of civil government into their legislation as they were commanded. As a result, the world has never seen just how well the "fully assembled package" of God's civil laws was designed to function!

Well, I believe that God's principles of civil government are clearly superior to the principles of civil government which our nation is using today! I further believe that nearly every major problem of our modern government and society can be traced to our government leaders' ignorance of the advantages which can be obtained by adopting God's principles into our national legislation (so America can have the type of sound and virtuous government which God intended for Israel as well as for all nations which trust in God's authority)! As a result, our nation is "destroyed from lack of this knowledge" (Hos. 4:6 NIV).

This "lack of knowledge" can be directly traced to our Christian leaders' inability to understand and correctly teach the superiority of these principles because of their unfamiliarity with the advantages underlying God's civil laws. Because of this, we have inadvertently raised generations of government leaders who are uninformed about the advantages of these principles. Therefore, we Christians have unknowingly allowed our former nation under God to slip away, never realizing that the answers to our nation's problems could always be found precisely in those scriptures about which we are least familiar (the biblical principles of civil law), while mistakenly thinking that the only cure for our nation's ills lies in more and more evangelism!

In the last half of this century, our nation has experienced a media explosion of evangelistic effort which has reached an all time high. We have more Christian radio, Christian TV, Christian videos, Christian magazines, Christian newspapers, and Christian books than we have ever had before. There are more Christian ministry organizations throughout the U.S. and more local and national Bible study groups than ever before, as well as more literature and groups focusing on discipleship training such as "Experiencing God," and "Promise-keepers."

Yet simultaneous to this great movement of God is an opposing, countermovement of both man and Satan that has had a hundredfold worse effect on this nation than all our "record-setting" evangelistic attempts could ever neutralize. While we Christians "slept," the biblical principles of having godly leadership and godly laws which foster godly peer pressure have been replaced by ungodly leadership, ungodly laws, and ungodly peer pressure throughout our land! At the same time, America's government and courts have either repealed or ignored nine of the biblical principles of civil law which were originally adopted by our Christian founders in the first place. So despite our evangelistic efforts being at an all time high, our unawareness of the simultaneous biblical mandate for godly leadership and godly laws has caused a hundredfold more destruction to our society than all our record-setting evangelistic efforts could ever oppose and neutralize with any degree of success!

Therefore, it is clear that we cannot correct the situation in America by evangelism alone. Evidently, the major reason for America's decline was never the lack of evangelism nor the lack of God's authority over the individual, but the lack of God's authority over the government. Unfortunately, the modern Church mistakenly teaches that only God's moral laws are valid today, and that God's civil laws have absolutely no value for the administration of sound and virtuous government! God's civil laws do indeed have value today. Although God's rules for *governing yourself* are his moral laws, God's rules for *self-government* are his civil laws!

You see, our society is now suffering the tragic consequences of believing that the principles underlying God's civil laws are no longer of any value for the administration of modern government. Indeed, America's fear of living in a theocracy (a society which adopts all the principles of God's civil law into government) has indirectly sponsored a "lawless society," where unrighteous men can now fully embrace the sins of the flesh, free from the restraining influences of God's principles of civil law.

As a result, "theocra-phobia" (fear of living in a theocracy) has indirectly sponsored America's rising rate of immorality, violence, crime, divorce, drunkenness, drug abuse, disease, and poverty! In fact, Americans are paying billions of dollars in extra taxes for big government to control America's problems using MAN'S civil laws, because of the mistaken belief that the principles underlying GOD'S civil laws are no longer useful for administering good government (as though these principles suddenly became invalid the moment Christ rose from the dead).

Unfortunately, the Church is oblivious to the huge tax burden resulting from our ignorance of the practical benefits that God's principles of civil law have for government. For without realizing it, evangelical Christianity has closed its eyes to the part of God's Word which concerns building better government with biblical principles, and now we find ourselves in the dark and unenlightened as to how to restore our country to a "nation under God." We have ignored the ways of the founders and have become lost without the guiding light of God's principles of civil law. So, while the focus of our churches must remain on evangelism, discipleship training, and service to our Lord Jesus Christ, our churches need to also begin teaching the *entire* Bible, which includes teaching that the principles underlying God's civil laws are still useful and practical for America's government to adopt and are superior to man's civil laws.

Some future day, when Christ returns to rule on earth for one thousand years, he will re-establish the preeminence of God's principles of civil law for the administration of sound and virtuous government for all the nations of the earth. Then we will finally understand the reality of how and why Christ's principles of civil law are superior to any of man's civil laws!

But let's not wait until Christ returns to learn this lesson! Let's borrow these principles from the Bible now and rebuild America today! Let's give Christ the same authority in our government which he already holds in the universe! For as King of Kings, he is also Lord of Lawmakers, and architect of the biblical blueprint for perfect government! Therefore, let America's leaders make a covenant with God, and once again pledge our loyalty to Jesus Christ—the Almighty Jehovah God—so that God's laws will once again and forever more be America's laws. Only then, when God reigns supreme in our government, can we truly obtain all of God's wonderful blessings upon our nation!

So let us exalt Christ as Savior of our citizens, Lord of our Lawmakers, and King of our Kings, so America's government can be lifted upon the shoulders of the "Prince of Peace!"

Chapter Two

HOW THE UNITED STATES BECAME AN ANTI-GOD NATION

Many people mistakenly blame our nation's ills on the Supreme Court decisions of 1962 and 1963 when prayer and Bible teaching were removed from our classrooms and our courtrooms. They cite evidence that many of the signs of our nation's wickedness, such as the rate of crime, divorce, violence, adultery, homosexuality, rape, murder, illegitimate births, and sexually transmitted diseases all started rising dramatically immediately after 1963. Certainly there is much evidence to show that our nation did begin an even more rapid decline into wickedness immediately after these abominable Supreme Court decisions.

The underlying problem did not start in 1962, for what happened at that time was only the inevitable consequence of a long series of previous legislative errors and ambiguities beginning nearly two centuries earlier, with Article VI in the Constitution and with the First Amendment. To understand the beginning of our nation's descent into wickedness we must go back centuries in time to the origins of our nation.

You see, more than two centuries ago, the vast majority of the founding fathers of our nation were dedicated Christians who wanted to create a Christian nation under God (this is well documented by Frank Marshall in his book, *The Light and the Glory*, and by Beliles and McDowell, in their book, *America's Providential History*, and by historian David Barton, in his videotapes entitled *America's Godly Heritage*, and *Keys to Good Government*). At that time, the Pilgrims and Puritans, as well as many other Christian groups, founded our nation upon the teachings of the Bible. As a result, our early statutes were based upon biblical principles of civil law. For instance, certain sins against God—such as fornication, adultery, homosexuality, and drunkenness—were also punishable crimes against the state. Because of this, the prevalence of these sins was very low when compared to the wickedness in our society today. Secondly, since the Fourth Commandment teaches us not to work on the Sabbath, many states passed various types of "Blue Laws" which prohibited citizens from doing certain types of labor or other activities on Sunday. As a result, we evolved a culture where there was a nationwide expectation that everyone should go to church, which produced very high rates of church attendance. Additionally, in 1776, the wording of the final sentence of the Declaration of Independence also revealed our growing allegiance to God.

> For support of this Declaration, with a firm reliance on the protection of Divine Providence, we mutually pledge to each other our Lives, our Fortunes, and our sacred Honor.

Also, years after the Revolutionary War, many of our first state constitutions required that only Christians be allowed to serve in our state governments. All these things were signs that our founders intended to create and maintain a "nation under God's authority"! In the decades which followed the Revolutionary War, we had an opportunity to turn the first thirteen colonies into a united "nation under God" by adopting all the rest of the biblical principles of civil law into our legislation and thus guarantee our nation's faithfulness to God forever.

But something went wrong! Despite such a noble beginning, our country has not been faithful to God, and we have removed nearly all God's principles of civil law which had been put into place by the founders of our nation. As a result, we have become a nation of wickedness! How could this have happened?

Well, as wonderful as the founders were, they were not perfect. For the precise wording chosen by the founders to be used in some of their most important legislation (such as Article VI of the Constitution and the First Amendment) has unfortunately turned out to be too ambiguous and misleading for us to easily understand their original intent two hundred years ago. Furthermore, the vagueness in the wording of the Fifth and Eighth Amendments has also allowed significant modern day misinterpretations. The Sixth Amendment actually violates biblical principles of civil law altogether. However, books such as *The Myth of Separation*, by David Barton, make the founder's intent abundantly clear concerning Article VI of the Constitution and the First Amendment. But, it is the exact wording of the Constitution and the amendments themselves (and not the founder's intent) upon which modern legal misinterpretations rest. The "poor choice of words" used by the founders in these areas has resulted in initiating the transformation of our country into an evil, anti-God nation with all our national sins.

The first major legislative problem was actually incorporated into the Constitution itself, in the last sentence of Article VI, which reads as follows:

... but NO RELIGIOUS TEST shall EVER be required as a qualification to any Office or public Trust under the United States. (emphasis added)

The intent of the founding fathers was that "you could test (and reject) a candidate for public office based upon whether he was indeed a Christian, but you could not test (or reject) him based upon which Christian denomination he was affiliated with! For they wanted to allow any Christian from any denomination to serve in the government whether Baptist, Methodist, Presbyterian, Lutheran, Episcopalian, etc. The lack of a "religious test" was not intended to allow atheists, agnostics, pagans, or those who were "anti-Christians" to serve in the government. How do we know this? Because many of the state constitutions, written about the same time, specified that only Christians could serve in government; yet simultaneously also specified that "no religious test" or "no other religious test" could be used to exclude participation in the government!

For instance, the 1796 Tennessee Constitution reads:

> Article VIII, Section 2. No person who denies the being of God, or a future state of rewards and punishments, shall hold any office in the civil department of this State.
>
> Article XI, Section 4. That no religious test shall ever be required as a qualification to any office or public trust under this State.

Historian David Barton says, "A fixed set of religious beliefs for an office holder is prescribed in Article VIII, and then a religious test is prohibited in Article XI. Obviously, in their view, requiring a belief in God and in future rewards and punishments to hold office was not a religious test" (David Barton, *The Myth of Separation*. Aledo, Texas: Wallbuilder Press, 1989). Barton goes on to quote from two other state constitutions to prove this point. Note that both constitutions require that only Christians serve in government, yet specify no religious test beyond this:

> Maryland, 1776, Article XXXV. That no other test or qualification ought to be required ... than such oath of a support and fidelity to this State ... and a declaration of a belief in the Christian religion.
>
> Vermont, 1786, Frame of Government, Section 9. ... And each member (of the legislature), before he takes his seat, shall make and subscribe the following declaration, viz: "I do believe in one God, the Creator and Governor of the universe, the rewarder of the good and punisher of the wicked.

And I do acknowledge the scriptures of the old and new testament to be given by divine inspiration, and own and profess the (Christian) religion."

And no further or other religious test shall ever, hereafter, be required of any civil officer or magistrate in this State.

Obviously, the founders wanted only Christians to serve in government but wanted to require no DENOMINATIONAL test, so that any Baptist, Methodist, Lutheran, Presbyterian, etc. could serve in government. They certainly would not have allowed atheists or idolators to run the federal government while simultaneously insisting that only Christians run the state governments!

Now if you ask someone today, "what religion are you?" many people will say, "I'm Baptist" or "I'm Lutheran" and tell you their denomination. Our society still retains traces of the historical definition of the word "religion" to mean "denomination." However, many people today also use the word "religion" to mean either "Christianity," "Buddhism," "Hinduism," "Islam," or "Judaism," etc. This is probably because modern Americans are more aware of the other major "world religions" than were our founders and so have a "broader world-view." Unfortunately, since our broader world view has given us a different definition of the word religion, we now misinterpret the founder's expression, "no religious test," to mean that we can no longer even specify that only Christians may serve in government. Yet the founders insisted that only Christians could serve in government but without specifying that you had to be from a specific denomination. For instance, John Jay, our first Supreme Court chief justice, is quoted as recommending that everyone should vote only for Christians:

> Providence has given to our people the choice of their rulers, and it is the duty as well as the privilege and interest, of a Christian nation to select and prefer Christians to be their rulers. (*Myth*, 118)

So it was clear two hundred years ago that we should vote for only Godly Christian elders to serve in our government. But generations later when we began to develop a broader world view and lose the meaning of the word "religion" to mean "denomination," we began to misunderstand the intent of the founders, and now we mistakenly interpret Article VI to mean that we can no longer require that only godly Christian elders serve in our government. Because the language chosen by the founders in Article VI was not specific enough to stand the test of time, we have now misinterpreted Article VI to mean that any atheist, agnostic, or pagan who wants to purge all Christian influence from our government can now become a senator, a supreme court judge, or even president of the United States. And, as the door began to open to allow evil men to enter our government, this set the stage for all future government scandals, corruption, and gridlock. Furthermore, modern politicians who have no fear of accounting to God for sins committed in office can even pass anti-biblical legislation to destroy the original Christian foundations of our government!

We must make an amendment to the Constitution specifying that only mature godly Christian elders (from any denomination) can hold political office or be judges anywhere in the U.S. at the federal, state and local levels. This is what the founders wanted, and more importantly, this is what the Bible teaches, so this is what we must do. This will end all our political scandals and all the government corruption, and re-establish the Bible as the foundational source of our principles of civil law.

The second major problem which caused our nation's demise occurred with the passage of the First Amendment, which reads:

> Congress shall make no law respecting an establishment of religion, or prohibiting the free exercise thereof; or abridging the freedom of speech, or of the press . . .

Now remember, to the founders, the word "religion" meant "Christian denomination." So, the First Amendment was originally designed only to keep the government from exalting one denomination of Christianity over another denomination of Christianity, so religious persecution against any denomination of Christians would never evolve in this country.

This is a laudable goal, and it is unfortunate again that we have become blinded to this original intention of the founders. In the mid-1900s, this Amendment began to be subverted to justify three abominable philosophies:

1. Completely Unrestrained Freedom of Speech and Press

According to this philosophy, there should be absolutely no censorship of any wicked and sinful ideas, regardless of the magnitude of their corrupting influence on society. Speeches and writings to promote anti-biblical ideas such as abortion, sexual promiscuity, gay lifestyles, feminism, drunkenness, drug abuse, prejudice, evolution, violence, revenge, anarchy, terrorism, and bomb-making can all be expressed without fear of prosecution because they are all "protected rights" because of "Freedom of Speech!" Also, artistic "Freedom of Speech" has caused so much pornography in movies, TV, magazines, as well as on stage with topless dancing and live sex acts, that it is very understandable why God's hand of judgement is heavy upon this country.

None of these wicked things can ever be stopped in this country as long as America fears censorship more than America fears God! Our motto should be: "FEAR GOD, NOT CENSORSHIP"—or our nation will suffer even more of God's potential wrath.

Our government's early legislation exalted obedience to God. However, because of our subsequent record of ungodly legislation, our nation today exalts every form of sin, blasphemy, and disobedience to God out of "fear of censorship"!

Surely you don't believe that our Christian founders felt that God wanted all the wicked, anti-biblical ideas to be presented openly and listened to eagerly! Nothing could be further from the truth. You see, the founders trusted in the teachings of the Bible, and the Bible is filled with references against completely unrestrained freedom of speech. In fact, the founders even outlawed blasphemous speech (*Myth,* 51-61). The loving God of the Bible does want certain ideas censored because of their corrupting influence on society (see chapter six). Unfortunately, many Christians today have adopted this anti-biblical doctrine against any form of censorship, as though God is pleased to hear blasphemy, gossip, foul language, and corrupt speech which encourages people to sin. Even famous Christian TV personalities have been heard to say that they don't want censorship either!

We will never be able stop pornography or all the other antibiblical influences in this country without first changing the First Amendment to be in accord with biblical guidelines and with the original intentions of America's founders! With this in mind, the First Amendment must be repealed and replaced with an amendment which prohibits blasphemy, foul language, or any language which exalts the sinful lifestyles of homosexuality, adultery, fornication, witchcraft, idol worship, drunkenness, terrorism, prejudice, etc. All entertainment which exalts sinfulness must be prohibited. Only these changes in the First Amendment will reflect the original intentions of the founders as well as encourage legislation which exalts obedience to God.

2. Freedom to Worship Idols and False Gods

Congress "shall make no law ... prohibiting the free exercise" of any "religion"! Remember, to the founders, the word "religion" originally just meant the "Christian religion" or "Christian denominations"! So, the founders meant to say that "Congress shall make no law restricting the Christian religion or any Christian denominations," implying that Congress could still make laws restricting the growth of non-Christian religions, such as idolatry. After all, the founders were already legally restricting the occupations which non-Christians could enter by prohibiting non-Christians from being elected as governors, etc. (according to the wording of many of the original state constitutions). This poor choice of wording for the First Amendment, which no longer reflects what the founders meant it to say, now has opened the door for the totally unrestrained worship of idols in America, something that neither the founders nor God would have wanted. Think of the many times God was infuriated at the Israelite governmental leaders for refusing to make any law "prohibiting the free exercise of" the worship of the idols of Baal, Molech, Chemosh, and Astoreth. It was an abominable mistake on the part of the Israelite leaders, and a very "poor choice of wording" on the part of our founders!

3. Separation of Church and State

This last problem resulting from the First Amendment has caused the greatest crisis of all. This "Myth of Separation" (also the title of David Barton's book) has slowly removed God and the Bible from influencing any future national legislation. It has also prompted the elimination of all God's biblical principles of civil law from our government, which has resulted in America suffering tragic national consequences for our national sins.

The above mentioned three categories of problems have all stemmed from the poor wording of the First Amendment, which has allowed for such modern misinterpretations of the founder's original intentions.

The next problem comes from the Fifth Amendment. The Fifth Amendment says that a person accused of a crime cannot "be *compelled* to be a witness against himself." The founders meant that a suspect could not be "physically compelled" (meaning by physical violence or by torture) to testify against himself. However, the Bible teaches that a man can be "verbally compelled" to "confess his sins" and testify against himself. Because the founders left out the word "physically" and just wrote the word "compelled," hundreds of years later the Miranda Act used this to interpret that a person could not be "*verbally* compelled to testify against himself" or confess his sins. In other words, the Miranda Act gives the accused the right to say in court, "I reserve the right not to confess my sins" (so to speak). This wording of the Fifth Amendment (together with the Miranda Act) has caused untold miscarriages of justice, has increased America's court costs, and has set the guilty free!

The Sixth Amendment grants us a trial by jury of twelve citizens who don't know God's laws, have no sense of God's mercy and justice, and who are biased by the procedures of jury selection which is performed by lawyers who are not seeking God's truth but are each seeking to advance their client's point of view at the expense of truth and justice! Thus, the trial becomes merely a sporting event for lawyers, and the jury is responsible to issue their appraisal of which lawyer won. This corrupt system was probably approved because we refused to insist on having only Godly Christian elders (who had a mature working knowledge of God's principles of civil law) to judge our cases! This is totally contrary to the Bible!

The Eighth Amendment says that "no cruel and unusual punishments" can be inflicted on a convicted criminal. As far as I know, the founders intended to forbid ungodly torture but not forbid godly justice and punishment as recorded in the Bible, such as whipping (Deut. 25:1-3 NIV). Once again, because the founders failed to specify that whipping (as explained in the Bible) can be allowed, this ruled out the simplest, quickest, most efficient, and most inexpensive method of punishment as a biblical alternative to an expensive, tax-sponsored prison system. By inadvertently ruling out whipping, this unfortunate lack of specificity in the Eighth Amendment created a need for an alternative "non-biblical" form of punishment. So, now our nation spends up to half-a-million dollars in taxes just to send one man to prison for ten years, all for the lack of a five dollar whip! This totals billions of dollars in taxes annually to pay for overcrowded, revolving door prisons where the inmates practice lifting weights and further corrupt themselves by educating each other on the finer points of crime so that when they are released, they are bigger, meaner, and more menacing than ever.

The Thirteenth Amendment says that "Neither slavery nor involuntary servitude, except as punishment for a crime whereof the party shall have been duly convicted, shall exist within the United States, or any place subject to their jurisdiction." This was ratified on 6 December 1865. The Bible also says that we can use slavery as a punishment for thieves who can not pay back a multiple of their debts. However, the slave owner was responsible to provide all the food, clothing, housing, and medical care for the slave-criminals (without the assistance of any tax money); also, he was required to set them free after six years, as well as provide them with a small subsidy (out of the slave owner's profits) to temporarily assist the criminal-slave to start life over again (see chapter ten). This tax-free biblical alternative to overcrowded prisons is technically still allowed by the Constitution but as far as I know has never been used in the U.S.

The next problem was that our *state* constitutions were changed to allow any non-Christians to serve in the government, presumably because of the last sentence of Article VI in the Federal Constitution which forbids a "religious test" of anyone who seeks public office. Formerly, many of our original state constitutions required that anyone who was seeking public office had to be a godly Christian elder (see Barton, *The Myth of Separation*). I have been told that these changes in our state constitutions began to occur sometime before the Civil War.

In 1947 the Supreme Court officially misinterpreted the First Amendment to mean "separation of Church and State" in the case of *Everson v. Board of Education*. Since that time many other court decisions have followed this mistaken path. But, this would never have happened if we had insisted that only godly Christian elders be allowed to serve as judges in the Supreme Court, which is what the founders wanted and the Bible commands. Also shortly after WW II, most states began to ignore and ultimately repeal their Blue Laws. This allowed all kinds of new money-making activities to spring up on Sunday, which gave people a greater incentive to stay away from church. Prior to this, our nation had a cultural expectation that everyone should be in church on Sunday. But, at this point, our governments were officially repealing this cultural expectation of church attendance.

Unfortunately, repealing the Blue Laws set into motion an inevitable series of catastrophic consequences for America. For instance, church attendance dropped dramatically in response to repealing the Blue Laws, because now there was a chance to make money on Sunday. Furthermore, as more entertainment businesses opened on Sunday, it became more "entertaining" just to stay away from church on Sunday and have fun! These cultural changes slowly began to occur during the 1950s. In response to declining attendance, churches had to make a greater effort to attract new members. Unfortunately, to accomplish this purpose, "church discipline" (as practiced according to Christ's instructions in Matt. 18:15-17) began to be "discarded" because it tended to inhibit church growth. You see, it is hard to "expel the wicked man from among you" (1 Cor. 5:13b NIV) while you are simultaneously trying to invite him into the church to hear the Gospel in the first place! Eventually, it was believed that "church discipline" was no longer an "essential" doctrine. As a result, some churchgoers began to realize that they could continue committing adultery or homosexuality, etc., and never be cast out of the Church, for church membership could no longer be "purified" as Christ intended now that the doctrine of "church discipline" had been abandoned. Furthermore, the Church had to tolerate behavior from its regular members which was formerly considered to be against God's Will, such as men with long hair and women with short hair who wore pants and who did not wear head coverings. To rationalize this pastors all over America began to de-emphasize God's "condemnation of sin" and "eternal damnation in hell" and began to preach that God's love and acceptance was "unconditional," and that many of these biblical regulations were meant only for Israel or for the "early Gentile Church." Verses such as:

> Do not judge, or you too will be judged. (Matt. 7:1 NIV)

began to be emphasized instead of verses such as:

> Are you not to judge those inside [the church]? . . . Expel the wicked man from among you. (1 Cor. 5: 12b, 13b NIV)

Eventually, Christian elders would forget how to go about "loving your neighbor as yourself" while simultaneously "rebuking them for their sins," and (if necessary) "casting them out of the church." Christians also began to believe that if we shouldn't "judge one another's sins" then maybe we should not "publicly rebuke one another for sins" either. As a result, the Christian church would eventually lose its desire to perpetually purify itself through church discipline as the Bible commands. I'm sure that the Apostle Paul would be infuriated at the "lack of church discipline" which exists in the modern church today. The expression, "Love the sinner, hate the sin, but don't judge him for his sins" seems to express this thought the best and is a sentiment which continues among Christians today. These changes started in the 1950s and still persist in modern churches everywhere. Shortly after American churches began to discard the doctrine of "church discipline" as a form of "legislating morality" within the church, American courts also began to discard the notion of "civil discipline" as a way to "legislate morality" within the community. After all, the church was now teaching "unconditional love," "unconditional acceptance," and "judge not"! While church congregations were taught to "stop judging our neighbor's immorality" inside the church, our REAL judges began to "stop judging our neighbor's immorality" inside the courtroom. Yet the laws against sexual immorality still remained "on the books." As a result, even though American citizens still thought immorality was wrong, it was no longer being "judged" in American churches or in American courtrooms!

Within a few years, the states began to slowly discard God's philosophy: that certain sins against God should also be considered crimes against the state. As a result, laws against adultery, drunkenness, and homosexuality began to be partially ignored, resulting in America moving one step closer to becoming a nation which embraces unrestrained immorality! All these problems were the inevitable result of repealing the Blue Laws and served to only exacerbate another disaster: that for the last three generations, Americans thought it no longer necessary to select only godly Christian elders to serve as their government leaders! As bad as things were up to this point, they were about to get much worse. The evil so far represented only Satan's preparation for the real battle, which would involve making sexual immorality, abortion, drunkenness, and divorce completely LEGAL throughout the entire United States! You see, even though the laws against such sins were being partially ignored by the courts, just having these laws "on the books" was enough to deter a tremendous amount of sin in this nation during the 1950s! So the "wheels of wickedness" were already in place but lacked the grease to do any significant damage. The grease Satan was about to add would change all that, for Satan was about to reveal his master plan: to repudiate the Bible as the foundation of all our legislation. This would force all the courts to totally disregard all God's laws against sin which were currently on America's law books, so sexual immorality, abortion, drunkenness, and divorce would suddenly become completely legal everywhere in the United States.

What is all the more remarkable is that Satan would accomplish this goal merely by striking down school prayer (in 1962) and school Bible teaching (in 1963), issues which were extremely symbolic of whether or not America thought it valuable to train future generations of citizens to worship God and to obey God's principles of moral and civil law. In other words, by the end of 1963 it would be "official"—that *God's Laws would no longer be America's laws.* This would set the legal precedent to symbolically "erase" all God's principles of moral and civil law from American law books and "force" the complete legalization of sexual immorality, drunkenness, and divorce to be accomplished practically overnight! As a result, what was considered completely illegal and immoral in the 1950s, would be completely legal and "acceptable" in the 1960s! What made his strategy even more amazing was that Satan's enemies (we God-fearing Christians) would not realize the impact of what had happened until twenty-five years later (while sexual immorality, drunkenness, and divorce rates were skyrocketing). Even then, those few Christians who would line up for battle would face the *wrong direction,* and attack the symbolic issue of school prayer, rather than the real issue that the sins of sexual immorality, drunkenness, and divorce had now become completely legal, and were no longer considered punishable crimes against the state, because God's laws were no longer to be considered America's laws. Even when we battle over school prayer, we only battle over getting the students to pray, rather than to get the teachers to be able to teach the Bible to all the students as the Word of God, whom all Americans must worship and obey. Furthermore, legal weapons used by the American Center For Law and Justice in our recent Supreme Court victory (and all our other lower courtroom victories), which have now guaranteed allowing "student initiated and student led prayers" to begin (again), have been won, not by persuading the High Court that "the God of the Bible wants the students to be able to pray and that we must obey all His commands," but because of the "freedom of speech" issue. But this strategy will ultimately backfire on Christianity for two reasons: First of all, any student who now wants to have a "student initiated and student led" prayer meeting to Satan or to "Mother Earth," or pray to pagan idols, either during lunchtime or after school, can now do so with the full approval of America's entire legal system, starting with the Supreme Court! As a result, the future corruption of America's children to an even greater degree has been virtually assured. Secondly, by setting the precedent of using the First Amendment ("Freedom of Speech and Religion") to achieve our courtroom victories, we have mistakenly endorsed the importance of *pluralism*— that America is now and should remain a nation where we can all think and speak as we please, and where we can worship and obey any false god we choose, and that the government should not force American children to pray to the God of the Bible or to obey God's moral and civil laws either. Therefore, we have now made it impossible to achieve the more important goal of getting America's teachers to be able to teach the Bible to all the students as the Word of God, whom all Americans must worship and obey, and that the Bible was and should always remain as the foundation for America's moral and civil laws!

America is now facing its darkest hour. For in addition to these problems, those Christians fighting against the anti-Christian forces are spread too thinly and are attacking the wrong areas and using the wrong weapons. For instance, Christians unite to get "student-initiated and student-led" prayer back into schools, but not to get an amendment passed to require the teachers to teach the students to worship and obey the God of the Bible. THIS is what America really lost in 1962 and in 1963, but this is not what we are fighting to regain. Secondly, Christians boycott sponsors of TV programs which feature sexual immorality, etc. But we never fight for an amendment to make sexual immorality and drunkenness punishable crimes against the state once again. THIS is what America really lost in 1962 and in 1963, but this is not what we are fighting to regain. Thirdly, Christians yearn to have church attendance increase all across America, and give large amounts of money to sponsor TV and radio evangelism as well as to home missions organizations. But, we never fight for an amendment to create a "National Blue Law" requiring businesses to be closed on Sunday, which would make Sunday "boring" and therefore dramatically increase church attendance again, hopefully to the same high levels of attendance achieved back before the Blue Laws were repealed. THIS is what we lost when the Blue Laws were repealed, but this is not what we are fighting to regain! Fourthly, Christians fight to get more Christians elected into government. But we never fight for an amendment to require that only godly Christian elders be allowed to serve in government. THIS is what we have lost over the last two hundred years, but again this is not what we are fighting to regain!

If we would only repeal and rewrite the First, Sixth, and Eighth Amendments, and clarify Article VI in the Constitution with another amendment, then all the national problems of sexual immorality, drunkenness, divorce, government scandals, and government corruption would begin to slowly disappear from our nation.

In conclusion, the American government has ultimately revoked and is now regularly breaking at least *nine* of God's principles of civil law which our founders had adopted during the birth of our nation, exactly as God commands in the Bible. These biblical principles of civil law are as follows:

1. Only godly Christian elders should ever be allowed to serve in government. This was the "command" that Jethro, the priest of

Midian, gave to Moses (Exod. 18:21-22). This same idea is mentioned a total of fifty times in the Bible in various ways. Our founders adopted this idea, but it was eventually ignored and ultimately "revoked" in the mid-1800s.

2. Work on Sunday should be outlawed and punished in order to get the voting majority of citizens back into church. This idea comes from God's civil laws as well as from God's Fourth Commandment. Our founders also adopted this idea but it was eventually ignored and ultimately revoked in different states at different times in the 1940s and 1950s.

3. All public schools should be Christian schools in order to discourage non-Christian religions and specifically to discourage the worship of idols. This idea came from God's civil laws as well as from God's First Commandment. To implement this idea, the founders decided to legally discourage non-Christian religions through public school education. Unfortunately, this idea was also "repealed" during 1962 and 1963, when school prayer, etc., was removed from our schools.

4-6. Fornication, adultery, and homosexuality should be illegal and punishable. This is based upon many biblical principles of civil law as well as upon God's Seventh Commandment. These ideas were also adopted by our founders, but eventually they were ignored and symbolically "repealed" in 1962 when the removal of school prayer indicated that God's laws would no longer be America's laws.

7. Non-biblical divorce should be illegal. This is based upon the biblical civil law which teaches that divorce is to be illegal unless one spouse has committed some serious sin (like adultery) for which he or she can be prosecuted. This biblical civil law was adopted by our founders, but was also symbolically "repealed" in 1962 as well.

8. Taking God's name in vain, blasphemy, sinful speech, and pornography were all against the philosophy of America's early laws, if not specifically illegal as well. These ideas also came from the biblical civil laws as well as from God's Third Commandment and were adopted by our founders, but eventually were ignored and ultimately "repealed" step by step throughout our nation during the 1960s and 1970s. This also resulted from the 1962 decision which made school prayer illegal because this meant that God's laws would no longer be America's laws.

9. Drunkenness should be illegal. The crime of being "drunk and disorderly" was evidently also adopted by our founders but was eventually ignored or "repealed" as well.

So, American legislators have repealed at least nine biblical principles of civil law which were adopted by our founders, and the devastating consequences of these abominable decisions have slowly transformed our nation from a Christian Republic into an atheistic, secular democracy which is hostile to Christian principles! Therefore, America can only be restored to her former "greatness" by adopting these *nine* biblical principles of God's civil law back into our nation's legislation once again. Anyone who says we can restore our nation to where we once were without adopting God's principles of civil law back into our government is not only ignoring God's commands, but ignoring the lesson of history, and ignoring the desires and objectives of America's original founders.

Unfortunately, there is one more problem facing America, which paradoxically, comes from the ranks of our Christian leaders themselves—the problem of "theocra-phobia." I have coined this term which is an "unrealistic fear of living in a theocracy." You see, many Christians are afraid to adopt any of God's principles of civil law back into our government, despite the fact that the founders had no trouble adopting these principles, and despite the overwhelming evidence that many of the major problems in our culture have been directly caused by the removal of these same nine biblical principles of civil law from our national legislation. What is even more startling is that the Christians who are most vigorously against the adoption of God's principles of civil law are frequently our Christian spiritual and political leaders—the very ones who are supposed to be teaching us the advantages of these laws, and encouraging our government leaders to readopt these same biblical principles of civil law back into our government. Because they are so reluctant to have God's principles of civil law in our government, God has also become reluctant to heal our land from the sickness of atheistic democracy to the health of a Christian Republic. Remember, in an atheistic democracy, God's laws can be removed from government simply by majority vote, whereas in a "Christian Republic," the Bible is the foundation of all civil laws and therefore God's laws can never be removed from government even by majority vote. This is what God wants for America—a Christian Republic, and he will not lead us to national victory just to be a silent partner in our government. In other words, for God to "heal our land," we must aim for God's target and play by God's rules.

A "theocracy" is a nation which adopts all God's principles of civil law into its legislation. But a "newborn " Christian Republic may have adopted just a few biblical principles of civil law into its legislation, and it could take generations of faithful obedience by Christian statesmen before it could adopt enough biblical principles of civil law into its legislation to finally call itself a "theocracy." America became a "newborn" Christian Republic under the leadership of our founders.

Why would our Christian spiritual and political leaders today not want America to adopt God's civil laws, when our Christian founders had the opposite attitude?

Well, our Christian leaders "claim" that God's civil laws were reserved by God for Israel alone, and that only God's moral laws are still valid and applicable for modern America (this is their "theological" argument). However, if you ask them to make a list of exactly which biblical civil laws God wanted to be reserved for Israel, and make another list of all the biblical civil laws which seem "unfair," or "don't make too much sense," or where "the potential benefits of a specific law do not clearly outweigh the drawbacks," it is likely that the two lists will be almost identical. You see, the real reason for their mistaken opinion is not theological at all, but practical. In other words, they conclude that "any law which has no obvious practical advantages must have been one of those laws which God wanted to be reserved for Israel alone," because, they further reason, "God surely wouldn't want America to adopt *that* particular law!" Their theological argument is chosen only to "pacify themselves" for not wanting to honor the biblical civil laws which seem so "disadvantageous" for America.

Likewise, practical arguments which demonstrate the superiority of God's principles of civil law can easily be very persuasive over theological arguments which claim that God wanted to exclusively reserve all His civil laws just for Israel. After all, once you learn the advantages God's civil laws have over man's civil laws, it's hard to imagine why God would deprive Christian nations of His wonderful principles of civil law, and save them just for Israel instead. Therefore, I believe our founders understood the advantages of biblical civil law better than our modern Christian leaders do today. Since Christian leaders today are unaware of the wonderful advantages God's principles of civil law have over man's principles for the administration of sound and virtuous government, it is natural that they would also be somewhat reluctant to encourage government leaders to adopt God's principles of civil law into our legislation. You see, since God's ways are higher and wiser than our ways, we often don't understand the wisdom underlying God's principles of civil law. Therefore, God's civil laws often sound so "foreign" to us that our natural conclusion is that God's laws would not benefit our society and may even harm our society. As a result, we may even delude ourselves into thinking that God himself would not want any nation other than Israel to adopt these laws—as if these laws would somehow magically benefit a Jewish society but do irreversible harm to a Gentile Christian society! Like the rest of us, our Christian leaders are still human, so they often have to see the true benefit of something before they will accept it as being God's Will. Therefore, they too often walk by sight and not by faith, until they can actually see the advantages of doing things God's way.

At one time or another, all of us have made the same mistake of thinking that man's ways are better than God's ways, only to find out that we were wrong and that once again, God's ways were right all along! In fact, it is not uncommon to eventually discover that God's ways had all kinds of advantages that we had never thought of before, but these advantages never came to mind until we had finally "tested" the ways of God as we should have done in the first place. We should realize, therefore, that God's ways will always prove themselves to be superior in every area in which they are tested. The problems are not within God's laws; the problems are within our perception of God's laws. All Christians (and especially Christian leaders) are supposed to have the faith that God's principles are superior to man's principles in every area of life. Of course, this would mean that all of God's principles of civil law would be superior to man's principles of civil law as well. Moreover, since God's laws of nature and God's laws of salvation are perfect and still applicable to all nations today, why should God's laws of government be any different? Did the architect of perfect natural law and perfect spiritual law deviate from his normal standards of perfection when he wrote his civil law? Of course not! In other words, since God's natural laws and God's spiritual laws still apply today, you can be sure that God's civil laws are also still valid, applicable, and superior to our current principles of civil law!

I've done an exhaustive study of the benefits and interactions between all of God's civil laws, and I can tell you that God's principles of civil law are the most wonderful, interactive, culture-changing, and compassionate laws that I can possibly imagine!

As Christians, our natural expectation must be that God's principles should always be better than man's principles anyway, and this same expectation should be true concerning God's civil laws! This book teaches you all the advantages of God's civil laws, so you'll realize that they are all still valid and superior to our current civil laws. Only when we are thoroughly convinced of the superiority of God's principles of civil law can we go about correctly readopting those principles of God back into our government and solve all the national problems of America today. Otherwise, the theocra-phobia of many of our Christian leaders reveals to God that they would rather continue to live in an atheistic, secular democracy than obey God and adopt His principles of civil law back into our national legislation so we can become a Christian Republic, where God's laws reign supreme and can never be repealed, even by majority vote, and where the Bible remains the foundation of all our legislation!

In summary, America has become an evil, anti-God nation precisely because of the devastating direct and indirect consequences of repealing nine of God's principles of civil law from our national legislation. This did not happen because of lack of evangelism, nor the lack of God's authority over the lives of individuals, but it happened because of the lack of God's authority over our government. Unfortunately, America is being held in this evil position with no foreseeable way out, because our Christian leaders mistakenly imagine that some harmful consequences will befall America if we attempt to adopt these nine biblical principles of civil law back into our national legislation once again. Because many of our Christian leaders are so determined to avoid having God's principles of civil law in our government, their rebellion has become the primary deterrent that keeps God from healing our land from the sickness of atheistic democracy to the health of a Christian Republic! This is the paradox which has been created by the "theocraphobia" of many of our Christian leaders.

The rest of this book is devoted to explaining both the natural and the supernatural advantages which can be obtained by Israel, or any other country which wants to become a "nation under God's authority" by adopting God's principles of civil law into its legislation. For, the best principles of civil law come from the Bible itself, and so we should never fear to adopt these principles of civil law into our national legislation!

Chapter Three

THE NATURAL AND SUPERNATURAL BLESSINGS OF BECOMING A "NATION UNDER GOD'S AUTHORITY"

When Jesus Christ walked on earth as the pre-incarnate Jehovah, he promised Israel that if they would obey him, he would bless them with a nearly crime-free, war-free, poverty-free, tax-free, inflation-free, natural-disaster-free, and disease-free society where nearly everyone lives to be 120-years-old and remains in near-perfect health. Furthermore, He also promised that they would dwell in the most peaceful and prosperous nation on the face of the earth. These are national blessings for national obedience—not individual blessings for individual obedience. God was not demanding that each Israelite citizen be "perfectly obedient" to His laws in order for God to grant them blessings to Israel. God knew that the percentage of citizens in Israel who would have the faith which inspires obedient surrender to His will would never amount to more than a small minority anyway. For it is written,

> . . . wide is the gate and broad is the road that leads to destruction, and many enter through it. But small is the gate and narrow the road that leads to life, and only a few find it. (Matt. 7:13-14 NIV)

Therefore, God knew that only a small, faithful minority of citizens would ever obey him because of "salvation and surrender" alone, and that the large unrighteous majority of citizens would never willingly yield control of their lives to Christ in obedient surrender to His will. Since God would never give Israel any command which he would not also somehow enable them to fulfill, how did God plan to keep the large unrighteous majority of Israelite citizens "on their best behavior" when they were so rebellious? Christ designed his civil laws to perfectly enable the small, faithful minority of God-fearing Israelites to rule over the large, unrighteous majority and keep them on their best behavior through the combined influences of indoctrination, culture, godly leadership, godly laws, and godly peer pressure. In other words, the large unrighteous majority of citizens would reluctantly obey God because of "training and tradition," even though they would never enthusiastically obey God because of "salvation and surrender." Quite simply, all Israel had to do was adopt ALL God's principles of civil law into their national legislation and regularly enforce them. This would empower the doctrines of "Christianity" with the legal muscle to keep the large unrighteous majority on their best behavior, as well as create a culture which would perpetually indoctrinate all future citizens of Israel into a tradition of obedience, encouraged by a culture of godly peer pressure, and perpetuated by godly leadership and godly laws. As a result of adopting ALL God's principles of civil law into their national legislation, the "aggregate righteousness" of all Israel would inevitably exceed the "threshold of righteousness" required by God so he could reward them by blessing their nation as a place where almost everyone lives to be 120-years-old and remains in near-perfect health, while dwelling in the most peaceful and prosperous nation on the face of the earth. These are incredible promises, yet Israel never received these blessings because they never completed the task God commanded them to finish. The exact nature of Israel's failure to obey God will slowly become apparent as you read this book.

But first, let's examine these majestic promises in detail. The first reference highlights God's promise to give Israel a nearly disease-free society. It is written:

> If you fully obey the Lord your God and carefully follow all his commands I give you today . . . the fruit of your womb will be blessed. . . . (Deut. 28:1a, 4 NIV)

This means that all babies will be born healthy, with no genetic illnesses whatsoever.

Furthermore, it is written that:

> "The Lord will keep you free from every disease." (Deut. 7:15)

Again it is written:

> I will take away sickness from among you. . . . I will give you a full life span. (Exod. 23:25-26 NIV)

These three verses reveal that if Israel had obeyed God, He would have blessed them with a nearly disease-free society, where their citizens would always be born healthy and they would never even get sick. But that's not all. For then, God promised to give them a full life-span, which, as it turns out, is 120 years.

How do we arrive at this 120-year life-span? Well, it turns out that God wants righteous men of faith to live forever (in heaven), but God believes the life-span of evil men sometimes seems too long. Yet because God allowed the average life-span of all men to be nine hundred years before Noah's Flood, in the following verse we hear God lamenting that . . .

"Evil men seem to live forever! So, since man is mortal, I'll shrink their life-span (from nine hundred years) down to only 120 years."

For it is written:

> The Lord said, "My spirit will not contend with man forever, for he is mortal; his days will be a hundred and twenty years." (Gen. 6:3 NIV)

As it turns out, this "full life span" will only be "available" for those nations which obey God's commands. Unfortunately, most Christians mistakenly believe that this 120 years either refers to the number of years to build Noah's Ark or refers to the number of years before Noah's Flood would come. If this were true, however, then Noah (who was 500-years-old before God's announcement Gen. 5:32) would have aged 120 more years to be at least 620-years-old by the time the ark was completed and the flood began. But, according to Genesis, Noah was only 600-years-old (and not 620) when the flood came. So this 120 years can not refer to the length of time to build the ark nor to the number of years before the flood would come, but can only mean that God was tired of contending with evil men who "seemed to live forever," so he intended to decrease the total life-span of mankind. Even this life-span would be "too long" for evil men living in nations which perpetually disobeyed God's commands. Israel never obeyed God completely enough to receive this blessing, for Moses himself wrote that the average life-span of the Israelites during his day was not 120 years, but was only seventy to eighty years, the same as it is today! For it is written:

> The length of our days is seventy years or eighty, if we have the strength (Ps. 90:10 NIV; this translation says that this is actually a Psalm of MOSES).

To demonstrate the reality of this promise, God allowed Moses himself to live to be exactly 120-years-old, even though the average life-span of everyone else at that time was only seventy- to eighty-years-old! Furthermore, the Bible reveals that Moses still had perfect eyesight and normal adult strength at the time of his death. For it is written:

> Moses was a hundred and twenty-years-old when he died, yet his eyes were not weak, nor his strength gone." (Deut. 34:7 NIV)

I believe this verse reveals that, even at age 120, Moses was still in "excellent shape" with no deterioration of any part of his body when he finally died. The longevity and perfect health of Moses provided the Israelites with the ideal object lesson to demonstrate the importance of obeying God and receiving his blessings of excellent health and a full life-span.

On the other hand, God also allowed Aaron to survive until he was 123-years-old (Num. 33:38 NIV) even though it was Aaron who built the golden calf which encouraged idolatry among the Israelites. However, this provided a different object lesson—that not everyone in Israel had to be as righteous as Moses to inherit the full life-span of 120 years. Since the promise of a full life-span is linked to the promise of a disease-free society (Exod. 23:26 NIV), then by implication, not everyone had to be as righteous as Moses in order for God to bless Israel with a disease-free society either. These national blessings were to be based upon national obedience, not individual obedience. In other words, the national blessings of a disease-free society would be based upon the sum total of all the obedience of everyone in the entire nation of Israel. And, if the sum total of the obedience of all the Israelites taken together exceeded the "threshold of national righteousness" which God had in his Divine Mind, then God would bless Israel with a disease-free society. The only way to get the aggregate righteousness of the entire nation of Israel to exceed the "threshold of righteousness" required by God was to adopt all God's principles of civil law into their legislation and regularly enforce these principles. Only this would empower the doctrines of Christianity with the legal muscle to keep the large unrighteous majority on their best behavior, so they would reluctantly obey God's commands because of godly leadership, godly laws, godly peer pressure, and "training and tradition," even if they would never enthusiastically obey God's laws because of "salvation and surrender"!

The next verse highlights God's promises of a nearly *poverty-free* society:

> If you follow my decrees and are careful to obey my commands, I will send rain in its season, and the ground will yield its crops and the trees of the field their fruit. Your threshing will continue until the grape harvest and the grape harvest will continue until planting and you will eat all the food you want . . . you will still be eating last year's harvest when you will have to move it out to make room for the new. (Lev. 26:3-5,10 NIV)

Additionally, it is written:

> If you fully obey the Lord your God and carefully follow all his commands I give you today. . . . All these blessings will come upon you and accompany you if you obey the Lord your God. You will be blessed in the city and blessed in the

country. The fruit of your womb will be blessed, and the crops of your land and the young of your livestock—the calves of the herds and the lambs of your flocks. Your basket and your trough will be blessed. You will be blessed when you come in and blessed when you go out. . . . The Lord will send a blessing on your barns and on everything you put your hand to. . . . The Lord will grant abundant prosperity. . . . The Lord will open the heavens, the storehouse of his bounty, to send rain on your land in season and to bless all the work of your hands. (Deut. 28:1a, 2-6, 8, 11a, 12a NIV)

This is God's promise to make Israel into a nearly poverty-free society. Furthermore, to show the eternal nature of these promises, a thousand years later God repeated a similar promise in Malachi. Here again God says that if Israel would obey all God's commands, he would bless them so greatly that all the surrounding nations would be envious because of God's blessings upon Israel. In this instance, God highlights Israel's failure to obey his commands concerning the "National Tithe!" It is written:

Bring the whole tithe into the storehouse, that there may be food in my house. "Test me in this," says the Lord Almighty, "and see if I will not open up the floodgates of heaven and pour out so much blessing that you will not have room enough for it. I will prevent pests from devouring your crops, and the vines in your fields will not cast their fruit," says the Lord Almighty. "Then all the nations will call you blessed, and yours will be a delightful land," says the Lord Almighty. (Mal. 3:10-12 NIV)

These are God's phenomenal promises to make Israel into a nearly poverty-free society if Israel would first obey God. Additionally, God also promised to make Israel into the richest nation on earth. For it is written:

If you fully obey the Lord your God and carefully follow all his commands I give you today, the Lord your God will set you high above all the nations on earth. . . . You will lend to many nations but will borrow from none. The Lord will make you the head, not the tail. . . . You will always be at the top, never at the bottom. (Deut. 28:1, 12b-13 NIV)

So it is clear that if Israel had done what God had asked, then God would have given them a nearly poverty-free society, as well as make them into the most prosperous nation on the face of the earth. However, God also promised he'd make Israel into a nearly *crime-free* and *war-free* society. For it is written:

> If you follow my decrees and are careful to obey my commands.... You will live in *safety* in your land. I will grant peace in the land and you will lie down and *no one will make you afraid*.... *the sword will not pass through your country*. You will pursue your enemies, and they will fall by the sword before you. Five of you will chase a hundred, and a hundred of you will chase a ten thousand, and your enemies will fall by the sword before you. (Lev. 26:3, 5b, 6-8 NIV; emphasis added)

In these verses, God promises to grant Israel both *internal* safety (relative freedom from the violence of crime) and *external* safety (freedom from ever being conquered in a war) in response to Israel's obedience to God. So in some sense, God had indeed promised Israel a nearly crime-free and war-free society if they would obey him.

God also promised to keep Israel free from all "natural" disasters. This is the implication of the verses which say that if Israel disobeyed God, then God would punish them with "natural" disasters. For it is written:

> ... if you do not obey the Lord your God.... The Lord will strike you with ... scorching heat and drought.... The sky over your head will be bronze, the ground beneath you will be iron. The Lord will turn the rain of your country into dust and powder ... the Lord will send ... harsh and prolonged disasters.... The Lord will also bring on you every kind of.... disaster not recorded in this book of the law. (Deut. 28:15a, 22-24, 59, 61 NIV)

You can see that the Lord promised to punish Israel with natural disasters such as scorching heat, drought (which of course causes famine), and many other natural disasters which are not even recorded in the Bible, if Israel failed to obey God. This implies that if Israel had obeyed God, then God would in turn protect them from natural disasters and give them a *natural disaster-free* society!

God also made two promises to Israel by implication alone. The first one was to give Israel a *tax-free* society. In First Samuel, God warned the Israelites that if they chose to disobey God and have a king, the king would force them to pay a tax of ten percent of their grain, vintage, and flocks to the king so he could finance the cost of building a new, large, centralized government. Furthermore, the Israelites would eventually become "slaves" to the financial burden of these same taxes. For it is written:

> This is what the king who will rule over you will do.... He will take a *tenth* of your *grain* and of your *vintage*.... He

> will take a *tenth* of your *flocks,* and you yourselves will become his *slaves.* When that day comes, you will cry out for relief.... (1 Sam. 8:11a, 15a, 17-18a NIV; emphasis added)

What God is really saying is:

> My laws are so complete and so perfect that Israel can use them to self-govern without the need for any taxes, and without the need for a large, centralized government.

Therefore, God was providing the Israelites with a tax-free form of self-government (which, unfortunately for them, they turned down).

The second promise God made only by implication is to give Israel an *inflation-free* society. Modern economists tell us that the rate of inflation is always linked to the prime rate of interest. But in the Bible, God says that the interest rate should always be zero, for God condemns the charging of any interest whatsoever, and calls this "the sin of usury." In other words, since God says the interest rate should always be zero percent, the rate of inflation should also be zero percent as well. This represents God's promise to give Israel an inflation-free society (see chapter twenty-one). The laws concerning lending money at interest (usury) are as follows:

> If you lend money to one of my people who is needy, do not be like a moneylender; charge him no interest. (Exod. 22:25 NIV);

> Do not take interest of any kind from him.... You must not lend him money at interest.... (Lev. 25:36a, 37a NIV)

Twenty-three times the Bible mentions usury (charging interest on loans) and in every instance God expresses his disapproval. In fact, in Nehemiah (5:7,11 NIV) God teaches us that charging even 1 percent interest is "too high." In addition, the Bible teaches that the other causes of inflation—natural disasters, war, poverty, economic collapse, etc.—would also be kept under divine control in a biblical society which is obedient to God's laws (for more details, see chapter twenty-one). If all the other causes of inflation are held in check and the interest rate is zero percent, then the inflation rate should be zero percent as well. Therefore, God indeed promised Israel an inflation-free society.

God's purpose for promising these blessings to Israel was to "spread the Gospel" (so to speak) and this notion is perfectly expressed by David. For it is written:

> God will bless us, and all the ends of the earth will *fear* him. (Ps. 67:7 NIV; emphasis added);

> May God . . . bless us . . . that your *ways* may be known on earth, your *SALVATION* among the nations. (Ps. 67:1a, 2 NIV; emphasis added)

One of the things God's "chosen people" were "chosen" for in the first place, was for Israel to become an international object lesson—to illustrate for all nations the magnitude of God's rewards for national obedience, or the magnitude of God's punishments for national disobedience. Unfortunately, one of the greatest tragedies of history is that Israel never completely adopted and enforced all of God's principles of civil law, so they never received these tremendous blessings. As a result, the world has never seen Israel as the recipient of God's majestic rewards for national obedience. Instead, the world has only seen Israel become an international object lesson of God's punishments for national disobedience. The fact that one thousand years later Malachi (3:10-12 NIV) prophesied the nearly identical promises of Moses indicates the eternal nature of these promised blessings and that Israel is still eligible to receive these blessings today, if they would only do what God has commanded. In the next chapter, you will see that America is also eligible for these same blessings!

Chapter Four

WHY GOD'S PROMISE TO BLESS ANCIENT ISRAEL CAN ALSO APPLY TO MODERN AMERICA

In this chapter we will learn why the same promises God made to ancient Israel thousands of years ago are also available to modern America today. "But," you say, "God made his 'Covenant Promises' with Israel, not with America. Since America is not a 'covenant nation,' how can America possibly be 'eligible' to receive any of the same blessings or punishments which God promised only to Israel?" Good question. Let's remember however, that Ninevah was neither a "covenant city" nor was Assyriah a "covenant nation," yet God intended to severely punish Ninevah (the capital city of Assyriah) for their many great sins against almighty God! In fact, the only reason they were "saved" from this punishment is because they repented at the preaching of Jonah for the wickedness of their sins.

In the Bible there is an implied covenant between God and all nations. For instance, in Micah 5:15, God promises to punish any nation "that has not obeyed him," and in Psalm 33:12 God promises to bless any nation "whose God is the Lord." In other words, just as God made all Gentile individuals potentially "eligible" for his promise of salvation, so also God made all Gentile nations potentially eligible for his promise of a peaceful and prosperous society. There are many biblical references about God punishing nations (other than Israel) for their disobedience of His commands. This means that many of God's ancient punishments for disobedient countries can apply to today's modern nations. This might explain why the nations which worship idols are generally also the poorest nations in the world (the third-world nations). However, if modern nations are eligible for God's punishments, then surely God has also made them eligible to strive for his blessings. This, of course, might explain why nations with Judeo-Christian backgrounds are generally the most wealthy nations in the world (the first-world nations). Therefore, we should realize that the ancient prophesies of God punishing (and blessing) nations (other than Israel) still apply today.

With this in mind, let us examine the verses in the Holy Scriptures which declare that God does indeed punish nations (other than Israel) for their disobedience of God's commands. It is written:

> I will take vengeance in anger and wrath upon the nations that have not obeyed me. (Mic. 5:15 NIV)

This verse alone should be enough to prove my point—that the God of the Bible will indeed punish nations other than Israel for their sins. This can only mean one thing—that God's "standards for national conduct" do not apply to Israel alone, but apply to all the nations of the world! If the nations don't obey God's standard for national conduct, then God punishes them!

But what is God's standard of conduct for all nations? And where do we find it? Well, God refers to his standard of conduct as "the ways of my people" and he records "these ways" in the Old Testament Mosaic civil law. God evidently also feels that all generations of all nations have had the chance to listen to God's "instructions" and learn "the ways of [His] people." And so, if certain nations do not listen and learn, then they will be slowly uprooted and destroyed. For it is written:

> "And if they learn well the ways of my people . . . then they will be established among my people. But if any nation does not listen, I will completely uproot and destroy it," declares the Lord. (Jer. 12:17 NIV)

This verse can only refer to nations other than Israel. It says that these particular nations must learn the ways of Israel (which actually come from God's principles of civil law) or be held accountable for not listening and learning to God's laws, and so they will be slowly destroyed.

Now here is a series of verses which illustrates the same point—that God does indeed punish nations other than Israel, implying that God holds all nations accountable to a certain "standard for national conduct." It is written:

> Son of man, if a country sins against me by being unfaithful and I stretch out my hand against it to cut off its food supply and send famine upon it and kill its men and their animals. . . ;
>
> Or if I send wild beasts through that country and they leave it childless and it becomes desolate so that no one can pass through it because of the beasts. . . ;
>
> Or if I bring a sword against that country. . . ;
>
> Or if I send a plague into that land and pour out my wrath upon it through bloodshed, killing its men and animals. . . . (Ezek. 14:13, 15, 17a, 19 NIV)

These four verses in Ezekiel again reveal that all nations are responsible to obey God or they will be punished. Therefore, God expects all nations to be faithful to him and not sin against him, for it says, "if a country sins against me by being unfaithful," I will punish it!

There are also times when God would like to destroy a nation, but if that nation repents, God will decide not to destroy it after all. For it is written:

> If at any time I announce that a nation or kingdom is to be uprooted, torn down and destroyed, and if that nation I warned repents of its evil, then I will relent and not inflict on it the disaster I had planned. (Jer. 18:7-8 NIV)

This is exactly what happened in the story of Jonah preaching to Ninevah. Furthermore, sometimes God wants to build up and exalt a nation, but he will reconsider this too if the nation begins to do evil in his sight. For it is written:

> And if at another time I announce that a nation or kingdom is to be built up and planted, and if it does evil in my sight and does not obey me, then I will reconsider the good I had intended to do for it. (Jer. 18:9-10 NIV)

Not only does God punish nations other than Israel for their wickedness, God also blesses nations other than Israel for their obedience! For it is written:

> Blessed is the nation whose God is the Lord, the people he chose for his inheritance. (Ps. 33:12 NIV)

This verse refers to any nation that God chooses to inherit his blessings. In fact, much of the rest of Psalm 33 tells of how God loves the righteousness and justice of good nations, but that he "foils the plans" and "thwarts the purposes" of evil nations. It is written:

> The Lord loves righteousness and justice; the earth is full of his unfailing love.... Let all the earth fear the Lord; let all the people of the world revere him.... The Lord foils the plans of the nations; he thwarts the purposes of the peoples; ... Blessed is the nation whose God is the Lord, the people he chose for his inheritance. From heaven the Lord looks down and sees all mankind; from his dwelling place he watches all who live on earth ... No king is saved by the size of his army; no warrior escapes by his great strength ... But the eyes of the Lord are on those who fear him, on those whose hope is his unfailing love, to deliver them from death and keep them alive in famine. (Ps. 33:5, 8, 10, 12-14, 16, 18-19 NIV)

This psalm clearly teaches that the Lord not only loves all generations of all nations, but makes them eligible for his punishments as well as his blessings. It is also written:

> Righteousness exalts a nation, but sin is a disgrace to any people." (Prov. 14:34 NIV)

> Through the blessing of the upright a city is exalted, but by the mouth of the wicked it is destroyed. (Prov. 11:11 NIV)

These two verses show that God will exalt and bless nations or cities if they are righteous and obey God's laws.

The founders of our nation knew that God loves all nations and that all nations were eligible for both God's blessings and his curses. More than two hundred years ago, George Mason, while he was a Virginia delegate at the Constitutional Convention of our country, said,

> ... As nations cannot be rewarded or punished in the next world, they must be in this. By an inevitable chain of causes and effects, Providence punishes national sins by national calamities. (Barton, *The Myth of Separation*, 217)

Ben Franklin believed the same:

> I have lived, Sir, a long time, and the longer I live, the more convincing proofs I see of this truth—that God governs in the affairs of men.... We have been assured, Sir, in the Sacred Writings, that "except the Lord build the house, they labor in vain that build it." I firmly believe this; and I also believe that without His concurring aid, we shall succeed in this political building no better than the builders of Babel: We shall be divided by our little partial local interests; our projects will be confounded; and we ourselves shall become a reproach.... (Ibid.)

In summary, the Bible tells us that many of the Old Testament promises of blessings and punishments for ancient Israel are actually available for all nations. And Malachi's prophesy teaches us that the potential to inherit God's national blessings is eternal and, therefore, still available today.

We see evidence for this biblical truth in our world history. The third-world nations are those whose government leaders and citizens worship idols or worship other things in nature. Because of their idolatry, these nations are punished with the worst economies, droughts, famines, floods, violence, plagues and diseases. The second-world nations are generally atheistic and are being punished as well, but often not as severely as nations which worship idols. According to the Bible, idolatry angers God much more than mere disbelief (atheism). These atheistic second-world nations generally have had better economies and fewer natural disasters than do the idolatrous third-world nations. The "first-world nations" were originally founded upon a Judeo-Christian world view, which included worshiping Jesus Christ. Because of this, almighty God has blessed the first-world nations with much better economies, as well as with climates which seem to have much fewer natural disasters than the third-world nations.

It appears as though God has blessed the Protestant "Christian" nations much more than the Catholic "Christian" nations, probably because so many of these Catholic nations participate in a great deal of idolatrous "Mary worship," which greatly angers God. This tells us that the more closely the citizens and government leaders of the first-world nations hold fast to the true teachings of the Bible, the more blessings almighty God will give to these same nations. However, since these same Judeo-Christian first-world nations have become more liberal and evil in the recent past, God has recently made their economies to become less prosperous as well. Generations ago, God blessed America with more economic prosperity than any other nation on earth, in large part because the founders of our government had the faith in Christ which inspired them to adopt and enforce nine of God's principles of civil law as part of America's legislation.

In recent years however, we have seen the removal of all nine of these biblical principles of civil law from our government. This action has released the unrighteous majority of citizens in America from the restraining influence of God's principles of civil law, resulting in America becoming a nation which embraces all kinds of sinful immorality. By doing this, America has disinherited herself from receiving God's blessings and has instead made herself eligible to receive God's wrath! In fact, since the Clinton administration has encouraged so much evil in our nation, God has punished America with more natural disasters during his term as president than our nation has ever experienced in such a short period of time. In order to end this continuing barrage of natural disasters upon America, our nation needs to readopt these same nine biblical principles of civil law back into our national legislation so we can avoid any more of God's almighty wrath and so we can become eligible to inherit some of God's national blessings once again. Surprisingly, our Christian leaders have willfully disregarded the importance that God's principles of civil law have for the administration of sound and virtuous government. They must repent of this sin, "turn from these wicked ways," and have the faith to adopt God's principles of civil law back into America's legislation once again. For God will not "heal our land" from the "sickness" of atheistic democracy to the "health" of a Christian Republic, until our Christian leaders are willing to aim for

His target, and play by His rules. Therefore, my interpretation of 2 Chronicles 7:14 is the following:

> ... if my people's *Christian leaders*, who are called by my name, will humble themselves and pray and seek my face and turn from their wicked ways *(of believing that God's principles of civil law have no value for the administration of good government)*, then will I hear from heaven and will forgive their sin and will heal their land. (2 Chron. 7:13-14 NIV; emphasis added)

Only by adopting these nine biblical principles of civil law back into our national legislation can the doctrines of Christianity again be empowered with the legal muscle to keep the large unrighteous majority of America's citizens on their best behavior. Then, America can become a nation under God's authority once again. In this way, God will truly bless us, in order that his ways (i.e., principles of civil law) can be made known on earth and his salvation among the nations. For it is written:

> May God ... bless us ... that your ways may be known on earth, your salvation among the nations. (Ps. 67:4 NIV)

Then, it will be known to the ends of the earth that God rules over America, just as God originally ruled over Jacob. For it is written:

> Then it will be known to the ends of the earth that God rules over Jacob. (Ps. 59:13 NIV)

So, let us remember that God's promise to bless ancient Israel can also apply to modern America today. Therefore, we too can strive to become an example (for all other countries) of a nation under God's authority hereby inheriting God's natural and supernatural blessings which result from adopting all of God's principles of civil law into our legislation.

Chapter Five

GOD'S VIEW OF GOVERNMENT REFORM AND GOD'S CURE FOR GOVERNMENT CORRUPTION, SCANDALS, AND GRIDLOCK

In this book, I have arranged most all God's principles of civil law into groups with similar laws. When God's civil laws are studied in this fashion, they begin to come alive with meaning and purpose. Moreover, some of God's civil principles can only be correctly understood after studying their interaction with other similar laws in the same group.

Some of the more unusual Mosaic laws are like pieces of a jigsaw puzzle. The meaning and purpose of a puzzle piece can not be fully appreciated until it is fitted perfectly into place within the big picture. This way, you can see how it touches and "interacts" with the other pieces. Likewise, the meaning and purpose of an unusual Mosaic law frequently can not be correctly understood until it too is fitted perfectly into place, so you can see how it "touches" and "interacts" with other similar laws to produce God's intended effect upon society. Therefore, many of God's laws which don't seem to make sense by themselves suddenly make perfect sense when viewed as interacting with other laws in a group. This is when the wisdom and hidden purposes of the Mosaic laws are revealed in all their splendor. Then you can see how the Mosaic laws of government interact together to form a Mosaic picture of "God's view of government reform." You can also see how the Mosaic laws of punishment interact together to form a Mosaic picture of "God's view of prison reform." Furthermore, the Mosaic laws of health care and welfare interact together to form a Mosaic picture of "God's view of health care reform and welfare reform." The list goes on and on!

Most of the following chapters highlight one specific category of biblical principles of civil law. In this particular chapter we will learn about God's view of government reform. This includes God's principles of *how* a government should run, and *who* should run it.

PRINCIPLE ONE—God's principles of civil law must be the foundation for all national legislation;

PRINCIPLE TWO—God's laws are both necessary and sufficient for sound and virtuous government;

PRINCIPLE THREE—Man's laws are inferior to God's laws and are largely unnecessary and superfluous for the administration of sound and virtuous government;

PRINCIPLE FOUR—All top government leaders must handwrite their own copy of God's civil laws, keep it with them at all times, and read it in depth each day.

Since Christ is Lord of lawmakers and architect of the biblical blueprint for perfect self-government, it is obvious that God wanted His civil laws to be the foundation for all legislation in Israel, as well as for the rest of the world. Even the "worst" laws of God are wiser than the "best" laws of man, as it is written:

> For the foolishness of God is wiser than man's wisdom. . . .
> (1 Cor. 1:25 NIV)

You see, Jehovah not only wanted God's men to rule the government, he also wanted God's laws to rule the nation! To help accomplish this, God wanted all top leaders to handwrite their own copy of all God's civil laws, keep it with them at all times, and read it in depth each day. For it is written:

> When he takes the throne of his kingdom, he is to write for himself on a scroll a copy of this law, taken from that of the priests . . . It is to be with him and he is to read it all the days of his life so that he may learn to revere the Lord his God, and follow carefully all the words of this law and these decrees and not consider himself better than his brothers and turn from the law to the right or the left. (Deut. 17:18-20a NIV)

In addition to helping the leaders focus upon God so that they would not consider themselves above God's laws and become corrupt, this law was also designed to provide all top leaders in Israel with a daily reminder that God's laws should be the *primary* civil laws of Israel. Also, it was a reminder that all man's laws should be subordinate to God's laws and should never contradict God's laws. Even the "best" laws of man can never hope to surpass any of the laws of God. However, the rulers in ancient Israel never accomplished what God commanded, and instead exalted *man's* principles of civil law over *God's* principles of civil law. When they did this, their nation became evil and so, God punished them. In fact, the Bible teaches that no one in Israel was wise enough to understand that God had "ruined the land and laid it waste like a desert" to punish Israel not because they had forsaken *good* laws, but because they had forsaken *God's* laws. It is written:

> What man is wise enough to understand this? Who has been instructed by the Lord and can explain it? Why has the land been ruined and laid waste like a desert that no one can cross?
>
> The Lord said, "It is because they have forsaken MY law which I set before them. They have not obeyed MY LAW!" (Jer. 9:12-13 NIV; emphasis added)

This problem has occurred in modern America as well: our government has denounced and forsaken God's civil laws and has exalted man's civil laws in their place. Furthermore, the tragic bias that modern leaders have against God's principles of civil law perpetuates the mistaken belief that "good government requires good laws" (and good leaders), whereas the Bible reveals that "good government requires God's laws" (and God's leaders)! Therefore, it appears that in modern America (just as in ancient Israel) no one in our country is wise enough to understand that the reason God is punishing America and refuses to "heal our land" is not because we have forsaken good laws, but because we have forsaken God's laws! Specifically, America has forsaken the nine biblical principles of civil law which the founders adopted, just as we have also forsaken all of the biblical principles of civil law which are listed in this book.

You see, just one of God's laws is worth more than a hundred of man's laws. In fact, in chapter two we learned that nine of God's principles of civil law have been removed from America's legislation over the last two hundred years and have been replaced by thousands of man's civil laws, yet America is now more evil than ever before! So also, if we would just reintroduce these nine biblical principles of civil law back into America's legislation, thousands of man's laws would slowly become unnecessary and obsolete. Furthermore, in chapter thirteen of this book you will learn how God's five biblical alternatives to imprisonment can provide a greater deterrent to crime, solve all our prison problems, save hundreds of billions of dollars in taxes, and (again) render hundreds of man's laws unnecessary, obsolete, and therefore superfluous.

"But," you ask, "how is it that these ancient legal principles can still function successfully in our high-tech society?" Well you see, the society may be high-tech, but the sins have not changed since ancient times. Modern technology only provides us with high-tech ways to commit the same old sins! For instance, stealing is still stealing, whether by "low-tech mugging" or by "high-tech embezzlement by computer." Likewise, murder is still murder (even if it's done by remote control explosives), and sexual immorality is still sexual immorality (even if done by pornography on the internet). God's principles of civil law are capable of stopping all these sin-crimes more efficiently than any of man's laws. What's more, with God's laws, society also saves hundreds of billions of dollars in taxes at the same time!

Our founders also believed that government should be founded upon God's principles of civil law, for they wrote that. . . .

> The judicial laws of God as they were delivered by Moses . . . [are to] be a rule for all the courts in this jurisdiction . . . (Barton, *Myth*, 88).

Additionally, in the first constitution of Connecticut, the people were instructed to make the laws: "as near the law of God as they [could] be" (Barton, *Myth*, 87).

PRINCIPLE FIVE—Only godly Christian elders should ever be allowed to serve in government.

Another of God's principles of government reform concerns the importance of character in choosing rulers. According to God, all government rulers are supposed to be godly Christian elders who know how to correctly apply all of God's principles of civil law in all situations. For instance, in the next verse, Jethro, priest of Midian, speaks to Moses:

> . . . select capable men from all the people- MEN WHO FEAR GOD, trustworthy men who hate dishonest gain . . . appoint them as officials. . . . Have them serve as judges. . . . (Exod. 18:21a NIV; emphasis added)

And, about five hundred years later, God spoke through King David at the end of David's life and said:

> The God of Israel said. . . . "He that ruleth over men must be just, ruling in the FEAR OF GOD." (2 Sam. 23:3 KJV; emphasis added)

And again, about 350 additional years into the future, God spoke through Ezekiel and said:

> But RIGHTEOUS MEN will sentence them to the punishment . . . (Ezek. 23:45 NIV; emphasis added)

So, according to God himself, all rulers in government should be capable, righteous men who fear God. These truths were spread out over 850 years, showing the eternal nature of these commands, and showing that they should still be obeyed today.

Six hundred additional years into the future—in the New Testament— God speaks through the Apostle Paul and teaches that if a man wanted to be a mere "overseer" or "deacon" in a church, he must be "above reproach." He must "first be tested" and only if there is "nothing against him" can he serve in a church as an overseer or a deacon (1 Tim. 3:2, 10 NIV). If this is how we are to evaluate all "overseers" and "deacons," how much more would God want us to test all our national leaders to make sure that they are "above reproach," and that there is "nothing that God himself would hold against them" which would disqualify them from serving in government!

Certainly the founders also knew the importance of having rulers who were themselves "ruled by God" and who knew they would be held accountable beyond the grave for sins committed while in office. William Penn said:

> If thou wouldst rule well, thou must rule for God, and to do that, thou must be ruled by him. (Barton, *Myth*, 89)

Additionally, many of the original state constitutions written by the founders specified that only Christians could ever be allowed to serve in government (see chapter two). Also, the Honorable John Jay, our first Supreme Court Chief Justice, strongly advised U.S. citizens to vote only for Christians to rule our nation. He said:

> Providence has given to our people the choice of our rulers, and it is the duty, as well as the privilege and interest, of a Christian nation, to select and prefer Christians for their rulers. (Ibid., 118)

It is too bad that the Supreme Court no longer says, "Vote only for Christians in every election!" Our nation would certainly be much better off if we would continue to elect only honest, godly Christian statesmen who hate dishonest gain and who understand all God's principles of civil law. For these principles were designed by God to prevent all government corruption and government scandal. Moreover, if all our statesmen had the Holy Spirit within them (as well as had within them a great understanding of all the principles underlying God's civil laws) and they joined together in fervent prayer before each political discussion and before each vote, then they would be divinely enabled to have God's perspective on every political issue and have a greater unity of mind and spirit when voting on new laws. Therefore, this would also help to prevent government gridlock. And, by ending government corruption, scandal, and gridlock, we can restore confidence in America's government!

PRINCIPLE SIX—All rulers should pray to God for the "gift of governments."

All rulers should pray and ask God for His wisdom to rule government, just like Solomon did. For it is written:

> "So give your servant a discerning heart to govern your people and to distinguish between right and wrong. For who is able to govern this great people of yours?" The Lord was pleased that Solomon had asked for this. The Lord said, "Since you have asked for . . . discernment in administering justice, . . . I will give you a wise and discerning heart. . . . " (1 Kings 3:9-12 NIV)

Notice that God was pleased that Solomon had asked for godly wisdom and discernment to govern the people. Therefore, one of the ways we can please God today is to ask him for godly wisdom and discernment to govern people as well, because God is still interested in having godly men administering justice. And, just as God gave Solomon the "gift of governments" in the Old Testament, so also the "gift of governments" is available today in the New Testament as well. For it is written:

> And God hath set some in the church, first apostles, secondarily prophets, thirdly teachers, after that miracles, then gifts of healings, helps, GOVERNMENTS, diversities of tongues. (1 Cor. 12:28 KJV; emphasis added)

Although the "gift of governments" (KJV) is available today for those who administer church "governments," this same "gift of administration" (NIV) can also be a wonderful blessing for those whom God "calls" to serve in national government as well, so they can receive wisdom and guidance from God to divinely enable them to work together to restore America to a "nation under God's authority."

PRINCIPLE SEVEN—Impeach, prosecute, and punish all leaders who have committed serious personal sins while in office, or who have approved legislation which clearly violates God's laws and which clearly increases national sins.

American culture no longer insists on having only godly Christian elders to serve at all levels of government, nor do we insist on purging known adulterers, homosexuals, or idolators from our government either. We now allow immoral people to rule us and to write our laws, even though their laws often exalt further immorality and godlessness throughout the land, such as laws which encourage atheism and a belief in evolution, while discouraging a belief in Christianity and in the Bible. Unfortunately, this has created an anti-biblical paradox, such that our culture now takes steps to purge godly men from government instead of purging the godless, the immoral, and those who approve of legislation which increases national immorality and godlessness. As a result, the godly have been swept from all levels of American government, which is exactly what happened in ancient Israel thousands of years ago. For it is written:

> The Godly have been swept from the land [the government], not one upright man remains ... the ruler demands gifts, the judge accepts bribes, the powerful dictate what they desire; they all conspire together. (Mic. 7:23 NIV)

This of course causes the citizens to be very miserable. For it is written:

> ... when the wicked rule, the people groan. (Prov. 29:2b NIV)

The people groan when the wicked rule because wicked rulers "make unjust laws" and "issue oppressive decrees." This makes God very angry, so he wants them to be punished. For it is written:

> Woe to those who make unjust laws, to those who issue oppressive decrees; to deprive the poor of their rights and withhold justice from the oppressed of my peoples. (Isa. 10:1-2 NIV)

But God would prefer not to punish the evil rulers himself. For he greatly prefers having his "saints" (his godly "Christian" elders) to do this for him.

You see, God evidently "calls" some of his "saints" to deal with these wicked leaders and purge them from government, prosecute them, and then punish them according to God's principles of civil law for the crimes these evil leaders have committed against God and men. God's principles of civil law are all recorded in the Bible—the written "Word of God"—which is also known in Hebrews 4:12 (NIV) as a "double-edged sword." God further says that the "glory of the saints" is the honor given to them by God for purging evil leaders from government in this way. It is written:

> Let the saints rejoice in this honor and sing for joy on their beds. May the praise of God be in their mouths and a double-edged sword [the Bible] in their hands, to inflict vengeance [God's Justice] on the nations; and punishment on the peoples, to bind their kings with fetters, their nobles with shackles of iron, to carry out the sentence written against them. This is the glory of the saints. Praise be the Lord. (Ps. 149:5-9 NIV)

According to Psalm 149 ("the impeachment Psalm") the "glory of the Christian saint" is to peacefully impeach ungodly rulers, remove them from office, jail them, prosecute them, and "carry out the sentence written against them" in God's principles of civil law for the crimes they have committed against God and men. So, God is "calling" some Christian saints to follow the instructions of the psalmist and change ungodly government into godly government and change ungodly nations into "nations under God"!

PRINCIPLE EIGHT—There are no term limits for godly Christian elders who serve well and who remain "above reproach." They can serve in government for their entire lives!

Since the Bible teaches that wicked men in government must be immediately removed, prosecuted, and punished, it becomes quite obvious that there are no term limits for godly Christian statesmen who vigorously encourage the government to regularly enforce all of God's principles of civil law, and who personally remain "above reproach." Evidently, according to God, the righteous should rule for life, but the wicked should be removed, prosecuted, and punished immediately.

PRINCIPLE NINE—It is the responsibility of Christian leaders to repeal all oppressive legislation and replace it with legislation based upon God's compassionate principles of civil law.

PRINCIPLE TEN—God does not consider laws against sexual immorality, drunkenness, non-biblical divorce, working on Sunday, etc. to be oppressive. Nor does God consider any of his other laws to be oppressive either.

According to Isaiah 10:1-2 (NIV), God hates it when leaders "make unjust laws," "issue oppressive decrees," or "withhold justice from the oppressed." To fix this problem however, God again says that it is the responsibility of the Christian saints to move into government and set the oppressed free, by loosening the chains of injustice and removing the yoke of man's oppressive laws which violate the principles of God's compassionate laws. For it is written:

> Is this not the kind of fasting I have chosen; to loose the chains of injustice; to untie the cords of the yoke, to set the oppressed free and break every yoke. (Isa. 58:6 NIV)

Again, this is the "glory of the saints"—to not only remove from government every *leader* who *violates* God's principles of civil law, but also to remove from government every *law* which *contradicts* God's principles of civil law! On the other hand, godly leaders and godly laws should be exalted and should continue to perform their function forever, without ever being removed from government.

Now, it is obvious that God does not consider his own civil laws to be "oppressive" in any way, so American legislators and voters should not consider any of God's civil laws to be "oppressive" either! Therefore, the outlawing of sexual immorality, drunkenness, non-biblical divorce, working on Sunday, abortion, idolatry, etc., should not be considered to be "oppressive," but should be considered to be part of God's "justice"!

PRINCIPLE ELEVEN—Government must be kept as small as possible;

PRINCIPLE TWELVE—Government must be kept as decentralized as possible;

PRINCIPLE THIRTEEN—Government must be kept as unintrusive as possible;

PRINCIPLE FOURTEEN—Government-owned real estate must be kept to an absolute minimum;

PRINCIPLE FIFTEEN—Taxes must be kept as small as possible. In fact, taxes are not an absolute necessity to administer good government. But, if the people must be taxed, this tax must be based upon a flat tax (on income only), and not a "graduated" tax, because God legislated a "flat" tithe (on income only) and not a "graduated" tithe.

In chapter eight of First Samuel, the Israelites have formally rejected God's form of government (which they had never wholeheartedly tried to adopt anyway). Instead, they wanted to be like all the other nations and have a government with a king. But, God tells Samuel to warn the Israelites that if they choose man's ways over God's ways, then they will inevitably end up with an expensive, large, centralized government, which will be very intrusive into their family lives and will take from them some of their sons, daughters, servants, animals, and real estate. For it is written:

> This is what the king who will reign over you will do; He will take your sons and make them serve with his chariots.... Some he will assign to be commanders ... and others to plow his ground and reap his harvest, and still others to make weapons of war and equipment for his chariots. He will take the best of your fields and vineyards and olive groves ... your menservants and maidservants and the best of your cattle and donkeys he will take for his own use. (1 Sam. 8:11-14, 16 NIV)

Clearly, God is warning Israel that when nations reject God's principles for self-government, then they will inevitably end up with an overly large, centralized government, which accumulates lots of property, equipment, and employees. This intrusive government will also prove to be a great disruption to their family life and to their economic stability, for many of their sons and daughters will no longer be working to build up their family's estate, but instead will be working to build up their government's bureaucracy. Furthermore, to finance this type of government, Israel will have to begin to pay taxes for the first time in their nation's four hundred year history. These taxes would come in the form of 10 percent of their grain, vintage, and flocks! For it is written:

> This is what the king who will reign over you will do; . . . He will take a tenth of your grain and of your vintage. . . . He will take a tenth of your flocks and you yourselves will become his slaves. When that day comes, you will cry out for relief . . . (1 Sam. 8:11, 15, 17, 18a NIV)

Israel was already supposed to pay a 10 percent tithe (which they did only halfheartedly anyway, according to Malachi 3:8-10) but now they would have to pay a 10 percent tax as well! And, as the costs of the large, centralized government would escalate, the Israelites themselves would become slaves to this new system of taxes and big government, which would ultimately prove to be very burdensome.

In contrast to the tremendous burden of man's thousands of intrusive laws, the mere few hundred laws of God are not burdensome at all! For it is written:

> This is love for God: to obey his commands. And his commands are *not* burdensome. (1 John 5:3 NIV; emphasis added)

In summary, God is opposed to big taxes and big, intrusive government and instead wanted Israel (and America) to have small, decentralized, unintrusive government with minimal (if any) state-owned property, and with minimal (if any) taxes. If taxes are to be collected at all, they must be based upon a "flat tax" (on income only), because God, in his infinite wisdom, chose to make the tithe a "flat tithe" (on income only) and not a "graduated tithe." Therefore, God is also opposed to property taxes and sales taxes, so these types of taxes should be eliminated as well.

PRINCIPLE SIXTEEN—God designed his system of government to enable the small, "Christian" minority to rule over the large, unrighteous majority.

PRINCIPLE SEVENTEEN—God's principles of civil law were designed to empower the doctrines of "Christianity" with the "legal muscle" to keep the large, unrighteous majority of citizens on their best behavior!

GOD'S INTENDED STRUCTURE FOR THE GOVERNMENT OF ANCIENT ISRAEL

PRINCIPLE EIGHTEEN—God designed a National Hierarchy of Judicial Authority to be staffed by appointees who freely volunteered to serve as judges over a progressively larger number of Israelite families. This would create a nationwide system of local accountability groups (comprised of one judge and ten families in each of the smallest groups), which would each be responsible before God to remain on their best behavior;

PRINCIPLE NINETEEN—This system of local and national accountability groups was designed by God to be the final step necessary to boost the aggregate righteousness of all Israel over the threshold which God had established as a standard requirement for all nations. This was done so God could finally bless Israel with a nearly crime-free, war-free, poverty-free, inflation-free, tax-free, natural disaster-free, and disease-free society where nearly everyone lives to be 120 years old while enjoying almost perfect health throughout their entire lives!

For it is written:

> But select capable men from all the people—men who fear God, trustworthy men who hate dishonest gain—appoint them as officials over thousands, hundreds, fifties, and tens. Have them serve as judges for the people at all times, but have them bring every difficult case to you; the simple cases they can decide for themselves. (Exod. 18:21-22 NIV)

The advice Jethro gave to Moses in Exodus 18:19-22 (NIV) of appointing judges over ten families, fifty families, one hundred families, and one thousand families was actually a command of God designed to create a National Hierarchy of Judicial Authority comprised of a nationwide system of local accountability groups, each of which would be held responsible before Jehovah (and his appointed Judges) to keep themselves free from serious sinful behavior. Each local accountability group would consist of ten families and a real judge. This judge would probably also be a father and family leader of one of the ten families in his group. He would have the legal authority to dispense true justice, tempered with mercy, and would decide all the simple cases himself. However, if he had a particularly difficult case, he could always appeal to a "higher judge." Thus, each judge would function as a catalyst to increase the group's accountability to God. Also, because the groups would be so small, their judges could know each of their families very well so that repetitive sinful behavior within each group could be dealt with on a very personal, yet professional, level. Moreover, the judge would also function as a shepherd keeping watch over his sheep, to keep them free from serious sin, and encouraging them to "love God with all their hearts" and to "love their neighbors as themselves." I'm sure that God also intended each judge and each accountability group to take some degree of pleasure in knowing that their group was particularly "well behaved."

Israel's original census at the time of Moses was about six hundred thousand males over age twenty. Presuming that each male over age twenty had his own wife and children (his own separate nuclear family), then this would be about six hundred thousand families in ancient Israel. Now remember, God's command to Moses was to appoint judges over all six hundred thousand families by dividing them into groups of ten families, fifty families, one hundred families, and one thousand families. Therefore, this would account for sixty thousand groups of ten families each, twelve thousand groups of fifty families each, six thousand groups of one hundred families each, and six hundred groups of one thousand families each. And, since there was supposed to be one single judge for every group of families, this would also account for sixty thousand "local" judges over each group of ten families, twelve thousand "mid-level" judges over each group of fifty families, six thousand "high-level" judges over each group of one hundred families, and six hundred "top-level" judges over each group of one thousand families. This would amount to 78,600 judges in Israel who would be involved in this National Hierarchy of Judicial Authority, or 13.1 percent of the total Israelite population of males over age twenty who would be involved in "judging their neighbor's sins"!

Now you are probably thinking, "This is too many judges who would have to know too many laws to be able to do this." However, you must remember four things:

(1) this was God's idea, not mine;
(2) the local and "mid-level" judges would probably only have to learn the most commonly broken principles of civil law, and God's five principles of civil law enforcement;
(3) the local judges could always ask for help from a "higher judge" if they needed to; and
(4) it would still be much easier for the "high level" and "top-level" judges to "master" the mere few hundred laws of God than to "master" the tens of thousands of federal, state, and local laws, regulations, ordinances, and codes which we have here in America!

According to Exodus 18:21 (NIV), the character of these appointed judges had to be above reproach. For to become a judge, you had to be a trustworthy, capable man who feared God and who hated dishonest gain. And, since there were no taxes collected to compensate these judges for their efforts (and they were not supposed to receive "dishonest gain" from those they were judging) then it is clear that God also wanted them all to be volunteers. Being a volunteer (local or lower level) judge was probably not too difficult because it was only a part-time job, and the cases were probably very few. However, being a "higher judge" over one hundred families or one thousand families was almost certainly a full-time job, yet even these "higher judges" were to receive no compensation at all for their more extended efforts. In fact, God most likely intended for this economic hardship to attract only the most righteous, dedicated, selfless, godly men into these positions of authority, where they could serve God by being true "public servants." Many of these dedicated, selfless volunteers, however, would be prepaid by the laws of inheritance which specified that the eldest sons must receive a double portion of inheritance (Deut. 21:17 NIV), in part so they could have the extra time to freely volunteer their services as judges throughout all Israel. As a result, most of the "higher judges" were probably either eldest sons ("supported" by a double portion of inheritance) or independently wealthy Israelites who also happened to be extremely righteous men. Also, by the time the "lower judges" rose to the position of a "higher judge" these men had to be godly "Christian" elders who had developed the expertise in "judging their neighbor" by applying all God's principles of moral law, civil law, and civil law enforcement to this task of judging their group of ten families, and later, after being "promoted," judging their group of fifty families.

So you see, this system was designed by God so the small, "Christian" minority could rule over the large, unrighteous majority. Furthermore, God's principles of civil law were designed to empower the doctrines of "Christianity" with the "legal muscle" to keep the large, unrighteous majority of citizens on their best behavior! Therefore, if the Israelites had obeyed God's commands and had implemented this National Hierarchy of Judicial Authority over the next four hundred years as the population of Israel was growing, then by the time Samuel became old and wanted to "retire" from being a "judge," the Israelite nation should have had well over six hundred godly "Christian" judges with many years experience in judging a thousand families each, who could easily have become judges over all Israel instead of Samuel's two evil sons.

Part of the reason why the Israelite elders asked to have a king to rule over them in I Samuel 8 is that they essentially had NO ONE to take Samuel's place, because they had neglected God's commands and had never built this National Hierarchy of Judicial Authority in the first place. Therefore, they had NO system of national accountability in existence, so it is no wonder that "every man did that which was right in his own eyes" (Judg. 17:6; 21:25 KJV) and that God punished Israel repeatedly for becoming so evil.

This is a great biblical paradox. Evidently, during the four hundred year period of the "Judges," Israel essentially had no judges at all! In other words, as the population grew during the four hundred year period of the "Judges," instead of Israel having 78,600 (or more) total judges to keep the nationwide system of local accountability groups righteous before God, evidently this divine system was never put into place by the Israelites at all—it appears that they only had one main judge at a time over all Israel! This is why (more than five hundred years later) God again reminds the Israelites that he has already "showed them what is good" and that God still requires godly "Christian" men to be involved in this National Hierarchy of Judicial Authority to administer both justice and mercy to those families over which they have been appointed. For it is written:

> He has SHOWED you, O Man, what is good. And what does the Lord require of you? To act justly and to love mercy and to walk humbly with your God. (Mic. 6:8 NIV; emphasis added)

Now the Hebrew word which is translated as "justly" is "mishpât," which means:

> to give a "verdict," pronounced "judicially" as a "formal decree," by either "Man's Law" or "Divine Law." (See *Strong's Exhaustive Concordance*, word # 4941: "mishpât").

In other words, God still required Israel to appoint thousands of righteous Israelite males to "administer justice, according to divine law by giving verdicts, and pronouncing sentences" so they could function as judges. And, the fact that God reminds Israel about this responsibility five hundred years later shows the eternal nature of these commands and that God still requires godly Christian elders to be involved in the administration of justice, tempered with mercy in some sort of voluntary, tax-free, National Hierarchy of Judicial Authority even today.

This same point is also made twice more in the New Testament several centuries into the future. The first time is when Jesus Christ is asked by "someone in the crowd" to "tell his brother to divide the inheritance with him." Jesus' response harkens back to this same ancient law—that God still wants righteous men to be appointed as judges over various numbers of families. For it is written:

> Jesus replied, "Man, who appointed me a judge or arbiter between you?" (Luke 12:14 NIV)

Jesus was perfectly willing to accept his "patriotic responsibility" of being a judge over a number of families (including this man's family), but first he needed to know who appointed him to this role. Everyone in the crowd knew that the National Hierarchy of Judicial Authority (NHJA) had been abandoned long ago and that the Pharisees of Israel had all but forgotten these laws, so there were basically no judges in the system who could have appointed Jesus of Nazareth to be judge over this man's family anyway! Therefore, since it was not this man's fault that the NHJA had been neglected for so many generations, Jesus simply changed the subject and taught a lesson about greed and the mistaken priorities of life.

But when it came to the Pharisees themselves, Jesus harshly rebuked them for allowing Israel to continue to neglect the commands of God concerning the administration of justice tempered with mercy. For it is written:

> You give a tenth of your spices-mint, dill, and cumin. But you have *neglected* the more important matters of the law— *justice, mercy,* and *faithfulness* ... You blind guides! (Matt. 23:23b, 24a NIV; emphasis added)

Here, Jesus teaches that Jehovah still requires the biblical principles of justice and mercy to be regularly enforced by men of faith, even though more than twelve hundred years have elapsed since Jethro first gave this idea of God to Moses. For, this is still the only way to have sound and virtuous government, and it is still the only way to establish this National Hierarchy of Judicial Authority within Israel as the key to voluntary self-government without the need for taxes. Therefore, this is an eternal command for Israel even today!

Jesus also says that those leaders who neglect the "more important matters of the law" are to be called "blind guides." Furthermore, Jesus also says that the "more important matters of the law" are divided into two parts: (a) "justice and mercy," and (b) "faith." The principles of justice and mercy which Christ is talking about in this verse are God's principles of civil law!

I recognize that our Christian leaders have great faith in Christ and are more surrendered to God than were the ancient Pharisees. Regardless of their great faith however, when Christian leaders act as the Pharisees and neglect the importance that God's principles of civil law (God's principles of justice and mercy) have for the administration of sound and virtuous government, then they are just as blind as the Pharisees were for ignoring the biblical principles of civil law which could have prevented the corruption of our government and our nation! Because of this, Christ would label them as "blind guides," just like he labeled the Pharisees two thousand years ago!

So, in both the Old and the New Testaments, the Bible teaches us that God's LAWS are both necessary and sufficient for the administration of sound and virtuous government and need to be adopted and regularly enforced by God's leaders. Furthermore, those who neglect the importance that God's civil laws have for the administration of sound and virtuous government are actually neglecting God's principles of justice and mercy and as such would be called "blind guides" by Christ, even today!

PRINCIPLE TWENTY—Christian leaders who neglect the importance that God's principles of civil law have for the administration of sound and virtuous government are considered by Christ to be "blind guides"!

PRINCIPLE TWENTY-ONE—All the other functions which modern government ordinarily provides are either somehow accomplished by the other biblical principles of civil law which are listed in this book, or have to be accomplished either through:

(A) community cooperation and voluntary participation,
(B) private enterprise, or
(C) supernatural divine intervention!

(All these other functions of government will be discussed in their respective chapters.)

In summary, God's view of government reform includes all the following principles:

1. God's principles of civil law must be the foundation for all national legislation;

2. God's laws are both necessary and sufficient for sound and virtuous government;

3. Man's laws are inferior to God's laws and are largely unnecessary and superfluous for the administration of sound and virtuous government;

4. All top government leaders must handwrite their own copy of God's civil laws, keep it with them at all times, and read it in depth each day;

5. Only godly "Christian" elders should ever be allowed to serve in government;

6. All rulers should pray to God for the "Gift of Governments," which is God's gift of a wise and discerning heart to enable God's leaders to administer God's laws;

7. Impeach, prosecute, and punish all leaders who have committed serious personal sins while in office, or who have approved legislation which clearly increases national sins;

8. There are no term limits for godly Christian elders who serve well and who remain "above reproach." They can serve in government for their entire lives;

9. It is the responsibility of Christian leaders to repeal all oppressive legislation and replace it with legislation based upon God's compassionate principles of civil law;

10. God does not consider laws against sexual immorality, drunkenness, non-biblical divorce, or working on Sunday, etc. to be "oppressive." Nor does God consider any of his other civil laws to be oppressive either;

11. Government must be kept as small as possible;

12. Government must be kept as decentralized as possible;

13. Government must be kept as unintrusive as possible;

14. Government-owned real estate must be kept to an absolute minimum.

15. Taxes must be kept as small as possible, and any taxes which must be collected should be based upon income only, for the Bible does not allow taxes on property or on sales. Furthermore, this tax must be a flat tax on income (not a "graduated" tax) because God's tithe was a flat tithe on "income" (not a "graduated" tithe).

16. God's civil laws are designed to enable the small Christian minority to rule over the large, unrighteous majority;

17. God's civil laws allow the doctrines of "Christianity" to be empowered with the "legal muscle to keep the large, unrighteous majority of citizens on their best behavior; and

18. Christian leaders who neglect the importance that God's principles of civil law have for the administration of sound and virtuous government are considered by Christ to be "blind guides" (just like the Pharisees).

If America can learn the importance of these first eighteen principles and adopt them into our national legislation, then we will have changed America from a secular, atheistic democracy into a Christian Republic! For then we will have a government without scandal, corruption, or gridlock, staffed by dedicated Christians who are "above reproach" and who know how to apply all God's principles of civil law in all political situations. We will also have small, decentralized, unintrusive government supported by a minimal flat income tax. Furthermore, the natural blessings of adopting God's principles of civil law into our government will be a nation of greater health, peace, and prosperity!

However, if we choose to adopt the remainder of God's principles of civil law which are listed in this book (and become a theocracy as well as a Christian Republic) then America can also develop a National Hierarchy of Judicial Authority—staffed totally by volunteers who are prepaid by the laws of inheritance, to administer a nationwide system of local accountability groups, each comprised of one real judge and ten families, who can begin to take pleasure in having a "well behaved" group. This system will so increase the aggregate righteousness of America that we can finally exceed the threshold of righteousness established by God as a requirement for all nations. Then we can become eligible for God to grant America the supernatural blessings of a nearly crime-free, war-free, poverty-free, tax-free, inflation-free, natural disaster-free, and disease-free society, where nearly everyone lives to be 120-years-old while enjoying perfect health!

And that is God's view of government reform!

 *Chapter Six*

GOD'S VIEW OF CENSORSHIP VERSUS THE FIRST AMENDMENT FREEDOM OF SPEECH
(SEE ALSO CHAPTER TWO)

An employee of mine told me a story which happened to her when she was only 4-years-old. With her permission, I am sharing this story with you because it illustrates the consequences of obeying the letter of the law (what someone *says*) while disobeying the spirit of the law (what someone *means*).

>Two little girls, ages four and six, were told by their mother, "You cannot go to swim in the pool until your older brother comes home." But the girls noticed that their mother did not say that their brother had to *accompany* them to the pool. So, when their brother came home (and did not want to take them to the pool), the little girls quietly left and went to the pool unaccompanied by their brother. This made their mother very angry when she learned of their disobedience, especially because only two years earlier their eight year old sister had wandered off and had accidently drowned in a local pond. And so the mother punished the little girls for their deliberate disobedience.

My employee (who was the 4-year-old girl) tells me that she and her 6-year-old sister knew they were deliberately disobeying their mother, but they thought they could "get away with it" because they did exactly what their mother *said*, even though they were not doing what their mother *meant*.

These two little girls obeyed the letter of the law (what their mother said) but disobeyed the spirit of the law (what their mother meant)! You see, because they had disobedience and rebellion in their hearts that day, they knowingly and deliberately misinterpreted their mother's rules to their own satisfaction. In other words, the idea that "the letter of the law is more important than the spirit of the law" is a motto for those who intend to deliberately disobey the spirit of the law and for those who want to get others to disobey it with them.

Unfortunately, our Supreme Court judges have adopted this same childish view of the law—that the letter of the law (what the founders *said*) is more important than the spirit of the law (what the founders *meant*)! Because of this childish bias, they have knowingly and deliberately misinterpreted several of the first ten amendments (the Bill of Rights) in order to legally allow our citizens to disobey the spirit of the law. This interpretation dishonors God and dishonors the intentions of our founders. In fact, the misuse of the Bill of Rights by our courts has indirectly either endorsed or encouraged a flood of pornography, sexual immorality, drunkenness, national violence, courtroom injustice, and overcrowded prisons. As a result, this same document which the founders designed to preserve America's Christian heritage is now being used to destroy it.

So, without further introduction, let us examine what the Bible says about God's view of censorship and the First Amendment freedom of speech. The First Amendment says (among other things):

> Congress shall make no law . . . abridging the freedom of speech, or of the press . . .

When our Christian founders wrote the First Amendment, they surely did not want this legislation to either dishonor God or to increase sinful behavior. In other words, they were not trying to legalize "sinful speech," nor were they trying to legalize speech or other forms of expression which would exalt, condone, or encourage sin. The philosophy of the founders was that the First Amendment should protect the kind of speech that God would want to protect, not protect the kind of speech which Satan would want to protect. We know this to be true because many of the writings of our founders exalted God's Word (the Bible) as the infallible source of eternal truth. Furthermore, many of our early court rulings exalted God's Word as the primary source of America's Christian form of government. So you would expect the founders to exalt what God would exalt, and condemn what God would condemn!

For instance, since God condemns blasphemy in the Bible, you would expect the founders to condemn blasphemy in the courts. And in fact, within the thirty-three years after the Bill of Rights was ratified in 1791, both the New York State Supreme Court (in 1811) and the Pennsylvania State Supreme Court (in 1824) still confirmed that "blasphemy" was NOT a protected right under the First Amendment (Barton, *Myth*, 51-58). So, it was clearly not the founders' intention to write an amendment to protect and exalt forms of speech which God himself would condemn. But, for those with childish rebellion and disobedience in their hearts (liberal judges and liberal voters), to this day they continue to deliberately misinterpret the First Amendment to their own satisfaction, because they want to legally be able to disobey the laws of God and encourage others to disobey with them!

According to twentieth century liberals, what the founders actually *said* is more important than what the founders *meant!* And so therefore, they claim that the actual wording of the First Amendment sounds like the founders wanted all citizens to legally be able to speak or write any conceivable evil thought which came to mind. Their bias to legally allow American citizens to sin against God has filled our nation with all kinds of sin, vice, and corruption. But the First Amendment was not designed to protect (and thereby promote) blasphemy, cursing, obscene language, obscene jokes, or pornography. Neither was it designed to protect speech which exalts sin or exalts anti-biblical ideas such as fornication, adultery, homosexuality, abortion, radical feminism, drunkenness, drug abuse, racial prejudice, evolution, violence, revenge, anarchy, terrorism, or bomb-making. For again, the founders wanted to protect the kind of speech, writing, or expression which God himself would want to protect. And they wanted to condemn the kind of speech, writing, or expression which God himself would condemn.

So, what types of speech does God condemn? Well, in the Bible, God condemns all the following types of "sinful speech":

1. "taking God's name in vain" (Exod. 20:7 KJV)
2. "blasphemy" & "cursing God" (Lev. 24:15, 16 NIV)
3. "cursing your parents" (Lev. 20:9 NIV)
4. "cursing your parents" (Matt. 15:4 NIV) (condemned in both the Old and the New Testament)
5. "swearing" (Matt. 5:34, 37 NIV)
6. "obscenity & dirty jokes" (Eph. 5:4 NIV)

Not only does God condemn "sinful speech" in the Bible, but God also condemns speech which encourages others to sin, or encourages others to "take sin lightly." For instance, in Deuteronomy 13:6-9, God condemns any speech which verbally encourages another person to sin by worshipping idols. God also condemns the type of speech you hear on TV shows which condone and exalt sinful lifestyles. More specifically, the Bible teaches that it is shameful and inappropriate to casually speak about sinful lifestyles (presumably because this implies that we condone them). For it is written:

> For it is shameful even to mention what the disobedient do in secret. (Eph. 5:12 NIV)

In other words, the Bible teaches that sinful lifestyles should not be spoken of casually without the biblical framework of identifying and condemning the sin, and encouraging confession, repentance, and justice (tempered with a love of mercy).

This means that God also disapproves of TV shows which condone or praise sinful lifestyles and discuss them as if God's condemnation of sexual immorality is irrelevant. In fact, some of these TV shows even encourage their audiences to take sin so lightly that they foolishly poke fun at sexual immorality, rather than condemn it as a sin against God and a crime against the state. For it is written:

> Fools make a mock at sin. (Prov. 14:9 KJV)

These TV shows also grieve God by encouraging obscenity, dirty jokes, or foolish talk (gossiping about sexual immorality rather than condemning it). It is written:

> Nor should there be obscenity, foolish talk or coarse joking, which are out of place. (Eph. 5:4 NIV)

> Do not let any unwholesome talk come out of your mouths. (Eph. 4:29 NIV)

> Put away perversity from your mouth; keep corrupt talk far from you lips. (Prov. 4:24 NIV)

In other words, the Bible gives our lawmakers and judges all the guidance they need to understand the limits which God himself would legally place on "Freedom of Speech." In fact, it is also equally clear that God wants our lawmakers to place legal restrictions on music and songs which contain words which encourage lust, fornication, adultery, homosexuality, drunkenness, drug abuse, suicide, homicide, anarchy, and Satan worship.

So you see, America's founders knew that God did not condone totally unrestrained "Freedom of Speech." Furthermore, they also knew that God will hold men accountable beyond the grave on Judgement Day for every careless word they have spoken (or written) in the name of "Freedom of Speech" or "Freedom of the Press"! For it is written:

> But I tell you that men will have to give account on the day of judgement for every careless *word* they have spoken. For by your *words* you will be acquitted, and by your *words* you will be condemned. (Matt. 12:36, 37 NIV; emphasis added)

In the 1990s, this verse means that God will now hold men accountable for every careless word they have spoken, written, filmed, or broadcasted, as well as every careless word which our lawmakers and judges have legally encouraged to be spoken, written, filmed, or broadcasted through their deliberate anti-biblical interpretation of the First Amendment.

Don't play the same game with God's Word which you play with the First Amendment! Don't think that the letter of God's law (the actual words Christ said) is more important than the spirit of God's law (what Christ meant)! If you mindlessly think that in this verse God only means the spoken word, and not the written word, the filmed word, or the broadcasted word, or that God will not hold you responsible for any other forms of expression (such as pornographic dancing, art, or movies) which is sinful and may cause others to sin, then you are being just as foolish as the little girls in the earlier story (who deliberately tried to misinterpret the words of their mother so they could get away with their disobedience). For they got punished for their disobedience, and so will you be!

It is clear enough in this verse that God will hold our lawmakers accountable beyond the grave for passing any bad law which exalts, condones, or encourages sin and will hold our judges accountable as well for every deliberate misinterpretation and distortion of the First Amendment which has had the same effect of exalting, condoning, or encouraging sin in our nation. He will also hold our TV show hosts, movie and stage actors, writers, directors, producers, and sponsors accountable for the part they have played in supporting and encouraging sinful speech and sinful lifestyles in America. For God's wrath on Judgment Day will be determined not just by what God *said*, but also by what God *meant!*

In summary, America's founders did not want to legalize blasphemy, cursing, obscenity, or pornography, or legalize speech, writing, or art which encourages fornication, adultery, homosexuality, or drunkenness. In fact, if our founders were alive today, they would immediately repeal and rewrite the First Amendment to outlaw all the above mentioned problems and so bring the exact wording of the First Amendment to be in line with God's commands. And, just as our founders would feel that their "godly mission" is to write God-honoring laws, so also our modern lawmakers need to be involved in this same "godly mission," and so outlaw all forms of speech, writing, songs, art, and movies which either represent "sinful speech" or which represent speech which condones, exalts, or encourages sin in our neighborhood and in our nation!

And THAT is God's view of the First Amendment, according to the Bible!

(The "Freedom of Religion" part of the First Amendment will be discussed in chapter sixteen.)

Chapter Seven

God's View of Sexual Immorality Versus The Fourth Amendment Right of Privacy

The Fourth Amendment reads:

> The right of the people to be secure in their persons, houses, papers, and effects, against unreasonable searches and seizures, shall not be violated, and no Warrants shall issue, but upon probable cause, supported by Oath or affirmation, and particularly describing the place to be searched, and the persons or things to be seized.

This amendment to the Constitution was originally designed to prevent "unreasonable search and seizure" of a man's property in his own home. However, modern lawmakers and courts now purposely exaggerate the Fourth Amendment "Right of Privacy" in order to permit fornication, adultery, and homosexuality with immunity from prosecution as a crime.

But is this what our founders really intended? Of course not!

You see, our Christian founders believed that God commanded Israel to regularly prosecute sexual immorality as a crime against the state. For it is written:

> If a man commits adultery with another man's wife—with the wife of his neighbor—both the adulterer and the adulteress must be put to death. . . . If a man lies with a man as one lies with a woman. . . . They must be put to death; their blood will be on their own heads. (Lev. 20:10, 13 NIV)

And again:

> If a man is found sleeping with another man's wife, both the man who slept with her and the women must die. (Deut. 22:22 NIV)

In this latter verse, you will notice that being "found" committing adultery "in private," does not provide any sort if immunity at all from being prosecuted for sexual immorality. God makes his point even more evident in a story about a married man who deliberately brings his lover into his house right in front of the tent of meeting where many Israelite elders were gathered together in mourning about the ongoing immorality in Israel. This story again illustrates the idea that man's notions about a "Right to Privacy" cannot provide immunity from prosecution for breaking God's laws about sexual immorality. This passage reveals that, as long as the authorities have a high degree of suspicion that an act of fornication, adultery, or homosexuality is occurring at that very moment within the privacy of a person's own house, that God himself is pleased when the local authorities enter that person's house in order to catch the couple, even if this requires that the authorities enter the house without the owner's consent, or even without the owner's knowledge. For it is written:

> While Israel was staying in Shittim, the men began to indulge in sexual immorality with Moabite women, who invited them to the sacrifices to their gods ... So Israel joined in worshipping the Baal of Peor. And the Lord's anger burned against them.
>
> The Lord said to Moses, "Take all the leaders of the people, kill them ..."
>
> So Moses said to Israel's judges, "Each of you must put to death those of your men who have joined in worshipping the Baal of Peor."
>
> Then an Israelite man brought to his family a Midianite woman right before the eyes of Moses and the whole assembly of Israel while they were weeping at the entrance to the Tent of Meeting. When Phinehas ... saw this, he left the assembly, took a spear in his hand, and followed the Israelite into the tent. He drove the spear through both of them—through the Israelite and into the woman's body. Then the plague was stopped ...
>
> The Lord said to Moses, "Phinehas ... has turned my anger away from the Israelites; for he was as zealous as I am for my honor among them ..." (Num. 25:1, 2a, 3, 4a, 5-8 NIV)

This story has direct application for America today. For the leaders of both ancient Israel and modern America have mistakenly concluded that man's "Right of Privacy" overrules God's commands against sexual immorality. The Lord's anger now burns against America just as hotly as it once burned against ancient Israel for allowing the rate of sexual immorality in America to skyrocket because of a nationwide lack of prosecution of sexual immorality as a crime against the state. Moreover, just as sexual immorality caused a plague in ancient Israel which killed twenty-four thousand Israelites, so also has sexual immorality caused a plague of sexually transmitted diseases in America, killing hundreds of thousands with AIDS and cervical cancer (cervical cancer is now known to be a sexually transmitted disease caused by the human papilloma virus).

Meanwhile, the leaders of both ancient Israel and modern America sit idly by, weeping over our national immorality and praying to God to give us an answer, while ignoring the solution which God gave us thirty-five hundred years ago:

> Make sexual immorality illegal again and regularly prosecute the offenders according to God's commands in the Bible.

But does America have any leader, lawyer, lawmaker, or judge who will be the first to make sexual immorality illegal again and start prosecuting this crime as the founders intended and as God commands? Who in America is willing to take the risk Phinehas took—the risk of being scorned, mocked, and ridiculed by his fellow leaders, priests, and judges, for doing what is right according to God's commands? Just as Phinehas had to take the first step in ancient Israel before the other leaders would follow in his footsteps and prosecute sexual immorality so God would stop the plague, so also America needs its own Phinehas to take the first step on our soil so other American leaders can follow his footsteps and prosecute sexual immorality so God will stop our plague of sexually transmitted diseases as well. And God will be so pleased with the American leader, lawyer, lawmaker, or judge who finally takes the first "leap of faith" to prosecute sexual immorality that God will credit this obedience as an act of righteousness to his "heavenly account." For it is written:

> But Phinehas stood up and intervened, and the plague was checked. This was credited to him as righteousness for endless generations to come. (Ps. 106:30-31 NIV)

Generally, we hear preachers say that only faith can be reckoned as righteousness, as in the case of Abram. For it is written:

> Abram believed the Lord, and he credited it to him as righteousness ... (Gen. 15:6 NIV)

However, rarely do we hear our preachers say that enforcing God's principles of civil law will also be credited as righteousness according to Psalm 106:30-31 (as noted above). In other words, both faith alone, and the faith which inspires obedience in our leaders to regularly enforce God's principles of civil law (to keep the unrighteous majority of

American citizens on their best behavior) will be credited by almighty God as righteousness to the "heavenly accounts" of the first faithful leaders who are willing to take these important steps. You see, if our preachers had always taught us the complete truth about this issue, and if our Christian leaders had always understood that enforcing God's principles of civil law would be credited to them as righteousness, then our leaders would never have become so deluded as to think that the Fourth Amendment "Right of Privacy" should provide immunity from prosecution for fornication, adultery, and homosexuality. Therefore, sexual immorality would never have gotten out of control in America because it would have been regularly prosecuted as a crime against the state as the founders intended and as God commands.

And so, just as the First Amendment Freedom of Speech was not designed to legalize blasphemy (see previous chapter) so also the Fourth Amendment "Right of Privacy" was not designed to legalize sexual immorality behind closed doors. Furthermore, there is actually nothing in the Fourth Amendment to prevent our ancestors from searching a house and seizing a couple caught in committing adultery or homosexuality anyway!

So, don't call yourself a Christian prosecuting attorney, or a Christian judge if you are willing to allow sexual immorality to go unprosecuted and unpunished in your jurisdiction. And don't call yourself a Christian lawmaker unless you are willing make sure that sexual immorality is illegal in your state and that there are laws to make sure that fornication, adultery, and homosexuality are regularly prosecuted as crimes. And of course, the same is true for drunkenness.

Our Christian leaders, lawyers, lawmakers, and judges must be willing to be mocked and scorned for Christ, just as Christ was mocked and scorned for them. Moreover, they must realize that the degree to which they are insulted, persecuted, and lied about for obeying the commands of Christ will to some degree increase their rewards in heaven. For it is written:

> Blessed are you when men insult you, persecute you and falsely say all kinds of evil against you because of me. Rejoice and be glad, because *great* is your reward in heaven, for in the same way they persecuted the prophets who were before you. (Matt. 5:11-12 NIV; emphasis added)

When will we finally see a leader of the House of Representatives say:

> Choose this day whom you will serve. If Christ is Lord, then serve him.
>
> Who is on the Lord's side today? Let him come forward now and publicly pledge his allegiance to serve God as a Christian lawmaker as long as he holds this office.

And let us all then make a public covenant with almighty God, that God's laws, will once again be America's laws!

I know not what course the Senate may take, but (in the words of Joshua) as for me and my House (of Representatives) we will serve the Lord!

Who is on the Lord's side? Are you?

In summary, the Fourth Amendment "Right of Privacy" was not intended by the founders to overrule God's command against sexual immorality, nor was it designed to provide sexual immorality with immunity from prosecution. Moreover, God wants every Christian leader, lawyer, lawmaker, and judge to risk the displeasure of his peers in order to gain the pleasure of God, and so take whatever steps are necessary within his own jurisdiction and sphere of influence to make sure that sexual immorality becomes a regularly prosecuted crime against the state. By doing this, God will credit this obedience as an act of righteousness to his heavenly account!

And that is God's view of sexual immorality and the Fourth Amendment "Right of Privacy"!

Chapter Eight

GOD'S VIEW OF MERCY FOR CRIMES "REQUIRING" EXECUTION

Many Christians mistakenly think that Jesus was against capital punishment simply because of His words to the woman taken in adultery. This debate is easily settled, however, by reading Matthew 15:3-4 or Mark 7:9-10. Here, Jesus reinforces the eternal validity of two of God's commands which concern parents and children, and at the same time reveals that he also condones and supports capital punishment. For it is written:

> Jesus replied, "And why do you break the command of God for the sake of your tradition? For God said, 'Honor your father and mother' and 'Anyone who curses his father or mother must be put to death.'" (Matt. 15:3-4; Mark 7:9-10 NIV)

In these verses Jesus is angry at the Pharisees for placing a higher priority on the traditions of man than upon the commands of God. So, he quotes two of God's commands which the Pharisees were evidently ignoring or breaking. Jesus declares that the same God who said "Honor your Father and Mother" also said, "Anyone who curses his father or mother must be put to death," thus teaching the Pharisees that both of these commands of God were still equally and eternally valid, even though more than a thousand years had passed since God gave these commands to Moses. Therefore, in this passage, Jesus clearly and unequivocally supports the death penalty.

What makes this verse even more interesting, however, is that Jesus is supporting the death penalty for the mere verbal sin of cursing your parents, which is the *least* of the death penalties in all recorded Scripture! To understand this point more clearly, I have prepared a list of the eighteen biblical death penalties in the approximate order of what might appear to be the "most criminal" physical sins down to "least criminal" verbal sins. These are as follows:

The Sin	The punishment	*Mercy?*	Reference
1. Idolatry	death	Show NO mercy*	Deut. 13:6-11
2. Murder	death	Show NO mercy*	Deut. 19:11-13
3. Kidnapping	death	May show mercy	Exod. 21:16
4. Adultery	death	May show mercy	Lev. 20:10
5. Promiscuity (fornication with at least one other person preceding marriage to someone else)	death	May show mercy	Deut. 22:13-21
6. Prostitution	death	May show mercy	Lev. 21:9
7. Homosexuality	death	May show mercy	Lev. 20:13
8. Bestiality	death	May show mercy	Exod. 22:19
9. Witchcraft	death	May show mercy	Exod. 22:18
10. Working on Sabbath	death	May show mercy	Exod. 31:15
11. Drunkenness	death	May show mercy	Deut. 21:18-21
12. Profligate	death	May show mercy	Deut. 21:18-21
13. Attacking your parents	death	May show mercy	Exod. 21.15
14. Reckless endangerment of an adult which causes death	death	May show mercy	Exod. 21:28-29
15. Reckless endangerment of the life of a fetus which causes its death (an accidental abortion)	death	May show mercy	Exod. 21:22-23
16. Cursing God/ Blasphemy	death	May show mercy	Lev. 24:15-16
17. Cursing a Judge (contempt of Court)	death	May show mercy	Deut. 17:12-13
18. Cursing your parents	death	May show mercy	Exod. 21:17

---

*Please note that it is written: "Show him NO pity" (NIV) in both Deuteronomy 13:8 and Deuteronomy 19:13 for the crimes of idolatry and murder, respectively. But this expression—"Show him NO pity"—is conspicuously *absent* for all other crimes involving the death penalty, with the possible exception of "bearing false witness," which will be discussed later on. Therefore, since the Holy Spirit purposely avoided using the expression—"Show him NO pity"— for any capital crime other than idolatry and murder, then God is confirming that judges should "Show mercy" if at all possible for all the other crimes associated with the death penalty. That is why I have concluded and therefore have written that the judge "May show mercy" for the crimes numbered three through eighteen.

After reading this list, it should become much easier to envision that, since Jesus supports the death penalty for the mere verbal crime of "cursing your parents," then he clearly supports all the other death penalties for the far more serious crimes as well.

God commands judges to love to show mercy. For it is written:

> ... what does the Lord require of you? To act justly and to love mercy ... (Mic. 6:8 NIV)

God also says that true justice actually involves showing mercy and compassion! For it is written:

> This is what the Lord Almighty says: "Administer true justice; show mercy and compassion to one another." (Zech. 7:9 NIV)

So, despite the fact that there are eighteen death penalties recorded in the Bible, God evidently does not take pleasure in the death of the wicked. Instead, God takes pleasure when the wicked repent in the courtroom so the judge can show God's mercy and allow the criminal to live. For it is written:

> Do I take any pleasure in the death of the wicked? declares the Sovereign Lord. Rather, am I not pleased when they turn from their ways and live? ... For I take no pleasure in the death of anyone, declares the Sovereign Lord. Repent and live! (Ezek. 18:23, 32 NIV)

God's purpose in creating these eighteen death penalties was not so he could execute every Israelite who committed adultery or homosexuality, etc. Rather, God's purpose was to prosecute them and provide them with the opportunity in court to recognize that they had sinned against God, so they could confess, repent, and be forgiven by God and the judge, in order that they might live, and not have to be executed. If this was the criminal's first offense or if he were extremely young, then the judge might send him home with no punishment at all, and only warn him to "go and sin no more." For it is written:

> In every case that comes before you ... you are to warn them not to sin ... (2 Chron. 19:10 NIV)

If, however, this was the criminal's second or third offense (yet he still appeared to be humbly repentant and was begging forgiveness from God and the judge), then the judge may still allow him to live, but may instead give him a whipping (from a mere one lash, up to a maximum of forty lashes) as a merciful alternative to execution. For it is written:

> When men have a dispute, they are to take it to court and the judges will decide the case, acquitting the innocent and con-

demning the guilty. If the guilty man deserves to be beaten, the judge shall make him lie down and have him flogged in his presence with the number of lashes his crime deserves, but he must not be given more than 40 lashes. (Deut. 25:1-3 NIV)

Here, God gives the command to whip those convicted of certain crimes, yet Scripture neither specifies which crimes deserve whipping, nor does it specify how many lashes should be given for each crime. Therefore, it is clear that God was allowing the Israelite judges to use whipping at their own discretion, either as a merciful alternative to execution, or for miscellaneous crimes where the Bible does not give a specific penalty. Moreover, God intended the whipping to be done right in front of the judge, probably so the judge could hear any further cries for mercy, and probably also so the judge could inspect the criminal's back to insure that no serious physical injury was occurring. In this way, the judge could stop the whipping at any point so he could demonstrate even more of the mercy of God. Therefore, because of God's emphasis on mercy, it is clear that God would not want these "biblical whips" to be designed as instruments of cruelty and torture—with stones, bones, metal, or glass sewn into the whip to tear and rip the flesh of their victims. Instead, God probably wanted these whips merely to serve as simple instruments of pain which would never cause any serious or permanent injury at all.

Man's philosophy for deterring crime reserves the threat of execution only for hard-core criminals, and completely hides the threat of execution from all the other lesser criminals. But God's philosophy for deterring violent crime and sexual immorality evidently involves bringing the death penalty "right up front" as the standard punishment for most serious crimes (except for stealing). In this way, the judges are required to show mercy if at all possible, unless Scripture absolutely forbids showing mercy (as in the case of idolatry and premeditated murder, where death was the mandatory punishment). In all other cases however, death was the maximum punishment, but not the mandatory punishment.

Thus, God's courtroom philosophy of "up front" death penalties not only provides a much greater deterrent to violent crime, sexual immorality, and drunkenness, but also transforms courtroom tradition from one of punishment to one of mercy in the face of a death penalty. In other words, after the sinner is convicted, instead of the judge trying to decide how much punishment to give, he now has to decide how much mercy to give. In this way, God intended each courtroom to develop a "Ministry of Mercy." Furthermore, in the next chapter you will learn how God intended each courtroom to develop a "Ministry of

Restoration" as well, by attempting to restore each criminal back into a right relationship with God and the community of believers.

In summary, Christ supported the death penalty in the context of a courtroom "Ministry of Mercy" and "Ministry of Restoration," creating a divine standard for all future courts to exalt mercy over execution, so "mercy can triumph over judgement" (James 2:13b NIV). Therefore, it is clear that Christ never abolished the death penalty, just as Christ never abolished any other laws of God, according to what is written:

> Do not think that I have come to abolish the Law ... I have not come to abolish them ... (Matt. 5:17 NIV)

Some Christians, however, mistakenly conclude that even though Christ never abolished the law, he still either voided it or made it worthless by "fulfilling" it—as if somehow the moment the law was "fulfilled," God's civil laws suddenly became powerless to keep the unrighteous majority on their best behavior and suddenly lost their superior advantages for the administration of sound and virtuous government.

Christ anticipated that Christians would distort what he was saying about the law. So, just after Christ stated (in verse seventeen) that he would never *abolish* the law, he then stated (in verse eighteen) that he would never *change* the law either! For in verse eighteen Christ specified that every single letter in the entire law would remain in effect forever, and would never be changed or nullified under any circumstances, until heaven and earth passed away at the end of the upcoming thousand-year reign of Christ on earth. For it is written:

> I tell you the truth, until heaven and earth disappear, not the smallest letter, not the least stroke of a pen, will by any means disappear from the Law. (Matt. 5:18 NIV)

If you change the words in a law, those words disappear from that law, and are replaced by other words. But Christ is saying that not even the smallest letter of a single word will disappear from the law until heaven and earth pass away. Therefore, Christ is teaching all generations of all Christians that no part of the law will ever be changed in any way whatsoever, but will remain in effect forever. After all, it was Christ himself who originally gave these laws to Moses in the first place (when Christ was in the form of the pre-incarnate Jehovah), so why would Jesus disagree with himself later on and change his mind? That doesn't make any sense, now does it? Moreover, it is blasphemy to think that Christ's work (of giving these wonderful laws to Moses) was flawed! For if Christ was only capable of writing an imperfect set of laws for Moses which he didn't realize would have to be changed later on, then this means that Christ was not "all-knowing"! Furthermore, if Christ deliberately gave us an inferior set of laws which he knew could not solve the problems of national government, and he purposely withheld his best laws (which he would only reveal to us during his upcoming thousand-year reign on earth), then Christ was not "all-loving"! In other words, if Christ changed any of the Mosaic laws at any time, then either Christ was not wise enough to write a perfect set of laws the first time, or he was not loving enough to give us the best of his laws which he had written, and therefore purposely gave us a defective set of laws which would have to be improved upon.

Thankfully, the Scriptures of both the Old and the New Testament reveal to us that God gave Moses a perfect set of laws which "he intended to be valid forever." For it is written:

> Long ago I learned from your statutes that you established them to last forever. (Ps. 119:152 NIV)
>
> All your righteous laws are eternal. (Ps. 119:160b NIV)
>
> Your statutes are forever right. (Ps. 119:144 NIV)

So, both David (in the Old Testament) and Christ (in the New Testament) say that all the principles underlying God's civil laws (even the smallest and least significant of these principles) are not only still valid today but will never be changed for any reason whatsoever and will remain in effect throughout all time until heaven and earth pass away.

With this in mind, let us re-examine God's laws of courtroom procedure so that we can set the stage for the story of the woman who was caught in the very act of adultery and who was brought to Jesus for trial (John 8:1-11). In doing this we can demonstrate how Christ could follow both the letter of the law and the spirit of the law and be both just and merciful at the same time!

(Please reread John 8:1-11 in your Bible (NIV) before continuing, because the story is too long to quote here.)

In this story, we must recognize that when Christ said, "If any one of you be without sin, let him be the first to throw a stone at her," he was not trying to skip the trial and go straight to the execution, for that would have been a grievous sin for any judge. Jesus was merely challenging the eyewitnesses to read the laws of God which he had just written on the ground. He was also warning them that during the trial they must obey these laws completely, which meant that they must "be without sin" against these laws. In this way, the eyewitnesses would be able to testify accurately and safely and not get themselves into trouble with the court, and therefore they could remain eligible to throw the first stones.

You see, more than five hundred years earlier, God spoke through Jehoshaphat and commanded judges to warn witnesses that they must be without sin during trial proceedings. For it is written:

> In every case that comes before you . . . you are to warn [the witnesses] not to sin against the Lord. (2 Chron. 19:10 NIV)

The reason for this command was simple: God did not want anyone to bear false witness against his neighbor in a courtroom. In fact, God's punishment for being a malicious witness was to "do to the witness, what the witness wanted to be done to his brother—life for life, eye for eye . . ." For it is written:

> If the witness proves to be a liar, . . . then do to him as he intended to do to his brother. . . . *Show NO pity:* life for life, eye for eye . . . (Deut. 19:18, 19, 21 NIV; emphasis added)

Please note that God's punishment for bearing false witness in a courtroom contained the command to "show no pity"—a command which was conspicuously absent from all God's other death penalties, with the exception of idolatry and murder, as we have discussed earlier. This extra phrase to "show no mercy" often made the crime of bearing false witness more serious than the crime for which the defendant was being accused in the first place. This was because ordinarily for most other crimes the judge was allowed, and actually required, to show mercy if at all possible. Furthermore, God also commanded that if a witness failed to tell the judge about something he had seen or learned about which could convict the defendant—especially after being instructed by the judge in a public charge to reveal what he knows to be the truth—then the witness could also be held responsible by the judge for failing to follow court procedure and give truthful testimony about what he really saw. For it is written:

> If a person sins because he does not speak up when he hears a public charge to testify about something he has seen or learned about, he will be held responsible. (Lev. 5:1 NIV)

Thus a witness could get into trouble for deliberately giving false testimony against a defendant, or for withholding true testimony against or for a defendant. Therefore, before any trial started, all judges had to "spell out" God's law to the eyewitnesses, or else the witnesses themselves might get into more trouble during the trial than the actual defendant was—if the eyewitnesses were caught either testifying about things which they *did not* see, or failing to testify about things which they *did* see.

Another law which Christ would have to "spell out" for the eyewitnesses would be:

> If a man commits adultery with another man's wife . . . both the adulterer and the adulteress must be put to death. (Lev. 20:10 NIV)

This would remind the eyewitnesses that both the woman and the man have to be prosecuted at the same time in all cases of adultery. This is actually the key issue in this case because the Jewish leaders brought the woman to trial, but did not bring the man!

In Deuteronomy 17:7 (NIV), the eyewitnesses were commanded by God to "throw the first stones." Of course, this would be done at the end of the trial—and only if the crime was associated with a death penalty, and if the judge found no reason to be merciful, or if this were a case of idolatry or murder where the judge was not allowed by God to show mercy in the first place. However, false witnesses would be ineligible to throw stones in any case, because they had sinned during the trial and would now be placed on trial themselves. So, only those truthful witnesses who were without sin during the trial would be eligible to throw the first stones.

After the judge revealed to the witnesses the specific laws of God which would be followed during the trial (by writing them on the ground so everyone could refer back to these laws throughout the trial) he would then say something like:

> If any one of you (can testify and) be without sin, (then at the end of the trial) let him be the first to throw a stone at the criminal.

This is exactly what happened when the Pharisees and the teachers of the law brought to Jesus the woman who was caught in the act of adultery by an eyewitnesses. Jesus had to write on the ground the specific laws of God which the eyewitnesses needed to obey so they could testify accurately and safely, and so they could provide Christ (the judge) with the information he needed so he could decide upon the innocence or guilt of the people being accused of adultery. This story is recorded in John 8:1-11, where the Pharisees challenged Christ to put the adulteress on trial to see if he would obey God's laws of justice and courtroom procedure. But the Pharisees themselves were not obeying the laws of courtroom procedure because they neglected to bring the man who was caught in adultery with them so he could be prosecuted along with the woman as the law required.

Now, since Christ generally paraphrased the truths of Old Testament Scriptures and rarely quoted them word-for-word, it is highly likely that what Christ wrote on the ground that day were also paraphrases of the specific laws of God which were most pertinent for courtroom cases about adultery. I believe what Christ wrote went something like this:

> Both the adulterer and the adulteress must be prosecuted and put to death.

> Eyewitnesses will be held responsible if they sin by withholding evidence about something they have seen.
>
> If the witnesses prove to be liars, . . . then do to them as they intended to do to their brother. . . . Show NO pity: life for life (paraphrases of God's laws recorded in Lev. 20:10; 5:1 and Deut. 19:18, 19, 21 NIV)

As the eyewitnesses were reading the three laws which Jesus was writing on the ground, they realized that they themselves were in serious legal trouble. In order to comply with God's laws, they had to tell the entire story and incriminate the man in addition to the woman. However, they did not bring the man to the trial, for evidently they did not intend to accuse him of anything. However, they already admitted to Christ that they caught this woman in the very act of adultery (John 8:4 NIV). If she was caught in the act, then so was he! Therefore, they must also identify him or be held responsible by the judge (Christ) for withholding evidence. Furthermore, if they could not identify the man, then they feared the judge would conclude that they did not truly catch her in the act of adultery. This would make them appear as false witnesses, for which they would all be sentenced to death without mercy.

Jesus then stood and said:

> If any one of you be without sin, let him be the first to throw a stone at her. (John 8:7b NIV)

By this Christ meant:

> If any one of you can tell the entire truth about what you've seen and still be without sin according to the laws I've written on the ground, then let him be the first to throw a stone at her after the trial is over, if I decide not to be merciful.

Christ then bent down again to write one last paraphrased law on the ground. In the meantime, the eyewitnesses began to leave quietly (while Christ was writing the last law on the ground), probably hoping that Christ (the judge) would not notice them leave and so he would not force them to choose between publicly implicating the man as an adulterer or implicating themselves as false witnesses! After the eyewitnesses left, Christ stood again. The final law which Christ had paraphrased on the ground then became visible to the Pharisees and teachers of the law who remained behind. I believe that this final law said:

> The testimony of at least two or three witnesses is required in order to condemn someone to death. (paraphrase of Deut. 17:6)

Then Christ said to the woman:

Woman, where are they? Has no one condemned you?

"No one, sir," she said.

"Then neither do I condemn you," Jesus declared. "Go now and leave your life of sin." (John 8:3a, 4-11 NIV)

By merely writing on the ground the laws of God which were pertinent to cases of adultery, Christ followed the letter of the law in every aspect of the trial. Furthermore, he followed the spirit of the law by looking for (and finding) a reason to show mercy to the woman as well (Mic. 6:8). In other words, Jesus neither abolished nor changed any of the Mosaic laws of justice during the trial. Had Jesus broken any of God's laws during the trial, then he couldn't have remained without sin himself, and therefore his death on the cross could not have atoned for our sins.

It is our ignorance of the details of the Old Testament laws which allows us to come to the erroneous conclusion that Jesus changed the law in this passage. Just as ignorance of God's law causes Christians to mistakenly conclude that Christ changed the law, so also ignorance of God's law caused the Pharisees to mistakenly conclude that Christ broke the law. In fact, the failure of the teachers of the law to anticipate the legal paradox of this story, as well as to foresee the obvious outcome of the trial shows how poorly they understood the practical applications of God's laws in the first place. It should have been obvious to any first year Israelite law student that any time a group of supposed "witnesses" brings a woman before a judge and accuses her of adultery (without bringing the man as well) that the eyewitnesses either have to publicly identify the adulterer, or drop the case before they publicly identify themselves as false witnesses. Evidently, the teachers of the law were only teaching their students to *recite* the law, and not teaching them how to *practice* the law in a courtroom the way God had intended. Hopefully, now that you understand the law better, you will realize that Christ never broke, abolished, or changed any portion of the law at any time, and that God has always wanted judges to show mercy if at all possible, except where the law says otherwise.

Before we end this chapter, I feel I must explain to you why Christ would support a standard penalty of death for children who merely curse or attack their parents (Matt. 15:3-4; Mark 7:9-10; Exod. 21:17; Lev. 20:9 NIV). You see, God encourages parents to physically discipline their children, even with the rod (a "hickory stick") if necessary, according to the book of Proverbs (Prov. 13:24; 22:15; 23:13-14; 29:15 NIV). It is during parental rebuke and/or physical discipline that the most rebellious offspring are tempted to curse or attack their parents.

Christ's plan was to link civil authority with parental authority. This was accomplished by having civil authority *support* parental authority to discipline our children, instead of *undermining* parental authority to discipline our children (which is one of the problems we have in America). God intended these civil laws to help to stop rebellion against parental authority, and to increase obedience and conformity to God's laws. In modern America, in an effort to avoid violent child abuse, our government is foolishly forbidding parents to physically discipline their children—a philosophy which undermines parental authority and can only exacerbate the cultural passion of our youth to further rebel against parental and civil authority. God's laws force both parents and offspring to realize that rebellion against parental authority (by attacking or even cursing parents), changes the nature of the sin from a "family crime" to a "civil crime." Now, the offspring must be brought into civil court for rebellion against authority and face a death sentence!

According to Micah 6:8, the judge is commanded by God to find a reason to be merciful if at all possible. Reasons to be merciful might include any of the following:
"Is the defendant just a child?"
"Is this his first offense?"
"Is he humbly repentant?"
"Is he begging for mercy?"
This means that if the offspring is convicted in court, then he must admit his guilt by confession, repent of his sin, and beg for the judge to show God's mercy on him in order to avoid execution. After going through this process once, you know that this particular offspring will probably never curse or attack his parents again and will be much more submissive to parental rebuke and physical discipline in the future. On the other hand, if this were the rare adolescent who is in court a second time for attacking or cursing his parents and is again facing a standard death sentence for this crime, the judge might give him a few lashes with a whip (as a merciful alternative to execution)—with a warning that if he cursed or attacked his parents again that he would again have to face the death penalty, or at best receive a much more serious whipping as a merciful alternative to execution the next time.

Suppose this was a very large sixteen-year-old boy who had been to court several times for cursing and attacking his father or mother while being physically disciplined. Further, suppose that he has already received as many as twenty lashes for previous convictions of drunkenness, working on the Sabbath, and blasphemy, as well as for actually beating up his father who was only half his size. It is clear that this boy despises parental discipline, but that he needs parental discipline in order to restrain the sins of the flesh. It is for such cases that Christ designed the law to link parental authority with civil authority—to bolster the effect of parental discipline in order to increase obedience and conformity to the laws of God. The judge has spared the boy's life each time in the past because the boy "feigned repentance" in the courtroom, but now he is in court again for cursing his father while being rebuked or disciplined, and he is clearly unrepentant in the courtroom. Furthermore, it is also clear that his previous efforts at repentance were fraudulent, and that he doesn't just disobey God's law, but that he despises God's law. In this case, the judge will likely not be able to find any reason to be merciful, and so this boy will be executed, long before he can become a true menace to society because of his escalating rebellion against the authority of both God and man.

As you can see, God's view of mercy for crimes "requiring" execution involves sixteen crimes which have a standard penalty of death. For each, the judges are required to look for a reason to show mercy, and only reluctantly execute those who willfully, repeatedly, and unrepentantly continue to violate God's laws; thus revealing that these criminals don't just disobey God's laws, but that they actually despise God's laws. For it was not those who merely *disobeyed* God's law, but those who *despised* God's law who were executed without mercy. It is written:

> He that despised Moses' law died without mercy under two or three witnesses . . . (Heb. 10:28 KJV)

God designed these "up-front" death penalties not only to create a much greater deterrent to violent crime, sexual immorality, and drunkenness, but to create a courtroom "Ministry of Mercy" and a "Ministry of Restoration," so sinners can be restored to a right relationship with God and with the community of believers!

And *that* is God's view of mercy for crimes "requiring" execution!

Chapter Nine

GOD'S VIEW OF COURT REFORM VERSUS THE FIFTH AMENDMENT RIGHT NOT TO CONFESS YOUR SINS

In the previous chapter, we discussed how adopting certain biblical laws of courtroom procedure will naturally transform court tradition from one of punishment into one of forgiveness. This results in the development of a courtroom "Ministry of Mercy" *during* the trial. In this chapter, we will discuss how adopting other biblical principles of courtroom procedure will encourage the natural development of a courtroom "Ministry of Restoration" *after* the trial.

The purpose for this courtroom "Ministry of Restoration" is twofold:

1. to restore as many as possible of the "lost sheep of Israel" (the criminals) back into a right relationship with God and with the community of believers; and

2. to provide the greatest additional deterrent to crime after the trial (and punishment) is over, by attempting to lead criminals to Christ and provide them with a constructive "Christian" environment, so they might slowly become righteous men (and women) of God.

Man emphasizes the secular idea of *rehabilitating* the criminal so that he will behave better and hopefully commit fewer crimes in the future. However, the Bible emphasizes the Christian idea of *restoring* a sinner to a right relationship with God and with other Christians, so he can inherit salvation in addition to behaving better. *Rehabilitation* involves just a change of behavior, while *restoration* involves a change of the heart and mind in addition to becoming a new creation by being born again and receiving the Holy Spirit. Of course, true rehabilitation can only occur when restoration comes first!

True justice is associated with restoration in 1 John 1:9. It is written:

> If we confess our sins, he is faithful and just to forgive us our sins and to cleanse us from all unrighteousness. (1 John 1:9 KJV)

In other words, when we confess our sins and repent, God feels that the just thing to do is to:

1. forgive us (which means to show us mercy); and,

2. cleanse us from all unrighteousness (which means to restore us to a right relationship with Him).

So, justice in heaven requires both mercy and restoration when a person confesses and repents! If this is true about justice in heaven, then it should also be true about justice on earth! Therefore, all courts on earth must develop both a "Ministry of Mercy" (during the trial) and a "Ministry of Restoration" (after the trial).

The notion that judges should be very concerned about what happens to a criminal after the trial is also noted by Christ in John 8:11-12. Immediately after the "trial," Christ tells the adulterous woman that she is "free to go," but that she must take care to "sin no more." This of course means not only to stop sinning, but also means to start obeying God with all her heart, soul, mind, and strength. The very next thing Christ says to her is not only about restoration, but is actually the key to restoration, and is so important that He wants to share it with the entire crowd! Christ then reveals that the key to filling the empty void in her life is to be *restored* to a right relationship with almighty God by having a personal relationship with Jesus Christ—the Light of the World. He says that by following Christ, she will no longer walk in darkness, but will have the "Light of Life" within her. For it is written:

> And Jesus said unto her, "Neither do I condemn thee: go, and sin no more."
>
> Then spake Jesus again unto them saying, "I am the light of the world: he that followeth me shall not walk in darkness, but shall have the light of life." (John 8:11-12 KJV)

Jesus' example shows us that all judges must attempt to restore all criminals to a right relationship with God after the trial (and punishment) is over. And if certain judges don't feel comfortable doing this, then maybe they shouldn't be judges in the first place!

Not only does the New Testament speak of this, but the Old Testament also speaks of the importance of judges warning criminals not to sin, presumably both during and after the trial. For instance, God spoke through Jehoshaphat and commanded all the judges, saying,

> In every case that comes before you . . . you are to warn them not to sin against the Lord . . . (2 Chron. 19:10 NIV)

In the previous chapter, we discussed why God wanted judges to warn eyewitnesses not to sin during the trial. This verse further implies that it is also the judge's responsibility to warn the convicted criminal not to sin after the trial (presuming that the criminal does not have to be executed). For (as noted above) God not only wanted criminals to stop sinning after the trial, but he also wanted them to start obeying with all their heart, soul, mind, and strength. You see, after the trial and punishment was over, God knew that the best way to maximize the deterrence of future crime was to attempt to restore the criminal to a right relationship with God and with the community of believers, and if possible, slowly turn him from a man of rebellion into a man of God.

Since each judge was supposed to be a godly "Christian" elder, they each should have known that the same things which keep them as "Christian" judges on their best behavior would also help to keep these criminals on their best behavior. These things are:

1. a personal relationship with Jehovah—the pre-incarnate Christ—who would later on return to earth as the Light of the World to become our Messiah, Savior, and Lord;
2. regular public worship, private prayer, and regular study of the Holy Scriptures; and,
3. belonging to a small "Christian" accountability group which meets regularly for Bible study and prayer, and to encourage each other to become as devoted and obedient to Christ as possible!

All judges know that criminals generally do not have any of these influences in their lives. For instance, drunkenness is considered a crime according to the Bible, and generally drunkards do not have a personal relationship with Christ, do not go to public worship or study the Scriptures, and do not have a group of Christian friends with whom they meet regularly as an accountability group (to help keep them away from alcohol, as well as to keep them on their best behavior by encouraging them to walk with Christ in daily moment-by-moment surrender to His Will). So, despite the tremendous crime deterrence of God's "up-front" death penalties and physical punishments (like whipping, etc.), after the trial and punishment is over, all criminals still need to be restored to a right relationship with God and with the community of believers. This will not only help to stop their unrighteousness, but will also assist them in becoming righteous, God-fearing citizens who (hopefully) will obey God because of salvation and surrender, or at least obey God because of training, tradition, and peer pressure. By giving judges the command to warn all criminals not to sin after the trial, God magnified the idea that all crime starts with a sinful heart that is disobedient to God. Therefore, for a criminal who confesses and repents of his sin, God's view of justice would require that the judge take steps to "restore" the criminal back into fellowship with God and with the community of believers, just as Christ did (John 8:11-12 KJV), and as our Father in heaven does regularly (1 John 1:9 KJV).

To accomplish this "Ministry of Restoration" after the trial and punishment is over, the Israelite judge must explain to the criminal how to have a personal relationship with Jehovah—a relationship characterized by confession, repentance, and walking with Christ daily in moment-by-moment obedient surrender to His Will (This is the same type of personal relationship with Christ which was enjoyed by Enoch, Abraham, Joseph, Moses, David, and others in the Old Testament.). After the judge has attempted to restore the criminal to a right relationship with God (by leading him to Christ, so to speak), the judge must try to restore the criminal to a right relationship with the community of believers as well. Therefore, the godly Israelite judge might "sentence" the criminal to go back to regular public worship, study the Holy Scriptures regularly, and join a small Christian accountability group which would attempt to keep him on his best behavior. In fact, the judge may even make his mercy contingent upon the criminal making a public commitment to do these things.

God desires to have a personal relationship with each criminal, so he calls each criminal back unto himself at the end of the trial. He enlists the help of the judge to enable the criminal to be restored to God in this personal relationship. For God wants to capture the criminal's *heart* by having the judge demonstrate God's mercy (in the face of a potential death penalty); and God wants to capture the criminal's *soul* by having the judge attempt to restore him to a right relationship with God and with other believers. As the judges would become more and more expert in:

—knowing all the practical applications of God's civil laws,
—judging cases exactly as Christ would judge them,
—showing God's mercy,
—showing God's love by leading the criminal back into a personal relationship with Christ, and
—restoring the criminal back into a right relationship with the community of believers, the courtroom was supposed to become a great vehicle to lead the lost sheep of Israel back to a personal relationship with the Lord. This is exactly how God wanted all courts of the world to function.

In a true "nation under God," there should always be three facets of society which continually confront citizens with the gospel of Jesus Christ. These three facets of society are:

—the church,
—the culture of godly peer pressure, and
—the courtroom!

The church reaches the "righteous," the courtroom reaches the "unrighteous," and the culture of godly peer pressure reaches "everyone in between." In all three places we should be confronted with the gospel of Jesus Christ—but this should be especially true in the courtroom. It is in the courtroom that the sinner is "caught" and his sinfulness is exposed to the community. Witnesses of his sin are summoned against him, and he realizes that the wages of his sin may possibly be death. Therefore, there is no more perfect place for the gospel of Jesus Christ to be presented and observed in action than in the courtroom! Furthermore, each judge was instructed to symbolically "stand in" for almighty God and prayerfully attempt to render the same kinds of verdicts which God himself would give in the courtroom (2 Chron. 19:6-7 NIV). This creates an incredible parallel between the sinner standing in front of an earthly judge (who is acting on God's behalf) and that same sinner standing before God's throne of judgement in heaven.

Evidently, God intended courtroom trials of sinners to symbolically represent each one of us as we finally stand at the judgement seat of God and are confronted with our sins as read from a "book" in which they are recorded. The judge, who represents God himself, should always be a godly Christian elder who loves to be merciful and compassionate; but if provoked, will prayerfully dispense either mercy or justice depending upon the sin, the testimony, and the presence or absence of the sinner's humble confession and repentance before God in the courtroom.

Hopefully, now you can see that the most important principles in God's system of justice are confession, repentance, and restoration. Modern justice, however, does not require repentance, restoration, or even confession! In fact, the Fifth Amendment guarantees a criminal the "right" not to confess his sins, which is totally in opposition to the Christian principles of civil law in the Bible, and undermines God's intended "Ministries of Mercy and Restoration" for the courts!

GOD'S VIEW OF THE FIFTH AMENDMENT (AND THE MIRANDA ACT)

The Miranda Act has distorted the original intention of the Fifth Amendment into an anti-biblical "right" not to confess your sins in a courtroom. Here's how the story unfolds: In Arizona in 1966, 23-year-old Ernesto Miranda kidnapped and raped an 18-year-old girl, who later identified him in a police lineup. After a two hour interrogation, Miranda admitted the details of his crimes and later signed a statement of confession, which was used in convicting him. Unfortunately, our Supreme Court felt that the Arizona police "compelled" Miranda to confess, so they overturned the conviction.

You see, the Fifth Amendment says,

> No person shall be . . . compelled in any criminal case to be a witness against himself.

Chief Justice Warren wrote that a suspect "must be warned prior to any questioning that he has the right to remain silent, that anything he says can be used against him in a court of law, that he has the right to the presence of an attorney, and that if he cannot afford an attorney one will be appointed for him prior to any questioning if he so desires" (*Academic American Encyclopedia*, vol. 13, 463, 1981). Police officers have recited these "Miranda warnings" ever since that time, otherwise a confession obtained from a suspect without being warned of his rights is not admissible in court.

Both the Fifth Amendment and the "Miranda warnings" say, "You don't have to confess your sins after you're arrested!" Does God agree with this? NO! For not only does God say, "Confess your sins to one other" as a general principle (James 5:16 NIV), but additionally, it is implicit in God's laws that a confession is supposed to be used to establish truth and to provide a rationale for punishment. According to the Bible, you have no right "not to confess your sins," but you do have the right not to have your confession "beaten out of you," because you are still innocent until proven guilty.

Where do we find these biblical principles? In Joshua 7, a man named Achan steals 2 hundred silver coins, a gold bar, and a beautiful robe from the town of Jericho during the battle, despite God's specific warning against doing this. Because of Israel's sin, God abandons the Israelites in the next battle against the city of Ai, and thirty-six Israelites die! God allows Joshua to discover that Achan, son of Carmi, is guilty. Then, with almighty Jehovah actually standing at the trial, Joshua asks Achan to confess his sins (without first "warning him of his rights"), saying,

> Give glory to the Lord, the God of Israel, and give him the praise. Tell me what you have done; do not hide it from me.
> (Josh. 7:19 NIV)

Achan confesses his criminal sins as well as where he buried the evidence, and the evidence is brought before the Lord. Achan is then executed by the Israelites.

Notice that Jehovah did not say to Joshua,

> I'm sorry Joshua, but you cannot convict and execute Achan, because you forgot to warn Achan that he had the "right to remain silent, and that anything he said could be used against him in a court of law."

Joshua only gave the strongest verbal inducements possible to "compel" Achan to confess, by saying,

> Give glory to the Lord, the God of Israel, and give him the praise (Josh. 7:19 NIV)

This means:

> Achan, you are caught and God is watching you, and he is standing right over there!

There was no conceivably stronger verbal inducement which could "compel" Achan to confess than being reminded that Jehovah, the God of the universe, was standing in front of him and knew what he had done.

In summary, Joshua did not "beat the confession out of Achan," but neither did he "warn Achan of his rights." Joshua only gave the strongest verbal inducements possible to "compel" Achan to confess. Yet the Lord felt that Joshua's actions were perfectly honorable and appropriate. Therefore, God's lesson for us from the Bible is:

1. Police should *never* warn a suspect of a supposed "right to remain silent" or that he doesn't have to confess his criminal sins, because the biblical teaching is that "there is no right to remain silent";

2. Obtaining confessions by the strongest "compelling" verbal persuasion can always be used as evidence for conviction and to provide a rationale for the administration of justice; and

3. You cannot "compel" someone to confess his criminal sins by "beating a confession out of him."

As a result of the vague wording of the Fifth Amendment and the unfortunate "Miranda warnings," our system of justice has had to spend millions of extra tax dollars to convict its criminals—all of which could have been saved by simply adhering to the principles underlying biblical laws. More importantly, since the "Miranda warnings" have undermined God's courtroom principles of confession, they have also interfered with the court's other goals of repentance, restoration, and salvation of criminals—goals which were also supposed to create the greatest possible degree of future crime deterrence after the trial for those who ordinarily would be the most likely to commit future crimes.

Therefore, with these principles in mind, the Fifth Amendment needs to be repealed and rewritten to be in accordance with the founders' intentions and God's commands, and the "Miranda Act" needs to be struck down in its entirety!

GOD'S VIEW OF PLEA BARGAINING

According to God's view of courtroom procedure, the only way to get a lesser punishment for a crime is for the judge to show mercy to the criminal after he confesses his sin, publicly repents in the courtroom, and begs the judge to have mercy on him (or if there are other mitigating circumstances such as are noted in chapter eight). If the defendant lies about his guilt during the trial, and it is proven that he is indeed guilty; then if the criminal finally does confess and repent, the judge may suspect that his repentance may be a lie as well. At this point the judge may not be as merciful as he ordinarily would have been.

Despite the fact that God considers public confession and repentance to be the key to obtaining a lesser punishment from the judge, man has designed an alternative, secular method to obtain a reduced sentence from the judge. This method, called plea bargaining, does away with any need for true confession and repentance, and implies that there is no need for restoration either. Plea bargaining allows the criminal (or the criminal's lawyer) to get the charges "lowered" by pleading guilty to a lesser charge. Pleading guilty does not imply feeling guilty or feeling repentant, or even an admission by the criminal that he may have sinned against God or against his neighbor. In other words, plea bargaining allows the criminal to get a reduced sentence without even having to admit that he feels badly about what he has done, much less admitting that what he did was actually wrong or sinful in the eyes of God! Furthermore, the concept of bargaining implies that the criminal deserves a reduced sentence because he earned it by bargaining. Earning a reduced sentence by bargaining is the complete opposite of obtaining a reduced sentence because of the unmerited grace and mercy of a godly judge whose actions are prompted by a sincere act of confession and repentance by the criminal. And, just as man does not readily embrace the idea of salvation by grace through God's unmerited favor (but prefers instead to earn and bargain his way into heaven by works), so has Satan again deluded mankind into thinking that it should be by works and not by grace that you get a reduced sentence in the courtroom. Therefore, plea bargaining violates God's principles of civil law, undermines God's philosophy of courtroom procedure, and attempts to eliminate the practice of true confession, repentance, and restoration of these criminals to a right relationship with God and with the community of believers. As a result of plea bargaining (along with these many other areas of courtroom disobedience), our society has become progressively blinded to the idea that the courtroom should be a major route to the salvation of criminals. Additionally, our leaders have become totally unaware of how God's system of restoration can maximize crime deterrence beyond that which trial and punishment can accomplish.

GOD'S VIEW OF PAROLE

Another way that man's laws oppose God's laws and undermine God's courtroom "Ministries of Restoration & Salvation" is through America's system of parole. In our parole system, the judge will sentence the criminal to meet regularly with a secular accountability individual, called a parole officer, who merely wants to keep the criminal from associating with known felons, carrying weapons, or doing other things which our secular society thinks will increase his likelihood of committing future crimes. Parole officers are generally only interested in a criminal's actions, and are not truly interested in the criminal's heart, mind, or soul. Because they are generally not interested in the salvation of criminals, they will neither lead them to Christ, nor encourage them to become more devoted to God by walking with Christ daily. They generally will neither pray with them, nor give them biblical counsel, nor encourage them to read the Bible, nor encourage them to go to church, to seek out godly Christian friends who will provide a good example of righteous obedience to the will of God.

How much better it would be for both the criminal and for society at large if we followed the commands of God in the Bible—instead of concentrating on rehabilitation, we concentrated on restoration! Instead of sentencing the criminal to periodically meet with a parole officer, the judge should sentence him to periodically meet with a Christian accountability group to lead him to Christ and to encourage him to develop an increased devotion to the Lord. This would surely be more successful at reducing future crime than our current system of parole, which opposes and undermines God's ideas. Furthermore, if our judges would make this process part of their routine sentencing procedure, then all criminals could be evangelized and discipled this way. In fact, this method of reaching "lost" criminals has the potential to become much more successful at accomplishing God's objectives than our wonderful prison ministries are currently doing.

By the way, Christ's command to "visit those in prison" (Matt. 25:36, 43) again shows the importance of God's command to attempt to restore criminals to a right relationship with God and with the community of believers after the trial. In chapter ten of this book you will see how God's five biblical principles of punishment can make our prison system obsolete, so that God's courtroom "Ministry of Restoration" can be accomplished by Christian accountability groups without the need for prison ministries (because there would be no need for any prisons).

God's View of Judges

According to God's commands (spoken through Jehoshaphat), Israel's judges were supposed to be men who were godly Christian elders who knew all of the principles underlying God's laws, hated dishonest gain, and recognized that they were not judging for men but were judging on behalf of almighty God, who shows no partiality. For it is written:

Consider carefully what you do, because you are not judging for man but for the Lord, who is with you whenever you give a verdict. Now let the fear of the Lord be upon you. Judge carefully, for with the Lord our God there is no injustice or partiality or bribery. (2 Chron. 19:6-7 NIV)

In other words, only godly "Christian" elders who were very serious about their responsibility of judging on God's behalf were eligible to serve as judges, so they could develop and carry out God's intended courtroom ministry of mercy and ministry of restoration and salvation.

If a judge himself became merciless and malicious, God commanded that he be impeached, prosecuted, and punished (Ps. 149:5-9 NIV; see also the section on impeachment in chapter five). Just as a malicious witness would be punished (Deut. 19:16-21 NIV), so would a merciless judge receive no mercy (James 2:13 NIV).

The men who were chosen to judge Israel had to do so for free, because according to 1 Samuel 8:11-18 (NIV) God designed his civil laws to work so well that Israel was to be able to govern herself without the need to collect any taxes (for more details, please reread the section on taxes in chapter five of this book). In order for a tax-free judicial system to work, Israel's judges either had to be independently wealthy, or they had to be able to support themselves through their family businesses because there were no taxes available to pay them salaries.

God designed the laws of inheritance to prepay the eldest sons of Israel to be able to participate in this tax-free judicial system as well. This law allowed the eldest sons to receive a double portion of inheritance from their parents (Deut. 21:17 NIV). In this manner, God would prepay the eldest sons to become leaders in their own family, so they could have the extra financial reserves to care for their aging parents, as well as to care for their younger siblings who were too young to leave the family and support themselves. When their parents passed away, hopefully these eldest sons would still have the benefit of these extra financial resources (including flocks and lands) so they would not have to work as hard as their younger brothers. This way, they would have extra time to be able to volunteer their services to serve as judges in their local community in Israel. I believe this law was not designed to show favoritism to eldest sons at the time of their parents' death, but to reveal God's amazing provision for a tax-free system of local justice and local government, something which could help any nation, and could only have been designed by a loving heavenly Father!

In summary, in order for a completely tax-free judicial system to work, all the judges would have to either be independently wealthy, or be able to support themselves from their family business, or at least be eldest sons who received a double portion of inheritance.

By the way, being either a local or a mid-level judge in Israel was probably only a part-time job anyway, because God designed the judicial system and the principles of civil law enforcement to be so efficient at deterring crime that there would not be many cases for them to judge (for more details, please reread the section in chapter five entitled "God's Intended Structure for the Government of Ancient Israel"). Furthermore, as you will see later in this chapter, God designed his system of justice so court cases can be decided very quickly in comparison to today's prolonged court cases.

GOD'S VIEW OF LAWYERS

In Exodus and Deuteronomy, Moses spoke to the entire nation of Israel and told them that no one participating in a courtroom trial (in any capacity) was ever allowed to take a bribe. For it is written:

> Do not accept a bribe, for a bribe blinds those who see and twists the words of the righteous. (Exod. 23:8 NIV)

> Appoint judges... in every town... they shall judge the people fairly. Do not pervert justice or show partiality. Do not accept a bribe, for a bribe blinds the eyes of the wise and twists the words of the righteous. Follow justice and justice alone... (Deut. 16:18-20 NIV)

It is extremely important to understand that in these verses, Moses is addressing the entire nation of Israel and not just judges and lawyers. This means that no one in all of Israel who participated in a trial could receive any money for any testimony or any argument he might say in a courtroom either for or against a defendant. This has profound implications for our entire legal system, because this means that no one who speaks either for you or against you in court can receive any payment of any kind—this includes lawyers. In other words, it is a sin to take money to eloquently defend someone in court and it is a sin to take money to eloquently accuse someone in court. Therefore, according to God, lawyers are not allowed to be paid one dime for either defending or prosecuting anyone, whether this dime comes as a salary paid by the government, a lawyer's fee paid by the client, or an actual bribe paid by someone else.

In Deuteronomy 16:19 (NIV), the Bible tells us that taking any payment to speak on behalf of someone else in court can "twist the words of the righteous!" So, when a lawyer (even a righteous lawyer) accepts payment from any source to either accuse or defend a client, God tells us that no one is immune from the influence of having his salary (from the government) or his fee (from the client) twist his words away from seeking God's truth and towards a one-sided presentation.

Therefore, when a lawyer is paid to either accuse or defend you in court, this is similar to the "bribe" mentioned in the Bible, for it causes him to be willing to distort the truth because he is being paid to deliberately focus the judge's attention away from discovering God's truth, and towards a biased presentation.

Today we have legalized this use of bribery in the courtroom and call it either a salary or a lawyer's fee. But, God's Word teaches us that this salary or fee will always have all the consequences of a bribe, because the lawyer is still being paid to represent only one point of view. Thus, the system we have chosen is corrupt, and over several generations the corruption has now become manifested.

For anyone who is paid to present only one side of the picture is not seeking God's truth to assist the judge in rendering the same verdict that God would give, but is seeking only to present his biased opinion of what happened—even if it blinds the judge to God's truth, and a guilty man goes free. There is already enough temptation to distort the truth in a courtroom without also having an economic incentive to do it as well. Evidently, the fastest, most efficient, least costly, and purest way of discovering God's truth is when everybody in the courtroom is dedicated to presenting and discovering God's truth. Alternatively, our modern system of "adversarial legalism" is not only a very unwholesome environment for discovering God's truth, but also ends up being slower, less efficient, more costly, and has built in incentives to stall the case. The "game" of "trivia, technicality, and legal correctness" has become more important than finding God's truth.

Modern American lawyers present and advance their client's point of view with every legal means possible at the expense of the truth, and on occasion may even defend people who they know are guilty. In fact, Philip K. Howard, practicing lawyer and author of the book *The Death of Common Sense (How Law Is Suffocating America)* writes:

> To Bazelon and most judges and lawyers, the purest form of process is our adversarial system, in which litigating lawyers make the best argument they can for their clients. You file a one-sided brief, and then I file one. But this procedure, as federal judge Henry Friendly once observed, is not designed for truth: 'Under our adversarial system the role of counsel is not to make sure the truth is ascertained but to advance his client's cause by any ethical means. . . . Causing delay and sowing confusion not only are his right but may be his duty (Howard, Philip K, *The Death of Common Sense*, 85-86, 1994).

There are two categories of problems which occur when lawyers get paid to argue in court: the distortion of the truth, and the generation of increased costs.

There are many reasons why allowing someone to be paid to argue on your behalf in court actually encourages a distortion of the truth. The first reason is that our system is based upon adversarial legalism. This system evolved out of the anti-biblical belief that lawyers should be paid to present a prejudiced opinion for either the defense or the prosecution. Paying lawyers encourages a skillful presentation of a one-sided perspective of the truth. This is not seeking God's truth but is actually distorting the truth. Alternatively, biblical civil principles imply that we should have *collegial* relationships in the courtroom which are friendly and cooperative, seeking only God's truth, rather than have *adversarial* relationships in the courtroom which present one-sided opinions and seek to "win" over your "opponent" (even at the cost of concealing or distorting God's truth). Just as paying lawyers money for services encourages adversarial legalism, so also the philosophy of adversarial legalism encourages lawyers to desire to "win" at all costs. This is the second consequence of having lawyers who are paid for their services.

Unfortunately, this attitude of courtroom *competition* (instead of courtroom *cooperation*) exalts the game of "procedure" and "legal correctness" over the truth. Thus, the "proper way to search for truth" becomes more important than actually "finding the truth." The "means" become more important than the "ends" as the procedure of the search becomes more important than the goal. This causes the *letter* of the law to become more important than the *spirit* of the law and is the third natural consequence of paying lawyers to argue for a particular point of view. The fourth consequence generated by paying lawyers money for their assistance is that "technicality" becomes more important than truth—a "good" lawyer can get someone off on a technicality even when his client is obviously guilty. A "good" lawyer can therefore be distinguished from a "bad" lawyer, not by how frequently he discovers the truth, but how frequently he gets his client "off" whether he was guilty or not! After all, if the truth is not enough to free your client, maybe a technicality will do the trick! Getting a criminal "off" on a technicality at the expense of the truth is an abomination to God.

The fifth natural consequence is that we have lost sight of our goal of "justice for all" when we allow someone to go free because of a technicality. The freed criminal certainly does not receive his "justice." Society does not receive justice in this way, and neither does the victim of the crime. The sixth natural consequence of paying lawyers is that, since criminals "get off" because of technicalities, there are more unrepentant criminals on the street who still have no concept that they did anything wrong.

The seventh natural consequence of paying lawyers is that lawyers are tempted to defend people they know are guilty because they are "rewarded" with money for doing so. It also tempts lawyers to encourage clients to sue innocent people, businesses, or the government, even when the lawyers know that their client's claims may be invalid or even fraudulent. Howard writes:

> The same lawyers who advertise for personal injury claims now seek out fired employees. It's just a business. (Howard, *Death of Common Sense*, 140)

Long trials also make a mockery of our legal system. Our system of "adversarial legalism" is a slower and less efficient way of discovering truth in a courtroom than God's system of "cooperative examination" where everyone is seeking the truth. The eighth consequence of having paid lawyers (which causes a natural desire to "win the case at all costs") is that lawyers try to pervert jury voting by their procedures of jury selection. In this way, lawyers try to "bias the jury vote" by selecting prospective jurors who might already be sympathetic with the lawyer's opinion of the case, hoping that the finally selected jury will vote in a way which will give a favorable verdict or a lesser punishment for their client.

Because of all the problems mentioned above, the tenth consequence of paying lawyers is that modern justice has now totally perverted and corrupted the concept of a "fair trial" by distorting God's truth, and abandoning His purpose for the court to bring sinners to confession and repentance, and restore them to a right relationship with God, the community of believers, and the rest of society.

The second category of problems which occur when lawyers get paid to argue in court is the creation of increased costs and the consequences of increased costs. First of all, because trials are longer, our legal proceedings require more time off from work, resulting in greater income loss for the participants in the litigation. Secondly, longer time spent in court also generates greater costs from lawyer's fees. Thirdly, this means that the U.S. does not provide "equal justice for all" but favors the rich over the poor, because the poor cannot afford to go to trial for as long a period of time as the rich can. In fact, another consequence of paying lawyers is that "rich" clients are more likely to get the "best" lawyers (who do not find the truth, but who can generate a prolonged trial, and ultimately find a technicality to force a dismissal, or a mistrial.) Thus, expensive trials tend to serve the rich much more than the poor. Howard writes:

> Staying power—who has the most money—is as important as the merits of the cases. (Howard, *Death of Common Sense*, 45)

The fourth problem is that citizens have more taxes to pay for the increased court costs generated by the state because of the prolonged trials. The fifth problem is that because lawyers have exalted the virtues of "technicalities over truth," mistrials can occur forcing the process to start all over, wasting all the money of the taxpayers, while the lawyers get rich on a second trial. Since it often costs the lawyers nothing if a mistrial occurs, a mistrial can pay the lawyer just as much as a "win." The sixth problem is that because technicality and trivia become more important than truth, business contracts are now written in a language which is understood only by lawyers, who charge hundreds of dollars to either write the contracts or to interpret them.

The seventh problem is that the philosophy of justice becomes perverted. Statements like, "I'll tie you up in court," reflect the philosophy that businesses can sue each other in an effort to "stall some project" or just to increase the overhead expenses of the other corporation to drive them out of business. The eighth problem is that the large lawyer bills for defending a criminal case pale in comparison to what they will charge for a potentially huge lawsuit, when they may actually demand a large percentage of the settlement amount as well! This can result in millions of dollars of lawyer's fees in a single case. This not only encourages huge fees for lawyers, but also further tempts lawyers to pervert the truth by encouraging frivolous lawsuits.

Howard writes:

> Congress encouraged more lawsuits by stiffening penalties, allowing claims for emotional injury, and increasing attorneys' fees.
>
> The same lawyers who advertise for personal injury claims now seek out fired employees. It's just a business. Defending the claim can easily cost an employer more than $100,000, so there is a powerful inducement to settle. (Howard, *Death of Common Sense,* 142)

Allowing lawyers to be paid for their services has encouraged so many lawsuits that ultimately these lawyers have "retrained" society to think that it is a reasonable and moral thing to initiate a frivolous or fraudulent lawsuit. Notice the following example from Howard:

> In 1993, a New York City Transit bus was hit by a garbage truck on 125th Street. Within a month, eighteen people filed lawsuits against the city, claiming injuries received when they were hurled down on the bus . . . no passengers were on the bus. The bus had gone out of service and was parked. But the eighteen claimants did not know that. They all claimed they had been passengers and had hobbled on home before the police arrived. Their scam, which often succeeds, was the result of their knowing that the city would typically settle

rather than bear the expense of trying to prove they weren't there." (Howard, *The Death of Common Sense*, 103-104)

Therefore, we would decrease lawsuits by decreasing lawyers' fees, and probably nearly eliminate frivolous lawsuits altogether if there were no legal fees whatsoever. The ninth problem is that these higher court costs also contribute to increasing the costs of goods and services because manufacturers, wholesalers, retailers, and service corporations have to now pay increased insurance fees to protect themselves from future lawsuits.

In summary, each year United States' citizens spend billions of dollars of extra taxes to support a legal system which has been failing for generations. On the other hand, God's system of justice is totally free, providing "equal justice for all" and without any tax burden to the public. This is true because the best system is one which entails collegial cooperation where everyone in the courtroom is only concerned with seeking God's truth—instead of adversarial legalism which, as we have discussed, ends up distorting the truth and generating increased costs for the plaintiff, for the defendant, and for the taxpayer.

So, America needs to slowly return to a system of justice where lawyers cannot receive any money to either accuse or defend someone in court. For example, in 1935, Jane Adams wrote:

> [When] the Juvenile Court was established . . . the child was brought before the judge with no one to prosecute him and with no one to defend him—the judge and all concerned were merely trying to find out what could be done on his behalf. (Howard, *The Death of Common Sense*, 126-127)

> But a system permitting understanding and flexibility, even if it works better in nineteen out of twenty cases, also carries with it the opportunity for abuse. (Ibid., 127)

This is an amazing admission! This legal expert says that a system of justice which has no juries and no paid lawyers to either prosecute or defend clients may work better than our current system of justice in nineteen out of twenty cases, which is 95 percent of the time! She implies that our justice system works *best* when the judge seeks the truth without the distraction of hearing opinions from lawyers who are not seeking God's truth, but are only seeking to advance their own client's point of view.

She then says that this wonderful system, which works better than our current system up to 95 percent of the time also carries with it the opportunity for abuse. Why? Because you don't always have a godly, Christian elder judge who prayerfully seeks God's truth and attempts to render courtroom verdicts as if God were looking over his shoulder!

But, if we always *chose* godly Christian elders to be our judges, then maybe there would be no abuse at all, and maybe this system would work better than our current system of justice 100 percent of the time! After all, that is the system designed by almighty God himself!

God's View of Jury Duty

Most people mistakenly feel that a trial by a "jury of your peers" represents the guarantee of "justice for all," as well as the guarantee that the responsibility for your future in the courtroom will not rest in the hands of a single judge who might be an ungodly, arbitrary dictator. On the surface, this idea sounds so good that you would think that God would have included it in the Bible as part of His principles concerning justice. But, God didn't include it. As a matter of fact, God disapproves of the jury system and is in favor of a much better idea.

God's better idea was to design a system of justice to be administered by a single judge who is required to be a God-fearing man, who hates dishonest gain, who loves mercy, and who will prayerfully attempt to administer justice as if God were watching over his shoulder (Deut. 16:18-20; 2 Chron. 19:5-10 NIV). As noted earlier, if a judge became merciless and malicious, God commanded that he be impeached, prosecuted, and punished (Ps. 149:5-9 NIV)—probably as a malicious witness would be punished (Deut. 19:16-21 NIV), which means that it would be the merciless judge who would receive no mercy. This of course, brings new meaning to the verses which say,

> ... judgment without mercy will be shown to anyone who has not been merciful. (James 2:13 NIV)

> ... in the same way you judge others, you will be judged, and with the measure you use, it will be measured to you. (Matt. 7:2 NIV)

You see, God's system has built-in safeguards to ensure that all citizens will have equal access to His divine system of merciful justice. In this way, placing your fate in the hands of such a judge would be similar to placing your fate into the hands of God himself—trusting in his mercy, but fearing his justice!

The jury system, on the other hand, was designed to avoid placing the fate of a person accused of a crime into the hands of a single person, who could be mistaken, misled, prejudiced, or bribed. Rather than solving this problem by obeying God's commands and insisting that all judges be righteous men according to God's standards, we impertinently thought we knew better than God and designed a jury system instead—a system composed of twelve citizens who are usually not "Men of God," and who know neither the laws of the state, nor the laws of God.

Moreover, since they are so unfamiliar with what goes on in a courtroom, they can easily be misled by lawyers to focus on the technicalities of a trial instead of focusing upon God's truth. Furthermore, the composition of the jury can be purposely "biased" by the lawyers during the procedure of jury selection in favor of whichever verdict the lawyer might hope for. We end up placing our fate into the hands of a group of twelve inexperienced people who are much more likely to be mistaken, as individuals or misled as a group, than if we had just followed God's commands and insisted on having only one, godly Christian judge in the first place. As a result, each year our federal and state governments waste millions of tax dollars on enforcing a jury system which is unnecessary, expensive, corrupt, and abuses the innocent jurors, their families, their employers, their coworkers, their creditors, their doctors, and the taxpayers.

The first abuse is that an official summons is mailed to the innocent, prospective juror, saying he must interrupt his life to "volunteer" to help the government decide if a criminal is innocent or guilty. If the innocent juror doesn't appear in court, he can be legally punished by the court. The "sick" prospective jurors must seek out a doctor's excuse and pay for an early medical exam to get a doctor's medical excuse from jury duty, which costs the juror time and money. Alternatively, the doctor must write the excuse for free (and document it in the patient's chart), which is a waste of the doctor's time. The "well" juror is in even worse shape, however. He has to rearrange his entire life, for who knows how long. He or she may have to get a baby sitter, which costs money, and take time off of work, which costs a lot more money, or else be punished for not honoring the jury summons.

Those who are self-employed may even risk bankruptcy from loss of business. Sometimes, if the judge orders the jury to be sequestered, they cannot even see their families (as if under house-arrest, or in this case, "hotel-arrest"). Sequestering a jury requires payment for the hotel, the food, and the extra police to patrol the hotel hallways, and generates increased inconvenience for the spouse and children of the juror. The hotel costs can be staggering, but are always passed on to the taxpayer, who is also abused by this jury system.

The juror may get compensated as little as $5.00/day (as in the O.J. Simpson trial) which is less than minimum wage, and which doesn't make a dent into the unnecessary expenses and loss of income incurred by the juror, or the inconvenience imposed on both the juror and his family. And of course, paying jurors even this small amount costs more taxes. The juror's creditors are also abused, as they are now asked to wait for payment on bills and loans, etc. Furthermore, the innocent employer of the juror is abused as well, for he loses a good employee and can't run his business as well without his presence. He may lose money from lack of sales or production during the absence of the juror (this may be especially true for the small businessman). Some businessmen are further abused by having to offer their employees "jury compensation" as part of their fringe benefit plan, which increases business expenses and drives up the prices of their products and services, which then abuses the consumer.

Additionally, the juror's coworkers are abused by this system, because during the juror's absence, they have to work harder to try to perform the absent juror's job as well as their own job. Furthermore, in very long trials, it is not impossible to have the judge dismiss many jurors for certain infractions (such as watching TV, listening to the radio, reading a newspaper, speaking to their own family about the case, or speaking to the press) that they run out of alternate jurors, which forces a mistrial. This costs the taxpayers even more money.

If these many abuses were not bad enough, the attorneys can now abuse justice itself by going through the process of "jury selection" to do their best to "bias the jury" in favor of their case. Lawyers who are "skillful" at jury selection believe they can definitely influence the verdict that a jury might give. But, creating a jury with a bias, either in favor of or opposed to conviction, cannot possibly safeguard true justice. And, of course, prolonged jury selections take even more time, which costs even more taxes!

Please don't think that the jury system renders perfect verdicts. On the contrary, our newspapers have recorded many of the stupid verdicts our juries have given from all parts of the United States over the last several decades!

In summary, the system of a trial by a jury of your peers is an abusive, anti-biblical system. It abuses the juror, his family, his employer, his coworkers, his creditors, his doctor, as well as abusing the taxpayers. This abuse occurs through inconvenience, expense, lost income, and emotional strain on the family. And, it is done all in the name of "freedom and justice for all!"

Every year, tens of thousands of innocent jurors are abused in this way, as well as hundreds of thousands of other people who know, love, or work with these jurors! It is no wonder that God doesn't mention this abusive system as part of his plan for perfect justice. For the jury system is an expensive, inefficient, and abusive system which needs to be abandoned in favor of God's simple system of having a single godly Christian elder decide all cases by himself, unless he feels he need to request help from a more experienced judge.

GOD'S VIEW OF WITNESSES

God wanted Israel to have a culture where the majority of citizens considered it patriotic to participate in purging sin-crime from their nation. To accomplish this task, God designed his laws to enlist community-wide support to rebuke sin, report sin-crime, and testify against strangers, neighbors, and even family members for any serious sin-crimes which they may have committed. The Bible records many laws of this kind which interact together to create a nationwide community watch against sin-crime. As long as all the laws which God designed to help create this culture were regularly enforced, then this system would become so efficient at suppressing crime within Israel, that Israel would never require a tax-sponsored system of justice, punishment, or police. Three of these laws concern witnesses and will be discussed in this chapter.

The first civil law reminds witnesses that they will be held responsible by the court if they withhold evidence (Lev. 5:1 NIV), especially if a judge has already issued a public charge to testify about anything they may know about a case. In fact, they may even be punished for withholding evidence depending upon how important the evidence is that they are withholding. God designed this law to prompt both righteous and unrighteous citizens to feel responsible before God (or at least before the state) to rebuke sin, report sin-crime to the authorities, and testify in court, thus laying the foundation for creating a culture of godly peer pressure.

The second civil principle was designed to encourage this same behavior of rebuking sin and reporting sin-crime, even if it means testifying against your own family members (Deut. 13:6-9; 21:18-21 NIV). In order to truly purge sin-crime from Israel, each family member must be taught the high and lofty goal of being personally and nationally at war with sin, so they can develop the commitment to willingly testify against their own family members in court if necessary. A third law which further encourages citizens to purge evil from their community is the law which says that witnesses are the ones who actually start the execution of murderers or others who are convicted by their testimony (Deut. 13:9; 17:7 NIV). This principle was designed by God to encourage fearful citizens to boldly testify about the truth which they have seen, without fear of criminal retribution. On the other hand, this same system which encourages true witnesses to testify in court will actually discourage false witnesses from testifying from in court, because of the guilt they will have to live with for testifying against a man they knew was innocent, and also for the guilt of personally executing a man they knew was innocent. This is just one more way in which God puts great pressure on the witnesses to tell the absolute truth. Together, these three biblical principles interact with many other civil laws to create a culture which is "at war with sin"—a culture where it is patriotic to purge sin-crime from the family, from the community, from the state, and from the nation.

The Bible records two additional biblical principles concerning witnesses. However, these other laws do not directly contribute to creating a culture of godly peer pressure, but instead were designed to prevent the execution or punishment of innocent people. With this in mind, the fourth principle for witnesses concerns the punishment for bearing false witness (Deut. 19:16-20 NIV) so trials can be based upon fairness and upon God's truth. This law was discussed in great detail in the previous chapter and is a perfect method for stopping anyone from being a false witness in a courtroom trial. In fact, this law would have stopped all the false witnesses from testifying at the Salem Witch trials, so that the terrible tragedy in Salem, Massachusetts, never would have occurred! The fifth biblical civil law requires at least two or three eyewitnesses to condemn someone to death (Deut. 17:6; 19:15 NIV), for God wants the strongest evidence possible before considering execution.

All five of these biblical laws concerning witnesses represent the legal guidelines that Jehovah required to avoid punishing and executing innocent people. I can imagine no better safeguards than these! Furthermore, the first three of these five laws concerning witnesses interact together with many other biblical laws to help develop a culture of godly peer pressure, where purging sin-crime from the nation actually becomes a form of patriotism. This is just one of the methods designed by Jehovah to legally discourage community apathy against sin-crime and replace it with community action.

God's View of the Defendant

There are five biblical principles concerning defendants which I would like to share with you. The first four principles address the same theme: "immunity from prosecution." The Bible teaches that no defendant can ever be granted immunity from prosecution, even if he is considered

1. a child or adolescent;
2. "mentally ill" (claiming insanity);
3. an ambassador (claiming diplomatic immunity);
4. a president (claiming executive privilege); or,
5. a criminal, who is bargaining to get the charges against him dropped in order for him to be willing to testify against someone who committed an even bigger crime!

There is no reference in the Bible which suggests that judges should grant children or adolescents immunity from prosecution. But, there are multiple biblical references which teach that God requires judges to love to show mercy if at all possible (Mic. 6:8 NIV). God would surely expect a great deal of mercy when it comes to prosecuting children, or even when prosecuting adolescents. However, receiving *mercy* is not the same as receiving *immunity* from prosecution, which means that the person can literally get away with murder. According to God's system of justice, even a child cannot get away with premeditated murder, because the punishment for premeditated murder is execution without mercy (Deut. 19:11-13 NIV). So, even though God wants judges to grant children and adolescents a lot of mercy, he does not want judges to make them immune from prosecution.

Additionally, in the Bible there is no such thing as juvenile court, for all children are prosecuted by the same rules as adults. In fact, there are four specific commands having to do with parents and their offspring, which appear to apply whether the offspring are still children or whether they have already become adults. For example, God did not specify any age limits in his law concerning "cursing parents" (Exod. 21:17; Lev. 20:9; Matt. 15:4; Mark 7:10 NIV) or in his law concerning "attacking parents" (Exod. 21:15). Also, there are no age limits specified in God's law concerning a son who is "stubborn, rebellious, a profligate, and a drunkard" (Deut. 21:18-21 NIV). When it comes to idolatry, Deuteronomy 13:6 specifically mentions sons and daughters as being brought to trial, and once again no age limits are mentioned. As mentioned above, if a child deliberately murders his parents, he is to be punished in the same way as an adult; because for murder, God's punishment is execution without mercy!

Therefore, the Bible teaches that God wants children to be prosecuted as adults, even though God commands judges to show more mercy to children to than they show to adults—unless it is a case of murder, where God forbids the judge to show any mercy at all (Deut. 19:11-13 NIV).

Secondly, according to the Bible, a defendant cannot get away with murder by having someone else claim that the defendant is insane and therefore not responsible for his actions. You see, insanity means that the defendant could not control his actions, and so he was tempted to sin beyond that which he could endure. The Bible teaches us that "God will not let us be tempted beyond that which we can endure" (1 Cor. 10:13 NIV). This means that no one (including those with true mental illnesses) can ever be tempted to commit murder beyond that which he can endure. Therefore, you can be sure that Jehovah would not allow any defendant to get away with murder just because someone else claimed the defendant was criminally insane, and should be immune from prosecution. For God made no provision in the Bible for an insanity defense because according to God, we are always legally responsible for our actions, especially when it comes to murder, for which God commanded the judge to show no mercy.

Thirdly (and fourthly) according to the Bible, no one is "above the law," so there is no such thing as having "diplomatic immunity" or "executive privilege," which can prevent either ambassadors or presidents from being prosecuted. God said that even the king must never consider himself better than his brothers because he may begin to think that he is above the law and immune from prosecution (Deut. 17:18-20 NIV).

Fifthly, the Bible teaches that you don't drop charges against one person just to get him to testify against another person. Rebuking sin, reporting sin-crime, and testifying in court is a God-given civil responsibility. If you fail to testify about what you have seen or heard about, then the judge will hold you responsible for withholding evidence (Lev. 5:1 NIV). The punishment will probably depend upon the seriousness of the evidence being withheld. American prosecutors, however, often violate this command of God and allow many unrepentant, unpunished, and unprosecuted criminals to go free as a result.

Finally, an additional miscellaneous biblical principle is that the defendant is expected to take part in defending himself, unlike in America, where we have created laws which have made procedure and technicality become more important than finding God's truth. In our mad rush to ensure a "fair trial" for everyone, we have made America's laws so complicated that a defendant can no longer defend himself in a court of law just based upon truth and innocence! In America today, if a defendant does not have a lawyer, and he knows neither the rules of courtroom procedure nor the laws of the state and he attempts to defend himself in court, then his chances of being declared guilty are probably very high even if he is truly innocent. In ancient Israel, God intended for the defendant to defend himself in court, perhaps with the assistance of others who believed in his truthfulness and character. God also intended that the judge alone would be responsible for questioning the defendant and the witnesses and deciding the case.

Now what does this say about our justice system in America? It says that we are more interested in the means to find the truth than in the truth itself. In other words, today our courtrooms exalt legal correctness and technicality over finding God's truth. This is just one more sign of how America's courts have become corrupted and why we would be better off by adopting God's principles of court reform.

Miscellaneous Laws of Courtroom Policy

There are four additional biblical principles of courtroom procedure which American courts violate repeatedly.

The first biblical principle of courtroom procedure is that there is no such thing as "night court." For it is written:

> This is what the Lord says, Administer justice every morning. (Jer. 21:12 NIV)

God says that we should make the administration of justice such a top priority that we should do it first thing in the morning. You see, this is when our minds are at our best, having been completely rested after a good night's sleep. Because we feel refreshed and have all day to listen to the legal cases being presented, we are less likely to make hasty decisions concerning justice and mercy. However, when we are tired and sleepy, we are more likely to render a hastily considered verdict and cause a miscarriage of justice. This is exactly what happened to Jesus during his "midnight trials" with Annas, Caiaphas, and the Sanhedrin. For there were ample false witnesses and corruptions of justice during Christ's "midnight trials."

If America would only abandon man's system of justice and punishment and adopt God's system of justice and punishment instead, then the backlog of criminal cases would decrease so dramatically that there would be no need for night court in any city in the United States. Unfortunately, America's system of justice and punishment fails more and more with each passing decade, which only serves to magnify the consequences of our mistaken belief that God's civil laws are not applicable for modern criminal justice.

The second principle of courtroom procedure is to carry out the criminal's punishment as quickly as possible after the trial is over. It is written:

> When a sentence for a crime is not quickly carried out, the hearts of the people are filled with schemes to do wrong. (Eccles. 8:11 NIV)

This principle implies that trials should commence and proceed as soon as possible, and that punishment should occur as quickly as possible after the trial. In other words, "justice delayed is justice denied!" Unfortunately, American justice violates this biblical principle constantly, so it is no wonder that our system of punishment does not deter crime as much as we would like.

The third biblical principle of courtroom procedure is that God hates "contempt of court," because showing contempt for the judge in God's courtroom of merciful justice implies a contempt for God himself! In fact, the standard punishment for contempt of court is execution! For it is written:

> The man who shows contempt for the judge or for the priest who stands there ministering before the Lord must be put to death. (Deut. 17:12 NIV)

Although death was the maximum punishment for "contempt of court," it was not the mandatory punishment. For God commanded all judges to love to be merciful (Mic. 6:8 NIV), and so, if the judge could find a legitimate reason to be merciful, then the judge could punish the criminal with a few lashes with a whip as a merciful alternative to execution. In other words, it is only when the Scripture says, "Show no mercy" or "Show no pity" that the judge was instructed to stick to the maximum punishment prescribed by God's laws (Deut. 13:8; 19:13, 21; 25:12 NIV).

The fourth biblical principle of courtroom procedure is that God expected every judge presiding in a courtroom to thoroughly understand the practical applications of all God's principles of civil law. Therefore, the Bible was to be the major legal reference for all judges in court, and God expected judges to read from the Bible and to quote the Bible in court as the foundation for all legal decisions concerning sin-crime. But today, if someone mentions the Bible in the courtroom, the case may turn into a mistrial because of a "religious technicality." So once again, our *Christian* bias against the potential usefulness of God's principles of civil law has ultimately propagated a *courtroom* bias against the use of the Bible in court.

Summary

The following chart is a list of thirty-two issues which relate to the corruption of our justice system in the United States. These thirty-two problems have occurred because mankind chooses to administer his system of justice in a way which is contrary to the principles underlying God's civil laws! Notice that none of these problems would exist if we chose to administer our system of justice according to the principles underlying God's civil laws!

Category of Corruption	Man's Court	God's Court
1. Judges, paid by taxes	Yes	No
2. State lawyers, paid by taxes	Yes	No
3. More taxes for more court costs	Yes	No
4. Private lawyers, paid by cash	Yes	No
5. Private lawyers, paid by commission	Yes	No
6. Commissions cause more lawsuits	Yes	No
7. System favors the "rich" client	Yes	No
8. Lawyers purposely stall for time	Yes	No
9. Delayed sentencing	Yes	No
10. Large backlog of legal cases	Yes	No
11. The abusive jury system	Yes	No
12. Lawyers select biased juries	Yes	No
13. Lawyers, paid to distort the truth	Yes	No
14. Lawyers defend people they know are guilty	Yes	No

15. Slow justice because lawyers are content to "drag their feet"	Yes	No
16. Delayed and more costly justice because of the Fifth Amendment	Yes	No
17. Criminals "get off" because of technicalities	Yes	No
18. Mistrials because of technicalities	Yes	No
19. Appealing cases because of technicalities	Yes	No
20. Plea bargaining	Yes	No
21. Criminals claim to be insane and not responsible for their actions	Yes	No
22. Occasionally, the court does not get a chance to question the defendant directly because his lawyers never allow him to take the witness stand!	Yes	No
23. Totally free justice for all	No	Yes
24. Totally equal justice for all	No	Yes
25 Judges who know God's laws	No	Yes
26. Judges who use God's laws in court	No	Yes
27 Lawyers who know and use God's laws in court	No	Yes
28. Courtroom encourages Confession	No	Yes
29. Courtroom encourages Repentance	No	Yes
30. Courtroom Ministry of Mercy	No	Yes
31. Courtroom Ministry of Salvation	No	Yes
32. Courtroom Ministry of Restoration	No	Yes

These are the thirty-two advantages which God's courtroom of merciful justice has compared to mankind's system of justice. We cannot honestly expect judges to consistently find God's truth through case after case and render verdicts which please God when our entire courtroom procedure violates the principles underlying God's civil laws, and substitutes an atmosphere where mentioning either God or the Bible has been made illegal.

In conclusion, mankind's method of justice as practiced in the United States is wasteful, inefficient, slow, and more costly, while it distorts the truth, and causes a backlog of cases. In contrast, God's courtroom of merciful justice has more than thirty advantages. God's system is faster, does not distort the truth, and is totally free. Furthermore, it encourages true confession, repentance, salvation, and restoration of the sinner to God and to his community.

Why are God's principles of civil law so much better than man's principles of civil law? Because they were written by Jesus Christ himself, when he was in the form of Jehovah, thirty-four hundred years ago! These principles should be expected to be still valid today, and should be expected to also be superior to our current principles of civil law.

Unfortunately, these lessons will in all likelihood remain a secret, because since we are not supposed to be "under the law" concerning salvation, Christians have mistakenly concluded that the Mosaic principles of civil law have also been disqualified for the administration of sound and virtuous government. Each year Americans continue to pay a trillion dollar tax burden as a result of mistakenly believing that we should neither study these principles, nor use any of these principles to remodel our government. This is likely never to change unless the readers of this book encourage their Sunday schools and Bible study groups to study the advantages of God's principles of civil law, and encourage their pastors to preach about these principles.

I agree that evangelism and salvation are ten times more important than the lessons in this book! They should be preached and studied ten times more frequently than the lessons in this book! Since there are fifty-two Sundays in each year, I suggest that having five Sunday sermons, five Sunday school lessons, and five Wednesday night Bible study lessons each year on the wonderful advantages God's principles of civil law have for the administration of good government would still leave 90 percent of the year for the more important lessons of evangelism and discipleship training.

Christians must be willing to use God's principles of civil law to guide us in amending our laws and amending our Constitution. Only by rebuilding America with biblical principles can we begin to create a true "nation under God" and create a courtroom environment which exalts confession, repentance, mercy, salvation, and restoration.

And that is God's view of court reform!

In the next chapter, you will see how God's system of punishment can reduce crime so greatly that God's system of court reform can easily handle the relatively tiny caseload which results from adopting God's very efficient form of punishment.

Chapter Ten

GOD'S VIEW OF PRISON REFORM AND HOW TO STOP CRIME IN AMERICA WITHOUT PRISONS

This chapter explains how ancient Israel was supposed to punish criminals by using God's principles of civil law enforcement. God gave Moses five biblical alternatives to imprisonment which were designed to function so well that, if implemented in America, we would. . . .

1. solve all our prison problems,
2. create the greatest possible deterrent to crime,
3. save hundreds of billions of dollars of taxes, and,
4. render hundreds of man's laws of punishment obsolete and superfluous!

God's principles of punishment for criminals are quick, simple, extremely effective, tax-free, and are designed to keep criminals out of an expensive tax-sponsored prison system where good character gets corrupted by bad character (1 Cor. 15:33 NIV) and where bad character gets corrupted even further. Since the criminals are kept out of prison by God's principles of punishment, then the judge can implement God's principles of restoration (see previous chapter), which include making the criminals regularly attend Christian accountability groups (the biblical alternative to secular parole officers), to assist the judge in carrying out God's plan of restoring criminals to a right relationship with God and with the community of believers. In this way, each criminal is immediately "joined" to a group of Christian men who meet regularly to study the Bible, pray, and to encourage one another to remain on their best behavior by walking with Christ daily in moment-by-moment surrender to God's Will. Hopefully, this will not only lead to the salvation of many of the criminals, but will also slowly turn them from men of rebellion into men of God!

So, with this in mind, let us examine God's five biblical alternatives to imprisonment.

I. WHIPPING AS A BIBLICAL ALTERNATIVE TO IMPRISONMENT

Three thousand four hundred years ago Jesus Christ (in the form of Jehovah) gave judges the option to punish criminals by whipping them from one to forty lashes. For it is written:

> If the guilty man deserves to be beaten, the judge shall make him lie down and have him flogged in his presence with the number of lashes his crime deserves, but he must not give him more than 40 lashes. If he is flogged more than that, your brother will be degraded in your eyes. (Deut. 25:2-3 NIV)

With this command, Jesus (the pre-incarnate Jehovah) clearly gives the Israelite judges the authority to have certain criminals whipped. However, the Bible neither says which crimes deserve this type of punishment nor does it say how many lashes should be given for each crime. Therefore, it is most likely that God was giving the judges discretion to use whipping either as a merciful alternative to execution, or as a flexible punishment for crimes which have no other specified penalty.

Moreover, as noted in chapter eight, God intended whipping to be done in the presence of the judge, probably so the judge could hear any further cries for mercy, and probably also so the judge could inspect the criminal's back to insure that no serious physical injury was occurring. In this way, the judge could stop the whipping at any point so he could demonstrate more of the mercy of God. Furthermore, because of God's emphasis on mercy, it is clear that God would not want these biblical whips to be designed as instruments of cruelty and torture—with stones, bones, metal, or glass sewn into the whip to tear and rip the flesh of their victims. Instead, God probably wanted these whips merely to serve as simple instruments of temporary pain which would never cause any serious or permanent injury. Therefore, God designed whipping to be a simple, effective, inexpensive system of punishment which could be used as a biblical alternative to expensive, tax-sponsored prison systems.

When a judge sentences a criminal to a full ten year prison term, this may cost the taxpayers between $300,000 to $500,000 in taxes, because prison expenses average between $30,000 to $50,000 per year of imprisonment for each inmate. This expense includes the cost of "renting" a jail cell for ten years, nearly eleven thousand meals over ten years, and ten years of electric, water, sewage, and fuel bills, ten years of medical care, and ten years of salaries for the warden, the guards, the maintenance mechanics, the janitors, and the cooks, all paid for by increasing your taxes. But that's not all! Since the criminal has now been taken away from his family, his family might be without any means of financial support for the next ten years. As a result, his family may now be welfare-dependent and may receive 120 months of welfare checks and food stamps over the next ten years. Furthermore, they may also be eligible to receive Medicaid benefits, which include free medicines, free doctor visits, free emergency room visits, free hospitalizations, and free surgical operations for the next ten years. Again, these are all paid by increasing your taxes. Thus, the total expenses for the innocent taxpaying citizens can easily exceed a third of a million dollars for every criminal who serves a full ten-year sentence!

Alternatively, according to the Bible, the criminal can be given perhaps ten lashes with a whip, sent home to recover from his wounds in a week, and be back at work, supporting his family almost immediately (presuming he had a job in the first place). In other words, when a criminal is sentenced to serve out a full ten year prison term, it costs the taxpayers more than $300,000 in taxes, all for the lack of a five dollar whip! Multiply this by the total prison population in all our federal and state prisons (1.8 million current prison inmates) and you can easily see how over the next twenty years Americans will pay over one trillion dollars in unnecessary taxes to feed, clothe, and house America's prisoners.

Unfortunately, instead of Christians studying these principles of civil law and enlightening the world with them, we have mistakenly concluded that the principles underlying God's civil laws are no longer valid. We have unwittingly left our country in political darkness because of our lack of familiarity with God's laws, and therefore God allows us to suffer for our willful ignorance, by letting us live under man's laws—statutes that are not good and laws we cannot live by! For it is written:

> [God said] . . . because they had not obeyed my laws but had rejected my decrees . . . I also gave them over to statutes that were not good and laws they could not live by. (Ezek. 20:24-25 NIV)

You see, by rejecting the principles underlying God's civil laws, we throw away a large part of the "abundant life" Jehovah had in mind for us as a society on earth, and instead inherit a nation of poverty, sin, violence, and crime.

II. An "Eye for an Eye" as a Biblical Alternative to Imprisonment for Violent Criminals Who Seriously Injure Their Victims

The courtroom legal principle of an "eye-for-an-eye" is a quick, simple, effective, and inexpensive method to administer justice to the violent criminal who causes serious injury to his victim. This represents the second biblical alternative to expensive tax-sponsored prisons. This principle was designed by God to be the most cost effective means of stopping violent assault and battery. For it is written:

> If anyone injures his neighbor, whatever he has done must be done to him: fracture for fracture, eye for eye, tooth for tooth. As he injured the other, so he is to be injured. (Lev. 24:19-20 NIV)

Christianity's misunderstanding of this Mosaic civil law has done more to deter Christians from embracing the advantages of God's other civil laws than any other line of reasoning. Specifically, it has caused us to ignore the best possible deterrent for violent crime-related injury. As a result of our deliberate unwillingness to obey God, He has again given us over to "statutes that are not good and laws we cannot live by," by allowing us to spend billions of dollars in taxes on ineffective imprisonment. Instead, we should be punishing violent criminals according to God's principles of civil law, creating the perfect deterrent to violent crime, and saving hundreds of billions of dollars in taxes at the same time.

One of the main reasons why Christians disapprove of this particular principle of civil law is because we have largely misunderstood Christ's teaching concerning "turning the other cheek." You see, most Christians have mistakenly concluded that Christ was *correcting* the written law, when in reality, Christ was merely correcting what was *said* about the law by the Pharisees and *clarifying* the intent of the law so the Jews could understand it better. You see, the concept of "an eye for an eye" is one of God's principles of "Fair and Just Punishment" which was to be implemented only by a judge (Exod. 21:22-25; Deut. 19:16-21 NIV), and this means only after a trial and *inside* of a courtroom (or inside a courtyard).

Unfortunately, rebellious man has a natural tendency to use this same principle *outside* the courtroom as a justification for revenge. This was not what God wanted, and Jesus condemns this practice. But just because Jesus condemns the use of the principle of an "eye for an eye" *outside* the courtroom (because it leads to violence and revenge) does not disqualify this principle for use *inside* the courtroom for administering God's justice, (according to the guidelines given to us in Lev. 24:19-20 NIV).

With this in mind, let us examine the words of Christ in Matthew 5:38-39 (NIV). Jesus declared,

> You have heard that it was SAID, "Eye for eye, and tooth for tooth." But I tell you, Do not resist an evil person. If someone strikes you on the right cheek, turn to him the other also. (Matt. 5:38-39 NIV; emphasis added)

Please notice that Jesus is *not* referring to what a *judge* should do when faced with this situation, but what the assaulted *victim* should do when faced with this situation. Jesus' instruction here concerns only a *personal* response to violent crime, not a *judicial* response to violent crime.

Please also notice that Jesus did NOT say, "You have heard that it was WRITTEN," but instead declared, "You have heard that it was SAID . . ." (Jesus repeated this same expression six times in chapter five of Matthew).

Is there a difference between "what was WRITTEN" and "what was SAID"? Of course there is! For when Jesus uses the expression "It is WRITTEN," He is referring to the infallible written Holy Scriptures of God. But when Jesus uses the expression, "You have heard that it was SAID," He is referring to the fallible oral traditions of men, and specifically to the mistaken oral teachings of the Pharisees.

Jesus never disagreed with what was written in the Scriptures, but he often disagreed with what was said about the Scriptures. Likewise, Jesus never corrected what was written in the Scriptures, but he often corrected what was said about the Scriptures.

In fact, Jesus always exalted the written Word of God. For example, when making a point about God's perfect truth, Jesus often declared,

1. "It is written.........."   Matthew 4:4 (NIV)
2. "It is written.........."   Matthew 4:7
3. "It is written.........."   Matthew 4:10
4 "It is written.........."   Mark 14:27
5. "It is written.........."   Luke 4:4
6. "It is written.........."   Luke 4:8
7. "It is written.........."   Luke 4:12
8. "It is written.........."   Luke 19:46
9. "It is written.........."   Luke 22:37
10. "It is written.........."   Luke 24:46
11. "Haven't you read......?"   Matthew 12:3
12. "Haven't you read......?"   Matthew 12:5
13. "Haven't you read......?"   Matthew 21:42
14. "Haven't you read......?"   Matthew 22:31
15. "Haven't you read......?"   Mark 2:25
16. "Haven't you read......?"   Mark 12:10
17. "Haven't you read......?"   Mark 12:26
18. "Haven't you read......?"   Luke 6:3
19. "Is it not written.....?"   Mark 11:17
20. "Is it not written.....?"   John 10:34
21. "What is written........?"   Luke 10:26

22. "You know not the scriptures...."	Matthew 22:29
23. "You know not the scriptures...."	Mark 12:24
24. "You know the commandments......"	Mark 10:19
25. "You know the commandments......"	Luke 18:20
26. "What did Moses command you?"	Mark 10:3
27. "What is the meaning of that which is written...........................?"	Luke 20:7

You see, Jesus insisted that what was already written in the Scriptures was an infallible source of God's eternal truth. For Jesus was always exalting the Scriptures, the commandments, and "that which was written"! Jesus was not *correcting* the written law; He was only *clarifying* the law and correcting what was said about the law by the Pharisees and others who were unrighteous.

The written law of "an eye for an eye" was supposed to *discourage* violence and revenge outside the courtroom, not *encourage* violence and revenge. However, what was said about the law, perverted the law's intent to motivate violence and revenge *outside* the courtroom and to justify a "slap for a slap," and a "punch for a punch."

So Jesus is not changing the law, but only clarifying the law and correcting the perverted oral tradition of the Pharisees. Notice, also, that Jesus did NOT say, "If someone puts out your right eye, turn to him the other also! If someone cuts off your right hand, offer him the left hand as well!" Jesus only said, "If someone merely strikes you on the cheek, turn the other cheek," because a strike (whether a punch or a slap) is not a form of serious or permanent injury. Remember, the law was "an eye for an eye," not "a slap for a slap"! The principle of an "eye for an eye" referred to serious injury, like putting out an eye, knocking out a tooth, or giving someone a serious wound, burn, or scar. For this law was designed by God to be used only as a courtroom punishment to discourage violence and revenge by making people fear that if they hurt another person seriously that they too would be restrained in the courtroom while the court-appointed strong-man would legally do the same to them.

Therefore, the law of "an eye for an eye" was not supposed to *negate* "turning the other cheek," but was supposed to *encourage* "turning the other cheek"! Jesus is merely reminding people that the true meaning of "an eye for an eye" (*inside* the courtroom) is to "turn the other cheek" (*outside* the courtroom). You see, offering the other cheek to your enemy was supposed to be a gentle but firm reminder that if he hurts you seriously, he may end up in court facing the same punishment.

Turning the other cheek was supposed to be a nonviolent response to aggression which gave your enemy time (and a reason) to calm down and consider making amends. Furthermore, this law was also supposed to turn the fear of being mugged while walking the streets into a bold confidence that whatever serious injury a mugger did to you would now be done to him in the courtroom. In fact, some people might defiantly "turn the other cheek" as if to say, "If you seriously hurt me, you're gonna be punished in court! So go ahead! Make my day!"

In summary, God designed the principle of an "eye for an eye" to. . . .

1. provide a quick, simple, effective, and inexpensive method to administer justice to the violent criminal who seriously injures his victim;
2. provide the perfect method for deterring violent crime, violent wife abuse, and violent child abuse;
3. encourage a gentle, nonviolent response to aggression;
4. replace fear of walking the streets with confidence and boldness;
5. provide the second biblical alternative to expensive, tax-sponsored prisons; and,
6. save society billions of dollars in taxes!

III. THE MARK OF JUSTICE AS ANOTHER BIBLICAL ALTERNATIVE TO IMPRISONMENT

In Genesis, it is written:

Then God put a mark on Cain so that no one who found him would kill him. (Gen. 15:4 NIV)

Cain, as you remember, had just murdered his brother, Able, so God banished Cain from his presence and from coming near the area surrounding the Garden of Eden. Cain complained to Jehovah that any of his brothers who found him, and knew that he had killed their brother, would now want to kill him. So, Jehovah put a mark on Cain to *inform* his brothers that God's justice had been done and that Cain's punishment by God was now complete, so they should not feel the need to punish Cain any further by killing him.

I believe that Cain's mark of justice was essentially a tattoo (of sorts) placed by God onto a perpetually exposed area of skin, such as on the back of the right hand, because the right hand is the dominant hand in most people, and this is where the mark could be most easily seen. In this way, the mark of justice could provide a quick reminder to his brothers of the punishment which Cain had already received from God.

In a biblical courtroom, since the judge is supposed to be prayerfully rendering justice on behalf of almighty God, then it is reasonable that God was giving us another tax-free form of crime deterrence—the placing of a mark of justice (a tattoo) on the back of the right hand of a criminal, indicating the date, the crime, and the punishment administered at that time.

Imagine the criminal having to live the rest of his life with the knowledge that everywhere he goes people will easily see the mark of justice on the back of his right hand, and immediately know what crime he has committed. Thus, the mark of justice can become a great deterrent to future crime all by itself.

Ordinarily, getting a tattoo is forbidden by God (Lev. 19:28 NIV), but in the context of punishment for a crime, receiving a mark of justice in court from a judge who is acting on God's behalf appears to be one more creative method which God has chosen to punish criminals, and is a third biblical alternative to expensive tax-sponsored prisons!

Before we study the fourth and fifth biblical alternatives to imprisonment, I'd like for you to consider for a moment the practical applications of God's first three principles of punishment.

Many years ago, a man raped a beautiful model and then cut both sides of her face with a knife. Let us suppose that an identical crime happened today, and that rather than sentencing him to serve ten years in prison at a cost to society of more than $300,000 in taxes, he was sentenced using God's principles of civil law. Let's see how this works!

First of all, the criminal would be tied to a post in the courtroom with his hands restrained. Then the victim would be brought in and her facial scars would be measured and then traced onto the criminals face. Next, the criminal's face would be cut in like fashion (without anesthesia) by the "courtroom strong man" (so to speak) to produce two facial wounds which are identical to the wounds which the rapist inflicted on the victim.

These two facial scars (and the story behind them) would become a warning to other violent criminals to "think twice" before injuring anyone. In other words, violent criminals would hopefully think,

> I might as well put away my brass knuckles, my knife, and my pistol, because if I seriously injure someone with any of these weapons, then the court-appointed "strong man" will injure me the same way with the same weapons in court!

Thus, violent individuals and gang members would begin to disarm themselves, because these "scars-of-justice" would provide a living testimony of God's justice. As a result, a surprising "culture of 'godly' peer pressure" develops within the ranks of the wicked, as they warn each other of God's command to never purposely injure anyone, or else they will be punished with an identical wound in court. In this way, God's system of justice provides the perfect deterrent to violent crime. Yet all that was required for this particular punishment was a knife to make the facial scars!

Next, if the victim's groin was bruised and abraded during her rape, then the rapist's groin must also be bruised and abraded in court (the bruises can be made by repeatedly striking his groin with mild to moderate force using a boxing glove until a similar sized bruise appears, while the abrasions can be made by gently rubbing a sandpaper over the area until a similar abrasion appears). Furthermore, if the rape injured the vagina by causing a small number of very tiny bleeding cuts in the vaginal wall, then the rapist must receive the same number of very tiny cuts to the shaft of his penis, which can be made using a very tiny knife. For God said:

> As he injured the other, so he is to be injured. (Lev. 24:19-20 NIV)

The rapist must not have his penis cut off, and he must not have his testicles cut off either, for that would be a far greater punishment than God commands!

Next, because being raped always leaves the female with nightmares, emotional scars, and difficulty with future intimate relationships, the rapist must now be whipped, from a maximum of forty lashes, down to a minimum of a mere one lash!

Finally, the judge could order the criminal to receive the mark of justice on the back of his right hand, indicating the date, the crime, and the punishment received. All this punishment would require only a tattooing needle.

Of course, the judge can always demonstrate the mercy of God by administering fewer lashes than deserved, fewer identical wounds on the groin than deserved, or only one facial laceration instead of two, or not placing the mark of justice on the criminal.

Instead of doing things God's way, we sentence him to serve ten years in prison at a cost of up to a half a million dollars in taxes, all for the lack of a knife, a whip, a needle, a boxing glove, and a piece of sandpaper!

In summary, God's principles of an "eye for an eye," whipping, and the mark of justice, are three quick, simple, and inexpensive alternatives to imprisonment for violent criminals who injure their victims. These principles would not only save America billions of tax dollars, but also provide the perfect deterrent to violent crime, gang wars, wife beating, and child abuse! Since God's ways are superior to man's ways, then we will never find a better way of deterring violent crime than the method Christ gave to Moses thirty-four hundred years ago.

By the way, despite the fact that the Eighth Amendment says there should be "no cruel or unusual punishments inflicted" in the United States, Jesus Christ certainly would not have considered his punishments to be cruel at all. I believe that our founders were not trying to use the Eighth Amendment to eliminate God's methods of punishment from being used here in America. However, if they were trying to do this (which I doubt), then they were simply wrong! Either way, the Eighth Amendment needs to be repealed and rewritten to accommodate God's methods of punishment as mentioned in the Bible and as described in this book. Otherwise, God will continue to allow America to suffer under "statutes that are not good and laws we cannot live by" (Ezek. 20:25 NIV).

IV. A SIX-YEAR PERIOD OF ENSLAVEMENT (INDENTURED SERVANTHOOD) FOR THIEVES WHO CANNOT PAY BACK A MULTIPLE OF WHAT THEY HAVE STOLEN

A fourth alternative to imprisonment which comes from God's principles of civil law is the concept of a six-year enslavement of thieves who cannot pay back a multiple of the amount they have stolen. There are seven advantages to this biblical principle of civil law. Let me explain how this works.

First of all, a thief is *always* required to pay back *double* the price of the item he has stolen, if the item still remains in his possession (Exod. 22:4 NIV). However, if the item no longer remains in his possession, then he is required to pay back an even *higher* multiple of the price of what he has stolen, for the Bible gives the example of paying back four sheep for a sheep and five oxen for an oxen (Exod. 22:1 NIV). This represented the difference between petty larceny and grand larceny, and gives the judges a "scale" to guide their recommendations for reimbursement.

In Proverbs (6:30-31 NIV), we are again reminded of God's system of multiple reimbursement which requires a "sevenfold" payback. "Seven" represents the "perfect" or "appropriate" amount which God would expect the Israelite judges to prayerfully conclude was "fitting" for any given theft, even if the thief had to sell all his possessions to pay back the debt (Prov. 6:31 NIV). Therefore, the thief risks impoverishing his family even further by knowing he might have to sell all he has to provide the twofold to sevenfold multiple reimbursement prayerfully required by the Israelite judges.

If the thief cannot repay the appropriate multiple of what he has stolen, he is to be SOLD as a slave to pay for his debt (Exod. 22:3b NIV). This money presumably goes to reimburse the victim of the crime for the specific item(s) which were stolen from him. This "slavery" is only to last six years (Exod. 21:2 NIV) and then the thief must be set free, having paid back his debt. This is Jesus' alternative to imprisonment—where the prisoner works for the slaveowner to pay for the free housing, meals, and medical care the slaveowner must provide during the six year enslavement ("imprisonment"). Notice that God's system of "imprisonment" requires no taxes to support it!

The six year period of enslavement is profitable for the slaveowner, for the Bible says he should average twice as much profit from the slave as he would from a hired hand (Deut. 15:18 NIV). Remember, if God had not made this system profitable for the slaveowner, then no one would ever purchase the poor thief, so the victim would not receive his reimbursement, and society would need to develop large, expensive, tax-sponsored prisons as a secular alternative to God's plan.

When the slaveowner releases the thief after six years, the slaveowner is to "supply him liberally from his flock, his threshing floor, and his winepress" (Deut. 15:12-13 NIV). This way, the thief can survive without having to steal before finding another job. If the thief can now purchase or rent some property, he can plant the grain and start a farm and raise the sheep, goats, or cattle which he may have received as his parting gift from the slaveowner.

This biblical system of enslavement has seven advantages over our current way of treating thieves, and includes advantages for the victim, for the slaveowner, for the thief, and for the taxpayer. These advantages are as follows:

1. The victim always gets reimbursed for his losses, unlike in America, where the victim rarely gets compensated at all, unless he is insured. Even then, the victim still loses his "deductible," and he may even have to fight his insurance company to compensate him for his losses.

2. The slaveowner gets an increased profit because the enslaved thief is worth twice what a hired hand is worth.

3. The thief (hopefully) will learn about Christ from the Christian slaveowner and become "rehabilitated" by the influence of the Holy Spirit in his life (after he accepts Christ as Savior and Lord), instead of going to prison, where "bad company would further corrupt his character" (1 Cor. 15:33 NIV).

4. The thief learns a skill or a trade from his six year period of "employment" with the slaveowner.

5. The thief (hopefully) gets a good reference from his "employer" so he can get a job elsewhere after the six year period of slavery is over. He may even get a job with the slaveowner as a hired hand.

6. At the end of his six year period of enslavement, the thief receives a small award of grain, wine, sheep, goats, cattle, or money as a parting gift to help supply his needs. With this he returns to his family, starts life over again, and looks for another job so he won't have to return to a life of crime.

7. Society's taxpayers don't have to pay *any taxes* to imprison the thief for six years, for it was the slaveowner himself who had to supply all the physical needs of the thief.

By the way, the thirteenth Amendment still allows this kind of punishment, probably because the authors knew that God himself ordained this kind of punishment in the Bible. For it is written:

> Neither slavery nor involuntary servitude, except as punishment for a crime, whereof the party shall have been duly convicted, shall exist within the United States . . . (Thirteenth Amendment)

V. EXECUTION AS A BIBLICAL ALTERNATIVE TO IMPRISONMENT FOR MURDERERS, KIDNAPPERS, AND OTHER HARDENED CRIMINALS

The biblical felonies "requiring" execution have been listed in chapter eight, and God's preferred method of execution will be discussed in chapter twelve. Here, it should suffice to say that execution is the fifth biblical alternative to imprisonment.

There are probably thousands of prisoners on death row in the United States who are not being executed because execution has become so unpopular in America. There are probably hundreds more in prison who have committed other serious crimes (such as kidnapping or raping a married woman) for which the Bible also has execution listed as one of the penalties. (Please understand that God's punishment for raping a virgin girl (Deut. 22:28-29) is not the same as God's punishment for raping a married woman, which is adultery, for which those is a potential death sentence.) In addition, there are also hundreds of hardened criminals who are not on death row but who are serving out life sentences in prison, who would also "qualify" for execution according to the biblical law of the profligate (the amoral hardened criminal who doesn't just *disobey* God's law, but *despises* God's law).

In other words, murderers, kidnappers, some rapists, and other hardened criminals who despise God's laws could also be executed according to God's fifth principle of civil law enforcement—execution—thus creating a much greater deterrent to crime as well as saving our citizens billions of dollars in taxes for unnecessary prisons.

In conclusion, God has given us five biblical alternatives to expensive tax-sponsored prison systems:

1. EXECUTION (for biblical felons; see chapter eight for the list of biblical death penalties.)
2. AN "EYE FOR AN EYE" (for violent criminals who seriously injure their victims);
3. WHIPPING as a merciful alternative to execution, a merciful alternative to an "eye for an eye," or for crimes with no other specified penalty (such as assault with a deadly weapon);
4. THE MARK OF JUSTICE (for those like Cain, who committed crimes worthy of execution but who received mercy instead,

and for those who have committed miscellaneous crimes); and,
5. ENSLAVEMENT FOR SIX YEARS (for thieves who cannot pay back a multiple of what they have stolen).

Now suppose, for example, that starting next year all potential *new* prison inmates were sentenced using biblical punishments (one through five) instead of being sent to prison. Further suppose that all *current* prison inmates who should have been executed according to God's principles of civil law were, in fact, executed and that all *current* inmates who had committed violent crimes were "resentenced" according to the biblical principles of an "eye for an eye," whipping, and the "mark of justice," and then released from prison. Let us also suppose that the rest of the current inmates were whipped according to biblical guidelines (but using a depreciated scale depending upon how much time they had left to serve in prison), and then, they were also sent home. As a result of implementing God's five principles of punishment, our prisons would finally be empty, and we would never need them again.

So, God's five biblical alternatives to imprisonment illustrate why God's principles of civil law are not only valid today, but are also superior to our current principles of civil law! If America would only implement God's principles of civil law enforcement into our national legislation, then we would:

1. solve all of our prison problems;
2. create the greatest possible deterrent for all forms of crime (but especially for violent crime);
3. save hundreds of billions of dollars of taxes; and,
4. render hundreds of man's laws of punishment to be obsolete and superfluous!

And that, is God's view of prison reform, and how to stop crime in America without prisons!

Chapter Eleven

GOD'S VIEW OF GUN CONTROL VERSUS THE SECOND AMENDMENT RIGHT TO BEAR ARMS

The Second Amendment was written to allow all citizens to "keep and bear arms," not so they could defend *themselves*, but so they could defend their *country*, and so that our nation's early military budget could be kept as small as possible by having the citizens use their own weapons in battle. For it is written:

A well regulated Militia, being necessary to the security of a free state, the right of the people to keep and bear Arms, shall not be infringed. (the Second Amendment)

A "militia" is a "body of citizens enrolled and drilled in military organizations other than the regular military forces, and called out only in emergencies" (*Funk and Wagnall's Standard Desk Dictionary*, 1969).

In Article I, Section Eight (paragraph 1, 12-16) of the Constitution, the founders allowed Congress to collect taxes to pay for a standing navy, but *NOT* for a standing army. Evidently, Congress was allowed only to collect taxes to support an army for a period of up to two years and only when such an army was actually needed. Otherwise, according to the Constitution, most military action was expected to occur by drafting the militia into active service for national emergencies. The militia in modern America is the National Guard, with an arsenal of weapons provided by the federal government through hefty income taxes. But in the 1700s, our early federal government did not have a whole lot of extra money to pay for weapons, for there were no federal income taxes during that time. Therefore, the Second Amendment to the Constitution was written to guarantee citizens the right to keep and bear arms, not so they could defend *themselves* individually, but so they could defend the *country* as part of a militia. In this way, our "penniless," newborn federal government could rather quickly raise an army of men most of whom could provide their own weapons for battle—so the federal government could use its meager financial reserves elsewhere (such as to pay for canons or ammunition, etc.). This would allow Congress to get by with a smaller military budget and control military spending more easily!

Today, our federal government has a massive military budget, thanks in large part to the Sixteenth Amendment (3 February 1913), which allows the federal government to collect income taxes. As a result, not only do we have a national guard with large numbers of armories which store military weapons for our modern militia, but also America now has a huge standing army, marines, and air force, in addition to our original standing navy.

Therefore, since our well-armed National Guard represent the modern equivalent of the ancient State militia of the 1700s and the 1800s, and since America now has a standing army and a standing marine force, the purpose for which the Second Amendment was originally written has now been rendered obsolete, for we no longer need to guarantee civilians the right to own weapons so they can bring them into battle with them. And, since the Second Amendment was not written so Americans could "keep and bear arms" to defend *themselves* individually from criminals, but so they could defend their *country* as part of a militia, then the Second Amendment cannot be "properly" used to defend the right for Americans to keep weapons any longer. At the very least, the Second Amendment should not be used to guarantee that all citizens have the legal right to own weapons for war (such as oozies, assault rifles, and grenades) as a pretense of being "ready" to defend our country. So also, the Second Amendment should not be used to justify owning handguns just for citizens to defend themselves, because this was not the original purpose of the Second Amendment either!

Any discussion about whether Americans should still be allowed to own handguns or assault rifles should be based upon truth, and not upon a perpetual distortion of the purpose and application of the Second Amendment. Otherwise, our nation will be plunged into violence and chaos because of a blind allegiance to a false understanding of the ideals of our founders.

With this introduction, you might think I'm going to say that America must have gun control. Surprisingly, the Bible does not teach that weapon control plays any role in God's plan for civil peace!

Let me explain. In the previous chapter—"God's View of Prison Reform, & Stopping Crime in America without Prisons"—we learned that if America implemented God's five biblical alternatives to imprisonment, then we would be able to:

1. eliminate all our prison problems;
2. save hundreds of billions of dollars in taxes;

3. have the strongest possible deterrent to crime (yet still have an emphasis on mercy); and,
4. render hundreds of man's federal and state laws which concern crime, punishment, prison, and parole to be obsolete and superfluous.

In other words, God provided mankind with five biblical principles of punishment which make the problem of overcrowded prisons disappear. So also, these same five biblical principles of punishment create the strongest possible deterrent to crime making the problem of gun control largely disappear as well. Therefore, the problems of overcrowded prisons and gun control are basically non-issues to almighty God, for these issues only arise when the governments of mankind are violating God's principles of civil law and civil law enforcement. Also, nearly *all* of the problems of governments today are only symptoms of the government's willful disobedience of God's principles of civil law, which could have prevented these problems in the first place.

You see, the issues which are important to God are issues which God discusses in the Bible at least once, if not several times. Generally, if a certain issue is not mentioned in the Bible, then to almighty God, it is a non-issue which could have been prevented from ever becoming a serious problem in the first place (if only the governments of mankind would just adopt and regularly enforce God's principles of civil law as part their legislation).

We can confirm that gun control is a non-issue to God because nowhere in the Bible is the concept of "weapon control" mentioned. For there are no civil laws in the Bible which infringe upon the Israelite's "right" to own and carry weapons—whether for hunting, for self-defense, or for war.

Although God never gave any laws which would restrict weapons, he had strict punishments for the person using the weapon. For God's laws regulate only the criminal, and not the criminal's weapon. You see, God knew thousands of years ago that when you have the proper punishment for the criminal, then you will not need to regulate the criminal's weapons. For instance, when a criminal deliberately brings a gun with him to commit a crime, then often he is willing to kill his victim with it. This means that the victim's death will either be first degree murder (deliberate and premeditated), or second degree murder (a crime of passion).

The biblical punishment for deliberate, premeditated first degree murder is execution without mercy. For it is written:

> ... if a man schemes and kills another man deliberately, take him ... and put him to death. (Exod. 21:14 NIV)

... if a man hates his neighbor and lies in wait for him, assaults and kills him ... hand him over to die. Show him NO PITY. (Deut. 19:11-13 NIV; emphasis added)

Moreover, there is still a death penalty even if the judge considers the crime to be second degree murder, although in this case, God does not say to "Show no mercy." For it is written:

If anyone injures his neighbor, whatever he has done must be done to him: fracture for fracture, eye for eye, tooth for tooth. As he has injured the other, so he must be injured ... but whoever kills a man must be put to death. (Lev. 24:19-20, 21b NIV)

Furthermore, whipping (Deut. 25:1-3; NIV) can be used as a merciful alternative to either execution or an "eye for an eye," and can also be used for crimes with no other specified penalty, such as assault with a deadly weapon. Finally, the "mark of justice" (a tattoo on the back of a hand indicating the date, the crime, and the punishment received) can also be creatively applied to deter further violent crime.

These four swift and extremely effective biblical punishments:

1. *execution* (for deliberate premeditated murder);
2. an *"eye for an eye"* (for purposeful serious violent injuries);
3. *whipping* (for assault with a deadly weapon); and,
4. the *"mark of justice"* ... will create the greatest deterrent to violent crime which can possibly be devised, and, if implemented, would make the problem of gun control to largely disappear!

For most of those convicted of first or second degree murder would be eliminated by execution, and those other criminals who had a propensity to violence would probably disarm themselves because they feared the "eye for an eye" statute of God's justice, therefore, honest, law abiding citizens would no longer feel the same need to purchase and carry handguns for self-defense because violent crime would slowly disappear in America.

This does not mean that it is *wrong* for a government to regulate weapons, only that the Bible teaches that it is *unnecessary* for a government to regulate weapons once it has adopted and is regularly enforcing God's principles of punishment. If a government is doing this, then its laws concerning weapon control will slowly become obsolete and superfluous. So, if a nation has a problem with violent crime and controlling the possession of weapons, then the government's priority should be to adopt God's principles of punishment long before considering any gun control, because gun control laws only delay the true solution to civil peace. For you see, if weapon control laws would work to deter violent crime as well as mankind thinks they should work, then God would have thought of this idea thousands of years ago, and would have given the Israelites more specific commands concerning the possession of weapons.

In conclusion, America should not distort the Second Amendment to guarantee citizens the right to own weapons of war, or even to own handguns for self-defense. These issues must be decided on their own merits, and not by a blind allegiance to a false understanding of the purpose of the Second Amendment.

On the other hand, the Bible teaches us that if we adopt gun control without God's principles of punishment, it will not work and will only delay the true solution to civil peace. Moreover, if America would regularly enforce God's principles of punishment for violent criminals, then the problem of gun control would fade away and become a non-issue, just as God intended all along!

And that, is God's view of gun control according to the Bible!

Chapter Twelve

HOW GOD'S RULES FOR EXECUTION MAXIMIZE THE DETERRENCE OF CAPITAL CRIME

It is written:

> You must certainly put him to death.... Then all Israel will hear and be afraid, and no one among you will do such an evil thing again. (Deut. 13:9a, 11 NIV)

It is clear by this verse that God intended execution to be a very strong deterrent to capital crime. However, God's rules for execution are entirely different from man's rules for execution. As usual, no matter what the problem, God's ways will always work, while man's ways will often fail. So, it is very important to understand how God's rules differ from man's rules on the subject of execution!

God gave Israel six guidelines concerning execution which were designed to maximize deterrence to capital crime to the greatest extent possible. This chapter explains the reasons why God's guidelines for execution will truly work to deter crime, while America's guidelines for execution will often fail to deter crime.

You see, in order for execution to deter capital crime as effectively as God intended, the Bible teaches that these particular criminals need to be executed.

1. <u>frequently</u> (not rarely, like in America),
2. <u>immediately</u> after the trial (not months and years later, like in America),
3. with <u>no possibility of retrial or stay of execution</u> (unlike the unlimited appeals and stays of execution we provide here in America),
4. <u>just outside</u> the <u>same crime-producing neighborhood</u> where the <u>offense was committed</u> (not in some distant city unrelated to the crime, like here in America),
5. <u>IN public</u> (not in private, like in America), and,

6. BY the public citizens themselves (not by a single executioner, like in America)!

Now let's examine these six issues by the eternal light of the Holy Scriptures.

I. LACK OF ENFORCEMENT OF THE DEATH PENALTY

America does not enforce the death penalty frequently enough because of three mistaken beliefs which are contrary to Scripture:

A. We mistakenly believe the death penalty is "wrong" or "immoral." God would not give the Israelites any command which was "wrong" or "immoral," and He did give the principle of the death penalty to the Israelites. For it is written:

> But if a man schemes and kills another man deliberately... put him to death. (Exod. 21:14 NIV)

B. We mistakenly believe Christ "abolished" the death penalty. But in the New Testament, Jesus declares to the Pharisees:

> For God said, "Honor your father and mother" and "Anyone who curses his father or mother must be PUT TO DEATH." (Matt. 15:4 NIV; emphasis added)

Here, we discover that Jesus still approves of the death penalty when he quotes from Exodus (21:17) and Leviticus (20:9). And of course, you remember from chapter eight of this book that the death penalty for cursing your parents was actually the least of all the eighteen biblical death penalties. Since Christ supported the least of the death penalties (for the mere verbal crime of cursing your parents), then he surely supported other death penalties for the far more serious crimes as well.

C. We mistakenly believe the death penalty does not deter crime. But the Bible says:

> You must certainly put him to death.... Then all Israel will hear and be afraid, and no one among you will do such an evil thing again. (Deut. 13:9, 11 NIV)

Clearly, the Bible says the death penalty (when carried out using God's guidelines of course) is a deterrent to crime.

Furthermore, the expression *"must* be put to death" (NIV) is used at least eight times in the Bible, indicating that God intended the standard penalty for capital crimes to be death, not life in prison. Therefore, God intended execution to be performed much more frequently than it is in America (that is, at least until the crime rate drops because of the tremendous effectiveness of God's system of justice).

In summary, according to the Bible:

A. execution is not immoral, for execution is God's idea;
B. execution was not abolished by Christ;
C. execution does deter capital crime (when carried out according to God's guidelines); and,
D. execution (not life in prison) is supposed to be the standard maximum sentence.

Therefore, the Bible teaches that the death penalty should be enforced frequently, not rarely, like we do in America.

II. DELAYED ENFORCEMENT OF THE DEATH PENALTY

America does not execute the criminal immediately after conviction, a practice which is also contrary to biblical teaching. For it is written:

> When the sentence for a crime is not quickly carried out, the hearts of the people are filled with schemes to do wrong. (Eccles. 8:11 NIV)

Our executions should be performed as quickly as possible after the conviction, because God says part of the deterrent of capital punishment involves the speed with which it is carried out. This is another reason why capital punishment in the U.S. does not deter crime as much as it would if we followed God's guidelines. Therefore, any law which postpones executions after the death sentence has been given (such as laws which allow court appeals, retrials, or "stays-of-execution") should be revoked. (See problem number three below.)

III. WE MISTAKENLY CHANGE OUR MIND ABOUT EXECUTING SOMEONE WHO HAS ALREADY BEEN SENTENCED TO DEATH

Even *after* a criminal is sentenced to death, America's legal system mistakenly grants retrials and appeals, and our state governors mistakenly grant stays of execution, totally contrary to the biblical teaching in Ecclesiastes 8:11 (see above) and Leviticus 27:29 NIV (see below). For it is written:

> No person devoted to destruction may be ransomed; he must be put to death. (Lev. 27:29 NIV)

In this context, the phrase "devoted to destruction" means "sentenced to being destroyed by execution," and the word "ransomed" means paying ransom money to someone (like the judge or lawyer) to "save the criminal from his death sentence."

In the United States, we pay millions of tax dollars in "ransom money" to save the criminals from their death sentence, which goes to pay for new trials or life imprisonment instead! But the Bible teaches us that no person who has already been "sentenced to death," can be "bailed out" with "ransom money" for any reason. In other words, once a death sentence has been given by the judge, the Bible teaches that you cannot change it for any reason. Therefore, it is a sin for a government ruler or judge to grant a retrial, or a stay of execution for anyone who has been already sentenced to death.

However, even though all death sentences are unchangeable, the Bible does teach that a judge can always ask for help from more experienced judges at any time before the case has been decided. For it is written:

> Have them serve as judges for the people at all times, but have them bring every difficult case to you; the simple cases they can decide for themselves. . . . The difficult cases they brought to Moses, but the simple cases they decided themselves. (Exod. 18:22a, 26b NIV)

In other words, a case can always be referred to a "higher court" *before* the case has been decided, and specifically before a death sentence has been given (Exod. 18:22a, 26b NIV). However, according to Leviticus 27:29, NIV, no one can ever appeal to a higher court, or order a stay of execution *after* the death sentence has been given without sinfully disregarding God's laws.

The purpose of these laws was to force all judges to ask for whatever judicial help they needed quickly, so they could reach the correct verdict during the first trial and never have to have a retrial. This also means that you can now "carry out the sentence for the crime quickly" so "the hearts of the people will not be filled with schemes to do wrong" (Eccles. 8:11 NIV). In other words, by forcing all death sentences to actually be carried out quickly, God maximizes the deterrence to crime and closes another loophole of hope for future criminals that they might avoid execution. For the judicial sins of granting retrials and commuting death sentences to life in prison have grossly undermined the death penalty's deterrent to future crime. These have also simultaneously cost society millions of dollars in taxes for needless court costs and for decades of needless incarceration.

IV. WE EXECUTE CRIMINALS AT THE WRONG LOCATION!

America mistakenly ignores God's commands that executions should generally take place outside the exact neighborhood, community, or town where the crime was committed, not in some far away capital city. For it is written:

> The man must die. The whole assembly must stone him outside the camp. (Num. 15:35 NIV)

> Take the man or woman who has done this evil deed to your city gate and stone that person to death. (Deut. 17:5 NIV)

> You shall take them both to the gate of the town and stone them to death. (Deut. 22:24 NIV)

This means that all executions must take place immediately outside the same neighborhood, community, or town where the crime was committed in order to create the greatest deterrent to crime in the place where it is needed most.

You see, part of the problem of crime deterrence involves the local community's apathy to the crime emerging from within its own neighborhood. Therefore, it is the crime-producing community itself which needs to be rehabilitated from community *apathy* to community *action*. This way, they will be more likely to follow God's commands to rebuke sin (Lev. 19:17b NIV) and report sin-crime (Lev. 5:1 NIV). This gives the citizens a sense of purging the wickedness from inside their neighborhood, which is symbolic of keeping their community swept clean from crime. This helps in the local deterrence of crime and is one more thing that we don't do in the U.S.

V. WE MISTAKENLY DON'T REQUIRE EXECUTIONS TO BE HELD IN PUBLIC!

America doesn't have public executions, despite God's command that He wants all executions to be public. For it is written:

> Then the Lord said to Moses, "The man must die. The whole assembly must stone him outside the camp." (Num. 15:35 NIV)

Since the Bible teaches us that executions using God's methods should deter crime, then executions IN public must also help in this deterrence to crime as well!

All executions in the Bible were commanded to be PUBLIC executions and were held OUTDOORS. This accommodates and affects the greatest number of spectators—to maximize the potential for transforming the way the citizens of the small community think about justice, and to increase the LOCAL deterrence of crime!

VI. EXECUTION BY PUBLIC PARTICIPATION— USING THE LARGEST NUMBER OF EXECUTIONERS POSSIBLE

God chose execution by public participation to be the standard method of execution for Israel according to nine verses in the Bible. For it is written:

Then the Lord said to Moses, "The man must die. The whole assembly must *stone* him outside the camp." (Num. 15:35 NIV)

The people of the community are to *stone* him. (Lev. 20:2 NIV)

You are to *stone* them. (Lev. 20:27 NIV)

... the entire assembly is to *stone* him. (Lev. 24:14 NIV)

... Then all the *men* of his town shall *stone* him to death. (Deut. 21:21 NIV)

... the entire assembly is to *stone* him. (Lev. 24:16b NIV)

(emphasis added, see also Lev. 24:16b; Num. 15:35; Deut. 17:5; 22:24)

These biblical references make it clear that God ordained execution by public participation to be the standard method of execution to be performed by the male Israelites for all time. These male community members are not just watching the execution, but are actually participating in executing one of their own wicked neighbors having been convicted of a biblical felony and the judge (or judges) could find no reason to be merciful in order to avoid the execution.

Since the principles underlying God's civil laws are valid today and superior to our current civil laws, then the principles underlying the laws of execution by public participation should also work better to deter crime in America than our current methods of execution.

But why would God choose a method of execution which requires a whole crowd of executioners? Why didn't God choose a form of execution which requires only a single executioner instead? After all, since Moses lived with the Egyptian princes for the first forty years of his life, as part of his education he probably learned at least eleven methods of execution (which did not require public participation, but which required only a single executioner), such as:

1. stabbing to death by a knife or sword,
2. stabbing to death by a spear,
3. stabbing to death by arrows (from a single archer),
4. cutting the throat,
5. cutting off the head,
6. strangling by hand,
7. strangling by a rope (hanging by the neck),
8. drowning,
9. whipping to death,
10. clubbing to death, and,
11. poisoning to death.

Since these eleven methods of execution should work very well (and require neither my participation nor even my presence), why would God purposely choose a method which forces me to participate in administering neighborhood justice when I'd much rather not be involved? Is there no way to purge evil from my neighborhood without having to involve the public? For the public would rather not have to be responsible for purging the evil from its own community. Surely it must be someone else's responsibility!

This attitude of apathy and indifference is actually one of the keys to the problem of crime. For our strong reluctance to be involved in community executions in part reflects a much deeper reluctance to rebuke our neighbor's sins (Lev. 19:17b NIV) and report our neighbor's crimes (Lev. 5:1 NIV) as part of an ongoing community effort to purge sin and crime from our own neighborhood. It is this community apathy and indifference towards the growth of sin and crime within our own neighborhood which actually encourages crime—passively at first, then actively later.

God's idea, therefore, was to take advantage of our natural revulsion against participating in a public execution, and redirect this passion to increase local crime deterrence. For after having participated in a public execution once, it is clear that those involved would now do whatever is necessary to avoid repeating such an unpleasant experience, including developing a missionary-like zeal to rebuke all sin and report all crime in their community while it is still in its early stages in order to stop it from escalating to a point where they'd have to be involved in another execution.

In this way, execution by public participation transforms community apathy and indifference (about local sin and crime) into community action and involvement. God knew that only execution by public participation would have this transforming effect upon communities whose profound apathy and indifference towards their own local sin and crime was providing a safe-haven for ongoing wickedness.

Put another way, God holds communities partially responsible for the behavior of their criminals, just as He holds parents partially responsible for the behavior of their children (Mark 9:42 NIV). Public stoning, therefore, symbolizes the idea that the local citizens are responsible before God for the death of the criminal by execution, just as God sees them as responsible for his death because they allowed his evil to continue for so long unrebuked, unreported, and unpunished by biblical principles (see chapters eight, nine, and ten) which could have stopped his growing evil long before it ever got far enough for him to be executed.

So in some sense, requiring male community members to participate in a God-ordained legal execution of one of their community members is God's method of disciplining and rehabilitating the entire community of their failure to obey God's commands concerning rebuking sin, reporting crime, and nipping crime in the bud by a merciful whipping long before execution would become necessary. Forcing the community leaders to participate in a public stoning would make them realize that:

> To some extent we are all responsible for the death of this criminal. For had we taught him better at home, at church, and at school, and had we all rebuked his sins and reported his crimes more vigorously, and had we punished him for his many well known earlier sins as God commanded, then maybe we wouldn't be here today publicly executing this man for what are (in part) our own failures to obey God as a family, as a church, as a school, and as a community! Therefore, let us all make a public covenant with God never to allow the emergence of such evil again in our community, and that from this day forward each one of us will do our part as God commands, not only to get ourselves right with God, but also to get (and to keep) our community right with God as well!

This is why the method of execution is much more important to God than it is to us. American society does not force local citizens to bear the responsibility of having to execute their own local criminals. But according to the Bible, having an entire crowd of reluctant executioners from the apathetic local community is essential in order to accomplish God's divine purpose of legislating godly peer pressure by transforming community apathy and indifference into community action and involvement to passionately purge sin and crime from their own community, as they should have been doing all along! And of course, this same passionate enthusiasm to purge sin and crime from the community was also designed by God to encourage them to lead their neighbors into a personal saving relationship with Jehovah, for this not only leads to greater crime deterrence, but more importantly, to salvation and eternal life.

To reiterate, this sudden community passion to keep the neighborhood clean from sin and crime should in turn create a community-wide culture of legislated godly peer pressure which should be so intense that the local crime-producing neighborhood would be transformed from a community of rebellion to a community of righteousness. Therefore, the greater the number of participating community executioners, the greater the degree of transformation of the community from an attitude of apathy to an attitude of action. This is why the method of execution (by public participation) is more important to deter future crime than is the actual death of the criminal.

What's more, God's method of execution by public participation is quick, simple, low-tech, tax-free, can be performed anywhere, does not require any skill from the participants, and causes minimal pain and suffering to the condemned individual during his execution.

Despite the New Testament stories where stoning appears to be a slow, painful torture of the criminal by hitting him with hundreds of small baseball sized stones, there is actually no biblical description of the way God intended stoning to be. Furthermore, just as the Pharisees corrupted all God's other commands, they probably corrupted God's intended concept of stoning as well. After all, the Jews stoned Paul without even giving him a trial (Acts 14:19) and they tried to stone Christ (twice) without giving him a trial either (John 8:59; John 10:31), and they stoned Stephen after producing false witnesses against him (Acts 6:13) and without even finishing his trial (Acts 7:56-58 NIV). So, why should we believe that the Jews got the procedure of stoning so right when they got everything else so wrong? It is much more likely that God did not intend his method of execution to be like the mob-vigilante stonings which are recorded in the New Testament verses above. In fact, it is very probable that God intended execution by public stoning to be as quick and as painless as possible. Had Israel followed God's commands and appointed only godly "Christian" men after God's own heart to be their judges—judges who truly loved mercy and who knew that God's civil laws emphasized mercy—these judges would have also emphasized mercy in their system of public stoning and made it as quick and as painless as possible.

To make stoning as painless as possible, I believe a godly judge would allow the criminal to receive enough strong drink to render him stuporous or even unconscious prior to his execution. For it is written:

> Give strong drink unto him that is ready to perish . . . (Prov. 31:6a KJV)

In this way, the criminal would "feel no pain" (so to speak). Even Christ was offered wine (twice) on the cross to "ease his pain," and, although he refused it the first time (Matt. 27:34), he actually requested it and drank it the second time it was offered (Matt. 27:48; John 19:28-30). Now you are probably thinking,

> But a painless execution will probably not provide the same deterrent towards future crimes that a painful execution will.

But remember, according to the Bible, the major deterrent of execution by stoning probably does not come from the death itself, but from the transformation of the local community leaders who participate in the stoning into leaders who are more likely to teach their neighbors about Christ, rebuke sin, and report crimes. And, as this process gets set into motion, the entire local community becomes restored to a better (but not perfect) fellowship with God and maintains an enthusiastic community spirit to preserve a society of righteousness. Thus, the major source of deterrence of future evil comes from the propagation of community-wide godly peer pressure for righteousness; and this part of crime deterrence is totally unaffected by whether the execution was painful or "painless."

With this in mind, imagine the condemned criminal to be nearly unconscious from strong drink and bound and lying face down at the bottom of a shallow pit. The pit is surrounded by the witnesses to the crime, the family of the victim of the crime, and many prominent neighborhood citizens, all holding very large stones, each weighing perhaps twenty-five to thirty pounds. After the witnesses throw the first stones (Deut. 17:7 NIV), twenty or thirty more massive stones are then thrown down on top of the criminal's head and body, and so he dies rather quickly. If however, the criminal does not die immediately, the procedure can be quickly repeated once or twice if necessary, and then, if the criminal is still alive, he can be quickly stabbed through the heart with a spear to ensure that there is absolutely no prolonged suffering.

As you can see, by adhering to God's commands for leaders to love mercy, execution by public stoning can be designed to be as quick and as "painless" as possible. Therefore, stoning does not have to be the extremely painful and prolonged torture that the New Testament Jews made it out to be.

Why did God choose stoning over having a firing squad of average local citizens with bows and arrows? Because shooting arrows with a bow requires too much skill, and so the criminal would be dead from the bull's eye into his heart by the local Robin Hood long before any of the rest of the citizens would have hit the target the first time. Therefore, community apathy would not be transformed into community action because the citizens never felt the responsibility for executing the criminal because all but one of them missed the target! So God chose stoning, because stoning requires no significant skill.

Why not publicly execute the criminal by having each citizen stab him simultaneously with his own knife or sword? Because emotions run so high at executions (as you can see from TV news coverage) and would run even higher in executions requiring public participation. It is not a good idea to have the entire community arrive armed to the teeth with weapons, because a riot might break out and endanger the participating executioners, especially if some citizens try to rescue the condemned criminal. So God chose stoning because stoning was a method of execution which would not endanger the participants.

Although modern science could probably design a high-tech system of execution which would require the simultaneous participation of twenty to thirty executioners, this system would surely be too expensive for small communities to afford. In addition, just having each citizen simply flip a switch (or something like that) would not generate the same emotional rage against sin and crime required to transform the community's apathy into community action.

Therefore, stoning is God's method of choice for execution because it requires no skill to perform, does not endanger the participants, does not require high-tech equipment, requires no tax dollars to implement, can generally be performed outside of any community, creates the greatest degree of emotional involvement in the execution and subsequent rage against local sin and crime, and therefore has the greatest potential to transform community apathy into community action. Because we refuse to follow God's six biblical guidelines for capital punishment, we end up using the wrong methods and procedures for execution. As a result, the methods we choose for execution do not deter crime as much as we had hoped. Modern methods of execution essentially do nothing to transform the neighborhood where the crime occurred from apathy to enthusiasm about purging the evil from within their community. As a result, the good people of America's neighborhoods will continue to passively encourage crime by their unwillingness to "get involved." If the criminal is one of their own family, they may even consider not reporting the crimes they have witnessed to the authorities at all. Both of these behaviors *passively* encourage crime.

The bad people of the community will continue to *actively* encourage crime by their unrestrained ungodly peer pressure. Moreover, they will continue not reporting the crimes they have witnessed to the authorities. They may lie to the authorities by providing false alibis for the suspects, and may also be willing to harbor known fugitives from justice. In other words, American neighborhoods appear to operate under a philosophy which actually functions to protect the criminal. The more corrupt the neighborhood, the more protection the criminal receives. As a result, criminals are encouraged to feel confident that they can safely begin (or continue) a life of sin and crime within their corrupted neighborhood because the threat of actually being caught, convicted, and executed by the state becomes so unlikely.

The best method of capital punishment must also rehabilitate the local community's self-destructive culture by transforming it into a culture where there is:

1. extreme involvement of each citizen in the neighborhood to eliminate evil from his community;
2. a refusal to hide, harbor, or assist any criminal in avoiding justice, even if the criminal is your best friend or is from your own family; and,

3. godly peer pressure to deter crime by biblical rebuke of all criminal behavior, followed by reporting all crimes to the authorities, even when the criminal is your best friend or is from your own family!

Only execution by public participation can involve enough local citizens as executioners and spectators to evoke the necessary emotional intensity and rage against crime, to reverse the neighborhood's counterculture which encourages crime. In other words, following God's guidelines for execution facilitates the destruction of the last stronghold of future emerging crime—public apathy and indifference. Remember, "all that is necessary for evil to triumph is that good men do nothing!" Only execution by public participation, as described in the Bible, has this thorough, complete, and well-rounded effect to deter local neighborhood crime. Ultimately, most crime (which involves capital punishment) is local neighborhood crime, or started years earlier as local neighborhood crime, where it should have been stopped before it escalated.

In summary, God gave Israel six guidelines concerning execution which commanded that those who were convicted of capital crimes (presuming that the judge found no reason to be merciful) were to be executed:

1. frequently (not rarely, like here in America),
2. immediately after the trial (not months or years later,
3. with no possibility of retrial or stay of execution (unlike the unlimited appeals and stays of execution we provide here in America),
4. just outside the same crime-producing community where the offense was committed (not in some distant city unrelated to the crime, like here in America),
5. IN public (not in private, like here in America); and,
6. BY the public, to transform the public attitude of community apathy into community action against sin and crime!

And that is how God's rules for execution can maximize the deterrence of capital crime!

Chapter Thirteen

GOD'S VIEW OF WITCHCRAFT & THE SALEM WITCH TRIALS

Many people fear that if American courts ever adopted the biblical principles of justice then we would have another disaster like the Salem witch trials. These people mistakenly believe that the tragedy in Salem resulted from judges following "out-of-date" Mosaic laws (including the Mosaic laws against witchcraft). And so, even more tragedies could occur if our courts enforced the Mosaic laws against homosexuality, adultery, or fornication. Therefore, they conclude that America should avoid using *any* of the Mosaic civil laws in our courts and in our government.

Thus, a misunderstanding of the tragedy at Salem has led Americans to the false conclusion that the Mosaic civil laws are "out-of-date" and have no practical application today. This conclusion is based upon the mistaken belief that the judges at the Salem witch trials *followed* God's laws, when in reality they *broke* God's laws. In fact, these judges violated at least *eight* biblical civil principles which God designed to safeguard true justice and to prevent such tragedies from happening. A better understanding of God's view of witchcraft and the Salem witch trials will clear up this confusion and exalt the value of the Mosaic civil laws, so we will realize that true adherence to God's civil laws will actually *prevent* tragedies of justice and not *cause* them.

With this as a background, let's examine God's laws against witchcraft and see what should have happened at the Salem witch trials if the judges had truly followed God's laws instead of breaking them.

The biblical punishment for witchcraft carries a maximum sentence of death. For it is written:

> Thou shalt not suffer a witch to live. (Exod. 22:18 NIV)

> A man or woman who is a medium or spiritist among you must be put to death. You are to stone them; their blood will be on their own heads. (Lev. 29:27 NIV)

Astrologers and false prophets also fall under this same category as witches, mediums, and spiritists. For it is written:

> Let your astrologers come forward, those stargazers who make predictions month by month . . . Surely they are like stubble; the fire will burn them up. They cannot even save themselves from the power of the flame. (Isa. 47:13, 14 NIV)

It is clear in this verse that God is planning an "eternal death penalty" in hell for astrologers. However, God also commanded an earthly death penalty for all false prophets, whether they prophesy on behalf of the arrangement of stars in space (as do astrologers), or they prophesy on behalf of "other gods." For it is written:

> . . . a prophet who speaks in the name of other gods, must be put to death. (Deut. 18:20 NIV)

Furthermore, "channellers" (and others who attempt to contact the dead and prophesy on their behalf) would also fall into this category. Therefore, according to the Bible, astrology and "channelling" are sins against God which should also be crimes against the state, and should still carry a maximum sentence of death.

Nearly five hundred years later God was still just as angry about witches, mediums, and spiritists. For instance, God was angry at King Saul for the sin of using the witch of Endor to attempt contact with the deceased prophet Samuel for advice. So, God told King Saul (through Samuel) that he would die in battle within the next twenty-four hours (1 Sam. 28:3-19, 29; 29:8 NIV). This story teaches us that God has not changed his mind and will continue to remain angry about witches, spiritists, mediums, and modern day "channellers" and will always want these sins to remain a crime against the state, and carry a maximum sentence of death.

Some of you may be wondering,

> But what about the Salem witch trials? Didn't those tragic executions at Salem teach us that witchcraft should not be prosecuted as a crime against the state, and that we should not use biblical guidelines for our courtroom proceedings? After all, the "witch hunt" hysteria in Salem during 1692 resulted in 150 people being accused of witchcraft—thirty-one of whom were actually executed. Isn't that why witchcraft is no longer a crime in America?

Actually, the reason why the tragedy at Salem occurred was not because the judges at the Salem witch trials *followed* biblical guidelines, but because the judges *violated* biblical guidelines for their courtroom proceedings during the trials. The only biblical principle which they did follow was that convicted witches should be executed (Exod. 22:18; Lev. 29:27). But they willfully ignored many other biblical courtroom principles which they needed to follow just as faithfully.

You see, God had given Moses eight additional biblical principles which He designed to safeguard against this type of tragedy, and these biblical safeguards were ignored by the judges at the Salem witch trials.

First of all, God does not allow hearsay to be used as evidence in cases which may bring a possible death penalty, and instead requires two or three eyewitnesses for any conviction. But in the Salem witch trials, the judge violated this principle by allowing something called "spectral evidence," which is evidence from "testimony given by witnesses about voices or apparitions perceived only by them" (*American Academic Encyclopedia*, vol. 17, 1981, 31). In other words, spectral evidence is nothing more than "supernatural hearsay," and therefore should have been disallowed by the judges at the Salem witch trials. So, by ignoring biblical guidelines, the judge allowed witnesses to claim they "saw a vision" or "heard voices" which revealed to them that the accused person was a witch. There is no biblical precedent for testimony based upon a vision—no command of God, Bible verse, or Bible story which allows such a travesty of justice. Additionally, when the court mistakenly trusts evidence based upon a "vision," it becomes harder to evaluate whether or not the person is deliberately bearing false witness. So, instead of *obeying* God's laws and disallowing spectral evidence to be used as testimony, the judges *defied* God's laws, and as a result, executed many people who were probably innocent.

Secondly, the judges allowed more than 150 people to be brought to trial and accused of witchcraft based "mainly on the evidence of children" (*Academic American Encyclopedia*, vol. 20, 1981, 192). Nowhere in the Bible does it say that you can use the evidence of children to make a case. Furthermore, it is written:

> When men have a dispute, they are to take it to court and the judges will decide the case, acquitting the innocent and condemning the guilty. (Deut. 25:1 NIV)

Notice that it does not say, "When children have a dispute . . ." In other words, eyewitnesses to a disputed event were expected to be adults and not children.

So when the Bible teaches that you need two or three eyewitnesses for a conviction (Deut. 19:15 NIV), the implication has always been that these eyewitnesses are adults and not children. This does not mean that God wants judges to ignore the testimony of children, but only that the major testimony should ordinarily come from adults. Therefore, it does not appear likely that God would allow the testimony of children to constitute the main body of evidence for a conviction under normal circumstances, but this is exactly what the judges allowed during the Salem witch trials.

Thirdly, the judges forgot that the heart of the law is *mercy*, not execution. For it is written:

> He has showed you, O man, what is good. And what does the Lord require of you? To act justly and to love *mercy* and to walk humbly with your God. (Mic. 6:8 NIV; emphasis added)

So, the judges at the trial were required by God to love mercy. Besides that, only two of the eighteen biblical death penalties (murder and idolatry) contain the words "show no mercy!" This expression is conspicuously absent from the sixteen other biblical death penalties, which means that for the crime of witchcraft, God required the judges to "look for a reason to be merciful if at all possible." Therefore, the judges in Salem were supposed to show mercy to any repentant individual who was convicted for the first time of witchcraft. In this manner, the local judges could provide a living demonstration of the grace, forgiveness, and mercy of the Supreme Judge, our Lord Jesus Christ (John 5:22 NIV).

Remember, God does not take pleasure in the death of the wicked, but prefers instead to have people repent of their sins and not be executed! For it is written:

> "Do I take any pleasure in the death of the wicked?" declares the Sovereign Lord. "Rather, am I not pleased when they turn from their ways and live?" (Ezek. 18:23 NIV)

So, God is pleased when those who are truly convicted of witchcraft can avoid being executed when they repent in the courtroom, and submit to the sovereignty of God's laws and his wisdom, and are restored to a right fellowship with God and with the community of Christian believers.

Fourthly, the biblical penalty for bearing false witness was to:

> do to him as he intended to do to his brother.... Show no pity: life for life ... (Deut. 19:16-20 NIV)

Thus, the judges were required to inform those participating in the trial that anyone convicted of deliberately giving false testimony with the malicious intent of getting that person executed by the court would result in the false witness being executed instead. The judges evidently neglected to remind the court that the penalty for deliberately falsely accusing an innocent person of being a witch could cost the malicious witness their life. If this warning had been given by the judge at the beginning of the trial, then there would have been no false witnesses at all. But, historical records indicate that there were false witnesses, so these biblical guidelines were clearly not followed.

Fifthly, the Bible teaches that "if the case is too difficult for you," then you can either ask someone else to help you judge the case, or you can give the entire case over to another judge (Exod. 18:22, 26 NIV). Therefore, judges could have been brought in from other parts of the state for assistance during the trials, and this would have helped prevent the mass hysteria which occurred. However, the judges in Salem did not do this and yet it is clear from the historical records that the cases being tried were "too difficult for the judge," especially when Judge Samuel Sewall confessed after the trial his guilt in having made these mistakes (*Academic American Encyclopedia*, vol. 17, 1981, 31).

Sixth, the defendants had no counsel. God encourages people to defend others if they believe in their innocence and believe their cause is right (Prov. 29:7; Isa. 1:17 NIV).

Seventh, it is probable that some of the "confessions" were obtained while the accused was "under duress." But nowhere in the Bible can you find any support that we are allowed to obtain confessions by torture or threats of torture, etc. (see chapter nine)

Eighth, it should have been evident from the very first sign of hysteria that the whole thing had gotten out of control, mainly because the judges were not following God's guidelines. Therefore, they should have stopped what they were doing until God's biblical principles of courtroom procedure had been properly explained to them and understood.

In summary, the judges did not obey God's principles of civil law in Salem in 1692 but violated biblical courtroom principles in eight different areas, and this is what caused the tragic mass executions resulting from the Salem witch trials.

So, if the judges at the Salem witch trials had followed all God's principles of courtroom procedure, then they would have:

1. required all testimony to be from eyewitnesses, and required two or three eyewitnesses for each conviction;
2. required the major testimony in all cases to be from adults, and not from children;
3. warned the court that the biblical punishment for being a false witness for a capital crime was death, and that this punishment will be enforced by the court;
4. eliminated the testimony of visions as mere hearsay;
5. eliminated confessions obtained under physical duress;
6. looked for a reason to be merciful to those who were truly convicted as witches, so they would not have to be executed;
7. asked for the help of additional judges when the cases became "too hard for them"; and,
8. stopped the trial proceedings when mass hysteria developed and prayerfully waited for God's leading.

Now, if the judges followed all eight of God's guidelines during the Salem witch trials, then probably no one would have been executed and at worse, only a few would have been whipped as a merciful alternative to execution.

In conclusion, although God still wants the sin of witchcraft to be a crime against the state which carries a maximum punishment of death, the Salem witch trials of 1692 were an abomination to God. This tragedy could have been entirely prevented if this trial were held using strict biblical guidelines and these eight biblical safeguards were adhered to by the judges during the trial. Furthermore, just as the abominations at the Salem witch trial occurred because of violating God's principles of courtroom procedure, the abominations in our courts and in our justice system today are also the result of deliberately violating God's principles of justice and mercy.

And that, is God's view of witchcraft and the Salem witch trials!

Chapter Fourteen

GOD'S VIEW OF UNRESTRAINED HOMOSEXUALITY AND ITS POLITICAL AND MILITARY CONSEQUENCES

The Bible teaches that:

1. God wants homosexual perversion to be a crime against the state, punishable by a maximum sentence of death;
2. The ultimate endpoint of generations of unrestrained homosexuality is to evolve a government which is so pro-homosexual that its rulers will be willing to go to war to defend the right of gays to commit gang rape, and leave their victims for dead;
3. God will not fight on behalf of an army of soldiers who practice the wickedness of homosexual perversion, and therefore many innocent soldiers will needlessly die in battle (if homosexuals are recruited into the military);
4. God does intervene in military affairs and therefore, a large homosexual army will lose the battle even if the odds are in their favor; but a small godly army will win the battle even when the odds are against them.

Now these are the most inflammatory four statements about homosexuality that most of you have ever read. I make no apology for them, for these are all God's ideas and not mine. Using these ideas as the outline for our discussion, let us examine God's view of unrestrained homosexuality and its political and military consequences.

PART I

The Bible teaches that homosexual perversion is a sin which is detestable to God. For it is written:

> Do not lie with a man as one lies with a woman; that is detestable. (Lev. 18:22 NIV)

The Bible also teaches that homosexual perversion should be a crime against the state which carries a standard punishment of death. For it is written:

> If a man lies with a man as one lies with a woman, both of them have done what is detestable. They must be put to death; their blood will be on their own heads. (Lev. 20:13 NIV)

As you have learned from chapter eight of this book, homosexual perversion is one of the sixteen biblical death penalties where the expression "show no pity" is conspicuously absent from the text, unlike for the sins of idolatry and murder (Deut. 13:6, 8-9; 19:11-13 NIV). Therefore, God allowed judges to show mercy to those convicted of homosexual perversion. Furthermore, since God commands judges to love to be merciful in Micah 6:8, then it is clear that God intended homosexual perversion to have a standard sentence of death from which the judges were required to be merciful if at all possible. This means that God's purpose in creating this law was not to execute everyone who ever had a homosexual encounter, but to *bring them to trial* and (if convicted) give them the opportunity to recognize that they have sinned against God, and confess, repent, and submit to God's laws, and then be forgiven by God and the court and set free. So, the purpose of this principle of civil law is to bring homosexuals to repentance, that they might live and not be executed. For it is written:

> "Do I take any pleasure in the death of the wicked?" declares the Sovereign Lord. "Rather, am I not pleased when they turn from their ways and live?" (Ezek. 18:23 NIV)

However, if he was convicted in court a second time for committing this same sin (and again he repents and begs for the court to have mercy upon him) he may again be fortunate enough to avoid the death penalty. But this time, he will most likely receive a whipping (from a mere one lash up to a maximum of forty lashes) as a merciful alternative to execution (Deut. 25:1-3 NIV) From then on, every time he is caught, prosecuted, and convicted for homosexual perversion, this merciful whipping will become progressively more severe until he eventually receives a maximum of forty lashes at one time. Then, he will be warned that because God's law forbids whipping a person more than forty lashes at a time, the judge will have no choice but to execute him if he is ever convicted again for the sin of homosexual perversion.

For after this many convictions for homosexuality, it is clear that his previous claims of repentance were fraudulent and that he doesn't just *disobey* God's laws, but he actually *despises* God's laws. The Bible teaches that generally it was not those who merely disobeyed God's law once or twice who got executed, but it was those who despised God's law who were executed. For it is written:

> He that despised Moses' law died without mercy under two or three witnesses . . . (Heb. 10:28 KJV)

Therefore, the Bible teaches that:

1. homosexuality should be a crime against the State;
2. those convicted of homosexual perversion should face a standard sentence of death;
3. those first time offenders who repent and beg for mercy may be totally forgiven and receive no punishment at all;
4. those repeat offenders may receive a whipping as a merciful alternative to execution, which becomes progressively more severe with each additional new conviction;
5. those who despise God's law and are never repentant, and those who continue to sin (even after receiving the maximum whipping of forty lashes) will eventually be executed without any more mercy.

Thus, God's principles of civil law enforcement were designed to nearly eliminate homosexual perversion from Israel. If America had been regularly enforcing these same biblical principles for the last several generations, then the open practice of homosexuality would be practically nonexistent in our nation and the closet practice of homosexuality would be suppressed to the lowest level possible.

However, most Americans today do not believe that God's principles of civil law should be adopted into our justice system. In fact, many Americans believe that gay men cannot control their homosexuality because they were born to be homosexuals. They should not be held responsible for their actions by the courts, or even by God himself. This mistaken philosophy makes God out to be a liar, for the Bible teaches that God will never allow men to be tempted to sin beyond that which they can endure. For it is written:

> And God is faithful; he will not let you be tempted beyond what you can bear. But when you are tempted, he will also provide a way out so that you can stand up under it. (1 Cor. 10:13b NIV)

In other words, no one is genetically programmed at birth to be tempted beyond his endurance to commit repetitive homosexual sins. Therefore, the gay male is not born to be a homosexual, any more than the heterosexual male is born to be an adulterer or a rapist, or the poor man is born to be a thief. So in God's mind, the homosexual should always be held responsible by the court for the sins of homosexuality.

PART II

When a government refuses to outlaw and punish sexual immorality using God's laws, and ignores or repeals man's laws against sexual immorality as well, then sexual immorality will move from the darkness into the light until aberration becomes acceptable and sodomy becomes the standard.

Just as unrestrained heterosexual perversion increases the frequency of fornication, adultery, rape, and gang rape, so also unrestrained homosexual perversion increases the frequency of homosexuality, homosexual rape and homosexual gang rape.

The Bible gives us two examples of how unrestrained homosexual and bisexual perversion leads to militant homosexuality where legalized homosexual gang rape becomes a protected gay right. These two stories are about an attempted gang rape in Sodom (Gen. 19:4-9 NIV) and a successful gang rape in Gibeah (Judg. 19:20-28 NIV). These teach us that gang rape is not just a problem which occurs with heterosexual perversion, but obviously occurs with homosexual perversion as well.

The first recorded episode is in Genesis 19:4-9 and is a story about an attempted gang rape of two angels by a large group of homosexual men. For it is written:

> The two angels arrived at Sodom in the evening, and Lot ... insisted ... that they go with him and entered his house. Before they had gone to bed, all the men from every part of the city of Sodom—both young and old—surrounded the house.
>
> They called to Lot, "Where are the men who came to you tonight? Bring them out to us so that we can have sex with them."
>
> Lot went outside to meet them ... and said, "No my friends. Don't do this wicked thing. ..."
>
> "Get out of our way," they replied ... "This fellow came here as an alien, and now he wants to play the judge! We'll treat you worse than them." They kept bringing pressure on Lot and moved forward to break down the door. (Gen. 19:1a, 3a, 4-9 NIV)

As you can see, this large group of homosexual men is attempting to break down the door of Lot's house so they can gang rape the two angels inside. Then, they threaten to gang rape Lot for condemning their actions, revealing that anyone in Sodom who condemns homosexual perversion will be silenced by the threat of gang rape.

Now Lot was actually an alien to Sodom because he was neither born nor raised in that city, and the Sodomites knew that aliens often condemned homosexuality. But the last thing these homosexuals wanted was an alien living in Sodom who suddenly had the courage to publicly condemn homosexuality to a crowd of hostile homosexuals. For this kind of courage might rally the real judges and the rest of the citizens to condemn homosexuality as well. That's one reason why the crowd of homosexuals wanted to silence him with the threat of gang rape.

The homosexuals in Sodom wanted to maintain the status quo, which gave them great confidence that they could routinely gang rape every new visitor to Sodom without fear of prosecution. The reason for this confidence was probably that none of the local judges would ever condemn them because the judges themselves were all practicing homosexuals or were at least pro-homosexual in their politics. In other words, this Bible story teaches that the inevitable result of many generations of unrestrained homosexuality is that violent gang rape of town visitors and strangers will eventually become a totally unpunishable cultural norm, and that all vocal opponents of this wickedness (whether they are citizens, rulers, or judges) will be silenced by the perpetual threat of homosexual gang rape.

The situation in Sodom probably developed because heterosexuals became unwilling to enforce any civil laws against sexual immorality, and eventually allowed homosexuals to infiltrate their government. Here they ultimately seized control, ensuring that no more antihomosexual laws would ever be passed again, and that no one would "play the judge" over them again either. Once the culture reaches this evil endpoint according to the Bible, the only way to cure it is to destroy it, which is exactly what God did. For it is written:

> Then the Lord rained down burning sulfur on Sodom and Gomorrah—from the Lord out of the heavens. Thus he overthrew those cities and the entire plain, including all those living in the cities—and also the vegetation in the land. (Gen. 19:24 NIV)

This is how angry God becomes when the voters or government rulers allow adulterers and homosexuals to enter the government and repeal laws against sexual perversion (including laws against fornication, adultery, or homosexuality), because it encourages the spread of sexual perversion throughout the entire nation—which will inevitably become more violent and militantly aggressive and will culminate by making homosexual gang rape into a protected gay right. In fact, as you are reading these words, our own government is already promoting the adoption of even more gay rights here in America. You can bet that as

God watches America—his "most favored Christian nation"—adopt the same political strategy that destroyed Sodom, he is equally angry at us as well!

Now the second biblical example also illustrates the same point: the natural history of unrestrained homosexuality involves a government which is so pro-homosexual and which will adopt so many gay rights that routine gang rape of town strangers will inevitably become a protected gay right as well. This second story is about a successful bisexual gang rape of a town stranger where the victim was left for dead in the city of Gibeah (in the tribe of Benjamin). For it is written:

> ... some of the wicked men of the city surrounded the house. Pounding on the door, they shouted to the old man who owned the house, "Bring out the man who came to your house so we can have sex with him." ... The man took his concubine and sent her outside to them, and they raped her and abused her throughout the night, and at dawn they let her go. (Judg. 19:22, 25 NIV)

The story goes on to indicate that the woman died. After the gang of bisexual men raped this woman to death, the rest of the nation of Israel learned about it. A large delegation from the other eleven tribes of Israel was sent to the tribe of Benjamin, demanding that the rulers of the tribe of Benjamin ...

> ... surrender those wicked men of Gibeah so that we may put them to death and purge the evil from Israel.
>
> But the Benjaminites would not listen to their fellow Israelites. From their towns they came together at Gibeah to fight against the Israelites. At once the Benjaminites mobilized twenty-six thousand swordsmen from their towns, in addition to seven hundred chosen men from those living in Gibeah. (Judg. 20:13-15 NIV)

The Benjaminites knew that God's law required them to bring those accused of gang rape to trial, and that if they were convicted they could possibly face a death sentence. Surprisingly, instead of obeying God's laws and capturing those accused of gang rape and murder and placing them on trial, the political leaders of the tribe of Benjamin decided to start a civil war to defend the right of the Gibeah bisexuals to gang rape town strangers—even to the point of death. In other words, this civil war was fought over the issue of gay rights!

I suspect that the reason the rulers of Benjamin were willing to start this gay rights civil war (to protect the right of homosexuals to routinely gang rape town strangers) was that the governments in all the cities in the tribe of Benjamin were probably infiltrated with homosexuals. Many of their leaders had probably become either practicing homosexuals or were at least pro-homosexual in their politics. More than likely, this started because the leaders ignored or repealed God's principles of civil law against homosexual perversion. This was followed by allowing gays in government, which inevitably prompted a progressive adoption of gay rights.

Both of these biblical stories serve to illustrate that "lack of vigilance by God-fearing men" to enforce the biblical principles of civil law concerning sexual perversion ultimately leads to government control by homosexuals, adulterers, and fornicators, who in turn will pass laws to protect any conceivable kind of sexual perversion.

In summary, God's laws against sexual immorality were not designed to execute every single homosexual any more than God wanted to execute every person convicted of adultery or prostitution. Instead, God's laws were designed to create wholesome, God-fearing, two-parent families (made up of one husband, one wife, their biological children, and possibly adopted children too). God's laws were also designed to help prevent the crippling physical, emotional, and financial costs of sexual immorality. These include:

- sexually transmitted diseases (STDS), as well as death and disability from STDS, and the associated increased taxes to support state and federal health care programs, welfare programs, and disability programs which result; and,
- the problems of single parents resulting from the sins of fornication, adultery, and non-biblical divorce, which also cause increased taxes to pay for state sponsored welfare programs, food stamps, and health insurance.

These increased tax burdens always result when the righteous pay the tax bill for the consequences of unrestrained sins of the unrighteous.

Rather than have our voters fighting about whether to make the sins of homosexuality, adultery, and fornication punishable crimes against the state, as they were many decades ago, our society continues to fight only about "gay rights."

Christian society will inevitably lose the battle over "gay rights" because the moment we impertinently decided that God's laws were wrong and that these sins against God should no longer be considered punishable crimes, we lost the entire war. All that remains is when and how we will ultimately surrender. You see, the two stories about Sodom and Gibeah were God's way of teaching us that

> when societies no longer prosecute sexual sins as punishable crimes against the State, their governments will eventually be run by those who embrace sexual perversion themselves. They will then pass laws to encourage all sexual perversions, and

"gay rights" will inevitably be accomplished and gays will be allowed to legally infiltrate and subvert all segments of society!

In other words, the Bible teaches us that without prosecution of sexual sins, sexual perversion cannot possibly be restrained by merely arguing about "gay rights." For the phase of "arguing about 'gay rights' " is only one of the last battles to fight before our society is entirely overwhelmed by sexual perversion. America is on the verge of having legislation which will turn us into another Sodom or Gibeah.

Christians are still fighting on the wrong battlefront of "gay rights" dispute. Our only real hope is to follow God's wisdom and initiate legislation which will make the sins of homosexuality, adultery, and fornication once again punishable crimes against the state.

PART III

When Moses fought against the Midianites, the Bible records that not one Israelite died in battle (Num. 31:48-49). This has great significance because this was the first battle fought by the new generation of Israelites after God allowed the previous generation to die in the wilderness (because of their sinful rebellion). God gave Israel this miraculous battle victory to teach them that if Israel continued to obey God in peacetime and maintain a righteous army during wartime, Jehovah would supernaturally protect them in battle, and would actually fight on their behalf. Therefore, Israel would win every battle (Lev. 26:7-8; Deut. 28:7 NIV) and no Israelite soldier would ever die during the fighting (Num. 31:48-49 NIV; this amazing promise is also discussed in chapter twenty-two).

Unfortunately, a soldier named Achan disobeyed God during the battle of Jericho and stole a robe, two hundred shekels of silver, and a gold bar (Josh. 7:20-21 NIV). As a result, God did not fight on behalf of Israel any longer, and so Israel lost the next battle and thirty-six innocent soldiers died (Josh. 7:3-5 NIV). This defeat was particularly humiliating for Israel because this time the size of the enemy was so small that Israel felt they needed to take only three thousand men into battle—which was less than 1/200th of their entire army of 601,730 men (Num. 26:2, 51 NIV).

God allowed this military defeat because of one soldier's sinful act of stealing. Homosexual perversion is a far greater sin in God's eyes than is stealing, because the Bible teaches that homosexuality carries a potential death penalty, while stealing does not. Therefore, recruiting homosexuals into the military will displease God far more than did Achan's sin of merely stealing. In other words, God will not fight on behalf of an American army of soldiers who are practicing the wickedness of homosexual perversion; and therefore, many innocent American soldiers will needlessly die in battle and America may lose some of its future battles as well. Furthermore, God will desert America in wartime if we desert him in peacetime. In fact, God punished America recently by giving us a humiliating defeat in the Vietnam War within a decade after we took prayer and Bible teaching out of the public schools. This decision indicated that America felt that we should no longer teach our youngest citizens to worship God and that God's laws should never again be the foundation for America's laws. So, right after America turned her back on God in peacetime, God turned His back on America in wartime.

Israel learned her lesson and purged the wickedness from her army. After this, God gave them an unparalleled winning streak of battle victories (Josh. 8-12). America also needs to purge the wickedness from our armed forces and from our entire nation if we ever want to gain God's blessings upon our armed forces and upon our nation once again.

PART IV

In Genesis (14:1-16) the Bible records a battle between a smaller army led by four kings and a larger army led by five kings. The Bible even describes this as "four kings against five" (Gen. 14:9b NIV). Now all armies in the Bible are presumed to be predominantly heterosexual unless the Bible states otherwise, and this is most likely the case with the smaller army of four kings. Two of the five cities of the larger army were Sodom and Gomorrah, which means that the larger army of five kings consisted of a large number of homosexuals.

In Genesis (14:8-11), God allows the larger homosexual army of five kings to lose the battle against the smaller heterosexual army of four kings, even though the odds were in favor of the larger homosexual army. But during the victory, the smaller heterosexual army made the mistake of capturing Lot, who was Abram's nephew. Abram then recruited 318 men who were all born in Abram's household and led them into battle to save his nephew. Abram's army presumably represents a small godly army with men of faith, and God allows Abram's small godly army to defeat the larger army even though the odds were against them (Gen. 14:14-16).

Because God does intervene in military affairs, a large homosexual army will lose the battle, even though the odds in are their favor; but a small godly army will win the battle even when the odds are against them. So, America dares not risk God's displeasure by recruiting homosexuals into the military or we too will not only lose more battles, but we will also lose the lives of more of our innocent soldiers.

This chapter was not intended to insult or demean homosexuals in any way, nor was it intended to verbally wound them. For the Bible not only teaches that God created us all equally, but that He loves us all equally, and that we are all equally in need of His grace and His forgiveness. Furthermore, Christians are commanded by God to love all sinners equally and are told to try to lead them all to accept Christ as Savior and Lord. However, the Bible also teaches that only a few will enter through the narrow gate and find salvation. The large unrighteous majority will choose to enter through the wide gate with the broad path and will never yield their hearts to the will of God and find salvation through the atoning sacrifice of Christ on the cross (Matt. 7:13-14 NIV). Therefore, very few of the world's inhabitants will ultimately obey God because of salvation and surrender, and the vast majority will obey only because of training and tradition, or because of prosecution and punishment, or will choose never to obey God at all.

In other words, the Bible teaches that a true "nation under God" can be created by love and legislation, but not by love alone! For the *Love* of Christ will change only a precious few (the small Christian minority), but it will take the *laws* of Christ to control the behavior of the large unrighteous majority.

In conclusion, the Bible teaches that:

1. God wants homosexual perversion to be a crime against the state, punishable by a maximum sentence of death;
2. The ultimate endpoint of generations of unrestrained homosexuality is to evolve into a government which is so pro-homosexual that its rulers will be willing to go to war to defend the right of gays to commit gang rape and leave their victims for dead;
3. God will not fight on behalf of an army of soldiers who are practicing the wickedness of homosexual perversion, and therefore many innocent solders will needlessly die in battle if homosexuals are recruited into the military;
4. Because God does intervene in military affairs, a large homosexual army will lose the battle even if the odds are in their favor, but a small godly army will win the battle even when the odds are against them.

Now if we don't heed the Bible's clear warning about the importance of making homosexual perversion into a regularly punishable crime against the state, then America will suffer for our disobedience exactly as the Bible describes—by falling into an abyss of sexual immorality and wickedness with no way out except for God to destroy our nation completely (just like he did with Sodom, Gomorrah, and Gibeah) and then start all over again.

And that, is God's view of unrestrained homosexuality and its political and military consequences!

I have only two more points to make before we end this chapter. First, the growth and acceptance of *heterosexual* immorality in America has also prompted the growth and acceptance of *homosexual* immorality. But Christians will never win the battle against the homosexual agenda if we are unwilling to attempt to outlaw both homosexual and heterosexual immorality at the same time. Why is this? It is because God will not lead us to victory unless we aim for *His* target and play by *His* rules, and *God's* rules involve *prosecuting* sexual immorality as a crime against the state!

Second, God's punishment for *hate crimes* which involve murder is "execution without mercy." For it is written:

> if a man hates his neighbor and lies in wait for him, assaults and kills him. . . . hand him over to . . . *die.* Show him *no pity.* (Deut. 19:11, 12b, 13a, NIV; emphasis added)

Therefore, anyone who calls himself a "Christian" but who *hates* and deliberately murders a homosexual should himself be executed without mercy, as an example for others who might follow in his steps. For if you sow the path, you'll reap God's wrath.

Furthermore, according to Leviticus 24:19-20, any believer who deliberately injures a homosexual in a fight should himself be injured in an identical fashion in the courtroom, according to God's law of an "eye for an eye!"

And that is God's view of how we should punish those who injure or murder homosexuals, even if the attackers claim to be "Christians"!

We must STOP THE HATE! STOP THE VIOLENCE! STOP THE GAY BASHING! STOP THE HATE CRIMES! Christ commands us to love the sinner and hate only his sins! I know this is difficult, but it can be done. For it is no different than loving one of your own disobedient children, yet hating his disobedience. God has called us to this kind of love.

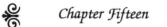 Chapter Fifteen

GOD'S VIEW OF ABORTION & THE CIVIL WAR AGAINST OUR UNBORN CITIZENS

According to the book of Judges, unrestrained homosexual perversion led to a civil war between the tribe of Benjamin and the rest of Israel. This civil war was actually fought over the issue of gay rights and altogether cost the lives of more than sixty-five thousand Benjaminites and Israelites (Judg. 19, 20).

In America however, it is not unrestrained homosexual perversion but unrestrained heterosexual perversion which has caused a civil war— a civil war against our unborn citizens by abortion! Whereas the civil war in Israel was fought over gay rights, the civil war in America is being fought over mother's rights. Furthermore, the death toll during Israel's gay rights civil war pales in comparison to the estimated thirty-eight million potential citizens who have died in the mother's rights civil war by abortion in America.

What is God's view of abortion and the civil war against our unborn citizens? Well, God illustrated his viewpoint in the following civil law concerning the accidental injury to an unborn child. According to this law, if the baby dies of the injuries it received before it was born, then the man who merely *accidentally* injured the unborn baby must be executed—life for life. For it is written:

> If men who are fighting hit a pregnant woman and she gives birth prematurely but there is no serious injury the offender must be fined whatever the woman's husband demands and the court allows. But if there is serious injury, you are to take *life for life,* eye for eye, tooth for tooth, hand for hand, foot for foot, burn for burn, wound for wound, bruise for bruise. (Exod. 21:22-25 NIV; emphasis added)

Therefore, the Bible teaches that God wanted abortion to be a capital crime against the state carrying a standard punishment of death.

Because the Israelites could not dismember or burn an unborn baby without seriously injuring or killing the mother, many Christians have mistakenly concluded that Exodus (21:22-25) concerns only the punishment for accidentally injuring the mother, and has nothing to do with accidentally injuring her unborn child.

There are five reasons why this passage concerns only injuries to the unborn baby and does not concern injuries to its mother at all. First of all, the offender's punishment for the mother's injuries comes from Leviticus (24:19-22)—a law which concerns injuring your neighbor. Therefore, if Exodus 21 referred only to the mother's injuries and had nothing to do with the unborn baby's injuries, then it would be unnecessary for God to stipulate that her injuries caused her to go into premature labor because the premature labor itself would not change the offender's punishment.

Secondly, the reason why the premature birth is important is so the newborn can be examined to determine what injuries it must have suffered before it was born.

Thirdly, the Bible teaches that fines are paid to compensate for serious injuries which cause temporary disability and transient inability to work resulting in an overall loss of income (Exod. 21:18-19 NIV). But in the law concerning the pregnant woman, a fine is allowed even though there is no serious injury. Since there is no disability or income loss (beyond that which would have happened anyway from the natural birth process, weeks or months later), then the fine demanded by the husband can only be for the increased expenses required to care for a healthy, but premature baby.

Fourthly, since it is clear that the first part of the verse focuses on the offender's punishment if the baby is *uninjured* in the womb, then the second part of the verse must by implication focus on the offender's punishment if the baby is *injured* in the womb.

Fifthly, because mankind frequently deprives the unborn of their civil rights and frequently deprives slaves and servants of their civil rights, God deliberately placed this law between those concerning accidental injury to slaves (Exod. 21:20-21) and servants (Exod. 21:26-27). This was done in order to highlight the importance of protecting the civil rights of slaves, servants, and the unborn, and to emphasize that these civil rights come from almighty God himself. This was also God's fifth way of emphasizing that this law refers only to injuring the unborn, and not to injuring the pregnant mother, for as noted above, the mother's injuries are covered under a separate law concerning injuring your neighbor.

For these five reasons it is clear that this law concerns punishing the offender only for accidentally injuring the unborn baby and does not concern the mother's injuries at all. With this in mind, let us examine God's civil law concerning the required punishment for a man who merely accidentally injures an unborn child (Exod. 21:22-25).

In this scenario a pregnant woman has just been accidently injured by one of two men who are fighting, so that she goes into labor and delivers her baby prematurely. When such a thing happens, the baby is either delivered healthy, but prematurely, and therefore requires more care, or the baby has suffered harm and may even die during childbirth.

If both baby and mother are healthy, the Bible commands that

> the offender be fined whatever the woman's husband demands and the court allows. (Exod. 21:22 NIV)

This means that the woman's husband gives his best estimate of the extra costs of caring for his healthy, but premature, baby. He then demands this fine to be paid by the offender, while the local court helps to decide whether his estimated costs are reasonable or excessive.

If the offender's mishap has caused serious injury to the premature infant (and the most likely serious injury would be that the baby is born dead), then God commands that "you are to take life for life" (Exod. 21:23 NIV). So God's punishment for a man who kills an unborn baby by accidently causing a miscarriage is that the offender must be placed on trial and face a possible death sentence. This also means that any doctor who causes an *accidental* abortion would face these same charges.

Notice that the expression "show him no pity" is conspicuously absent from this law, unlike for the capital crimes of idolatry and deliberate murder, recorded in Deuteronomy (13:8; 19:13 NIV). This means that for the crime of causing an accidental abortion, not only is the judge allowed to be merciful, but according to Micah (6:8 NIV) the judge is actually required to love mercy, and therefore required to look for a reason to be merciful.

Furthermore, God's punishment for either injuring or killing an unborn child in Exodus 21 is identical to his punishment for either injuring or killing an adult in Leviticus. For it is written:

> If anyone injures his neighbor, whatever he has done must be done to him: fracture for fracture, eye for eye, tooth for tooth. As he has injured the other, so he is to be injured ... whoever kills an man must be put to death. You are to have the same law for the alien and the native-born. (Lev. 24:19-22 NIV)

This law would also apply to any injuries received by the pregnant woman spoken of in Exodus. Notice again that the expression "show him no pity" is conspicuously absent from this text as well, which again means that the judge is not only allowed to show mercy, but is also required to show mercy if at all possible (Mic. 6:8). Therefore, God treats the accidental death of an unborn child in the same way he treats the accidental death of an adult. In either case, the criminal must face a standard sentence of death, but may still receive mercy.

It is important to realize that the above verse (Lev. 24:19-22) does not refer to deliberate, premeditated murder because God forbids the judges to show mercy in cases of deliberate, premeditated murder. For it is written:

> But if a man hates his neighbor and lies in wait for him, assaults him and kills him . . . hand him over to . . . die. Show him no pity." (Deut. 19:11, 12b, 13a NIV)

Since God's punishment for accidentally killing an unborn child is clearly identical to his punishment for accidentally killing an adult, then surely God's punishment for purposely killing an unborn child is identical to his punishment for purposely killing an adult—by execution—with God's additional command to "show him no pity!" (Deut. 19:13a NIV).

Therefore, it is reasonable to conclude that God equates purposeful abortion with deliberate, premeditated murder, and wants it to be punished in our courts in the same way. In other words, for doctors who purposely murder the unborn by abortion, God wants American courts to punish them by execution, with no possibility of mercy at all. This is the inescapable conclusion of examining Exodus 22:22-25, Leviticus 24:19-22, and Deuteronomy 19:11, 12b, 13a NIV).

If the baby dies from the purposeful injuries it received before it was born, then God's punishment is for the court to take "life for life." Therefore, by implication, if the baby survives the injuries it received before it was born, then the court is to take "hand for hand, foot for foot, burn for burn, wound for wound," etc. For it is written:

> If men who are fighting hit a pregnant woman, and she gives birth prematurely . . . if there is serious injury, you are to take life for life, eye for eye, tooth for tooth, hand for hand, foot for foot, burn for burn, wound for wound, bruise for bruise. (Exod. 21:22a, 23-25 NIV)

This again confirms that God's punishment for injuring the *unborn* (Exodus 21) is identical to his punishment for injuring the *born* (Leviticus 24). Therefore, if the baby survives the injuries it received before it was born, God wants the offender to be punished in court by an identical wound, dismemberment, or burn.

Even though the ancient Israelites could neither dismember nor burn the unborn without seriously injuring or killing the mother, modern doctors dismember and chemically burn the unborn all the time by various methods of abortion. Therefore, I believe God's command foreshadows the advent of modern techniques of abortion and provides divine legal guidance to prevent modern technology from being used in this abominable way. Thus God is commanding American lawmakers to create legislation stipulating that any doctor convicted of purposely dismembering or chemically burning a baby in the womb in a case where the baby *survives* its injuries, should himself be dismembered or chemically burned in court as his punishment. However, since the expression, "Show him no pity" is *not* in this particular law of God, then the judge can offer a whipping as a merciful alternative to dismemberment for those doctors who are repentant, etc.

If the baby *dies* of its injuries, then the doctor should be executed without mercy (Deut. 19:11, 12b, 13a NIV). According to Exodus (21:22-23 NIV), the Bible teaches that purposeful abortion is equivalent to premeditated murder. Of course, the woman who requests and pays for her abortion is guilty as well. It is possible that the judge may prayerfully conclude that her conspiracy to commit murder deserves the same punishment as the doctor who actually caused the death of the unborn baby.

You may say that God's method of punishment is cruel and that America is too "civilized" to carry out this type of punishment. But remember, our society has been chemically burning and dismembering unborn babies continually over the last several decades. So, we have not become truly civilized, but have instead become one of the most cruel nations which has ever existed. So let us not imagine that God is cruel in his justice, because it is really man who is cruel, and God is merely matching the punishment to the crime. Over the last several decades American doctors (in the name of "freedom of choice") have dismembered or chemically burned thirty-eight million unborn babies to death (*World Magazine*, 16 January 1999). This is many times more than the millions of Russian citizens who were killed by Stalin or the six million Jews who were killed by Hitler. Furthermore, American doctors have killed more unborn babies than the combined populations of the following states:

State	Population (1990 census)	Page
1. Wyoming,	455,975	772
2. Alaska	551,947	19
3. Vermont	564,964	734
4. North Dakota	641,364	530
5. Delaware	668,696	195
6. South Dakota	699,999	676
7. Montana	803,655	475
8. Rhode Island	1,005,984	625
9. Idaho	1,011,986	336
10. New Hampshire	1,113,915	510

CREATING A NATION UNDER GOD

11. Hawaii	1,115,274	308
12. Nevada	1,206,152	504
13. Maine	1,233,223	423
14. New Mexico	1,521,779	515
15. Nebraska	1,584,617	502
16. Utah	1,727,784	728
17. West Virginia	1,801,625	754
18. Arkansas	2,362,239	41
19. Kansas	2,485,600	374
20. Mississippi	2,586,443	462
21. Iowa	2,787,424	355
22. Oregon	2,853,733	551
23. Oklahoma	3,157,604	545
24. Connecticut	3,295,669	164

total population 37,237,651

(The above table was constructed from *The Young People's Encyclopedia of the United States*, Ed. William E. Shapiro, Millbrook Press, Brookfield Connecticut, 1992, from the 1990 Census.)

In other words, over the last several decades American doctors have murdered thirty-eight million unborn babies, a figure which is so huge that it approximates the combined populations of the twenty-four states mentioned above (according to the 1990 census). In fact, the number of babies aborted in the United States exceeds the entire population of Canada (population 27,296,859—according to the 1991 Canadian census; Ibid., 114).

So, God's principles of civil law provide the perfect and fitting punishment for the abominable practice of killing the unborn. Therefore, God wants American legislators to attempt to adopt God's civil principles into our legislation to make abortion a sin-crime which must be punished by execution without mercy if the baby *dies*, or by dismemberment or chemical burning if the baby *survives*. God knows that only this type of legislation will truly end the abortion civil war in America. No doctor would dare risk his own life (or limb) just to perform an abortion once these biblical civil principles became the "Law of the Land"!

Unfortunately, our Christian leaders are merely attempting to ban partial birth abortion and stop government funding of abortion—actions which would still allow the vast majority of abortions to remain completely legal. Furthermore, Christian leaders forget that *fornication* is the mother of abortion, and God will not help us to outlaw abortion while we allow fornication (and adultery) to remain completely legal as well! So as usual, Christians are lined up for battle but are facing the wrong direction. This is why year after year, and decade after decade,

God refuses to give us the victory for which we have so long prayed.

You are probably thinking, "We could never pass that kind of legislation in the U.S., even if we tried." To accomplish God's goal, we must depend upon God's help. For adopting this law into our national legislation requires an obvious political miracle—such as a national revival—during which time the hearts of the nation's voters will be rendered soft enough, and for long enough, to vote to live under God's principles of civil law. It will be during such a national revival that many of God's other principles of civil law will be able to be adopted into our national legislation.

As long as we depend upon our own political strength and reach only for goals we believe are achievable without divine intervention, then God leaves us on our own and allows us to fail repeatedly while we pray for divine help which is never coming. God will not assist us in passing legislation which does not accomplish His goals. And God will not heal our land unless we aim for his target and play by His rules. In other words, we cannot expect God to fully bless our legislative efforts as long as we intend to allow those who practice abortion to remain unpunished, for this reflects our target and not His.

On the other hand, if we do this God's way, then God will supernaturally assist us in passing His type of legislation. Remember, God would not give America any command which He would not enable America to fulfill. Therefore, we can pass this legislation, but only with God's miraculous help. So, if you believe in a God who still grants miracles and who is very interested in legislation, trust Him for His assistance and blessing, and attempt to initiate the types of legislation which Jesus Christ wrote for all nations to use so we can stop the abortion war in our nation for all time.

And that is God's view of abortion and the war against our unborn citizens!

This bears repeating! God's punishment for *hate crimes* which involve murder is "execution without mercy." For it is written:

> if a man *hates* his neighbor and lies in wait for him, assaults and kills him. . . . hand him over to . . . *die*. Show him *no pity*. (Deut. 19:11, 12b, 13a NIV; emphasis added)

Therefore, anyone who calls himself a "Christian" but who *hates* and deliberately murders an *abortionist* should himself be executed without mercy as an example for others who might follow in his steps. God wants courtroom justice, not vigilante violence. And any believer who destroys an abortion clinic by bombing must replace the entire value of the clinic. For it is written:

> If a fire breaks out and spreads into thornbushes so that it burns shocks of grain or standing grain or the whole field,

the one who started the fire must make restitution. (Exod. 22:6 NIV)

This also means that if a bomb causes damage by explosive fire so that it destroys private property (such as an abortion clinic), the one who planted the bomb which started the explosive fire must make full restitution.

And that is God's view of how we should punish those who murder abortionists and those who bomb abortion clinics!

Chapter Sixteen

GOD'S VIEW OF THE FIRST COMMANDMENT (WHICH OUTLAWS IDOLATRY) VERSUS THE FIRST AMENDMENT (WHICH LEGALIZES IDOLATRY)

The sin of idolatry angers God more than any other sin. An idol is a lifeless statue of wood or stone fashioned into the imagined likeness of a god. Idolatry (as described in the Old Testament) involves the worshipping of an idol—by bowing down to it, praying to it, praising it, thanking it for blessings, and occasionally offering sacrifices to it. Both Buddhism and Hinduism involve idolatry, and that part of Catholicism which involves kneeling in prayer and worship to a statue of Mother Mary (or to any other saint for that matter) is also a form of idolatry.

When I use the term idolatry in this chapter, I am always referring to true idolatry as defined in the Old Testament and for which God's laws prescribe a courtroom penalty of execution without mercy (Deut. 13:6-10 NIV). I am not referring to *covetousness,* which is merely *symbolic* idolatry as defined in the New Testament (Col. 3:5 KJV), and for which there is no courtroom penalty at all, because you cannot summon eyewitnesses to testify about sins which are expressed only in the mind.

True idolatry is an abomination to God, and so God outlawed idolatry in many places in the Bible. In fact, when God gave Moses the Ten Commandments, his First Commandment outlawed idolatry by saying:

Thou shalt have no other gods before me. (Exod. 20:3 KJV)

On the other hand, America's First Amendment "legalizes" idolatry, by saying:

Congress shall make no law respecting an establishment of religion or prohibiting the free exercise thereof . . .

Herein lies one of the paradoxes of Christianity in America: the zeal of our founders to ensure "Freedom of Religion" (so that any denomination of Christians could worship Christ in their own fashion) has now been corrupted to include legal protection for any individual or group who wants to worship nature, worship other gods, or even worship Satan himself. Therefore, modern society has allowed America's First Amendment (which "legalizes" idolatry) to overrule God's First Commandment (which outlaws idolatry).

"Does a jealous God bless nations which legalize idolatry, or does he curse them?" Well, in the Old Testament, whenever the nation of Israel disobeyed God and allowed idolatry to flourish, Jehovah cursed them with drought, poverty, or military defeat. Furthermore, whenever nations other than Israel disobeyed God, Jehovah punished them for their disobedience as well. For it is written:

> I will take vengeance in anger and wrath upon the *nations* that have not obeyed me." (Mic. 5:15 NIV; emphasis added)

> Son of man, if a *country* sins against me by being unfaithful and I stretch out my hand against it to cut off their food supply and send famine upon it and kill its men and their animals . . . (Ezek. 14:13 NIV; emphasis added)

> Or if I bring a sword against that *country*. . . . (Ezek. 14:17a NIV; emphasis added)

> Or if I send a plague into that *land*. . . . (Ezek. 14:19a NIV; emphasis added)

> "And if they learn well the ways of my people . . . then they will be established among my people. But if any *nation* does not listen, I will completely uproot and destroy it," declares the Lord. (Jer. 12:17 NIV; emphasis added)

> If at any time I announce that a *nation* or *kingdom* is to be uprooted, torn down and destroyed, and if that *nation* I warned repents of its evil, then I will relent and not inflict on it the disaster I had planned. (Jer. 18:7-8 NIV; emphasis added)

So, the Bible makes it clear that almighty God curses nations other than Israel for their disobedience. Therefore, God surely punishes nations for their idolatry, because idolatry is the greatest disobedience of all.

But God blesses nations other than Israel as well, especially when a nation legislates that Jehovah will be their nation's God and that God's laws will be their laws. For it is written:

> Blessed is the nation whose God is the Lord . . . (Ps. 33:12 NIV)

So, it is clear in the Old Testament that our jealous God curses nations which do not obey Him and He blesses nations which do obey Him (for further details, see chapter four). However, since Christ rose from the dead, many Christians have mistakenly concluded that God no longer punishes nations for their idolatry. In fact, many believe that our jealous God will not be angry and will not punish America even if our leaders use the First Amendment to legalize all forms of idolatry as a sign of the "Freedom of Religion" which is available in the United States.

But if God no longer punishes nations which worship idols, then why are the "third-world nations" so poor? After all, the "third-world nations" are generally those whose citizens and leaders worship idols or worship nature. According to the Bible, we would expect that their idolatry would prompt God to give them more droughts, famines, floods, plagues, diseases, and poverty than the nations which are not idolatrous. And that is exactly what has happened, for the idolatrous "third-world nations" are generally the poorest nations in the world. On the other hand, the first-world nations were originally founded upon a Judeo-Christian world view, which included worshipping Jesus Christ and obeying God's moral and civil laws. Because of this, you would expect that God would bless the "first-world nations" with better economies and better climates with fewer natural disasters than the idolatrous third-world nations. And again, history records that this is exactly what has happened. The second-world nations are generally somewhere in between, for these nations neither have Judeo-Christian backgrounds, nor are they frankly idolatrous. As a result, you would expect that God would neither bless them as much as the first-world nations, nor curse them as much as the idolatrous nations. Once again, it appears as though this is true.

Additionally, God appears to have blessed the Protestant nations much more than Catholic nations, probably because many of these Catholic nations have encouraged the idolatrous "Mary worship" which angers God so greatly. This also helps explain why Central and South America have remained so poor—because their "Christianity" has been doubly corrupted. These areas were contaminated not only by the original pagan idolatry which was native to these countries long before the white man came to America, but also by the idolatrous "Mary-worship" which has attempted to replace it. This confirms that God still punishes nations which embrace idolatry, and also tells us that the more closely a nation's leaders and citizens hold fast to the true teachings of the Bible, the more blessings their nation will receive from almighty God.

Generations ago, God blessed America with greater economic prosperity than any other nation on earth in large part because the founders of our government had the faith in Christ which inspired them to legislate that Christianity should be the "Law of the Land." You see, the founders adopted two biblical civil principles which greatly discouraged idolatry through a program of nationwide education in both churches and schools.

First of all, because of the Fourth Commandment, the founders outlawed working on Sunday—a principle which God knew would greatly encourage nationwide church attendance so that our country could effectively discourage idolatry through the continuous education and indoctrination of its adults. This nationwide weekly worship and education in Christian doctrine would also encourage most Americans to behave better by combining the influences of salvation and surrender (for the small Christian minority) with training and tradition (for the large, unrighteous majority).

Secondly, our founders legislated that all public schools must be Christian schools so that our youngest citizens would be forever indoctrinated in the principles of Christianity as well. Furthermore, nearly all of the first one hundred colleges and universities in America were Christian schools. This meant that the entire system of higher education in America was designed to encourage Christianity and to suppress idolatry.

Additionally, the founders adopted six other principles of biblical civil law into our legislation, including, the outlawing of fornication, adultery, homosexuality, drunkenness, blasphemy, and non-biblical divorce. This had the effect of creating a culture which felt that:

—Christ should be exalted (and idolatry should be suppressed); and that . . .
—God's laws should be America's laws!

Lastly, many of the original constitutions of the early states stipulated that only godly Christian elders could serve in government. Having a government composed only of mature Christian statesmen who understood the advantages of God's principles of civil law was supposed to guarantee that America would keep all nine of these biblical principles in our government, and that we would slowly adopt even more of God's principles into our legislation with each passing generation. This would also guarantee that the nationwide discouragement of idolatry would never diminish but would get stronger in the future.

In other words, when all was said and done, through the laws which our founders had chosen to be the foundation for our government, America had officially declared that we would only worship the one true God in prayer, and obey his principles of moral and civil law.

America's greatness was a direct result of the founder's obedience to God's commands and their faith that God would bless America for officially declaring that Jesus Christ—the pre-incarnate Jehovah—would forever be our nation's God, and that he would be Lord of our laws,

Lord of our government, Lord of our culture, and Lord of our hearts. For it is written:

> Blessed it the nation whose God is the Lord ... (Ps. 33:12 NIV)

Unfortunately however, once America accomplished this goal, I believe our churches eventually stopped teaching their congregations that God's civil principles had any advantages for the administration of good government. As a result, the small amount of attention God's civil principles were being given by preachers slowly disappeared, and this set the stage for America to be "destroyed from lack of knowledge" (Hos. 4:6 NIV).

Once America forgot the importance of having godly laws, we then forgot the necessity of having godly leaders to regularly enforce God's laws. This was followed by allowing non-Christians to serve in our government for the first time. But without God's men to enforce God's laws, all nine of God's principles of civil law were eventually removed from legislation over the next several generations. This effectively released the large unrighteous majority of citizens in America from the restraining influence of God's principles of civil law, resulting in America becoming a nation which now embraces all kinds of sinful immorality (including idolatry). By doing this, America disinherited herself from receiving God's blessings and instead made herself eligible to receive God's wrath. For example, since the Clinton administration has encouraged so much evil in our nation, God has punished America with more hurricanes, floods, droughts, severe snowstorms, and firestorms during his terms as president than our nation has ever experienced in such a short period of time.

God is still in the business of punishing nations for their evil, and of course the greatest evil in God's sight is the worshipping of idols. For Jehovah is still a jealous God who is unwilling to continue to pour down blessings upon a nation which protects the "right to worship other gods" as an example for other nations to follow. Therefore, if we want God's blessings upon this nation, then America must adopt and enforce God's Ten Commandments—the first two of which mandate that idolatry must be outlawed! For it is written:

> You shall have no other gods before me. You shall not make for yourself an idol ... You shall not bow down to them or worship them. (Exod. 20:3, 4 KJV)

Furthermore, it is written:

> These are the LAWS you are to set before them ... Whoever sacrifices to any other god must be destroyed ... do not curse God ... do not invoke the names of other gods; do not let

them be heard on your lips . . . do not bow down before their gods or worship them or follow their practices. You must demolish them and break their sacred stone to pieces. Worship the Lord your God. (Exodus 21:1; 22:20, 28; 23:13, 24, 25 NIV; emphasis added)

It is clear that Jehovah wants idolatry to be outlawed. But when it comes to the punishment for idolatry, most Christians do not realize that God emphasizes execution without mercy even more for idolatry than he does for deliberate murder. You see, for a murderer, God says that the elders must "hand him over . . . to die. *Show him no pity*" (Deut. 19:12b, 13a NIV). But for idolatry, notice the many additional expressions God uses to emphasize the absolute necessity of executing every single idolator without mercy. For it is written:

If your very own brother, or your son or daughter, or the wife you love, or your closest friend, secretly entices you, saying, "Let us go and worship other gods" . . . do not yield to him or listen to him. Show him no pity. Do not spare him or shield him. You must certainly put him to death. Your hand must be the first in putting him to death, and then the hands of all the people. Stone him to death. (Deut. 13:6a, 8-10a NIV)

For the crime of murder, God merely says to "hand him over . . . to die" and "Show him no pity." But when it comes to idolatry, God not only says to "show him no pity," but also mentions the death penalty three times.

Secondly, for punishing idolators God also adds the expression "You must certainly put him to death."

Here, God uses the word "certainly" to highlight the importance of the death penalty for idolatry even further, for neither this word nor this expression appear in any of the seventeen other biblical death penalties.

God also says to us, "Do not spare him or shield him," another expression which does not appear in any of the other seventeen death penalties. This expression again magnifies how important it is to God for the state to legislate that all idolators should be executed.

Fourthly, God specifies that you must always report the crime of idolatry to the authorities so that the idolator can be executed—even if the offender turns out to be your very own brother, son, daughter, wife, or best friend.

In other words, for the sin of idolatry, God starts with the same penalty as for murder—"put him to death" and "show him no pity"—and then, using four different ways, God further emphasizes that there should be absolutely no exceptions to this rule.

With this kind of biblical evidence, you can be sure that the execution of idolators is not something about which God would ever change his mind.

Now, . . .

— since it is clear that God has not changed his mind about the importance of executing idolators,
— and since God still punishes idolatrous nations even today,
— and since America is slowly making herself eligible to inherit the same punishments that the "third-world nations" are receiving,

then it becomes very important for Christian statesmen to know exactly which potential blessings America is losing, and which potential curses America is inheriting for our deliberate refusal to outlaw idolatry. But in order to understand this, we must realize that more than any other single law, the laws against idolatry were directly tied to the supernatural blessings of a nearly poverty-free, disease-free, and war-free society. For it is written:

> Do not bow down before their gods or worship them or follow their practices. You must demolish them and break their sacred stone to pieces. Worship the Lord your God, and his blessings will be on your food and water. I will take away sickness from among you, and none will miscarry or be barren in the land. I will give you a full life span.
>
> I will send my terror ahead of you and throw into confusion every nation you encounter. I will make all your enemies turn their backs and run! (Exod. 23:24-27 NIV)

In these verses, God not only outlaws idolatry but also commands the Israelites to destroy the actual idols themselves. God then says that if they do these things and worship only Jehovah (which means of course, that they would also adopt and enforce all God's other civil laws), then God will supernaturally bless their entire nation with all the food they need, heal all their diseases, and win all their wars.

Now God's promise of giving them all the food and water they would ever want is explained further in Deuteronomy 28, where it becomes more clear that God is actually promising to give Israel a nearly poverty-free society (if Israel can accomplish all that God has required of them). For it is written:

> The Lord will send a blessing on your barns and on everything you put your hand to . . . the Lord will grant you abundant prosperity in the fruit of your womb, the young of your livestock and the crops of your ground . . . the Lord will open the heavens, the storehouse of his bounty, to send rain on

your land in season and to bless all the work of your hands. (Deut. 28:8,11-12)

Therefore, if in addition to obeying God's other principles of civil law, Israel also finally outlawed, punished, and nearly eliminated the worship of idols and worshipped only Jehovah (who is the pre-incarnate Jesus Christ anyway), then God promised Israel that he would:

1. "grant you abundant prosperity," "bless your food and water," "bless all the work of your hands" (the blessings of a nearly *poverty-free* society),
2. "take away sickness from among you," "take away barrenness from among you," "give you a full life span" (the blessings of a nearly *disease-free* society),
3. "terrorize your enemies," "throw them into confusion," "make them turn their backs and run" (the blessings of a nearly *war-free* society)!

God's purpose in outlawing idolatry was so he could eliminate poverty, disease, and war in Israel and showcase His blessings on them to the rest of the world so the Gentile nations could follow suit and learn to worship and obey the one true God as well.

Remember, God has made all nations eligible to receive both his punishments for disobedience as well as his blessings for obedience. For it is written:

> I will take vengeance in anger and wrath upon the nations that have not obeyed me. (Mic. 5:15 NIV)

> Blessed is the nation whose God is the Lord... (Ps. 33:12 NIV)

Therefore, America is also eligible to receive all the supernatural blessings of a nearly poverty-free, disease-free, and war-free society, if we are willing to change the First Amendment to outlaw idolatry and also adopt most of God's other principles of civil law into our legislation as well, so we can eventually become a true "nation under God"!

How dare we think that it is too much for God to ask us to outlaw idolatry in this nation when He promises America a nearly poverty-free, war-free, and disease-free society as a supernatural reward for our obedience? When viewed in this manner, the outlawing of idolatry suddenly becomes one of the most practical and profitable things America can do!

On the other hand, when Israel legalized idolatry (and disobeyed God's other civil laws), God promised Israel that He would curse them with "natural disasters," hunger, poverty, and plagues. Just as America is eligible to inherit all God's blessings for national obedience, we are just as eligible to inherit all God's curses for national disobedience.

The plagues that I refer to are identified in Leviticus and Deuteronomy, and involve the following:

—"wasting diseases and fever that will... drain away your life" (Lev. 26:16 NIV). These are diseases like tuberculosis, cancer, leukemia, and AIDS;
—"blindness" (Deut. 28:28 NIV). These are diseases such as diabetes, glaucoma, macular degeneration, and cataracts;
—"madness... and confusion of the mind" (Deut. 28:28 NIV) These are neurologic and psychiatric diseases like Alzheimer's disease, strokes, psychosis, panic attacks, convulsions, etc.;
—"the itch from which you cannot be cured" (Deut. 28:27 NIV) These are diseases such as eczema, psoriasis, and other forms of dermatitis;
—"afflict your knees and legs with painful boils that cannot be cured" (Deut. 28:35 NIV) and "inflammation" (Deut. 28:22 NIV) Actually the Hebrew word for "boils" means inflammation and probably would be better translated as "arthritis." This would include osteoarthritis, rheumatoid arthritis, gout, traumatic arthritis, etc.

As you can see, America is currently inheriting all of these same biblical plagues because of our national disobedience to God's clearly stated commands. In fact, all of the other nations of the world appear to be inheriting these same plagues for their national disobedience to God as well. Unfortunately, we have gotten so used to living in a society which has all of these diseases that we have mistakenly concluded that they are just the price a nation pays for living in the twentieth century. However, according to the Bible, all these diseases represent curses from God as a sign of national wickedness.

God's promise is that if a nation obeys him by outlawing idolatry and worshipping only Christ (the pre-incarnate Jehovah), as well as implementing all of God's other principles of civil law , then God will not only prevent all the diseases noted above, but also will completely "take away sickness from among you and... give you a full life span" (Exod. 23:25b, 26b NIV).

So, how dare we claim that America "enjoys" freedom of religion (which translates into a "legal right to worship idols which is protected by law") when this same philosophy of rebellion against God's laws has caused our nation to inherit the divine retribution of war, poverty, and disease (Ezek. 14:13, 17a, 19a NIV). You see, America has literally thrown away God's protection from poverty, disease, and war, and instead must now pay hundreds of billions of dollars in taxes to provide for national welfare, health care, and military defense—blessings which God was willing to provide for free, if we would have followed his commands!

God's laws against idolatry are also foundational to all God's other principles of civil law. This is because when idolatry spreads, it has a corrosive effect which dissolves the influence of all teachings of the Bible and therefore, the entire fabric of a "nation under God" melts away, and we become a nation of wickedness where none of God's principles of civil law are applied at all!

Finally, "freedom to worship idols" is a slap in the face of God by a country which was once founded upon worshipping the one true God, and depending upon his continued blessings and favor. How can our nation sing "God Bless America" (which implies that our country depends upon his continual blessings), while we simultaneously legislate the "freedom to worship idols," a philosophy which showcases our rebellion against God to the world? This reveals that our country has rejected dependence upon God for any blessings at all, feeling that we are self-sufficient (we can succeed without God's continued favor), and that we have no desire to ever become a true "nation under God" at any time in the future!

COMMON OBJECTIONS TO OUTLAWING IDOLATRY

There are five common objections to outlawing idolatry in America.

Objection One: "But what about the *First Amendment?*"

The First Amendment says:

> Congress shall make no law respecting an establishment of religion or prohibiting the free exercise thereof . . .

In writing this amendment, the founding fathers wanted to ensure that the government would not make a law which would either restrict Christian worship or elevate one denomination of Christianity over another denomination (see chapter two).

The purpose for the First Amendment was not to condone idolatry, nor was it to encourage idolators to immigrate to this country. I believe the subject of the emergence of non-Christian religions and idolatry was never addressed in the First Amendment because the vast majority of the Founding Fathers and citizens of our new nation were either true Christians by faith, or were at least "Christians" by tradition. They concluded that Christianity was already the "law of the land" and therefore never felt threatened by the remote possibility of non-Christian religions beginning to get a foothold on American soil.

A second reason why idolatry and blasphemous speech may not have been mentioned in the First Amendment might have been that the

First Amendment only restricts what the *federal* congress can legislate, and not what the *state* congresses can legislate. According to the Tenth Amendment, the state congresses could still pass any law not prohibited by the Constitution. For the Tenth Amendment says:

> The powers NOT delegated to the United States by the Constitution, nor prohibited by it to the states, are reserved to the states respectively, or to the people.

Therefore, the states could still restrict freedom of speech and religion if they chose to. The founders may have been saying, "The *state* governments reserve the RIGHT to restrict freedom of speech or religion, but we don't want that type of power to be in the hands of the *federal* government!"

Thirdly, the purpose of the First Amendment was not to remove Christianity and the Bible from being the source of inspiration for all our laws, a philosophy which is the offspring of our modern mistaken idea of "separation of church and state." The founders certainly would not want to keep the influence of Christianity and the Bible out of the federal government, because many of the state constitutions written at that time insisted that only Christians could administer the state governments. Unfortunately, the final version of the First Amendment, which was eventually ratified by the founding fathers, left a lot of room for modern misinterpretations of "separation of church and state," and "freedom to worship idols" (see chapter two).

Since God's First Commandment ("Thou shalt have no other gods before me") contradicts the mistaken modern misinterpretation of our First Amendment, which one is right: the First Commandment, or the First Amendment?

The First Commandment of God, of course! If we want to be a "nation under God," and sing "God Bless America," then our government must enforce these same principles of civil law in our country as well!

Objection Two: "But the Jews had laws against idolatry and it didn't help them!"

Actually, the Jews had *all* God's laws "on the books," but they were not being enforced. You see, it doesn't help to have laws "on the books," and not enforce them. For instance, many states still have laws "on the books" against fornication, adultery, and homosexuality, but they are not enforced, so they do not work. As a result, we live in a land filled with fornication, adultery, and homosexuality. The fault is not within God's laws, but with the *lack of enforcement* of God's laws.

In other words, if the Israelites had only enforced the laws against idolatry, then idolatry would have disappeared. Instead, after each "revival," the Jews never continued to enforce their laws against idolatry. So, when idolatry began to spring up all over again, it was never nipped in the bud when it was still controllable.

Objection Three: "But God doesn't force us to worship him! And doesn't the execution of idolators force us to worship God?"

No, it doesn't! Executing people who worship idols is not the same as forcing them to worship the one true God. God never says that people should be converted by "the edge of the sword," but he does demand the death penalty for worshipping idols. The fact is that the Bible never gives any courtroom penalty for not worshipping God, or for not going to the temple or the synagogue on the Sabbath, etc. There was only a punishment for worshipping idols. Therefore, the Israelites were never forced by any courtroom punishment to worship Jehovah; they were only forced not to worship idols.

This is no different than what happened in America generations ago when society punished people who worked on Sunday based upon God's Blue Law—the Fourth Commandment! Outlawing work on Sunday had the effect of dramatically increasing church attendance. Yet outlawing money-making work on Sunday did not force people to go to church, it only forced them not to engage in money-making work on this day. They could still choose not to go to church and stay home without fear of being punished!

Likewise, outlawing idolatry does not force you to worship Christ. You could still become an atheist or an agnostic, etc. and not be punished at all, just as long as you did not worship idols.

Objection Four: "But it was "Freedom of Religion" that made this country great!"

No, it wasn't! America has more "freedom of religion" now than ever before in our nation's history. Yet during this same time our nation has fallen into a pit of wickedness, crime, sexual immorality, rising taxes, rising suicide rates, and bigger and more intrusive government than ever before. In fact, America is now in worse shape than it has been at any time since the late 1950s.

You see, "freedom of religion" did not make this country great, nor did it make Israel great. On the contrary, "freedom of religion" destroyed Israel time and time again because God is a jealous God who hates the idea that Israel would legislate the protection of idolatry. So, God punished Israel every time they allowed idolatry to flourish. Just as "freedom of religion" did not make Israel great, (but destroyed her over and over), so also "freedom of religion" and "freedom of speech" did not make this country great (but has practically destroyed us as well).

Actually it was God who made this country great as a reward for our faith and obedience (we originally worshipped God, and God alone) and because we initially implemented at least nine of God's principles of civil law into the building of our government centuries ago. We need to do this all over again if we want God to restore His blessings upon this nation, but we must do the job more completely than the Puritans. You see, the Puritans implemented only a small portion of God's laws into the government, yet God still blessed us immensely. In this book, you have been reading about how we should implement *all* God's principles of civil law into our government so we can receive *all* his blessings.

For God will not grant America a nearly disease-free, crime-free, poverty-free, war-free, inflation-free, tax-free, and natural disaster-free society (as discussed in chapters three and four) if we allow "freedom of religion" to "protect the right to worship idols" in America. Even if the U.S. faithfully adopted 99 percent of all the biblical civil laws into our legislation, yet at the same time allowed idolatry to flourish in our land, God would surely minimize the natural benefits of implementing His laws, just as He would also deny us the supernatural blessings of a disease-free, poverty-free, war-free, and "natural disaster-free" society. For God would never showcase his blessings on us to the rest of the world and exalt us as an example for other nations to follow, while America was allowing idolatry to flourish and while our citizens were giving praise to false gods for all our blessings.

Suppose that the U.S. also began to outlaw and prosecute idolatry (as well as obey God's other principles of civil law). We could not even begin to measure the blessings which we would receive as a result of our obedience to almighty God! For in Exodus (23:24-27 NIV) God promised Israel that He would heal all of their diseases, end their poverty, and win all of their wars if Israel would do this—and it is clear that God is willing to do the same for America as well!

Unfortunately, given the state of our nation, where Christianity is America's official religion "in name only," it is understandable why America has been disinherited by God for any further natural or supernatural blessings. You see, a "fallen nation" (such as America) cannot expect God to continue to provide it with national blessings based solely upon the faith and obedience of its ancestors. Eventually, God makes no distinction between a "fallen" nation and a nation which was always wicked.

Objection Five: "But how can you decide who should be executed for idolatry, when being covetous can cause even money to be an idol?"

Do you really think that Jehovah would have created a law that could not be correctly enforced because the definition was so vague that anyone in Israel (who merely coveted anything at all) must be executed? That would make Jehovah a very poor lawmaker, wouldn't it?

In truth, the New Testament does, in fact, say that "covetousness is idolatry" (Col. 3:5 KJV). But there is no courtroom punishment for covetousness recorded anywhere in the Bible. Therefore, covetousness is "symbolic" idolatry, but clearly is not "punishable" idolatry.

Covetousness is a sin of the mind, and, since no witness can ever testify as to what another person has merely thought in his mind, covetousness can never be punished in a court of law. Only actions or words which spring from covetousness (like stealing or telling someone of your plans to steal) can be actually witnessed and therefore punished in a court of law. So, covetousness may be "symbolic" of idolatry (in the sense that a man may love something else in his heart more than he loves God) but covetousness is not the same as idolatry which can be punished in a courtroom. True "punishable" idolatry must be able to be witnessed and attested to in a court of law (such as witnessing someone praying on his knees in worship to a statue of a false "god").

If mere covetousness were considered to be punishable idolatry during the time of Moses, then Paul's confession in Romans (7:7-8 NIV) could have gotten Paul convicted and executed for idolatry. Rather than holding Paul up as an example of Christian righteousness, Paul would have been executed as an example of wicked idolatry instead. Surely it was never the intention of Jehovah (who became our Messiah and Savior, Jesus Christ) to treat godly Christian elders like Paul as though they were wicked idolators.

So, since Jehovah does not consider covetousness to be punishable idolatry, please do not think that covetousness would be punished by execution! Just because God knows what you are thinking, does not mean that God wants you to be executed for thinking it.

God's Laws against Idolatry Do More Than Just Eliminate Idolatry from a Nation

God, in His wisdom, knew that His laws against idolatry do not just eliminate idolatry from a country, but refocus the whole culture to exalt God as sovereign authority over the entire nation. This makes it dramatically more likely that God's other principles of civil law will also eventually be adopted into legislation!

You see, most all of God's other principles of civil law are still "secular" in nature, and enforcing them can easily become nothing more than "tradition" for society, while it slowly forgets that these were God's laws to begin with.

The law concerning "executing idolators" is one of the rare biblical civil laws which is directly tied to worshipping God. Because of this, the command concerning the execution of idolators keeps our entire system of laws focused upon God's ways rather than focused upon man's ways. In other words, the execution of idolators reminds us that God is (and should be) the author of all our laws, and this philosophy becomes the superglue which holds all these biblical principles together as one massive body of Christian legislation. This also keeps them all enforced, and much more resistant to being repealed in the future. For without executing idolators, the national enthusiasm for exalting God as Sovereign Authority over the country inevitably dwindles to a point of national apathy where the culture couldn't care less that God's principles of civil law are slowly being removed from their legislation.

When cultures change, certain laws may be repealed even though they still accomplish their original purpose. This is because the citizens no longer like the purpose of such laws, or they forgot that these were originally God's laws and not man's laws. For instance, for hundreds of years many sins against God were crimes against the state (such as fornication, adultery, homosexuality, and drunkenness), because God said it should be this way. Eventually the churches stopped teaching the advantages of God's principles of civil law, and after many generations passed, we forgot that these were originally God's laws. Later on, the Blue Laws were repealed so the majority of the population no longer went to church, so the degree of our national ignorance concerning the origin of these laws increased even further.

By this time, it had long been forgotten that the laws against sexual immorality and drunkenness were actually laws of God and not merely laws of man, so these laws began to be ignored or repealed as well. After this, since the majority of the nation was no longer "churched," it was just a short step for our country to develop a secular, pluralistic society with a tolerance for sin and an intolerance for Christian principles. So, it is to be expected that the laws of Christian morality would eventually make no sense at all to the modern "unchurched majority" living in the 1990s and beyond.

God planned that the periodic execution of idolators should give the entire country a renewed understanding of the importance of exalting God as Sovereign Authority , so that the rest of society's laws would continue to be based upon the Bible, generation after generation! As a result, it would be much harder to develop a secular, pluralistic society which tolerates sin and is intolerant to Christian principles. Furthermore, the only law which has the capacity to demonstrate to the world that our laws are based upon the Bible is the "execution of idolators"! The periodic execution of idolators should generate international attention as a divine reminder that the Bible is the source of all the laws in the U.S. And, with the possible exception of the laws concerning "blasphemy" and "cursing God," no other laws can provide this international witness that our nation is committed to serving the one true God of the Bible, and that this is why God will perhaps someday give us a nearly disease-free, poverty-free, and war-free society as a reward for our national obedience. Finally, not having laws against idolatry in this nation has had a destructive effect upon America which is comparable to the destructive effect seen when America repealed the Blue Laws.

The execution of idolators by our judicial system is supposed to provide the perfect opportunity for our government leaders to periodically remind us that America's God is a jealous God, and so we must obey his laws. Therefore, God's laws must be America's law, or else America will eventually become wicked and then we will be punished by God. The lack of laws against idolatry has allowed America to become apathetic and indifferent towards the philosophy that "God's laws should be America's laws," and so ultimately the philosophy of complete "separation of church and state" has taken its place.

This is similar to what happened when America repealed the laws against working on Sunday. For this mistake encouraged so many people to stop going to church that the Christian influence in our culture was drastically reduced. As a result, this helped to create a secular, pluralistic society with liberal theology, liberal politics, tolerance to wickedness, and intolerance to biblical principles.

GOD HOLDS CONGRESSMEN, SENATORS, AND JUDGES ACCOUNTABLE BEYOND THE GRAVE FOR ALLOWING IDOLATRY TO GO UNPUNISHED IN FAVOR OF FREEDOM OF RELIGION

The Scriptures reveal God's anger at each individual Israelite king who refused to outlaw idolatry and instead encouraged "freedom of religion" and made the worship of idols and false gods into a protected right. In fact, the books of I and II Kings and II Chronicles are filled with examples of how almighty God "evaluated" each king based upon his "voting record" concerning this issue of legalizing idolatry. In these books, nearly every story about these kings records whether the king encouraged "freedom of religion" by protecting idolatry, or discouraged "freedom of religion" by outlawing idolatry. For example, it is written:

> In the thirty-first year of Asa king of Judah, Omri became king of Israel, and he reigned twelve years. . . . But Omri did evil in the eyes of the Lord and sinned more than all those before him. He walked in all the ways of Jeroboam . . . and his sin, which he had caused Israel to commit, so that they provoked the Lord, the God of Israel by their worthless idols. (1 Kings 16:23a, 25-26 NIV; see also 1 Kings 16:29-33; and 2 Kings 15:32-35)

Accounts just like this one abound in these books and reveal that God takes great notice when a ruler allows idolatry to go unpunished because of "freedom of religion." Likewise, you can be sure that God takes equal notice of the voting record of America's congressmen, senators, and judges who also believe God will not care if idolatry remains legal in favor of "freedom of religion."

Just as God recorded the voting record of the ancient Israelite kings in God's book on earth (the Bible), you can be equally sure that their voting record is also recorded in God's books in heaven, which will be opened on the day of judgment. For it is written:

> And I saw the dead, great and small, standing before the throne, and books were opened. Another book was opened, which is the book of life. The dead were judged according to what they had done as recorded in the books. (Rev. 20:12 NIV)

So, you can be sure that God also holds America's congressmen, senators, and judges accountable beyond the grave for their voting record concerning the issue of legalizing idolatry and that their voting record is also written in the books out of which the dead are judged. Now some of you are probably thinking:

> But I am a Christian congressman and so I won't have to go through the judgment anyway. So I shouldn't even be concerned about having to give an account to God for my voting record on this issue.

But remember, even if you are saved by grace through faith in Christ and you bypass the great white throne judgment of God, you will still have to stand before Christ to give an account and to "receive what is due ... for the things done in the body." For it is written:

> So we make it our goal to please him.... For we must all appear before the judgement seat of Christ, that each one may receive what is due him for the things done while in the body, whether good or bad. (2 Cor. 5:9a, 10 NIV)

But wouldn't Christ be delighted on the day we stand before him if our voting record were like the "voting record" of good King Josiah, who clearly pleased God by outlawing idolatry and legislated that the worship of Jehovah was the only acceptable practice within Israel. For you see, King Josiah

> called together all the elders of Judah and Jerusalem ... He read in their hearing all the words of the Book of the Covenant ... The king stood by his pillar and renewed the covenant in the presence of the Lord-to follow the Lord and

keep his commands, regulations, and decrees with all his heart and all his soul . . . then he had everyone in Jerusalem and Benjamin pledge themselves to it . . . Josiah removed all the idols from the territory belonging to the Israelites, and had all those who were present in Israel serve the Lord their God. As long as he lived, they did not fail to follow the Lord, the God of their fathers! (2 Chron. 34:29-33 NIV; see also 2 Kings 18:1-4)

In conclusion, since the political sins of allowing "freedom to worship idols" are recorded in God's books on earth, you can be sure that they are also recorded in God's books in heaven out of which the dead are judged (Rev. 20:11 NIV), and that even Christian rulers will someday have to stand before Christ and give an account for things done in the flesh.

In other words, you can be sure that the voting record of each ruler (on every issue which is important to almighty God) has consequences beyond the grave, and that this is just one more reason why American legislators must outlaw idolatry.

IMPLEMENTING GOD'S LAWS AGAINST IDOLATRY IN A NATION OF "FREEDOM OF RELIGION"

There are two different ways to go about eliminating idolatry in this nation, but they each involve either restricting the application of the First Amendment only to the federal government and not applying it to the states, or repealing and rewriting the First Amendment altogether.

The first alternative should be the easier of the two to accomplish, for the mechanism for its implementation is already in place. You see, the first word of the First Amendment is . . .

> CONGRESS shall make no law respecting an establishment of religion, or prohibiting the free exercise thereof; or abridging the freedom of speech, or of the press; (emphasis added)

This means that it is the federal government's congress which cannot make a law that prohibits "free speech" or "freedom of religion," but the states' governments still can make such laws. Furthermore, the Tenth Amendment guarantees that the states still retain this power. For the Tenth Amendment says,

> The powers not delegated to the United States by the Constitution, nor prohibited by it to the states, are reserved to the states respectively, or to the people.

This tells us that the states have always had the power to restrict certain religious practices and outlaw idolatry, as well as the power to pass laws against totally unrestrained freedom of speech or the freedom of the press. It is a violation of Tenth Amendment state's rights for the federal government to say that a state government cannot do so. In other words, the Tenth Amendment guarantees that the states still have the right to outlaw idolatry, and the First Amendment guarantees that the federal government's congress cannot stop them or interfere in this process.

Furthermore, any U.S. Supreme Court Judge who decides a case in such a way that his verdict denies a state its Tenth Amendment rights (such as applying the First Amendment to the states) has violated his oath of office to uphold the Constitution and the amendments and therefore could be impeached. Therefore, Christian statesmen should be able to write and pass all kinds of new state legislation based entirely on Christian morality, tradition, and biblical principles of civil law, and know that the U.S. Supreme Court is powerless to do anything about it because of the Tenth Amendment! Slowly, using this strategy generation after generation, the laws of state governments could be based entirely upon the Bible and God's principles of civil law.

If our Christian statesmen could be reeducated concerning the need to eliminate idolatry from our nation—and that the founding fathers gave them the power to do so—then we may indeed be able to inherit trillions of dollars worth of medical, economic, and military blessings from God, and be granted a nearly disease-free, poverty-free, and war-free society as a reward for our obedience.

Now the second method of eliminating idolatry in our nation is more difficult, for it involves repealing and rewriting the First Amendment altogether, to make it clear that idolatry is unwelcome in our nation and that anyone caught worshipping idols (statues) would be executed without mercy. Of course, given the political window of opportunity, the new version of the First Amendment should also be designed to restrict foul language, blasphemy, and pornography on TV, radio, movies and print.

I believe that this second alternative would be a much harder political goal to accomplish than the first alternative mentioned, but would be very worthwhile indeed! If we can implement this strategy, eventually the laws of federal government could be based entirely upon the Bible and God's principles of civil law as well!

The modern interpretation of the First Amendment implies that our government should no longer base our laws upon the Bible, for that would be elevating Christianity above all other religions, and "violate" the First Amendment. Therefore, the First Amendment practically forces us to use only secular sources for our laws, resulting in the immediate rejection of any proposed legislation which sounds even remotely Christian or biblical. As a result, the standard twentieth-century misinterpretation of the First Amendment practically eliminates any chance of ever becoming a true "nation under God." For we can no longer use God's infallible wisdom and God's perfect laws to run our country, but can only use the fallible wisdom of man and man's laws!

We need to consider striking down the original First Amendment and rewriting it to allow freedom of all "Christian denominations" to worship Christ in their own way (except for worshipping the statue of "Mother Mary," which constitutes punishable idolatry) and striking down all other forms of idolatry. Furthermore, we must recognize the need to base all our laws upon the Bible, and restrict speech by outlawing foul language, pornography, and blasphemy, etc.

If all the money which has been spent attempting to get prayer back into schools had been spent on attempting to change the First Amendment, by now we would have successfully won a much larger victory. If we could repeal and rewrite the First Amendment, we could legally outlaw all the pornography, foul language, and blasphemy in movies, magazines, TV, and radio. It would also eliminate the philosophy of "separation of church and state" so we could again use the Bible as the foundation for our laws, and therefore again outlaw fornication, adultery, homosexuality, drunkenness and abortion. Finally, by eliminating the "separation of church and state" problem, we could not only get prayer and Bible study back into the public schools, but we could also attempt to legislate that all public schools become Christian schools once again, as the founders wanted and the Bible commands. This would allow prayer, Bible reading, and all doctrines of Christianity to be taught in all the nation's schools by mature Christian teachers. This would result in a much greater impact for Christ than merely having the student-initiated and student-led prayers and Bible reading which we have today! So, it is clear that repealing and rewriting the First Amendment is a good and worthwhile goal for Christian statesmen!

Conclusion

I'm sure that God is greatly angered by the hypocrisy of a nation which sings "God Bless America" yet at the same time throws God and the Bible out of the classroom, the courtroom, and the government, and uses the First Amendment to protect the right to worship idols!

Is this what God really wants us to do? No! Of course not! For if we really want to be a "nation under God" and sing "God Bless America," we must follow the biblical guidelines for national government which were given by God to Moses thirty-four hundred years ago, in order for us to receive God's blessings upon our nation. This includes the outlawing of idolatry.

Now there are ten reasons why America should outlaw idolatry.

First of all, it is God's command.

Second, God does not change his mind. For it is written:

> I the Lord do not change. (Mal. 3:6 NIV)

> He who is the Glory of Israel does not . . . change his mind; for he is not a man, that he should change his mind. (1 Sam. 15:29 NIV)

> Jesus Christ is the same yesterday and today and forever. (Heb. 13:8 NIV)

Third, the principles underlying God's civil laws were established to last forever. For it is written:

> Your statutes are forever right . . . all your righteous laws are eternal. . . . Long ago I learned from your statutes that you established them to last forever." (Ps. 119:144, 160, 152 NIV)

Fourth, according to Deuteronomy 13:6a, 8-10a (NIV), God evidently hates idolatry more than he hates deliberate murder, for God added four extra commands to his law against idolatry (which are not present in his law against murder) in order to emphasize for all time that idolators should be executed without mercy no matter what the circumstances.

Fifth, America must outlaw idolatry because historically, God blessed America at least in part because our ancestors suppressed idolatry through the continuous education and indoctrination of adults (in church) and children (in schools). Since we have stopped doing this, our nation has become more evil with each passing decade.

Sixth, America must outlaw idolatry because it is clear the founders wanted us to continue to suppress idolatry in one form or another. Therefore, they designed the First Amendment to limit only what the federal congress can do not limit what the state congresses can do at all. They also designed the Tenth Amendment to guarantee all states the right to do whatever is not specifically forbidden in the Constitution. Therefore, states have always had the right to outlaw idolatry.

Seventh, God will not bless America any longer unless we begin to redesign our laws and our culture to focus the attention of the international community onto *who* is blessing America and *why*. This means that all nations must see unmistakable evidence that:

> —America worships only the one true God in prayer, and that we have outlawed idolatry by prosecution and punishment (or at least have greatly suppressed idolatry by education and indoctrination), and

> —America obeys God's principles of moral and civil law (by progressively implementing more and more of God's principles of

civil law into our legislation with each passing generation in order to become a nation under God).

Eighth, according to Exodus 23:24-27 (NIV), God promised Israel that if they would eliminate idolatry from their nation (in addition to implementing all God's other principles of civil law) that he would:
—heal all their diseases,
—end all their poverty, and,
—win all their wars!
So consider the question,

> What would Jehovah do (WWJD) for America, if America became a true nation under God?

Well, there are seven verses in the Bible which reveal that the same blessings God promised to Israel are also available to America if we will also outlaw idolatry in our nation and progressively implement most of God's other principles of civil law into our legislation. For the emotional and economic value of inheriting a nearly disease-free, poverty-free, and war-free society would have such an important impact upon American culture, that it would be worth doing *anything* God would ask us to do to receive these blessings, even if we had to outlaw idolatry.

Ninth, America must outlaw idolatry because God is still in the business of punishing idolatrous nations, and this is why the idolatrous third-world nations have so much more poverty, diseases, plagues, droughts, floods, famines, and other natural disasters than do the first-world nations. Furthermore, because the Clinton administration has encouraged so much evil in our nation, the national sin burden in America is beginning to reach levels seen only in the idolatrous third-world nations. As a result, God has punished America with more hurricanes, droughts, floods, firestorms, snowstorms, and earthquakes in a shorter period of time than at any other point during our nation's history. These "natural disasters" have cost hundreds of billions of dollars in extra taxes, and have left thousands of Americans bankrupt and homeless.

And tenth, America must outlaw idolatry because the Scriptures teach that God holds each ruler accountable beyond the grave for his voting record on this particular issue. According to the Scriptures, each ruler (even if he is saved) will someday have to stand before Christ and "receive what is due him for the things done in the body, whether good or bad" (2 Cor. 5:10 NIV).

And that, is God's view of the First Commandment (which outlaws idolatry) versus the First Amendment (which "legalizes" idolatry)!

Chapter Seventeen

GOD'S VIEW OF REINTRODUCING THE BLUE LAWS TO OUTLAW WORK ON SUNDAY

The term "Blue Laws" refers to laws which prohibit money-making work and certain other types of activity from occurring on Sunday. It is believed that hundreds of years ago the New England colonists printed their version of such laws on blue paper and had them posted at various public places throughout their towns, thus giving rise to the term (*Academic American Encyclopedia*, vol. 3, 343).

The original idea to prohibit working on one day of the week came directly from the Ten Commandments. For instance, the Fourth Commandment reads:

> Remember the Sabbath day and keep it holy. Six days you shall labor and do all your work, but the seventh day is a Sabbath to the Lord your God. On it you shall not do any work, neither you, nor your son or daughter, nor your manservant or maidservant, nor your animals, nor the alien within your gates. For in six days the Lord made the heavens and the earth, the sea, and all that is in them, but he rested on the seventh day. Therefore, the Lord made it holy. (Exod. 20:8-11 NIV)

So, you see, it was originally God's idea for people not to work on one day of the week, but God chose Saturday (the seventh day of the week) for us to rest, not Sunday (the first day of the week).

However, after Christ rose from the dead on the first day of the week, Christians occasionally met together on this day to worship Christ in commemoration of this event. This was not done to replace Sabbath worship, because the Bible teaches that Paul was still worshipping on the Sabbath long after Christ rose from the dead (Acts 13:14, 42, 44; 16:13; 17:2; 18:4 NIV). Therefore the other Christians living during Paul's day were most likely still worshipping on the Sabbath day as well.

Slowly, this tradition of meeting for worship on Sunday to commemorate Christ's resurrection began to become more and more popular, and for this reason (as well as for other reasons which will not be discussed here) our day for Christian worship became Sunday. Yet Saturday has always been the real Sabbath day in God's eyes.

Our Christian ancestors inherited this tradition of "Sunday worship and rest," and so they outlawed working on Sunday in response to God's Fourth Commandment. This action had a marvelous effect upon this country. By outlawing work on Sunday, the Blue Laws were able to maximize voluntary church attendance, allowing the Bible to mold and maintain our culture for nearly two hundred years—from their inception by the Puritans (before the Revolutionary War) up until shortly after World War II.

After our victory in WWII however, our leaders evidently felt that as long as we had international allies and modern weapons to help us in battle, then we no longer needed almighty God's assistance to help us win our wars. Therefore, I believe that America's leaders subconsciously concluded that if we didn't need God during wartime, then we didn't have to obey Him during peacetime. For ever since WWII, the states have either ignored or repealed the Blue Laws. Shortly after the war, they began to ignore or remove all God's other biblical principles of civil law from our legislation as well.

As a result, America has become an object lesson which illustrates for the rest of the world the dramatic positive effect America's Blue Laws had on our culture *before* they were repealed compared to the destructive impact on America's culture which occurred *after* they were repealed.

So, we need to prayerfully examine the lessons of history in order to understand what practical advantages resulted generations ago when our nation outlawed work on Sunday. We then need to prayerfully ask God to reveal to us what *additional* natural benefits He intended America to have if we would have followed His command more closely and made *Saturday* our day of Christian rest and worship (instead of *Sunday*). Finally, we need to ask God to reveal to us what *supernatural* blessings He would have given to America if we had also punished Sabbath-breakers *God's* way instead of *man's* way.

In other words, we need to understand all the advantages God intended America to inherit if we would have implemented the entire Fourth Commandment exactly as God originally intended.

I. THE FOUR EXCEPTIONS TO THE FOURTH COMMANDMENT

There are four exceptions to the Fourth Commandment which are mentioned in the Bible. These four exceptions define what type of "work" is allowed on the Sabbath, and they are as follows:

1. "preparing food" for people (Exod. 12:16 NIV) and "giving water to animals" (Luke 13:15 NIV). Gathering food (i.e., shopping for food) is outlawed, however (Exod. 16:27, 29 NIV);
2. "healing" people or animals—meaning, to be involved in the medical, nursing, paramedical, pharmacy or veterinary professions (Matt. 12:10-12 NIV);
3. "rescuing" people or animals from danger (Luke 14:5 NIV). This includes firefighters, rescue squads, etc.;
4. "ministering" to others, as a priest (Matt. 12:5 NIV).

So, the Fourth Commandment outlaws all work on the Sabbath except in the preaching, healing, and rescuing businesses, and outlaws all chores on the Sabbath, except for feeding family and animals. All of the rest of the Sabbath regulations that the Jews had were merely traditions of man, and were not the laws of God.

II. THE PRACTICAL ADVANTAGES OF HAVING A NATIONAL "DAY OF REST"

There are many practical advantages of having a nationwide "day of rest."

For instance, if America outlawed all money-making work on Sunday except in the preaching, healing, and rescuing businesses, then your TV and radio would only carry Christian worship services etc., on Sunday. This is the only type of programing where all the participants would be willing to donate services free-of-charge as a ministry for Christ.

Imagine having no radio, TV, movies, or any other type of paid entertainment (including professional sporting events) available to watch on Sunday. Further imagine that there wouldn't be any restaurants, food stores, or gasoline stations open, and imagine that the only people working on Sunday would be in the preaching, healing, and rescuing business. In other words, only preachers, doctors, nurses, pharmacists, rescue squads, paramedics, EMT's, employees of hospitals, nursing homes, and rest homes, as well as policemen and firemen would be working on Sundays. I believe that God's wisdom and compassion can be observed and "measured" (so to speak) by examining all the following advantages that this kind of "day of rest" would have for America.

For instance, as a physician I can tell you that our bodies would be healthier because our stress levels would be lower. We would probably live longer and have less medical problems, such as heart attacks, strokes, high blood pressure, peptic ulcers, and stomach spasms.

Secondly, because of our lowered stress levels, our minds would also be healthier, and there would probably be less anxiety, panic attacks, depression, nervous breakdowns, neurosis, and psychosis.

Thirdly, our families would become more important to us because we could spend more time together. We would be better able to raise our children in "nurture and admonition of the Lord," and teach them more thoroughly about salvation and Christian values. Additionally, there would be less divorce, and more "abundant life."

Fourthly, there would be a much greater degree of community fellowship at church. You see, the idea of going to church becomes much more attractive to non-Christians when there isn't a whole lot of other things that they can do on Sunday. As a result, the vast majority of our population would return to church. For at church they would find all the fellowship, singing, and worship necessary to make Sunday more enjoyable and fulfilling. And, since there wouldn't be a whole lot of activity at home (for the Fourth Commandment also outlawed most household chores), then it becomes much more likely that the community would gather after the worship service for food, fellowship, fun, singing, and even more Bible study and worship.

In other words, simply by having a national "day of rest," we would probably be healthier (both physically and mentally), and we would have a greater opportunity to develop better relationships with our family, with our friends, with our community, and with our God.

III. WHAT ADDITIONAL NATIONAL BLESSINGS DID AMERICA INHERIT WHEN OUR NATION OUTLAWED WORKING ON SUNDAY?

As noted in the beginning of this chapter, by outlawing money-making work on Sunday, the Blue Laws were able to maximize voluntary church attendance. Nationwide church attendance before the Blue Laws were repealed was far greater than church attendance after the Blue Laws were repealed.

Simply because the great majority of Americans went to church generations ago does not mean that the great majority of Americans were saved. You see, the Bible teaches that those who enter through the narrow gate of salvation and surrender will never be more than just a few (a small minority) of the nation's population. For Jesus said:

> Enter through the narrow gate. For wide is the gate and broad is the road that leads to destruction, and many enter through it. But small is the gate and narrow is the road that leads to life, and only a few find it. (Matt. 7:13-14 NIV)

In other words, because "only a few find life", Christ is saying that the number of true believers at one time in any given society will never amount to more than a small Christian minority of the total population.

Even though this remains true, Christians must still share the gospel with everyone anyway, so that we may continue to obey the Great

Commission of Christ and find all the lost sheep (who will ultimately follow the Good Shepherd).

Although spreading the gospel of Christ is the most important mission of the Church, we know from our history that much more was accomplished by the Blue Laws than simply getting the vast majority of Americans into church to hear the gospel. For instance, before the Blue Laws were repealed, the voting majority of Americans still believed that fornication, adultery, homosexuality, drunkenness, non-biblical divorce, blasphemy, foul language, and pornography were wrong, even though these same citizens may not have had a personal relationship with Christ as Savior and Lord. In other words, by teaching Christian doctrine and Christian morality to the great majority of Americans each week in church, the Blue Laws made it easier for the principles of Christianity to prompt most Americans to think and behave better—even if they still refused to surrender to Christ as their Lord and Savior. Therefore, one of God's purposes for the Fourth Commandment must have been to empower the doctrines of Christianity with the muscle of training and tradition to help keep the large unrighteous majority of citizens on their best behavior. It worked amazingly well!

It is important at this point to add the fact that before the Blue Laws were repealed, America had actual laws against blasphemy, fornication, adultery, homosexuality, drunkenness, and non-biblical divorce. Our founders adopted these six principles of civil law directly from the Bible and placed them into our legislation. In addition to the Blue Laws, these also helped to keep the large unrighteous majority of citizens on their best behavior—but this time it was by the threat of prosecution and punishment.

In other words, God intended that the small Christian minority of citizens (and voters) would be kept on their best behavior by salvation and surrender. The large, unrighteous majority of citizens (and voters) would be kept on their best behavior by combining training and tradition with the threat of prosecution and punishment. This also teaches us that God's Fourth Commandment does not act in isolation, but interacts with many other biblical principles of civil law. Therefore, God's Fourth Commandment is understood best by carefully examining its interaction with these other biblical principles.

In summary, when America outlawed work on Sunday (and also outlawed fornication, adultery, homosexuality, drunkenness, blasphemy, and non-biblical divorce) by combining training and tradition with prosecution and punishment, these seven biblical principles of civil law interacted in a way to prompt the large, unrighteous majority of Americans to act better and to believe that God's ways were always right, even if they didn't yield their hearts in submission to Christ as Savior and

Lord. As a result, before the Blue Laws were repealed, the large unsaved majority of citizens still exhibited a more uniform view of Christianity, creation science, morality, and conservative politics.

After the Blue Laws were repealed however, the majority of Americans left the Church and slowly lost their culture of Christian training and tradition. And so, the second and third generation "unchurched majority" developed a *secular* world view by default—a view that morality, politics, and science should be understood as if their were no God, which meant that there was no ultimate right and wrong. As a result, the "unchurched majority" of our nation developed much greater diversity in their thinking, and as part of their pluralism began to exalt evolution, sexual immorality, liberal politics, and a liberal view of Christianity.

By examining our nation's descent into wickedness since the Blue Laws were abandoned, we can see more clearly that God's intended purpose of the Fourth Commandment was not just to set aside one day a week to rest and to worship God, but also to maximize voluntary church attendance. This was so the unrighteous could be trained to habitually think and act as the righteous, even if they never willingly yielded their hearts in submission to Christ as Savior and Lord. In this way, nationwide weekly education in Christian doctrine and morality would prompt more conformity of action and unity of thinking, such as encouraging all citizens to have a more *biblical* world view of creation, morality, and politics. At the same time, nationwide weekly education in these same principles would tend to suppress the development of a nationwide *secular* world view which would exalt evolution, sexual immorality, and liberal politics.

In other words, the Blue Laws functioned to help preserve America's Christian heritage, and to prevent the disintegration of our Christian culture into:

1. a secular society, with a secular world view and a secular view of politics, which would eventually evolve into a
2. pluralistic society, with a
3. liberal view of politics and government,
4. which would successfully repeal God's laws against sexual immorality, drunkenness, non-biblical divorce, and blasphemy,
5. and allow the development of a progressively more evil and immoral society,
6. which God would be forced to punish with hurricanes, tornados, floods, droughts, firestorms, blizzards, earthquakes, diseases, pestilence, and poverty.

For you see, God has always wanted the Bible to mold nations and shape cultures, not just mold and shape the Christians within those cultures. Unfortunately, by repealing the Blue Laws we have dishonored both God and our founders, and have legislated that the Bible's influence be restricted only to those Christians who still continue to faithfully attend church (which is a much smaller proportion of the total population than attended church before the Blue Laws were revealed).

IV. HOW WORSHIPPING ON THE SABBATH (SATURDAY, INSTEAD OF SUNDAY) WOULD ADD TO THE EFFECTIVENESS OF THE BLUE LAWS TO HELP KEEP THE UNRIGHTEOUS MAJORITY ON THEIR BEST BEHAVIOR

God declared in his Fourth Commandment that the real day of worship and rest for the Israelites was to be the SABBATH day (Saturday, instead of Sunday). Since God's other civil laws have such wonderful practical applications for American government and culture, the question is:

> Could switching our national day of worship from Sunday to Saturday further improve the effectiveness of the Blue Laws in keeping the large, unrighteous majority on their best behavior?

Well, as noted earlier, Matthew 7:13-14 teaches that those who enter the "narrow gate" of Salvation and Surrender will never amount to more than a small minority of the total population in any nation. As a result, the vast majority of citizens in any nation will never choose to accept Christ as Savior and Lord and therefore never have the Holy Spirit's influence in their lives to help control their behavior from within.

Jehovah (who personally became our Savior—Jesus Christ) knew that the large, unrighteous majority would never obey him out of love for a Savior who wants to forgive their sins. Jehovah also knew that this same rebellious majority would often obey him out of fear and trepidation, even if they would never obey him out of love and surrender. Therefore, Jehovah deliberately connected Sabbath worship with a weekly reminder to all people that they have a Creator who commands their obedience. For it is written:

> Remember the Sabbath day by keeping it holy. . . . For in six days the Lord made the heavens and the earth, the sea, and all that is in them, but he rested on the seventh day. Therefore, the Lord made it holy. (Exod. 20:8, 11 NIV)

You see, by connecting weekly Sabbath-worship to the Creation, Jehovah motivated the Israelites to remember that they had a Creator-God who commands their obedience. This would help to maximize a nationwide fear of the Lord (Prov. 9:10 NIV), which he knew would also help to keep the large, unrighteous majority on their best behavior, especially when added to the principles of training and tradition (in combination with the threat of prosecution and punishment).

For God created our minds in such a way that every seven days all mankind needs to be reminded that they have a Creator to whom they need to be obedient, or else they will slowly forget their Creator and begin to believe in evolution, disbelieve the Bible, and disobey God's commands. And, evidently God felt that reminding the unsaved masses every seven days that they have a Creator (who warns them not to sin) works better to control their behavior, than reminding the unsaved every seven days that they have a Savior who wants to forgive them for their sins. Therefore rather than have a weekly celebration on the first day of the week in honor of "forgiveness," Jehovah decided that it was even more important to have a weekly celebration on the seventh day in honor of "obedience"—to remind the "unsaved masses" of their obligation to fear God and to obey the laws of their Creator. After all. . . .

> The fear of the Lord is the beginning of wisdom, and knowledge of the Holy One is understanding. (Prov. 9:10 NIV).

America should once again outlaw working on Sunday, as well as outlaw sexual immorality, drunkenness, and blasphemy. By doing so, the voting majority would be more likely to return to church and stay on their best behavior because of the combined influences of training and tradition (learned in church) with prosecution and punishment (learned in the courts). Then, if we made the nationwide switch from Sunday-worship to Sabbath-worship of a Creator who commands our obedience, this would add even *more* incentive for the large, unrighteous majority to remain on their best behavior.

But that's just the *first* advantage of Sabbath-worship. In the next section, you will see that Sabbath-worship was also designed to suppress liberal theology and liberal politics, as well as to motivate greater trust in the potential application of God's other civil laws. This would prompt Christian rulers to adopt even more of God's principles of civil law into our national legislation.

V. HOW WORSHIPPING ON THE SABBATH (SATURDAY INSTEAD OF SUNDAY) HELPS TO PREVENT THE EMERGENCE OF LIBERAL POLITICS AND LIBERAL THEOLOGY

If America used the Blue Laws to outlaw work on the Sabbath, in addition to outlawing sexual immorality, drunkenness, blasphemy, pornography, and non-biblical divorce, and we also switched our national day of worship from Sunday to Saturday, then our citizens would eventually develop a cultural tradition which taught that:

> when God rests, we rest, and when God works, we work. So every seven days we are reminded that the STANDARD for

our obedience as a nation is to do exactly what God says. And because of this tradition, our voting majority has slowly become more inclined to favor adopting God's other principles of civil law into our national legislation as well!

In other words, when America begins to obey the Fourth Commandment more completely, we will be much more likely to look for, and to recognize the potential advantages of, adopting God's other principles of civil law into our legislation as well. As we then begin to witness the benefits of adopting additional biblical principles into our legislation, the Bible will inevitably be exalted as the primary resource for all our future civil laws for generations to come.

If America's early churches had taught the advantages that God's principles of civil law had for the administration of good government (as part of their commitment to teach the entire Bible completely), then the majority of American citizens would have eventually begun to favor having God's laws in our government. Therefore they would have voted only for godly leaders to adopt and enforce God's laws. So, if our ancestral Christian rulers had followed these biblical guidelines correctly, then each subsequent generation would have naturally developed a more biblical world view as well as a more biblical view of politics. In other words, adopting nationwide *Sabbath*-worship, in addition to adopting God's other principles of civil law, develops the capacity to create and perpetuate a very fundamentalist theology and a biblical view of politics, while simultaneously preventing the development of liberal (non-biblical) politics. Alternatively, worshipping on the *first* day of the week tends to do just the opposite, for *Sunday*-worship so violates the Fourth commandment week after week, and generation after generation, that this automatically reinforces the false idea that the Fourth Commandment principle of Sabbath worship may no longer be valid today! This naturally undermines our faith in God's other principles of civil law as well!

As a result, our poor national compliance with the Fourth Commandment (by worshipping on Sunday instead of the Sabbath) now sets a NEW STANDARD for future poor national compliance with the other biblical principles of civil law (by creating and perpetuating our mistaken customary belief that the other biblical principles of civil law may be equally faulty, unreliable, or no longer applicable for modern society)! Furthermore, our preachers unfortunately *teach* this bias against God's civil laws to their congregations by regularly implying that the evil behavior of the Pharisees resulted from their "*overcommitment*" to the law (rather than their "*undercommitment*" to the Lord). This mistaken idea unfortunately ties the evil of the Pharisees to the Mosaic laws—as if God's laws somehow contributed to the evil of the Pharisees. As a result of repeatedly painting the Pharisees and the Mosaic laws with the same broad brush, modern pastors have taught their congregations to doubt that the Mosaic civil laws could have any value at all.

Therefore, traditional Sunday-worship sets in motion a process which eventually causes us to inadvertently *prejudice* ourselves against God's principles of civil law and *repudiate* the value that these principles might have for the administration of sound and virtuous government. By the time we get around to voting, we have so little faith left in God's principles of civil law that these principles are never considered by Christian politicians or by the Christian voters themselves, much less by the non-Christian politicians and voters.

You see, reinterpreting the Fourth Commandment in light of Christ's resurrection, and therefore worshipping on Sunday instead of Saturday opens the door to allow the Church to reinterpret all of God's other laws in light of the resurrection as well. In practical terms, this "reinterpretation" amounts to nothing more than motivating a general distrust of all God's other principles of civil law. Furthermore, nationwide Sunday worship repeatedly reinforces and "confirms" the mistaken prejudice that all God's principles of civil law are suspect and open to rejection as a group without any prior evaluation of their individual merits (simply as good laws).

By undermining the believers' faith in the eternal value of God's laws, and instead substituting a prejudice against any practical application of these civil principles, traditional Sunday-worship promotes a national deterrence to adopting God's civil laws into government. On the other hand, Sabbath-worship promotes faith that there might be some additional benefits to be gained by adopting more of God's principles of civil law into our national legislation. In other words, by undermining the value of the principles underlying God's civil laws, traditional Sunday worship promotes a liberal view of politics. This view tends to disregard the practical value of God's civil laws and tends to repeal any biblical civil laws which might already be in place (such as the laws against fornication, adultery, homosexuality, drunkenness, blasphemy, non-biblical divorce, and even working on Sunday).

For these same reasons, traditional Sunday-worship also promotes a more liberal theology as well. By educating the Church to believe that all of God's laws should be reinterpreted in light of Christ's resurrection, we undermine the eternal validity of God's laws while promoting speculation that these are spurious laws which may not have come from God in the first place—but may have been written by either Moses himself, or by someone else entirely, or may have come from a totally different source such as from the (law) Code of Hammurabi.

In any case, when the divine authorship of God's laws is suspect, then by logical extension, the entire authenticity of God's Word comes into question. This destructive process is encouraged at least in part by traditional Sunday-worship, which repeatedly violates and undermines the authority of the Fourth Commandment, and reinforces the mistaken idea that some of the principles underlying the Fourth Commandment may no longer be valid.

After generations of not worshipping on the Seventh Day and not following God's command to rest on the Sabbath (just as God himself rested after he created the heavens and the earth) some Christians probably began to think,

> Well, if the Fourth Commandment is NOT to be taken literally (and is only a symbol of a weekly pattern of worship), then maybe the story of the Creation is not to be taken literally either (and is only a symbol of man's origins)!

So, the inevitable consequence of not worshipping on the Sabbath and therefore not being reminded each week of the truth of the Creation story and the Garden of Eden, is that some churches developed a liberal theology. Eventually, they stopped teaching that the Creation was true, and began to compromise biblical teaching with the theory of evolution. This false belief in evolution further encourages a liberal theology and a liberal view of politics. For as Ken Ham says:

> If Adam is in your ancestry, God sets the rules! But if an Ape is in your ancestry, man sets the rules!

Therefore, it is clear that Sunday-worship perpetuates a more liberal theology and a more liberal view of politics (which ignores God's principles of civil law), than if we practiced Sabbath-worship (which would cause us to favor God's principles of civil law, thereby perpetuating a more biblical view of politics and a more fundamental view of theology)!

What are the practical implications of this idea for the individual Congressman? Well, if a congressman learns a theology which ignores God's civil laws, then his politics will also ignore God's civil laws. For politics which ignores (or deplores) God's principles of civil law always has as its foundation in a theology which ignores (or deplores) God's principles of civil law. On the other hand, national politics which exalt God's principles of civil law can only spring from a national theology which exalts God's principles of civil law. And of course, a national theology which exalts God's principles of civil law can only spring from large numbers of pastors who periodically teach their congregations about the practical advantages that God's principles of civil law have for administering American government. So, before Christianity can even consider creating a "nation under God," it is absolutely essential for churches to first develop a theology which exalts God's principles of civil law over man's principles of civil law, so we can then develop a culture whose politics also exalts these principles.

This is exactly the kind of society the Fourth Commandment was designed by God to produce, by being a catalyst to create a culture which would exalt God's principles of civil law while at the same time presenting the gospel of Jesus Christ to the entire nation. But nowadays, the Fourth Commandment has become only a symbol of the importance of worshipping every seven days, and has become powerless to prevent the secularization of our society, the progressive emergence of pluralism, and the rapid decay of our nation caused by liberal theology and liberal politics.

(By the way, worshipping on Sunday also teaches our nation's non-Christians that if Christians don't obey the literal interpretation of the Fourth Commandment, then non-Christians need not obey the literal interpretation of the Seventh Commandment about adultery, or obey the literal interpretation of the Tenth Commandment (about lust and pornography), or obey the literal interpretation of the Sixth Commandment (about killing, and by implication, about abortion)?

You see, traditional Sunday worship has caused many problems which God intended to be easily prevented by simply following his commands to worship on the Sabbath day.

VI. HOW REPEALING THE BLUE LAWS FURTHERS THE DEVELOPMENT OF THE SAME LIBERAL THEOLOGY AND LIBERAL POLITICS WHICH ORIGINALLY STARTED BY WORSHIPPING ON SUNDAY INSTEAD OF SATURDAY

Another reason that liberal churches and liberal politics develop when a nation ignores the Fourth Commandment and repeals the Blue Laws, is because church attendance declines dramatically (as a consequence of allowing people to work on Sunday). As a result, the church must now compete with the world to increase attendance, and so liberal doctrine and liberal preaching often develop to "improve" the church's ability to "compete" successfully with the rest of the world.

We once lived in a climate where the church molded its members' behavior through good biblical teaching, "church discipline," and a doctrinal emphasis on obedience. But now we live in a climate where the lack of attendance dictates that doctrines such as "church discipline" and an emphasis on obedience are discarded in favor of "cheap grace" (in order to increase church attendance). Churches are now "consumer-driven" to become acceptable to the community, whereas in the past consumers were "driven by biblical principles" to become acceptable to God. As a consequence of this, our modern churches have moved from "Christ-conscious" to "consumer-conscious," and from "master-driven" to "market-driven." So today, when a person hears a doctrine in church which steps on his toes, rather than think, "Am I really right with God?" instead he now feels comfortable to think, "Is this church really right for me?" As a result, perpetually unrepentant sinners can switch churches whenever their toes are stepped on, or even stay home altogether and never go to church. By repealing the Blue Laws, we also repealed the stigma of not going to church. Because there is no longer any stigma attached to "not going to church," they never have to change their ways in order to be allowed back into church again, for they no longer have fear of being "cast out of the church" by "church discipline!"

As a result, the church has lost its premier position to mold society into a biblical framework, and has now become impotent to do nearly anything except lead sinners to Christ (which is, however, its most important task). However, the church could lead sinners to Christ more efficiently if we brought back the Blue Laws to get everyone back into church in the first place.

There are four reasons why church attendance should be expected to decline after repealing the Blue Laws. They are as follows:

1. The government is officially condoning and sanctioning the idea that you can now undertake gainful employment without punishment on Sunday. As a result, the national expectation that "everyone should go to church" gets "repealed" as well. After all, "if our government leaders say it's OK not to go to church, then it must be true!" Eventually, Christians mistakenly believe that even God himself "changed his mind" about working on Sunday, just like they mistakenly believe He "changed his mind" about worshipping on Saturday.

2. Although generally the Blue Laws didn't cover doing "household chores" on the Sabbath, many church members probably realized that the Fourth Commandment also forbids doing household chores (Exod. 34:21, 35:2-3; Num. 15:32-36 NIV), with the exception of preparing (but not "gathering") food (Exod. 12:16b NIV). As a result, people have begun to feel that the government has overturned the Fourth Commandment and so, they can stay home on Sunday and not go to church in order to do household chores that they did not get done during the week.

3. Furthermore, slowly employers began to open their businesses on Sunday and eventually began requiring their employees to work on Sunday. Now, laws have begun to appear which prohibit employees from refusing to work on Sunday—even for religious reasons—if their employer requires them to work on Sunday as a condition of their employment.

4. Then, businesses specializing in entertainment began to open up on Sunday such as restaurants, movies, bowling alleys, etc. Even professional sports began occurring on Sunday! Furthermore, TV was invented at about the same time the Blue Laws were being repealed, and

the TV producers eventually decided to place entertaining movies and sports programs on during church time, which also decreases church attendance.

In other words, America slowly developed a culture where "Sunday-fun" became "required," and "Sunday-church" became "unnecessary." Now, church wasn't supposed to be "fun" or "entertaining" in the usual sense of the word. But originally, it didn't matter that church was not "fun" because there weren't a whole lot of "fun" things which were competing with church attendance on Sunday mornings to keep people away!

In summary, there are so many other things which can now be legally done on Sunday which were forbidden in the Bible, that there is no longer any national expectation that American citizens should go to church at all on Sunday!

By the way, all these things had a much greater effect in keeping men away from church than women, because men are much more likely to avoid going to church if they have chores to do, money to earn, entertainment to pay for, or professional sporting events to watch. Because repealing the Blue Laws caused so many men to stop going to church, women have now become the spiritual head of the home instead of men! This also violates God's commandments and causes even further deterioration of our society.

So, in order to compensate for the lack of attendance in the "Post Blue Law Era," I believe that many pastors either deliberately or subconsciously changed the emphasis of their preaching. This was followed by an inevitable slow change in doctrinal emphasis by entire denominations.

Here's how I believe it happened. In the "Post Blue Law Era", instead of preaching sermons which condemn sins and make people "feel bad" about themselves, I believe that it was discovered that making people "feel good" about themselves was helpful to increase attendance. As a result, many churches probably stopped preaching about the realities of hell and even "the wages of sin." After this however, it was probably only a short step to stop preaching that man is a sinner or that he needs a Savior! And so some ministers probably stopped preaching the gospel message altogether and preached a "social gospel" instead. Furthermore, both church discipline for immorality as well as civil discipline for immorality began to vanish from our nation. This probably occurred because attendance dropped in our churches after repealing the Blue Laws, so it became harder to attract new members while the churches continued to practice church discipline by "casting out" perpetually unrepentant immoral people who attended church! So to attract new members, churches had to eventually discard the doctrine of church discipline (Matt. 18:15-17; 1 Tim. 5:19-20; 1 Cor. 5:11-13, etc.).

As church discipline for immoral behavior began to disappear from the Christian scene, civil discipline for immoral behavior begin to disappear from the secular scene as well. In other words, after our Christian leaders stopped judging immorality in the Church, our real judges stopped judging immorality in the courts. For when you no longer see the benefits of church leaders enforcing God's principles of morality in the church, then you will also become blinded to the benefits of government leaders enforcing God's principles of morality in society. As a result, all across our nation, certain sins against God were no longer considered punishable crimes against the state, so the original laws against fornication, adultery, homosexuality, and drunkenness were all ignored or revoked (since the Blue Laws were repealed, and were replaced by the mistaken non-biblical belief that "You can't legislate morality"). In retrospect, it has become clear that in large part it was the repealing of the Blue Laws which paved the way for the further development of this type of liberal theology and liberal politics!

Liberal theology has been around as long has theology itself has been around, and there has always been a struggle to resist its appeal. However, when church attendance dramatically dropped liberal theology finally had a practical value—it provided the justification for discarding any doctrine which might prove to lower church attendance as well as lower tithes and offerings. And so, thousands of liberal churches have now flourished in the "Post Blue Law Era" by discarding important biblical doctrines which might discourage church attendance.

VII. HOW REPEALING THE BLUE LAWS HAS ALSO CREATED A NATIONWIDE SECULAR WORLD VIEW AND A SOCIETY WHICH EXALTS PLURALISM

Repealing the Blue Laws was the government's official sanction that U.S. citizens were no longer expected to go to church on Sunday to learn about salvation or to learn about God's principles of civil law. This also represented our government's official declaration that America's laws no longer needed to be based upon the Bible, and that American citizens would no longer benefit from having a culture based upon Christian morality and biblical principles. Unfortunately, decades later an unexpected consequence of repealing the Blue Laws also emerged. You see, we didn't realize that it only takes two generations to go from a Christian culture to a secular culture. As a result, America's "second-generation-unchurched" no longer have a biblical world view. This is because in the absence of a biblical framework to organize their thinking, they inevitably developed a secular world view by default and embraced man's ways of doing things over God's ways.

In other words, after the Blue Laws were repealed, the population of "unchurched citizens" grew into the tens of millions; and so, for the first time in our nation's history, the majority of our citizens began to develop a secular world view—that all of life, including our government, should be reckoned without biblical influence. Without a biblical foundation to guide our non-Christian citizens, nationwide pluralism developed, and with pluralism came the doctrine of tolerance—that all opinions about life were equally valid and legitimate. In fact, the main reason we have a secular society today is because we repealed the Blue Laws a generation ago! With each passing decade, the state became more secular and society became more sinful, eventually spawning an attitude of tolerance of sin, and intolerance of biblical principles! As a result, even our politicians have developed a legislative bias that:

> Religion and Christianity should be restricted to the Church, and its influence on the state should be minimized or eliminated!

And slowly, when our state governments decided we would no longer live in a culture where all our laws would be based upon the Bible, all the other biblical principles of civil law began to fall into disrepute.

Even the New Testament concepts of women wearing dresses, head coverings, and keeping silent in church fell into disfavor because of the mistaken belief that these principles are no longer valid and applied only to Christians during the time of the Apostle Paul. As "women's lib" occurred inside the churches by women removing their hats, cutting their hair, wearing pants, and teaching, preaching, and having authority over men, we began to notice woman's lib occurring outside the church as well. Woman's lib occurred both outside the church and inside the church probably within a generation after the Blue Laws began to be ignored or repealed by our government!

In summary, repealing the Blue Laws just to allow people to work on Sunday, has ultimately culminated in a totally secular state and in a government which is hostile to biblical principles and openly embraces anti-biblical, liberal political ideas. And, this is just one more problem that God was trying to prevent by the Fourth Commandment!

VIII. HOW REPEALING THE BLUE LAWS HAS MINIMIZED THE POLITICAL RELEVANCE OF CHRISTIANITY AND HAS DIRECTLY LED TO THE DESTRUCTION OF OUR CHRISTIAN CULTURE

The Fourth Commandment was designed by God to encourage nationwide church attendance in order to teach us about the gospel of Jesus Christ, and to give the majority of our citizens a biblical world view concerning morality, politics, science, and religion. God wanted to engineer our culture in this fashion so that it would have the capacity to create and maintain a Christian Republic—which would eventually develop into a true "nation under God." In addition however, it would also have the capacity to prevent the development of a secular society with its pluralism and hostility to biblical principles. In other words, by enforcing the Fourth Commandment and by teaching the entire Bible in America's churches, God's civil, moral and spiritual principles would keep Christianity perpetually relevant for solving all society's civil, moral, and spiritual problems through Bible-based legislation as well as through a personal relationship with Christ as Savior. For example, by adopting the biblical principles in this book, Christianity would remain perpetually relevant to solve all the problems concerning America's system of government, justice, punishment, welfare, health care, economics, education, military policy, and foreign policy. And because of this, America's newborn Christian Republic would slowly evolve into a true "nation under God."

This is what American society was supposed to be like after generations of living under the Blue Laws, and after teaching the entire Bible (including the principles in this book) to our American ancestors generation after generation. Unfortunately, our churches did not teach the entire Bible completely (and therefore did not teach the lessons of this book). As a result, the modern Church totally disregards God's civil laws and censures those who attempt to suggest that the principles underlying God's civil laws might still have practical advantages to help to solve the civil, social, and moral problems of America today. In fact, today's conservative Church vigorously declares,

We are not supposed to live under God's civil laws,

and also says,

America's real problems can not be solved by *legislation*, but only by *salvation*.

And so, by saying that the principles underlying God's civil laws are essentially worthless for the administration of government, the Church has unwittingly chosen to make Christianity irrelevant to the problems of national economics, justice, healthcare, welfare, foreign policy, and military policy, and has rendered Christianity almost impotent to do anything other than lead sinners to Christ. For instance, Christianity has become progressively irrelevant to our problems of crime, inflation, and taxes—largely because churches do not teach the biblical principles of civil law which could help America to lower its rates of crime, inflation, and taxes. Furthermore, Christianity has become progressively irrelevant to our problems of disease, war, and poverty, again largely because churches do not teach the biblical principles of civil law whereby God can bless us with national health, peace, and prosperity.

Since the churches concentrate only on the message of salvation and have discarded the notion that the biblical principles of civil law can be useful and relevant to improve society, then it is no wonder that non-Christians frequently perceive Christianity to be irrelevant for solving any of the problems in America which are not directly spiritual in nature. For when Christianity and salvation by grace distance itself from God's principles of civil law, Christianity loses its power to create and maintain a "nation under God," even though it retains the ability to lead sinners to Christ.

Today, the large "unchurched" majority has become so secular and pluralistic that they do not want America to ever become a true "nation under God" anyway. You see, nowadays most Americans say:

> America can not obey God's laws today because our culture has changed and has become pluralistic!

But God responds by saying:

> Yes, American culture has changed and has become pluralistic, precisely because you haven't obeyed my laws!

You see, these changes would never have occurred if America would have continued to obey God's laws as we were commanded. For God's laws were supposed to encourage conformity and national unity concerning religion, morality, politics, and creation, and were supposed to prevent pluralism on these same issues from ever emerging.

In other words, God designed the Fourth Commandment to interact with God's other civil laws to help prevent cultures from becoming pluralistic. By keeping the vast majority of citizens in church weekly so they will be provided with a standard frame of reference for their thinking, they can develop a biblical world view. God's laws also help society preserve what was "good" about the "good old days" while helping to prevent society from disintegrating into a culture of wickedness. For God intended his Fourth Commandment to influence the Church, culture, government, and to help both Christians and non-Christians to be able to conform to God's commands.

IX. HOW REPEALING THE BLUE LAWS HAS CAUSED AMERICA TO BE WORSE OFF ECONOMICALLY

The Bible teaches that America would be better off financially if we did not work on the Sabbath, because it is actually God himself who controls our national income, expenses, and profit, based in large part upon our national obedience to him (in addition to our hard work). For instance, the Bible teaches that God makes our national expenses increase when our nation doesn't obey him. For it is written:

> You earn wages, but only to put them in a purse with holes in it.... What you brought home, I blew away. (Hag. 1:6b, 9b NIV)

Secondly, God also makes our national resources vanish when we don't obey him. For it is written:

> When anyone came to a heap of twenty measures, there were only ten. When anyone went to a wine vat to draw fifty measures, there were only twenty. (Hag. 2:16 NIV)

Thirdly, God makes our national income decrease when we disobey him. For it is written:

> "You have planted much, but have harvested little... You expected much, but see, it turned out to be little... I struck all the work of your hands with blight, mildew and hail, yet you did not return to me," declares the Lord. (Hag. 1:6a, 9a; 2:17 NIV)

These verses declare that when Israel disobeyed God, He:

—increased their national expenses,
—decreased their national resources, and,
—decreased their national income!

Therefore, if America disobeys God (and one of the ways America can disobey God is by legalizing work on the Sabbath), then God may punish America in this same fashion. The paradox is that if a nation tries to better itself economically by disobeying God and by making it legal to work on the Sabbath, then God will punish that nation economically, and see to it that this national sin has just the opposite effect.

So, if we want a nearly poverty-free nation so our citizens can have the maximum income with the least expenses, America should obey God in all ways. Therefore, if America would obey God and not work on the Sabbath (in addition to obeying God's other commands) then our citizens would probably have more money to spend because God would stop punishing our nation economically. Furthermore, if God blessed America economically for our obedience, then our nation's families would be less likely to require two incomes to support them, and so our wives wouldn't have to work outside the home any longer. Therefore, our wives could spend more time at home, raising our children in the "nurture and admonition of the Lord."

X. WHY THE FOURTH COMMANDMENT IS THE MOST IMPORTANT COMMANDMENT FOR NATIONS AND WHY GOD CHOSE EXECUTION TO BE THE STANDARD PUNISHMENT FOR SABBATH-BREAKERS

According to Mark 12:29-31, the greatest Commandment (for *individuals* is:

> Thou shalt love the Lord thy God with all thine heart, and with all thy soul, and with all thy might. (Deut. 6:5 KJV)

Unfortunately, most people choose to disobey this "Greatest of all Commandments" by never yielding their heart in submission and surrender to Christ. In fact, the Bible teaches (Matt. 7:14) that those who enter through the small gate of salvation and surrender will never amount to more than a small minority of the total population. Because of this, creating a "nation under God" involves much more than just keeping the small Christian minority on their best behavior by salvation and surrender, but also involves keeping the large, unrighteous majority on their best behavior too, by combining training and tradition in church with prosecution and punishment in court.

The Greatest Commandment for *nations* therefore, has to be the Fourth Commandment, because only the implementation of this principle can initiate such wide spread cultural changes in a nation. God's Blue Law, the Fourth Commandment, has a greater effect on all areas of society than any other biblical principle of civil law. Therefore, this one biblical principle of civil law is indispensable for nations and foundational to the implementation of all God's other principles of civil law. For the Fourth Commandment is the one law which causes the entire population to obey God every seventh day, thus creating a standard for national obedience to all of God's other principles as well.

Now, according to Leviticus 26 and Deuteronomy 28 (as explained in chapters three and four) God's earnest desire is ultimately to get America's aggregate righteousness to exceed a certain threshold so He can bless America with a nearly crime-free, poverty-free, war-free, inflation-free, natural disaster-free, tax-free and disease-free society where nearly everyone lives to be 120 years old while enjoying excellent health the entire time. Therefore, it should be clear that any sin which interferes with God's sublime objective to bless nations in this way must be dealt with swiftly and decisively. For you see, unrestrained Sabbath-breaking destroys a nation's chances to receive God's blessings of an utopian society free from disease, poverty, war, crime, taxes, and natural disasters.

It is little wonder then, that God chose execution to be the standard penalty for Sabbath-breakers. Unrestrained disobedience to the Fourth Commandment rapidly destroys a nation's capability of keeping its large, unrighteous majority on their best behavior, so they will inevitably become ineligible to receive God's supernatural blessing of nationwide "abundant life" in a healthy, peaceful, prosperous, and moral society of God's design.

So, God felt that the national consequences of allowing individuals to work on the Sabbath were so serious and extended over so many generations, that God wanted the death penalty to be the standard punishment. As a result, a sinner who did break the Fourth Commandment by working on the Sabbath could still repent and ask the judge to show mercy. At this point he might be totally forgiven or he might instead receive a few lashes with a whip as a merciful alternative to execution (Deut. 21:1-3 NIV).

For God's philosophy is that execution should be the standard from which you show mercy, based upon repentance, forgiveness, and circumstances. It was only those who despised God's law, refused to repent, and continued to break the law by working on the Sabbath who were ultimately executed.

The biblical punishment for breaking the Sabbath does not say, "Show him no pity" as it does for idolatry, deliberate murder, and for deliberately bearing false witness in court. For it is written:

> Observe the Sabbath ... Anyone who desecrates it must be put to death, Whoever does any work on that day must be cut off from his people ... Whoever does any work on the Sabbath day must be put to death. (Exod. 31:14-15 NIV)

In other words, when it comes to executing Sabbath-breakers, God deliberately left out the expression, "Show him no pity" from the law. For God not only expected judges to show mercy if possible, but he would later command them to love mercy (Micah 6:8).

By the way, God also said that you shouldn't have your animals work for you or have anyone else work for you on the Sabbath. For it is written:

> Remember the Sabbath day by keeping it holy. Six days you shall labor and do all your work, but the seventh day is a Sabbath to the Lord your God. On it you shall not do any work, neither you, nor your son or daughter, nor your manservant or maidservant, nor your animals, nor the alien within your gates. (Exod. 20:8-10 NIV)

Since the Fourth Commandment also forbids animals to work alone on the Sabbath (i.e., to turn the stones in a grinding mill), then most likely both the "semi-automated" as well as "fully-automated" businesses of today would not be allowed to operate on the Sabbath either.

XI. How the Modern Church Has Unintentionally Helped to Destroy America's Christian Traditions

Traditional Sunday-worship has so undermined our faith in the literal interpretation of the Fourth Commandment and has so biased the Church against God's other biblical principles of civil law that the Church has long ago lost their knowledge and curiosity about the practical advantages that God's principles of civil law might have for the administration of Christian government. In fact, the Church today actively discourages Christians from seriously investigating God's laws by saying,

Don't get bogged down in the Law, for this leads to "legalism" and a "works theology."

We certainly don't want anyone to be "legalistic" about God's principles of Salvation by grace through faith. However, this does not mean that the Church should go so far as to ignore the practical advantages that God's principles of civil law have for the administration of Christian government.

Modern pastors never seem to want to teach that part of the Bible which contains God's principles of civil law. For instance, although most pastors can easily make a preachable list of practical reasons why "husbands should love their wives as Christ loved the Church" (Eph. 5:25), these same talented pastors never have the inclination to make a preachable list of the practical applications of God's civil laws against fornication (Exod. 22:16). Such a list could include how God's laws against fornication can dramatically:

1. decrease the number of unwed mothers—which would also save Americans billions of dollars in taxes on welfare, food stamps, and Medicaid;
2. decrease the number of sexually transmitted diseases—which would also save America billions of dollars in taxes on health care; and,
3. decrease the number of children raised in homes without a father, and who are statistically more likely to get into trouble in school and with the law—which would save us billions of dollars in taxes on education costs (for extra security guards, metal detectors, and dogs to sniff out drugs), as well as save us taxes on our justice system (for the costs of extra police, prosecution, prison, and parole).

In other words, church leaders never teach us any of the practical advantages of God's laws against fornication, and never teach us the practical advantages of any of God's other principles of civil law. Without the perceived need to have God's principles of civil law in our legislation, Christians inevitably develop a secular view of government, which means they believe that government can be run without godly laws and without godly leaders to enforce these laws.

This inevitable secular view of government on the part of Christians is very unfortunate, because having godly laws enforced by godly leaders is necessary to empower the traditions of Christianity with the legal muscle to help keep the large, unsaved majority of Americans on their best behavior. This type of social engineering is supposed to be accomplished by combining prosecution and punishment (enforced in the courtroom) with training and tradition (learned in the church). In other words, America's courts and America's churches must be in agreement so that the lessons learned in court will be the same as the lessons learned in church (see also chapters eight and nine).

For instance, marital fidelity is one of these Christian traditions. Before the Blue Laws were repealed, this Christian tradition was also the law of the land, because (according to Deut. 22:22) adultery is also supposed to be a punishable crime against the state. Generations ago, when our ancestors legislated that marital fidelity should be the law of the land, this Christian tradition was suddenly empowered with the legal muscle to control the behavior of non-Christians, and keep them from committing adultery as well. In this way, the traditions of America's Christians became the traditions for America's non-Christians too. And since America's courts and America's churches were in agreement, then America's non-Christians were able to learn about morality in the churches and were able to see immorality punished in the courts. Unfortunately, by repealing the Blue Laws (and by repealing the civil laws against adultery as well), the Christian tradition of marital fidelity has now become a tradition only for Christians again, just like it is in the rest of the world.

Premarital virginity is a second Christian tradition. When some of our Christian ancestors legislated that premarital virginity should also be the law of the land, and that fornication should also become a crime against the state (i.e., the shot gun wedding), then suddenly the Christian tradition of premarital virginity was also empowered with the legal muscle to control the behavior of non-Christians. This also helped to insure their premarital virginity. And so again, the traditions of Christians became the traditions of non-Christians, at least in part because the courtroom was again punishing the sins that the church was preaching against. Unfortunately, churches no longer teach the practical advantages of making fornication into a crime against the state, or that according to Exodus 22:16-17, God's punishment for fornication is to get married. And, without the restraining influence of God's principles of civil law, fornication has skyrocketed, which causes the innocent citizen to pay billions of dollars in extra taxes on welfare, health care, education, and justice. This again is why God gave civil laws which were designed to make certain Christian traditions become the "law of the land."

A third Christian tradition is that Christians should not get divorced. The Bible teaches in Deuteronomy (24:1-4) that divorce was supposed to be illegal unless one spouse committed a sin which was also a crime against the state, as adultery once was. And, when our Christian ancestors made this principle into the law of the land, then our Christian traditions were again empowered with the legal muscle to keep the non-Christians from getting divorces as well. And as a result, divorce was practically unheard of many generations ago, because the traditions of Christians had become the traditions for non-Christians. For again, what was taught in churches was enforced by the courts.

A fourth Christian tradition is that there was no "right of privacy" when it came to sexual immorality. In other words, sexual sins done in the privacy of your own home were still punishable by the state. Once again, our Christian ancestors turned this biblical principle into the law of the land. Therefore, our Christian traditions were once again empowered to control the behavior of non-Christians as well (see also chapter seven). Unfortunately, by never teaching churchgoers the advantages of these biblical principles of civil law, after the Blue Laws were repealed, the unrighteous majority left the church and developed a secular view of government by default. Then, they somehow decided for us that our Fourth Amendment "right of privacy" should protect their sexual immorality from prosecution.

A fifth Christian tradition is that drunkenness is a sin, but which should also be a punishable crime against the state (Deut. 21:18-21). When our Christian ancestors turned this biblical principle into a law against becoming drunk and disorderly, our Christian traditions were again empowered to control the behavior of non-Christians, to help prevent them from committing the sin of becoming drunk. But today, this appears to be a tradition for Christians only, for not only is drunkenness no longer a crime, but churches no longer teach the biblical principle that drunkenness is supposed to be a punishable crime against the state.

There are many more Christian traditions which our nation *should* have developed as well, but unfortunately, we never did.

In other words, before the Blue Laws were repealed, the large majority of our citizens went to church and were indoctrinated with these biblical principles of moral law. By having our courts put into practice the biblical *civil* laws which corresponded to God's *moral* laws, the traditions of non-Christians became the same as the traditions of Christians, because the courts practiced what the church preached. As a result, these Christian traditions functioned extremely well to keep the behavior of the masses under control in America.

As Christianity and "salvation by grace" slowly distanced itself from God's principles of civil law, Christianity rejected its God-given empowerment to control the behavior of the nation's non-Christians so we could all live together in a healthy, prosperous, and moral society. It is by this process of rejecting the value of God's civil laws that the modern Church has unintentionally assisted in destroying the Christian traditions that helped keep the large majority of non-Christian Americans on their best behavior.

Summary

The Fourth Commandment should not be viewed as acting alone, but should be understood by examining its interaction with God's civil laws against sexual immorality, drunkenness, blasphemy, and non-biblical divorce.

You see, the object of the Fourth Commandment was that, through legislation which would maximize voluntary church attendance, the entire nation would not only learn about the gospel of Jesus Christ, but would also learn about the practical advantages of God's principles of civil law. And so, they would eventually develop a biblical world view and a biblical view of politics. This nationwide biblical view of politics would exalt the value that God's principles of civil law had for administering government. Since it takes godly leaders to adopt and enforce godly laws, then the voting majority of Americans would naturally be encouraged to select only godly leaders to rule over us. These godly leaders would also adopt and enforce God's laws against sexual immorality, drunkenness, divorce, and blasphemy. After witnessing the practical benefits that God's civil laws have for administering good government, these same godly leaders would be prompted to consider adopting even more biblical principles of civil law into our national legislation in the future.

By combining training and tradition with prosecution and punishment, the Church and the court would join forces to keep the large, unrighteous majority of citizens on their best behavior. Together, they would create a nationwide culture of Christian traditions and godly peer-pressure. The final glorious "Mosaic picture" represents at least part of what a true "nation under God" should look like according to Christ Jesus (the pre-incarnate Jehovah who gave these principles of civil law to Moses 3400 years ago). This culture would have all the "social armor" in place to keep Christianity relevant to all aspects of society forever, as well as to prevent the development of pluralism, with its inevitable tolerance to sin and intolerance and hostility to biblical principles.

God did not design the Fourth Commandment just to mold and shape the worship schedule of Christians within non-Christian cultures, but to mold entire nations of non-Christians and shape their entire cultures into healthy, prosperous, and moral societies so God could bless them.

If America can adopt these biblical principles of social engineering, then we will have started on the road towards raising the aggregate righteous of our nation over the threshold required by God so he will bless us with a nearly disease-free, crime-free, poverty-free, war-free, inflation-free, natural disaster-free, and tax-free society as a reward for our obedience (according to God's promises in Lev. 26 and Deut. 28).

Since God's purpose for the Fourth Commandment is so sublime, it becomes clear why God feels that anything which interferes with His grand objective should be dealt with swiftly and decisively. It is little wonder then, that God required the death penalty (from which the judges were commanded to show mercy) as a standard punishment for Sabbath-breakers. For you see, unrestrained disobedience to this commandment has such destructive consequences upon the future of our nation that our chances of developing this utopian Christian "nation under God" become essentially zero.

In conclusion, America needs to bring back the Blue Laws, and at some future time we need to phase in the entire Fourth Commandment and enforce it fully. For the Fourth Commandment was originally designed by God as the single, most fundamental legal principle to help create and preserve a "nation under God," and which would also help to prevent the disintegration of our Christian culture into a:

1. secular society, with a secular world view, and a secular view of politics, which would eventually evolve into a . . .
2. pluralistic society with its . . .
   —liberal politics,
   —liberal theology,
   —tolerance of sin, and,
   —intolerance and hostility to biblical principles!

And that is God's view of reintroducing the Blue Laws to outlaw work on Sunday, increase church attendance, and reintroduce Christian doctrine and Christian morality to America!

In the next chapter, you will see how these same biblical principles also form the foundation for God's view of pro-family legislation.

Chapter Eighteen

GOD'S VIEW OF PRO-FAMILY LEGISLATION

Many Christians are concerned about the breakdown of the family and what can be done to reverse this national trend. Since 1962, there has been an increased incidence of violence in the home, drunkenness, wife abuse, child abuse, child molesting, rape, murder, disrespect for parental authority, cursing parents, attacking parents, sexual infidelity, separation, and divorce (see also chapter two).

The reaction of the Church to this deterioration of the American family has been to say that there needs to be more love, prayer, and salvation in the home in order to stop these thirteen problems. Of course, it's a wonderful idea to have more love and prayer in the home, but it's hard enough to get this to occur in the homes of Christians, much less in the homes of non-Christians. Also, since the Bible teaches that the large majority of families in each nation will be composed of non-Christians (Matt. 7:13-14), then how can these thirteen problems be remedied in the families of non-Christians, when the influence of Christ in these homes is minimal to none?

Well, the Holy Scriptures teach that Bible-based *legislation* can solve all thirteen of these problems which occur in the families of non-Christians. You see, there are certain biblical principles of civil law which can empower traditional Christian morality with the legal muscle to keep the large, unrighteous majority of citizens on their best behavior even when they are members of non-Christian families. For instance, there are biblical principles of civil law which can practically guarantee premarital virginity and marital fidelity, as well as practically insure that there will be no drunkenness, wife abuse, child abuse, child molesting, rape, murder, disrespect for parental authority, cursing parents, attacking parents, separation, or divorce.

Furthermore, God's version of pro-family legislation takes advantage of a large body of biblical principles of civil law which foster the inevitable development of large, extended families as training grounds for submission to God—each with hierarchies of spiritual and moral authority, and with triple economies of scale from shared expenses, shared labor, and shared possessions. These large families were designed to be economically stable and relatively self-sufficient so that they could easily provide for their own occasionally sick, poor, retired, or disabled family members without the need for tax-sponsored government health care, welfare, retirement, or disability programs to support them.

Because of the triple economy of scale provided by large, extended families, the need for heavy tax burdens to fund government agencies to supply these benefits is drastically reduced. As taxes are reduced overall, then taxes on businesses are reduced as well, which means that businesses have more profits and can create more jobs and reduce the unemployment rate. This also reduces poverty and reduces taxes for welfare support even further, while creating a more prosperous society at the same time. Furthermore, since the Bible teaches that these large families don't have to pay property taxes, inheritance taxes, or huge interest payments on home mortgages (for God's laws outlaw charging any interest on loans), then the wealth and security of the large, extended family increases with each generation. Surely this is pro-family legislation at its best! And hopefully, by the time you finish reading this chapter, you will be convinced that God's perfect principles of pro-family legislation can effect a wonderful change in the entire culture, and demonstrate a dramatic superiority over man's narrow view of pro-family legislation.

God designed the following five categories of biblical principles to interact in such a way as to create a culture where all these benefits should occur naturally.

1. GOD'S BLUE LAWS AND GOD'S CIVIL LAWS AGAINST IMMORALITY, ETC.

As you learned from chapter seventeen, God's purpose for the Fourth Commandment was to maximize voluntary church attendance so the large, non-Christian majority would attend church along with the small Christian minority. This way, the majority could learn about the gospel of Christ as well as learn about God's principles of moral and civil law. Additionally, God's civil laws against immorality, etc., were designed to get the court and the Church to join forces so the large, non-Christian majority would be kept on their best behavior by combining the influences of training and tradition (learned in church) with prosecution and punishment (learned in court).

It is these same biblical principles which we discussed in chapter seventeen which also form the foundation for God's view of pro-family legislation.

2. SYMBOLS WHICH STRENGTHEN SURRENDER

The second and third categories of biblical principles interact together to transform the family into a training ground for submission to God. This second category includes the laws which reveal the best "symbols which strengthen surrender" to generate a godly influence on the behavior of both Christians and non-Christians at home, at work, in private, and in public. These laws also pressure men to become spiritual heads of their home, and provide citizens with a double protection against the sins of sexual immorality and drunkenness. Furthermore, these laws also encourage men to freely volunteer to serve as godly Christian leaders and judges in a system of government which is designed to require no taxes to fund its operation, so we can all live in a tax-free society.

3. LAWS PROMOTING FAMILY DISCIPLINE

This third category includes laws which encourage respect for elders and encourage the formation of a hierarchy of spiritual authority in the family. This category also reveals the biblical principles which promote the use of physical discipline for children, and those principles which create civil punishments for those parents who abuse the right to discipline their children.

4. LAWS WHICH KEEP THE NUCLEAR FAMILY TOGETHER

This fourth category includes laws which practically guarantee premarital virginity and marital fidelity, as well as laws which prevent divorce. Also, there are laws to prevent drunkenness, drug abuse, child molesting, rape, and other forms of family violence.

5. LAWS WHICH PROMOTE THE DEVELOPMENT OF LARGE, EXTENDED FAMILIES

This fifth category reveals the biblical principles which function to maintain a harmonious hierarchy of authority in large, extended families which contain three or more generations. It also reveals the biblical principles which outlaw property taxes and inheritance taxes in order to preserve the wealth of the family. Since the Bible also outlaws usury, then the money saved on home mortgage interest payments can create a larger inheritance for the children. This category also reveals how God's guidelines for dividing the children's inheritance help to preserve the family homestead and promote large, extended families. Finally, these same laws of inheritance also "prepay" the eldest sons to be able to freely volunteer to serve as judges in a tax-free system of justice and government.

So, as a result of the interaction between these five categories of biblical principles, the thirteen problems mentioned above virtually disappear; and in their place, large, extended families emerge as training grounds for submission to God, with triple economies of scale, enabling them to support their own poor, elderly, disabled, or unemployed. This allows for smaller government and less taxes on citizens and business, the latter of which allows business to hire more employees, which decreases national unemployment and increases national prosperity.

This is surely pro-family legislation at its best.

Most Christians would like to see traditional Christian families for everybody, but generally we are unwilling to adopt God's principles of civil law into our legislation as a means to obtain these benefits. Man's principles of pro-family legislation are totally impotent when it comes to accomplishing the goals mentioned above, while God's principles can give a 100 percent guarantee that these goals will be achieved for society at large and practically guarantee the same for the individual family as well.

With this as an introduction, let us investigate God's view of pro-family legislation!

SYMBOLS WHICH STRENGTHEN SURRENDER

Since the fall of man, God wanted the family to be a training ground for submission to God. You see, after Eve sinned, God told her:

> Your desire shall be for your husband, and he will rule over you. (Gen. 3:16b NIV)

Please notice the difference between Eve's punishment and Adam's punishment. For God punished Eve by commanding her to submit to her husband, while God punished Adam by saddling him with the responsibility to guide his wife's behavior like a good shepherd. You see, in God's eyes, Eve's sin was different than Adam's, and He wanted the punishment to fit the crime. For Eve's sin was that she did not want to submit to God's Will, so God designed her punishment so that she would practice submitting to her husband as if she was submitting to God, which is why Scripture says,

> Wives, submit to your husbands as to the Lord. (Eph. 5:22 NIV)

The Bible further says,

> Children, obey your parents in the Lord, for this is right. (Eph. 6:1 NIV)

This means, "Children, obey your parents as if you were obeying the Lord himself." In this way God laid the foundation for making the family a training ground for submission to God.

While Eve's sin involved a lack of submission to God's Will, Adam's sin involved a lack of responsibility for Eve's behavior. For notice that Adam said,

> The woman whom THOU gavest to be with me, she gave me of the tree, and I did eat. (Gen. 3:12 KJV; emphasis added)

Adam was essentially saying,

> You gave me this woman God, so you are responsible for her behavior. You are responsible to make sure that she won't sin and that she won't tempt me to sin either.

As a result, God basically replied,

> You think you're NOT responsible for her behavior, Adam? Well, you are NOW! From now on, you will be responsible to guide Eve as a good shepherd and to do all the things you failed to do to keep Eve from sinning in the first place!

In this way, God made the punishment fit the crime by saddling Adam with the responsibility for the physical and spiritual well-being of Eve, and that's why God wanted Adam to rule over Eve!

What did Adam fail to do in the Garden of Eden? Adam failed to:

1. *identify the sin* (for he didn't say, "Eve, You have sinned.")
2. *instruct in righteous obedience* (for he didn't say, "I told you not to eat from that tree or even go anywhere near that tree.")
3. *provide a godly example* (for Adam ate the forbidden fruit also.)

As a result of Adam's lack of feeling any responsibility for Eve's behavior, God punished Adam by giving him and all future men, the instinct to "rule over" their wives and "feel responsible" for their behavior.

After first getting ourselves "right with God," we men were supposed to . . .

1. *identify sin;*
2. *instruct in righteous obedience;* and,
3. *provide a godly example* for our wives and children to follow, and be the spiritual head of the family, which is the very thing that Adam failed to do.

In other words, God wanted each family to be led by a righteous man who would hand down God's commands to his family. In turn, wives and children were supposed to practice submitting to this righteous man as if they were submitting to God himself. Out of this mutually beneficial relationship, the family was to become a training ground for submission to God.

Unfortunately, men have forgotten why we have this instinct, for generally we have not been taught that the reason we were given this instinct by God is so we can do what Adam failed to do in the garden of Eden. Our spiritual headship is therefore essentially restricted to these three areas only, for God did NOT originally give men this instinct to boss our wives around in ANY other areas. We were only placed in charge of their physical and spiritual well-being, and not placed in charge of any other area of their lives.

In summary, since the Garden of Eden, men have been commissioned to first get themselves "right" with God, and then to identify sin, instruct in righteous obedience, and provide a godly example for their wives and families to follow, and so assume the role of spiritual head of the home. At the same time, wives were instructed to practice submitting to their husbands as if they were actually submitting to God himself (Eph. 5:22 NIV). Children also have been instructed to obey their parents as if they were obeying God himself (Eph. 6:1 NIV).

This is a perfect match: a godly husband who lovingly hands down God's commands to his wife while she in turn practices submission to her husband as if she were submitting to God himself. These lessons were so important that God gave women pain in childbearing as a sign that it is now time to reteach these same lessons to each new child, and to each new generation.

Because Adam was given the subtle instinct to rule over Eve, all Adam's male descendants have inherited this same subtle instinct to rule over their wives as well. Even though men have inherited this instinct to rule, we don't seem to want to become righteous rulers for our family, or even to choose righteous rulers for our community. However, in order for society to build future nations under God, Jehovah knew that men needed to be "pressured" into taking responsibility for righteous leadership of their families, of their governments, and of their future churches. Since Adam denied responsibility for Eve's actions (and chose not to be the righteous spiritual leader of the world's first family), men have been reluctant to take seriously this role of righteous leadership.

God knew that if the family did not remain as a training ground for submission to God, that this would ultimately lead to the destruction of the family, the government, and the society, despite the influence of the future church. So, to keep the family functioning as a training ground for submission to God, one of the things Jehovah did was to give mankind a biblical dress code to help remind men that everything they think, say, and do should be guided by God's Will. Then, to multiply the usefulness of the biblical dress code, Jehovah gave mankind an instinct which prompts us to "act the part if we dress the part". This God-given instinct can be nurtured and developed by our culture to empower the Mosaic dress code with the symbolic authority to influence both the wearer and the observer to remain on their best behavior.

Let me illustrate this idea by pointing out the influence of some non-biblical dress codes. For example, many people who see a man wearing the "backwards collar" of a priest respond by stopping all their bad language and dirty jokes. Also, many people who see the uniform of a police officer respond by slowing their car to the normal speed limit. In the army, seeing someone wearing the uniform of a higher rank causes you to stop what you are doing, stand up at attention, and salute. So it is very clear that certain dress codes can influence people to behave better.

Of course, since it was God who originally gave us this instinct to respond to symbols and dress codes, you would think that God himself would give us the most powerful and influential symbolic dress codes to keep both the wearer and the observer on their best behavior. For if man can come up with some good symbolic dress codes, then surely almighty God should be able to come up with the best symbolic dress codes, and create a scriptural standard for the church and for the country at the same time.

In fact, God's chosen symbolic dress codes not only help to regulate the behavior of Christians, but they empower Christian morality and doctrine to control (in part) the behavior of non-Christians as well. This is accomplished by helping to focus peer pressure on the issue of whether or not we (and they) are obeying God's commands. This helps to create nationwide *godly* peer pressure while reversing the natural tendency for nationwide *ungodly* peer pressure to grow and develop, which has unfortunately happened in the U.S. as well as in all the other countries.

The dress code God chose for men included wearing headbands and wristbands! For it is written:

> These commandments that I give you today are to be upon your hearts. Talk about them when you sit at home and when you walk along the road, when you lie down and when you get up. Tie them as symbols on your hands and bind them on your foreheads. Write them on the door frames of your houses and your gates. (Deut. 6:6-8 NIV)

The symbols on foreheads and hands actually represent headbands and wristbands, which God is commanding all men to wear. These were supposed to have Bible verses written on them to remind the wearer to both love and obey God. More specifically, the purpose of the headband is to remind the wearer that:

everything I *think* (in my head) and *say* (with my mouth) should be guided by God's Will!

And the purpose of the wristbands is to remind the wearer that:

everything I *do* (with my hands) should also be guided by God's Will!

Imagine the effect on society if all men were required by law to wear symbols on their heads and wrists to remind them that everything they *think, say,* and *do* should be guided by God's Will! These ancient headbands and wristbands were supposed to encourage the wearer to ask himself, "What would Jehovah Do?" This is very much like the new Christian fashion of wearing a wristband with the letters (WWJD) on it as a symbol of the question, "What would Jesus Do?"

God did not stop there. He also said that the Israelite nation must have a law requiring men to always wear clothing which had tassels sewn into its "corners." For it is written:

Throughout the generations to come you are to make tassels on the corners of your garments, with a blue cord on each tassel. You will have these tassels to look at and so you will remember all the commands of the Lord, that you may obey them and not prostitute yourselves by going after the lusts of your own hearts and eyes. Then you will remember to obey all my commands. (Num. 15:38b-40a NIV)

Despite the fact that we are saved by grace and not by works of the flesh, I know that my personal behavior as a Christian would improve further if everyday I wore headbands, wristbands, and tassels which constantly reminded me that everything I think, say, and do should be guided by God's Will. Moreover, these dress codes would have an even greater effect upon me through peer pressure if I saw that all the other men around me were dressed the same way. For when my faith was weak and I might have a tendency to disobey God, I would probably still obey Him because of the godly peer pressure all around me.

Additionally, these nationwide dress codes would also encourage men to give "biblical rebukes" to each other when they witness disobedience to God's commands. For it is written:

Rebuke your neighbor frankly so you will not share in his guilt. (Lev. 19:17b NIV; also, Ezek. 3:20; Matt. 18:15; and 1 Tim. 5:1, 20 NIV)

Imagine the godly peer pressure that would develop in our nation if we had a law requiring all of America's men to wear headbands, wristbands and tassels. The pressure on the men to assume their God-given Christian roles of spiritual head of the family would increase dramatically.

Again, God did not stop there. He wanted to make sure that both our clothing and our hair styles would always point out the difference between men and women in order to further emphasize the difference between the roles of spiritual headship of the husband and the submission of the wife. For it is written:

> A woman must not wear men's clothing, nor a man wear women's clothing, for the Lord your God detests anyone who does this. (Deut. 22:5 NIV)

Now in America, pants and dresses have traditionally represented the differences between the types of clothing worn by men and women. But since the Church has blinded itself to the practical advantages and spiritual applications of God's principles of dress codes and hair length, Christians have mistakenly concluded that after Christ rose from the dead, He must have changed his mind about the value of these principles. For the modern Church largely ignores these commands of God, just as it ignores many of the other commands of God which are listed in this book.

As a result of our prejudice against God's principles of civil law, the Church has unwittingly deprived our nation of the practical benefits of behavior which God intended these principles to provide for the nation. So, just as we need to re-establish obedience to God's commands in other areas, we also need to go back to a dress code of pants for men only, and dresses, hats, and earrings, etc. for women only, for these were the dress codes worn by Americans when God's hand of displeasure was not so heavy upon our nation.

This next verse makes it clear that God wants women to wear hats (head coverings) as well as have long hair, and for men to wear short hair and no hats. For it is written:

> If a woman does not cover her head, she should have her hair cut off; and if it is a disgrace for a woman to have her hair cut or shaved off, she should cover her head. A man ought not to cover his head ... the woman ought to have a sign of authority on her head ... Does not the very nature of things teach you that if a man has long hair, it is a disgrace to him, but that if a woman has long hair, it is her glory? For long hair is given to her as a covering. If anyone wants to be contentious about this, we have no other practice nor do the churches of God. (1 Cor. 11:6-7a, 10b, 14-16 NIV)

So, the divine dress code (for clothing and coverings) is complete. Women are to wear long hair and head coverings and men are to wear headbands, wristbands, and tassels, and have short hair and no head covering. Again, this is to put pressure on them to assume their role as spiritual head of the home, the government, and the church.

By the way, the man's headbands and the woman's head coverings may also be symbolic of the future crowns we will wear in heaven. For the man's future crown may very well be an "open" crown (which does *not* cover the top of the head) while the woman's crown may very well be a "closed" crown (which *does* cover the top of the head).

In addition, wearing the appropriate hair style, head covering, and clothing also helps to teach the lesson that "God is Lord of my body," as an extra precaution against the sexual sins of fornication, adultery, and homosexuality, plus the sins of drunkenness, drug abuse, and getting tattoos. For once again, when we dress the part we also act the part. This divine dress code helps generate the peer pressure required to empower Christian doctrine and morality to control the behavior of the non-Christians, and keep them from committing these same sins by creating a constant reminder that God is Lord of their entire body too.

Modern Christianity also tries to teach sexual purity using the doctrine that "God owns your body" but without using any symbols whatsoever to help us, as if we will somehow magically act the part even without dressing the part. Most Christians today repudiate the value of all the God-given symbols (clothing, hair length, hair covering, headbands, wristbands, and tassels) which God designed to help remind us that since God owns our body, we should avoid sinning against our bodies. You may think,

> But Christians have the Holy Spirit within them to guide their behavior without the need of dress codes!

This is true! But first of all, the non-Christians do not have the Holy Spirit within them to help control their behavior. So, they would still benefit from the influence of biblical dress codes which encourage godly peer pressure, biblical rebuke, and remind them that God is not only supposed to be Lord of their bodies, but that everything they think, say, and do should be guided by God's Will.

Secondly, many people who profess to be born-again Christians often fail to heed to guidance of the Holy Spirit within them. And still, they have committed these sins, which they might not have done if they (and the others around them) were wearing this divine dress code which generates godly peer pressure, biblical rebuke, reminds us that God is Lord of our bodies, and that everything we think, say, and do should be guided by God's Will.

Since this dress code is guaranteed to improve everyone's behavior (both non-Christians and Christians), it makes sense that God commanded this dress code to be worn by everyone, to remind us all to ask the question, "What would Jehovah do?" But, since modern Christian doctrine no longer takes advantage of these symbols which strengthen surrender to assist us in remembering that God is Lord of our bodies, it is no wonder that so many people who claim to be Christians end up sinning sexually. For Christian tradition says that it is okay to use symbols such as the dove, fish, cross, Bible, or praying hands to remind us to obey God, so long as they are not the Old Testament symbols of headbands, wristbands, tassels, hair length, or head covering, or else other Christians will mistakenly conclude that you have "embraced the Old Testament law" and are "trying to be saved by works."

These symbolic dress codes were designed by God mainly to put pressure on men to always act as righteous leaders whenever they were at home, work, play, church, or shopping. The symbolic dress code for the woman was designed by God, not only to assist the woman in maintaining an attitude of practicing submission to a husband, but also to champion the husband's role to be a righteous spiritual leader in the family and in the local community, by participating in the National Hierarchy of Judicial Authority as discussed in chapter five (principles number eighteen and nineteen).

Finally, God commands men to assume all the positions of teaching and authority in the church, and indirectly commands men to teach the Bible to their wives and family at home. For it is written:

> As in all the congregations of the saints, women should remain silent in the churches. They are not allowed to speak, but must be in submission, as the Law says. If they want to inquire about something, they should ask their own husbands at home, for it is disgraceful for a woman to speak in the church. (1 Cor. 14:33b-35 NIV)

Because of man's natural reluctance to be spiritual head of the home, the church, and the government, God has to curb the enthusiasm of women for assuming these same roles in order to provide additional practice opportunities for all the men to cultivate and nurture their spiritual headship.

To be more specific, the Bible teaches that the woman must not allow her husband to get out of his responsibilities of teaching his family about God's love and God's commands at home. So, instead of having her natural curiosity about Christ, the Bible, and other spiritual things to be satisfied by asking questions at church, she is commanded to "keep silent at church" and focus all her questions onto her husband at home, to lovingly "pressure" him to teach the Bible to her and the children.

Otherwise, if he cannot answer her questions by his own Bible study, he may have to ask these same questions on behalf of his wife at church. In this way, he again gets an opportunity to practice developing his spiritual headship both at home and at church. Before you know it, it will become much easier for him to talk about spiritual things at home, at church, at school, at work, at stores, at play, and wherever else he goes.

This is exactly what God wants of man, but all of God's ordained influences must be in place in order to get the average rebellious non-Christian man to be "pressured" into doing this. Therefore, society needs men to wear headbands, wristbands, tassels, pants, and short hair, while women should wear dresses, hats, and have long hair.

God's restrictions on clothing and covering are necessary in order to create a biblical culture where *all* men (both non-Christian and Christian) will more naturally take on the role of spiritual headship in their own families. Furthermore, these same biblical principles were designed by God to prompt men to more naturally consider freely volunteering as judges in the tax-free National Hierarchy of Judicial Authority (chapter five), where they will decide who is innocent, who is guilty, who gets executed, who gets whipped, and who is totally forgiven.

(Remember, the biblical system of government was designed by God to be totally tax-free. To maintain this tax-free status, it required thousands of godly Christian elders as unpaid volunteers to be involved administering justice to the entire nation at a local level. But these volunteers more naturally develop within a culture which practices the biblical principles of civil law which require its men to wear headbands, wristbands, tassels, "pants," and short hair, while requiring its women to wear "dresses," hats, and have long hair.)

So you see, God's principles of clothing and covering were designed to interact with God's principles of salvation and surrender, training and tradition, and prosecution and punishment in order to:

1. create a nationwide culture of godly peer pressure;
2. prompt the large, unrighteous majority of citizens to stay on their best behavior;
3. urge all men to accept the role of spiritual authority in their homes;
4. inspire all men to want to participate in the National Hierarchy of Judicial Authority (as discussed in chapter five);
5. provide a double protection against the sins of sexual immorality, drunkenness, drug abuse, and getting tattoos (where the individual sins against his own body); and,
6. encourage the family to remain a training ground for submission to God.

Hopefully, you can now see how the synergistic interplay of God's principles of civil law is capable of creating a Mosaic picture of what biblical pro-family legislation can accomplish for America (and could have accomplished for ancient Israel, if the Israelites would have implemented all these principles as God commanded).

So, this divinely chosen symbolic dress code accomplishes not only the same basic purpose as a lapel pin of a cross, a dove, an open Bible, or a fish, but also has the capability of doing the other six things mentioned above.

Now in the Bible, we learn that the Pharisees used headbands, wristbands, and tassels, not as symbols to *strengthen* surrender, but as symbols to *substitute* for surrender. As a result of the Pharisee's misuse of these symbols, these symbols fell into disrepute among Christians. Consequently, the scriptural symbols which strengthen surrender have been slandered by saints for centuries, as being displeasing to God and a sign that the wearer believes in salvation by works of the law, and not by grace.

Simply because the Pharisees misused God's symbols does not mean we should discard them. We merely discard the Pharisees' bad example and try not to misuse these symbols ourselves. For it is possible to believe in salvation by grace through faith in Christ and still take advantage of God's "symbols which strengthen surrender," because of the ability of these symbols to generate a national culture of godly peer pressure so both Christians and non-Christians will behave better, and so we can all live together in a better world.

Lastly, God said that all of the door frames in our houses and on our gates should have Bible verses on them concerning God's commands (Deut. 6:8 NIV). Now in the average home, this would probably be about seven or eight door frames which God required to have verses engraved upon them. This is to keep reminding family members, as they pass from room to room, about God's love and his commands, as well as their individual relationship with God, and his provision for atonement of sin by grace through faith in Christ's death on the cross, and to encourage all families to maintain a "household of faith" so the family could always be a training ground for submission to God. Of course, by extension, all government buildings and other public buildings, as well as all buildings housing private businesses could also benefit by having God's commands engraved on all their door frames.

Therefore, this architectural "law of the land" for Israel should be the "law of the land" for America as well.

Laws Promoting Family Discipline

The biblical principles revealed in this section were designed by God to supplement the laws concerning dress odes, hair length, and head coverings to extend the family hierarchy of spiritual authority beyond the parents to the grandparents.

To this foundation, God added laws to encourage parents to physically discipline their children, and added other laws concerning criminal punishment for children who curse or attack their parents out of rebellion against this discipline. Then, God added another law to punish parents if they seriously injured their children while disciplining them by using unnecessary violence.

The result is a culture which encourages the development of families which are training grounds for submission to God, where God's authority and parental authority are both revered, and where government laws encourage and support the use of physical discipline at home to assist God's plan to build a nation where Christian morality has been empowered to control behavior of the non-Christians masses.

With this in mind, let us consider the paradox that God's requirement for parents to teach God's principles of submission and obedience to their children often creates rebellion and disobedience within the children.

There are two extreme potential outcomes for this paradox. One is that the society fosters a culture which mocks parental authority, and which magnifies this natural tendency for rebellion and division until it causes a national breakdown of the family. In other words, the side of rebellion wins, creating a culture just like the culture we have in America today. Alternatively, society could evolve a culture which exalts parental authority, and which magnifies the importance of submission to this authority as a sign of "growing up," which in turn causes a national devotion to the family. In other words, the side of authority wins, creating a culture similar to the culture that ancient Israel was supposed to have developed but never did.

God, of course, wanted the side of authority to "win," so a culture could develop where children would submit to parental authority as if they were submitting to God, while parental authority, in turn, would teach their children about God's principles of Love and Salvation by Grace, as well as about God's principles of moral and civil law. By doing this, our biblical traditions would bring us one step closer to becoming a true "nation under God."

That is why thousands of years ago, God, in his wisdom, gave us laws to encourage both children and adults to always regard their parents and grandparents with high esteem, honor, and respect, so that this would exalt the virtues of submission to parental authority (and by implication, submission to God's authority as well) For it is written:

> Honor thy father and mother. (Exod. 20:12 KJV)

and,

> Rise in the presence of the aged, and show respect for the elderly. (Lev. 19:32 NIV)

These laws were designed by God get the government, Church, family, and school to teach the same lesson: we must become a people who give honor to our fathers and mothers, as well as give honor to the elders in our family and community.

To accomplish this goal, we must also develop a culture which exalts the virtue of submissive obedience to elder authority, and praises adolescents and young adults when they consistently demonstrate the ability to give honor, respect, and homage to their elders. In other words, our culture must learn to:

—*honor* those who give honor to their elders, and

—*exalt* those who demonstrate submissive obedience to their parents and elders.

In this way, a culture can more easily maintain its family hierarchy of spiritual authority as well as more naturally develop large, extended families with extremely strong bonds of loyalty and devotion, and where its members depend upon each other emotionally and financially. As a result, the younger, middle, and older generations would all enjoy living together, and benefit from the resulting triple economy of scale which is inherent in the large extended family.

You may think God would not want us to punish someone who violates God's guidelines for hair length, head coverings, and dress codes, and not want us to punish someone who doesn't treat his parents with honor and respect, or rise in the presence of his elders. But if a culture does not enforce any punishments for this type of disobedience whatsoever, and begins to allow disrespect of parents, elders, and others of spiritual authority, then the Christian traditions of that nation will ultimately be destroyed and their chance to become a true "nation under God" will disappear along with the chance to inherit God's supernatural blessings of a society free from disease, crime, poverty, war, taxes, inflation, and natural disasters.

The Fifth Commandment—"Honor thy father and mother" (Exod. 20:12 KJV)—implies that dishonoring and mocking one's father and mother should become a crime against the state. But in America, we have allowed our First Amendment "Freedom of Speech" to overrule God's Fifth Commandment in order to legalize the mocking of parental authority.

When you allow society to perpetually slander its role models of godly leadership (and slander the importance of having godly laws), then the enthusiasm to become a godly Christian role model of spiritual authority ultimately dies. When this happens, the role of the family as a training ground for submission to God to teach each generation the importance of having godly leadership and godly laws, will eventually be destroyed.

Finally, out of the resulting ignorance of society's need to have godly leadership and godly laws, certain sins against God (such as fornication, adultery, homosexuality, and drunkenness) will no longer be prosecuted as crimes against the state, and society will rapidly become just as wicked as it is today.

It is impossible to develop a culture which openly mocks parental authority if the youth of that culture also "rise in the presence of the aged" (Lev. 19:32 NIV). For you see, God intended this practice to help prevent the deterioration of society to the point where it mocked parental authority and destroyed the family as a training ground for submission to God.

Some elders dislike it when young people immediately stand up when they come into a room. So, out of humility they may say, "Please, don't get up just for me." Encouraging the younger generation to violate God's command to "rise in the presence of the aged" (Lev. 19:32 NIV) undermines and subverts God's intended plan to transform the family into a training ground for submission to God with a hierarchy of spiritual authority.

For example, suppose nobody in the army wore uniforms, and suppose all the officers told their enlisted men to address them by first names only, and never stand to salute them. This would eventually undermine their authority to command effectively as leaders. And as a result of ignoring the importance of dress codes and due honor, the service provided by the armed forces for national defense would slowly be rendered less effective. Likewise, the service God intended for the family to provide a national training ground for submission to God, is also rendered less effective because of our lack of attention to the importance of dress codes and due honor, to bolster and to maintain a family hierarchy of spiritual authority to train Christian soldiers and commanders to help transform our secular democracy into a Christian Republic. To this end, God also gave us four laws of child discipline. It is from these four laws that America got its tradition (no longer in much use) of disciplining children with a "hickory stick"! For it is written:

> Folly is bound up in the heart of a child, but the rod of discipline will drive it far from him. (Prov. 22:15 NIV)

> Do not withhold discipline from a child; if you punish him with the rod, he will not die. Punish him with the rod and save his soul from death. Prov. 23:13-14 NIV)

> The rod of correction imparts wisdom, but a child left to himself disgraces his mother. (Prov. 29:15 NIV)

The fourth verse however, reveals that parents need to be "full of care" and love to attempt to discipline correctly, according to God's guidelines. For it is written:

He who spares the rod hates his son, but he who loves him is careful to discipline him. (Prov. 13:24 NIV)

It is clear from this verse that God wants us to discipline children with a loving heart, but that we may actually use a "stick" if necessary.

To further encourage the family to remain a training ground for submission to God, God gave the government two additional civil laws designed to support the parent's right to discipline their children. By doing this, God linked the four laws of family discipline (as noted above) with two additional laws of civil discipline in order to prevent children from either cursing or attacking their parents as a form of rebelling against the authority of their parents and rebelling against the authority of God himself. For it is written:

> Anyone who curses his father or mother must be put to death. (Matt. 15:4; Mark 7:10; Exod. 21:17; Lev. 20:9 NIV)

> Anyone who attacks his father or mother must be put to death. (Exod. 21:15 NIV)

These laws were designed by our loving heavenly Father to perpetuate parental authority, respect, and honor, by adding the power of civil law to family discipline, thus ensuring that the extreme rebellion of cursing or attacking your parents would also be a crime against the state. In other words, Jehovah commanded the government to *support* the parent's right to physically discipline their children, unlike in America today, where our government tries to *thwart* the parent's right to discipline their children instead.

Furthermore, by quoting from these laws in Matthew 15:4 and Mark 7:10, Jesus is publicly supporting the practical applications of these Mosaic civil laws. More specifically, Jesus reveals the natural link between God's moral laws and God's civil laws by implying that if the proper implementation of God's civil laws ("Anyone who curses his father or mother must be put to death") had empowered God's moral laws ("Honor your father and mother") as they should have—to bolster the moral laws and make them more effective—that the Pharisees probably would not be dishonoring their parents through the tradition of "Corban" (Matt. 15:4 NIV). You see, in this verse Christ appears angry that the sin of dishonoring your parents is no longer a crime in Israel, having been overruled by the traditions of men, because God's moral laws were not being supported by God's civil laws. So also, Christ is angry at America because the sin of dishonoring parental authority is not a crime in our nation either. This is because God's principles of civil law are being ignored in our country as well, again having been replaced by the "courtroom traditions" of men, which legalize the mocking of parental authority and destroying the family as a training ground for submission to God.

For God's laws which say "Honor your father and mother" and "Children, obey your parents," were supposed to be empowered by God's four laws of parental discipline with the rod. In turn, these were supposed to be empowered by God's laws of civil discipline, like a potential death penalty, for either "attacking" or "cursing" your parents (Exod. 21:15, 17 NIV) in response to parental discipline with the rod.

Remember, the object of these laws was not to execute every child or adolescent who merely cursed or attacked his parents, but to prosecute them in a civil court so they would learn the seriousness of their crime and never do this again. In this way, the merciful judge would obviously let the child or adolescent go free after the child demonstrated his fearful repentance, and so his parents would have regained the authority they needed to once again discipline their child effectively. However, adult offspring who curse or attack their parents may fare less well, and may be whipped anywhere from one to forty lashes, as a merciful alternative to execution (see chapter eight for further details).

Although the Bible teaches us that our civil laws should support parental authority to physically discipline a child at home (with our hand, or even a "rod" if necessary), any serious child abuse from excessive physical punishment by the parents would result in the parents being punished by the court in the same way—an "eye for an eye, a fracture for a fracture" (Lev. 24:19-20 NIV).

I hope you can see how the laws of dress codes, hair length, and head coverings interact with the laws of due honor, rising in the presence of the elderly, family discipline, and civil discipline, to create a hierarchy of spiritual authority and form the basis for family members being more devoted to each other. For it is in this way that God designed the large extended family to not only be a training ground for submission to God, but also provide a triple economy of scale of shared labor, shared possessions, and shared expenses, so the family could more easily provide support for its own members. Therefore, family members would not have to depend upon the government to provide a tax-sponsored source of welfare income, disability income, or retirement income, and would not have to depend upon the government to provide a source of tax-sponsored health care benefits in the form of Medicare or Medicaid.

LAWS THAT KEEP THE NUCLEAR FAMILY TOGETHER

PREMARITAL VIRGINITY

To start the family off right, it is best that both bride and groom remain virgins until the wedding night, for the following five reasons:

1. to eliminate any chance of spreading sexually-transmitted diseases to the unsuspecting spouse,

2. to prevent any emotional scars from previous sexual relationships from being brought into the new marriage and to prevent comparisons and jealousies over previous lovers,
3. to know that premarital virginity predicts a greater commitment to marital fidelity,
4. to be able to teach your children to imitate your example by remaining virgins until their wedding night, and
5. to start a tradition that your family is a training ground for submission and obedience to God.

There are four biblical principles of civil law which interact in such a way as to practically guarantee that both bride and groom will still be virgins until after the wedding.

1. The punishment for a virgin boy who seduces a virgin girl is that "they are to get married" (unless the girl's father absolutely forbids the marriage). For it is written:

> If a man seduces a virgin who is not pledged to be married and sleeps with her, he must pay the bride-price, and she shall be his wife. If her father absolutely refuses to give her to him, he must still pay the bride-price for virgins. (Exod. 22:16-17 NIV)

This law reveals God's understanding of the passions of youth, but implies a stern warning that:

> With sexual intercourse comes the responsibilities of marriage and raising a family! This command is to be the law of the land!

This law also demonstrates to the community that it is the father's responsibility to ensure that his family lives in obedience to God's principles of civil law (this is a practical application of spiritual authority).

Furthermore, since this biblical law outlaws fornication, then this would save us billions of dollars in taxes on health care for sexually transmitted diseases. And, since all pregnant girls would have to get married under this law (unless their father objects), it would also eliminate the problem of unwed mothers and save us billions of dollars in taxes on welfare as well.

2. The punishment for rape of a virgin girl by a virgin boy is also that "they are to get married"—presumably also unless the girl's father absolutely forbids the marriage (Deut. 22:28-29 NIV). This law allows the girl's father to try to discern whether his daughter has a genuine affection for the boy, but was "date raped" (in which case they are "to get married"), or whether his daughter was actually stalked, attacked, and violently raped.

3. If the father forbids the marriage because his daughter claims she was stalked, attacked, and violently raped, then the father may present the case in court. As a result, the rapist may be whipped from one to forty lashes if he is convicted (Deut. 25:1-3 NIV).

4. The standard punishment of a new bride who turns out not to be a virgin because she did not bleed from intercourse on her wedding night is death from which we are encouraged to show mercy (Deut. 22:13-21 NIV). This is God's law against promiscuity.

Now, God's intended purpose for these four laws was to generate godly peer pressure among young adults so they would encourage each other to remain virgins until marriage. For instance, after learning about these laws, the boys would now say to each other,

> You better not have sex before marriage, because if you get caught, you have to marry the girl. And if she accuses you of rape, you might be brought to trial by her father and whipped. But even if you're not caught, you still have to marry the girl, for if she marries someone else and doesn't bleed on her wedding night, she could be executed for promiscuity. So if you really love the girl, you better not have sex with her before marriage.

Likewise, after knowing these laws, the girls would now say to each other:

> You better not have sex before marriage because if you get caught or get pregnant you have to either marry the boy or accuse him of rape which might get him whipped. But even if you don't get caught, you still have to marry him, because if he breaks up with you later on, and you marry someone else and you don't bleed a little after having sex on your wedding night, then you might be placed on trial and face a possible death penalty for promiscuity. So you better not have sex before marriage.

So, as a result of the interaction of these four laws, premarital virginity is practically assured for the entire nation and unwed mothers would be rare as well! (Obviously, the use of tampons or the use of any form of legalized premarital birth control undermines the effectiveness and interaction of these principles.)

DIVORCE IS ILLEGAL

The second principle which keeps the family together is the biblical principle which outlaws divorce (Deut. 24:1-4 NIV). Most Christians mistakenly believe that this law made divorce very easy to obtain for any reason at all. This command actually makes divorce *illegal* unless a "righteous" spouse found some "uncleanness" (NIV) or "indecency" (KJV) in the other spouse. This most likely represented a biblical "felony" which had execution as the standard punishment, from which the judges were commanded to show mercy. In other words, if a "righteous" spouse discovered that his or her spouse had committed adultery, homosexuality, or drunkenness, etc., (sins which were associated with death penalties), God held him or her responsible for bringing the case to trial (Lev. 5:1 NIV), because each spouse was responsible before God for keeping the family pure from sin, so the righteous spouse and the children would not be corrupted by repeated exposure to the sins of the unrighteous spouse.

In this way, if convicted, the guilty spouse would face the standard punishment of execution. However, by the grace of Jehovah (the preincarnate Christ) God not only commanded the judges to love to show mercy (Mic. 6:8 NIV), but also provided them with three merciful alternatives to execution: whipping, total forgiveness, and divorce. If the spouse was totally forgiven in court, he or she would never commit adultery, homosexuality, or drunkenness again for fear that if they were convicted a second time in court they might either be whipped or executed.

But God wanted Moses to allow divorce as an additional merciful alternative to execution. This was because people had such "hardness of heart" against God and against their spouses that they often refused to forgive their spouse after the trial and live together again. As a result, it would be God (and not man) who would "put asunder" the marriage through a divorce (as a merciful alternative to executing the convicted spouse). And, since God wanted divorce to be a punishment which was a merciful alternative to execution for the spouse who was convicted of a sin which carried a potential death penalty, then the convicted spouse would definitely not be allowed to keep the children as part of the divorce settlement. This was because the object of the divorce was to protect the children from being exposed to the influence of the sinful lifestyle of the convicted spouse. Furthermore, the convicted spouse was probably not allowed to take any of the estate with him (or her) but was most likely forced to go back to live again with his or her own parents or brothers. Additionally, if someone divorced you, the community would immediately recognize that you had committed some sin unto death for which you received a divorce as a merciful alternative to either an execution or an extended whipping. So, the chances of you marrying again would be much less because any future spouse would have to chance whether you would commit the same sin again which got you divorced in the first place, thereby exposing his or her future children to that same sinful lifestyle.

There are three reasons why we know that the "uncleanness" (NIV) and the "indecency" (KJV) mentioned in Deuteronomy 22:1 represents serious sinfulness.

The first reason is that the divorced woman is not allowed to remarry the first man who originally divorced her under any circumstances (Deut. 24:2-4 NIV). This was because this would mean that the man divorced her on a whim, and not because of an attempt to purge serious sinfulness from the family. Therefore, it is clear that God hates frivolous divorce (Mal. 2:16 NIV) and that divorce was supposed to be a punishment for serious sins and another merciful alternative to execution.

The second reason is that a convicted rapist who is punished by having to marry the girl he raped can never divorce her as long as he lives (Deut. 22:28-29 NIV). This is because the rapist has already been convicted of the sin of rape, and therefore has lost the right to ever bring his wife to trial (for any future sin she may commit) in hopes to divorce her.

Thirdly, a man who was convicted of bearing false witness against his new bride by saying she did not bleed on her wedding night also can never divorce her as long as he lives (Deut. 22:19 NIV). This is because he is no longer righteous enough to present a case for divorce.

In other words, the principle is that anyone convicted of a biblical crime against his spouse (i.e., rape or bearing false witness about his new bride's virginity) loses the right to even divorce his wife for any reason whatsoever in the future. Therefore, it becomes more clear that divorce was supposed to be illegal unless a righteous spouse discovered that his or her spouse had committed a serious act of unrighteousness which was also a crime against the state. Instead of always executing the unrighteous spouse, God allowed divorce to be used as a third merciful alternative to execution.

So, it is clear that although God hates divorce, he gave these laws to Moses so the righteous would have an additional merciful alternative method of purging the evil from their marriage, if the sinful marital partner refused to repent in the courtroom. Far from making divorce easy and common, this law was designed to make divorce very rare, because you had to first bring your spouse to trial for a serious sin, in which case, your own righteousness might be cross-examined during the trial as well.

Violent Wife Abuse and Child Abuse

Since violence in the home can cause physical and emotional harm to the spouse and children, God decided that this problem should be punished in the courtroom using the biblical principle of an "eye for an eye." For it is written:

If anyone injures his neighbor, whatever he has done must be done to him: fracture for fracture, eye for eye, tooth for tooth. As he has injured the other, so he is to be injured. (Lev. 24:19-20 NIV)

This system of "identical wounding" would stop all the violent physical wife abuse and child abuse in this nation. Furthermore, it would not only teach the husband or boyfriend a valuable lesson, but would also allow battered wives to no longer live in fear of further bruises, black eyes, broken bones, or live in fear for their lives. Once again, this is a valuable type of biblical pro-family legislation. (By the way, neither spanking nor "beating with a rod" is considered by God to be child abuse.)

SEXUAL HARASSMENT OF CHILDREN

Sexual harassment can also harm the family (and especially the children), so God dealt with this issue as well, and commanded that the maximum punishment for sexual harassment would be to cut off the offending hand! For it is written:

If two men are fighting and the wife of one of them comes to rescue her husband from his assailant, and she reaches out and seizes him by his private parts, you shall cut off her hand! Show her no pity! (Deut. 25:11-12 NIV)

As you can see, sexual harassment is not always an attempt to be seductive, but can be just a purposeful, offensive, inappropriate touching of someone (who is not your spouse) on their "private parts" without "invitation." God says that in the context of a "fight" when the person being harassed is restrained and helpless so he cannot even defend himself that the punishment for this offense is to cut off the hand.

In the case mentioned above, the man is helpless to defend himself. But women who are the objects of sexual harassment often feel helpless as well, because of fear or weakness. However, because the woman is still not being restrained by others in a "fight," the standard punishment of cutting off the hand no longer carries the requirement to "show no mercy." Therefore, for all other forms of physical sexual harassment, the judges are still required to "love mercy" (Mic. 6:8 NIV), and therefore cutting off the hand becomes the maximum punishment, but not the mandatory punishment, and the convicted sinner is still eligible to receive a merciful whipping of from one to forty lashes instead, or be totally forgiven and not punished at all.

I repeat, cutting off the hand is the maximum punishment, but not the mandatory punishment for all forms of sexual harassment, except when the sexual harassment occurs in a fight when the victim is physically restrained and so cannot defend herself or himself in which case cutting off the hand becomes the mandatory punishment according to almighty God.

Other than this exception, in the ordinary case of sexual harassment, the punishment could still be "total forgiveness" upon repentance, or a whipping (from as little as one lash up to a maximum forty lashes) as a merciful alternative to cutting off the hand. This law gets cutting off the hand on the law books as the standard punishment for sexual harassment—a punishment from which the judges could still show mercy. This was to instill fear in the hearts in those who would consider sexually harassing someone.

Now Jesus actually quotes from this law concerning sexual harassment when he says,

> You have heard that it was said, "Do not commit adultery." But I tell you that anyone who looks at a woman lustfully has already committed adultery with her in his heart . . . if your right hand causes you to sin, cut it off and throw it away. (Matt. 5:27-28,30 NIV)

Now remember, there is only one possible place where Jesus could be quoting from when he speaks of "cutting off the hand" and that is from the Old Testament law concerning sexual harassment, recorded in Deuteronomy (25:11-12), because this is the only place in the entire Old Testament which speaks of such a punishment.

You see, the Pharisees evidently must have been teaching the false doctrine that:

> as long as you don't commit adultery, you can lust as much as you want and put your hands on a woman's private parts and not be prosecuted for adultery.

Jesus reminded them that although they were not committing adultery, they would still be held responsible by God for their sexual harassment. Also, they should still be prosecuted by man for their sexual harassment, implying that:

> Just because no one caught you or is willing to prosecute you when you did your sexual harassment, doesn't mean that you have gotten away with it! For God knows what you have done, and that the standard punishment for your sin is still for you to have your hand cut off. You have still neither repented nor made yourself right with God, nor have you asked the woman to forgive you, and therefore, God will still hold you accountable if you continue in sin and don't make things right again with the woman and with God!

Therefore, even in the New Testament, Jesus says that the laws concerning sexual harassment are still in effect and that he approves of these laws wholeheartedly.

Furthermore, in the book of Mark, Jesus again quotes the Mosaic punishment for sexual harassment (Deut. 25:11-12); this time he applies this law to the sin of child molesting—the sexual harassment of children. For it is written:

> And if anyone causes one of these little ones who believe in me to sin, it would be better for him to be thrown into the sea with a large millstone tied around his neck. If your hand causes you to sin, cut if off. (Mark 9:42-43 NIV)

There are many ways to teach a child to sin. One of the most abominable ways is to molest the child sexually, for this may lead the child to a lifestyle of sexual perversion. So, in this verse Jesus applies the law of sexual harassment to child molesting and gives His divine New Testament approval that this same Mosaic law should be applied today to those who molest children (because of the emotional scars left with the children who suffer from this, and because the little boys who are victims of this become more likely to adopt a homosexual lifestyle in the future).

Therefore, it is clear that this principle is still valid today and is superior to the way the U.S. handles sexual harassment and child molesting. If the U.S. handled sexual harassment and child molesting with a maximum punishment of cutting off the hand, this problem would disappear in our nation for as long as this law was in force. Viewed in this way, this law also becomes a form of "pro-family legislation."

Alcohol and Drug Abuse

Since alcohol and drug abuse can destroy the family, the Bible teaches us that the maximum punishment for alcohol and drug abuse is death. For it is written:

> They shall say to the elders, "This son of ours is stubborn and rebellious. He will not obey us. He is a profligate and a drunkard." Then all the men of his town shall stone him to death. You must purge the evil from among you. All Israel will hear of it and be afraid. (Deut. 21:20-21 NIV)

Notice that in this passage, God deliberately left out the expression, "Show him no pity," unlike consequences for the sins of idolatry, murder, bearing false witness in court, etc. (see chapter eight). Therefore, the maximum (but not the mandatory) punishment for drunkenness is death. Of course, by implication, death would be the maximum punishment for drug abuse as well.

In actuality however, God wants death to be the standard punishment from which judges are required to show mercy if at all possible. So, after being convicted of drunkenness or drug abuse and facing a death sentence, the criminal would be given a chance to publicly repent and ask for mercy. In this way, he or she might receive a whipping, from one lash up to a maximum of forty lashes as a merciful alternative to execution, or he or she might be totally forgiven without punishment at all. This would solve all the problems of alcohol and drug abuse in the home as well as in the entire nation. This illustrates the compassion, wisdom, and love of Jehovah's principles of pro-family legislation!

LAWS THAT PROMOTE THE DEVELOPMENT OF LARGE EXTENDED FAMILIES

God wanted to design a culture which did not have to depend upon a large, tax-sponsored centralized government to provide its social and welfare services, but one where these services would come through other divinely designed biblical alternatives. Therefore, because of his infinite love and compassion for mankind, God designed some of his laws to have an economic impact on cultures to help them to develop large, extended families with triple economies of scale. This would be done in order to be able to provide for the security and financial needs of their own disabled, widowed, elderly, or poor, and so society wouldn't need to develop large, tax-sponsored governments with multiple agencies to do this job for them.

Whereas God's laws promote the development of large, extended families, America's laws do just the opposite and promote the development of single parent families and even encourage people to live by themselves. The "marriage penalty" tax problem is just one of the more infamous examples of this problem of the government financially sponsoring the breakup of families. But in reality, all of the tax-sponsored government programs of welfare support, disability income, and even social security retirement income financially sponsor the ability of individuals to live apart from their families without having to depend upon them for financial support. Therefore, all these government programs represent types of "anti-family" legislation.

With this in mind, let us look at the Mosaic laws which encourage the natural development of large, extended families, which in turn can provide most of the social and welfare services society needs, without costing Americans billions of dollars in taxes for additional government services.

BE FRUITFUL AND MULTIPLY

God gave Adam and Eve the divine command to "Be fruitful, and multiply" (Gen. 1:28 KJV).

About fifteen hundred years later, God gave this same command to Noah and his family. For it is written, "Be ye fruitful, and multiply" (Gen. 9:7 KJV). This was not just a command to populate the earth, but was also a command for us to enjoy the benefits inherent in large extended families. You see, God knew that life in the future would be hard for mankind, and that large families which depend upon each other emotionally and financially would have an easier time surviving.

Generations ago, American farmers thought this way as well and discovered the advantages of having larger families to help run the farm. But you don't have to live on a farm to still enjoy the triple economy of scale obtainable in large, extended families.

Honor Thy Father and Mother

Earlier in this chapter we discussed how God's Fifth Commandment ("Honor thy father and mother") helps to promote discipline in the family. In this section however, we will discuss how this same command helps to promote the development of large, extended families as well.

When a society develops a culture which exalts the importance of citizens perpetually honoring their fathers and mothers, this tradition nurtures within each generation of children the desire to continue to live with, and to provide for, their parents and grandparents in their old age. The elderly, in turn, enjoy this extreme respect and therefore they are more likely to want to continue to live with their children, even in their golden years. This illustrates God's idea that cultures which exalt the virtue of honoring their fathers and mothers can more easily develop large, extended families.

On the other hand, American culture mocks parental authority, a point which is well illustrated on modern TV sitcoms. This anti-biblical attitude of mocking parental authority encourages giving dishonor and disrespect to our elders, which in turn, promotes the breakdown of the American family. You see, mocking parental authority encourages an attitude of independence within the children and disrespect for parental authority so they will not want to care for their parents and grandparents in their old age. In addition, American elders often do not want to live with their offspring either, because of the many years of disrespect they have received from the lips of their children.

If America can develop a culture which

—honors those who give honor to their elders, and
—exalts those who demonstrate submissive obedience to their parents and elders,

then this obedience to God's command will not only promote better discipline in the family (to assist the family to become a training ground for submission to God), but will help America to develop a culture of large, extended families with triple economies of scale. It is this triple economy of scale which increases family prosperity so that it makes our government programs of welfare and social security become largely unnecessary.

By the way, the larger the extended family, the greater the necessity to adhere to God's commands in order to maintain a harmonious hierarchy of authority so the large family can live together peacefully. This is where God's symbols which strengthen surrender (i.e., dress codes, hair length, head coverings) really begin to have an impact by encouraging submission to the family hierarchy of spiritual authority. This is one of the reasons why modern American Christians (with our small nuclear families) have difficulty seeing the practical applications of God's civil laws concerning dress codes, etc.

TAXES

In the eighth chapter of First Samuel, God makes it abundantly clear that he detests large, centralized governments which create heavy tax burdens on their citizens and which confiscate their properties (see chapter five; principles 11-15 for details). So, it is no wonder that the Bible never mentions inheritance taxes or property taxes as part of God's perfect plan for civil government, because these types of taxes undermine God's view of government, and especially undermine the large extended family.

You see, inheritance taxes tend to divide up the estate upon the death of the parents because you often have to sell part of the estate to pay the taxes on the inheritance. As a result, all the efforts to build up an estate for future generations may be destroyed, at least in part, when the estate passes into the hands of the children. God knew that laws concerning inheritance taxes become an "anti-family legislation" and that laws against inheritance taxes actually become a type of "pro-family legislation."

Furthermore, God mentioned nothing about property taxes in the Bible. You see, having property taxes means that the government really owns your land and that they are just leasing the land to you as long as you pay the "rent," which is in the form of a property tax. Therefore, the land never permanently belongs to you or your family, because you can always lose it to the government if you owe "back taxes." But according to the Bible, God owns all land, not the government, and God allows us to live on His land because it pleases Him.

Another biblical principle which clearly demonstrates God's desire to encourage the development of large, extended families has to do with the "Year of Jubilee" which is celebrated every fifty years. You see, the land was not to be sold permanently, for in the "Year of Jubilee," all properties revert back to their original family owners, which descended from the first Israelites who received the gift of land from Joshua centuries earlier (Lev. 25:23-28 NIV). As a result, there would always be an economic incentive to stay on the original land which God gave to your ancestors, because anything you built up on anyone else's property could be lost after fifty years.

So God wanted the Israelite to develop a philosophy which sounded like this:

> I cannot build up my estate on another man's property if I am going to lose the entire thing in the "Year of Jubilee"! For I may be able to move my cattle and my flocks back home, but that beautiful house I might build would have to stay on the other man's property!

As a result, God provides an economic incentive to build up large, extended families on the same family estate which was inherited from your ancestors, and which would not be handed back to someone else's family during the "Year of Jubilee."

One of the reasons that God said that "the family's land should not be sold permanently, but must be returned to the original owners at the Year of Jubilee" (Lev. 25:23-28 NIV) was to provide an object lesson to illustrate the economic disadvantages to the family when children move away from home to "seek their fortune." This was to teach all nations the value of "keeping the land in the original family" and to give them an example of how to develop laws of economics designed to discourage children from moving away from home (so they would want to remain on their ancestor's original property instead, and continue to live in their own large, extended families).

This is one law which we can not adopt in the U.S. I include this law only to illustrate the biblical idea that God's laws promote the development of large, extended families as a hedge against poverty, unemployment, bankruptcy, and homelessness. The eternal principle underlying this law, however, can be adopted in the U.S. America should also design laws which should provide an economic incentive to encourage the development of large, extended families with their triple economies of scale.

INHERITANCE LAWS

Christians should be very concerned about inheritance laws, for it is written:

> A good man leaves an inheritance for his children's children. (Prov. 13:22a NIV)

Surprisingly, God commanded the Israelites to give their inheritance only to the sons—unless the parents only had daughters (Deut. 21:15-16; Num. 27:8-10 NIV). Ordinarily, the females were supposed to inherit through marriage.

Why would God choose a mode of inheritance which gives the property only to the men, when this does not result in either any overall increase or decrease in the total amount inherited by the next generation?

God did this because, when you divide the inheritance into fewer pieces, the family is much more likely to stay together as a large, extended family. This is because the inheritance is transferred as one, two, or three large pieces. Alternatively, when the total inheritance of property has to be divided into many pieces, it becomes much more likely that the entire inheritance must be sold and turned into cash to be split up equally. As a result, since there is no more homestead, the entire family splits up and each member goes his own way. You see, when a nation includes the females as recipients of the inheritance, it is far more likely to lead to the break up of the large, extended family. So dividing the inheritance into fewer pieces results in a divine economic incentive to keep families together as larger groups which can enjoy greater economies of scale. Therefore, God's method of dividing the inheritance of wealth and property becomes a another method of "pro-family legislation" whereas the method in America has become a form of "anti-family legislation!"

As if this wasn't enough, God in His wisdom decided to give a *double* portion of the inheritance to the firstborn male child (Deut. 21:17 NIV). This makes the family even more likely to stay together because the younger males and females may not have enough of an inheritance to move away immediately. They must wait a few years until the estate grows larger in order to be able to afford to move away. Meanwhile, they begin to realize that it is much easier to stay at home and continue to build up the estate than to move away and start over.

Giving a double portion of the inheritance to the firstborn male child also encourages a hierarchy of spiritual authority, thereby providing an additional form of pro-family legislation. You see, this same law allows the firstborn male child to be "prepaid" by the laws of inheritance to be able to care for his elderly parents as well as to care for the extremely young children who haven't been able to move out on their own yet. After his parents have passed away, the eldest son will now have more free time so he can volunteer to be involved in local politics (as a local judge, etc.) which is the primary mechanism God chose to establish a tax-free form of self-government. Therefore, this law of inheritance not only encourages the firstborn son to be spiritual authority of the entire extended family, but also prepays him to be able to freely volunteer to become a local judge over ten families, fifty families, or one hundred families, etc., as he enters the National Hierarchy of Judicial Authority (discussed in chapter five).

In modern America, we unfortunately encourage our teenagers to live elsewhere when they turn eighteen, or when they finally get a job or get married, thus breaking down the potential for a large, extended family to develop (with its triple economy of scale). We also encourage our teenagers to "get an education" so that they can have any kind of job they want and live anywhere they want, as if somehow that will make them happier and more prosperous than living at home and building up a large, extended family.

Now please don't hear me wrong. I'm not saying that "getting an education" or "moving away from home" is sinful, nor am I saying that "having a job which forces you to live away from home" is sinful. I'm merely saying that our culture teaches that the large, extended family has essentially *zero* value in our society, and that it has become much more important to have the kind of job you want and to live wherever you want, than to live at home out of family loyalty and build up the large, extended family with its triple economy of scale.

In other words, our culture exalts freedom to "be all you can be"— to get an education and move away from home and start all over again financially, and try to build a home from "scratch." Our culture exalts a lifestyle which encourages each generation to move into an economically disadvantageous position by having to start all over again to pay for a new house, rather than exalt the virtues of living at home and building up a large, extended family.

In summary, God gave the Israelites the law specifying that "a double portion of the inheritance goes to the eldest son" to encourage the development of large, extended families. Furthermore, one of the reasons God gave the Israelites the law concerning the "Year of Jubilee" was so they would be more motivated to concentrate upon building large, family estates, rather than building houses on another family's property which he would have to turn over to the other family each generation. Thus the Law of Jubilee was at least partially designed to give additional economic incentive to create and maintain large extended families as a cultural way of life. God probably chose to do it this way because economic incentives motivate people better than just giving them a command which says, "Thou shalt have large, extended families."

And of course, these large extended families help provide the triple economy of scale which allows us to provide for our own widows, poor, sick, disabled, and our elderly, and obviate the need for a large centralized tax-sponsored government to do this job for us.

The Bride Price

Another of God's pro-family legislations is the bride price, which is fifty silver coins paid by the fianceé to the family of the bride (Exod. 22:16-17; Deut. 22:19 NIV). The bride price also causes a mild financial hardship on the male fianceé so he has a harder time affording to move away from home. As a result, he may have to build a couple of extra rooms onto the family homestead for his bride until they can afford to move out on their own. But in the meantime, they will be able to enjoy the benefits of starting married life in a large family with a triple economy of scale, so the newlyweds won't be so poor.

Another way that the bride price helps to create large extended families is that the groom may have to borrow the money for the bride price from the family estate. Therefore, the rest of the family may insist that they continue to live together after the wedding so the bride's extra labor can help repay the bride price which the family lent to the groom. In this manner, the family's loan for the bride price can be viewed as an "investment" in the bride's future labor and productivity for the family. Viewed in this way, the bride price generates a culture of hard work to discourage laziness and welfare dependency.

The bride price also provides an economic incentive to "get along" with your in-laws, because of the social pressure to become a happy, healthy, and prosperous family. Furthermore, having to pay such an investment makes it even less likely that the bridegroom will consider divorcing his wife in the future.

Corban

God's view of pro-family legislation is also illustrated in the New Testament in the story about "Corban." One of the lessons of the story of "Corban" was that children should financially support their parents in their old age so that their parents would not have to be welfare dependent and supported by the state through the national tithe.

You see, in Matthew 15:3-6, Jesus was angry at the Pharisees and the teachers of the law for pretending to put aside money in a "savings account for God" (so to speak) while their own parents needed money to help with their physical needs—this tradition was called "Corban." Thus Jesus says that no money was ever supposed to be set aside in a "savings account" as a pretense to be "saving for God" when you first should be supporting your own family. First, provide for the needs of your large extended family (in this case, your parents) before opening up a "savings account" for yourself. And remember, according to God's laws, usury (earning interest in a savings account) is supposed to be illegal anyway.

In other words, if children don't support their parents in their old age, the parents may become "welfare-dependent" and the state must support them through the national tithe. Therefore, to avoid a "welfare-state," Jesus is saying that children must support their parents in their old age. This is another way of saying that God favors the large extended family. For it is written:

> If anyone does not provide for his relatives, and especially for his immediate family, he has denied the faith and is worse than an unbeliever. (1 Tim. 5:8 KJV)

Likewise, if American children don't support their parents in their old age, their parents will become dependent upon social security retirement income to support them, and this increases our tax burdens and unnecessarily increases the size of our government.

LAWS AGAINST USURY
(SEE ALSO CHAPTER TWENTY-ONE FOR FURTHER DETAILS.)

The word *usury* refers to the practice of lending money in order to receive a profit of interest. In the Bible, God outlawed the practice of loaning money to make a profit of interest, regardless of whether the Israelite receiving the loan was rich or poor. God only allowed non-Israelites (foreigners) to be charged interest on their loans, as it is written:

> Do not charge your brother interest, whether on money or food or anything else that may earn interest. You may charge a foreigner interest, but not your brother Israelite. (Deut. 23:19-20 NIV; see also Exod. 22:23; Lev. 25:36a, 37a; Neh. 5:7-11 NIV)

Our nation however, violates God's laws against usury by giving interest-bearing loans to the poor, to the rich, or to anyone else who wants them. In fact, our culture not only *borrows* money at interest (in the form of credit cards and home mortgages) but we also *save* money at interest (in the form of savings accounts and savings bonds). For savings accounts and savings bonds use this same principle of interest-profit to encourage you to lend your money to the bank. The bank can make an interest-profit which is large enough to share some of it with you so you can both make money.

Moreover, in the last few generations, creative businessmen have invented three different ways to return this interest-profit to the "lender":

1. as *cash* (such as in a savings account);
2. as *payment* for health care, funerals, or for automobile body repair (such as in health insurance, life insurance, or car insurance); and,

3. as a *monthly stipend* (such as a retirement income).

As a result, this same principle of interest-profit has now produced even more usury-related businesses such as the health insurance, life insurance, car insurance, and pension plan businesses, and has also led to legalized gambling. These forms of insurance have so inflated the costs of health care, funerals and automobile body repair, that insurance is no longer considered to be an advantage, but is now considered to be a necessity. Because of this problem, the federal and state governments have responded by creating their own form of usury-related health insurance (Medicare and Medicaid), as well as usury-related government pension plans (Social Security Retirement and Disability programs) and usury-related welfare programs, but are funding them through mandatory taxes, rather than by voluntary "loans."

All of these usury-related businesses have created some very serious problems for our culture, but two of these philosophies have directly contributed to the breakdown of the American family by providing a financial incentive to loosen the economic ties that bind the large extended family together. You see, ordinarily it is difficult to leave the family behind and move out on your own because it is so expensive to start life all over again. However, legalizing usury in the form of credit cards and loans affords the discontent young family member with the financial capability to buy or rent major appliances, furniture, cars, and homes, etc. This not only leads to the breakup of the large extended family, but also to the beginning of a lifetime of interest payments which may total $50-100,000 or more before retirement, and which deprive the next generation of their rightful inheritance. In this way, nationwide usury has empowered disgruntled young family members with the financial capability of moving away from their families and living on their own, rather than staying together in large extended families with triple economies of scale, where everything is already paid for.

Additionally, nationwide usury has empowered the elderly, disabled, and poor family members with the financial capability of moving away from the family and living on their own through social security, disability, and welfare benefits—three government programs which are also linked to the sin of usury as well as to the sin of having a large, centralized government (see chapter five, principles number 11-15). This again leads to the further breakdown of the American family.

Therefore, laws which allow usury are actually "anti-family laws," while laws which forbid usury are actually "pro-family laws." Furthermore, usury impoverishes the family in the long run and over several generations makes it much less likely for the family to afford to care for its own occasionally sick, disabled, unemployed or elderly family members. For instance, the average family may pay as much as $100,000 in interest payments throughout the lifetime of the family, mostly from home mortgage interest and car loan interest payments. More specifically, because of interest payments, a house can cost you perhaps 2 to 2.5 times as much as the original purchase price if it is mortgaged over thirty years, depending upon the interest rate! Therefore, families throw away a large percentage of their children's inheritance through interest payments—money which could easily provide a great foundation for continuing a large extended family, and to pay to care for its own occasionally sick, disabled, unemployed, or elderly family member so the federal government won't have to collect billions of dollars in taxes to do this for us.

The benefits of having a nation which outlaws usury include developing a culture which prefers *saving* money to *borrowing* money. In the long run, it is always financially advantageous to save money until you can afford what you want, rather than borrowing money at interest to buy whatever you can not yet afford to purchase with cash. And, living in a large extended family where everyone gets along well and enjoys the benefits of its triple economy of scale, can allow you to save money easier and faster than living on your own. Furthermore, this same triple economy of scale so decreases the per capita expenses of each family member that wives are no longer needed to work outside the home, so they can stay home and raise the children. The principles of the hierarchy of spiritual headship and family discipline create a greater devotion to the family anyway, so living at home is not the burden you might think it to be.

In summary, God has given mankind at least eight biblical principles to encourage the development of large extended families. These families would live in a large house where everything is already paid for, and with a triple economy of scale to obviate the need for a large, centralized government with multiple agencies to support those who should be supported by their own families instead. Therefore, since the building of large, extended families is such a high priority for God, why is it such a low priority for today's Americans, and especially today's Christians? For again, God's idea promotes family togetherness and prosperity, whereas the traditions of America promote independence and poverty.

To this end, America needs to invent and exalt laws which promote the development of large, extended families which have the financial capability of supporting all their own family members in times of need. America needs to stop exalting the destructive philosophies which tend to break down the large, extended family, such as:

—"Be all that you can be;"
—"Look out for number one;" and,
—"To thine own self be true."

CONCEALED PURPOSE COMMANDS AND DOUBLE PRECAUTION COMMANDS

As you have seen from this chapter, God has many commands in the Bible which have concealed purposes. Some of these concealed purpose commands are actually double precaution laws which are supposed to provide a double precaution against individual or national sins. Other concealed purpose commands have entirely unexpected purposes and provide hidden benefits to society by interacting with other Mosaic laws to provide a synergistic impact.

Double precaution commands are twice as effective in preventing sin and disobedience as the usual single precaution commands. For example, we don't tell a three year old child, "Watch out for cars when you play in the street" (a mere single precaution command). Instead, we tell the child, "Don't play in the street" (for double precaution), or better yet, "Don't go near the street" (for triple precaution). In fact, we have such faith in the superiority of double and triple precaution commands, that even our lawmakers have designed laws using this same philosophy. For instance, to prevent car accidents, lawmakers don't just say, "Drive safely" (a single precaution law), but instead they say, "Don't drink and drive" (for double precaution), or, "Don't even have an open beverage container in your car while driving" (for triple precaution).

Likewise, God's commands concerning our dress code, our diet, and our hair length all function as double precaution commands to help prevent sexual sins. You see, obedience to these commands gives us a perpetual reminder that "God is Lord of what goes *on* my body" (my clothing), what goes *in* my body (my diet), and my actual *body* (my hair)," and strengthens the conviction that "my body is a temple of the Holy Spirit"! In this way, obedience to God's dress codes, dietary laws, and hair laws provides a double precaution against sexual sins, drunkenness, and drug abuse.

For any man who is wearing headbands, wristbands, and tassels should experience great conflict within himself if he attempts to either get drunk or seduce a future sexual partner while also being dressed this way. Attempting to first remove his headbands, wristbands, and tassels to obtain "peace of mind" so he can commit these sexual sins will serve only to magnify his intentions to violate God's Will in the first place. As a result of providing a heightened awareness of his intention to sin, this dress code is again serving to provide a double precaution against sexual sins.

Furthermore, this dress code also helps to sponsor a man's role as spiritual head of the home (purpose number two), and additionally helps to champion his involvement in local politics as a future Christian statesman and judge over "thousands, hundreds, fifties, or tens" as noted in Exodus 18:21-NIV (purpose number three). Yet none of these three hidden purposes are immediately obvious to the casual reader.

Also, it is not immediately obvious that God's laws of inheritance actually function to sponsor the development of large extended families which can care for their own occasionally sick, poor, retired, or disabled family members, and so obviate the need for tax-sponsored government health care, welfare, retirement, or disability programs to support them instead.

Unfortunately however, since we have neither understood God's wisdom nor understood the hidden purposes for many of his civil laws, we have mistakenly concluded that these civil laws are neither applicable nor beneficial for our society. Just as a child frequently cannot understand his father's wisdom when he is told to "stay away from the bad kids" (a double precaution command), so also a child of God frequently cannot understand his heavenly Father's wisdom when he is told to "wear headbands, wristbands, and tassels" (a double precaution command) with concealed purposes as well. But, just like a child's lack of understanding neither invalidates his father's wisdom nor abolishes his father's commands, so also the lack of understanding of a child of God neither invalidates his heavenly Father's wisdom nor abolishes his heavenly Father's commands either.

Our government leaders and judges however, remain in the dark concerning the benefits and practical applications of God's civil laws because they were not properly instructed in Church and Sunday school concerning these issues. Therefore, our leaders have allowed our culture to evolve without the wonderful hidden benefits of God's concealed purpose commands, which were supposed to perpetuate large extended families in a healthy, peaceful, and prosperous "nation under God." By neglecting the proper teaching of these laws, modern Christianity has unwittingly taught generations of government leaders that God's concealed purpose commands either have no obvious benefit for Gentiles or for Christian America, or were "fulfilled in Christ's coming," so we can ignore them and not incorporate them into our society's laws and culture.

America's bias against God's laws goes even further than this. For instance, many non-Christians (as well as Christians) would say that a society which "forces" females to wear dresses, have long hair, head coverings, keep silent in churches, and not teach or have authority over men is a male-dominated, repressive society.

However, in this biblical society which appears on the surface to be so "repressive," there is a paradox of extreme "freedom." For you see, in a biblical society, a woman would have the freedom to never worry about being married to an alcoholic, drug abusing, bisexual or adulterous husband who beat her or sexually abused her children. Why? Because these sins against God would also become crimes against the state with serious punishments, such as an "eye for an eye" (for wife abuse and child abuse), possibly cutting off the hand (for child molesting), and whipping (as a merciful alternative to a possible execution) for adultery, homosexuality, drunkenness, and drug abuse!

Also, the women would never have to worry about being married to a man who wouldn't go to church, read the Bible, or be the spiritual head of the family. You see, there is tremendous peer pressure to be a good husband in a society where the men wear headbands, wristbands, and tassels to remind them to obey God, and where women have the right to insist that their husbands teach them the Bible at home, and where money making work on the Sabbath is illegal. This way, 95 percent of the population ends up going to church once a week, even if it's just to find something to do!

Furthermore, if our country could eventually become a true "nation under God" so God would bless America with a nearly crime-free, poverty-free, war-free, tax-free, inflation-free, natural disaster-free, and disease-free society where nearly everyone lives to be 120 years old while enjoying excellent health (see chapters three and four for details), then the extreme freedom females can experience in this "repressive" society includes never worrying about crime, poverty, war, taxes, inflation, natural disasters, diseases or premature death from breast cancer, etc. Given this possible option, most women would probably say, "If this is 'repressive,' then please repress me"!

Let us not think that a biblical society gives all the freedoms and benefits to the male. Quite the opposite, for in addition to restricting the male's tendency to sin just as much as the female's, there are an host of *additional* commands for men—to pressure them to become spiritual head of the home, as well as to generate a patriotic tradition of volunteering to serve in a tax-free system of justice and government which requires the participation of a large minority of godly Christian elders in order to function correctly.

Hopefully you can now see how God designed his civil laws to provide the legal and cultural muscle to keep the small Christian minority and the large unrighteous majority on their best behavior (by combining the influences of salvation and surrender, training and tradition, prosecution and punishment, and clothing and covering.

So, wouldn't it be nice to have a society like this, where non-Christians acted as Christians (rather than Christians acting like non-Christians)? Of course! Unfortunately, we've removed all the God-given cultural motivations which would encourage this type of society to evolve, all in the name of "freedom in Christ," which we mistakenly believe has given us the license to violate God's Old Testament principles concerning justice, government, and family.

Summary

The modern Christian movement for pro-family legislation appears to have limited its goals to include only the following:

1. stopping abortions;
2. stopping special gay rights legislation and gay marriages;
3. stopping sex education in our public schools; and,
4. limiting access to pornography.

Contrast this with God's view of pro-family legislation. For as you have read in chapters seventeen and eighteen, God has given us all the laws necessary to practically guarantee premarital virginity and marital fidelity, while nearly eliminating fornication, adultery, and homosexuality (which would stop pornography as well), in addition to stopping nearly all the violence in the home, drunkenness, drug abuse, wife abuse, child abuse, child molesting, rape, disrespect for parental authority, cursing parents, attacking parents, separation, and divorce!

Furthermore, God has given mankind laws requiring a specific dress code, diet, and hair length to teach all Americans that God is Lord of what goes *on* my body, *in* my body, and my actual body *itself,* in order to provide a double precaution against sexual sins, drunkenness, and drug abuse. These dress codes were also designed by God to sponsor the man's role as spiritual head of the home as well as champion his role as a godly statesmen and judge of his community.

Thirdly, God has given us all the laws necessary for America to develop a nationwide culture where we honor those who honor their father and mother, and exalt those who demonstrate submissive obedience to their parents and elders, so the families of both Christians and non-Christians can more naturally develop a hierarchy of spiritual authority, and become training grounds for submission to God. Moreover, God's principles encourage the development of a culture where the parents can physically discipline their children without government interference and where the government supports (rather of thwarts) this God-given right of parents to discipline their children in this way.

Fourthly, God has given us at least eight economic principles to help America encourage the development of large, extended families with triple economies of scale from shared labor, shared expenses, and shared possessions which can better provide for their own occasionally sick, poor, retired, or disabled family members, rather than requiring tax-sponsored government health care, welfare, retirement, or disability programs to support them. For God's plan was that a culture of large, extended families would obviate the need for large, centralized government, so that taxes on citizens and businesses would decrease, which would increase national employment and prosperity.

Therefore, God's Principles of Pro-Family Legislation encourage our leaders to design laws to develop large, extended families to obviate the need for big government and hefty taxes, instead of designing laws to develop big government and hefty taxes to obviate the need for large, extended families.

In conclusion, by adopting the civil principles of Jesus Christ (the Lord of Lawmakers) America can solve all its problems concerning the family, which in turn will allow for smaller government, less taxes, and a more peaceful and prosperous society at the same time.

And that, is God's view of Pro-Family Legislation!

Chapter Nineteen

HOW GOD'S VIEW OF WELFARE REFORM CAN SAVE AMERICA HUNDREDS OF BILLIONS OF DOLLARS IN TAXES

The foundation of America's system of welfare rests upon our large, centralized, tax-supported federal and state governments. They use our tax dollars to fund large welfare programs to help the poor. This financial aid may include welfare checks, food stamps, aid for dependent children, social security disability income, Medicaid, and emergency payments for medicines, electricity, and heating fuel.

However, in recent years it has become apparent that our system of welfare needs to be reformed. There are some deserving applicants for whom there is no money available, and there are applicants receiving welfare benefits who should not even be eligible for benefits in the first place. Some of these welfare regulations actually encourage married people to separate and live apart so they can receive more benefits, or encourage young couples to live together and not get married (because getting married would decrease their welfare benefits). These regulations have also encouraged thousands of young women to have multiple babies out of wedlock just so they can get more welfare benefits. In fact, the laws concerning welfare benefits are actually discouraging people from finding a job and getting off welfare. Furthermore, our system of welfare appears to have sponsored an entire culture of welfare-dependent citizens who pass this philosophy down to their children and grandchildren. In summary, America's system of welfare encourages sexual immorality, fraud, and welfare-dependency. You can see, the U.S. is badly in need of welfare reform .

Yet no one ever seems to ask, "What is God's view of welfare reform?" or, "What does the Bible have to say about welfare reform?" Well, because God so loved the poor, He had a great deal to say about how a society should help the poor. The Bible clearly teaches how welfare reform can be accomplished without any taxes and without requiring the government to even be involved.

To begin with, in chapter eight of 1st Samuel, the Bible teaches that God did not want the Israelites to have a king who would create a large, centralized government which required taxes to support its function. But without such a government, how did God plan to provide financial aid for the citizens of Israel who were poor?

This chapter reveals how God originally intended for the Israelites to be able to provide for the poor of their nation—without a large, centralized government, without paying any taxes, and without developing a welfare state within Israel. Furthermore, any country (such as the U.S.) which desires to become a "nation under God" can adopt these same biblical principles to provide for the needs of the poor within its own country, without the need for a large, tax-sponsored welfare system, and without creating a large minority of welfare-dependent citizens. As usual, God's view of welfare reform requires a cultural reorientation of values which can only be accomplished by the implementation of many of God's principles of moral law, civil law, and civil law enforcement.

Briefly, the foundation of God's system of welfare reform comes from the more than thirty different laws discussed in chapter eighteen which interact together to promote the development of large, extended families throughout all of Israel. These large families were expected to "take care of their own" elderly, disabled, unemployed, and poor so those individuals would not have to become dependent upon others outside their family. Thus, most citizens were supposed to have large, extended families to help them if they became unemployed, sick, disabled, elderly, or poor.

However, the Bible also mentions a special class of citizens which it refers to as "the widows and the fatherless," implying that these people do not have large, extended families which they can depend upon to provide for them if they become impoverished. So, God gave Moses five additional laws to help the poor, specifically designed for those citizens who did not have families to help them out.

These five laws were divided into three categories:

1. Pre-welfare laws,
2. Tithe-sponsored welfare,
3. Work-Programs—the last resort of welfare support!

Now the three pre-welfare laws allowed some of the "poor" to:

1. purchase food "at cost";
2. obtain zero-interest loans (the balance of which is canceled every Sabbath year); and,
3. go onto a farmer's property and pick corn, grain, and grapes, etc. and eat them on the farmer's premises for a single meal (items can NOT be carried off the farmer's property).

The fourth law concerns tithe-sponsored welfare and involves having the poor person (and his family) go to the "storehouse" in the local town (a collection point for the national tithe) and receive food or other type of assistance. Since tithe-sponsored welfare is for the "innocent" and not the "immoral," then an applicant who is perpetually immoral can be "cut off" from being eligible to receive financial support from the tithe.

The fifth law concerns the last resort of welfare support and requires the healthy citizen (who is only poor because he is too lazy to work) to enter a six-year work program on a farm or in a business where his master would provide him with free housing, food, clothing, and medical care, but he would not receive any money at all for his work until the day he leaves (at the end of his six-year "contract"), at which time he receives a "discounted" salary for the entire six years work in one lump sum.

These five biblical principles of economics were designed by God to help those poor Israelites who had no families to care for them, which the Bible often refers to as "the widows and the fatherless"! These laws were also applicable for the poor aliens as well, although the loans for the aliens were neither canceled nor were they interest-free, and the work program was not six years but was life long.

In summary, the thirty-plus laws which promote the development of large, extended families (which are expected to help their own poor) would also dramatically decrease the number of Israelites without families who still needed welfare assistance. This smaller, more manageable number of poor Israelites would now be more than adequately provided for by the five other welfare laws which God gave to Moses more than three thousand years ago.

Let us now discuss of these categories individually.

The Large, Extended Family

Generally, the people who help you when you're "down and out" are those from your own family. You see, somehow God built an instinct into mankind's genetic code so that people within each family would feel a natural responsibility to care for one another. Not only can this instinct be modified by the environment of your own family, but, by adopting God's principles of pro-family legislation, this instinct for family responsibility can be *magnified* by any culture so it can form the *foundation* for a biblically-based welfare system for the poor. Any system of successful welfare reform must take full advantage of these natural instincts of family responsibility which already exist and bolster them even further by approving lots of pro-family legislation which *encourages* these instincts, and by revoking all anti-family legislation which *discourages* these instincts.

Paradoxically however, welfare reform in America does just the *opposite*, by revoking all the pro-family biblical principles of moral and civil law adopted by our founders (such as laws against premarital sex, adultery, homosexuality, drunkenness, and non-biblical divorce) while approving many anti-family principles such as "legalizing" premarital sex, adultery, homosexuality, drunkenness, no-fault divorce, allowing single mothers and gays to adopt children, and allowing gays to marry. All of these bad laws which encourage "alternate lifestyles" and "nontraditional families" create a culture which grows "numb" to the biblical concept that the large, extended family was God's original plan for mankind. And so, now it becomes harder to publicly state that these "alternate lifestyles" are sinful and offensive to God, and harder to publicly state that laws which encourage "nontraditional families" are actually counterproductive to successful welfare reform.

The many laws of pro-family legislation (discussed in chapter eighteen) were designed by God not only to prevent the emergence of "alternate lifestyles" to begin with, but were also designed to keep people off welfare by providing their needs through their own large, extended family.

Just as laws which increase participation in large, extended families *decrease* those on welfare, so also, laws which promote the breakdown of the family *increase* those on welfare. Let me give you six examples which demonstrate how the number of citizens on welfare increases when America ignores or revokes God's principles of pro-family legislation.

The first category of examples involves the notion that every law which promotes an increase in the number of single parents in this nation, also promotes an increase in those on welfare. This is because a very large proportion of those on welfare are also single parents of young children. This includes unwed mothers as well as divorced single parents, and there are four illustrations of this problem within this first category.

A. First of all, when America ignores the biblical principle that "The punishment for fornication is to get married" (Exod. 22:16-17 NIV), then the number of unwed mothers increases on the welfare roles of society.

B. Secondly, American congressmen and senators ignore biblical principles which teach that "Adultery, homosexuality, and drunkenness are sins against God which must also be punished as crimes against the state" (as America's founders believed centuries ago), and instead make sexual immorality and drunkenness completely legal. The resulting increased drunkenness and sexual immorality also promotes an increase in divorce and again increases those on welfare.

C. Thirdly, American judges do not punish wife abuse and child abuse according to the biblical principle which teaches: "Use an 'Eye for an Eye' as a biblical alternative to imprisonment for those criminals who violently injure their victims" (Lev. 24:19-20 NIV). As a result, family violence escalates, promoting even more divorces, and which again increases the number of single parents on welfare.

D. Fourthly, when American judges ignore the biblical principle that says "Divorce should be illegal except in cases where one of the spouses has committed a serious sin which must be prosecuted as a crime against the state" (see chapter eighteen), and instead allow no-fault, frivolous divorces, this again increases the number of single parents of young children who now need welfare.

So, the first category of examples demonstrates the great numbers of unwed mothers and divorced single parents which result when America ignores God's principles of moral law, civil law, and civil law enforcement. These four examples represent sins which cause *healthy* people (who *can* work) to end up on welfare anyway, because of their need to stay home to care for their young children.

The next category refers to sins which cause people to be so *unhealthy* that they can *not* work, so they end up on welfare also. Laws which do not punish drunkenness and sexual sins as crimes against the state also lead to an increase in the number of *unhealthy* citizens who are disabled by alcoholism and AIDS, which increases the number of citizens dependent upon government welfare to support them. In fact, citizens who are disabled by the consequences of the sins of drunkenness and sexual immorality are not mentioned in the Bible as even being *eligible* for receiving financial assistance from the national tithe. The only applicants mentioned in the Bible which are eligible for receiving the tithe are the "widows," the "fatherless," and the "alien." You see, the expression "the widows, the fatherless and the alien" implies that they have no immediate family to take care of their financial needs, and that their own sins have not contributed to their poverty or disability. So, in God's system of welfare reform, the sexually immoral and the drunkards are dealt with by the *justice* system so they won't ever be a burden to the *welfare* system. In fact, in the U.S., the thousands of citizens who have become disabled by alcoholism and sexual immorality and are burdening our welfare system represent God's sign to America that our society has not been dealing with drunkenness and sexual immorality according to the biblical principles of *justice* and *punishment* to begin with.

The third category does not refer to the sinfulness of individuals, but refers to the evil of certain government laws. Every law which financially supports the ability of the elderly and the disabled to live apart from their families (such as social security retirement income and social security disability income) also increases the number of citizens who begin to depend upon the government instead of their families for financial aid. This also increases the number of children who grow to expect that the government will care for their parents' needs so that they won't have to.

All the examples and categories mentioned represent forms of anti-family legislation. As you can see, anti-family legislation increases those on welfare, while pro-family legislation decreases those on welfare. So, the foundation of God's principles of welfare reform comes from all of the laws mentioned in chapter eighteen which interact together to promote large, extended families throughout all Israel. You see, the large extended family has a triple economy of scale: shared labor, shared possessions, and shared expenses. Therefore it provides the most cost-effective way of managing family finances. In this way, the large extended family, which has an occasional widow, elderly, disabled, sick, or healthy unemployed family member, can easily care for them from their own resources, without requiring a tax-sponsored welfare system to financially assist them.

So, God's view of welfare reform begins by encouraging us once again to adopt God's principles of moral law, civil law, and civil law enforcement as they relate to pro-family legislation!

More specifically, enforcing God's moral and civil laws against premarital sex will dramatically decrease the number of new unwed mothers on welfare. Secondly, enforcing God's moral and civil laws against adultery and homosexuality will lead to a decreased rate of separation and divorce which should also decrease the number of new single parents on welfare. Thirdly, enforcing the biblical punishments for wife abuse, child abuse, and sexual harassment of children should nearly eliminate these problems and thus dramatically decrease the resulting separation and divorce rates. This will again decrease the number of new single parents on the welfare roles. Fourthly, making drunkenness illegal and punishable (as well as drug abuse) according to biblical principles will nearly eliminate such problems from our society. This way, there would be no new applicants for welfare who have been disabled by their drunkenness or by their drug abuse. Lastly, we need to follow the Bible principle of making divorce illegal except when a spouse has committed a sin against God which is also a crime against the state, and for which he or she would be prosecuted and possibly executed or whipped. This would nearly abolish the category of "single parents" as applicants for welfare because divorces would be so rare under this system in comparison to the rate of divorce in America today.

In other words, enforcing God's principles of moral and civil law against the sins of premarital sex, adultery, homosexuality, wife abuse, child abuse, sexual harassment of children, drunkenness, drug abuse, and frivolous divorce should dramatically decrease those victims of uncontrolled sin which are on welfare.

Furthermore, eliminating usury (lending money at interest) would cause young married couples to find it harder to move away from their parent's home because of the unavailability of large loans without interest to finance their first car or their first house, etc. As long as the couple is living with their parents (and therefore not having to pay as much money for bills), they are much less likely to end up on welfare if one or both of them is unemployed temporarily.

Also, according to the Bible, children are responsible for caring for their aging parents, not the government, not the welfare system, and not the national tithe! In fact, Jesus gets angry at the Pharisees for not using their money to care for their parents. Instead, they pretend that their money is "devoted to God"—concept the Pharisees called "Corban." For it is written:

> But you say that if a man says to his father or mother: "Whatever help you might have received from me is Corban" then you no longer let him do anything for his father or mother. Thus you nullify the word of God by your tradition that you have handed down. And you do many things like that. (Mark 7:11-13 NIV)

It is also written:

> If anyone does not provide for his relatives, and especially for his immediate family, he has denied the faith and is worse than an unbeliever. (1 Tim. 5:8 NIV)

Clearly, the Bible teaches that children must be financially responsible for the care of their aged parents and grandparents, and that this is neither the responsibility of the state, nor the national tithe.

The most cost-effective way to do this is to have the grandparents live with their children and grandchildren. But the government, through social security retirement income, sponsors the ability of grandparents to live apart from their children, and by so doing, underwrites the breakup of the large extended family, so families don't have to try as hard to get along with one another. This eventually changes our culture into believing that it is the government's responsibility to financially care for our elderly. This is totally anti-biblical and is a form of anti-family legislation. And it is because of this mistaken legislation that so many thousands of elderly citizens are solely dependant upon the government for financial support.

Furthermore, in our society, the elderly often don't want to live with their children anyway, because of the many years of disrespect they have received from the lips of their children. However, other biblical laws which help to create a hierarchy of spiritual headship (such as "Honor thy father and mother" and "Rise in the presence of the elderly") make it more likely that the grandparents will want to live with, and be supported by, their children and grandchildren. Therefore, the grandparents won't end up living apart from their children and possibly becoming welfare dependent in the future. Added, the biblical law which grants a double portion of the inheritance to the eldest son so he can care for his parents in their old age also accomplishes the same thing by creating larger, extended families and keeping the elderly off the welfare rolls.

In summary, there are thirty-plus laws in the Bible which were designed by God to interact together to create large extended families with such a good economy of scale that they can care for their own sick, unemployed, disabled, and elderly. These laws were originally given to Moses by Jesus Christ, the Architect of this biblical blueprint for perfect self-government. They were given so Israel (as well as America) would not create a society with a large minority of welfare-dependent citizens, or have to pay lots of taxes to support a large, centralized government to care for our poor (when their own families should be caring for them instead).

POOR CITIZENS WITHOUT FAMILIES

The large, extended family was supposed provide for the needs of the vast majority of poor Israelites. But what about the poor Israelites who had no families? Well, remember that God gave Moses five additional principles to provide for the needs of those Israelites who had no families to care for them. We will now examine each of these principles.

The first three principles are what I call pre-welfare laws, and they are as follows:

1. SELLING FOOD (AND OTHER NECESSITIES) TO THE POOR "AT COST" (WITHOUT MAKING ANY PROFIT)

God commanded merchants to make no profit off of the poor but to sell them their food "at cost." For it is written:

> If one of your countrymen becomes poor and is unable to support himself among you, help him.... You must not ... sell him food at a profit. (Lev. 25:35, 37 NIV, selected portions)

In this verse, God commands businessmen and farmers to give discounts to poor families for food and (by implication) for other necessities as well. These discounts should be approximately equivalent to selling these items "at cost," so the merchant and farmer would not "make a profit" on the poor. And as usual, this method of welfare assistance to the poor costs no taxes to implement.

2. Lending Money to the Poor without Requiring Interest

God not only said to sell food (and other necessities) to the poor at cost, but God also said to lend money to the poor at cost. In other words, the Israelites were not supposed to make a profit off of the poor on food, merchandise, or money. For instance, in the full version of the above quote, notice that God commands the Israelites to be generous to the poor and lend them money for their necessities at zero interest. For it is written:

> If one of your countrymen becomes poor and is unable to support himself among you, help him as you would an alien or a temporary resident, so he can continue to live among you. Do not take interest of any kind from him, but fear your God, so that your countryman may continue to live among you. You must not lend him money at interest or sell him food at a profit. (Lev. 25:35-37 NIV)

Again it is written:

> Do not charge your brother interest, whether on money or food or anything else that may earn interest. You may charge a foreigner interest, but not a brother Israelite. (Deut. 23:19-20 NIV)

Evidently, giving interest-free loans is one of God's ways of providing financial assistance to the poor without requiring any taxes, and without requiring a large, centralized government to create a tax-sponsored system of welfare. So, when it comes to poor families, God says we should neither sell them food at profit, nor lend them money at a profit.

As a result of the availability of substantial discounts on food and other merchandise, as well as the availability of zero-interest loans, the poor man can hopefully recover from his poverty and indebtedness without placing him further in debt because of unnecessary interest payments.

These small interest-free loans are only for the bare necessities of life. They are not to be given so the poor can purchase nonessentials (such as alcohol and cigarettes), and neither are they to be given so the poor can purchase luxuries. For it is written:

> ... be openhanded and freely lend him whatever he NEEDS. (Deut. 15:8 NIV; emphasis added)

Notice that God says to lend him whatever he *needs*, not whatever he *wants*.

As if giving small interest-free loans to the poor wasn't enough, God went even further and said to *cancel* the payments required on these interest-free loans every seventh year. For it is written:

> At the end of every seven years you must cancel debts . . . Every creditor shall cancel the loan he has made to his fellow Israelite. He shall not require payment from his fellow Israelite or brother, because the Lord's time for canceling debts has been proclaimed. You may require payment from a foreigner, but you must cancel any debt your brother owes you . . . If there is a poor man among your brothers in any of the towns of the land the Lord your God is giving you, do not be hard hearted or tight-fisted toward your poor brother. Rather be openhanded and freely lend him whatever he NEEDS. Be careful not to harbor this wicked thought: "The seventh year, the year for canceling debts, is near," so that you do not show ill will toward your needy brother and give him nothing. He may then appeal to the Lord against you, and you will be found guilty of sin. Give generously to him and do so without a grudging heart; then *because of this the Lord your God will bless you in all your work and in everything you put your hand to.* There will always be poor in the land. Therefore, I command you to be openhanded toward your brothers and towards the poor and needy in your land. (Deut. 15:7-11 NIV; emphasis added)

Please observe that God also says in this passage that if the Israelites were to freely lend to the poor, and be willing to cancel debts every seven years, then God would "bless them in all their work and in everything they put their hand to!" In other words, God says, "Don't worry about the money you will lose when you cancel the loan, for I the Lord, will pay you back several times over." It is almost as if God were saying, "Test me in this!" (Mal. 3:10b NIV) I believe, therefore, that God is declaring,

> When Israel finally develops a culture which generously gives interest-free loans to the poor to help supply them with their necessities, and is willing to cancel those loans every seven years, then I, the Lord your God, will reimburse my people Israel for their generosity to the poor with blessings from above on their crops, cattle, flocks and herds, etc. to pay them back several times over for their obedience of canceling their loans to the poor.

I believe that the year for canceling these debts was actually the Sabbath Year, which, of course, occurred every seven years. You see, if the Israelites followed God's command and promised not to either sow their fields or reap any harvest during the Sabbath year and only eat what the land produced on its own (Lev. 25:2-7 NIV), then God promised to send them a triple harvest in the sixth year which would last until the ninth year's harvest comes in (Lev. 25:20-22 NIV). By doing this, God may also be using this bumper crop of harvest in the sixth year to prepay the Israelite's generosity in canceling the payments on their zero-interest loans during the seventh year. So, God was actually underwriting the generosity of the Israelite farmers, which would more than make up for their lost money. Surely this same type of blessing overflowed to the merchants for their generosity as well (Deut. 15:10 NIV).

American banks give interest to depositors, which encourages more customers to lend their money to the bank so the bank can lend it to others at higher rates of interest and make even more profit. Unfortunately, this violation of God's laws against usury encourages Americans to believe that the purpose of extra money in America is to use it to make more money—otherwise the money sits idle, and is of no use to anyone. However, the Bible teaches that charging interest on loans is supposed to be illegal. Therefore, the purpose of extra money within Israel was to use it to lend to the poor, otherwise the money sat idle, and was of no use for anyone.

Charging interest on loans tilts our economy towards a posture of lending money for profit to those people who can easily pay back the loan. As a result, we grant much larger loans to people for nonessentials—for luxuries—and for business expansion. Rather than let our money sit idle, we place it in interest-bearing savings accounts, money market funds, certificates of deposit, government bonds, or in the stock market, instead of being willing to lend some of it to the poor in small loans for the bare essentials of life.

On the other hand, having laws which outlaw the charging of interest on loans would tilt our economy into a posture of granting small, zero-interest loans for the bare necessities of life, to those who often can not afford to pay you back at all. Why? Because since your money can't be used to "make more money" by gaining interest, then the money of private individuals will sit idle and accumulate nothing. Therefore, you might as well lend it to the poor, for at least then you will have the fulfillment of helping the poor, obeying God, and knowing that God will somehow bless your generosity even more. For it is written:

> Give, and it well be given to you. A good measure, pressed down, shaken together and running over, will be poured into your lap. (Luke 6:38 NIV)

So, a culture which has zero-interest loans encourages generosity to the poor and a giving spirit; a culture which has interest-bearing loans encourages a selfish spirit and encourages the hoarding of money where we can make more money from interest. When viewed in this way,

God's laws against usury become divine laws of welfare reform to help the poor without requiring any taxes or government bureaucracy.

3. THE "PICK AND EAT" LAWS

The third pre-welfare law is what I call the "pick and eat" law. It refers to allowing the poor to go onto a farmer's property and pick some corn, grain, apples, grapes, etc., and eat them on the farmer's premises for a single meal (but these items can not be carried off the farmer's property. For it is written:

> When you enter a neighbor's vineyard, you may eat all the grapes you want, but do not put any in your basket. If you enter your neighbor's grainfield, you may pick kernels with your hands, but you must not put a sickle to his standing grain. (Deut. 23:24-25 NIV)

This is a wonderful law for the wanderer or for the poor citizen living in or traveling through the country, as he/she is able to obtain a small fruit or grain meal *before* the harvest. In fact, even *after* the harvest, farmers were required by God to leave a small area around the four edges of their fields "unreaped" so the poor could be able to find a little extra to eat. God also said not to go over their fields a second time or gather the gleanings (the "leavings" which they had missed earlier), but to be sure to leave them for the poor to eat! For it is written:

> When you reap the harvest of your land, do not reap to the very edges of your field or gather the gleanings of your harvest. Leave them for the poor and the alien. (Lev. 23:22 NIV)

And again:

> When you reap the harvest of your land, do not reap to the very edges of your fields or gather the gleanings of your harvest. Do not go over your vineyard a second time or pick up the grapes that have fallen. Leave them for the poor and the alien. (Lev. 19:9-10 NIV)

And, a third time:

> When you are harvesting in your field and you overlook a sheaf, do not go back and get it. Leave it for the alien, the fatherless, and the widow so that the Lord your God may bless you in all the work of your hands. When you beat the olives from the trees, do not go over your branches a second time. Leave what remains for the alien, the fatherless, and the widow. When you harvest the grapes in your vineyard, do not go over the vines again. Leave what remains for the alien,

the fatherless, and the widow. Remember that you were slaves in Egypt. (Deut. 24:19-22 NIV)

Now as you can see, there were no laws against trespassing on another's property (for all land was the Lord's anyway). Also note that many of these laws helped the wandering traveler so he would be able to find food for himself while on his journey. This is what Jesus and his disciples did in the New Testament (Matt. 12:1 NIV). This is also why Ruth was able to gather grain in the fields of Boaz even before he befriended her (Ruth 2:2-3 NIV).

Now these laws would only help during the few weeks each year when certain crops were "ripe," and they would help mostly the poor who lived in the countryside and not the poor who lived in the cities. So, God needed to create laws which would help the poor within the city, as well as create laws which would provide assistance throughout the entire year. He did just that, for the first two pre-welfare laws do, in fact, assist all the poor throughout the year, whether they live in the city or the country.

3. Tithe-Sponsored Welfare Reform

The fourth principle God gave to Moses to help the poor people who had no families to support them was the use of the national tithe as a form of welfare support. Every adult Israelite, individual or family, was supposed to set aside a tithe (meaning a tenth) of their income each year according to God's command. This was supposed to be true whether the income was in the form of crops, vintage, flocks, herds, or money. For it is written:

> Be sure to set aside a tenth of all that your fields produce each year. (Deut. 14:22 NIV)

> ... the Israelites ... brought a great amount, a tithe of everything ... a tithe of their herds and flocks ... (2 Chron. 31:5b, 6b NIV)

> ... thou shalt bring forth all the tithe of thine increase ... (Deut. 14:28 KJV)

So, whether their increase was in the form of crops, flocks, or money, the Israelites had to bring a tithe of their increase to the storehouse in their local towns.

The Bible speaks of the tithe as being an inheritance of the Levites (Num. 18:21, 24; Deut. 14:28-29; 26:12). However, the Bible also speaks of the tithe as being for the aliens, the widows, and the fatherless orphans as a form of welfare support (Deut. 14:28-29; 26:12). Evidently, God wanted the tithe to be divided in such a way as to support the poor, but at the same time be an "inheritance" for the Levites. But how much of the tithe did God want to reserve for the poor, and how much was to go to the Levites?

I believe the tithe was God's welfare system for the poor, and that the poor were supposed to receive 80 percent of the tithe. The Levites who collected, protected, and distributed the tithe in the non-Levite cities and towns were supposed to receive 10 percent, and the last 10 percent of the tithe went to the temple in Jerusalem to provide financial support and food for the Levites, priests, gatekeepers and singers who lived in the temple.

Now, what is the biblical evidence to support such a conclusion?

Well, since the tithe was supposed to be an "inheritance" for the Levites, it appears as though none of them were required to pay the tithe in the first place (for it wouldn't make a whole lot of sense for the Levites to collect the tithe from one other just to give it back again). Since the tithe was supposed to belong to God to begin with, then for the Levite tribe not to have to pay the tithe was like God's gift to each Levite family (as if it were an extra 10 percent inheritance). This would allow the resources of the Levites to be 10 percent higher than "non-Levites."

However, the tribe of Levites actually *did* have an inheritance from God of forty-eight towns and cities along with pastures surrounding each town. These forty-eight towns and cities were spread throughout all Israel. For it is written:

> ... the Lord said to Moses, "Command the Israelites to give the Levites *towns* to live in from the *inheritance* the Israelites will possess. And give them *pasturelands* around the towns. Then they will have the *towns* to live in and the *pasturelands* for their cattle, flocks, and all their other livestock. The pasturelands around the towns that you give the Levites will extend out fifteen hundred feet from the town wall. Outside the town, measure three thousand feet on the east side, three thousand feet on the south side, three thousand feet on the west and three thousand feet on the north, with the town in the center. They will have this area as pastureland for the towns." (Num. 35:1b-5 NIV; emphasis added)

> The towns of the Levites in the territory held by the Israelites were forty-eight in all, together with their pasturelands. Each of these towns had pasturelands surrounding it. (Josh. 21:41-42 NIV)

So, the Levites did, in fact, have an inheritance among the Israelites. Therefore, the Levites generally did not have to depend on receiving a tithe from the other tribes of Israel to meet their needs. And, since the

Levites also did not have to pay the tithe in the first place, this provided an extra 10 percent to their income which they could keep.

Since the Levites did receive an inheritance from God of forty-eight cities and towns with their surrounding pasturelands spread throughout all Israel, what does it mean when the Bible says:

> ... bring all the tithes ... and store it in your towns, so that the Levites (who have *no* allotment or inheritance of their own) and the aliens, the fatherless and the widows ... may come and eat and be satisfied ... (Deut. 14:28, 29 NIV; emphasis added)

This verse reveals that there was indeed a special group of Levites who had NO allotment or inheritance of their own. This was probably because they willingly *gave up* their inheritance by leaving their homes in the Levite towns to serve God in Jerusalem, or in one of the non-Levite towns. As a result, these men did become:

> ... Levites (who had no inheritance of their own) ... (Deut. 14:29a NIV)

You see, just like Christian missionaries today often give up any inheritance they may have in America for a lifetime of missionary work in a foreign country, so also there was a special group of Levites who were willing to voluntarily leave their homes in the Levite cities, give up their inheritance, and travel to a foreign city to serve God. This special group of Levites was actually composed of two subgroups.

The *first* subgroup of Levites traveled to Jerusalem and became the priests, gatekeepers, and singers in the temple of God. This subgroup of Levites indeed received no inheritance in Israel as a result of their lifetime commitment to God to serve at the temple. Because of their dedication to serving God at the temple, God wanted them to be supported by the national tithe. For it is written:

> I give to the Levites *all* the tithes in Israel as their inheritance in return for the work they do while serving at the Tent of Meeting ... They will receive *no* inheritance among the Israelites. Instead, I give to the Levites as their inheritance *the tithes that the Israelites present as an offering to the Lord.* That is why I said concerning them: "They will have *no* inheritance among the Israelites." (Num. 18:21, 24 NIV; emphasis added)

Notice that these Levites did not receive all the tithes in Israel, but actually received only those tithes "that the Israelites presented as an offering to the Lord" at the temple in Jerusalem. This was only 10 percent of the total tithes collected at the local storehouses in all the towns throughout Israel. For it is written:

> ... the Levites are to bring a *tenth* of the *tithes* up to the house of our God, to the storeroom of the treasury ... where the gatekeepers and the singers stay. (Neh. 10:38b, 39b; see also Num. 18:26 NIV; emphasis added)

Therefore, my interpretation of Numbers 18:21, 24 is the following:

> I give to the particular Levites who serve at the Tent of Meeting a portion of all the tithes in Israel as their inheritance. Otherwise, these particular Levites would receive no inheritance among the Israelites. So instead, I give to these Levites, as their inheritance, that portion of the tithes that the Israelites present as an offering to the Lord in Jerusalem, which is 10 percent of the total tithes collected throughout all Israel!

In this way, the Levites who left their homes and gave up their normal inheritance to serve God in the temple at Jerusalem (as priests, gatekeepers, and singers) would receive 10 percent of the national tithe as their inheritance from God. This would support them during their entire lifetime, or at least during the months or years which they served at the temple of God.

There was a *second* subgroup of Levites who left their homes and became a special class of:

> ... Levites (who had no inheritance of their own) ... (Deut. 14:29a NIV)

You see, many Levites probably felt called by God to leave their homes and families to serve God in the many other non-Levite cities by collecting, protecting, and distributing the local tithe to the poor. For it is written:

> And we will bring a tithe of our crops to the Levites, for it is the Levites who *collect* the tithes in all the towns where we work. (Neh. 10:37b NIV; emphasis added)

In other words, the tithe again became a special inheritance for those particular "Levites who had no inheritance of their own" because they had given it up (possibly for the rest of their lives) to serve God with "missionary zeal" in one of the other non-Levite towns to collect, protect, and distribute the local tithe to the poor. These particular Levites also had no inheritance which they could leave to their children. Therefore, they were entirely supported by the gifts of God through the local tithe. For it is written:

> And do not neglect the Levites living in *your* towns for they have *no* allotment or inheritance of their own. (Deut. 14:27 NIV; emphasis added)

Since 10 percent of the national tithe was reserved by God for the Levites who were the priests, gatekeepers, and singers serving at the temple in Jerusalem as a payment for their services (Neh. 10:38b, 39b), it's highly likely that God intended for another 10 percent of the tithe to be reserved for the local priests and other Levites who would collect, protect, and distribute the tithe to the poor in the non-Levite cities and towns throughout Israel. This would leave approximately 80 percent of the national tithe to be reserved for the poor, the widows, the fatherless orphans, and the aliens who became poor after living in Israel for a while, and if he had no family in Israel to support him.

So, I believe this was the way God originally intended the tithe to be collected and "spent." According to the Bible, the process entails:

1. reserving 10 percent of the tithe (as the "inheritance") for those Levites who served in the temple at Jerusalem,
2. reserving another 10 percent of the tithe (as the "inheritance") for the local priests and Levites who collect, protect, and distribute the tithe to the poor in the non-Levite cities and towns, and,
3. reserving the final 80 percent for the widows, the orphans, and those poor who did not belong to any large extended families in Israel who could support them.

And of course, since the tithe was supposed to be an "inheritance" of the Levites, it appears as though none of the Levites themselves were required to pay the tithe in the first place. This would allow the income of the Levites to be 10 percent higher than non-Levites. This "extra" 10 percent would also be God's gift to each Levite family as if it were an inheritance.

Some of the tithe which was brought by the Israelites to the temple was actually supposed to be eaten by the Israelites before the Lord as a celebration of their commitment to Him and the Lord's commitment to them. For it is written:

> Eat the tithe of your grain, new wine and oil, and the first-born of your herds and flocks in the presence of the Lord your God at the place he will choose as a dwelling place for his name . . . you and your household shall eat there in the presence of the Lord your God and rejoice. And do not neglect the Levites living in your towns, for they have no allotment of their own. (Deut. 14:23a, 26b, 27 NIV)

God did not want the entire tithe to be eaten at Jerusalem, but only a small portion of it. The rest of the tithe was supposed to be left with the Levites in a person's local town. Unfortunately, there was a great temptation to bring only the required 10 percent of an individual's tithe to Jerusalem and eat a portion of it in front of the priests while merely *pretending* to have left the other 90 percent at the local storehouse. As a result, God said that the Israelites were "robbing him" and that there wasn't enough food in the local storehouse to feed the poor because of the disobedience of the tithers. For it is written:

> ... you are robbing me. Bring the whole tithe into the storehouse, that there may be food in my house. (Mal. 3:9b, 10a NIV)

Now the Levites were evidently supposed to distribute about 80 percent of the tithe to those widows, fatherless, and poor aliens who did not have any family in Israel to care for them. In this way, these poor would have access to fresh fruits and vegetables at harvest, as well as a more regular supply of food made from stored grains. They would also be eligible to receive money from the tithe to help them pay other bills.

The tithe was supposed to be brought to the storehouse every three years. For it is written:

> At the end of three years, even the same year, you shall bring forth all the tithes of your increase and shall lay it up within your gates. (Deut. 14:28: Green Sr., Jay. *The Interlinear Bible*, second ed.)

As a practical matter however, the tithe itself was probably divided into two parts: the nonperishable tithe, and the perishable tithe. The nonperishable tithe consisted chiefly of money and animals, such as sheep, goats, cattle, horses, donkeys, camels, and chickens. These nonperishable items most likely represented that portion of the tithe which was supposed to be brought to the Levites every three years (Deut. 14:28 NIV). The perishable tithe consisted of fruits, vegetables, grains, and grape juice ("new wine"). Generally, these items needed to be brought to the Levites on a more regular basis—probably with every harvest.

Some tithable items could be extremely perishable—such as milk, eggs, and fish. It would be very impractical for every farmer or fisherman to bring a daily tithe of milk, eggs, or fish to the local storehouse if they lived too far away. God's laws appear to allow a great deal of flexibility for the tithers and Levites in following these principles. For instance, suppose there were seven chicken farmers, seven cattle farmers, and seven fishermen, all living in the same local area. The Levites could then assign each farmer or fisherman a different day of the week on which to bring a fresh tithe of their weekly production of milk, eggs, and fish (with a double amount on Friday so the tithers won't have to transport their tithe on the Sabbath) into the storehouse. In this way, the Levites would have fresh milk, eggs, and fish available to eat each day and to distribute to the widows, the fatherless, and the poor aliens. With this in mind, the Levites might also suggest to the local tithers that the storehouse is in more need of some things and less of others. This would allow the Israelites the option of bringing in a tithe composed of a greater amount of the requested items, as long as it was approximately of equal value to the tithe they owed anyway.

So, imagine that each local storehouse would be run in some way like a modern rescue mission. Most local rescue missions are administered by godly Christian elders who feel that God has called them to enter this type of ministry—just as the ancient Levite might feel God has called him to be a missionary, so he moves to a non-Levite town to run the local storehouse as a form of tithe-sponsored welfare support for the poor. Moreover, the ancient Levite (just like the modern rescue mission administrator) must also develop an in-depth knowledge of the *needs* of the local poor, as well as a knowledge of the local *resources* to help the poor. Therefore, both the ancient Levite and the modern rescue mission administrator would probably also inform their tithers and donors to consider matching the types of donations with the specific needs of the poor being served.

Most importantly, these dedicated godly Levite men of faith could also share the gospel while they share the food, etc.—a gospel of salvation by grace through faith in Jehovah, a God who loves to forgive the sins of repentant Israelites who walk in contrite, obedient surrender to His Will. So also, Christian volunteers at modern rescue missions can share this gospel message, with the additional revelation that it was this same Jehovah God who personally returned to earth to become our Messiah and Savior—Jesus Christ—to die on the cross as the perfect atonement for all the sins of mankind.

I expect that this God-given welfare program would not only work very well for ancient Israel, but would work even better for modern America. Our twentieth-century methods of refrigeration, preservation, and computer information exchange, would give modern America the capacity to administer a tithe-sponsored welfare program far more efficiently and with even greater flexibility today than in the days of the ancient Levites.

Who is Eligible to Receive Financial Support from the National Tithe?

The Bible gives us three categories of poor people who are eligible to receive the tithe (other than the Levites, whose job it is to collect, protect, and distribute the tithe to the poor in the first place). These three categories of recipients are: the widows, the fatherless, and the aliens. For it is written:

> When you have finished setting aside a tenth of all your produce . . . you shall give it to the Levite, the alien, the

fatherless and the widow, so that they may eat in your towns and be satisfied. (Deut. 26:12 NIV)

And,

... bring all the tithes ... and store it in your towns, so that the Levites ... and the aliens, the fatherless and the widows who live in your towns may come and eat and be satisfied ... (Deut. 14:28-29 NIV)

When the Bible says that the tithe was to provide the needs of the orphans, the widows, and the aliens, so they "may come and eat and be satisfied (Deut. 14:28-29 NIV), it is clear that the poor are not coming to eat once every three years, or once a year at harvest, but are coming to eat regularly and be satisfied. Therefore, this verse is referring to a source of food and/or financial aid which was supposed to be regularly available, to be used as needed by the poor, either on a temporary or a permanent basis. Whether this would be a temporary or a permanent source of assistance for any given citizen was to be decided by the Levites who are in charge of distributing the tithe.

TITHE SUPPORT FOR WIDOWS AND ORPHANS

The use of the national tithe in the Old Testament parallels the use of the gifts of the church in the New Testament, for a portion of these New Testament gifts were also used to support the poor widows in the church. It is interesting, however, that not all widows were eligible to receive support from the church. In fact, there were two classes of widows who were not eligible to receive permanent financial support from the church: the "young" widows who were less than sixty years old, and those widows (young or old) who had families which could support them.

If the widows were less than sixty years old, the Bible teaches that they should not be placed on the list of widows who would permanently be supported by the church, for evidently they were "too young." These widows may have been able to be supported by the gifts of the church temporarily until they had a chance to marry again (or move back in with their parents or siblings, or find some kind of work to support themselves), but they would not be placed on the list of those who would be supported permanently by the church. For it is written:

No widow may be put on the list of widows unless she is over sixty ... As for younger widows, do not put them on such a list ... So I counsel the younger widows to marry, to have children, to manage their homes ... (2 Tim. 5:9a, 11a, 14a NIV)

As I mentioned, if the widows had families to support them, then again they should not be supported by the church, but should be supported by their families instead. For it is written:

> If any woman who is a believer has widows in her family, she should help them and *not* let the church be burdened with them, so that the church can help those widows who are really in need. (1 Tim. 5:16 NIV; emphasis added)

And again it is written:

> But if a widow has children or grandchildren, these should learn first of all to put their religion into practice by caring for their own family and so repaying their parents and grandparents, for this is pleasing to God. (1 Tim. 5:4 NIV)

So, God wants the younger widows (those less than sixty-years-old) to try to get married again, so their future husbands will support them instead of the church. And, God wants the older widows (those more than sixty-years-old) to be taken care of by their families (if they have families), so the church can take care of those widows who are really in need because they have no families to help support them.

Since "God doesn't change his mind" (Num. 23:19 NIV), it is also clear that God would use these same guidelines for administering the Old Testament tithe as well as the New Testament gifts of the church—only widows who are greater than sixty-years-old and who have no families to support them would be eligible to receive the tithe on a permanent basis.

Notice that the elderly per se (who are not widows or widowers) are not mentioned as being eligible to receive financial support from either the Old Testament tithe or the New Testament gifts of the church. This is because God wants the elderly who have families (whether or not they are widows or widowers) to be taken care of by their own families, and not become a burden to the church or to the local tithe.

Apparently, at that time there were societies of unbelievers who did provide for their own relatives, and the Bible teaches that any Christian who does not follow these biblical commands has "denied the faith and is worse than the unbelievers." For it is written:

> If anyone does not provide for his relatives, and especially for his immediate family, he has denied the faith and is worse than an unbeliever. (1 Tim. 5:8 NIV)

One of God's high priorities is for each family to provide financial support for their own family members who cannot support themselves. This would include temporary support for those family members who are temporarily sick or unemployed, and permanent support for family members who are permanently disabled by injury, illness, or extreme age. The most cost-efficient way to implement this pro-family legislation is for the entire family to live together so they can enjoy a triple economy of scale: shared possessions, shared labor, and shared expenses.

Notice that these commands represent a biblical form of pro-family legislation which also should promote the development of larger families, as well as promote a culture which encourages a strong feeling of responsibility for taking care of those within your own family. However, when the American government gives away tax-sponsored social security money to the elderly, this sponsors the ability of the elderly to live apart from their family. This encourages the mistaken belief that it is the role of government (not the family) to take care of our nation's elderly.

THE TITHE SHOULD SUPPORT THE "INNOCENT"— NOT THE "IMMORAL"

The poverty of the widows and the fatherless occurs through no fault of their own—they are innocent victims of circumstance. For it is not the fault of the widow that she is a widow, nor is it the fault of the orphan that he is an orphan. In other words, presumably neither the widow nor the fatherless orphan did any punishable sinful activity which resulted in the circumstances which caused their poverty.

So, by reserving the tithe for the widows and the fatherless, the Bible teaches that the tithe is to be given only to the *innocent* poor, and *not* to be given to those citizens whose punishable sinful activity has in some way caused them to become poor. In fact, in Deuteronomy (14:29 and 26:12) there is no indication that God ever wanted tithe-sponsored welfare to be given to citizens who were impoverished as a consequence of their own sins.

For example, the Bible does not say to give the tithe to unwed mothers who have become impoverished as a result of becoming pregnant through the sin of premarital sex or adultery with a married man. In addition, the Bible does not say to give the tithe to those who are disabled by the consequences of their sins either, such as those who suffer from advanced liver disease (as a result of repetitive drunkenness), or those who suffer from advanced syphilis (from sexual immorality). In fact, if AIDS had existed in ancient Israel, it would also have been against God's Will to give tithe-sponsored welfare support to those who became permanently disabled by AIDS—*if* their illness was the result of the sin of homosexuality, adultery, fornication, prostitution, or intravenous drug abuse! (AIDS could never flourish in a biblical society anyway because those sins against God which help to spread AIDS would also be punishable crimes against the state!) So according to the Bible, all these groups would be ineligible to receive financial support from tithe-sponsored welfare when they became either impoverished or disabled as a natural consequence of their sins. As a result, the number of citizens on tithe-sponsored welfare would be drastically reduced in a biblical society.

Furthermore, most people who have become single parents as a result of divorces in America would also probably not have been eligible to receive financial support from the Old Testament tithe. Since all divorces were supposed to be the result of one spouse committing serious sins against God—which were also crimes against the state (for which the "guilty" spouse could receive a "merciful divorce" as an alternative to being executed or whipped)—then the *innocent* spouse (who would still be eligible for tithe support) would probably *not need* tithe support in the first place. This is because he or she would still retain possession of all the family's property, which could be used as a source of income. However, the *guilty* spouse (who has lost the property rights) would *not be eligible* for tithe support, and so would have to go back to his or her parents or siblings for financial assistance.

The Bible teaches that tithe-sponsored welfare was not to be given to those people whose sins caused them to be poor. Furthermore, I believe the Bible teaches that if a person was already receiving tithe-sponsored welfare and then started to commit fornication, adultery, homosexuality, or drunkenness, that God would want that person's financial support from the tithe to be cut off. He would want him or her to be prosecuted for his crimes of immorality and drunkenness as well.

For certainly in the Old Testament, if a spouse became either sexually immoral or a drunkard, he or she could be divorced (Deut. 24:1 NIV) with the implication that the family would no longer financially support him or her. Since the spouse is being "punished" by receiving a divorce (as a merciful alternative to execution or whipping), he or she certainly would no longer be eligible to receive financial support from the ex-in-laws. Likewise, he or she certainly is not eligible to be a burden on society by receiving a portion of the tithe either.

For the tithe was not designed by God to support sinners who ordinarily should have been executed or whipped for their sins, but instead received a merciful divorce. You see, if divorced sinners could be eligible for financial support through the tithe, this would encourage further sexual immorality and drunkenness, not discourage it. And all God's principles were divinely designed to discourage sin, not to encourage it.

In the New Testament, since Paul warns about withholding financial support from those young widows who merely "get into the habit of being idle and . . . become gossips and busybodies . . ." (2 Thess. 5:13

NIV), then you can be absolutely sure that God would want those who began to commit more serious sins (such as fornication, adultery, homosexuality, or drunkenness) to also be cut off from receiving any permanent financial support from either the gifts of the church or from tithe-sponsored welfare.

By ignoring God's commands, America has mistakenly developed a welfare policy which has no moral restrictions at all and which encourages welfare-dependency. So, Americans are burdened by having to pay billions of dollars of unnecessary extra taxes to support a welfare-dependent society. Such a society is made up, in large part, of:

1. unwed mothers (from the sin of fornication),
2. other single parents (from the sin of "leaving your wife or husband" without biblical grounds),
3. those permanently disabled by AIDS (from the sins of homosexuality, adultery, fornication, and prostitution), and
4. those permanently disabled by the natural consequences of the sins of drunkenness and drug abuse.

In fact, the large numbers of welfare recipients today who are either unwed mothers, drunkards, drug addicts, or those disabled from diseases caused from the sins of fornication, adultery, and homosexuality, would not even exist in a biblical society. This is a sign that God's laws against these sins are not being enforced. These problems should be taken care of by God's justice system, so they will not have to be taken care by God's welfare system. But, because America has chosen to ignore God's principles of moral law, civil law, and civil law enforcement, her burden of sin has become burden of taxes for welfare support!

The Bible teaches that a person's character is important in deciding who gets supported by "tithe-welfare." Therefore, the Levites were supposed to withhold food or tithe support from certain applicants if they refused to live a good, moral life.

No Tithe Support for the "Lazy"

If applicants for the tithe were just lazy and would not work, the Bible says they should not be eligible to eat a portion of the food provided by church gifts. For it is written:

> For even when we were with you, this we commanded you, that if any would not *work*, neither should he *eat*. For we hear that there are some which walk among you disorderly, working not at all, but are busybodies. Now them that are such we command and exhort by our Lord Jesus Christ, that with quietness they work, and eat their own bread. (2 Thess. 3:10-11 KJV; emphasis added)

If lazy people who did not work were ineligible to receive financial support from the Church in the New Testament, then you can be equally sure that they would also be ineligible to receive tithe-sponsored welfare assistance from the Levites in the Old Testament.

Therefore, the biblical principles of tithe-supported welfare *discourage* laziness and irresponsibility. In contrast, the principles of American welfare *encourage* laziness and irresponsibility.

TITHE SUPPORT FOR THE "ALIEN"

Since the local tithe was meant to be distributed to those people who could not take care of themselves (like fatherless orphans and older widows who have no family to care for them), it becomes clear that the only aliens who would be eligible to receive the tithe would not be rich aliens (like "the Wise Men" who visited baby Jesus, or the Queen of Sheba who visited Solomon), but would be poor aliens who had no family within Israel to support them. However, this does not imply that Israel was to become an international magnet to attract all the world's poor to emigrate to Israel. You see, God told the Israelites that they should help the alien (just like one of their own countrymen) if he *becomes* poor, not if he *arrives* poor. In other words, when an alien has been living in Israel, supporting himself and his family, and then becomes poor through no fault of his own, then the alien and his family would become eligible for receiving support from the local tithe. For it is written:

> If one of your countrymen *becomes* poor and is unable to support himself among you, help him as you would an alien or a temporary resident, so he can continue to live among you. (Lev. 25:35 NIV; emphasis added)

I believe this means that they were supposed to help the Israelite who *becomes* poor the same way they should help the alien who *becomes* poor, so they could continue to live in Israel. God was saying that the Israelites were to help aliens who *became* poor while living in Israel, not those aliens who just *arrived* and were already poor. Otherwise, this would cause a massive immigration of poor immigrants to enter Israel which would totally consume Israel's tithe-sponsored welfare system, so there would be nothing left for any of the poor Israelites themselves.

The only aliens eligible for financial assistance from the tithe would be those aliens who were already living within Israel, supporting themselves, and paying their tithes to the Levites to support others who were poor, and then they themselves became poor sometime later on. Only these aliens would be eligible to receive support from the local tithe, probably at the discretion of the Levites. If the aliens were just lazy and would not work, the Bible says then they should not be eligible to eat a portion of the tithe either. Remember it is written:

> ... if any would not work, neither should he eat. (2 Thess. 3:10 NIV)

Therefore, everyone living in Israel (whether Israelite or alien) must work hard and learn to support himself and his family in order to avoid becoming dependent upon the tithe for prolonged periods. For the tithe was designed to be only a temporary provision for those who were temporarily unemployed, temporarily too sick to work, or a permanent provision for those who were permanently disabled or too elderly to work and yet had no family to care for them. So, if the Levites felt the Israelite (or the Alien) was just lazy and was inappropriately prolonging his dependence upon the tithe, then the Levites could refuse to support him.

America however, violates these biblical principles, and as a result, our tax-supported welfare system spends billions of dollars to support millions of impoverished immigrants who continue to overflow our borders and inundate our system of welfare. We have become an international magnet to attract all the impoverished people of the world, and this was one of the very things that God's principles of immigration and welfare were designed to prevent.

ADVANTAGES OF TITHE-SPONSORED WELFARE COMPARED TO TAX-SPONSORED WELFARE

What are the advantages of administering the national tithe as a form of welfare support for the poor in comparison to the way we do it in America today?

First of all, the tithe is administered locally, by people who actually know you personally. They know if you are truly poor or truly disabled, so it's much harder to fool them and get away with "tithe fraud" than it is to get away with "welfare fraud." After all, the Levites who collected, protected, and distributed the tithe were the very neighbors of the applicants for the tithe. So, it would be much harder to pretend to be disabled without your own neighbors eventually "catching you" at it.

Secondly, the local citizens would feel much more guilt if they fraudulently took tithe money given by their own neighbors (as a gift to God to support the poor), than to fraudulently take money from the government. So once again, there are natural restraints in place in God's system which help to avoid fraud, while in our current system (in America) there are no natural restraints, but only regulations, paperwork, and penalties to help avoid welfare fraud.

Thirdly, the poor man can now say, "My God supplies all my needs through the local tithe given generously by my own neighbors, and I am humbled and grateful for the grace extended to my family and me in our time of need." This good attitude may encourage him and his family to attend church more regularly. He is sure to recognize his dependence upon God to supply his needs, and this will encourage him to develop a better relationship with Christ and with others who attend his church. However, currently in America the poor man thinks, "My atheistic and corrupt government supplies all my needs by forcing everybody to pay a huge tax burden, so I deserve whatever I can get, because my government owes me!" This bad attitude will certainly not teach him or his family to depend upon God for their needs, nor will it help them to build a closer relationship with Christ or with those in the church.

Fourth, after implementing God's view of court reform and justice reform, sins against God—such as premarital sex, adultery, homosexuality, drunkenness, drug abuse, wife abuse, and child abuse—would become rare because of the stiff penalties associated with these crimes. Divorce would again become illegal unless the spouse had committed one of these sins for which he or she would be prosecuted and possibly executed, whipped, or divorced as a merciful alternative to execution. As a result, there would be very few applicants for tithe-sponsored welfare who would be unwed mothers, divorced, or permanently disabled by the consequences of the sins of drunkenness or drug abuse. This is because these sins are dealt with first by the justice system so they won't have to be dealt with by the welfare system!

Fifth, once an applicant is approved by the Levites to become a recipient of the local tithe, he or she will notice that these same moral restrictions still apply. You see, there are moral restraints in God's system of tithe-sponsored welfare, but there are no moral restraints in man's system of tax-sponsored welfare. For instance, a previously approved recipient of the local tithe cannot begin to live in sin or get pregnant by committing fornication or adultery and expect that he or she will continue to be eligible to be a recipient of the local tithe. Nor can any recipients expect future financial support if they begin to commit homosexuality, drunkenness, or drug abuse, for they not only risk losing any consideration of financial support from the tithe, but also risk criminal prosecution for committing these sins. So, not only are there moral restrictions for applicants to be eligible for tithe-sponsored welfare, but there are also moral restrictions for recipients to continue to participate in tithe-sponsored welfare. In other words, God's system of tithe-sponsored welfare *discourages* sin, while man's system of tax-sponsored welfare *encourages* sin.

Lastly, God's system of tithe-sponsored welfare reform encourages families to stay together, whereas man's system of tax-sponsored welfare reform financially sponsors the ability of the poor, disabled, and elderly to live separately from their own families and therefore becomes a form of anti-family legislation.

These are the six advantages of God's system of tithe-sponsored welfare compared to man's system of tax-sponsored welfare.

THE *SIX-YEAR* WORK PROGRAM FOR THE POOR *ISRAELITES*

This last means of welfare support was designed by God probably for those poor Israelites whom the Levites felt should no longer be eligible to receive tithe benefits. This was because they were perceived to be healthy enough to easily find work, yet always remained unemployed and impoverished, probably in part because of their laziness. Allowing such healthy people to continue receiving a share of the tithe would eventually encourage a culture of tithe welfare dependent citizens which would consume the entire national tithe, so there would be nothing left for those who were truly in need.

Therefore, God gave the Levites the discretion to decide whether certain healthy applicants would possibly be better off in a "work program" than being perpetually dependent upon the tithe for support. This divinely creative means of supporting impoverished individuals or families involved commanding some of the rich businessmen (whether farmers, merchants, or cattlemen) to be willing to enroll the poor Israelite in a six-year work program in their own businesses. During this time, the wealthy businessman would pay for all the costs of shelter, food, clothing, and medical care (possibly for his family as well), because the poor man could not afford to pay for these things on his own. In return, the poor man would work very hard for the wealthy man, but would receive no wages at all—that is, until the day he was "released from his six-year commitment." At the time of release, he was to receive a large departing bonus from the wealthy businessman, so he could start life over again with a "small savings." This way, he would not immediately become poor again. In this manner, the work program became a hand-*up*, and not a handout!

In addition, after working six days a week for six years, he probably would never be lazy again because of his "reformed work habits" and would probably continue to work hard for the rest of his life. He also had the option to request to continue to work for the employer as a hired hand, and from then on receive regular wages—although he would no longer receive free shelter and free food, etc.

This "work program" actually involved the "buying" of Hebrew servants for a period of six years, after which time they were to "go free, without paying anything." For it is written:

> If you buy a Hebrew servant, he is to serve you for six years, but in the seventh year he is to go free, without paying anything. (Exod. 21:2 NIV)

Again, it is written:

> If a fellow Hebrew, a man or a woman, sells himself to you and serves you six years, in the seventh year you must let him go free. And when you release him, do not send him away empty handed. Supply him liberally from your flock, your threshing floor and your winepress. Give to him as the Lord your God has blessed you . . . Do not consider it a hardship to set your servant free, because his service to you these six years has been worth twice as much as that of a hired hand. (Deut. 15:12-14, 18 NIV)

Please notice that the poor man, woman, or family is given a large departing bonus at the end of the six years, so they can start life over again without being poor and without having to steal. In addition, the man probably has developed much better work habits which I just mentioned, so he will be less likely to ever again allow himself to become lazy, unemployed, and impoverished. Also notice that this six year work program becomes very profitable for both the servant and employer (as long as the program continues for the required six years), yet it does not require any public taxes to run it!

So here we have a divinely designed work program to provide welfare for the poor which:

1. costs no taxes to implement,
2. restores a stronger work ethic to the servant and to the entire culture, and,
3. makes a profit for both the employer and the servant!

Only our all-wise Lord Jesus Christ could have designed such a wonderful system of welfare, as part of His biblical blueprint for perfect self-government.

(By the way, this same type of six-year work program was also designed by God to be an alternative to a tax-sponsored prison system for thieves who could not pay back double (or up to sevenfold) the price of the item or animal which they had stolen! For further details, please review chapter ten.)

If however, the year of Jubilee (the fiftieth year) comes before the six year work program is finished, then the businessman is to set the servant free, and not wait until his six-year work program is finished. For it is written:

> If one of your countrymen becomes poor among you and sells himself to you, do not make him work as a slave. He is to be treated as a hired worker or a temporary resident among you; he is to work for you until the year of Jubilee. Then he and his children are to be released, and he will go back to his

own clan and to the property of his forefathers. Because the Israelites are my servants . . . they must not be sold as slaves. Do not rule over them ruthlessly . . . (Lev. 25:39-43 NIV)

Since the servant will be returning to his own large, extended family and to his family's property in the year of Jubilee, it is no longer an absolute requirement for the master to send his servant away with a large, departing bonus of flocks, herds, or vintage, etc. It is expected that he will now be supported by his own family, so he will not immediately become poor again or again become dependent upon tithe-sponsored welfare.

The only exception to this rule would probably be the thieves who are sold as servants to pay off a debt for stolen goods (Exod. 22:3 NIV). Thieves would probably have to work the entire six years to pay back their debt, regardless of whether this overlapped with the year of Jubilee. If thieves knew that, if caught, they would only serve a maximum of a few days, weeks, or months in a work program because by law they had to be freed as soon as the year of Jubilee began, the crime rate for theft would increase markedly immediately prior to the year of Jubilee.

The poor Israelite servant (who was not a thief) was only required to work either six years or until the year of Jubilee (whichever came first), and the Israelite always retained his right to demand to be "set free" at any time (Lev. 25:48 NIV). However, if he is "set free" before the six-year work program is completed, he will probably lose his departing bonus as well as his chance to be "set free" without payment. This is because God evidently feels it takes six years of work to make the system profitable enough to pay for itself. Otherwise, no Israelite businessmen would be willing to risk paying the purchase price for the Israelite (by paying off the Israelites's debts) plus the cost of six years of free shelter, food, clothing, and medical care for any healthy, poor stranger, if the stranger could be released for free at any time, without having to work long enough to make a reasonable profit for the businessman.

So, even though the poor Israelite servant could demand to be set free, he (or his family) would still have to buy his freedom for whatever price "the employer demands and the court allows." The precedent for this "price bidding" involves a biblical story where a man accidently injures a pregnant woman who goes into premature labor but still delivers a healthy, but premature baby. Of course, since there are increased costs involved in caring for a premature infant, God commanded that "the offender must be fined whatever the woman's husband demands and the court allows" (Exod. 21:22 NIV). As a result, I believe that the price to free an Israelite servant (as well arbitrating other types of business contracts) would also be based upon the same precedent of "whatever the employer demands and the court allows." The price requested by the employer would probably be based upon the expenses incurred by the employer—the original purchase price for the servant plus the expenses of providing free shelter, food, clothing, and medical care for the servant up to that time.

In addition, it is probable that judges may not even allow the Israelite servant to be set free early, if the Levites (who administer the local tithe) testify that this servant would have no other visible means of support; and the Levites would again refuse to provide tithe support for this man because of his history of chronic laziness.

THE *LIFE LONG* WORK PROGRAM FOR POOR *ALIENS*

The concept of work programs was designed by God to not only provide the last resort of welfare support for poor Israelite citizens, but also for poor aliens from foreign countries as well. However, there are some significant differences between the way God commanded these work programs to be administered for the poor Israelites as compared to how He instructed these programs to be administered for aliens who had come from foreign nations.

The work program for aliens did not last a mere six years, but the Israelite "owner" had the option to make it last an entire lifetime. God did not require him to set his *alien* servants free in the year of Jubilee, yet was required to set only his *Israelite* servants free during that year. In this way, although the Israelite servant remained a servant for only six years, the alien servant could actually become a slave for life at the discretion of the slave owner. For it is written:

> Your male and female slaves are to come from the nations around you; from them you may buy slaves. You may also buy some of the temporary residents living among you and members of their clans born in your country. You can will them to your children as inherited property and can make them slaves for life, but you must not rule over your fellow Israelites ruthlessly. (Lev. 25:44-46 NIV)

Generally, the only way that an alien family would be willing to sell some of their members as slaves would be if they were too poor to support themselves. So, I believe that this type of slavery was designed by God also as an alternative to a tax-sponsored form of welfare support for poor aliens living within Israel's borders, who otherwise might starve, or live in poverty and squalor.

In addition, this philosophy of welfare was designed to not only encourage a strong work ethic within the Israelites, but also within the aliens who would want to come to Israel. The aliens who were either lazy or poor had to realize that they could not just go to Israel and become welfare dependent on the national tithe. By doing so, they and their family could risk becoming slaves of the Israelites for life if they became impoverished and dependent upon the state.

If the Levites discovered that some of the aliens were impoverished because they were merely lazy and refused to work hard and hold down a job, then those who were lazy (just as any lazy Israelite) would be cut off from receiving the tithe as a form of welfare support, and required to enter a work program to survive. Then, the future master would most likely purchase the servant through the courts and the purchase price would be designed to pay off the debts that either the Israelite or the alien owed to his creditors. So generally, (up until the time they were sold to a master) both Israelites and aliens were treated in the same way if they became impoverished and welfare-dependent as a result of refusing to find steady work.

However, there are two important differences between what happens to the Israelite and the alien after they are sold to a master. The Israelite must be set free either at the end of six years, or (if he is not a thief who was sold to pay off double what he had stolen) he must be set free in the year of Jubilee (whichever comes first). In other words, the Israelite could not be forcibly made a slave for life. But, the alien could (at the discretion of the master) actually be made a slave for the rest of his life and even willed to the master's children.

This welfare policy was also to function as an immigration policy which provided a warning to all of the surrounding nations of the serious consequences of immigrating to Israel and "allowing" yourself and your family to become impoverished and dependent upon the support of others. The proclamation of these consequences among the nations would drastically limit the number of undesirable aliens who were lazy and who would want to immigrate into Israel. This was God's protection to Israel—to keep them from becoming a welfare state as the United States has become! America, however, ignores God's immigration policy and so, we are overrun by immigrants who are idolatrous, immoral, and idle. So, our welfare system is overburdened by them as well.

Briefly, God's immigration policy involved keeping the three "I's" out of Israel: idolatry, immorality, and idleness. By strictly enforcing God's laws against these, the aliens who were idolatrous, immoral, or idle would choose never to move to Israel. For they knew that if they committed these sins within Israel's borders, they would be executed (idolatry), whipped or forgiven (immorality), or possibly enslaved (idleness) if they allowed themselves to become poor, overwhelmingly in debt, and cut off from tithe-sponsored welfare support.

When we consider God's view of servanthood and enslavement as the last resort of welfare support, it becomes clear that a poor person's financial security is more important to God than is his personal freedom. Americans believe that personal freedom—to "be all you can be" and "go where you want to go, and do what you want to do"—is more important than financial security. As usual, man is more interested in what happens to the *individual* than what happens to the entire *nation!* Since God wants to love and to care for the entire nation as his family, it is natural that He wants to do what is most loving for the entire nation—even if it is at the expense of an individual's freedom.

(This is similar to God's view of prison reform. America's view is to punish criminals in a way which also punishes the innocent public (by increasing their tax burden to pay for expensive, dangerous, and overcrowded prisons). However, God's view is to punish criminals without imposing any tax burden at all on the innocent public. You see, God wants to do the most loving thing for the entire nation, even if it requires punishing unrepentant sinners in a way which most Americans do not like.)

WHY DID GOD ALLOW SLAVES AND SERVANTS TO BE BEATEN WHEN THEY DID NOT WORK?

Remember, it is the healthy, but lazy and idle Israelite or alien who is so poor and so overwhelmingly in debt (because he refuses to hold down a steady job), who ultimately is the one who is forced to enter these work programs and become an Israelite servant or alien slave to begin with.

Why does God allow them to get beaten if they become servants or slaves and continue to be lazy and not work? First of all, because of their laziness, these men have been punishing their wives and families by unnecessary impoverishment and public humiliation for months, or even years. The public humiliation comes when the wives have to repeatedly ask the merchants to allow them to purchase food and other merchandise at cost because of their unnecessary impoverishment caused by their husband's laziness.

Secondly, the laziness of these father figures also punishes the businessmen of the community, for the farmers and merchants are required by God to make no profit off the poor when selling them food and other merchandise (Lev. 25:37 NIV). Hopefully, these farmers and merchants are willing to make no profit off the poor when their poverty has resulted from disability, illness, or death of the "breadwinner." When the family is poor because the breadwinner is merely lazy, idle, and refuses to hold down a job and support his family, then the farmers and merchants will become angry. This is because the breadwinner's laziness is now punishing the businessmen by costing them money and profit.

Thirdly, the entire community is punished as well because they are required to give zero-interest loans, which must be canceled every Sabbath year, to a family which is impoverished solely because of the husband's laziness.

Fourthly, other poor people are also punished when the lazy and idle poor inappropriately consume portions of tithe-sponsored welfare, which should be reserved for those who are more deserving of welfare support, whose poverty is not the result of their own idleness or sin.

As a result, this man's laziness is punishing everybody but himself! His family is punished by poverty and humiliation; the businessmen are punished by having to sell food and other merchandise to them at cost; and, the entire community is punished by having to give them periodic, small zero-interest loans which must be canceled every Sabbath year. Even the poor are punished because this man's family may now be using up the tithe and preventing the Levites from supporting those poor families who are truly in need.

Since the law does not make laziness a punishable crime, then the man cannot be punished because of his laziness. So, everyone gets punished, but the lazy one gets off "Scot-free."

God designed these work programs as a last resort of welfare support to reverse this injustice. For, in these work programs:

1. the *family* is provided for by the master;
2. the *businessmen* get their losses back from the purchase price of the servant or slave, and also no longer have to sell the family food and other merchandise at cost;
3. the *community* no longer has to provide small zero-interest-loans for the family which must be canceled every Sabbath year;
4. the *truly poor* are no longer deprived of their rightful portion of tithe-sponsored welfare, now that the lazy and idle poor are provided for by the six-year work program, and finally,
5. the *lazy bum* can now get punished by a whipping if he continues to be lazy!

In other words, this terrible injustice—where a man's laziness can financially punish his family, the merchants, and the entire community—has now been totally reversed by divine justice, which restores financial security to the family, the merchants, and the community, and focuses the punishment on the lazy bum instead.

America has the same problems that Israel had, for the laziness of some of our American men also:

1. punishes their *families* with poverty and welfare dependency;
2. punishes the *truly poor* by depriving them of precious welfare resources which were unnecessarily consumed by families who are impoverished only because of the laziness of the "breadwinner"; and,
3. punishes *society* with an ever increasing tax burden to support an ever-expanding tax-sponsored welfare system!

America, like Israel, has the same problems for which God gave Israel these principles of welfare reform. And America, like Israel, continues to ignore God's solutions.

One last reason why God allowed the lazy servant or slave to be whipped if he does not work is that this will eventually get the servant to work hard enough so that the master can make enough money to recoup the purchase price of the servant, as well as continue to provide free shelter, food, clothing and medical care for the servant and his family, and make a profit as well. And remember, the master must also make enough profit off of the Israelite servant so that he can put aside a large, departing bonus for the Israelite and his family (to be given to them when he sets them free at the end of six years). (This last part does not apply to the alien slave however.)

God's Laws to Prevent Cruelty to Alien Slaves and to Israelite Servants

God gave the Israelites seven laws which were designed to prevent masters from being cruel to their alien slaves. These laws were created so the kindness shown to the alien slaves by their Israelite masters would be an example for all the world to follow. Furthermore, these seven guidelines and restrictions would change the purpose of slavery within Israel from one of *cruelty* to provide *wealth* for the rich slave owner, to one of *kindness* to provide *welfare* for the poor alien and his family.

Taken in this manner, slavery within Israel was supposed to be viewed as a last resort of welfare support for impoverished alien families whose father figure never held down a steady job, and who the community was tired of supporting them with:

1. multiple interest-free loans which were never paid back,
2. selling them food and merchandise at cost (without making any profit),
3. and letting them live off the tithe for many months without any sign that the father wanted to change his ways and begin to work!

As a result of the father's laziness, the Levites were expected to eventually cut off the alien family from the tithe. For it is written:

> ... if any would not work, neither should he eat. (2 Thess. 3:10 NIV)

Therefore, the last resort of welfare support was for a businessman to pay off the alien family's debts (which was probably the purchase price to "buy" the debtor and his family), and pledge that he would take the risk of supporting this family—getting them off the tithe and removing them from being a burden to the community—by setting up a work program for them, which (for the aliens) the Bible calls "slavery."

God so hated slave abuse that he gave to the Israelites a golden rule for slave owners. This required the masters to always treat their slaves as they would wish to be treated if they were the slaves instead. Furthermore, if the slave refused to work, the punishment given to the slave could never be so severe as to cause the slave either death or disability. There were also laws to prevent forcing a slave to work on the Sabbath, as well as laws to punish masters if they had sex with their slaves.

How can we be absolutely sure that the type of slavery God had in mind for Israel was a form of welfare support of last resort? Well, God's philosophy of slavery is revealed in the many laws he gave concerning the treatment of slaves, seven of which we will discuss below.

These seven laws were designed by God to prevent the kind of slave abuse which occurred in America more than a century ago. Many American slave owners perpetually broke all seven of these laws. As a result, America treated its slaves with terrible cruelty. America's slave abuse was one of the major reasons why God punished America with the Civil War, from 1861 to 1865.

The first law said that if an alien slave escaped from the slave owner's property, he could not be forcibly recaptured or returned to his master under any circumstances, and he was to be considered a free man. For it is written:

> If a slave has taken refuge with you, do not hand him over to his master. Let him live among you wherever he likes and in whatever town he chooses. Do not oppress him. (Deut. 23:15-16 NIV)

So, this law says that you can not legally return a runaway slave to his ex-master, but that instead, you must welcome him and allow him to live among you anywhere he wants.

The second law goes even further and says that anybody who kidnaps someone (such as a runaway slave) to sell him back into slavery could face a maximum punishment of execution. For it is written:

> Anyone who kidnaps another and either sells him or still has him when he is caught must be put to death. (Exod. 21:16 NIV)

These first two laws taken together make it practically impossible to develop a culture of cruel slavery for profit, because it is illegal to recapture your own runaway slaves without being charged with kidnapping and facing a maximum sentence of death, or at least a whipping as a merciful alternative to execution.

If a master was cruel to his slaves so that they would want to run away, then there are only two things the master can do to stop this. First of all, he could hire one taskmaster for every slave in order to be able to chase after each of them every time they tried to run away. However, this would cost the slave owner so much extra money to pay for the extra manpower just to watch each slave that it would not be worth having the slaves in the first place. Alternatively, the master could place a ball and chain, or some other type of restraining device, on the slaves to slow them down so they couldn't run away as easily. The problem here is that it limits the slave's productivity and limits the types of different jobs to which he can be assigned. So, once again it becomes no longer profitable to own slaves in the first place, since you cannot recapture them if they run away.

In other words, *cruel* slavery for profit becomes a *money-losing proposition* once it becomes *illegal* to recapture your own runaway slaves. So, these two laws would not only prevent the growth of slave trading within Israel, but would tend to eliminate cruelty to slaves, for sooner or later the slaves would be provoked to try to escape, by simply stepping over the boundaries of your property.

However, if the slave's relationship with his master was one of love and kindness, with the generous provision of free shelter and food for him and his family, then he could even send the slave off of his property (i.e., into town to get food and supplies), knowing that his loyalty and his obligation to you would always bring him back without any temptation to run away.

As a result, the only really profitable type of slavery would not be based upon cruelty and coercion, but would be based upon commitment and cooperation, where the slave understands that his master is supplying him with free shelter, food, clothing, and medical care, and that in turn the slave must supply his master with hard work six days each week. So, slavery within Israel was supposed to be the form of welfare support of last resort.

The third law which prevented cruelty to slaves said that if a master beat a slave to death, the master also had to be punished (most likely by a severe whipping). For it is written:

> If a man beats his male or female slave with a rod and the slave dies as a direct result, he must be punished. (Exod. 21:20 NIV)

Furthermore, according to the fourth law of slavery, if a master caused any permanent injury to his slave (by beating him too severely), then the master had to set the slave free immediately. For it is written:

> If a man hits a manservant or maidservant in the eye and destroys it, he must let the servant go free to compensate for

the eye. And if he knocks out the tooth of a manservant or maidservant, he must let the servant go free to compensate for the tooth. (Exod. 21:26-27 NIV)

You see, God so hated it when masters were cruel to their slaves that he wanted the slaves to be immediately set free if the slave was ever beaten to the point of having a permanent disability. But if the slave was beaten to death, then God wanted the master severely punished. I believe this punishment would probably be a severe whipping (Deut. 25:1-3 NIV). Furthermore, such action against a slave owner (such as severely whipping him for beating a slave to death) would probably also be followed by an investigation by the godly judges. This would be to determine whether or not the slave owner was being cruel to his other slaves, and whether or not the rest of his slaves should be set free or transferred to a "kinder" slave owner.

The fifth law regulating slavery said that "no one, whether master or slave, was ever allowed to work on the Sabbath day." For it is written:

Remember the Sabbath day by keeping it holy. Six days you shall labor and do all your work, but the seventh day is a Sabbath day to the Lord your God. On it you shall not do any work, neither you, nor your son or daughter, nor your manservant, or maidservant, nor your animals, nor the *alien* within your gates. (Exod. 20:8-10 NIV; emphasis added)

Again it is written:

Six days do all your work, but on the seventh day do *not* work, so that. . . . the *slave* born in your household, and the *alien* as well, my be refreshed. (Exod. 23:12 NIV; emphasis added)

So, slavery in Israel was supposed to be unlike slavery in any other country in the world. For in Israel, God gave the alien slaves one day each week to rest and relax and spend time with their families, and possibly even learn about the importance of worshipping Jehovah—who would later on personally become our Messiah and Savior, Jesus the Christ. Also, since the maximum punishment for working on the Sabbath was death, then any master forcing his slaves to work on the Sabbath might possibly face a death sentence, or at least a whipping as a merciful alternative to execution.

The sixth law regulating a master's treatment of his slaves is actually a series of laws which deal with having sex with slaves. These laws are complicated, but basically mean the following:

1. If an *unmarried* slave owner had sex with an *unmarried* virgin slave, the master had to either marry her or set her free—if he was displeased by her and didn't want to marry her (Deut. 21:10-14 NIV). The reason he had to set her free if he didn't marry her is probably

because the master had caused a permanent injury to her vaginal hymen during intercourse. (Remember, Exod. 21:26-27 teaches that if a master causes a permanent injury to a slave through violence, he must set the slave free.)

2. If an *unmarried* slave owner had sex with a *betrothed* slave girl (who had not yet been ransomed or set free, because the bride-price had not yet been paid to buy her freedom—so the betrothal process has been initiated but not yet completed), the master had to be punished (Lev. 19:20-22 NIV). This was probably accomplished by a whipping, which appears to be the biblical standard alternative to execution (Deut. 25:1-3 NIV). Since the master had to be punished, the godly judges would probably interview all of his other slaves, to make sure he was not being cruel to them either. And, if cruelty was found, the master would be prosecuted.

3. If a *married* slave owner had sex with an *unmarried* slave, or an *unmarried* slave owner had sex with a *married* slave, this was considered to be adultery, and the slave owner may have had to face execution (Deut. 22:22 NIV), or at least a whipping as a merciful alternative to execution. Also, he would have to let the single slave girl go free because he had permanently damaged her virginity. Once again, since the master had to be punished, this probably motivated the godly judges to interview all the rest of his slaves, to ensure they were being treated well. And if they had been victims of cruelty (such as rape, adultery, or permanent injury from beatings, or being forced to work on the Sabbath) then the master would be prosecuted by the godly judges, and any slave which had a permanent injury from the master would have to be set free.

The seventh law regulating slavery was the golden rule for slave owners! You see, the Israelites were not only commanded to "love your *neighbor* as yourself" (Lev. 19:18b NIV) but also to "Love the *alien* as yourself." For it is written:

> When an alien lives with you in your land, do not mistreat him. The alien living with you must be treated as one of your native-born. Love him as yourself... (Lev. 19:33-34 NIV).

This *golden rule for slave owners* required the Israelite slave masters to treat all aliens (including their own alien slaves) as the slave master himself would want to be treated if he were the slave. This commandment provided the seventh safeguard against cruel slave abuse.

In addition to these seven safeguards to prevent cruel slave abuse, God gave another command which (if Israel had obeyed it) would have motivated God to bless Israel with so much wealth that it would not be worth the trouble to own slaves in the first place, unless it was done as a generous form of welfare support of last resort. For if the Israelites had obeyed God and brought the entire tithe into the local storehouses so the widows, the orphans, the aliens, and the poor could be fed, then God promised to open up the windows of heaven and pour out such a blessing upon their nation that there would be no room to receive it ((Mal. 3:10 NIV). As a result, there would no longer be any incentive to go to the trouble to cruelly enslave aliens for profit, because you would already be about as well off as you would want to be. For it is written:

> "Bring the whole tithe into the storehouse, that there may be food in my house. Test me in this." says the Lord Almighty, "and see if I will not throw open the floodgates of heaven and pour out so much blessing that you will not have room to receive it. I will prevent pests from devouring your crops, and the vines in your fields will not cast their fruit," says the Lord Almighty. "Then all the nations will call you blessed, for yours will be a delightful land," says the Lord Almighty. (Mal. 3:10-12 NIV)

So, it is obvious that there would be absolutely no incentive to develop a cruel form of slavery for profit in such a delightful land, where you are already about as well off financially as you would want to be.

God never wanted the Israelites to develop a cruel slave trade, but he did want the Israelites to be willing to care for the healthy impoverished aliens living within Israel who could not support themselves. To do this, God allowed the Israelites to enslave the healthy, impoverished aliens if they became overwhelmed with debt and eventually were thought by the Levites to no longer be eligible to receive tithe-sponsored welfare because of an unwillingness to work. This was to be the last resort of welfare support. However, the slaves must still work hard so the slave owner can get back his investment. You see, the slaveowner had to pay the original purchase price for the slave (which probably matched the amount the slave had previously owed to his creditors), also, the slaveowner is now obligated, before God, to continue to provide ongoing free shelter, food, clothing, and medical care for them as well.

Remember, the primary purpose of slavery in Israel was not so the slave owner could make a profit, but so the slave owner could help the poor person. This person was healthy enough to work, but was unemployed and overwhelmingly in debt. Also, the Levites had probably decided he was no longer a candidate to receive financial support from the tithe. So, if the servant (whether Israelite or alien) was lazy and refused to work, God allowed for the servant to be beaten, but never hard enough or long enough to be permanently injured, otherwise the servant would have to be set free (Exod. 21:26-27, 20-21 NIV).

For the Israelite servant to be redeemed, someone *must* assume responsibility for their care—either from within their own family or from other citizens who also cared about the servant's welfare. He would not be redeemed just so he could become a bum again, living under a bridge and being supported by the tithe, but so he could have gainful employment elsewhere (so he would not be tithe-welfare-dependent). The alien slave, however, generally had no family within Israel who might have an interest in redeeming him; so therefore, when an alien became a slave in Israel, it was for life, and his master could will his slaves to his offspring.

God's purpose for these work programs was not to encourage the Israelites to keep slaves (far from it!), but to provide an alternative to an expensive tax-sponsored welfare system for the poor. These people were healthy enough to work, but overwhelmingly in debt, and were either too lazy to find a job (and stick with it), or there were no jobs available. (Actually, if Israel had been obeying God in the first place, there would always have been plenty of jobs available because of God's promised blessings upon the harvest and everything else the Israelites "put their hands to" (Deut. 28:1-6, 8, 11-13 NIV).

So, in a nation of such blessings from God, there is no incentive to own slaves for increased profit, but only to help the poor—which both Jehovah and Jesus said "would always be with you" (Deut. 15:11; Matt. 26:11 NIV), as if to continue to test the Israelites to see if they would continue to help the poor.

So in summary, God allowed slavery in Israel as part of His loving plan to do three things:

1. provide a form of welfare support of last resort for poor aliens,
2. provide a strong work ethic within Israel so the Israelites (and aliens) would work hard and not have to become Israelite servants or alien slaves; and,
3. discourage any aliens who would be lazy from leaving their country and coming to Israel to live and become tithe-welfare dependent.

This would also be part of God's immigration policy which was noted earlier.

SUMMARY

In summary, God's view of welfare reform starts with the thirty-plus laws which promote the development of large, extended families throughout all Israel. These large, extended families have a triple economy of scale so they can more easily provide for their own elderly, disabled, or unemployed family members, to obviate the need for expensive, tax-sponsored federal social security retirement, disability, or welfare programs to do this for them. Furthermore, God's laws against sexual immorality and divorce practically *eliminate* these problems as the major source of applicants for welfare, so that the number of applicants for welfare support (who had no families to support them) would decrease to only a fraction of what it would have been otherwise.

Those remaining poor (who have no families to support them) would now have access to "financial support" made possible because of three pre-welfare laws, which allow the poor to obtain:

1. small, zero-interest loans for bare necessities, the balance of which is canceled every Sabbath year. For aliens, however, these loans are neither interest-free, nor are they cancelled in the Sabbath year;
2. purchasing food and other absolute necessities at cost from merchants and farmers; and,
3. the "pick and eat" laws, where the traveler and the poor can legally "trespass" onto a farmer's property and pick and eat fruits (including grapes), grains (including corn), or other vegetables, but they can't take them off the farmer's property.

For those people who cannot afford to purchase food even at cost, they can obtain support from the local tithe and receive tithe-sponsored welfare. The tithe is collected and protected by the Levites for a mere 10 percent overhead, and 80 percent is reserved for the poor, with the last 10 percent being transported to Jerusalem by the "tither." A small part of this is eaten before the Lord by the tither and his family, and the rest is given to the Levites and priests serving at the temple.

But remember, tithe-sponsored welfare is reserved for the *innocent*—not the *immoral*. Repetitive immorality cancels one's eligibility to receive the tithe, and makes one subject to criminal prosecution for immorality. This again decreases the number of recipients and new applicants for tithe-sponsored welfare. Therefore, those recipients and applicants who continue to remain eligible for the tithe because of their high moral standard can more easily be provided for, without the need of collecting taxes to start a tax-sponsored system of welfare instead.

The last resort of welfare support for the healthy poor who continue to remain idle and never seem to want to work, is a six year period of servanthood for the Israelite or a potential lifetime of slavery for the alien. This system costs no taxes to implement, perpetuates a good work ethic within all Israel, and may even rehabilitate the idle, as well as keep any aliens who might want to be idle from emigrating into Israel and becoming welfare-dependent.

There are six advantages of tithe-sponsored welfare compared to tax-sponsored welfare. This reveals that God's principles of welfare reform are not only still valid today, but are superior to our current ways of managing our welfare system. Furthermore, these principles illustrate the love that Jesus Christ has for nations and for poor individuals—in designing laws which prevent the innocent majority from having to pay extra taxes to provide the welfare support necessary because of the sinfulness of the immoral and idle minority.

What Christ wants our nation to do is to adopt God's view of pro-family legislation along with all of his other biblical principles. These principles can help us to generate a culture of large, extended families which have not only the desire, but the financial resources to take care of their own elderly, disabled, unemployed, and poor.

Secondly, we need some pre-welfare laws which can accomplish the same things as God's pre-welfare laws.

Thirdly, we need to create a mandatory, locally controlled, tithe-sponsored welfare system. This would be accomplished by first delegating the administration of all federal welfare programs back into the hands of the states, and then into the hands of the counties, and eventually back into the hands of the cities, towns, and local communities themselves. Then, the funding of this program must be slowly converted from *tax*-sponsored to *tithe*-sponsored. This tithe-sponsored welfare program must be administered by dedicated volunteers for only a 10 percent overhead with a 10 percent surplus which can be sent to a national collection center to be disbursed to specific local areas with extreme burdens of poverty.

Fourthly, there must also be enforceable moral restraints for continued eligibility to receive tithe-sponsored welfare.

Finally, we must develop a tax-free system of servanthood as the last resort of welfare support for those who are healthy, but perpetually unemployed because of their idleness. This system must also be more restrictive for foreigners who are not yet citizens of the United States, so America won't become an international magnet to attract any immigrants who would like to come to America and be idle and lazy and a further burden to our welfare system.

Remember God's command and challenge to Israel thirty-four hundred years ago (and by implication, God's challenge to America today) was to earnestly support the tithe-based system of welfare, so God could "rain down blessings" upon Israel in response to their obedience. For it is written:

> ... bring all the *tithes* ... and store in your towns, so that the Levites ... and the aliens, the fatherless and the widows who live in your towns may come and eat and be satisfied, and so that the Lord your God may *bless you in all the work of your hand.* (Deut. 14:28-29 NIV; emphasis added)

A thousand years later it was again written:

> "Bring the whole *tithe* into the storehouse, that there may be food in my house. *Test me in this*," says the Lord Almighty,

"and see if I will not throw open the floodgates of heaven and *pour out so much blessing that you will not have room for it.* I will prevent pests from devouring your crops, and the vines in your fields will not cast their fruit," says the Lord Almighty. "*Then all the nations will call you blessed,* for yours will be a delightful land," says the Lord Almighty. (Mal. 3:10-12 NIV; emphasis added)

These commands and promises were spoken by God to Moses and Malachi, and were written down a thousand years apart from each other. These holy words of God reveal that Jehovah's message to Israel was (and is) the same, showing the eternal nature of these commands and the eternal nature of these promises as well.

So, it is clear from these verses that part of God's blessing on Israel (and therefore on America as well) is directly linked to whether or not we can legislate a national tithe to care for our poor, using dedicated volunteers to cut administrative expenses and using moral constraints to regulate who is eligible to receive the tithe. Then, and only then, will God fulfill his promise that he will "pour out so much blessing upon *our* nation that we will not have room enough for it!"

It is also just as clear from these verses that Jehovah (the pre-Incarnate Jesus Christ) has challenged Israel (and therefore America as well) to "*Test him in this!*" So, let us rise to God's challenge, and follow God's commands. For only God's principles of welfare reform can truly . . .

1. provide for the needs of the poor,
2. solve our problems of welfare fraud and abuse,
3. end our culture of immorality, idleness, and welfare dependency, and,
4. save America hundreds of billions of dollars in taxes at the same time.

And that, is God's view of welfare reform!

Chapter Twenty

HOW GOD'S VIEW OF HEALTH CARE REFORM CAN SAVE AMERICA HUNDREDS OF BILLIONS OF DOLLARS IN TAXES

Although God's greatest promise to *individuals* is the promise of eternal life, God's greatest promise to *nations* is the promise to Israel that He would bless them with a disease-free society where everyone lives a full lifespan, if only they would follow His commands as outlined in this book. For it is written:

> If you pay attention to these laws and are careful to follow them . . . the Lord will keep you *free from every disease*. (Deut. 7:12, 15 NIV; emphasis added)

And again:

> Worship the Lord your God . . . I will *take away sickness* from among you, and none will miscarry or be barren in your land. I will give you a *full lifespan*. (Exod. 23:25-26 NIV; emphasis added)

In these two verses God made a pledge to the Israelite nation that if they would obey him completely, he would "keep the Israelites free from every disease" by "taking away sickness from among them" and "giving them a full lifespan"!

Imagine that almighty God promised your nation that you and your loved ones would never be seriously ill at any time during your lives, and that none of you would ever die prematurely as a result of illness, and that you would all live a full lifespan. Isn't that an amazing promise? This is exactly what Jehovah guaranteed he would do for the nation of Israel if they would obey him completely by following all the principles outlined in this book.

How long is a full lifespan? Well, God wanted a full lifespan to be *120 years*. For it is written:

The Lord said, "My Spirit will not contend with man forever, for he is mortal, his days will be a hundred and twenty years." (Gen. 6:3 NIV)

Because of man's appalling wickedness before Noah's flood, God announced that He was about to gradually shorten the lifespan of all people—from the nine hundred year average lifespan prior to Noah's flood, to a brand new average lifespan, which God said would now be 120 years. This 120 years is the full lifespan which God intended for all mankind!

Unfortunately, most Christians mistakenly believe that this 120 years either refers to the number of years to build Noah's ark, or refers to the number of years before Noah's flood would come. If this were the case, then Noah (who was already 500-years-old before God's announcement, according to Gen. 5:32) would have aged 120 more years (to be at least 620-years-old by the time the ark was completed and the flood began). But according to Genesis 7:11, Noah was only 600-years-old (and not 620) when the flood came. So, this 120 years can not refer to the length of time to build the ark, nor to the number of years before the flood would come. It can only refer to a change in the intended total lifespan of mankind from an average of nine hundred years down to an average of 120 years.

Israel never obeyed God completely enough to receive this blessing, for Moses himself wrote that the average lifespan of the Israelites during his day was not 120 years, but was only seventy to eighty years, the same as it is today! For it is written:

The length of our days is seventy years-or eighty, if we have the strength. (Ps. 90:10 NIV; this translation says that this is actually a psalm of Moses)

To demonstrate the reality of this promise, God allowed Moses to live to be exactly 120-years-old, even though the average life span at that time was only 70- to 80-years-old. Furthermore, the Bible reveals that Moses was still in good shape with good eyesight and strength at the time of his death. For it is written:

Moses was a hundred and twenty-years-old when he died, yet his eyes were not weak, nor his strength gone. (Deut. 34:7 NIV)

I believe this verse reveals that, even at age 120, Moses was still in "good shape" with no significant deterioration of any part of his body when he finally died. So, the longevity and excellent health of Moses provided the Israelites with the ideal object lesson to demonstrate the importance of obeying God and receiving his blessings of excellent health and a full lifespan.

On the other hand, God also allowed Aaron to survive until he was 123-years-old (Num. 33:38 NIV) even though it was Aaron who built the golden calf which encouraged idolatry among the Israelites. However, this provided a different object lesson: that not everyone in Israel had to be as righteous as Moses to inherit the full lifespan of 120 years. Since the promise of a full lifespan is linked to the promise of a disease-free society (Exod. 23:26 NIV), then by implication, not everyone had to be as righteous as Moses in order for God to bless Israel with a disease-free society either.

These national blessings were to be based upon national obedience, not individual obedience. In other words, the national blessings of a disease-free society would be based upon the sum total of all the obedience of everyone in the entire nation of Israel. If this sum total reached or exceeded the "threshold of national righteousness" which God had in His divine mind, then He would begin to bless Israel with a nearly disease-free society.

Furthermore, Jesus taught that the number of true Christians of any nation would never account for more than a small minority of the total population when compared to the large majority of non-Christians. For it is written:

> But small is the gate and narrow is the road that leads to life, and only a few find it. (Matt. 7:14 NIV)

Obviously then, the total righteousness of the small Christian minority can never compensate for the tremendous wickedness of the large unrighteous majority.

So, how could Israel (or America, for that matter) ever reach the threshold of righteousness required by God in order for Him to bless them (or us) with a disease-free society, when Jesus said that the number of true Christians will never represent more than a small minority, regardless of how hard we try to win the lost to Christ? Well, the only other way to increase the total obedience of the entire nation of Israel would be to keep the unrighteous on their best behavior by adopting all of God's principles of moral law, civil law, and civil law enforcement into the legislation of every community, so the unrighteous would begin to obey God, however reluctantly. For God designed his principles of civil law with this same goal in mind—to keep the large unrighteous majority on their best behavior by combining the influences of:

—salvation and surrender,
—training and tradition,
—prosecution and punishment,
—clothing and coverings,
—legislated godly peer pressure, and
—nationwide accountability groups.

By doing this, God could indeed be able to bless Israel with a disease-free society, as well as a society which is nearly crime-free, poverty-free, war-free, tax-free, inflation-free, and natural-disaster-free. So, the key to obtaining the blessing of a disease-free society was not to win the entire nation to the Lord, for even though this should be our main focus and is a laudable goal, Jesus himself says that we will never be successful in winning more than a small minority of any nation to Christ. Therefore, the key to obtaining these blessings was to have the small Christian minority rule over the large, non-Christian majority and adopt all of God's principles of health care law, moral law, civil law, and civil law enforcement into the national legislation of Israel. In this way, these biblical principles would be empowered to control the actions of nearly all the Israelites, keeping both the righteous and the unrighteous on their best behavior. And as a result of the influence of godly peer pressure and godly legislation, the reluctant obedience of the unrighteous majority would increase so dramatically and reach such a high level that when added to the true submissive obedience of the Christian minority, the aggregate righteousness of the entire nation would inevitably exceed the threshold required by God so he could supernaturally bless Israel with a disease-free society.

So, even though, generation after generation the majority of Israelites would still never seek to have a personal relationship with Jehovah (just as most Americans don't seek to have a personal relationship with Christ), the entire nation of Israel would still end up obeying him anyway, because of the social engineering which inevitably results when God's legal principles are adopted by godly leadership.

Unfortunately, Israel never at any time in their history truly adopted these principles of godly leadership, godly laws, and godly peer pressure into their legislation. So, they never had a disease-free society, and ended up frequently being cursed instead of being blessed.

Now I believe the Bible teaches that these same potential blessings of a disease-free society with a full life span of 120 years are still available to America, if America can do what Israel failed to do: adopt all God's principles as recorded in this book into the legislation of our government. For I believe America will then finally reach the threshold of righteousness required by God so he can give America a nearly disease-free society, as well as a nearly crime-free, poverty-free, war-free, tax-free, inflation-free and natural disaster-free society. Modern America, just like ancient Israel, is also eligible for these tremendous blessings (for complete details, please see chapter four).

How can I be so sure of this? Well, all that you have to do is look at the many verses which prove that God holds all nations of the earth accountable for obeying his principles of moral and civil law, and that he either rewards or punishes them depending upon their obedience or disobedience. For instance, there are many verses in the Bible which clearly indicate that throughout all time God curses entire nations (other than Israel) as a result of their national disobedience of His laws. For it is written:

> I will take vengeance in anger and wrath upon the nations which have not obeyed me. (Mic. 5:15 NIV)

> Son of man, if a *country* sins against me by being unfaithful and I stretch out my hand to cut off its food supply... Or if I bring a sword against *that country*... Or if I send a plague into *that land*... (Ezek. 14:13, 17a, 19a NIV; emphasis added)

> And if they learn well the ways of my people... then they will be established among my people. But if *any nation* does not listen, I will completely uproot it," declares the Lord. (Jer. 12:17 NIV; emphasis added)

Not only does God punish entire nations which have disobeyed His commands in the Bible, but when a nation repents, then God says that he "will not inflict on that nation the disaster he had planned." For it is written:

> If at any time I announce that a nation or kingdom is to be uprooted and destroyed, and if that nation repents of its evil, then I will relent and not inflict on it the disaster I had planned. (Jer. 18:7-8 NIV)

Furthermore, God also heals the land of nations when they repent. For it is written:

> When I shut up the heavens so that there is no rain, or command locusts to devour the land or send a plague among my people, if my people, who are called by my name, will humble themselves and pray and seek my face and turn from their wicked ways, then will I hear from heaven and will forgive their sin and will heal their land. (2 Chron. 7:13-14 NIV)

Lastly, God says that when a city or nation is righteous, that he will exalt that city or nation, and he will "bless that nation whose God is the Lord." For it is written:

> Through the blessing of the upright a city is exalted... (Prov. 11:11 NIV)

> Righteousness exalts a nation. (Ps. 14:34 NIV)

The Lord loves righteousness and justice . . . Let all the earth fear the Lord; let all the people of the world revere him . . . the Lord foils the plans of nations; he thwarts the purpose of the peoples; But the plans of the Lord stand firm forever, the purposes of his heart through all generations. Blessed is the nation whose God is the Lord. (Ps. 33:5a, 8, 10-12a NIV)

In summary, just as God makes all nations of the earth eligible for his curses, so also God makes all nations of the earth eligible for his blessings—including the greatest blessing of all, the blessing of a nearly disease-free society with a full lifespan of 120 years! If America wants a nearly disease-free society with a full lifespan, then we have to pay much closer attention to God's view of health care reform, which includes the adoption of God's principles of health care.

Even if America never exceeds the threshold of righteousness required by God in order for Him to supernaturally bless us with a disease-free society (where everyone lives to be 120-years-old), there are still abundant natural blessings obtainable for America if we adopt God's principles of health care reform. Simply by adopting God's principles of health care reform, we can prevent millions of Americans from suffering from many diseases, as well as save America hundreds of billions of dollars in taxes and health care costs every year.

How Adopting God's Health Care Laws Can Naturally Make Us Healthier and Decrease the Cost of Health Care in America

There are seven sins which cause 50 percent of the health care expenses in the United States each year, and these seven sins are:

1. smoking,
2. alcohol abuse,
3. drug abuse,
4. sexual immorality,
5. violence,
6. abortion, and
7. food abuse (bad eating habits).

Surprisingly, the Bible teaches (directly or indirectly) that the first six of these sins were also supposed to be punishable crimes against the state (in ancient Israel); and therefore, should also be punishable crimes against the state in modern America. If America would just make the first six of these sins into punishable crimes against the state as the Bible commands, then not only would we keep millions of Americans from becoming ill, injured, or dying from these causes, but we would also save hundreds of billions of dollars in health care expenses each year. That savings would probably come in the form of the largest tax cut in America's history as well as dramatically lowered costs of medical insurance, prescription drugs, hospital bills, and doctor's bills.

Smoking is a major risk factor for all four of the top causes of mortality in America: heart attacks, cancer (certain forms), strokes, and lung disease. Each year, smoking accounts for approximately four hundred thousand deaths, which makes smoking the number one risk factor for health problems in America. In fact, in 1993 alone, the total cost of health care attributable to smoking was fifty billion dollars, according to (MMWR, 8 July 994, vol. 43, no. 26, publication of the U.S. Department of Health and Human Services).

Not only is smoking the major cause of heart attacks, strokes, chronic bronchitis, emphysema, and lung cancer, but smoking (along with other forms of tobacco abuse) is also the major cause of cancer of the mouth, tongue, and vocal cords. Smoking can also cause cancer of the kidney, bladder, and pancreas and is one of the causes of high blood pressure as well. All of these problems would dramatically decrease if America treated smoking as a sin against God which was also a crime against the state, and therefore, made it illegal to manufacture, distribute, import, or sell cigarettes. If we had done this generations ago, America could have saved fifty billion dollars in health care costs in 1993, and in every year thereafter.

But how can we *prove* that God would condemn smoking as a sin, and that God would want us to make smoking illegal? Well, first of all, we need to identify the two main health care problems caused by smoking. They are:

1. Smoking is unhealthy, even in the tiny doses inhaled in passive smoking, and this risk to health increases with the intensity and the duration of exposure;
2. Smoking is *addictive*, even when smoking as little as a third of a pack of cigarettes daily.

Next, we need to find the closest approximation to these issues in the Bible to see what God's guidance is concerning the consumption of items into the body which He considers to either be *unhealthy* (even in small amounts) or *addictive* (in larger amounts).

The answer to the first part is found in God's laws concerning eating fat, while the answer to the second part is found in God's laws concerning drunkenness. In the Bible, eating fat (specifically animal fat) is the exact parallel of smoking, because the scientific evidence reveals that both smoking and eating animal fat are harmful even at low doses, and both cause increasing harm at increasing doses. The Bible teaches that eating animal fat is supposed to be illegal—against God's laws in the bible (Lev. 7:23 NIV). Therefore, since the laws in the Bible are general principles designed to be applicable in all other similar circumstances, then smoking should also be illegal (against God's laws) as well. This is, again, because both smoking and eating animal fat are harmful at low doses with increasing harm at increasing doses. Secondly, smoking is also addictive, and its addictive properties are the exact parallel to drunkenness in the Bible. Since God intended that repetitive drunkenness (which leads to alcohol addiction) should be a punishable crime against the state (Deut. 21:18-21 NIV), then this would also generalize to smoking as well, such that the repetitive smoking of cigarettes in amounts high enough to become addictive would also be a punishable crime against the state. So, according to the Bible, smoking is a sin which should be made illegal, and smoking enough to cause you to become addicted should actually be made a punishable crime against the state.

This means that God would command our government to make the manufacture and sale of cigarettes illegal as well. And, since this would destroy the tobacco industry in the United States, our government must take responsibility to organize the slow dismantling of the entire tobacco industry. For according to the Bible, government rulers are responsible before God to pass laws to legally dismantle any industries or businesses which encourage citizens to sin. You see, the tobacco industry encourages our citizens to commit the sin of smoking, just as the "idol industry" encouraged the ancient Israelites to commit the sin of worshipping idols. Just as God commanded the kings of Israel and Judah to destroy the idols and demolish the pagan temples of idol worship (thereby destroying the "idol industry" to help stop the Israelites from committing the sin of idolatry), so also God would have us dismantle the tobacco industry so Americans would no longer be encouraged to commit the sin of tobacco abuse either.

This can easily be accomplished by taking the twelve billion dollars in foreign aid which America gives away yearly (while pretending these are foreign "loans") and use this money to:

1. subsidize the tobacco *farmers* for two years to start farming a different crop,
2. subsidize the tobacco *industry* for two years to convert it to another industry,
3. subsidize all the *employees* in the entire tobacco industry for two years to look for a different type of work!

If we need more money to underwrite this national project, then we can also shut down NASA and save another seven billion dollars annually to help fund this two year conversion. Both foreign aid and NASA are offensive to God anyway, and neither of these government programs would exist in a biblical society (the reasons for this are discussed in detail in chapters twenty-three and twenty-four, respectively).

Once the tobacco industry is dismantled, smoking in America would become rare, because in order to smoke, you'd have to plant your own tobacco in secret, fertilize it, water it, harvest it, cure it, cut it, and roll it into cigarettes. Most Americans would never go to this much trouble just to smoke.

This biblical plan will pay for itself over and over. For after the two year subsidy ends, America will not only continue to save the twelve billion dollars every year by stopping the foreign aid program, but as noted above, America will also eventually save the annual fifty billion dollar expense directly attributable to the health care costs of smoking. Furthermore, Americans would also save in health insurance premiums, etc. as well as prevent millions of Americans from suffering from smoking related diseases.

Alcohol abuse is the second sin which is a major contributor to health care costs in the United States. For instance, in 1985, alcohol abuse caused 95 thousand deaths—the health care costs of alcohol abuse totaled 58.2 billion dollars, not including 4.3 billion dollars for crime expenditures and 2.6 billion dollars for motor vehicle accidents (according to a government publication entitled "The Economic Costs of Alcohol and Drug Abuse and Mental Illness: 1985").

Repetitive drunkenness and alcohol abuse cause alcoholic hepatitis, cirrhosis, liver failure, dementia, and pancreatitis. Alcoholism is also associated with certain types of cancer and is one of the causes of heart rhythm problems and heart failure.

If America would make the sin of drunkenness once again be a crime against the state as the Bible commands, and punish drunkenness and alcohol abuse in the manner prescribed by God in the Bible, then all the health care problems associated with alcoholism would vanish and America could have saved 58.2 billion dollars in health care costs in 1985 alone! By the way, in the Bible, the punishment for drunkenness (and, by implication, drug abuse) is a maximum sentence of death, a whipping (from one to forty lashes) as a merciful alternative to execution, or total forgiveness (for first time offenders who are extremely repentant). (For details, see chapters eight, ten, and eighteen.) This differs from prohibition (which made drinking illegal) because according to God's laws, drinking should still be legal, but drunkenness should be a crime. By implication therefore, regularly drinking alcohol in excess (i.e., chronic alcoholism) would be a crime as well.

Drug abuse is the third major sin which contributes heavily to health care costs in America. Drug abuse caused 6,100 deaths in 1985 and cost 44.1 billion dollars in health care expenditures, and another 13.2 billion dollars for crime expenditures, according to the same publication noted above. As usual, if America would punish drug abuse the way God commands us to punish alcohol abuse in the Bible, then this problem would practically disappear in America, and again America would have saved 44.1 billion dollars in health care expenses in 1985 alone.

The total medical expenses for the entire nation was reported to be 308.7 billion dollars in 1987 (MMWR, 8 July 1994, vol. 43, no. 26). Yet in 1985, the medical expenses for the sins of alcohol abuse and drug abuse together already accounted for 102.3 billion dollars (as noted above) which is approximately one third of all the health care expenses which probably occurred in 1985. Can you imagine the percentage of health care costs accounted for when we add to this the health care expenses caused by the sins of smoking, sexual immorality (which causes both AIDS and cervical cancer, violence, and abortion)? To this we must also add the sins of bad diets (food abuse). I'm sure that these sins together account for at least one half of all America's medical expenses annually!

Sexual immorality is the fourth major sin which costs America billions of dollars in health care expenditures each year. For the treatment of AIDS alone costs billions of dollars and is in the top ten causes of mortality annually in the United States. Furthermore, other sexually transmitted diseases (such as gonorrhea, chlamydia, syphilis, herpes, and the human papilloma virus—the cause of cervical cancer) have begun to rise to epidemic proportions since 1964.

You see, 1964 was the year after prayer and Bible teaching were removed from public schools (in 1962 and 1963) by the Supreme Court. This meant that our government officially decided that our youngest citizens should never again be publicly taught to either worship God or obey God's principles of moral or civil law, for knowledge of these principles was no longer considered to be of value to become good American citizens. This symbolized for our lawyers and judges that God's laws would no longer be America's laws, and so the sins of sexual immorality would no longer be considered crimes against the state, but would instead be suddenly "legalized" and officially "acceptable" to our government. As a result, the "free love" generation began, and in the latter half of the 1960s this caused an epidemic of sexually transmitted diseases, including cervical cancer, and set the stage for the epidemic spread of AIDS (beginning in the mid and late 1980s).

So, if America legislated that the sins of fornication, adultery, and homosexuality should once again become punishable crimes against the state (with the same penalties as recorded in the Bible), then we would prevent millions of Americans from suffering from all of these diseases, as well as save billions of dollars in health care expenses.

Violence is the fifth major sin which contributes to health care costs, whether in the form of rape, domestic violence (wife abuse and child abuse), assault and battery, or attempted suicide. Much of this violence involves the misuse of firearms. In fact, in 1994, there were 17,866 homicides, 18,765 suicides, 1,356 accidental injuries, and 518 undetermined injuries, all caused by firearms. This totals 38,505 injuries and deaths by firearms in the United States during just 1994 (according to the Monthly Vital Statistics Report, vol. 45, no. 3.[S], 30 September 1996).

I'm sure the health care costs for firearm to related injuries also totals millions, if not billions, of dollars. Some of these health care costs have already been accounted for under the alcohol abuse related and drug abuse related health care costs, because many (but not all) firearm injuries are directly or indirectly related to drug abuse and alcohol abuse.

From what I have read, the vast majority of firearm injuries are from handguns. The inadequacy of man's wisdom has led to the perpetual controversy of whether or not to outlaw handguns altogether, or just to severely punish those who use handguns to commit crimes. Because no one has yet resolved this controversy, our government neither outlaws the handguns nor punishes the criminals severely enough to solve the problems of handgun related violence.

The Bible resolves this controversy by giving us the answer. And, the Bible reveals that God's answer on this issue is that:

> Severe punishment (not gun control) is to be the primary deterrent to prevent violent crime associated with the use of deadly weapons. (see chapter eleven for details)

You see, in the Bible, God commands that anyone who commits deliberate, premeditated murder must be executed without mercy (Deut. 19:11-13 NIV). Furthermore, anyone who deliberately seriously injures someone else was to receive an identical wound in the courtroom, presumably from the "courtroom strongman" (Lev. 24:19-20 NIV). This latter punishment of "identical wounding" is called "an eye for an eye." God even allowed the judges the discretion to use whipping (from one to forty lashes: Deut. 25:1-3 NIV) for miscellaneous crimes which fell into no other category of punishment. Being threatened with a deadly weapon, such as a sword, spear, knife, or modern handgun, would probably fall into this category.

To reiterate, these three swift and extremely inexpensive biblical punishments are:

1. *execution* (for deliberate, premeditated murder);
2. *"an eye for an eye"* (for purposeful, serious, violent injuries); and,
3. *whipping* (for threatening people with deadly weapons).

These are just three of the five biblical alternatives to expensive tax-sponsored prison systems, and they provide the greatest deterrent to violent crime which can ever be devised. How do we know this? Because after God "considered" all the different ways to deter violent crime, He gave us the five principles of civil law enforcement which He decided were the absolute best. (see chapter ten for details.)

In summary, if we would punish violence the way God commands in the Bible, then violent crime would practically cease to exist in the United States. Thousands of victims and their families would be spared the consequences of this violence annually, and America would be spared the billions of dollars in expenses associated with these violent acts.

Abortion represents the sixth major sin which adds significantly to our health care expenses. According to the National Right to Life, the abortion industry received ninety million dollars from public funding (tax money) in 1994. This was to pay for 203,200 abortions for low income women, which was only a fraction of the total 1,287,416 abortions performed nationwide that year. Since the total number of abortions is more than six times the number of abortions which received the public funding of ninety million dollars, I would therefore estimate that the total dollars spent on abortions annually would be more than six times this figure—or approximately five hundred million dollars. This is especially true since abortions paid for by insurance companies or by the patients themselves generally cost more than abortions which are paid by tax-sponsored government programs. By the way, from 1973 (the year of *Roe v. Wade*) through 1998, approximately 38 million abortions have occurred in the United States (*World Magazine* 16 January 1999). And, at about 5 hundred dollars per abortion, this should total to about 19 billion dollars which America has spent to kill its babies.

If America would make the sin of abortion a punishable crime against the state the way God commands in the Bible (Exod. 21:22-23 NIV), then not only would we spare two hundred thousand "pre-infants" from being aborted each year, but America would save nearly five hundred million dollars annually in health care costs.

Now let's review. The two sins of alcohol abuse and drug abuse together cost America about 102.3 billion dollars in health care expenses in 1985, yet the total cost of health care in the U.S. in 1987 was 308.7 billion dollars. So, the sins of alcohol and drug abuse together accounted for about a third of all our health care expenditures in the mid-eighties. And when we add on top of this figure the expected costs of the sins of smoking, sexual immorality, violence, and abortion, then I believe that these six sins together account for probably fifty percent of our national health care expenses annually.

If our Senators and Congressmen made these six sins against God punishable crimes against the state—and punished these crimes the way God commands in the Bible—then millions of Americans would be prevented from getting the illnesses related to these sins. It would also save America hundreds of billions of dollars in health care expenses annually.

How then, can America justify any course of action other than this one? Instead of punishing sin in the manner prescribed by God, America embraces and exalts the "freedom to sin" more with each passing decade. America's "love affair" with the freedom to sin has given us both a great national burden of diseases, as well as a great national burden of taxes to pay for the health care costs involved in treating these same diseases.

In other words, American legislators refuse to obey God's commands to put an end to these particular sins by making them punishable crimes against the state. As a result, our entire nation gets punished, through the natural consequences of these sins. These consequences involves allowing millions of people to suffer from preventable diseases which cost hundreds of billions of dollars each year for diagnosis and treatment.

Now in addition to the sins of:

1. Smoking,
2. Drunkenness,
3. Drug Abuse,
4. Sexual immorality,
5. Violence, and
6. Abortion,

there are at least five other sins which also cause serious disease and which together further increase our nation's health care costs by billions of dollars. These are as follows:

7. the sins of food abuse (dietary sins),
8. the sins which cause increased stress on the heart,
9. the sin of not placing certain contagious patients in quarantine,
10. the sins of delaying pregnancy until late in life,
11. the sin of not being circumcised.

When God created Adam and Eve in the Garden of Eden, his original intention was that they should have a strictly vegetarian diet, (Gen. 1:29 (NIV). And it wasn't until after Noah's flood that God allowed mankind to supplement this strictly vegetarian diet by eating a little meat (Gen. 9:3 NIV). Finally, God told the Israelites (through Moses) that they should never eat any fat (Lev. 3:17 NIV), and then clarified his meaning further by saying that it is specifically animal fat that mankind should avoid eating. For it is written:

> The Lord said to Moses, "Say to the Israelites, 'Do not eat any of the *fat* of cattle, sheep or goats." (Lev. 7:22-23 NIV; emphasis added)

So, the biblical diet is primarily a vegetarian diet, supplemented with small amounts of meat, with the instructions to avoid eating any fat—specifically animal fat. Finally, thousands of years later, science has begun to "catch up" with the Bible and discover that the best diet is a primarily vegetarian diet, supplemented with only a little meat. Added, we should avoid eating fat as much as possible, and it is specifically the fat of animals which is bad for us. Animal fat is "saturated fat" and is very harmful to us, but vegetable fat is "unsaturated fat" and is not very harmful to us.

Americans frequently do just the opposite of what God commands and what science teaches us. Instead, we consume diets which are high in fat and meat, and low in fruits and vegetables. These bad eating habits represent the sin of *food abuse,* the seventh sin which is known to account for a high percentage of diseases as well as a high percentage of medical expenses annually. In fact, it has been estimated that three hundred thousand people die annually as a result of poor diet and activity patterns—a sedentary lifestyle. (*JAMA* 270 (18):2207-12, 10 November 1993).

According to the Bible, having a sedentary lifestyle is not a sin, but "gorging yourself on meat" (Prov. 23:20 NIV) and eating lots of animal fat is. While this reference in *JAMA* did not isolate the contribution of bad diets towards these three hundred thousand annual deaths (separately from the contribution of sedentary lifestyles), I'm sure the sin of eating high fat, high meat diets by itself still contributes heavily towards a large percentage of these deaths.

Science teaches us that some serious diseases are associated with bad diets. Conversely, there is also scientific evidence that biblical diets (diets high in fruits and vegetables, low in meat, and extremely low in fat) help improve, control, or prevent constipation, hemorrhoids, diverticulosis, diverticulitis, high cholesterol, high triglycerides, obesity, diabetes, hardening of the arteries, high blood pressure, heart attacks, and strokes. More specifically, a diet high in fruits helps protect us from cancer of the oral cavity (i.e., cancer of the mouth, tongue, and tonsils), and also helps to protect us from cancer of the larynx and esophagus. Furthermore, a diet high in both fruits and vegetables helps protects us from cancer of the stomach, colon, rectum, pancreas, bladder, cervix, ovary, and breast. Conversely, a diet very low in fruits and vegetables doubles your chances of developing these same cancers (Block, G., Patterson, B., and Sublar, A. "Fruit, Vegetables, and Cancer Prevention: A Review of the Epidemiological Evidence." *Nutrition and Cancer,* 1992, vol. 18, no 1, 1-29).

In the Bible, these dietary sins are not associated with any particular punishments. Therefore, it is probable that God intended that these dietary sins be "enforced" primarily by education and godly peer pressure. So, if America would officially place the biblical diet (a primarily vegetarian diet, with small amounts of meat and zero animal fat) into the "law of the land" (as God commanded Moses to do for the health of the Israelite nation), then our legislators would help prevent millions of Americans from suffering from all the diseases just mentioned. This would also save Americans from the unnecessary burden of having to pay billions of extra dollars for health care expenses directly related to disobeying biblical dietary principles. This legislation should make it illegal to buy or sell foods high in animal fat and make it illegal for restaurants to cook foods in grease made from animal fat as well.

The eighth problem is that many sins place increased *stress* on the heart and on other parts of the body. If we developed the type of biblical society which is described in this book, then there would be very little stress in our lives because our nation would be more healthy, peaceful, prosperous, and free from the problems of immorality, drunkenness, drug abuse, divorce, violence, inflation, poverty, natural disasters, and big government with its huge tax burden. Also, the stress of working seven days a week would not exist because it would be illegal to work on the Sabbath. Therefore, we would all be much healthier, and again, we would save billions of dollars in health care expenses. For taken together, all the major sins in our culture increase the stress in our lives and therefore increase heart attacks, strokes, ulcers, etc. Therefore, this represent the eighth sin (or set of sins) which cause increased diseases and increased expenses for health care in the U.S.

The ninth national sin which increases diseases and health care costs in America is the violation of God's principles concerning *quarantine*. This biblical concept of quarantine is referred to as living "outside the camp" and is repeated many times in the books of Leviticus and Numbers. These quarantine laws were designed by God to prevent the epidemic spread of certain contagious infectious, including leprosy, sexually transmitted diseases, and possibly tuberculosis, by combining the concepts of *separation* and *stigma*.

A modern day application of these same principles of quarantine would be that each state should set aside a large area of land where all its patients with certain serious contagious infections should live until they are cured. Such legislation would help to prevent the epidemic spread of the plague of sexually transmitted diseases via *separation*. Also, because of the *stigma* of having to live in a quarantine area if they contracted a sexually transmitted disease, millions of people would no longer dare to commit the sins of fornication, adultery, or homosexuality.

In other words, in designing his principles of quarantine, God incorporated both concepts of separation and stigma in order to help prevent the epidemic spread of disease. Of course, our legislators ignore these biblical principles of quarantine. At least as a partial consequence of this disobedience, America ends up suffering from the plagues of sexually transmitted diseases, including gonorrhea, chlamydia, syphilis, herpes, cervical cancer (a sexually transmitted disease) and AIDS. So, if our nation had started following the biblical principles of quarantine generations ago, then surely far fewer Americans would be suffering from these diseases, and again America would save billions of dollars in health care expenses.

God told man to "be fruitful and multiply"—in the context of marriage, of course (Gen. 1:28, 9:7 NIV)—and this command has never been rescinded. Violation of this command represents the tenth sin which increases diseases and health care costs in America. Only now, thousands of years later, has science discovered that *delaying pregnancy* until late in life (or avoiding pregnancy altogether) causes an increased chance of developing breast cancer and endometrial cancer.

You see, it is known that the more frequently the breasts and uterus undergo their monthly cycles, that changes can occur in the breast and uterus which can unfortunately give rise to cancer of those organs. But by becoming pregnant, these cycles are given a rest period for nine months, and, when followed by breast feeding, this rest period is prolonged even further. It is these prolonged rest periods which make it less likely to develop cancer of the breast and cancer of the womb (endometrium).

So, by disobeying God's command to "be fruitful and multiply," our nation has unwittingly increased the health care costs of cancer of the breast and cancer of the womb. Therefore, America needs to develop a culture which exalts the important health benefits of obeying God's commands concerning early marriage and multiple pregnancies, and denounces the custom of delaying pregnancy until later in life.

Therefore, if America would lose its love affair with birth control and learn the value of obeying God's command to "be fruitful and multiply," then perhaps thousands of women would be less likely to develop breast cancer and endometrial cancer. And of course, America would again save money and taxes on national health care.

Science teaches us that *circumcision* on the eighth day of life prevents 100 percent of cancer of the penis, and violation of this principle represents the eleventh sin which increases diseases and health care costs in America (for details, see S.I. McMillen, M.D., *None of These Diseases*, 1984, 87-96). As usual, if America would legislate that circumcision must be performed on every baby boy on the eighth day of life, then cancer of the penis would all but disappear in the U.S. And, while this is an uncommon cancer in America, it should still prevent many Americans from suffering this dreaded disease and again save on our national health care costs.

In summary, according to government data in 1985, the sins of alcohol and drug abuse together accounted for one third of America's annual health care expenses at about that time. When we add the costs of health care resulting from the sins of smoking, sexual immorality, violence, abortion, high fat/high meat diets, delaying pregnancy until late in life, not being circumcised, not having a national quarantine policy, and the many sins which cause more stress on the heart, it is clear that at least one half of our entire nation's health care expenses result directly or indirectly from America's failure to make these eleven sins against God illegal, and from America's failure to make the first six of these sins into punishable crimes against the state.

It has been estimated that in 1993, the health care costs in the U.S. would reach approximately 9 hundred billion dollars (McGinnis and Foege. "Actual Causes of Death in the U.S." *JAMA*, 10 November 1993, vol. 270, no. 10; 2221). If one half of America's health care costs are directly or indirectly related to these eleven sins, and if we followed the principles which I have outlined from the Bible, America could prevent millions of Americans from suffering illness or death from these diseases. We could also save American citizens a total of 450 billion dollars annually in health care expenses. This is the second facet of God's view of health care reform.

The third part of God's view of health care reform involves the sin of usury (lending money at interest). Usury causes health care costs to increase by two different methods. The sin of usury is one of the keys to:

1. general inflation, and,
2. industry-specific inflation (caused by health insurance and other third-party payment systems, such as federal Medicare and state-sponsored Medicaid).

Now the sin of usury is one of the causes of general inflation, and this will be discussed in detail in the next chapter. Here it should suffice to say that although inflation can be caused by many things (such as supply and demand, political instability, war, plagues, droughts, and natural disasters), most of these things are either naturally or supernaturally prevented or controlled in a biblical society. For God has promised to supernaturally prevent all these problems for any country which becomes a true nation under God and whose aggregate national righteousness exceeds the threshold required by God (for details, see chapter three).

The last remaining cause of inflation is when banks lend money to other businesses and charge them interest payments in return. This extra expense of paying off interest on business loans is passed on to the consumer by inflating the cost of the product or service. In this way, the rate of interest is directly related to the rate of inflation.

Unfortunately however, nationwide usury has also gotten Americans out of the good habit of saving money for expensive items, and has gotten us into the bad habit of taking out interest-bearing loans to pay for these items instead. So, as a result of the sin of usury, our culture has developed a mind set of spending money instead of saving it. And today, our usury-dependent culture is populated with citizens who have a tendency to spend all the extra money they have as soon as they get it. In other words, a usury-dependent culture inevitably becomes a spendthrift culture. Whenever the national money supply temporarily increases in a spendthrift culture, then demand for products and services increases, causing further inflation.

Knowing this, our Federal Reserve Bank—created from the sin of big government (see chapter five)—has begun to take advantage of our usury-dependent spendthrift culture and has created policies allowing the government to purchase massive amounts of interest-bearing bonds whenever they think it is necessary. This has the effect of lowering interest rates while increasing the national money supply, which in turn, causes a greater demand for products and services, which increases their prices and raises the rate of inflation.

In other words, the national sin of having big government (and the subsequent power of the Federal Reserve Board) has created a society where the rate of interest has now become *inversely* related to the rate of inflation. Whereas, without big government (and therefore without a Federal Reserve Board regulating our nation's money supply) the rate of interest would ordinarily be *directly* related to the rate of inflation. So any way you look at it, the rate of inflation is linked to the rate of interest.

But God says that the interest rate should always be *0 percent* when we lend money to our own citizens (Deut. 23:19-20; Exod. 22:23; Lev. 25:36a, 37a; Neh. 5:7-11 NIV). If the interest rate always remained at zero percent, then the inflation rate should always remain at zero percent as well. After all, if the interest rate was always zero percent, then the government would no longer have any interest-bearing bonds available to buy or sell. Therefore, the Federal Reserve Board could no longer control the rate of inflation by changing the nation's money supply in order to suddenly increase or decrease consumer demand for products and services. As a result, prices of goods and services would eventually stabilize and general inflation would cease to exist. In other words, if America outlawed the sin of usury (lending money at interest) then inflation itself would stop (providing that all the other factors effecting inflation were equally well controlled, as of course they would be in a biblical society).

If America can stop general inflation, then this will also slow the rising cost of health care in the United States. Unfortunately, the cost of health care in America always seems to rise even faster than the rate of general inflation. The reason for this is that our usury-dependent, spendthrift culture has given birth to a usury-dependent health insurance industry as well.

You see, when you lend someone money at interest, you hope to eventually get your interest-profit returned to you. Over the last few generations, creative businessmen have invented new methods of returning your interest-profit to you, and one of these methods involves their promise to take the risk of paying all of your medical bills as long as they can keep the rest of the interest-profit for themselves. In this manner, the sin of usury has given birth to the health insurance industry. This makes all types of third-party payment programs (such as federal Medicare and state-sponsored Medicaid) related to the sin of usury as well, except that these government programs use mandatory taxes rather than voluntary loans.

Unfortunately, the usury-related health insurance industry and the usury-related third-party payment programs of Medicare and Medicaid have sponsored the financially deep pockets of the health care industry and have been directly responsible for the skyrocketing costs of health care in America. For when a nation carries health insurance, this inevitably causes the cost of health care to skyrocket. When a nation carries life insurance, this causes the costs of funerals to soar; when a nation carries car insurance, then America's body shops naturally raise their prices to repair cars involved in motor vehicle accidents; when a nation encourages physicians to carry malpractice insurance, this naturally increases settlement fees for medical malpractice, as well as increases the number of malpractice lawsuits.

To prevent all these problems, 3,400 years ago Jehovah outlawed the sin of usury, because he knew that all these problems would inevitably arise if our nation began to lend money at interest. By outlawing the sin of usury, Jehovah not only made a law which would help to stop general inflation, but he also outlawed the sin of health insurance and government third party payment programs, which God knew would otherwise become the primary cause of skyrocketing health care costs.

So once again, if America had outlawed usury long ago, as God commanded us to do in the Bible, then we wouldn't be having these skyrocketing health care costs today.

THE UNNECESSARILY HIGH COST OF ATHEISTIC RESEARCH

The fourth part of God's view of health care reform involves the sin of atheistic research. You are probably thinking:

> Modern medical research is very expensive, and this contributes to the high cost of medicines and diagnostic medical equipment in America. Therefore, if America is to continue to have high quality medical care, then we must have medical insurance so we can afford to offset the expensive research

costs involved in developing modern medicines and diagnostic medical equipment. But if America abandons its system of health insurance, then Americans will not be able to afford good quality health care. And, America will no longer be on the cutting edge of medical research because there will no longer be any financial incentive to develop high-tech diagnostic medical equipment and modern medicines.

Now this is a good point, but only if America continues to have the kind of wasteful, inefficient, expensive research that we have today. You see, the Bible teaches that God will curse our efforts at medical research if our nation does not obey God. For in the Bible, God promised that if Israel truly obeyed God, he would:

> send a blessing on your barns and on everything you put your hand to . . . The Lord will . . . bless all the work of your hands. (Deut. 28:8, 12 NIV)

On the other hand, God said that if Israel disobeyed God:

> The Lord will send on you curses, confusion, and rebuke everything you put your hand to . . . You will become unsuccessful in everything you do. (Deut. 28:20, 29b NIV)

Now, according to these verses, if ancient Israel were to have pursued medical research, God would have either blessed their efforts (with efficiency, discovery, and success), or cursed their efforts (with delay, expense, and failure), depending upon whether their nation was obedient or disobedient to God's commands in the Bible.

So, when it comes to medical research in modern America, it is clear that our national disobedience to God's commands has provoked the Almighty to curse our medical research with delay, expense, and failure (whether we realize it or not). When God "curses all the work of our hands," this increases the cost for America to develop its future medicines and diagnostic medical equipment.

There are three things our nation does to prompt God to curse our research with delay, expense, and failure. First of all, we anger God by legalizing the eleven sins mentioned earlier which increase our nation's diseases and health care costs. Secondly, some of our research goals are to find cures for the diseases caused by our own sexual immorality, not just so we can cure the sick, but also so we can continue to embrace our sexual immorality without the risk of disease. Thirdly, we magnify our rebellion against God by having our medical research frequently performed by scientists who believe that God did not create man (evolutionists), or by scientists who do not believe in God at all (atheists)!

So why should God bless our attempts at medical research, when most of our research is performed by evolutionists or atheists, and when the goal of some of our research is to make it medically safer for America to continue to commit the sins of sexual immorality with reckless abandon so we won't risk contracting the very diseases which might ordinarily prompt us to repent and ask God's forgiveness?

Additionally, since most scientists today are either atheists, evolutionists, or both, this means that they believe the human body was put together by an infinite series of accidents spread out over millions of years. Also, they believe that there was essentially no premeditated logic behind how the body was originally assembled, and that any logical workings within the human body which may be apparent today are only the result of "what worked out best" for evolution. In this manner, their research (in practice) becomes essentially atheistic, meaning that "no God" was ever involved at any point in designing the human body. And so, they believe there is no need to attempt to understand the philosophy of the design process since there was never any God involved to design our bodies.

Therefore, essentially no consideration is given to the possibility that there could actually be a logical, premeditated, purposeful design behind all the inner workings of our bodies (as the result of an infinitely intelligent divine mind). So, there are no attempts in research to "recreate the thinking processes of the Master Builder," to help us in understanding how He put our bodies together. As a result, atheistic research closes its eyes to what perhaps could be the primary source of important insights into understanding human health and disease. Moreover, there is generally no prayer by the researcher to ask God to reveal His truth about the inner workings of the human body. If he did, this could help develop more accurate hypotheses, so that fewer, less costly experiments could yield more positive, accurate, and consistent results.

I'm not saying to give up on good scientific research—far from it! I'm just saying that when a scientist believes in a Creator and actively tries to recreate the Creator's thought processes when choosing a hypothesis to be tested, actually prays for guidance from the Creator to help him understand the workings of the human body, then the hypotheses are more likely to be inspired. Therefore, his research is bound to be more productive, efficient, and applicable to America's health care needs.

As a consequence of this atheistic research, the medicines being discovered generally show such a small advantage over other medicines currently in existence that the experiments have to be quite large and involve thousands (if not tens of thousands) of patients to be able to demonstrate any small significant improvement in effectiveness over medicines currently being used. If God would begin to "bless all the work of our hands" (Deut. 28:8b, 12b NIV), then I believe we would be led to discover medicines which are not only much more effective, but much safer as well. This way, smaller, less expensive experiments would still be able to demonstrate the advantages of these new medicines.

So, atheistic research is costly, wasteful, and inefficient, whereas prayerful research done by men of great faith in God (specifically seeking His truth) can be much more efficient and cost-effective. Also, prayerful research could probably save America billions of dollars in research costs, and therefore the cost of medical care would again be much less. Currently, America is spending billions of dollars on research which often yields negative or contradictory results instead of spending only millions of dollars on research which could yield positive and consistent results.

I believe we should formulate our research hypotheses based upon the idea that we are created beings and that if we "think God's thoughts after him" (as Sir Isaac Newton put it), then our research hypotheses are bound to be more accurate, and our experiments will be more fruitful.

Let me give you an example of a hypothesis which a creationist might think of before an evolutionist would:

> When a bacteria develops resistance to a modern antibiotic, the genetic machinery now devoted to creating this resistance might have simultaneously become defective in performing its original God-given purpose.

Why might this be so? Because, bacteria were also created by God according to a specific premeditated design. Therefore, it is impossible for a bacteria to "better" God's plan by improving its genetic machinery without that machinery simultaneously becoming less effective in performing its original function. Therefore, if a bacteria has mutated to become stronger in one way, it must also have become weaker in another way. This new weakness can be exploited by designing a medicine to capitalize on this frailty to kill the bacteria.

Generally, this type of hypothesis is not even considered, presumably because our scientists often do not believe in a Creator whose designs cannot be improved upon unless God performs the "improvements." And, while creationist hypotheses will not always win the day, they should prove useful now and then to help make our experiments more productive. In addition to this, God will actually help us in our quest for scientific wisdom and knowledge. This will happen if we worship Him and ask Him for this knowledge, and if we remove the wickedness from our nation and attempt to become a true nation under God, so God will "bless all the work of our hands" (Deut. 28:8b NIV). For instance, in the Bible, God took two men and miraculously...

> filled them with skill to do all kinds of work as craftsmen, designers, embroiderers ... and weavers ... (Exod. 35:35 NIV)

Furthermore, God miraculously gave Solomon scientific knowledge concerning plants and animals. For it is written:

> God gave Solomon wisdom and very great insight, and a breadth of understanding . . . He described plant life, from the cedar of Lebanon to the hyssop . . . He also taught about birds, reptiles and fish. (1 Kings 4:29, 33 NIV)

Does God do this today? Well, maybe not as dramatically as in the Bible, but he does still give scientific wisdom, knowledge, and insight to those Christians who prayerfully do scientific research, and earnestly seek his will in their own lives as well as in their scientific work. For instance, did you know that all the founders of all the major scientific fields were Bible-believing Christian creationists, and that (in comparison to today) they used minimal research money and obtained maximal results? Many of them looked to God for guidance in their research. In other words, the faith in God which leads to prayerful research is much more efficient and cost-effective than atheistic research.

Now there is a book entitled, *The Biblical Basis for Modern Science*, written by Henry Morris, which contains an appendix which lists all of the founders of our major scientific disciplines. As it turns out, all of them were Bible-believing Christians. Their contributions to mankind's understanding of science was immense, and yet the cost of their research was minuscule in comparison to research costs today. The following table is taken from that book which I highly suggest that you purchase and read.

BIBLE-BELIEVING SCIENTISTS OF THE PAST

Scientific Disciplines Established by Bible-Believing Scientists (from Henry M. Morris' *The Biblical Basis for Modern Science*; 1984, 463-465)

1. Antiseptic Surgery	Joseph Lister (1822-1912)
2. Bacteriology	Louis Pasteur (1822-1895)
3. Calculus	Isaac Newton (1642-1727)
4. Celestial Mechanics	Johann Kepler (1571-1630)
5. Chemistry	Robert Boyle (1627-1691)
6. Comparative Anatomy	Georges Cuvier (1769-1832)
7. Computer Science	Charles Babbage (1792-1871)
8. Dimensional Analysis	Lord Rayleigh (1842-1919)
9. Dynamics	Isaac Newton (1642-1727)
10. Electrodynamics	James Clerk Maxwell (1831-1879)
11. Electromagnetics	Michael Faraday (1791-1867)
12. Electronics	Ambrose Fleming (1869-1945)
13. Energetics	Lord Kelvin (1824-1907)
14. Entomology of Living Insects	Henri Fabre (1823-1915)
15. Field Theory	Michael Faraday (1791-1867)

16. Fluid Mechanics	George Stokes (1819-1903)
17. Galactic Astronomy	William Herschel (1738-1822)
18. Gas Dynamics	Robert Boyle (1627-1691)
19. Genetics	Gregor Mendel (1822—1884)
20. Glacial Geology	Louis Agassiz (1807-1873)
21. Gynecology	James Simpson (1811-1870)
22. Hydraulics	Leonardo da Vinci (1452-1519)
23. Hydrography	Matthew Maury (1806-1873)
24. Hydrostatics	Blaise Pascall (1623-1662)
25. Ichthyology	Louis Agassiz (1807-1873)
26. Isotopic Chemistry	William Ramsay (1852-1916)
27. Model Analysis	Lord Rayleigh (1842-1919)
28. Natural History	John Ray (1627-1705)
29. Non-Euclidean Geometry	Bernard Riemann (1826-1866)
30. Oceanography	Matthew Maury (1806-1873)
31. Optical Mineralogy	David Brewster (1781-1868)
32. Paleontology	John Woodward (1665-1728)
33. Pathology	Rudolph Virchow (1821-1902)
34. Physical Astronomy	Johann Kepler (1571-1630)
35. Reversible Thermodynamics	James Joule (1818-1889)
36. Statistical Thermodynamics	James Clerk Maxwell (1831-1879)
37. Stratigraphy	Nicholas Steno (1631-1686)
38. Systematic Biology	Carolus Linnaeus (1707-1778)
39. Thermodynamics	Lord Kelvin (1824-1907)
40. Thermokinetics	Humphrey Davy (1778-1829)
41. Vertebrate Paleontology	George Cuvier (1769-1832)

So you see, the Bible-believing Christians in the past have been greatly responsible for the origin and foundation of many of our scientific disciplines today. So, it is obvious to me that even today, prayerful research by those who believe in a Creator can produce more positive results than can atheistic research by those who believe in evolution. Added, prayerful research can save America millions, if not billions of dollars in research costs, which ultimately will lower the cost of health care in America. As a result, the medicines and high-tech diagnostic medical equipment which America would develop in the future—if we became a biblical society, and God "blessed all the work of our hands" Deut. 28:8b NIV)—would hopefully end up costing us only a fraction of the current projected costs.

America would no longer have to be dependent upon a usury-related health insurance business just to be able to afford the high cost of medicines, treatment, and diagnostic medical equipment. This is because the costs of these items would eventually become much more affordable than they are today. But because America allows such completely unrestrained evil in our nation, and our scientists are often atheists or evolutionists who frequently do not seek God's guidance in their own lives nor do they seek God's guidance in their scientific research, it is no wonder that God, instead of helping our scientific research, will frustrate our efforts instead (Deut. 28:20).

CPR, FEEDING TUBES, AND THE GOLDEN RULE

I have been told (by personal communication with a government representative) that there are approximately 1.5 million nursing home patients in this nation and that approximately 7.1 percent of these patients are being fed by feeding tubes inserted directly into the abdomen into their stomachs or their intestines. Since the vast majority of these tube-fed patients are also vegetative, this means that over one hundred thousand patients in this nation are vegetative and are being kept alive by tube feeding alone. This costs taxpayers about one hundred dollars per day to pay for nursing home beds. Multiply this by 365 days per year and by one hundred thousand patients: this totals to about 3.65 billion dollars annually!

In other words, America spends more than three billion dollars each year in tax-sponsored benefits to pay nursing homes to keep terminally demented elderly patients alive. Prior to the insertion of the feeding tube, frequently these patients already could not think, speak, move, often had bedsores, and were repeatedly admitted into the hospital. This is either because these bedsores often became infected, or because their terminal anorexia and inability to correctly swallow caused repeated episodes of dehydration, kidney infections, constipation with fecal impaction, or aspiration pneumonia.

These patients often cannot complain of their pain to others and cannot feel the pain of their bedsores, but they can still feel the pain of needles being used on them either to draw blood, to start intravenous lines, or to give intramuscular injections. In addition, since they are demented and often mute, they cannot complain of their arthritis pains, and so nurses don't know when to give them medication for pain relief. They cannot complain of their abdominal pains from a bladder infection or from terrible constipation, even though their bowels may feel like they are about to burst. They cannot complain about the pain of having to be turned about in bed every two hours to prevent bedsores, nor can they complain about the pain of having to have their bedsores cleaned or dressed twice or three times daily. Most of these patients have an absolutely miserable existence, without any possibility of pleasure; yet they can still experience pain, dizziness, headache, and nausea, but are physically incapable of expressing their agony. This is what we call a "vegetative state."

Because many of these patients will ultimately stop eating altogether (or eat so little that they cannot survive, and what they do eat often goes down their windpipe into their lungs giving them repeated episodes of choking with pneumonia), the physician will eventually ask the family,

> Considering all the suffering your grandmother is currently going through, if your grandmother's heart stops beating or if she stops breathing, do you think your grandmother would want us to revive or resuscitate her, or do you think she would prefer to pass away peacefully?

Very frequently one of the family members replies by saying,

> Although I personally would not want to be resuscitated if I were in her place, I do, in fact, want you to try to revive and resuscitate my grandmother if her heart stops beating or if she stops breathing. And furthermore, while I personally would never want to be kept alive by a feeding tube if I were in such a condition, I still want you to put a feeding tube in grandma anyway (even though grandma would not want this either), because I cannot take the personal responsibility of letting her die.

You see, often a family member may insist on having the medical profession resuscitate (perform CPR on) his aged grandmother, or having a feeding tube placed into her stomach, even though the patient may be more than 95-years-old and in a completely vegetative state. That same family member will often say that he would never want to be resuscitated or have a feeding tube placed into himself if he were in a vegetative state like his grandmother.

These decisions are very hard for some families to make. But God has not left us without guidance, for he has given us the Golden Rule to help direct us in making these types of difficult decisions. It is the Golden Rule which reveals to us that it is a sin for family members to insist on resuscitating their terminally ill *vegetative* grandmother (who may be only hours from death), or put a feeding tube into their *vegetative* grandmother, if the family members themselves would not want to be resuscitated or have a feeding tube placed into them if they were in the grandmother's place. So therefore, we all must follow the Golden Rule in deciding whether or not to either resuscitate or place feeding tubes into our family members who are already in a *vegetative* state. For it is written:

> Do to others as you would have them do to you. (Luke 6:31 NIV; Matt. 7:12)

And, the Golden Rule is just another way of saying the second greatest commandment, which is:

> Love your neighbor as yourself. (Mark 12:31 NIV)

In other words, God commands you to . . .

> Do to your vegetative grandmother what you would have her do to you (if she were well and it was you who were vegetative, and you could not speak, think, move, etc.)!

So, if you would not want to be kept alive by a feeding tube if you were in grandma's situation, then God commands you not to keep grandma alive by a feeding tube. The same lesson applies in deciding whether or not to resuscitate a vegetative grandmother if her heart stops beating, or if she stops breathing. If you would not want to be resuscitated and restored back into a mere vegetative state, then you are commanded by God not to resuscitate your grandmother if she will merely be restored to a vegetative state as well.

Let's look at this from a spiritual point of view. One of the primary purposes of life is so we can accept Christ as Savior. Then we can grow in faith and obedient surrender to Christ, so he eventually becomes Lord of all of our life's priorities as well. But for the person who is already in a vegetative state, God's purpose for that patient's life on earth is now over. The aged and terminally demented vegetative patient already has such brain damage that he can no longer accept Christ as Savior (if he has not already done so), and can no longer grow in faith through prayer, etc., to build up treasures in heaven any more either. On the other hand, neither can this patient actively sin any more to lose rewards (if he is "heaven-bound") or to increase any punishments (if he is "hell-bound")! Therefore, this patient's eternal destiny (heaven or hell) is fixed, and his eternal rewards (or punishments) are fixed as well. Nothing the patient can do can change any of this, because the patient is no longer capable of either praying or sinning. Therefore, God allows them to linger in this vegetative state, not for their own benefit, but for the benefit of others around them—as a reminder to deal with these same issues of life after death, and get themselves right with Christ before it is too late. God also allows "mindless" vegetative patients to linger and suffer as a prophetic reminder and warning that God still punishes wicked nations by choosing some of their citizens to be cursed with "madness . . . and confusion of the mind" (Deut. 28:28 NIV), regardless of that person's individual righteousness. This serves as a sign that their nation has deliberately chosen to allow ungodly leadership to adopt ungodly laws which encourage immorality, wickedness or idolatry to flourish throughout their land.

Therefore, using a feeding tube to keep the remains of this patient alive long after God would have ordinarily called them home is not an act of faith and obedience, but is an act of doubt and disobedience. It reveals that we honor the life of the body more than the purpose for life, which is to accept Christ as Savior and then grow in faith to make him our Lord as well.

So, if America would legislate that family members must abide by the Golden Rule in making the decision of whether or not to resuscitate or place a feeding tube into their loved one, then America would prevent about one hundred thousand patients yearly from receiving this terribly cruel treatment. It would also save more than three billion dollars in tax-sponsored health care costs which ordinarily goes to pay nursing homes to keep vegetative patients alive with feeding tubes.

THE SIN OF EUTHANASIA

Choosing to neither resuscitate nor to place a feeding tube into an aged, vegetative, terminally ill patient with advanced Alzheimer's disease or multi-infarct dementia is *not* a form of euthanasia. You see, I would never advocate euthanasia, because the Bible would classify euthanasia as deliberate, premeditated murder. In the Bible, God says that the court should execute murderers for their crimes and show them no mercy (Exod. 21:14; Deut. 19:11-13 NIV).

The Golden Rule should never be misused to overrule God's commands against murder (Exod. 21:14; Deut. 19:11-13) in an attempt to justify euthanasia ("compassionate murder"). And, neither should the Golden Rule be misused to overrule any other biblical principle of civil law enforcement for that matter. For imagine what would happen if convicted criminals could distort the Golden Rule by telling the judge that:

> since you would not want to be punished if you were convicted of idolatry, murder, adultery, or homosexuality, then you should do to me as you would want me to do to you, and set me free!

You see, if the Golden Rule were allowed to overrule God's other principles of civil law, then the entire code of Mosaic punishments dissolves into a puddle of contradictions. So the idea that the Golden Rule can be used as a compassionate excuse for murdering a terminally ill patient by euthanasia is ridiculous. Euthanasia is deliberate premeditated murder and is mankind's cruel alternative to a more biblical form of loving care for the terminally ill, such as "comfort care only" and keeping the patient free from any pain.

An Additional Way that the Sin of Usury Increases the Cost of Health Care in America

Decades ago these family decisions over life and death were much easier, and it was common to allow the grandparents to die in their own beds in their own homes instead of in nursing homes with feeding tubes. When the mind of our aged grandparents deteriorated to the point that they stopped eating or drinking, then it was clear to all concerned that there was no hope and that they would soon die. Attempting to resuscitate them after they stopped breathing, or putting a feeding tube into them to keep them alive would have been considered sinful and cruel. Also, the families could never have afforded the high cost of keeping a vegetative grandparent alive in this manner, and this financial burden helped to continuously provide them with the proper moral perspective concerning these things. In other words, families came to the right conclusion (of allowing their terminally ill loved one to die at home without the benefit of inappropriate resuscitation or inappropriate surgical implantation of a feeding tube), even though it may have been for the wrong reason (financial considerations).

But now, in the latter half of the twentieth century, the national sin of usury has allowed the creation of large, third party payment systems, (such as Medicare, Medicaid, Blue Cross, etc.), which do have the resources to pay for inappropriate resuscitation and inappropriate implantation of feeding tubes. So now, families no longer have to face the financial burden of paying for inappropriate feeding tubes, and therefore these same families are now free to make all the wrong decisions with reckless abandon without any financial constraints whatsoever.

In other words, in the past, financial pressures helped families follow the Golden Rule. But now, since someone else "pays the bill"—through medical insurance and/or tax-sponsored Medicare and Medicaid, families often no longer follow the Golden Rule in these situations. Because of these problems, the cost of health care in America has risen to more than three billion dollars annually just to pay nursing homes to keep vegetative patients alive by feeding tubes. This is just one more way that usury-related businesses (i.e., health insurance, Medicare, and Medicaid) have unwittingly increased the cost of medical care in America.

Cost Shifting

The biblical principles of pro-family legislation and welfare reform also function to shift the burden of health care expenses off of the shoulders of the American taxpayer and onto the lap of the large, extended family, where this burden belongs. In other words, adopting the biblical principles of pro-family legislation (see chapter eighteen) into our legislation would cause the creation of large, extended families throughout all America. These families could more easily afford to pay the cost of medical care for their own elderly family members, so American taxpayers would no longer need to pay hundreds of billions of dollars in taxes to support our federal Medicare program. Furthermore, since these elderly patients could now be cared for at home (instead of placing them in nursing homes), this could also save America as much as 54.75 billion dollars annually—a sum which currently goes to pay for America's 1.5 million nursing home patients at one hundred dollars per day for 365 days a year.

Likewise, adopting the biblical principles of welfare reform would so dramatically decrease Medicaid health insurance enrollment that the American taxpayers would again no longer need to pay the billions of dollars in taxes to support our state-sponsored Medicaid programs. This is because the combination of the biblical principles of welfare reform, justice reform, and pro-family legislation function to nearly eliminate alcohol and drug abuse, wife and child abuse, homosexuality, adultery, fornication, and divorce. As a result, there would be no significant numbers of unwed mothers or single parents on the Medicaid rolls, and neither would there be any Medicaid recipients who had become disabled as a consequence of their own sins. Additionally, those remaining elderly, disabled, poor, unemployed, and sick citizens were supposed to have their healthcare paid for by their large, extended families. Therefore, the number of remaining eligible Medicaid recipients would shrink to only a small fraction of what it is currently. Of course, this would entail a dramatic culture change in our nation as well.

How much tax money could be saved in this way? Well, the state of North Carolina alone spent 3.5 billion dollars in Medicaid in 1995 ("Medicaid in North Carolina Annual Report State Fiscal Year 1995," 29, 36), so I presume that the total Medicaid cost for the nation would be about fifty times that much, or approximately 175 billion dollars annually. Imagine American citizens saving a large fraction of this 175 billion dollars in state taxes each year by simply creating a culture where families would naturally take care of their own sick, disabled, and poor, instead of having the state do it for them! And this is just the savings on the state-sponsored *health* care programs alone (i.e., Medicaid) and does *not* include the tax savings on state-sponsored *welfare* programs at all.

In addition, implementing God's view of immigration policy would dramatically decrease our medical bills to pay for the medical care of poor *illegal aliens* and poor *legal* aliens (see chapters nineteen and twenty-three). How much would this save? Well, the Medicaid Program in North Carolina alone spent 4.4 million dollars in 1995 on aliens and refugees, so I presume that the total expenditure nationwide would be many times that much as well (Ibid., 533).

CONCLUSION

God's view of health care reform involves the interaction of all the biblical principles of Justice reform, welfare reform, economic reform, and pro-family legislation.

How does this work? Well, *first* of all, the biblical principles of justice reform and health care reform combine to outlaw the eleven sins which cause the diseases responsible for up to fifty percent of the healthcare costs in America today. By also making the first six of these sins into punishable crimes against the state, America can prevent millions of citizens from becoming ill from these diseases. This would also save us up to fifty percent of our healthcare costs nationally, which would be about 450 billion dollars in savings each year.

The *second* step takes these even smaller costs of health care and shrinks them even further. By switching from "atheistic research" to "creation-based, God-honoring, prayerful research," almighty God is more likely to "bless all the work of our hands" (Deut. 28:12 NIV) and by doing so enable our scientific research to be more productive and less expensive. Therefore, the future medications, treatments, and diagnostic testing equipment developed from this research would be less expensive for patients to use, and so the remaining health care costs would decrease even further.

Then, the *third* step takes these remaining smaller costs of providing health care and shrinks them even further by eliminating general inflation, health care inflation, and insurance fraud and abuse. You see, the yearly inflation of health care costs in America is stopped by outlawing the sin of usury. This has three important implications. First, this helps to stop general inflation; and second, this also outlaws third party payment systems (i.e., Medicare, Medicaid, and private medical insurance) which will eliminate the "deep money pockets" of insured medical care, so health care costs don't skyrocket any longer. Third, the elimination of health insurance and third party payers also stops insurance fraud and abuse. This eliminates unnecessary visits to the emergency room by patients with insurance for conditions which could easily be handled at a doctor's office for a mere fraction of the cost (while also eliminating inappropriate placement of feeding tubes into terminally ill vegetative patients). At this point, the remaining costs of healthcare should become small enough to begin the process of shifting the cost from the government back to our culture of large, extended families. These large extended families have such beneficial economics of scale that they can more easily pay for the health care costs of their own elderly, disabled, sick, unemployed, or poor. This is the *fourth* step of God's view of healthcare reform. The fifth aspect of God's view of healthcare reform is that those citizens without large, extended families to pay for their healthcare needs can be provided for by tithe-sponsored welfare (see chapter nineteen). The *sixth* aspect of God's view of health care reform is that it is God who is the ultimate source of the health or sickness of our nation's citizens. The Bible teaches that if Israel (or any other nation) sends only godly Christian elders into their government—who legislate that their citizens must obey and worship only the one true God of the Bible, and adopt and implement all God's principles of moral law, civil law, and civil law enforcement—then God promised to respond by granting that nation a disease-free society where nearly everyone lives to be 120-years-old while enjoying excellent health the entire time (Deut. 7:12, 15; Exod. 23:25-26; Genesis 6:13 NIV).

The Bible also teaches that if a nation does not obey God, then God instead will *curse* that nation with all kinds of diseases, which of course will increase the health care costs of that nation. For it is written:

(In the following reference, the words written in [*italics*] are *my* words for the modern medical illnesses which could be associated with these biblical prophecies.)

> ... if you do not obey the Lord your God and do not carefully follow all his commands ... all these CURSES will come upon you and overtake; you ... The fruit of your womb will be cursed [i.e., *genetic illnesses*] ... The Lord will plague you with diseases ... The Lord will strike you with wasting disease [i.e., *cancer, leukemia, AIDS, tuberculosis*], with fever and inflammation [i.e., *Rheumatoid arthritis or Lupus*] ... The Lord will afflict you with the boils of Egypt [i.e., *severe dermatitis*], and with tumors [i.e., *cancers or benign tumors*], festering sores and the itch, from which you cannot be cured [i.e., *eczema, psoriasis, seborrheic dermatitis*]. The Lord will afflict you with blindness [i.e., *cataracts, glaucoma, macular degeneration, diabetic eye hemorrhages*], madness and confusion of the mind [i.e., *Alzheimer's dementia, schizophrenia, phobias, panic attacks, strokes*] ... The sights you see will drive you mad [i.e., *nervousness and depression*]. The Lord will afflict your knees and legs with painful boils that cannot be cured [i.e., *painful swelling in the knees, from arthritis, gout, and skin lesions*], spreading from the soles of your feet to the top of your head ... The Lord will send fearful plagues on you and your descendents, harsh and prolonged disasters [i.e., *"natural" disasters, such as hurricanes, floods, droughts, earthquakes, famine, and pestilence*], and severe and lingering illnesses. He will bring upon you all the diseases of Egypt that you dreaded, and they will cling to you. The Lord will also bring on you every kind of sickness and disaster *not* recorded

in this Book of the Law [i.e., *every kind of disease that will ever be described in any nation at any time in the future*] . . . " (Deut. 28:15, 18a, 21a, 22a, 27-28, 34-35 NIV; the words "madness" and "blindness" in the above passage are reversed for simplicity; see also Lev. 26:14, 16a NIV; emphasis added)

So, God promised to curse Israel with all kinds of diseases and "natural" disasters if Israel failed to obey God's commands to become a true nation under God by adopting all God's principles of moral law, civil law, and civil law enforcement into their national legislation. But America, just like Israel, has also failed to adopt these laws into our national legislation. Therefore, we too are suffering from all of the same kinds of diseases mentioned in this prophecy.

Most all American scientists have "naturalistic explanations" for all known diseases which affect U.S. today. I too have been educated to believe these same "naturalistic explanations," but I also believe that the God of the Bible created mankind and that His promises concerning blessing or cursing nations with health or disease (depending upon their national obedience or disobedience) are no less valid than his promises concerning salvation by grace through faith in Jesus Christ! It is a strange paradox that so many people today pray to God for personal *healing*, yet so few believe that God would have purposely made the Israelites *sick*, specifically because their leaders refused to implement the civil laws of God which outlawed fornication, adultery, homosexuality, drunkenness, non-biblical divorce, idolatry, etc., as a way to eliminate wickedness from Israel. We must therefore recognize that the same God who heals and provides can also harm and punish. We must also recognize that God still sends diseases upon the citizens of every nation whose leaders refuse to adopt the biblical principles of civil law which outlaw the sins that so greatly anger God.

With this in mind, America must consider the importance of creating a nation which worships and obeys the God of the Bible and adopts all God's principles of moral law, civil law, and civil law enforcement into our national legislation. For only then can America become a true "nation under God," so that we can be blessed with a nearly disease-free society where nearly everyone lives to be 120-years-old while enjoying excellent health for their entire lives.

And imagine the international witness for Christ that a nearly disease-free state of Israel (or America) could have today. All of the nations of the earth would marvel at this supernatural form of health care. This perpetual blessing of divine intervention would also provide an everlasting declaration to all the world that there truly is a God, and that he is the God of the Bible, whose "truth endureth to all generations!" Therefore, international evangelism would be more successful, as all nations would open their doors and welcome the ambassadors for

Christ sent from Israel (or America) to tell them how they can not only receive salvation by grace through faith in Christ, but also have a true "nation under God," which God would bless as a disease-free society. This international reputation of being the world's first disease-free nation under God represents the seventh and final piece of the Mosaic picture of God's view of health care reform.

Why should our leaders persist in using mankind's ineffective methods of health care reform, when mankind's methods only anger God and provoke him to punish us with even more diseases which result in even more costs each year for health care? Instead, our Christian political leaders should make a covenant with God to create a nation which will:

1. outlaw the sins which cause fifty percent of our health care expenses,

2. switch to prayerful, God-honoring, medical research, so God will "bless all the work of our hands" with greater medical discoveries at minimal research cost,

3. outlaw usury and usury-related businesses (in order to stop general inflation, health care inflation, insurance fraud and abuse),

4. shift the remaining smaller costs of health care to a culture of large, extended families,

5. have tithe-sponsored welfare pay the cost of healthcare for those without large, extended families,

6. create a "nation under God" which God will bless as a disease-free society where nearly everyone lives to be 120-years-old while remaining in excellent health, which in turn would

7. create an international witness for Christ among the nations, as the world's first disease-free nation under God, so all nations of the world would want to worship the Lord of lawmakers and God of America—Jesus Christ!

And *that*, is God's view of healthcare reform!

Chapter Twenty-One

GOD'S VIEW OF ECONOMIC REFORM, NATIONWIDE PROSPERITY, AND THE CREATION OF A NEARLY POVERTY-FREE SOCIETY

Thirty-four hundred years ago God promised Israel that if they became a true "nation under God" by adopting all of God's principles of moral law, civil law, and civil law enforcement into their legislation, that He would bless them with a nearly poverty-free society and make them the richest nation on earth! This is one of the greatest promises ever made by God to Israel. For it is written:

> If you fully obey the Lord your God and carefully follow all his commands I give you today, the Lord your God will set you high above all the nations on earth. All these blessings will come upon you and accompany you if you obey the Lord your God: You will be blessed in the city and blessed in the country. The fruit of your womb will be blessed and the crops of your land and the young of your livestock—the calves of your herds and the lambs of your flocks. Your basket and your kneading trough will be blessed. You will be blessed when you come in and blessed when you go out.... The Lord will send a blessing on your barns and on everything you put your hand to. The Lord your God will bless you in the land he is giving you.... The Lord will grant you abundant prosperity—in the fruit of your womb, the young of your livestock and the crops of your ground.... The Lord will open the heavens, the storehouse of his bounty, to send rain on your land in season and to bless all the work of your hands. You will lend to many nations but will borrow from none. The Lord will make you the head, not the tail... you will always be at the top, never at the bottom. (Deut. 28:1-6, 8, 11-13 NIV)

In these verses, God promises to bless Israel with a nearly poverty-free society and make them into the richest nation on earth if only Israel would obey God's commands completely. More specifically, God promised that Israel would become the top nation, at the head of the list of prosperous nations, and have so much reserve riches that they could lend money to many other nations. Furthermore, about a thousand years later, God made the same type of promise again to the Israelites through the prophet Malachi, revealing the eternal nature of these promises. For it is written:

> "You are under a curse—the whole nation of you—because you are robbing me. Bring the whole tithe into the storehouse, that there may be food in my house. Test me in this," says the Lord Almighty, "and see if I will not throw open the floodgates of heaven and pour out so much blessing that you will not have room enough for it. I will prevent pests from devouring your crops, and the vines in your fields will not cast your fruit," says the Lord Almighty. "Then all the nations will call you blessed, for yours will be a delightful land," says the Lord Almighty. (Mal. 3:9-12 NIV)

There are at least five references in these two verses about blessing groups of people, not individuals! Three references concern blessings upon the nation or the country, while one refers to a delightful land, and one refers to blessings upon cities and rural areas. It is clear that these are national blessings for national obedience, not individual blessings for individual obedience.

It was only when the aggregate righteousness of the entire nation of Israel exceeded the graduated threshold of national righteousness which God had in his divine mind that God would begin to bless Israel with a nearly poverty-free society and make them into the richest nation on earth. But since Jesus taught that:

> small is the gate and narrow is the road that leads to life, and only a few find it. (Matt. 7:14 NIV)

then it is clear that the large majority of citizens in any nation will never become Christians. They will continue to live their lives in rebellion to the will of God. Therefore, only by keeping the large, unrighteous majority on their best behavior could Israel ever hope to receive the wonderful blessing of a nearly poverty-free society and become the richest nation on earth. The only way to accomplish this goal would be to have the righteous rule over the unrighteous and adopt all God's principles of civil law into the national legislation of Israel in order to empower the doctrines of Christianity with the legal muscle to keep the large, unrighteous majority on their best behavior. This is what it takes foreign nations. In the meantime, God's system of laws would guarantee that the nation of Israel would be healthy, peaceful, and prosperous, with the best possible system of government, justice, welfare, health care, and economics.

To summarize, the secret of national prosperity and a poverty-free society is to have a government which adopts all God's principles of moral law, civil law, and civil law enforcement into its national legislation in order to keep the large unrighteous majority on their best behavior. But even if the aggregate righteousness in America never exceeds the graduated threshold required in order for God to bless us with a nearly poverty-free society, there are still abundant natural blessings available for America if we would only adopt God's principles of economic reform into our national legislation.

How Implementing God's Principles of Economic Reform Can Solve Most of the Economic Problems in America Today

Now we will discuss a few of the principles of economics which are mentioned in the Bible. Here is the outline we will follow:

I. God's Condemnation of Usury (loans with interest)
  A. How easy credit can cause financial irresponsibility, overwhelming indebtedness, and occasional bankruptcy.
  B. How decades of large interest payments decrease total family net worth, decrease the children's future inheritance, increase emotional stress, generate the need for the wife to work outside the home, and leave the children to raise themselves under the corrupting guidance of the television set.
  C. How usury causes nearly every single product or service in America to increase in price. Also, how usury causes general inflation, and how usury-related businesses cause business-specific inflation.
  D. How usury causes gambling.
  E. The two methods by which usury takes interest money from the poor and gives it to the rich, spreading out the economic distance between them, creating national discontent and covetousness, which in turn increases national crime.
  F. How the philosophy of usury in our government has caused a three trillion dollar national debt, a government on the verge of bankruptcy, and a monstrous threat to the entire American way of life.
  G. How usury allows big business to expand further and unfairly compete with small businesses, causing small busi-

nesses to often go bankrupt. Also, two reasons why usury causes labor strikes.
  H. How usury breaks up the American family by sponsoring our ability to live apart from each other.
  I. How usury causes taxes to increase.
  J. How interest-free loans help the poor.
  K. How laws against usury help to create a debt-free society by encouraging us to save money.
II. How national disobedience to God's commands increases the national unemployment rate.
III. Why God told Israel (and by implication, America as well) that they did not need a large centralized government which collected taxes.
IV. How national usury causes God's commands to be removed from the government.
V. How the biblical standard for government to recruit and promote only righteous men sets the standard for businesses to do the same.
VI. What will happen to the national economy without usury?
VII. What will happen to the stock market without usury?
VIII. God's view of true wealth—measuring our standard of living by His priorities and not our priorities.
IX. Conclusion: How adopting God's principles of economics will allow America to be more blessed economically than we are today, with an even more advanced technology.

Hopefully, when you have finished reading this chapter, you will agree that if America had followed God's principles of economics over the last two hundred years, then our entire nation would now be much better off, and that America would now have:

1. a much better standard of living,
2. a nation of debt-free families,
3. a debt-free government,
4. a much slower, more relaxed lifestyle,
5. less poverty,
6. no inflation, and
7. a more advanced, high-tech society than we have today.

I. God's Condemnation of Usury

Usury is the charging of a profit (or, interest) when lending money to someone. America's economy is based in large part upon the legal ability to make a profit on the lending of money. Mankind appears to see many advantages in lending money in this way, but in the Bible,

God says it is illegal to make a profit through the lending of money, presumably because this is bad for the country. For it is written:

> If you lend money to one of my people who is needy, do not be like a moneylender; charge him no interest. (Exod. 22:25 NIV)
>
> Do not take interest of any kind from him . . . You must not lend him money at interest . . . (Lev. 25:36a, 37a NIV)

The Bible mentions usury twenty-three times, and in each reference there is evidence of God's disapproval. Some Christians however, have mistakenly concluded that God only outlawed interest on loans to poor Israelites, but that He allowed interest to be charged on loans to rich Israelites who might have wanted to expand their businesses. But the Bible allows interest to be charged only to foreigners, and expressly forbids interest to be charged on loans to "brother Israelites." For it is written:

> Do not charge your brother interest, whether on money or food or anything else that may earn interest. You may charge a foreigner interest, but not a brother Israelite, so that the Lord may *bless you in everything you put you hand to* . . . (Deut. 23:19-20 NIV; emphasis added)

This last reference reveals that if Israel were to outlaw usury (and follow God's other economic policies as well) that God would "bless them in everything they put their hand to." In other words, God's economic blessings for the entire nation of Israel are linked (at least in part) to whether or not Israel would outlaw usury on loans for fellow Israelites.

Since God's promise to Israel of national economic blessing as a reward for national obedience is still available to all nations today (see chapter four), then it is clear that America would have been blessed even more by almighty God—if our nation could somehow have guaranteed that usury would have remained illegal over the last 2 hundred years.

Unfortunately, many Christians, including Christian economists, accountants, and financial planners (whose jobs depend, in part, on knowing how to use interest-bearing vehicles to "work to your advantage") have mistakenly concluded that "usury" really means "the taking of *excessive* interest" rather than "the taking of *any* interest." Therefore, they mislead others to believe that God would *allow* Israel (and America) to lend money at interest, as long as the interest rate is not too high!

How high is "too high?" Is 20 percent interest too high? How about 15 percent, 10 percent, or even 5 percent? Well, the Bible teaches that even 1 percent interest is too high! For it is written:

> I accused the nobles and officials. I told them, "You are exacting usury from your own countrymen! . . . I and my brothers and my men are also lending the people money and grain. But let the exacting of usury stop! Give back to them immediately . . . the usury you are charging them—the *hundredth part* of the money, grain, new wine and oil." (Neh. 5:7, 11 NIV; emphasis added)

It is clear in this passage that charging any interest at all, even interest as low as 1 percent (the "hundredth part"), is against the will of God. God prefers that the wealthy people (such as Nehemiah, his brothers, his men, and the nobles and officials) lend money and grain to the poor people without any interest whatsoever.

Most secular American economists would disagree with the Bible on this point. So who is right: man or God? Why, God, of course!

I'm sure God gave due divine consideration to every conceivable advantage of lending money at interest before he decided that usury was ultimately bad for the nation!

What are the advantages of usury, as man sees it? Since God disapproves of usury, what then must be the disadvantages of usury, as God sees it?

American economists teach us that usury has a great many advantages. For instance, usury allows individuals to take out loans to buy furniture, major appliances, automobiles, houses, and boats, without having to first save up the entire purchase price of these items. So, not only would American economists claim that usury allows our citizens to buy many things that we could not ordinarily afford, but also that this raises America's standard of living! Furthermore, usury also allows businessmen to take out loans to finance the expansion of their businesses, or to finance the cost of research and product development. In summary, most economists believe that usury fuels the economy, raises our standard of living, and raises America's gross national product, and that without usury, our entire economy would suffer.

Viewed in that context, who in his right mind would dare oppose the idea of having interest-bearing loans to stimulate our economy? Even I myself would never dare oppose the idea of usury if it were not for just one thing—God himself opposed the idea of usury for the Israelite nation, and by implication, for all other nations as well. You can be sure that only almighty God can see all the true problems for society which develop directly or indirectly from usury, many of which ordinarily remain obscure to men, but are obvious to almighty God, who can truly weigh the advantages and disadvantages of usury over many generations!

For you see, usury is actually the single most destructive economic policy in America. In fact, it not only indirectly causes the unemployment rate in America to increase, but also contributes to the removal of God's commands from our government. It also directly or indirectly causes all the problems lettered A through K listed earlier in this chapter, which we will now examine one by one.

A. How Easy Credit Can Cause Financial Irresponsibility, Overwhelming Indebtedness, and Occasional Bankruptcy

The Israelite's ambition to "get ahead" was supposed to be translated into saving money for any large purchases. This is because the unavailability of usury-credit teaches financial responsibility, patience, hard work, and self-control to save money and not to spend it wastefully. In America many generations ago (when usury-credit was much less available than it is today), our grandparents and great-grandparents also learned the financial responsibility to work hard and have the patience to save money for nearly everything they purchased. For you see, these biblical economic principles which God gave to Moses 35 hundred years ago work equally as well in the modern, crowded, high-tech societies of America as they were designed to work in the ancient, rural, primitive societies of Israel.

Easy credit, on the other hand, causes financial irresponsibility by undermining our desire to be frugal and to save money, and leads to a society which practices wasteful self indulgence. After all, why develop the good habit of regularly saving money for all our needs (large and small), when instead you can buy with usury-credit and pay low monthly payments?

A second problem is that easy access to usury-credit also tempts us to buy higher quality items rather than what we really need, and for more money than we can really afford. You see, usury-credit lures us into paying more (sometimes much more) for an item (over a period of time) than the item is actually worth, just to have that item immediately. As a result, it is all too frequent for families to get overextended on their credit cards and loans. The family becomes so deeply in debt that they cannot pay off their loans and so, face repossession of their car, foreclosure on their house, and personal bankruptcy.

So you can see how easily usury credit can cause financial irresponsibility, overwhelming indebtedness, and occasional bankruptcy.

B. How Decades of Large Interest Payments Decrease Total Family Net Worth, Decrease the Children's Future Inheritance, Increase Emotional Stress, Generate the Need for the Wife to Work Outside the Home, and Leave the Children to Raise Themselves under the Corrupting Guidance of the Television Set

Because usury has encouraged our citizens to live beyond their means, American families are now more in debt than ever before. In fact, when a young family buys their first new house or mobile home, for several years thereafter the amount of money they owe will often greatly exceed the total value of their possessions. In other words, their assets (the value of their possessions) minus their liabilities (the total amount of money they owe) is actually a negative number, which means that the net worth (assets minus liabilities) of these young, upwardly mobile families actually is *negative* for many years. If the net worth of the fortunate, young, upwardly mobile families is negative, then the net worth of less fortunate families may also be very low.

American politicians like to claim that since we have a better standard of living today, that our citizens are therefore much better off than in generations past. However, because usury causes us to live up to and beyond our means, our national standard of living is being maintained by a cash flow which is barely adequate to sustain the payments for the debts accumulated by most American families. As a result, if the family income were to be suddenly cut off, then within a matter of months many would go bankrupt and lose their house and cars through foreclosure.

I suggest that a better way to evaluate the total wealth of American families is to estimate the purchasing power of the average family's total net worth. In other words, in light of inflation and the large accumulated debts of the average family, how many months can the average family survive buy selling their assets to pay off their past debts and their current monthly expenses before they become welfare-dependent?

You see, because of usury-dependency, I believe that the average family's net worth is probably so low that the "time to welfare dependency" is shorter now than in generations past (when our ancestors saved their money and did not always borrow money to buy whatever they wanted). This becomes even more true when you consider that inflation has raised the cost of living to be much greater today than in generations past. Viewed in this way, America's families may actually be poorer now than our ancestors were generations ago.

So, if America would measure our prosperity by our "time to welfare dependency," rather than by our standard of living, then we would discover that America is much poorer than we realize. This type of poverty is measured by the stress and speed of America's rat race, which we run in order to keep up with the huge monthly interest payments required to maintain our standard of living.

Let me give you an example. If you buy a one hundred thousand dollar house with an interest-bearing loan, it may very well cost you two hundred thousand dollars before it is actually paid. For if you count up all the interest you will pay out from mortgaging a house over fifteen to twenty-five years, you end up paying practically double the original price of the house (or more), depending upon the interest rate. So in some sense, if you pay cash for your house, you are getting as much as 50 percent (or more) off the total purchase price for the house which you would end up paying out over twenty years to the bank. This extra one hundred thousand dollars of interest could have purchased other things or could have gone for your children's inheritance.

These increased expenses for interest-bearing loans cause increased emotional stress on the family, as they begin to worry about paying off an ever-increasing debt. This frequently prompts the wife to find employment outside the home to increase the family income in order to pay off the debt. This causes the children to have less "quality time" with their parents than before. Unfortunately, the corrupting influence of the television fills this void in the vast majority of homes, so our children are tempted by television programming to become more violent and immoral with each succeeding generation.

This is certainly not how God intended family life to be. Yet this is often the natural history of families which have overextended themselves and now are overwhelmingly in debt because of the temptation of easy availability of usury-credit. Furthermore, there is often no easy way out of such circumstances without suffering repossession, foreclosure, or bankruptcy. Such families would have been much better off if they had just saved their money until they could pay cash for all their major purchases, exactly as the Bible teaches.

C. HOW USURY CAUSES NEARLY EVERY PRODUCT OR SERVICE IN AMERICA TO INCREASE IN PRICE. ALSO, HOW USURY CAUSES GENERAL INFLATION, AND HOW USURY-RELATED INDUSTRIES CAUSE INDUSTRY-SPECIFIC INFLATION

The sin of usury is one of the causes of general inflation, and, since this subject was already discussed in the previous chapter, some of this discussion will be repetitious.

Basically, inflation can be caused by many things (such as supply and demand, political instability, war, plagues, droughts, and natural disasters) but most of these things are either naturally or supernaturally prevented or controlled in a biblical society. For God has promised to supernaturally prevent all these problems for any country which becomes a true nation under God and whose aggregate national righteousness exceeds the threshold required by God (for details, see chapter three).

The last remaining cause of inflation is when banks lend money to other businesses and charge them interest payments in return. This extra expense of paying off interest on business loans is passed on to the consumer by inflating the cost of the product or service. In this way, the rate of interest should ordinarily be *directly* related to the rate of inflation.

Unfortunately however, nationwide usury has also gotten Americans out of the good habit of saving money for expensive items, and has gotten us into the bad habit of taking out interest-bearing loans to pay for these items instead. So, as a result of the sin of usury, our culture has developed a mind set of spending money instead of saving it. Today, our usury-dependent culture is populated with citizens who have a tendency to spend all of the extra money they have as soon as they get it. In other words, a usury-dependent culture inevitably becomes a spendthrift culture. And whenever the national money supply temporarily increases in a spendthrift culture, then demand for products and services increases and this causes further inflation.

Knowing this, our Federal Reserve Bank—created from the sin of big government (see chapter five)—has begun to take advantage of our usury-dependent, spendthrift culture and has created policies allowing the government to purchase massive amounts of interest-bearing bonds whenever they think it is necessary. This has the effect of lowering interest rates while increasing the national money supply. In turn, this causes a greater demand for products and services which increases their prices and raises the rate of inflation.

In other words, the national sin of having big government (and the subsequent power of the Federal Reserve Board) has created a society where the rate of interest has now become *inversely* related to the rate of inflation. Whereas, without big government (and therefore without a Federal Reserve Board regulating our nation's money supply) the rate of interest would ordinarily be *directly* related to the rate of inflation. Any way you look at it, the rate of inflation is linked to the rate of interest.

God says that the interest rate should always be zero percent when we lend money to our own citizens (Deut. 23:19-20 NIV; see also Exod. 22:23; Lev. 25:36a, 37a; Neh. 5:7-11 NIV). If the interest rate always remained at zero percent, then the inflation rate should always remain at zero percent as well. After all, if the interest rate was always *zero percent,* then the government would no longer have any interest-bearing bonds available to buy or sell. Therefore, the Federal Reserve Bank could no longer control the rate of inflation by suddenly changing the nation's money supply in order to immediately increase or decrease consumer demand for products and services. Furthermore, business would no longer have to inflate their prices to compensate for interest payments. As a result, prices of goods and services would eventually *stabilize* and general inflation would *cease to* exist. In other words, if America outlawed the sin of usury (lending money at interest), then inflation would stop. This would happen providing that all of the other factors effecting inflation were equally well controlled, as of course they would be in a biblical society.

These other causes of inflation include the wage-price spiral, political instability, economic recession and depression, wars, national involvement in unfavorable or collapsing foreign markets, and natural disasters. However, all of these problems are either naturally prevented or supernaturally controlled by God as an actual divine blessing upon any nation which regularly enforces all of God's principles of civil law. The problem of "supply and demand" however, may continue to exist, but this should only affect the price of whichever specific product is in short supply, and usually should have no affect on general inflation!

In addition to causing general inflation, usury also causes business-specific inflation (a concept which was discussed in chapter twenty). For example, recall how the cost of health care in America always seems to rise faster than the rate of general inflation. The reason for this is that our usury-dependent, spendthrift culture has given birth to a usury-dependent health insurance business. You see, when you lend someone money at interest, you hope to eventually get your interest-profit returned to you. Over the last few generations, creative businessmen have invented new methods of returning your interest-profit back to you, and one of these methods involves their promise to take the risk of paying all of your medical bills as long as they can keep the rest of the interest-profit for themselves.

In this manner, the sin of usury has given birth to the health insurance business. This makes all types of third-party payment programs (such as federal Medicare and state-sponsored Medicaid) related to the sin of usury as well. The difference is that these government programs use mandatory taxes rather than voluntary loans. Unfortunately, the usury-related health insurance business and the usury-related third-party payment programs of Medicare and Medicaid have sponsored the financially deep pockets of the health care industry and have been directly responsible for the skyrocketing costs of health care in America.

When a nation carries health insurance, this inevitably causes the cost of health care to skyrocket. When a nation carries life insurance, this causes the costs of funerals to soar; when a nation carries car insurance, then America's body shops naturally raise the prices to repair cars involved in motor vehicle accidents; and when a nation encourages physicians to carry malpractice insurance, this naturally increases settlement fees for medical malpractice, as well as increases the number of malpractice lawsuits. So, to prevent all of these problems, 34 hundred years ago Jehovah outlawed the sin of usury, because he knew that all these problems would inevitably arise if our nation began to lend money at interest. By outlawing the sin of usury, Jehovah made a law which would help to stop both general inflation and industry-specific inflation, which God knew would otherwise cause skyrocketing costs of health care, funerals, auto body repair, and lawsuit settlements.

D. HOW USURY CAUSES GAMBLING

Imagine that I lent you some money and you promised to pay it back—plus all of the interest—in sixty days. And so, you *gave* me your IOU as your personal guarantee. Well, suppose that instead of my returning in sixty days, I came back in five minutes and said,

> Let me flip this IOU onto the ground. If it lands face up, then you can keep all the money without owing me anything. But if it lands face down, then you owe me all the money plus all the interest right now!

This is gambling! Since gambling is related to usury, then when God outlawed usury, he also outlawed gambling. For gambling not only causes organized crime to flourish, but also tempts gamblers to waste their entire life savings—money which should have instead gone towards their retirement and their children's inheritance. These are just two more reasons why God commanded usury to be made illegal throughout the entire nation of Israel.

E. THE TWO METHODS BY WHICH USURY TAKES MONEY FROM THE POOR AND GIVES IT TO THE RICH, SPREADING OUT THE ECONOMIC DISTANCE BETWEEN THEM, CREATING DISCONTENT AND COVETOUSNESS, WHICH IN TURN INCREASES NATIONAL CRIME

There are two methods by which usury spreads out the economic distance between the rich and the poor. The first involves taking interest payments from the lower classes and giving part of these payments to the rich. The second method involves banking bias and preferential lending to those who can easily pay back their loans, rather than lending money to the unemployed poor who can not pay back their loans.

You see, in a true "nation under God," loans are given for the benefit of the poor, unlike in America, where loans are given for the benefit of the bank—to increase their profits so they can pay interest on the interest-bearing savings accounts, money market accounts, and CDs, of the middle class and the wealthy. In this way, the poor families (who are generally borrowing and not saving) are paying high interest, and the very rich families (who are generally saving and not borrowing) are being paid a portion of this same interest profit in their savings accounts, (after the bank takes out its share for being the middleman). So, the bank makes the greatest profit, the rich make less, the middle class may break even or possibly lose money, and the poor lose a lot of money. So, as a consequence of national usury, money is slowly taken from the poor (through interest payments from the poor to the bank), and given to the rich (through interest payments from the bank to the rich), which spreads out the economic distance between the poor and the rich. In other words, because of nationwide usury, the poor get poorer and the rich get richer!

With national usury, the unemployed very poor don't qualify for any loans whatsoever (because of their inability to pay back the loan), yet these were the very people to whom God commanded the Israelites to give their interest-free loans. In a biblical society, lending money is a money-*losing* endeavor and is mostly done out of generosity to the poor and out of duty to almighty God. But in America, lending money is a money-*making* endeavor and is done mostly by banks, and always for the purpose of making money for the bank, and never out of compassion for the poor.

Therefore, a society which allows usury discourages lending money to the unemployed poor (who may not be able to pay you back), but instead encourages the lending of money only to the middle class and upper class (people who can pay you back). In this way, lending money *with* interest again TILTS the economy in the direction of the wealthy to increase their riches, whereas lending money *without* interest TILTS the economy in the direction of the poor, to decrease their poverty.

So you see, there are two ways in which national usury spreads out the economic distance between the poor and the rich even further, and makes the rich richer, and the poor, poorer. The first method involves interest payments, and the second method involves lending bias. This progressively uneven distribution of wealth breeds covetousness, jealousy, greed, and crime.

God's laws however, stop this process. Since there are no interest-bearing loans available, we all learn to save money, become more financially responsible, and eventually become debt-free. The debt-load of society ultimately becomes essentially zero, so all Americans are much better off (because 10-20 percent of their income is no longer going for interest payments), and the rich are less rich than they would have been (because they no longer have access to the extra income generated from interest-bearing sources). In other words, society may still have millionaires, but no billionaires!

In America today, people have grown out of the habit of being generous to the poor by directly lending money to them, because nowadays there are banks to do this lending for us. Unfortunately for the poor however, the banks will either charge them interest (which may increase their impoverishment even further), or not lend them any money at all (if the banks fear that the unemployed poor cannot repay the loan).

In a society without usury, no one's extra money ever goes into an interest-bearing checking account, savings account, certificate of deposit, stock or bond. As a result, since your extra money is not making you any interest, it doesn't "cost you anything" to lend a small part of it to the poor, presuming you eventually get your money back again. By doing this, you are not only helping the poor, but are pleasing almighty God as well. If the entire nation obeys God in this way, then even if you don't get your money back, at least you will be obeying God's commands, and God promises that He will reimburse your nation for its obedience by blessing all the work of the hands of all its citizens. So, because of God's condemnation of usury, and God's promised blessings for national obedience, people are more likely to lend their money to the poor for their basic necessities of life.

Since banks cannot make a profit on lending money to either rich or poor, then the poor have nowhere to turn to get their small loans except to other friends and strangers. So, society once again learns to be more personally involved in helping the poor through loans as God intended. This makes society more friendly and less indifferent to the plight of the poor. This is exactly what God wanted—for the citizens of Israel (and America) to open up their hands and be generous to the poor by lending money to them without charging them any interest payments.

Furthermore, not only does usury-credit teach people *not* to save money, but also gives people increased opportunities and temptations to *steal*—such as credit card fraud, insurance fraud, Medicare fraud, and Medicaid fraud. This is just one more way that usury increases national crime.

F. How the Philosophy of Usury in Our Government has Caused a Three Trillion dollar Debt, a Government on the Verge of Bankruptcy, and a Monstrous Threat to the Entire American Way of Life

Generations ago, most of our great grandparents were taught in the churches of America that God hates it when citizens allow themselves to accumulate debt without paying it off. For it is written:

> Give everyone what you owe him ... Let no debt remain outstanding ... (Rom. 13:7a, 8a NIV)

They also remembered, from the Great Depression, that the family which saves money is better off when financial tragedy strikes than the family which has accumulated significant debt. As a result, our ancestors learned to hate being in debt and tried very hard to save their money so they could always pay cash, or else go without. Not only did our great grandparents hate for their families to be in debt, but our government leaders at that time hated for the government to be in debt as well. As a result, the government did not accumulate any really significant debt until the last several decades.

As time went on, America's increased participation in usury-credit as a way of obtaining our "needs" and "wants," eventually spawned the notion of "acceptable indebtedness." Consequently, as American citizens became more willing to allow themselves and their families to be greatly in debt, so also our governmental leaders became more willing to allow our government to develop this same indebtedness as well.

The increased prevalence of usury in America has prompted our citizens to change their priorities and purchase things we cannot afford out of the mistaken belief that we really "need" these things. Also, the philosophy of "acceptable indebtedness" has prompted our government leaders to "purchase" an unaffordable military, as well as an unnecessarily large and intrusive government, in the mistaken belief that America "needs" these things!

It is no wonder therefore, that we have "governmental fiscal irresponsibility" when our leaders are raised in a society which encourages "family fiscal irresponsibility" by encouraging debt through usury-credit, which in turn, discourages the saving of money. So today, usury-credit and the subsequent philosophy of "acceptable indebtedness" has caused our government to develop a staggering debt, bringing us near the verge of bankruptcy. Consequently, taxes must remain very high in order to keep our government from defaulting on all their loans and going broke. And so, for the last three or four decades Americans have been willing to allow our families (and our government) to get heavily into debt just so we can get what we want now, for our families, and from our government.

In summary, embracing usury as a nation has discouraged its citizens from saving money, and has sponsored a spendthrift attitude of financial irresponsibility in the hearts of both our citizens and our rulers. This has created a three trillion dollar national debt and a government on the verge of bankruptcy, which has guaranteed that taxes must remain perpetually high and burdensome for our own families and for the families of our children and our grandchildren. This is just one more part of the terrible legacy which results when a nation embraces usury.

G. How Usury Allows Big Business to Expand Further to Unfairly Compete with Small Business, Causing small Businesses to Often Go Bankrupt. Also, Two Reasons Why Usury Causes Labor Strikes.

Usury-credit allows interest-bearing loans to be given to some businesses to either finance their expansion or help them to purchase smaller businesses. These much larger businesses can now unfairly compete with small, family businesses and drive them out of business. As a result of usury, thousands of small businesses and farmers have had to close because of the unfair advantages for competition which can be obtained through interest-bearing loans.

However, in a biblical society, any business which wants to expand would have to save up the money to do so. Furthermore, business expansion would generally be slow enough to allow the smaller (non-growing) businesses to accommodate more readily, so as to not be driven into bankruptcy. As a result of the lack of interest-bearing loans available in society, there may be bigger businesses, but probably no giant corporations. Small family businesses would probably be much more common in America today.

Also, when some family businesses did manage to save enough money—to finally expand, or purchase some expensive new piece of equipment to help their business grow—any price increases charged by them would only reflect the cost of the equipment and would not include any interest payments. This means that future price increases after business expansion would always be less, because the expansion occurred without using any interest-bearing loans. And, since any future business expansion would be much slower, the smaller businesses wouldn't lose as much profit to the larger corporations. This way, they wouldn't have to increase their prices as much just to stay afloat. Competition between businesses would be much more fair and cordial, because you couldn't afford the expense to compete unfairly anyway.

Additionally, America's labor force would be much less likely to ever go on strike. Why? Because there would be no general inflation to continually raise the cost of living each year, and neither would there be any business-specific inflation to make the cost of health care skyrocket, or the cost of funerals soar! Therefore, labor would no longer have to seek a new "cost-of-living-raise" each year. Furthermore, without interest-bearing loans, none of the larger businesses would have any significant debt, so they could afford to pay laborers what they truly deserve.

H. How Usury Breaks Up the American Family by Sponsoring Our Ability to Live Apart from Each Other

God's commands in the Bible indicate that He wanted Israel (and by implication, America as well) to have large, extended families with triple economies of scale (shared labor, shared possessions, and shared expenses) as the basic economic unit of society. Grandparents were expected to live with their children, and most frequently with the eldest son, who received a double portion of the inheritance to assist him in supporting them. Children and young adults were also expected to continue to live at home and support their family until they got married. In fact, out of duty and responsibility to their parents, even after getting married, spouses would probably still be expected to move in with the large, extended family and to help support them for years, even after they could afford to move out and start their own household.

Because of this cultural emphasis on the duty and responsibility to support your family, inevitably there would be an increased emphasis on the importance of getting along with one another to make the large, extended family a viable reality. Those families who got along well would be able to maintain large, extended families longer and therefore, would enjoy the benefits of higher income and lower expenses because of the triple economy of scale.

In America however, there has been a progressive emphasis on "freedom-freedom-freedom-freedom!" Freedom from God's laws, freedom from tradition, freedom from your responsibility to your family, and freedom to "be all that you can be"! And so eventually, "loyalty to family" has been replaced by "loyalty to self." In America today, we no longer encourage large, extended families. In fact, most Americans are not only glad to move away from their parents, but are also glad when their children grow up and move away from them. America has generally rejected the idea of trying to get along with one another just to keep large, extended families together, no matter what may be the economic and emotional advantages of larger families.

Usury has affected both the *opportunity* to leave the family and the *means* to leave the family by sponsoring our ability to live apart from each other. You see, the opportunity to find work outside your city or state has increased. At the same time, there are fewer and fewer small, family businesses, which might keep the children at home working for (and with) the family. The availability of usury-credit is partially responsible for causing this problem by allowing interest-bearing loans to be given to some businesses to either finance their expansion or help them to purchase smaller businesses. These much larger businesses can now unfairly compete with small, family businesses and drive them into bankruptcy. As a result, since the family business is gone, the children have less loyalty to stay in the same city to find work. Now, there is increased temptation to find work in other cities and other states, which results in the children moving away from home and decreases the number of large, extended families. These problems result at least partially from usury-credit, even though there are certainly other causes of this problem.

Additionally, the usury-related third-party payor of social security retirement income has provided the means of breaking up the large, extended family by sponsoring the ability of our grandparents to live apart from their children and grandchildren. Usury-credit also provides the means to help finance the ability of our newly married children to move away from home without having to first save up money to start a new home.

In summary, usury tends to destroy the large, extended family by providing the means to finance both newlyweds and grandparents to live apart from their families. Usury also provides the interest-bearing loans which allows big businesses to squash small family businesses; so the commitment to live at home and work with the family business decreases, and the opportunity to find work with big businesses in other cities and in other states increases.

I. How Usury Increases Taxes

As you have read, usury increases bankruptcies through overwhelming indebtedness from interest bearing loans, credit cards, and gambling (see sections A and D). These bankruptcies increase those on welfare which increases taxes. Secondly, usury causes inflation (section C) and also makes the poor poorer (section E); and therefore, again increases those on welfare which also increases taxes. Thirdly, the government participates in usury-related social security retirement and disability programs as well as federal pension plans, which also increases our taxes. Fourthly, government participation in usury has caused and increased our national debt to three trillion dollars, and paying off this debt has also increased our taxes.

Therefore, I would estimate that about a quarter of the average family's income goes to pay for the consequences of participating in usury as a family and as a nation, namely:

1. paying interest on family loans,
2. paying insurance premiums to usury-related businesses,
3. paying increased taxes on usury-related social security retirement income, disability income, and federal pension plans,
4. paying increased taxes for welfare because of usury-induced poverty, and
5. paying increased taxes caused by a three trillion dollar government debt.

So, it is clear that our nation's families pay much more in interest and in taxes because of nationwide usury than we have ever received in benefits from usury to increase our standard of living. Therefore, if America could outlaw usury, then our citizens would save so much money with decreased taxes and without any interest payments, that within a few generations our standard of living would become much higher *without* usury than it currently is *with* usury.

J. How Interest-Free Loans Help the Poor

God wanted the Israelites to develop a culture where God would bless the entire nation economically. Therefore, its citizens would be more inclined to be generous to the poor, and "freely lend them whatever they needed." For instance, in the following verse concerning lending money to the poor, it is written:

> ... be openhanded and freely lend him whatever he *needs*. (Deut. 15:8 NIV; emphasis added)

Notice that God says to lend the poor man whatever he *needs*, not whatever he *wants*. This is God's way of saying that these loans are to be small, and are to be used only for the bare necessities of life.

In addition to this, these loans were to be canceled every seven years if they had not already been paid back. This is God's "bankruptcy law" to prevent perpetual impoverishment generation after generation. For it is written:

> At the end of every seven years you must cancel debts ... Every creditor shall cancel the loan he has made to his fellow Israelite. He shall not require payment from his fellow Israelite or brother, because the Lord's time for canceling debts has been proclaimed. You may require payment from a foreigner, but you must cancel any debt your brother owes you. (Deut. 15:1, 2b-3 NIV)

God designed this system so the canceling of these loans by creditors every seven years was not supposed to cause a great hardship on the creditor. These loans were only supposed to supply the poor man's actual "needs," and therefore would be generally very small loans.

God's purpose in canceling debts every seven years was to avoid developing a culture of perpetual indebtedness (like we have in America today). Furthermore, the idea that you can become debt-free and "start life over again" (economically speaking) not only decreases bankruptcies, but also decreases national crime. This occurs by raising the hopes and the ambitions of the poor, so they can anticipate a better life in the future without indebtedness and without having to resort to stealing. It is highly probable that once the poor become debt-free (every seven years), they will do their best to avoid getting into debt again, probably by working harder and saving money. This biblical ethic of hard work, saving money, and not allowing yourself to get too much into debt would be regularly reinforced as a result of the godly peer pressure which naturally develops in a biblical society (for reasons which are covered in earlier chapters).

Part of God's purpose for the "year of canceling debts" was to create an incentive within the poor community to work hard, to save money, and to avoid creating a family tradition of perpetual indebtedness. This encourages a nationwide attitude of financial responsibility throughout society, by giving each citizen a desire to be debt-free.

A system of loans from private individuals (the balance of which would be "canceled" every seven years) is the system which would provide the strongest encouragement to develop a culture of financial responsibility with maximal "internal" motivation to return to work. This is the kind of culture which would naturally develop if our government adopted God's principles of civil law. Alternatively, a tax sponsored welfare system provides the strongest encouragement to develop a culture of welfare dependency because the recipients eventually come to believe they deserve every penny they can get, so there is minimal "internal" motivation to go back to work. This is the kind of welfare-dependent culture we have had in America—a society which has rejected all of God's civil laws (for details, see chapter nineteen).

Furthermore, by following God's economic principles, society once again learns to be more personally involved in helping the poor through loans as God intended. This makes society more friendly and less indifferent to the plight of the poor. This is exactly what God wanted—for the citizens of Israel (and America) to open up their hands and be generous to the poor by lending money to them without charging them any interest payments.

Can you see the wisdom and love of Jehovah as revealed through these laws?

K. HOW GOD'S LAWS AGAINST USURY ENCOURAGE US TO SAVE MONEY AND CREATE A DEBT-FREE SOCIETY

In a society which does not allow usury, we must pay cash for everything, because credit is generally unavailable. Consequently, we have to save up all of the money required for large (and small) budget purchases. So, we stop buying what we want, and only buy what we need. As a result, we get into the good habit of saving money and avoiding impulse buying, while at the same time enjoying the benefits of debt-free living. This same attitude carries over to our rulers, who also would begin to run our government with a balanced budget.

We have all heard the expression:

> Don't wait until you save enough money to buy it! Buy it now with credit!

This has been the mistaken advice Americans have been hearing for more than half a century. Although usury-credit may initially jump-start a family's finances or a nation's economy, a philosophy of paying interest on every major purchase will severely limit the total net worth a family can pass to their grandchildren as inheritance. Also, usury may jump-start a government's economy, but a generation of interest payments ultimately limits the total net worth of our government as well, This can only be passed on to our subsequent leaders as a government on the verge of bankruptcy, owing the world's largest national debt, and ruling over a nation whose citizens owe more money to each other than any other nation in the world! In fact, our national debt of over three trillion dollars (in a nation of 260 million people) amounts to almost 12 thousand dollars for each man, woman, and child in America today, which somehow each of our children and grandchildren will have to pay off, through higher taxes.

Usury-dependent societies teach us not to save money. So as society's citizens age, they begin to realize they have no savings for their retirement. As a result, they pressure our government to save for them (through higher taxes to fund social security retirement income) and pressure our businesses to save for them (through higher prices of products and services to fund pension plans for us). How much simpler it would be if we did it God's way and just saved money for our own retirement to begin with, and lived with our children when we retire, and enjoyed the benefit of paying less taxes to the government and less prices for our products and services!

But how do you buy or build a house without taking out an interest-bearing loan? Well, generations ago, our ancestors would build their own houses. After they laid the foundations and set up the floor plan, they would hold a "house-raising party" where the entire community would come and help them build their house while having a picnic during the day, and a party at night. In this way, not only would you get your house built more quickly, but the entire community would grow closer together and be more neighborly to one another.

The house which would be built would be smaller than the house you may live in today, but you could expand the house by yourself later on as your family grew. If we still had this kind of tradition, then we would be much less in debt, and we would all learn to be content with smaller houses, and we would all be healthier because we would all be more physically active.

Surprisingly, nearly all of the things you want you can still afford if you just save your money for them. Furthermore, you won't have to save up as much money for expensive items, because things will not cost as much, because inflation will not exist. Additionally, you won't have to pay quadruple insurance and benefits for all the products and services you buy. Also, you would have much more to start with because your family would already have been debt-free and would be enjoying a triple economy of scale. So, as a result of beginning and remaining debt-free and living with increased income and decreased expenses, you can save up your money to purchase expensive things much more easily than you would have expected.

Furthermore, you may have thought you couldn't afford luxuries in a society without interest payments, but, as a result of living in a usury-free society you have also saved an average of possibly 50 thousand dollars of interest payments which ordinarily you would have had to pay for your house. This 50 thousand dollars which would be saved by each family would go a long way to pay for that new car, boat, mobile home, or other luxury item.

II. HOW NATIONAL DISOBEDIENCE TO GOD'S COMMANDS CAUSES NATIONAL UNEMPLOYMENT

Many of God's commands in the Bible are indirectly related to business expenses. When a nation develops a culture which violates these specific commands, this will often cause businesses to have increased expenses resulting in decreased profits. Such decreased profits sometimes force businesses to downsize and to lay off employees, which increases unemployment in the nation. So, any command in the Bible which indirectly effects business expenses, can also influence the national unemployment rate.

There are seven principles which illustrate this point.

PRINCIPLE ONE: WHEN TAXES GO UP, UNEMPLOYMENT GOES UP!

Let me give you an example of this: When crime increases, taxes (including business taxes) must increase to fight crime. By our government ignoring God's principles concerning *crime and punishment* (see chapter ten), crime skyrockets. This raises business expenses through increased taxes, resulting in decreased business profit, decreased hiring, increased layoffs, and increased unemployment. See how it works?

Let's try another example: When our government ignores God's principles concerning *health care* (see chapter twenty), health care costs skyrocket, resulting in increased taxes on businesses to fund Medicare and Medicaid, which increases business expenses, and which increases unemployment again!

When our government ignores God's principles concerning *sexual immorality, drunkenness, and divorce* (see chapter nineteen), this dramatically increases the number of impoverished unwed mothers, and impoverished divorced single parents of young children. This results in an equally dramatic rise in taxes to support America's welfare system, which results in further unemployment because much of these taxes are paid by businesses as increased business expenses. This in turn causes decreased profits, decreased hiring, and increased layoffs.

Further, when our government ignores God's principles concerning *limiting the size of our armed forces* (see chapter twenty-two), taxes rise to pay for an unnecessarily large military. This forces businesses to pay more taxes which increases their business expenses and again causes unemployment.

Finally, when our government ignores God's principles concerning *usury* and *usury-related industries,* then America develops a system of ENTITLEMENTS, consisting of a pension plan for government workers as well as a pension plan for the entire nation called social security. This sponsors the breakup of the family even further by subsidizing our elder's ability to live apart from his own family, so families don't want to support their own parents and grandparents in their old age (see chapter eighteen).

Both pension plans and social security are a violation of God's commands concerning usury and usury-related industries, and as such, will always cause more national harm than good. Yet American politicians have said that each person is "entitled" to these benefits. In this case, these ENTITLEMENTS form the largest part of our federal government's budget. In other words, our government's anti-family, pro-usury legislation has caused taxes to increase dramatically just to pay for the usurious business of government pension plans and social security retirement income. It is these increased taxes which increase business expenses and decrease profits, which in turn, decrease hiring, increase layoffs, and increase the rate of unemployment.

In summary, taxes increase when our nation violates God's commands. Because of these increased taxes, business expenses increase and this causes unemployment.

PRINCIPLE TWO: USURY CAUSES GENERAL INFLATION, WHICH INCREASES UNEMPLOYMENT

Usury causes general inflation, which increases the prices paid for business supplies. This increases business expenses, which decreases business profits, so business owners must lay off some of their employees. And so, national unemployment increases. Furthermore, the inflation caused by usury also has caused labor to organize and develop unions which dispute with management each year over wages so the employees' paycheck can keep up with inflation. And of course, when businesses have to pay more in wages and salaries, then business expenses increase, profits decrease, hiring decreases, layoffs increase, and unemployment increases.

Unfortunately, the business owner must now increase his prices to compensate for his increased expenses. However, higher prices sometimes decreases sales, which decreases profits. This in turn decreases hiring, increases layoffs, and increases the rate of unemployment.

So, general inflation (which is caused by usury) causes unemployment by increasing business expenses in two ways:

1. by annually increasing the cost of business supplies, and
2. by annually increasing the cost of labor.

In addition, inflation causes unemployment by decreasing sales of products which now cost too much to purchase.

Principle Three: Usury-related Businesses Causes Unemployment

Because inflation has created an annual battle between labor and management, it was inevitable that labor unions would eventually insist on getting fringe benefits for all employees of the large businesses. As a result, we now have a culture where all large and medium-sized businesses are expected to provide fringe benefits for all their employees, and even some small businesses are having to do the same. These benefit packages almost always include health insurance, but may also include dental insurance and life insurance, and on rare occasions, may include disability insurance as well. These fringe benefits may sometimes cost an employer as much as one third (or more) of a worker's entire salary. So, if an employee earns nine dollars per hour, it may cost the employer an extra three dollars per hour (or more) just to pay for the insurance benefits for that employee.

If a business has three employees, the fringe benefits may be costing the employer the same amount as if he hired a forth employee. Likewise, if a business has 3 hundred employees, the employer would have been able to hire 1 hundred more employees to increase his production if he did not have to pay for all the fringe benefits for the first 3 hundred employees. In other words, when a business has to pay for fringe benefits for its employees, this increases its business expenses, which decreases profits, which causes decreased hiring, increased layoffs, and increased unemployment. Since insurance companies are usury-related businesses (and it is medical, dental, and life insurance which form the largest part of these benefit packages), then this means that usury is again causing unemployment.

In summary, usury causes both inflation and the rise of usury-related businesses (such as the insurance business). Inflation itself also causes labor unions to insist that employers pay for these expensive fringe benefits, which come from the usury-related insurance industry in the first place. Remember, anything which increases business expenses also increases unemployment.

Principle Four: Usury-financed Mergers Cause Layoffs which Increases Unemployment

Large interest-bearing loans allow big businesses to swallow up small businesses more easily, without having to first save up enough money to purchase the smaller businesses with cash. When two businesses have merged, it is very common for layoffs to occur in order to take advantage of the better economics of scale for the new, larger business. Unfortunately, these layoffs cause further unemployment. This type of situation would happen far less frequently if usury were illegal and therefore, interest-bearing loans were unavailable.

Furthermore, these larger businesses (whose growth has been financed by usury) now unfairly compete with smaller businesses to drive them out of business, and this again increases unemployment.

PRINCIPLE FIVE: USURY CAUSES BUSINESS DEBT WHICH INCREASES BUSINESS EXPENSES AND CAUSES UNEMPLOYMENT

It's pretty obvious that usury causes debt, and it is the paying out of all the interest payments which increases business expenses. In fact, for some businesses, just like for some families, the interest paid on their debt can actually be a very large fraction of their budget.

Consider our government as an example of a business. It has a three trillion dollar debt and a large part of its budget goes to pay just the interest on this debt. Of course, no business could avoid bankruptcy if it operated as wastefully as our government.

It should suffice to say that businesses should attempt to remain, or become, debt-free if at all possible because this decreases their businesses expenses. If a business needs to expand, it should attempt to do so based upon its own profits, and not take on further debt. In other words, profit-growth is better for business than debt-growth, even though it may take longer initially. Interest-bearing loans may jump start the economics of your business at first, but decades of interest payments will often come back and bite you later on, when you realize that your total payout on the loan may be as much as double the amount you borrowed originally.

Don't just chalk up huge interest bearing loans as the absolutely necessary price of running a family or of doing business, for there are occasional families and occasional businesses which insist on remaining debt-free. These businesses will only indulge in debt-free growth and do there best to achieve it. It is these businesses which should be held up as examples for us to follow.

PRINCIPLE SIX: VIOLATING GOD'S FOREIGN POLICY BY LINKING AMERICA ECONOMICALLY WITH POOR FOREIGN NATIONS ALSO CAUSES UNEMPLOYMENT IN AMERICA

God became angry with righteous King Jehoshaphat (ruler of the righteous southern Kingdom of Judah) for linking himself and his nation economically with wicked King Ahab (ruler of the evil northern kingdom of Israel). This unholy economic alliance involved the building of several ships designed to carry heavy cargo so that both nations could together make money through the importation of gold. But God destroyed all their ships in the harbor before they could first set sail (2 Chron. 20:35-37; 1 Kings 22:48 NIV).

God wanted to bless the kingdom of Judah for its righteousness, yet punish the kingdom of Israel for its evil idolatry. He could not do both at the same time, since they were now linking themselves together economically. So, God destroyed the link. Basically, the Bible is teaching that when God is blessing a righteous nation with riches, that if that nation links itself economically with an evil, idolatrous nation which God is punishing with poverty, then the rich righteous nation will suffer as well. For example, American businessmen occasionally pay money to build factories in poor, foreign nations so they can make their product more cheaply and then import this same product back into the United States. This creates unfair competition between this inexpensive imported product and the more expensive American-made product, and drives the other American competitor bankrupt. So, Americans lose jobs to foreign nations because we have violated this biblical principle and linked ourselves economically with poor nations which God is punishing economically, often because of their idolatry.

In other words, when either America's government or America's businesses violate God's principles of foreign policy by linking us economically with poor, pagan nations (through the building of American factories in foreign nations and giving them our advanced technology), this unfair competition decreases sales of similar products made at home in the U.S. and causes unemployment. By doing this, America is basically underwriting a foreign nation's ability to make products which put Americans out of work (see chapter twenty-three).

PRINCIPLE SEVEN: UNNECESSARY GOVERNMENT REGULATION CAUSES UNEMPLOYMENT

Unnecessary government regulations cause unemployment by increasing business expenses to comply with these regulations, and by decreasing productivity because of the unnecessary paperwork. The increased expenses and decreased productivity combine to decrease profit, which of course, decreases hiring and increases unemployment.

In summary, if national *disobedience* to God's commands causes national *unemployment,* then national *obedience* to God's commands should cause national *prosperity* by allowing all Americans to easily find jobs. With such obedience, America would have full, 100 percent employment for all, and we would again become a true land of opportunity!

III. WHY GOD TOLD ISRAEL (AND BY IMPLICATION, AMERICA AS WELL) THAT THEY DID NOT NEED A LARGE CENTRALIZED GOVERNMENT WHICH COLLECTED ANY TAXES

Remember, in I Samuel 8, God warned the Israelites that if they decided against God's wishes to have a king, that this new king would also charge them a 10 percent tax on their grain, their wine, and their flocks of animals in order to build a large, centralized government. This is what God means when he says the king will take their sons, their daughters, and their servants—as if he were forcibly drafting them to serve in this new large centralized government (1 Sam. 8:11, 13, 15-17). Then, God says the king will use their sons to create a large army, to make weapons of war, and to work as farmers on the king's own property. The king will also take their daughters and make them work as cooks and maids for the new government. In addition, the king will take their servants and the best of their cattle and donkeys for his own personal use. Finally, the king will also confiscate the best of their private property and make it the property of the state, and let his new government officials use it for their own personal use (1 Sam. 8:11-14, 16).

In other words, God warned the Israelites of the evils of having a large centralized government, and that this government would do a lot of unnecessary things. Some of these would be: charging taxes (the Israelites never had to pay taxes before), creating large state properties (like the large state parks in America today, for which we pay unnecessary taxes to maintain), and creating an unnecessarily large standing army (which costs us even more unnecessary taxes). God's lesson was that Israel had the capability of actually governing itself and defending itself without having to charge its citizens any taxes, and without having to financially support an unnecessarily large standing army—as long as they adopted all of God's principles of civil law (as outlined in this book) into their government.

But without taxes, how could Israel build its courthouses, libraries, jailhouses, firehouses, and other public or government buildings? Well, remember that in America's distant past, our communities occasionally got together to build churches by having a "church-raising", the same way people would have a house-raising or a barn-raising. By the same token, Israelite (or American) communities could also get together to build their own courthouses, libraries, and firehouses without the use of any taxes.

Remember that Nehemiah and the Israelites rebuilt the entire wall of Jerusalem in fifty-two days with help of forty-two groups of people (most of whom appeared to be just large, extended families), who all freely volunteered their services (Neh. 2:17; 3; 4:6,16-23; 6:15 NIV). The actual lumber for the gates and for other parts of the wall came from the forest of King Artaxerxes as a donation from the king himself (Neh. 2:1, 8 NIV).

This is a perfect biblical example of how entire communities can work together to build public projects by freely volunteering their time without having to require any taxes to fund their projects. Furthermore, those who can not donate their time and strength to work on the project (because of reasons of age, disability, or disposition) can still donate money and material for the project just as King Artaxerxes did (by donating lumber for the wall) and just as the Israelites did earlier (by donating money and other items for building the temple) in Jerusalem (Ezra 1:5-6 NIV) as well as for building the tabernacle in the wilderness (Exod. 35:20-29; 36:3-7 NIV).

This type of community effort was supposed to be made all the easier in Israel, when you realize that every seven years God provided for an approximately one year long partial vacation for all the farmers and vineyard owners in Israel. He called this blessing "the Sabbath Year" (Lev. 25:1-7, 20-22 NIV). This Sabbath year would easily provide the farmers and the vineyard owners enough free time every seven years so the Israelite community could come together for "courthouse-raisings" or "town hall-raisings," or "public library-raisings" or to build or repair any public project, such as roads or dams. You see, God said that He would give Israel:

> such a blessing in the sixth year that the land will yield enough for three years. While you plant during the eighth year, you will eat from the old crop and will continue to eat from it until the harvest of the ninth year comes in. (Lev. 25:21-22 NIV)

There are at least two obvious blessings related to the Sabbath year. The first one is that every seven years, God prepays the Israelites in the sixth year with such a bountiful harvest, that they are easily able to forgive all their debtors any residual moneys still owed on those zero-interest loans which they had been giving to the poor on and off over the last six years. In this way, God is subsidizing his zero-interest loan program, which also helps keep God's welfare program running smoothly, because the zero-interest loan program is also one of God's three pre-welfare laws (see chapter nineteen).

Secondly, during the Sabbath year, the farmers were not allowed to sow their fields or to reap their fields, and the vineyard owners were not allowed to prune their vineyards or harvest the grapes from the vineyards (Lev. 25:4-5 NIV). Therefore, every seven years, the farmers and vineyard owners, suddenly had a lot more extra time on their hands to relax, go on vacations, visit relatives, and to participate in community building projects.

But, since the farmers and vineyard owners would undoubtedly need help in their fields and vineyards during the triple harvest in the sixth year, then the whole town probably would have to assist in the harvest for a week or two, knowing that this particular harvest would feed the whole local community for the next two or three years. And, since the farmer himself probably couldn't store three years worth of harvest on his own property, then he probably had to sell some of it immediately to merchants and to the other citizens. Therefore, when the harvest was over, the entire town had enough food to eat and wine to drink for the next two to three years. And, since their needs for food and drink for the next two to three years were now met, most of the community now had a lot of extra time on their hands to relax, to visit each other, and for community projects.

This means that the entire community could participate in community building projects or repair projects on and off during the Sabbath year. Imagine the closeness of that community as they worked together and enjoyed each other's company during each Sabbath Year. God thought this Sabbath year was so important, that more than 9 hundred years later, God mentions how angry he was at Israel for not continuing to obey His commands concerning the Sabbath year (2 Chron. 36:21 NIV). This shows the eternal nature of God's commands concerning the Sabbath year, and that this promised blessing is still available to Israel today. Of course, by implication, America (as well as all other nations), should also be eligible for these same wonderful promises if our nation begins to obey God completely, by adopting all God's commands into our legislation.

How did God intend for the Israelites to pay their rulers for their duties without collecting any taxes? Well you see, the Israelite rulers were actually supposed to work for FREE. By creatively designing the laws of inheritance, God, in his infinite wisdom, actually "prepaid" all the eldest sons in Israel to be able to donate their time as volunteer rulers if appointed (see chapter five).

You see, the eldest sons were supposed to receive a double portion of inheritance according to God's command in Deuteronomy (21:17 NIV). This double portion of inheritance helped the eldest son carry out his responsibilities to care for his aging parents and also care for his youngest brothers and sisters who could not yet financially provide for themselves. This double portion of inheritance also prepaid him to freely volunteer to be a public servant as a judge or elder.

Nehemiah is a perfect example of a governor of Israel who did not charge the Israelites any salary at all to pay for his rulership. For it is written:

> when I was appointed to be their governor . . . twelve years—neither I nor my brothers ate the food allotted to the governor. But those earlier governors—those who preceded me—placed a heavy burden on the people and took forty shekels of silver from them in addition to food and wine. Their assistants also lorded it over the people. But out of reverence for God I did not act like that . . . I never demanded the food allotted to the governor, because the demands were heavy on the people." (Neh. 5:14b-15, 18b NIV)

So evidently, when Nehemiah became governor he gave the people a tax-cut. He appears not to have charged them any salary at all for his services to rule over them.

Furthermore, it is probable that the judges and rulers over Israel would have only had to work part-time anyway and yet still have been able to do their jobs very well. For if all God's principles of moral law, civil law, and civil law enforcement were to have been adopted into Israel's legislation, then there would essentially be no significant crime, poverty, or war, which otherwise would have required a lot more of the ruler's time and involvement to run the local and national government!

IV. How National Usury Causes God's Commands to be Removed from Government

In a biblical society, only godly Christian elders are allowed to serve in government. They are usually the eldest sons in each family, because they are the ones who received a double portion of inheritance so they might have some extra time to freely volunteer to be public servants. Consequently, the elders in government usually have more money than the average citizen.

These elders were responsible before God to establish a government which regularly enforced all of God's principles of moral law, civil law, and civil law enforcement. Of course, this included making specific sins against God (such as fornication, adultery, homosexuality, and drunkenness) into regularly punished crimes against the state. This would be done in part because it would uphold the sanctity of marriage, as well as decrease the number of poor unwed mothers and impoverished divorced single parents, which in turn, would decrease poverty and welfare dependence within Israel.

God also commanded the wealthy to lend money without interest to poor citizens who temporarily could not afford their basic needs (see chapter nineteen; 1 Tim. 6:17a, 18b NIV). This is exactly what Nehemiah, Nehemiah's brothers, and Nehemiah's employees did (Neh. 5:7, 9-11 NIV). It would not be very long before the wealthy rulers would notice that when they regularly enforced God's commands against fornication, that fornication would decrease throughout all Israel, and there would be less impoverished unwed mothers who needed these loans from the wealthy rulers and businessmen. They would also notice that when they regularly enforced God's commands against adultery, homosexuality, and drunkenness, that these sins would also decrease throughout all Israel. As a result, there would be less impoverished divorced single parents who needed these loans from the wealthy rulers and businessmen. For single parenthood (whether through unwed motherhood, or through divorce) is always one of the greatest and most easily preventable sources of poverty, whether in ancient Israel, or in modern America.

So, God's commands were supposed to force the wealthy, godly rulers of Israel to realize that there was an economic incentive to keep God's principles of moral law, civil law, and civil law enforcement in their government, by making each of the Israelite rulers feel personally financially responsible for lending money to the poor for their basic necessities.

Now there is also an economic incentive to keep God's principles of morality in America's government as well, but this incentive goes largely unnoticed. You see, in America, the politicians have shifted the burden of helping the poor away from themselves and the wealthy merchants, and placed this burden onto all the taxpayers in the nation. So, when sexual immorality or drunkenness increases the number of poor unwed mothers in America or increases the number of poor divorced single parents in America, it is the taxpayer who pays more taxes to subsidize the poverty resulting from the sins of immorality and drunkenness. Since the politicians and wealthy merchants are not personally held financially responsible for paying for America's growing welfare-dependent society, then it is very easy to have a liberal attitude in Washington about enforcing God's principles against immorality in America, which is one of the major causes of poverty in the first place.

So you see, in a usury-*independent,* biblical society, the rich will automatically care more about both the marriage and the morality of all their neighbors, for they have become more sensitive to the ideas that sexual immorality and drunkenness cause poverty through disease, disability, divorce, and unexpected pregnancy out of wedlock. The wealthy will be much more inclined to ensure that these specific sins against God will always remain as regularly prosecuted crimes against the state, so there will be less poor families asking the rich for loans. Thus, God ordained a government which was designed to encourage the traditional conservative American values (of money, marriage, and sobriety) which originally came directly from God.

On the other hand, a usury-*dependent* society (which uses money from either the banker or the taxpayer to support the poor), can more easily develop an attitude of apathy towards their neighbors and a tolerance towards their sexual immorality, drunkenness, and divorce (liberal politics). This is at least partially because it doesn't see any direct financial consequences of this apathy and tolerance, nor does it see any financial incentive to interfere with the neighbor's immorality and drunkenness. We even have laws preventing any invasion of privacy concerning these "private" matters.

In summary, a society which encourages national usury, high taxes, and non-Christians in government will eventually cease to notice the economic advantage of keeping God's laws in government, and therefore all of God's laws will slowly be ignored or repealed. The paradox of allowing God's laws against immorality, drunkenness, and non-biblical divorce to be erased from our government is that the rich will end up paying much more in taxes to support the very large numbers of unwed mothers and divorced single parents impoverished by immorality, drunkenness, and divorce than they would have ever given out in loans for the very small numbers of remaining poor citizens whose poverty may have been caused merely by accidents and diseases unrelated to immorality or drunkenness (once sexual immorality, drunkenness, and non-biblical divorce have been outlawed)!

By the way, the same principle which prompts godly leaders to keep God's laws in government to decrease the sins which lead to impoverishment (in order to avoid having to lend money to the poor at zero-interest), also functions to prompt community members to encourage each other to avoid any sins which might lead to impoverishment so they too can avoid the responsibility of giving a zero-interest loan to their neighbors who have become impoverished by the consequences of their own sins! In other words, God's zero-interest loan program for Israel was also designed to create godly peer pressure within the Israelite community so they would all try to keep each other on their best behavior and avoid committing any of the sins which would lead to impoverishment!

V. How the Biblical Standard for Government to Recruit and Promote Only Righteous Men Sets the Standard for Businesses to Do the Same

The Bible clearly teaches that only godly Christian elders will have the determination required to adopt, implement, and keep God's own laws as the permanent national legislation of ancient Israel (or of modern America). Furthermore, God's blessings upon the nation are directly proportional to the degree to which these laws can successfully keep the large, unrighteous majority of citizens on their best behavior. This success is directly proportional to the number of godly leaders involved and the number of God's laws adopted and regularly implemented.

Of course, when the business community observes that God rewards righteous leadership and righteous laws in government with supernatural success and blessing upon the nation, then these businessmen will inevitably conclude that their businesses also need to be administered by righteous men implementing righteous business practices. To this end, business owners will begin to recruit and promote only "capable men ... who fear God, trustworthy men who hate dishonest gain..." to run their businesses. This is the exact advice Jethro gave to Moses concerning those who should become judges and leaders in the growing volunteer government of ancient Israel (Exod. 18:21 NIV).

As a result, the biblical standard for government to recruit and promote only righteous men now sets the standard for businesses to do the same thing.

VI. WHAT WILL HAPPEN TO THE NATIONAL ECONOMY WITHOUT USURY?

So far we have discussed many of the bad things which happen to a nation when it becomes usury-dependent. You are probably still wondering,

> But what will happen to our nation's economy as a whole without usury? Won't the economy slow down? Won't we have an economic depression? Won't our standard of living drop? And won't our children be worse off in the future?

These are all good questions. But before I answer these questions, let me first ask you a question: Don't you think that God considered all these possibilities before he concluded that outlawing usury was still best for the nation? It was God, who outlawed usury (Exod. 22:25; Lev. 25:36a, 27a; Deut. 23:19-20 NIV), yet later on, God still promised that if Israel obeyed God, that he would make them the richest nation on the face of the earth. He would do this as an object lesson for the rest of the world to consider the blessings which can be had by nations which worship and obey Jehovah—the one true God of the universe (Deut. 28:1-6, 8, 11-13 NIV).

Doesn't this answer all your questions? For these verses teach us that God would bless Israel, America, and any other nation which obeyed God in these same ways. Therefore, America could become far richer than we are today, and have a nearly poverty-free society as well, despite outlawing the sin of usury (for complete details, please reread the first section of this chapter).

So, let's stop worrying about the question, "How bad will the American economy get if we outlaw usury?", and start getting excited about the question, "What does America need to do in order to accomplish the adoption of all God's principles into our national legislation?" We should do this in order to receive God's richest blessings upon our nation. In the meantime, however, I'll try to explain what God may have had in mind concerning how our nation's economy should function if America became a true "nation under God" with a usury-independent biblical society.

First of all, I believe our economy may very well slow down, for without usury, there would be essentially no interest-bearing loans available for people to buy houses, cars, boats, and other large, budget items. Since the economy appears to be measured in part by the number of "new housing starts," then it would appear as if the economy was slowing down. This "slow down" of the economy would not be a bad thing, but actually a good thing!

You see, the Gross National Product (another measure of our economy) is in some way also a measure of the current speed of America's rat race. This in part, reflects American's desire to live beyond our means, and to get so deeply into debt that we spend a large part of our children's inheritance for interest payments on loans for things we should have saved up and paid cash for in the first place.

We all want the rat race to slow down, but we must realize that if we stop overspending, live within our means, and only purchase true necessities so we can all work less and have a more relaxed life style, then the GNP will inevitably go down, and so will many other measures of our economy. But to have the advantages of a slower rat race in our nation, Americans need to learn to be more content with less material possessions. When we do this, we will have much less stress in our lives, and probably begin to be healthier and live longer. For instance, people work all of their lives to pay off the house and the car, etc. so they can feel less stress. But if you remained debt-free your entire life, then you would have much less stress and probably live longer, with less chance of heart attack, stroke, ulcers, and anxiety.

Furthermore, since we have just discussed how disobedience to God's laws causes high unemployment, then national obedience to God's laws would not only allow the rat race to finally come to an end, but also allow America to have 100 percent employment as well. This 100 percent employment rate would tend to raise the GNP, or at least keep it from going down too much further.

But how can we afford to purchase new cars or new houses without interest-bearing loans? Well, you see, when people can't afford new cars, they will either buy used cars or repair the cars they have and keep them in better shape. Also, if the younger generation cannot afford to buy new houses, out of necessity they will probably begin to expand or remodel their parent's old houses to accommodate their needs. In other words, there would be a balance in the national marketplace, such that, as new car sales begin to decrease across the nation, old car sales and repairs would begin to increase. As construction of new houses would begin to decrease across the nation, old house expansion, remodeling, and repair would naturally begin to increase in America.

Therefore, although the loss of usury in our nation would decrease the overall gross national product, American creativity and ingenuity would find a way to adapt and survive without usury, and so the American economy would merely change its shape and balance out.

Furthermore, America would go back to the time when we had "house-raisings" and "barn-raisings" as a method of house building and barn building, etc. The family would lay the foundation of the house or the barn, and then invite the whole community to visit on the weekend to have a picnic during the day and a party at night, during which time the visitors would help build the house or the barn. There would be lots of food, fun, and music, as well as lots of hard work, community interaction, and community spirit. After the "house-raising" picnic/party was over, the family could now move into their new house. But this didn't mean that the house was totally completed—just that it was completed enough to move into and have shelter. It was expected that from here on in the family would now be able to complete the rest of the building of the house as time went on.

If America gave up usury and we had to go back to "house-raisings," then we'd have to make our building codes more "user-friendly" with less restrictions and less bureaucratic interference (without compromising safety however). Furthermore, in order to ensure that America's future families knew how to build their own homes and give competent assistance in "house-raisings," high school students would take "shop," and instead of learning how to build a *bird* house, they would learn how to build a *real* house. Each class could spend time actually building a house for the poor. There could be freshman carpenters, sophomore plumbers, junior electricians, and senior supervisors, so to speak, where in each year you would work on a different house and play a different role in doing so. Then, when our teenagers graduate, they would all be able to either remodel and expand their parents' houses or be able to start building their own houses. This type of education would be extremely helpful, since our future homeowners would no longer have access to interest-bearing loans to pay someone else to build their house for them. Also, for those who would *still* prefer paying cash to professionals to build their house, they would find the costs of housebuilding to be surprisingly *affordable*. For in a biblical society, there would be no inflation, no taxes, and no insurance benefits, so the cost of labor and materials would be much lower than they are today!

But how can businesses expand without being able to obtain interest-bearing loans? Well, all business expansion would have to come from cash flow without incurring any debt, and obviously would have to occur more slowly than it does today. However, all other things being equal, a debt-free business can raise money out of their own profits for business expansion faster than a business which is burdened by increased expenses because of interest payments. Furthermore, profit margins would be much greater because none of the businesses would have to pay any loan-interest. And, since none of their suppliers would have to pay any loan-interest either, then the cost of their supplies would be less. Also, the cost of labor would be about one-third less because the employer would no longer have to pay any insurance benefits for his employees (because insurance is a usury-related business). There would also be less expenses for security, and theft, and there would hardly be any business taxes to pay once the government outlawed all of the sins which cause increased taxes.

Therefore, since profit margins would be much higher, it would be much easier for businesses to expand using their own profits, so they would no longer need to resort to interest-bearing loans to finance their expansion. And, growing your business from your profits (profit-growth) is more healthy for a business than growing your business using debt (debt-growth). For debt-growth is actually false growth initially, and debt-growth takes a long time to become true growth, because you have to pay off so much interest.

Finally however, what most ancient Israelite businessmen never realized is that whenever the government of ancient Israel rejected and spurned God's principles of moral law, civil law, and civil law enforcement, that God himself would punish the Israelite BUSINESSMEN by dramatically decreasing their profits! He did this by reducing their business income and by increasing their business expenses. You see, Scripture teaches us that it is God himself who actively controls business profits. For it is written:

> You will plant but not harvest; (Mic. 6:15 NIV)

> They will sow wheat but reap thorns; they will wear themselves out but gain nothing. (Jer. 12:13 NIV)

> Now this is what the Lord Almighty says; "Give careful thought to your ways. You have planted much, but have harvested little . . . You expected much, but see, it turned out to be little." (Hag. 1:5-6a NIV)

Not only does God himself reduce business *income* in nations who disobey God, but God also increases business *expenses* as well because of this same national disobedience. For it is written:

> You earn wages, only to put them in a purse with holes in it . . . What you brought home, I blew away. (Hag. 1:6b, 9 NIV)

> You will store up but save nothing. (Mic. 6:14 NIV)

On the other hand, God decreases the expenses of nations which please him. For it is written:

> During the forty years that I led you through the desert, your clothes did not wear out, nor did the sandals on your feet. (Deut. 29:5 NIV)

So, what will really happen to America's economy if our government finally outlaws usury and begins to adopt all God's other principles of moral law, civil law, and civil law enforcement into its national legislation? Almighty God will respond to this obedience by fulfilling his promises and bless American businesses by *increasing their income* and *reducing their expenses,* so America will become a nearly poverty-free society with 100 percent employment, and zero inflation! You can't beat that!

VII. WHAT WILL HAPPEN TO THE STOCK MARKET WITHOUT USURY?

In a society which forbids the charging of interest on loans, the stock market would eventually diminish in size, activity, and influence because of a loss of investment capital from banks and pension plans—the two largest sources of stock market investment. Here's why.

First of all, if banks can no longer charge interest on loans, then they will lose billions of dollars in profits which they would ordinarily make from lending this money to customers. So, banks would no longer have the surplus of profits to pay its customer interest to hold their money in accounts, and neither would banks have the extra profits to offer "free checking" to their customers for their personal checking accounts. Trillions of dollars in interest-bearing *saving* accounts would be withdrawn from the banks because they would now have to *bill* you to hold your money instead of paying you to hold your money. In addition, trillions of dollars in *checking* accounts would be withdrawn because the banks would now have to charge you too much to hold your money. Many customers would not find this fee to be worth it to keep their checking accounts open in the first place.

As a result, banks could only make profits on large personal checking accounts and on business payroll accounts. Therefore, banks would have too little business and too little profits to invest in the stock market, so stock market trading would decrease.

But banks are not the only industries based upon usury which invest in the stock market. You see, pension plans are basically large group savings accounts which can often generate even higher interest rates than individual savings accounts because of their large size. This means that pension plans are actually usury-related businesses as well, and these pension plans would also cease to exist in a society where usury is illegal. And, since the stock market would now lose the trading which now comes from both the pension plans and the banks, then the stock market would begin to decrease in size, activity, and influence because there would be such a loss of investment capital.

VIII. GOD'S VIEW OF TRUE WEALTH— MEASURING OUR STANDARD OF LIVING BY HIS PRIORITIES AND NOT OUR PRIORITIES

God does not measure true wealth using a standard of living rooted in materialism. God measures true wealth based upon His priorities and not our priorities. God's priorities include his commands to:

1. Love God;
2. Love your spouse;
3. Love your children and your parents; and,
4. Love your neighbors in your community.

In other words, God prizes quality time spent in building loving relationships with God, with your family, and with your neighbors in your community. God also knows that the only source of true wealth and happiness comes from these relationships—especially the relationship with Jesus Christ.

For instance, when a couple first falls in love, they measure their happiness and their success by the amount of time they can spend together and by the quality of their relationship (this is much closer to God's view of true wealth). Decades after they have been married, they will frequently remember these early years of "poverty" as being some of the happiest years of their lives.

But America exalts a materialistic standard of living, which prizes the accumulation of conveniences and possessions, such as a house, two cars, a dishwasher, a clothes washer and dryer, a swimming pool, a boat, a vacation home, and the like. Because materialism is the yardstick by which we measure our standard of living, the collection of possessions has become both the means and the end of our goal. As a result, American families are frequently willing to accumulate tremendous debt in order to be successful in obtaining these possessions and conveniences. To pay off this debt, American families often have both spouses working multiple jobs outside the home. This leads to a more frantic, stressful lifestyle. This is the cause of America's rat race.

Unfortunately, by entering America's rat race, families frequently begin to destroy the very foundation of their happiness by terminating the quality time that the couple was spending together to build up their relationship. As a result, their lives become filled with discontent and depression, which they attempt to relieve by acquiring even more possessions with even more debt. Eventually, this journey towards materialistic success will frequently destroy their marriage, their relationship with their children, and their relationship with almighty God.

From God's point of view, a society which develops a rat race just to accumulate conveniences and possessions is actually a *poor* society, with:

1. a *poverty* of relationships with your parents, your spouse, and your children,
2. a *poverty* of relationships with the neighbors in your community,
3. a *poverty* of relationships with almighty God,
4. a *scarcity* of fulfillment and contentment, and
5. a *shortage* of time.

God however, has presented mankind with a biblical standard of living, by which we should:

> ... seek first his kingdom and his righteousness, and all these things will be given to you as well. (Matt. 6:33 NIV).

Put another way, if the measure of our standard of living is rooted in obedience to God's commands, then we will be much happier and more content. Furthermore, God doesn't mean for our families to be poor, but that America's families can indeed be rich. However, America must first stop being materialistic and outlaw usury, as well as adopt and regularly enforce all God's other principles of moral law, civil law, and civil law enforcement into our national legislation. This way God can and will honor His promises and bless America with a nearly poverty-free society and make us into the richest nation on earth.

In other words, America can have its cake and eat it too! By outlawing usury and creating laws which encourage the development of large extended families which can spend lots of quality time together to build loving relationships, America will again have the time to enjoy these relationships as the source of true happiness and wealth. Furthermore, because of the triple economy of scale inherent in large, extended families where the homestead is already paid for, and because of all the nationwide economic advantages obtainable by adopting God's principles of economic reform into our national legislation, American families will now able to afford all the possessions and conveniences that we can possibly need.

However, as long as American culture exalts the sin of usury as a way to obtain our materialistic standard of living, then God will allow our nation's families to persist in running a frantic, frustrating rat race which will continue to injure the only true source of happiness and wealth—the relationships with our family, with our neighbors, and most importantly, with Jesus Christ.

IX. CONCLUSION

If our federal and state governments adopted all of God's principles of moral law, civil law, and civil law enforcement into our legislation, then America would reap a large number of economic advantages. In fact, this would solve most of the economic problems in America today.

Furthermore, God promised Israel that if they did this, he would bless Israel with a nearly poverty-free society as well as make it into the richest nation on the face of the earth. Of course, by implication, these promises are also available to America, as well as being available to any other country which succeeds in becoming a true nation under God.

Two of the wonderful changes which would occur is that family expenses would *decrease* while family income would *increase*. First, family expenses would decrease because nearly every product and service in America would eventually decrease in price, and there would also be a zero-percent inflation rate. Furthermore, there would be decreased taxes, no interest charges to pay off, and no insurance premiums to pay. There would also be no significant expenses for security because there would be minimal crime. Additionally, since there would be no interest-bearing loans available to buy expensive items which are not really necessities, we would purchase less of these things. And so, American society would eventually return to a culture of less covetousness and more contentment.

Therefore, Americans would more frequently repair, restore, and expand their old houses, instead of always wanting to buy new houses. The building of new houses would more frequently be accomplished by purchasing the supplies with cash and building it yourself with the help of your entire family, or with community involvement in a "house-raising", guided by someone familiar with the new "user-friendly" building codes. In this way, the average American home-owning family would save perhaps between 25 to 100 thousand dollars in interest payments. Therefore we would have a lot more money with which to enjoy life and to pass on to their children as inheritance. We'd also be more content to repair our old cars and not always feel the need to buy new ones. Since everything we'd buy would be with cash instead of loans, our culture would begin to emphasize greater responsibility with our money and encourage us to do more saving and less spending. Family life and family values would be encouraged once again and Americans would again enjoy a triple economy of scale by living together in large, extended families.

Also, God promised to supernaturally decrease the expenses of citizens in a true nation under God, by miraculously making things last longer and not wear out as quickly. So, because of all these changes, family expenses would dramatically decrease.

In addition to this, Americans would also begin to enjoy a higher average income, because our nation would have full, 100 percent employment. Furthermore, our employers would pay us higher wages because American businesses would have less expenses for supplies, taxes, insurance, and security. Also, God promised to "bless all the work of our hands," which means that in addition to having the benefits of a *natural* increase in wages, Americans would also have the benefit of a *supernatural* increase in wages.

So, having obeyed God by implementing all of His laws, and therefore having received all of the natural as well as the supernatural blessings of this obedience, Americans would now have much less stress because of having less expenses and a greater income. We could work less and enjoy life more, which would also cause us to be more healthy and happy, so we would be able to live longer. This would finally bring America's rat race to an end!

Furthermore, by removing usury from society, the economy would tilt once again back towards the poor, shrinking the distance between the poor and the rich so there would be less class envy, more contentment, and less crime. There would be better family life with more quality time with our spouses and our children. There would also be a better community life and we'd know many more of our neighbors because of the many "house-raisings" and community projects we had worked on together. There would no longer be community apathy towards our neighbor's problems or towards the crime in our local communities. Rich rulers would be more concerned about the marriage, morality, and sobriety of all of our citizens and be more likely to keep God's commands in government. Our government would never have developed a three trillion dollar debt, and our economy would be more stable because it would also be independent from a sudden decline in the economy of foreign nations through world trade.

All of these wonderful changes would occur because, in a society without usury, American culture could be more easily molded by God's Will to adopt even more of God's commands. As a result, God would supernaturally "bless all the work of our hands" and give us a nearly poverty-free society as well as make America into the richest nation on the face of the earth. We'd be the envy of all the other nations and be held up by God as an example for all of the other nations to learn what divine blessings God will grant to a country when it successfully becomes a true nation under God.

Best of all, America would develop a new international reputation of having a culture which reflected true Christian morality and obedience, which resulted in the supernatural blessing of a nearly poverty-free society, as well as a nearly disease-free, crime-free, war-free, tax-free, inflation-free, and natural disaster-free society. Because of this, all nations of the earth would be awed by the power of our God, and would eagerly welcome American Christian missionaries by the thousands, so we could teach all nations about salvation by grace through faith in Jesus Christ, and about the blessings of individual and national obedience to the will of almighty God. We'd even be able to create a national 1 percent voluntary contribution (over the mandatory 10 percent tithe) to be earmarked just for international evangelism, so we could send even more missionaries around the world than ever before, just to obey the great commission of Jesus Christ.

In conclusion, adopting God's principles of economic reform can solve most of the economic problems in America today. More specifically, God's principles of economics can:
1. increase family income while decreasing family expenses;
2. increase total family net worth, and increase the inheritance for children;
3. decrease nationwide stress, discontent, covetousness;
4. prevent unfair competition between big business and small business;
5. decrease the prices of nearly every product and service in America;
6. eliminate general inflation and industry-specific inflation;
7. decrease taxes and eliminate our federal debt;
8. decrease unemployment, decrease bankruptcies, and end America's rat race;
9. help to create a debt-free society by encouraging us to save money;
10. tilt the economy and culture back towards helping the poor;
11. encourage God to transform America into a nearly poverty-free society and the richest nation on earth, a blessing which will in turn . . .
12. exalt America as an object lesson to the rest of the world so that all other nations will want to abandon their pagan idolatry and worship the God of America—Jesus Christ—the Lord of lawmakers and architect of the biblical blueprint for perfect self-government, a motivation which will . . .
13. encourage the spreading of the gospel of salvation by grace through faith in Jesus Christ, to all the nations of the world.

And that, is God's view of economic reform!

Chapter Twenty-Two

GOD'S VIEW OF MILITARY POLICIES WHICH CAN GIVE AMERICA A STRONGER DEFENSE AND DRAMATICALLY REDUCE AMERICA'S MILITARY BUDGET

It is an amazing paradox that America, a nation once founded on biblical principles, has developed military policies which are so contrary to the military policies God gave to Israel thousands of years ago. But America's record of disobedience is actually not too much worse than Israel's record of disobedience, for ancient Israel faced the same temptations that America faces today—to escalate their weapons and to increase the size of their nation's military, as well as to break most all the rest of God's military principles which are listed below.

Now the military strategies of the Prince of Peace are clearly presented in the Bible, and I believe they are for Israel, for America, and for the rest of the world. These policies are as follows:

1. God wanted Israel (and therefore all other nations) to live in peace with their neighbors.
2. Israel should never be the first one to start a war.
3. Israel should only attack an enemy if the enemy first attacks Israel, or is preparing to attack.
4. Israel is not to trust in foreign armies as allies to help her achieve victory, but is to trust in God alone.
5. Israel is not to trust in her weapons or technology to help her achieve victory, but is to trust in God alone.
6. Israel is not to escalate her weaponry to match that of her enemies.
7. Only righteous MEN of faith can serve in the armed forces of Israel, and their faith is of greater importance than their skill.
8. Israel is not to trust in the size of her armed forces to help her achieve victory, but is to trust in God alone.

9. If any of Israel's soldiers died in battle, it was not a sign of heroism, but it was a sign that God had abandoned their army because of serious sinful activity either within the army or within the nation which had not yet been dealt with.
10. Israel must never count the size of her army.
11. Israel must maintain a righteous army and a righteous nation in order for God to fight on her behalf. Therefore, Israel must obey God in peacetime in order for God to fight for Israel in wartime.
12. No homosexuals are ever to serve in the armed forces of Israel.
13. No women are ever to serve in the armed forces of Israel.
14. Israel is never to intervene militarily in the affairs of foreign nations, either in their own private wars or because of "human rights violations" in foreign countries.
15. Israel's military is not expected to be the policeman of the world.

However, America's military policies include:

1. trusting foreign armies as allies,
2. trusting in large armies, which . . .
3. include female and homosexual soldiers,
4. trusting in high-tech weaponry,
5. escalating our weapons yearly,
6. being the "policeman" of the world,
7. to justify military intervention in foreign countries which have not attacked us.

America also has other military policies which are contrary to God's Will for any country attempting to be a true nation under God.

This chapter will discuss how America's military policies are entirely the opposite of what God wants for America, and also will reveal how the military policies of Jehovah (who became our Messiah and Prince of Peace—Jesus Christ) are superior to the military policies of America today. This means, that if the United States could somehow become a true nation under God, Americans would no longer have to pay billions of dollars in unnecessary taxes each year to support a vast military buildup of men and weapons spread all over the world.

God's purpose for the military in ancient Israel was not just for defense, but more importantly, to demonstrate the power and the pageantry of the repeated overwhelming supernatural victories of God's tiny armies against overwhelming odds; to serve as a dramatic witness to all nations of the earth that the one true God rules over Israel; and, that all other nations should therefore abandon their pagan worship and worship this same Jehovah, who would later become the Messiah and Savior of the entire world—Jesus Christ!

You see, Israel watched as God defeated the enemies of righteousness by either blinding them, drowning them, cremating them with firefall, stoning them with hailstones, causing the ground to swallow them in an earthquake, or causing an entire army of soldiers to die in their sleep! They also watched as God would send both hallucinations and delusions upon the enemies of God, which would either lure their armies into a fatal trap, cause them to flee from the Israelite soldiers, or cause them to attack each other instead of attacking the Israelites. Imagine what a strong impression such battles would have on all the other nations of the earth—to prompt them to abandon their pagan idolatry and instead worship Jehovah (the God of the armies of ancient Israel).

You don't need a very large military budget when God fights on your side. For even the weapons of modern twentieth century technology are no match for the power of the almighty Master of the Universe—Jesus the Christ. For if God can control the infinite complexity of the eyes, the ears, and the minds of the enemies of Israel (by sending upon them blindness, auditory hallucinations, or delusions) then he can certainly control the relatively simple radar, sonar, and missile guidance systems of the enemies of America today. Yet, America spends billions of dollars on escalating our weaponry and financially supporting a vast army of soldiers. Does God approve of all these expenditures? Are we, as a former Christian nation, being good stewards of God's blessings upon us to spend our money this way?

With these thoughts in mind, let us consider the military strategies of Jesus Christ—the Prince of Peace, who (as the pre-incarnate Jehovah) commanded the armies of ancient Israel, leading them from one supernatural victory to another. Let us also consider what Israel needed to do to always have the confidence that God would defend their nation with supernatural military victories over their enemies, so they would not have to spend a huge amount of tax dollars for an enormous military with high-tech weapons to defend themselves.

1. GOD WANTS ALL NATIONS TO LIVE IN PEACE WITH THEIR NEIGHBORS

For the purposes of this discussion, let me first make a distinction between a peace treaty and a war treaty. A peace treaty means:

I won't attack you if you don't attack me!

But a war treaty means:

I'll help you fight your enemies, if you help me fight my enemies!

The Bible teaches us that God wants peace treaties, but never wants war treaties. It was Jehovah who became our Prince of Peace—Jesus Christ—

and one of His promises to Israel was to grant her peace with her enemies, if she would obey him.

The only time Jehovah actually told the Israelites *not* to make a peace treaty was concerning the Canaanites, who were not only worshipping idols, but were also sacrificing their babies as part of the worship practice. For it is written:

> Be careful *not* to make a treaty with those who live in the land where you are going, or they will be a snare to you . . . Be careful *not* to make a treaty with those who live in the land . . . (Exod. 34:12, 15; see also Deut. 7:2 NIV; emphasis added)

And also,

> . . . do not learn to imitate the detestable ways of the nations there. Let no one be found among you who sacrifices his son or daughter in the fire . . . (Deut. 18:9-10 NIV)

So, it is clear that the Canaanites should be the one exception to the rule that Israel was supposed to live at peace with its neighbors as long as they were not first attacked by their enemies. For God appears to condone war only if a nation either attacked Israel first, or was preparing to attack. Unfortunately, Israel was attacked so often by her neighbors that she appeared to be perpetually at war with some of them, without attempting any diplomatic "cease-fire" or a peace treaty.

2. ISRAEL SHOULD NEVER BE THE FIRST ONE TO START A WAR

3. ISRAEL CAN ONLY ATTACK AN ENEMY IF THE ENEMY FIRST ATTACKS ISRAEL OR IS PREPARING TO ATTACK

There are some battles in the Bible where it is not clear who started the original war in the first place. Despite this fact, we can still be absolutely sure that God never wanted the Israelites to be the first ones to start a war.

God allowed King Josiah to die in battle when he deliberately disobeyed God by attacking an army which had not attacked him first. The army was marching away from Israel on their way to attack Assyria, and so was clearly not posing any immediate threat to the Israelites (2 Chron. 25:20-24 NIV). Because of this story (as well as other biblical principles) we can be absolutely sure that God does not want any nation even today to start wars with its enemies, but rather wants each nation to live in peace with all other nations.

In the tenth chapter of 2 Samuel, the Ammonites hired thirty-three thousand mercenary soldiers from Aram, Maacah, and Tob. Because of this, it was clear to King David that they had declared war against Israel and were *preparing* to attack. So, King David attacked the Ammonites and their mercenaries before they attacked Israel. God gave Israel the victory, presumably because this was still a defensive war.

This is the only case where it is clear to me that Israel attacked another nation before they were attacked by the enemy. In all other cases (2 Sam. 11, etc.) it appears as though Israel and her enemies were perpetually at war and it is not clear who attacked whom when the war first started. Because of this lack of clarity, I believe it is appropriate to give God the benefit of the doubt (so to speak) and still conclude that God wanted Israel to be at peace with her enemies; and also, would not have blessed Israel with battle victory if Israel had indeed been the first one to start the war. This idea is consistent with the conclusion that one of the reasons God allowed righteous King Josiah to die in battle is because King Josiah violated these military principles of God and started a war with an enemy who had not attacked Israel first.

4. Israel Is Not to Trust in Foreign Armies as Allies to Help Her Achieve Victory, But Is to Trust in God Alone

God wanted the Israelites to depend solely upon him in their battles. Otherwise, the Israelites would claim credit for themselves and mistakenly believe that they won the battle with their own skill and strength. Therefore they would not learn to depend upon the Lord. So, God warned them never to make any war treaties with foreign countries to obtain military allies, and there are four stories in the Bible which reveal this to us.

First of all, King Amaziah of the southern kingdom of Judah made an "unholy alliance" with one hundred thousand mercenary soldiers from the northern kingdom of Israel (which was an evil, idol-worshipping kingdom at that time) so they would join forces with the army of Judah against the Edomites. But, God sent a prophet to declare that this was an "unholy alliance," and that He would not fight for Judah as long as Judah had joined its forces with the wicked northern kingdom of Israel. For it is written:

> ... a man of God came ... and said, 'O king, these troops from Israel must not march with you, for the Lord is not with Israel ... Even if you go and fight courageously in battle, God will overthrow you before the enemy, for God has the power to help or overthrow. (2 Chron. 25:6-8 NIV)

Secondly, good king Jehoshaphat of Judah mistakenly allied himself with wicked king Ahab of Israel (at Ahab's request) to help Ahab fight the Arameans. After the battle, God sent the prophet Jehu to declare that this too was a wicked, "unholy alliance." For it is written:

> When Jehoshaphat king of Judah returned safely to his palace in Jerusalem, Jehu the seer . . . went out to meet him and said to the king, "Should you help the wicked and love those who hate the Lord? Because of this the wrath of the Lord is upon you." (2 Chron. 19:1-3 NIV)

(Remember, if King Ahab was a righteous king and the northern kingdom of Israel was a righteous nation to begin with, they wouldn't have needed to ask for Judah's help in the first place. This is because they should have known that God would fight the battles for them, so they wouldn't need any additional military assistance!)

Thirdly, King Asa relied upon God for peace and freedom from war up until the thirty-fifth year of his reign. In 2 Chronicles 16:1-3 (NIV) however, instead of continuing to rely upon God to defend his kingdom against the wicked kingdom of Israel, King Asa of Judah relied instead upon the king of Aram (Syria). Together, a war treaty is made so together they can fight the king of Israel. This made God angry, so he sent a prophet to speak to King Asa. For it is written:

> Hanani the seer came to Asa king of Judah and said to him, "Because you relied on the King of Aram and not on the Lord your God, the army of the King of Aram has escaped from your hand. Were not the Cushites and Libyans a mighty army with great numbers of chariots and horsemen? Yet, when you relied on the Lord, he delivered them into your hand. For the eyes of the Lord range throughout the earth to strengthen those whose hearts are fully committed to him. You have done a foolish thing, and from now on you will be at war. (2 Chron. 16:7-9 NIV)

Fourthly, instead of relying upon God to defend the kingdom of Judah, King Hezekiah mistakenly made a war treaty with Egypt to assist her in an upcoming battle against Assyria. God was angry about this, so he inspired Isaiah to prophesy against King Hezekiah's "unholy alliance" with Egypt. For it is written:

> Woe to those who go down to Egypt for help, who rely on horses, who trust in the multitude of their chariots and the great strength of their horsemen, but do not look to the Holy One of Israel, or seek help from the Lord. (Isa. 31:1 NIV)

> Egypt will no longer be a source of confidence for the people of Israel, but will be a reminder of their sin in turning to her for help. (Ezek. 29:16; see also Isa. 30:1-2; 20:5-6 NIV)

So, four times Israel made a war treaty with other nations and each time God sent a prophet to declare God's anger about this. This should make it clear enough that God hated it when Israel made an alliance with a foreign power and did not depend purely upon almighty God for her military defense. Furthermore, as you will see in sections seven and eight of this chapter, God's method of defending Israel was so spectacular, that in comparison, the mere assistance of foreign allies was useless. In fact, King David once lamented that God would sometimes stop fighting for Israel (whenever Israel became wicked), but that using foreign allies to assist Israel in battle during these times was worthless. For it is written:

> Is it not you, O God, you who have rejected us and no longer go out with our armies? Give us aid against the enemy, for the help of man is worthless. (Ps. 60:10-11 NIV)

5. ISRAEL IS NOT TO TRUST IN HER WEAPONS OR TECHNOLOGY TO HELP HER ACHIEVE VICTORY, BUT IS TO TRUST IN GOD ALONE

6. ISRAEL IS NOT TO ESCALATE HER WEAPONRY TO MATCH THAT OF HER ENEMIES

The United States spends billions of dollars each year on nuclear missiles, smart bombs, aircraft carriers, battleships, destroyers, nuclear submarines, military jets, helicopters, tanks, hand weapons, and spy satellites, yet the Bible teaches us that we should not place our confidence and trust in our military weaponry for assurance of military victory. For it is written:

> Some trust in chariots and some in horses, but we trust in the name of the Lord our God. (Ps. 20:7 NIV)

Also, each year our military asks Congress for more and more money to escalate our weaponry even further, yet the Bible teaches us that we should not escalate our weaponry to equal that of the surrounding nations. For it is written:

> The Lord said to Joshua, "Do not be afraid of them, because by this time tomorrow I will hand all of them over to Israel, slain. You are to hamstring their horses and burn their chariots." (Josh. 11:6 NIV)

You see, God was guaranteeing that the following day Israelites would defeat a much larger army who also had superior weapons technology (a large number of chariots and horses). By comparison, the

Israelite weapons technology was clearly inferior to that of their enemy. But after this battle, the Israelites confiscated the superior technology of their enemy (the large inventory of horses and chariots).

Ordinarily, this escalation of their weaponry would give the Israelites confidence to be able to achieve military victory over even larger enemies who had even better weapons technology. So, to prevent the Israelites from depending upon themselves for future military victories (instead of depending upon God), God told Joshua to hamstring the horses and burn the chariots to ensure that the Israelites would not escalate their weaponry to equal that of the surrounding nations.

For God knew that there is much more incentive to remain a righteous nation if you have to depend upon God for your military victories because you only have a small army with insignificant weapons. You see, once the Israelites felt they didn't need God's help during wartime, they would soon feel they didn't need to obey God during peacetime, so their government would no longer think it necessary to regularly enforce God's commands. In other words, just as children sometimes think,

> Once I'm no longer dependent upon my parents, then I will no longer have to obey them either,

so also Israel would begin to think,

> Since we are no longer dependent upon God in wartime, then we no longer have to obey God in peacetime either!

Therefore, God did not want Israel to escalate their military weaponry because they would inevitably develop an attitude of independence followed by disobedience.

Unfortunately, the Israelites all too often disobeyed God's military policies. As a result, rather than develop a submissive attitude of *obedient dependence* upon God and His commands, they instead developed an antagonistic attitude of *disobedient independence* from God and His commands. And, at least partly because of our own rebellious military policies, America has also developed this same shameful attitude of disobedient independence from God and God's commands.

God thought it was very important for the Israelite men to learn warfare, because they would begin to understand what it meant to have an almighty God fight for them on the battlefield. For it is written:

> These are the nations which the Lord left to test all those Israelites who had not experienced any of the wars in Canaan (he did this only to teach warfare to the descendants of the Israelites who had not had previous battle experience). (Judg. 3:1-2 NIV)

As a result of participating in these battles, the Israelites would learn to depend upon God in wartime. This meant that they would therefore have to obey God in peacetime by regularly enforcing God's principles of moral and civil law. In the process, they would begin to transform Israel into a true nation under God.

7. ONLY RIGHTEOUS MEN OF FAITH CAN SERVE IN THE ARMED FORCES OF ISRAEL, AND THEIR FAITH IS OF MUCH GREATER IMPORTANCE THAN THEIR SKILL

8. ISRAEL IS NOT TO TRUST IN THE SIZE OF HER ARMED FORCES TO HELP HER ACHIEVE MILITARY VICTORY, BUT IS TO TRUST IN GOD ALONE

Americans are proud of the large size of our military, with thousands of soldiers serving in the Army, Navy, Air Force, and Marines. But the Bible teaches us that we should not place confidence in the size of our armed forces for victory over our enemies. For it is written:

> No king is saved by the size of his army. Ps. 33:16 NIV

You see, the Bible teaches that victory is not related to the size of a nations's army, but that victory is more related either to the nation's relationship with God, or to the army's relationship with God.

For instance, Gideon had recruited only 32 thousand soldiers for his battle against the enormous army of the Midianites, the Amalekites and the other eastern peoples. However, God told Gideon that he had too many soldiers and that he must send some away. For it is written:

> The Lord said to Gideon, "You have too many men for me to deliver Midian into their hands. In order that Israel may not boast against me that her own strength saved her, announce now to the people, 'Anyone who trembles with fear may turn back and leave Mount Gilead.'" So twenty-two thousand men left, while ten thousand remained. (Judg. 7:2-3 NIV)

God knew that the remaining group of ten thousand men (who did not "tremble with fear") was actually composed of two subgroups:

1. those who did not tremble with fear because they had *confidence in themselves* and their own skills and "knew what they were doing" and,

2. those who had *no confidence in themselves* or their own skills and had "no idea what they were doing," yet who still did not tremble with fear because of their tremendous faith in God's skills and in God's power to protect them in battle.

It was this latter group (of unskilled and incompetent "rookies" with great faith in God's promises) that God was pleased to choose to use to fight the battle, so he could demonstrate his power and his glory to the Israelites, the Midianites, and all the other surrounding nations. So, with this in mind,

> ... the Lord said to Gideon, "There are still too many men ... (Judg. 7:2-4 NIV)

God then proceeded to tell Gideon how to "sort out" the men, based upon whether or not each man knew the "safest way" to drink water during a battle. This simple test would reflect each man's "common battle sense" as well as set a minimal standard for competency in battle. This was because it was supposed to be obvious to every soldier that you don't "drop your guard" in a battle just to get a drink.

The safest way to drink water during a battle is to kneel down to drink, cupping the water in the left hand while holding your drawn sword in your right hand, so you can be ready to defend yourself, should you be ambushed while drinking the water. On the other hand, the dangerous way to drink water during a battle, is to lie down on your belly and use both hands to cup the water into your mouth. If you are ambushed while you are in this position you will die, because you are lying face down with your back to the enemy, so you can neither see the enemy nor defend yourself, for neither hand is on your sword, but both hands are near your mouth instead! God called this, "lapping" the water "like a dog" (Judg. 7:5 NIV), and only a "foolish soldier" would risk his life to drink water this way during a battle.

God tells Gideon to choose the men who "lap the water with their tongues like a dog ... with their hands to their mouths" (Judg. 7:5, 6 NIV). This reveals that God wants to use the men who are "rookies" with no "common sense" of how to act in battle. For it is written:

> The Lord said to Gideon, "With the three hundred men who LAPPED I will save you and give the Midianites into your hands." (Judg. 7:7 NIV; emphasis added)

Now God has given Gideon an army of three hundred men who are potentially the worst soldiers in all of Israel, with no significant battle skills, battle experience, or even "common sense" for battle! Gideon, of course, makes the "perfect" leader for these "rookies" because Gideon himself has no battle skills or experience either (Judg. 6:14-15 NIV). In fact, "Gideon's rookies" probably represent the most incompetent army which has ever assembled for battle throughout all time. Yet, despite their lack of skill and experience, all 301 of them had the perfect faith that God would deliver the enemy into their hands. To God, only righteous men of faith should serve in the armed forces of Israel, and their faith in God's power and in God's protection was of greater importance than their skill for battle.

Let me give you another example. Prince Jonathan, the son of King Saul, was a man who had great faith in the power of God to miraculously defeat Israel's enemies. He surely knew the story of "Gideon's Rookies" as well as the story of how one lone soldier named Samson, defeated an entire army of one thousand Philistines by himself, using nothing more than the jawbone of a donkey (Judg. 15:15-16 NIV). It was stories like these that inspired Jonathan's great faith that God would miraculously deliver twenty Philistines into his hands and into the hands of his armor bearer, even though there was only one sword between the two of them (1 Sam. 13:22 NIV). For it is written:

> Jonathan said to his young armor-bearer, "Come, let's go over to the outpost of those uncircumcised fellows. Perhaps the Lord will act in our behalf. Nothing can hinder the Lord from saving, whether by many or by a few."
>
> "Do all that you have in mind," his armor-bearer said. "Go ahead; I am with you heart and soul."
>
> Jonathan said, "Come, then; we will cross over toward the men and let them see us. If they say to us, 'Wait there until we come to you,' we will stay where we are and not go up to them. But if they say, '"Come up to us,"' we will climb up, because that will be our sign that the Lord has given them into our hands."
>
> So both of them showed themselves to the Philistine outpost. "Look!" said the Philistines. "The Hebrews are crawling out from the holes they were hiding in." The men of the outpost shouted to Jonathan and his armor-bearer, "Come up to us and we'll teach you a lesson."
>
> So Jonathan climbed up, using his hands and feet, with his armor-bearer right behind him. The Philistines fell before Jonathan, and his armor-bearer followed and killed behind him. In that first attack Jonathan and his armor-bearer killed some twenty men in an area of about half an acre. (1 Sam. 14:6-14 NIV)

So again, it is clear that God wants soldiers to be righteous men who have great faith in God, and who believe that victory in battle is in the hands of God alone.

This story of Jonathan represents how God defeated an enemy using only a *two-man army*. You may wonder how Jonathan came to have such great faith in God's abilities to lead in battle, especially since his father, King Saul, was so unrighteous and so disobedient to God during this time in Jonathan's life. Well, as I mentioned above, I believe Jonathan surely knew the story of Samson, which is as follows:

> The Spirit of the Lord came upon [Samson] in power. The ropes on his arms became like charred flax, and the bindings dropped from his hands. Finding a fresh jawbone of a donkey, he grabbed it and struck down a thousand men. Then Samson said, "With a donkey's jawbone, I have made donkeys of them. With a donkey's jawbone I have killed a thousand men." (Judg. 15:14b-16 NIV)

This story of Samson is the first of five stories in the Bible which describe *one-man armies*. The story of Samson surely inspired Prince Jonathan, and probably also inspired a man who was to later become Jonathan's best friend—David, the shepherd boy.

David had already killed a lion and a bear as a shepherd boy (1 Sam. 17:34-37 NIV), and knew well the power of God to lead in battle. When David killed the giant Goliath (1 Sam. 17:47-51 NIV), this revealed to Jonathan and everyone else David's great faith that victory over the enemy was in the hands of God alone—regardless of the weapons used. For David said:

> All those gathered here will know that it is not by sword or spear that the Lord saves; for the battle is the Lord's, and he will give all of you into our hands. (1 Sam. 17:47 NIV)

It was probably the killing of the giant Goliath which brought David and Jonathan together to be best friends. I believe that Jonathan surely told David of how years earlier God led Jonathan (and his armor bearer) in victory over the twenty Philistines with only one sword between them.

So it is no accident that the stories of the other four *one-man armies* occurred to David's "mighty men"—probably because these same men were inspired by King David himself and his great faith in God to deliver victories in battle. For it is written:

> Josheb-Basshebeth, a Tahkemonite, was chief of the Three; he raised his spear against *eight hundred men*, whom he killed in one encounter. (2 Sam. 8 NIV; emphasis added)

> Next to him was Eleazar, son of Dodai the Ahohite. As one of the three mighty men, he was with David when they taunted the Philistines gathered at Pas Dammim for battle. Then the men of Israel retreated, but he stood his ground and struck down the Philistines till his hand froze to the sword. The Lord brought about a great victory that day. The

troops returned to Eleazar, but only to strip the dead. (2 Sam. 23:9-10 NIV)

Next to him was Shammah son of Agee the Hararite. When the Philistines banded together at a place where there was a field full of lentils, Israel's troops fled from them. But Shammah took his stand in the middle of the field. He defended and struck the Philistines down, and the Lord brought about a great victory. (2 Sam. 23:11-12 NIV)

Abishai the brother of Joab son of Zeruiah was chief of the Three. He raised his spear against *three hundred men,* whom he killed, and so became as famous as the Three. (2 Sam. 23:8 NIV; emphasis added)

Because Josheb-Basshebeth defeated eight hundred men and Abishai defeated three hundred men, the chronological order of this presentation (2 Sam. 23:8, 18), reveals that Eleazar and Shammah probably killed more in one encounter than Abishai killed, but less than Josheb-Basshebeth killed. Therefore, I believe that Eleazar and Shammah probably killed about five hundred men each in their respective battles (2 Sam. 23:9-12).

David also has evidently had these same experiences of defeating large armies by himself, with the help of God! In fact, 2 Samuel twenty-two records not what David's army can do, but what David himself can do in battle with the help of God! This passage reveals that (with God's help) David gets the strength and speed to do the impossible:

1. Bend a bow made of bronze,
2. Run with the speed of a deer,
3. Use his sword and spear with the speed and accuracy of almighty God, for God has "trained his hands for battle" and divinely guides David's sword and spear to find its mark every time; and finally,
4. David can advance against a troop (an entire army) by himself!

For it is written:

With [God's] help I can advance against a troop; with my God I can scale a wall ... [God] is a shield for all who take refuge in him ... It is God who arms me with strength ... He makes my feet like that of a deer; he enables me to stand on the heights, He trains my hands for battle; my arms can bend a bow of bronze. You give me your shield of victory, and your right hand sustains me; you stoop down to make me great ... You armed me with strength for the battle" (2 Sam. 22:30-40 NIV selected passages; Ps. 18:29-39 NIV, selected passages).

Furthermore, the Holy Spirit records this entire passage twice in the Bible (practically word-for word)—once in Psalm 18, and again in 2 Samuel twenty-two! Now why would God want a huge, forty-nine verse passage about war to be written in the Bible twice? Because it is extremely important to God to have righteous men of faith (like David) to lead Israel's armies into war, so God can perform these battle miracles for all the world to see. For this not only was supposed to make Israel more obedient to God in peacetime (by making Israel more dependent upon God in wartime), but also win other nations to the Lord by the awesome display of the power of God to win battles.

David, of course, knows that his miraculous strength, speed, and skill in battle come directly from God and that ordinarily he cannot do these things unless the Holy Spirit empowers him in battle. This is why David goes on to say:

> I do not trust in my bow, my sword does not bring me victory; but you give us victory over our enemies, you put our adversaries to shame. (Ps. 44:6-7 NIV)

As a result, David knows first hand of the fulfillment of the Mosaic military promises, which say,

> You will pursue your enemies, and they will fall by the sword before you. Five of you will chase a hundred, and a hundred of you will chase ten thousand, and your enemies will fall by the sword before you. (Lev. 26:7-8 NIV)

These battles where God empowered *small* armies, *two-man* armies, or *one-man* armies to defeat the much larger armies of the enemy clearly illustrate the fulfillment of the following prophecy:

> The Lord will grant that the enemies who rise up against you will be defeated. They will come at you from one direction but flee from you in seven. (Deut. 28:7 NIV)

Even in the New Testament, the author of the book of Hebrews wants all Christians to be aware of the military policies of Jesus Christ, the Prince of Peace, and how he empowered men of great faith (in small armies, two-man armies, or one-man armies) to defeat much larger enemy forces, because "faith conquers kingdoms"! For it is written:

> I do not have enough time to tell about Gideon, Samson, Jepthah, David, Samuel, and the prophets, who through faith conquered kingdoms . . . escaped the edge of the sword, whose weakness was turned into strength; and who *became powerful in battle* and routed foreign armies! (Heb. 11:32-34 NIV; emphasis added)

We've discussed God's small armies, his two-man armies, and his one-man armies. But the battles involving his *"NO-man armies"* are the most interesting of all! For this is where God wins the entire battle by Himself, without the assistance of any soldiers at all! These are the battles where Israel merely watched as God defeated the enemies of righteousness. This was done by either drowning them, blinding them, cremating them with firefall, stoning them with hailstones (or meteorites), causing the ground to open up and swallow them in an earthquake, giving them hallucinations and delusions to make them either flee from the Israelites or attack each other (instead of attacking the Israelites), or causing an entire army of soldiers to just die in their sleep.

DROWNING THE ENEMY

In the "Battle of the Red Sea," God drowns Pharaoh's entire army in the Red Sea. For it is written:

> ... the Lord swept them into the sea. The water flowed back and covered the chariots and horsemen—the entire army of Pharaoh that had followed the Israelites into the sea. Not one of them survived. (Exod. 14:27b-28 NIV)

Imagine hearing the testimony of the Egyptians who were watching from the shore of the Red Sea, as they reported witnessing the power of the God of the Israelites, to inspire them to throw away their idols, repent of their sins, and worship only the God of the Israelites.

BLINDING THE ENEMY

In the story of "Elisha Traps the Blinded Arameans" (NIV), a "great host" of the Syrian army surrounded the city of Dothan to capture Elisha. But God blinded the entire Syrian army, and Elisha himself led them many miles to the capital city of Samaria, where once inside, God restored their sight and they suddenly realized that they had been captured. Although the idolatrous King of Israel wanted to execute the entire Syrian army, Elisha (speaking on behalf of God) evidently wanted to forgive them instead, so they were all set free to return home, after being served a great feast by the Samaritans—their "former enemies" (2 Kings 6:8-23).

Imagine the testimony of the thousands of Syrian soldiers returning home to their own country, as they tell of the power, grace, and mercy of the God of the Israelites, to inspire them to throw away their idols, repent of their sins, and worship only the God of the Israelites.

CREMATING THE ENEMY

Because of the evil homosexuality which had overrun these cities, God cremated all the citizens of Sodom and Gomorrah in one huge firefall, which was so hot that it destroyed all the buildings as well as everything else in both cities (Gen. 19:24-25, 28).

Secondly, in the story of "Elijah and the Captains" (NIV), Elijah called down fire from heaven. As a result, 102 men were cremated, in two separate "firefalls." For it is written:

> Elijah answered the captain, "If I am a man of God, may fire come down from heaven and consume you and your fifty men!" Then fire fell from heaven and consumed the captain and his fifty men.
>
> At this the king sent to Elijah another captain with his fifty men. The captain said to him, "Man of God, this is what the king says, 'Come down at once!' "
>
> "If I am a man of God," Elijah replied, "may fire come down from heaven and consume you and your fifty men!" Then the fire of God fell from heaven and consumed him and his fifty men. (2 Kings 1:10-12 NIV)

Thirdly, in the story of the "Cremation of the 250," Jehovah—the pre-incarnate Christ—stood at the entrance to the tabernacle, and fire came directly out of the body of Christ and consumed (cremated to ashes) 250 Israelite men. These men were usurping the authority of Aaron by offering "unapproved incense," and trying to "steal the priesthood." This was a conspiracy to overthrow Moses and Aaron to take away the command of the Israelites (Num. 16:35 NIV).

Fourthly, when Christ returns, he will cremate (or set on fire) the bodies of his enemies while they are still alive. They will watch each other burn up ("consume away" KJV) from the inside outward. For it is written:

> They will look aghast at each other, their faces aflame. (Isa. 13:8b NIV)
>
> Their flesh shall consume away while they stand upon their feet, and their eyes shall consume away in their holes, and their tongues shall consume away in their mouth. (Zech. 14:12b KJV)
>
> All the arrogant and every evil doer will be like stubble, and that day that is coming will set them on fire ... the wicked ... will be ashes under the soles of your feet. (Mal. 4:1, 3 NIV)

And finally, in the story of "Satan's Final Battle," Satan is released from Hades ("for a short while") after serving a 1 thousand year sentence in hell. The first thing he does is to lead all the world's armies to surround Jerusalem to attack and destroy Jesus Christ and his followers.

Christ responds by cremating all the world's armies simultaneously in one massive firefall (Rev. 20:9).

Stoning the Enemy with Hailstones or Meteorites

There are several places where God destroys his enemies by stoning them with either hailstones or meteorites (burning sulfur). Now the idea of destroying enemies by stoning them with hailstones is first mentioned by God in a conversation with Job thousands of years ago, about the time of Abraham. For it is written:

> Have you . . . seen the storehouses of hail, which I reserve for times of trouble, for days of war and battle? (Job 38:22-23 NIV)

The first time God actually used the hailstones in battle was more than five hundred years later, when He helped Joshua to destroy the Amorite idolators who practiced child sacrifice. For it is written:

> . . . the Lord hurled huge hailstones down on them from the sky, and more of them died from the hailstones than were killed by the swords of the Israelites. (Josh. 10:11 NIV)

Furthermore, God intends to use hailstones again to destroy the enemies of righteousness when Christ returns. However, these hailstones appear to actually be meteorites instead. For it is written:

> I will pour down torrents of rain, hailstones and burning sulfur on him and on his troops and on the many nations with him. (Ezek. 38:22b NIV)

The expression "burning sulfur" implies "rocks from the sky which are on fire" which most likely represent meteorites. In another passage it is revealed that these same meteorites are extremely heavy, and weigh "about a hundred pounds each." For it is written:

> From the sky huge hailstones of about a hundred pounds each fell upon men. (Rev. 16:21 NIV)

"Swallowing" the Enemy In an Earthquake

In the story of "Korah, Dathan, and Abiram" (NIV), God caused the . . .

> ground under them to split apart, and the earth opened its mouth and swallowed them, with their households . . . and all their possessions. They went down alive into the grave, with everything they owned; the earth closed over them and they perished and were gone from the community. (Num. 16:31-33 NIV)

There are other earthquakes recorded in the Bible which destroy the enemies of God also (see also Rev. 16:17-20 NIV).

AUDITORY HALLUCINATIONS AND DELUSIONS

In the story of "Famine in Besieged Samaria" (NIV), the entire Syrian army surrounded the city of Samaria and would not let any food come into the city. So, the Samaritans began to starve. However, God sent a strong delusion and an auditory hallucination into the minds of the Syrian army. They fled in terror back to Syria, leaving all their food, clothes, weapons, tents, horses, and riches behind. Their absence was first discovered by four men with leprosy (2 Kings 7:5-8, 15, 16). For it is written:

> At dusk [the four men with leprosy] got up and went to the camp of the Arameans. When they reached the edge of the camp, not a man was there, for the Lord had caused the Arameans to hear the sound of chariots and horses and a great army, so that they said to one another, 'Look, the king of Israel has hired the Hittite and Egyptian kings to attack us!' So they got up and fled in the dusk and abandoned their tents and their horses and donkeys. They left the camp as it was and ran for their lives. (2 Kings 7:6-7 NIV)

Later, the king sent soldiers to confirm the story of the four men with leprosy. It is written:

> They followed them as far as the Jordan, and they found the whole road strewn with the clothing and equipment the Arameans had thrown away in their headlong flight. (2 Kings 7:15 NIV)

Also, in the "Battle of Jehoshaphat" three nations (the Moabites, Ammonites, and Edomites) gather to attack Israel. But God sends upon them a delusion, so they attack and destroy each other instead, so that every single enemy soldier of all three armies dies in the battle. The Israelites then arrive and strip the dead and gather the plunder. For it is written:

> As they began to sing and praise, the Lord set ambushes against the men of Ammon and Moab and Mount Seir who were invading Judah, and they were defeated. The men of Ammon and Moab rose up against the men from Mount Seir to destroy and annihilate them. After they finished slaughtering the men for Seir, they helped to destroy one another.

> When the men of Judah came to the place that overlooks the desert and looked toward the vast army, they saw only dead bodies lying on the ground; no one had escaped. So Jehoshaphat and his men went to carry off their plunder, and they found among them a great amount of equipment and clothing and also articles of value—more than they could take away, There was so much plunder that it took three days to collect it. (2 Chron. 20:22-25 NIV)

BATTLE PANIC

Here, God causes the enemy to panic and the enemy ends up either fleeing from the Israelites or betraying and destroying each other. This is not too different from the "Battle of Jehoshaphat" which you just read. For instance, the Midianites panic in their battle with Gideon:

> ... the Lord caused the men throughout the camp to turn on each other with their swords. The army fled ... (Judg. 7:22 NIV)

The Philistines panic in their battle with King Saul and Prince Jonathan:

> Then panic struck the whole army—those in the camp and field, and those in the outposts and raiding parties—and the ground shook. It was a panic sent by God. (1 Sam. 14:15 NIV)

Even in the future God will once again send battle panic upon the enemies of righteousness. For it is written:

> Every man's sword will be against his brother. (Ezek. 38:21b NIV)

> On that day men will be stricken by the Lord with a great panic. Each man will seize the hand of another, and they will attack each other. (Zech. 14:13 NIV)

In summary, since God can control the eyes, ears, and minds of our enemies, then he can certainly control their comparatively simpler radar, sonar, and missile guidance systems as well. In fact, God controlled the ancient "guidance systems" (the "chariot wheels" of the Egyptians) by making the wheels come off when they chased the Israelites into the Red Sea, just to show us that he can do the same thing today with modern "guidance systems." For it is written:

> He made the wheels of their chariots come off so they had difficulty driving. (Exod. 14:25 NIV)

THE ENEMY DIES IN THEIR SLEEP

Finally, in the "Battle of Hezekiah," God kills 185 thousand Assyrian soldiers in just one night, and they presumably all died in their sleep. For it is written:

> That night the angel of the Lord went out and put to death a hundred and eighty-five thousand men in the Assyrian camp. When the people got up the next morning—there were all the dead bodies! (2 Kings 19:35 NIV; see also 2 Chron. 32:21, Isa. 37:36)

In summary, God glorifies Himself and exalts Israel's reputation through supernatural military defense using very small armies—including one *two-man* battle, five *one-man* battles, and at least eight *no-man* battles. These stories were included in the Bible at least in part to clearly demonstrate to all generations of all nations that no army of any century, regardless of their high-tech weaponry, can ever stand up to God's almighty power.

Moreover, the international testimony provided by the power and the pageantry of these miraculous military victories should prompt all other nations to consider giving up their pagan idolatry and instead, begin to worship the one true God—the pre-incarnate Jesus Christ—leader of the armies of ancient Israel!

9. ISRAELITE SOLDIERS WERE INVINCIBLE AS LONG AS GOD WAS FIGHTING FOR ISRAEL—HOWEVER, WHEN ISRAELITE SOLDIERS DIED IN BATTLE, IT MEANT THERE WAS SERIOUS SIN EITHER IN THE ARMY OR IN THE NATION OF ISRAEL ITSELF

The power of almighty God turned ordinary men into incredible warriors, each one with the supernatural strength, speed, and divine skill to easily kill several hundred enemy soldiers by themselves at one time. Also, these mighty men were actually invincible on the battlefield and could not be killed.

After Moses destroyed the Midianites, the Israelite commanders went through their command to count the soldiers who were either dead or missing (and therefore presumed dead). To their surprise, not a single Israelite soldier of thousands had been killed in battle because God was fighting on their side. Evidently, God had made the Israelite soldiers temporarily invincible. For it is written:

> Your servants have counted the soldiers under our command, and not one is missing. (Num. 31:49 NIV)

This verse reveals the doctrine of *the invincible soldier,* and sets the standard for all future battles by revealing that when God fights on the side of Israel, that *no Israelite soldiers will ever die!*

David knew firsthand the doctrine of the invincible soldier for he had seen hundreds, if not thousands of enemy soldiers die around him, and yet he knew that God had made him temporarily invincible on the battlefield. For it is written:

> You will not fear the terror of night, nor the arrow that flies by day . . . A thousand may fall at your side, ten thousand at your right hand, but it will NOT come near you. (Ps. 91:5, 7 NIV; emphasis added)

So, if Israelite soldiers were ever killed in combat, this was not a sign of the misfortunes of war, but a sign of serious sin either within the army or within the nation.

This is why Joshua was so upset when thirty-six Israelite soldiers were killed unexpectedly in "The Battle of Ai" (Josh. 7:4, 5, 10-12 NIV). This meant that God was no longer fighting on Israel's side in the battle because there was wickedness in the army (Josh. 7:11-12 NIV).

One of the Israelite soldiers named Achan had deliberately disobeyed God and had stolen the following items during the previous battle of Jericho:

> a beautiful robe from Babylonia, two hundred shekels of silver and a wedge of gold weighing fifty shekels. (Josh. 7:21 NIV)

As a result of having wickedness and rebellion in the Israelite army, God allowed thirty-six Israelite soldiers to die in the very next battle (Josh. 7:1-5, 11-12).

Because of this, God views America's celebration of Memorial Day with disdain. The honoring of our dead soldiers is paradoxical in the eyes of God because dead soldiers are a sign that God did not fight the battle for us either because we did not have a righteous army or we did not have a righteous government. Since God wins the battles, he also views Veteran's Day with disdain because we give praise, honor, and glory to the veteran as if the *veteran* soldiers won the battles, and not God himself.

Even our flag does not give honor to God but instead gives honor to ourselves. The red stripes represent the shed blood of our own soldiers, and the fifty stars represent the power we find in our own fifty states—which we mistakenly believe is the true source of our strength to keep our nation free. Instead, we ought to have designed a flag which gives glory to God for HIS power to win battles, and for HIS shed blood on the cross as a sacrifice for our sins.

10. ISRAEL MUST NEVER COUNT THE SIZE OF HER ARMY

David, a "man after God's own heart," once said that:

No king is saved by the size of his army. (Ps. 33:16 NIV)

As a result, counting the army was not only a colossal waste of time and effort, but also was a sin against God. This was because it gave credit and honor to the size of the army for military victories instead of giving credit and honor to the power of God.

Unfortunately however, one day even King David himself began to trust in man instead of God, and ordered Joab (commander of the army) to count all the fighting men in Israel. It was as if he began to believe that an army of larger size would offer more safety and protection. This made God very angry, so He sent a plague, and seventy thousand people died (2 Sam. 24:1, 10, 15 NIV). This is probably a representative number of the people who "should-have-died-but-didn't" in those battles where God did miraculously protect all David's men so that "not one of them was missing," just as God miraculously protected Moses' men against the Midianites (see Num. 312:48-49 NIV).

In the mid-1960s however, America proudly violated this same military principle by repeatedly boasting on TV about the size of our army compared to the Russian army. While we were making a public display of our arrogance, America also began to invade Viet Nam (which also violated God's military principle number 14) and so God punished us by allowing approximately 50,000 American soldiers to die in battle, just like God punished ancient Israel by allowing 70,000 soldiers to die just because Israel had counted the size of her army.

In fact, the U.S. Supreme Court also played a role in setting the stage for the defeat in Viet Nam by removing prayer and Bible study out of the public schools a few years earlier in 1962 and 1963. This symbolized to the world that America no longer thought it advantageous to train our youngest citizens to either worship the one true God in prayer or to obey his moral and civil laws. Thus "*God's laws* would no longer be *America's laws*," an action which symbolically "erased" God's laws against sexual immorality from our law books, and started the sexual revolution of the mid and late 1960s. But since our nation had now "officially" abandoned God in peacetime (violating God's military principle number 11) God would now abandon us in Viet Nam.

11. ISRAEL MUST MAINTAIN A RIGHTEOUS ARMY AND A RIGHTEOUS NATION IN ORDER FOR GOD TO FIGHT ON HER BEHALF, THEREFORE, ISRAEL MUST OBEY GOD IN PEACETIME IN ORDER FOR GOD TO FIGHT FOR ISRAEL IN WARTIME

12. NO HOMOSEXUALS ARE EVER TO SERVE IN THE ARMED FORCES OF ISRAEL

We learned, in the stories of the "Sin of Achan" and the "Battle of Ai," that God refused to fight on behalf of Israel when there was sin in the army. This sin caused thirty-six innocent soldiers to die in battle (Josh. 7:1-26). This becomes very important when we consider the idea of recruiting homosexuals into the army. *Homosexual perversion* is a far greater sin in God's eyes than is *stealing* (the "sin of Achan"). (Homosexuality carries a *death* penalty in the Bible and *stealing* does *not*.) Therefore homosexuality will eventually cost more lives in America's army than stealing cost in Israel's army!

God gave us a dramatic example in the Bible of how He will influence victory or defeat in battle depending upon the righteousness of the leaders and the soldiers fighting in battle. By the way, in the Bible, all the characters are all presumed to be heterosexual ("straight") unless the Bible clearly identifies them as homosexual ("gay").

In chapter eighteen of Genesis, the homosexual orientation of the citizens of Sodom and Gomorrah is revealed. Because of this, the armies of Sodom and Gomorrah (recorded in Genesis 14) must have been largely homosexual armies in comparison to the usual armies of other kingdoms, which were probably heterosexual armies.

The three kings of Admah, Zeboiim, and Zoar (three presumably heterosexual cities) had mistakenly joined forces in an unfortunate military alliance with the two kings of Sodom and Gomorrah (two clearly homosexual cities). As a result of the wickedness of homosexuality and this unholy military alliance, God allowed these five kings and their subjects to be conquered and to pay tribute for twelve years to their enemies—four heterosexual kings.

In the thirteenth year however, these cities rebelled against their conquerors, and the following year there was another war—four kings against five! The smaller heterosexual army of four kings reconquered the larger homosexual army of five kings, and captured Abram's nephew Lot as well. This was to teach us that a larger army of homosexual men will lose, even when the odds are in their favor.

But . . .

> When Abram heard that his relative had been taken captive, he called out the 318 trained men born in his household and went as far as Dan. During the night Abram divided his men to attack them and he routed them, pursuing them as far north as Hobah, north of Damascus. He recovered all the goods, and brought back his relative Lot and his possessions, together with the women and the other people. (Gen. 14:14-16 NIV)

So, a large army representing the evil homosexuality of Sodom and Gomorrah will lose, even when the odds are in their favor. But, a small army representing the righteousness of Abram will win, even when the odds are against them!

This teaches us that America (just like Israel) should never purposely recruit homosexuals into our military either, or God may humiliate America on the battlefield just as he did to Sodom and Gomorrah. In fact, God would be pleased if America would purposely exclude homosexuals from serving in the armed forces. After all, homosexuality is a sin against God which is supposed to be a crime against the state as well (Lev. 20:13; 18:22 NIV). Clearly God would not want homosexuals in the military!

13. NO WOMEN ARE EVER ALLOWED TO SERVE IN THE ARMED FORCES OF ISRAEL

A common theme throughout the Bible is that only men can serve in the army. For it is written:

> You and Aaron are to number by their divisions all the *men* in Israel twenty years or more who are able to serve in the army. (Num. 1:3; see also Deut. 20:7-8 NIV concerning "rules for going to war;" emphasis added)

"But," you ask, "how about Deborah, Jael, and the woman who dropped a large stone on a soldier's head and killed him? Didn't they fight in battle and doesn't that prove that women can serve in the army?"

No, it doesn't! You see, while it is true that there are three times a woman is mentioned in the context of a battle, in none of these cases was the woman actually *recruited* by God to fight or to lead! So this does *not* prove that God approves of women serving in the army.

For instance, Deborah was asked by "General" Barak (a spiritual wimp) to come into battle as an observer to give confidence to Barak that God would be with Israel in battle. You see, Barak felt that his faith and his obedience was so weak that God would not fight on Israel's behalf, if Deborah didn't also go into battle with them. For it is written:

> Barak said to her, "If you go with me, I will go; but if you don't go with me, I won't go." (Judg. 4:8 NIV)

Barak was supposed to be the bravest and most skilled warrior in all of Israel, else he wouldn't have become commander of the entire Israelite army. Yet it is clear he is a spiritual wimp, for he is afraid that God will not fight on behalf of the Israelite army without a spiritual giant (like Deborah) at the scene of the battle. This story does *not* say it's okay for women to be recruited to serve in the army, but teaches instead just the opposite, that God wants only righteous men of great faith to serve, not spiritual wimps like Barak. But at that time, no righteous men of great faith could be found in all of Israel, so instead they had to settle for Barak, a spiritual wimp.

In fact, to make this point even more strongly, God embarrasses Barak further by saying (through Deborah) that if He does not go into battle without Deborah's presence (like he is supposed to do) that God will hand over the enemy commander (Sisera) to a woman. For it is written:

> "Very well," Deborah said, "I will go with you. But because of the way you are going about this, the honor will not be yours, for the Lord will hand Sisera over to a woman." (Judg. 4:9 NIV)

Sure enough, a woman named Jael kills Sisera by hammering a tent peg through the temple of his skull while she found him asleep (Judg. 4:21). Again, the only reason God allowed Jael (a woman) to kill Sisera was to embarrass Barak (and all the other Israelite men) into realizing that in all of Israel, not one righteous man of great faith could be found to lead the Israelite army into battle and trust that God would give them the victory.

The only other recorded time a woman ever participated in a battle was as follows:

> But as he approached the entrance to the tower to set it on fire, a woman dropped an upper millstone on his head and cracked his skull. (Judg. 9:53 NIV)

This woman was not recruited to serve in the armed forces of Israel, but as you can see, she was only trying to help save herself and the others hiding in the tower from being burned alive.

Just as women are never supposed to serve in the armed forces of Israel, so also, if we are to please God, women should never serve in the armed forces of the United States either. You see, it is irrelevant to God how skilled or how brave the woman might be in battle, for when it comes to issues of national importance, the only thing that matters to God is national obedience.

14. ISRAEL IS NEVER TO INTERVENE MILITARILY IN THE AFFAIRS OF FOREIGN NATIONS, EITHER IN THEIR OWN PRIVATE WARS OR BECAUSE OF "HUMAN RIGHTS VIOLATIONS" IN FOREIGN COUNTRIES

King Josiah was perchance the most righteous king Israel ever had. In fact, nothing bad is ever said about Josiah in the entire Bible. That is perhaps, with one possible exception.

You see, King Josiah made the fatal mistake of military intervention in foreign countries when he attacked a nation on foreign soil which had not attacked Judah first, and which had no intention of harming Judah at all. This is the only mistake or sin ever recorded in the Bible about Josiah. Because of this sin God took Josiah's life on the battlefield. For it is written:

> ... Neco king of Egypt went up to fight at Carchemish on the Euphrates, and Josiah marched out to meet him in battle. But Neco sent messengers to him, saying, "What quarrel is there between you and me, O king of Judah? It is not you I am attacking at this time, but with the house with which I am at war. God has told me to hurry; so stop opposing God, who is with me, or he will destroy you."
>
> Josiah, however, would not turn away from him, but disguised himself to engage him in battle. He would not listen to what Neco said at God's command but went to fight him on the plain of Megiddo.
>
> Archers shot King Josiah, and ... he died. (2 Chron. 25:20-24 NIV)

This story was to teach us that God does not want Israel (or the U.S.) to intervene in the military affairs of other nations.

You see, Neco was marching to fight the Assyrians (not Israel) and his intended place of battle was 380 miles north of the northernmost border of Judah. Somehow the entire Egyptian army had silently passed through the kingdom of Judah, and was now all the way up to Megiddo, which was nearly fifty miles north of the northernmost border of the kingdom of Judah. In fact, by the time Josiah caught up with the Egyptian army at Megiddo, Pharaoh Neco was evidently still marching even further away from Judah, clearly intending no harm to Judah at all.

Furthermore, since the Assyrians were the official rulers of the former northern kingdom of Israel since conquering it about 118 years earlier, the Egyptians were technically already well inside the borders of "Assyriah" by the time Josiah caught up with them at Megiddo. So, when King Josiah finally caught up with Pharaoh Neco at Megiddo,

Josiah was technically no longer defending his own country but was now intervening in the military affairs of a foreign nation, Assyriah. God is teaching us that we should not do this unless we have been attacked. Since Judah had not been attacked by Egypt, God wanted Josiah not to intervene in the military affairs of another nation.

So also, the United States should never intervene militarily in the affairs of foreign nations, or else risk the displeasure of God as well. Therefore, according to the Bible, America should never have intervened militarily in Vietnam, Korea, World War I, Somalia, Rowanda, or even Desert Storm, because the United States was never attacked first in any of these wars. However, we were allowed to participate in World War II because Japan attacked America first.

15. ISRAEL'S MILITARY IS NOT EXPECTED TO BE THE POLICEMAN OF THE WORLD

God did not want Israel's military to be the policeman of the ancient world, and he does not want America's military to be the policeman of the modern world either.

You see, historians tell us that Assyria was one of the most evil nations which ever existed, because of their repeated human rights violations. Yet in the Bible, God never asked Israel to attack Assyria because of this or to join forces with Egypt or any other nation against the Assyrians because of this problem. So, God did not want Israel to police the ancient world for international violations of human rights.

Just as God did not want Israel's military to be the policeman of the ancient world, neither does he want America's military to be the policeman of the modern world.

But, America's military not only polices the modern world to purge it from human rights violations (against God's Will), but we also police the world to attempt to keep it free of any other system of government except democracy.

You see, Americans have this idea that communism, socialism, fascism, Naziism, and all dictatorships are all enemies to democracy. However, according to the Bible, *all* systems of government (including democracy) which exalt the foolish ways of man and suppress the principles of GOD are really the enemies of any country attempting to become a true nation under God.

Yet we do our utmost to prevent communism from conquering the world in the ultimate belief that if communism becomes too big and powerful, that communism will conquer democracy as well. We reject the biblical principle that . . .

no enemy's army (regardless of its size or high-tech weapons) could ever harm Israel, as long as Israel was a righteous nation which obeyed God in peacetime so that God would supernaturally defend Israel in wartime!

In other words, if the United States became a true nation under God (by carrying out all of God's principles of moral and civil law), then God would supernaturally defend our nation just like He defended Israel in the Bible. As a result, America would not need to be the policeman of the world to stop other forms of government because no matter how strong communism became, a true nation under God could never be defeated in battle. This is because God would miraculously defend us just as He promised to defend Israel.

In this way, America would be exalted by God as an international object lesson to magnify the supernatural rewards which can be received by any nation which successfully enforces all of God's principles of moral and civil law as part of their national legislation—principles which not only promote nationwide righteous behavior, but more importantly, promote nationwide worship of Jesus Christ! And as a result, instead of displeasing God by spending billions of tax dollars to support a large, high-tech army spread all over the world, we would only need a tiny army—if that.

Just think what we could do with the tax savings! For as other nations marvel at how God has blessed America with righteousness, prosperity, and peace and therefore begin to open their doors to our Christian missionaries, if just 1 percent of our entire military defense budget went to support Christian missionaries in those "enemy" countries, we could win a small minority of citizens in *those* nation to Christ. We could also help them change *their* governments so they too can become "nations under God" by incorporating some of the Mosaic laws into their constitutions. Helping to transform "enemy nations" into Christian nations under God would go a lot further to protect America from future attack than our current military and foreign policies do.

The Bible teaches that (with very few exceptions) all of the blessings God promised to Israel are still available to all nations today. This means that God is willing to miraculously defend the United States (in the same ways He defended Israel thousands of years ago) if we first implement all of God's principles of moral law and civil law into our national legislation. America must first obey God completely in peacetime in order to guarantee that God will miraculously defend us in wartime.

Let's briefly re-examine just a few of those promises. (A detailed discussion of this topic has already been presented in chapter four.)

God's Promised Blessings to Israel Are Still Available to America Today

1. God promises to bless any nation which obeys Him. (Ps. 19:33)
2. Any country which is unfaithful to God will be punished (see Jer. 18:7-10 and Ezek. 14:12-14).
3. Any country which nationally repents of its sin and turns from its wicked ways will be blessed (Jer. 18:7-10; Ezek. 14:12-14 NIV).
4. Any nation can "learn the ways of [God's] people" and become "established among [His] people" (Jer. 12:14-17 NIV); and therefore be "called by [His] name" and reap the rewards of a political and national relationship with Christ (2 Chron. 7:14 NIV).
5. God's truth endureth to all generations (Ps. 100:5b NIV).

(Please reread chapter four for complete details of why God's promises to Israel are still available to America today.)

Since God promises to miraculously defend any nation which attempts to become a nation under God, let us see how God has already demonstrated some battle miracles during the French and Indian War, as well as during the Revolutionary War, to confirm that indeed these promise are truly still available to the United States today.

The following story has been called "The Bullet-Proof George Washington" and originally came from an 1856 Maryland history textbook entitled, *Tragic Scenes in the History of Maryland and the Old French War*, by Joseph Banvard, (Boston: Gould and Lincoln, 1856, 142-159). My reference however, comes from a transcript of a videotape/audiotape entitled *America's Godly Heritage* by David Barton (1993, Wallbuilders, Inc.). According to Barton, stories like this one continued to appear in our public school history textbooks before the late 1940s but were purged from our educational system more than forty years ago.

Briefly, this

> is a story of how Washington's life hung in the balance for over two hours and how that only by the direct intervention of God it was spared. (Barton, 3).

You see, during the French and Indian War, George Washington was in the middle of the battle when the French and Indians massacred the British and American soldiers. Barton records this as follows:

> ... while marching through a wooded ravine, they walked right into an ambush; the French and Indians opened fire on them from both sides.
>
> But these were British veterans; they knew exactly what to do. The problem was, they were veterans of European wars.

European warfare was all in the open. One army lined up at one end of an open field, the other army lined up at the other end, they looked at each other, took aim, and fired. No running, no hiding. But here they were in the Pennsylvania woods with the French and Indians firing at them from the tops of trees, from behind rocks, and from under logs.

When they came under fire, the British troops did exactly what they had been taught; they lined up shoulder to shoulder in the bottom of that ravine—and were slaughtered. At the end of two hours, 714 of the thirteen hundred British and American troops had been shot down; only thirty of the French and Indians had been shot.

There were eighty-six British and American officers involved in that battle; at the end of the battle, George Washington was the only officer who had not been shot down off his horse—he was the only officer left on horseback.

Following this resounding defeat, Washington gathered the remaining troops and retreated back to Fort Cumberland in western Maryland, arriving there on July 17 1755.

The next day, Washington wrote a letter to his family explaining that after the battle was over, he had taken off his jacket and had found *four bullet holes* through it, yet not a single bullet had touched him; several horses had been shot from under him, but he had not been harmed. He told them: "By the all powerful dispensations of Providence, I have been protected beyond all human probability or expectation."

Washington openly acknowledged that God's hand was upon him, that God had protected him and kept him through that battle.

However, the story does not stop there. Fifteen years later, in 1770—now a time of peace—George Washington and a close personal friend, Dr. James Craik, returned to those same Pennsylvania woods. An old Indian chief from far away, having heard that Washington had come back to those woods, traveled a long way just to meet with him.

He sat down with Washington, and face-to-face over a council fire, the chief told Washington that he had been a leader in that battle fifteen years earlier, and that he had instructed his braves to single out all the officers and shoot them down. Washington had been singled out, and the chief explained that he personally had shot at Washington *seventeen different times,* but without effect. Believing Washington to be under the care of the Great Spirit, the chief instructed his braves to cease firing at him. He then told Washington: "I have traveled a long and weary path that I might see the young warrior of the great battle... I am come to pay homage to the man who is the particular favorite of Heaven, and *who can never die in battle."*

That account appeared in American history textbooks for nearly a century and a half; today it has disappeared! (Barton, 3-5; emphasis added)

This story reveals to us that God still makes great men of faith to be temporarily INVINCIBLE on the battlefield. For God still honors the promises he gave to Israel thirty-five hundred years ago, by performing battle miracles even for "Christian" nations who are attempting to become true nations under God by implementing God's principles of moral law, civil law, and civil law enforcement. It also reveals the great international impression that non-Christian nations could receive upon observing or hearing about such battle miracles. This can create a foundation to build upon to draw entire nations to begin to understand the importance of worshipping Christ, as well as using these same biblical principles to create their own nation under God.

But that is not all! The following are quotes from William J. Federer's, *America's God and Country Encyclopedia of Quotations* (Fame Publishing, Inc., Coppell, Texas, 1994, 645-646; emphasis added).

> On January 1, 1781, circumstances were desperate for the Continental Army. The Pennsylvania line troops being paid with worthless paper currency, revolted. Short enlistments threatened the discipline of the ranks.
>
> In a bold move, on January 17, 1781, George Washington's southern army, led by General George Morgan, defeated the entire detachment of British Colonel Tarlton's troops at Cowpens. Lord Cornwallis was infuriated and immediately began pursuing the American troops. He decided to wait the night at the Catawba River, where the American troops had crossed just two hours earlier, but to his distress, a storm began during the night, causing the river to be *uncrossable* for days.
>
> On February 3, Lord Cornwallis nearly overtook the American troops again at the Yadkin River, watching the American troops getting out on the other side. But before they could cross, a *sudden flood* ran the river over its banks, preventing the British from crossing.

On February 13, only a few hours ahead of the British, the American troops crossed the Dan River into Virginia. When the British arrived, again the *river had risen,* stopping the British from pursuing. British Commander-in-Chief Henry Clinton wrote, explaining the incident:

Here the royal army was again stopped by *a sudden rise of the waters,* which had only *just fallen* (almost *miraculously*) to let the enemy over, who could not else have eluded Lord Cornwallis' grasp, so close was he upon their rear.

This story illustrates the principle of the Red Sea and the Jordan River—that God will control the rise and fall of rivers, and the like, to enable an army led by godly men of faith to escape its enemies, and to safely go where God wants them to go. In other words, God still honors the promises He gave to Israel thirty-four hundred years ago which teach that God will control all of nature if necessary to give miraculous victory for any army of any nation which intends to honor God by building better government with biblical principles.

This next story occurred on 26 December 1776, and comes from Beliles and McDowell's *America's Providential History,* (Province Foundation, Charlottesville, Virginia, 1989, 161-162; emphasis added):

In a desperate move, Washington decided to cross the Delaware River in predawn hours in order to surprise the enemy. He chose the early morning of December 26 to attack the Hessian garrison quartered at Trenton, for he knew their accustomed drinking on Christmas would help assure their deep slumber on that early morning.

As the troops prepared to cross the Delaware River, a violent snow and *hailstorm* suddenly came up. This hardship, however, worked in their favor by inducing the enemy's sentries to take cover and reducing the visibility to near zero.

The Americans entered so unexpectedly and with such surprise to the Hessians that about 1 thousand prisoners were taken captive after only forty-five minutes of battle. Only three Americans were wounded in the fighting. Two had died, but not in the fighting, they froze to death on the march.

This story teaches us about the *hailstones* which occurred in one of the battles of Joshua, and reminds us that "no one dies in battles when God is doing the fighting for us." Certainly, God's Old Testament promises to fight Israel's battles for them are still available to us today. Therefore, since this is true, we should slowly (over the next few decades or generations) change the policies of our military to match all fifteen of the military policies of Jesus Christ, the Prince of Peace, as written at the beginning of this chapter.

These fifteen military policies can save our nation billions of tax dollars which could be better spent elsewhere. For, America would no longer need a large army with high-tech weapons for deployment all over the world, to police the world of human rights violations and for military intervention in foreign countries. This is because, if America first redesigns our culture to implement all God's principles of moral law, civil law, and civil law enforcement—and therefore becomes a true nation under God—then God would miraculously defend America through supernatural divine intervention. He would do this by either blinding our enemies, drowning them, cremating them with firefall, stoning them with hailstones, causing the ground to swallow them in an earthquake , or causing an entire army of soldiers to die in their sleep. Or, God would send upon our enemies hallucinations and delusions so they are either lured into a fatal trap, flee from us in battle, or develop battle panic, causing them to attack each other instead of attacking America. And, since God can control the eyes, ears, and minds of the enemy, then he can certainly control the relatively simpler missile guidance systems of our enemies, or destroy all their missiles in midair with firefall.

Furthermore, on the battlefield itself, our men could be made temporarily invincible so they would never die in battle, so that "not one of them would be missing-in-action"! They could be made into mighty warriors like Samson, Josheb-Basshebeth, Eleazar, Shammah, Abishai, and David, who all killed hundreds of men at one time by themselves, and, as the writer of the book of Hebrews says:

> whose weakness was turned into strength, and who became *powerful in battle* and routed foreign armies. (Heb. 11:34b NIV; emphasis added)

You see, God can overthrow any kind of weaponry. However, it was very hard for the Israelites to imagine how God was going to enable them to achieve victory against their enemies without a "balance of power" which could be measured by counting soldiers, horses, and chariots.

But is there really any difference between the Israelite desire to count soldiers, horses, and chariots, and the American desire to count soldiers, aircraft carriers, battleships, submarines, and nuclear missiles? Don't we, in America, have the same fear as the Israelites (that even God cannot stop chariots or nuclear missiles)? Yet perhaps we believe God *can* stop them but we don't trust that he *will* stop them.

Well, this was the same problem the Israelites had. You see, because of their sinful idolatry, God allowed them to be conquered thirteen times over 4 hundred years during the period of the judges. As a result, they no longer felt they could trust God to protect them, either because they felt God *couldn't* or God *wouldn't*. They probably felt that God expected too much of them and that they could never be righteous enough as a nation for God to protect them. I'm sure that the Israelites felt that God was giving their nation a command which He would not enable them to fulfill. I'm sure most Americans feel God would never enable America to have enough national righteousness for us to trust that God would miraculously stop an armed invasion of hundreds of incoming nuclear missiles.

Well, God would not give Israel any command which He would not also enable Israel to fulfill. He required Israel to obey his military policies thirty-four hundred years ago and He requires the same of Israel today. By the same token, God would not give America any command which He would not enable America to fulfill as well. God requires America to carry out His commands; and He will enable America to carry out these same commands if we make the effort to become a nation under God by rebuilding America with biblical principles. Now don't say this is impossible, for God himself will do the enabling if America's leaders aim for God's target and play by God's rules.

Let us also realize that, when we (as a nation) follow the military strategies of Jesus Christ, that this can become a great tool for evangelism. For it is written:

> We have heard how the Lord dried up the water of the Red Sea for you when you came out of Egypt, and what you did to Sihon and Og, the two kings of the Amorites east of the Jordan, whom you completely destroyed. When we heard of it, our hearts melted and everyone's courage failed because of you, for the Lord YOUR GOD IS GOD of heaven above and on the earth below. (Josh. 2:10-11 NIV; emphasis added)

You see, the military strategies of Jesus Christ can actually work for EVANGELISM by making citizens of other nations understand that the God of the Israelites IS the one true God of heaven and earth. They will also see that it was this same Jehovah who became the world's Messiah and Savior—Jesus Christ.

Furthermore, when other nations fear you, they will not attack you, so you will be at peace with all your neighbors. As a result, Israel (or America) would have PEACE with its enemies, which is the natural end-result of following the military strategies of Jesus Christ—the Prince of Peace.

Other nations are not interested in learning to worship the God of an evil nation, a poor nation, or a conquered nation. But God's plan was for America to be a righteous nation, a prosperous nation, and a nation supernaturally defended by the Prince of Peace—Jesus Christ. Therefore, if America followed God's plan for righteous Christian elders to rule over the unrighteous, and adopt God's principles of moral and civil law into our national legislation, then both the righteous and the unrighteous would be kept on their best behavior. This would so increase the aggregate righteousness of our nation that God would bless America with great prosperity and would defend America supernaturally.

America would then be neither evil, nor poor, nor conquered, but instead would be righteous, prosperous, and supernaturally defended by almighty God. This would put all other nations on notice: that there is a God in America, and his name is Jesus Christ! This proclamation would throw open the doors to international evangelism which were previously closed to our missionaries.

In conclusion, God wants America's military to:

1. dismiss all homosexuals and women from serving in the armed forces;

2. stop trying to be the military policeman of the world;

3. stop all military intervention in foreign countries;

4. stop using Veterans Day to exalt our veterans as though they have been responsible for our military victories (and that God played no military role at all);

5. stop using Memorial Day to give honor to our dead servicemen (because when a soldier dies in battle it is a sign that America has angered God and so He is not fighting on America's behalf);

6. recognize that America must obey God completely in peacetime before He will be willing to supernaturally defend America in wartime;

7. look for progressive evidence of God's supernatural blessing in our military affairs, as a reward for America becoming more righteous and obedient to His Will;

8. have the faith to slowly taper our military size, weaponry, and budget to a small fraction of its current size (once progressive evidence of God's supernatural military blessings becomes obvious to our rulers and to our military commanders); and then,

9. have the faith to slowly remove our military presence from around the world, and have the faith to end all our war treaties with all our allies and begin to trust in God alone to defend America,

10. give God all the praise, honor, and glory for his military intervention when it occurs,

11. marvel in worship as Christ exalts America as a true nation under God and creates an international fearful reverence of America's God, an action which will . . .

12. open up all the doorways to international evangelism which were previously closed to Christian missionaries, which in turn, will . . .

13. lead millions more to accept the gospel of salvation by grace through faith in Christ's atoning sacrifice on the cross!

And that, is God's view of military policy reform!

Chapter Twenty-Three

GOD'S VIEW OF FOREIGN POLICY AND IMMIGRATION REFORM

There are at least nine biblical principles involving foreign policy which God designed for Israel and for any other country which seeks to become a nation under God.

1. FEARFUL REVERENCE

Israel's foreign policy was divinely designed to magnify the reputation of Jehovah in order to generate an international fearful reverence of the God of the Israelites. This was to be accomplished, in large part, by combining the influences which God's military and economic policies have on foreign nations.

The first part of God's foreign policy involves the international reputation Israel would develop once they successfully implemented the military policies of the Prince of Peace—Jesus Christ. For, if the Israelites had obeyed God, he would have given them such miraculous supernatural military victories, that all the other nations would begin to fear Israel and Israel's God, which would lead to peace. For it is written:

> The fear of God came upon all the kingdoms of the countries when they heard how the Lord had fought against the enemies of Israel. (2 Chron. 20:29 NIV)

And . . .

> The fear of the Lord fell on all the kingdoms of the lands surrounding Judah, so that they did not make war with Jehoshaphat. (2 Chron. 17:10 NIV)

You see, part of Jehovah's military policy involved putting the fear of God into all of the surrounding nations so they would not attack Israel. Therefore, Israel could live in peace with her neighboring countries, which is one of the reasons why Jehovah (the pre-incarnate Christ) would eventually be called the "Prince of Peace."

In addition, if Israel would have obeyed God, His economic policy would have involved giving Israel so much wealth and prosperity, in such a miraculous fashion, that this also would cause all of the other nations of the earth to fear Jehovah—the God of the Israelites. For it is written:

> God will bless us, and all the ends of the earth will fear him." (Ps. 67:7 NIV; see also Mal. 3:9-12 and Deut. 28:9-10)

And, as the other nations began to witness Israel's surprising production of wealth, they would have realized that such unexpected wealth was too improbable to have occurred naturally. This could only have occurred supernaturally, with the help of God. That is why they would begin to fear Jehovah.

In other words, Jehovah wanted to bless Israel with such supernatural military victories in wartime, and with so much miraculous prosperity in peacetime, that all the other nations of the world would learn to fear the God of the Israelites. As these nations learned to FEAR the Lord, they would also learn to REVERE the Lord. For it is written:

> Let all the earth FEAR the Lord; let all the people of the world REVERE him. (Ps. 33:8 NIV; emphasis added)

So, by magnifying the reputation of Israel's God throughout the entire world, an international fearful reverence develops, which can be used for evangelizing foreign countries.

You see, God's foreign policy has been (and always will be) very evangelistic. For God has always wanted all of the nations of the world to fear, honor, and worship him, as well as to "crown" him as their "king," by adopting his principles of moral and civil law into their legislation. This way, all nations could become nations under God and receive God's blessings of health, happiness, peace, and prosperity.

By the way, developing a true nation under God (in order to receive all of God's blessings) does not mean that each citizen is "saved" or righteous. It does mean that the righteous minority rules the nation, and has made certain sins against God (such as adultery, homosexuality, premarital sex, drunkenness, etc.) to always remain punishable crimes against the state. This allows the moral doctrines of the small Christian minority to be empowered with the legal muscle to control the actions of the unrighteous majority to keep them on their best behavior.

In fact, the well-behaved unrighteous will always make up the majority of the citizens in a true nation under God. However, their actions are "kept under control" by a much smaller Christian minority. This is because the Christian minority has developed a society where the reluctant righteous are automatically drawn into (or are pushed into) positions of authority. Here, they can exercise their godly leadership by enforcing the godly laws which generate the godly peer-pressure to keep the unrighteous majority on their best behavior in the first place.

2. INTERNATIONAL FEARFUL REVERENCE OF JEHOVAH HELPS TO SPREAD THE GOOD NEWS OF SALVATION

As a result of God's foreign policy of creating an international fearful reverence of the God of the Israelites, the nations would also begin to learn about *salvation* by grace through faith in Jehovah (who would later on become our Messiah and Savior—Jesus Christ, and die for our sins on the cross). For it is written:

> May God be gracious to us and bless us and make his face shine upon us, that your *ways* may be known on earth, your *Salvation* among the peoples. (Ps. 67:1-2 NIV; emphasis added)

> The Lord has made his *Salvation* known and revealed his righteousness to the nations . . . all the ends of the earth have seen the *Salvation* of our God. (Ps. 98:2-3b NIV; emphasis added)

So you see, this foreign policy of international fearful reverence helps to carry the message of salvation around the entire world!

Jehovah then gave the Israelites an Old Testament "Great Commission" to spread this good news of salvation all over the world. For it is written:

> *Proclaim* his Salvation day after day. *Declare* his glory among the nations, his marvelous deeds among all peoples . . . *Say* among the nations, "the Lord reigns." (Ps. 96:2b-3, 10; see also: 1 Chron. 16:23-24; Ps. 105:1b; and Jer. 31:10 NIV; emphasis added)

This command, of course, represents the forerunner of the "Great Commission" given by Christ, which is as follows:

> Therefore go and make disciples of all nations, baptizing them in the name of the Father and of the Son and of the Holy Spirit, and teaching them to obey everything I have commanded you. (Matt. 28:19-20 NIV)

So you see, in both the Old and the New Testaments, God's foreign policy is very evangelistic. This is because God has always wanted the entire world to come to know Him as Savior (of individuals) and as King (over nations).

Now, if you are wondering whether the "salvation" spoken about in these verses is the same as the "salvation" spoken about in the New Testament, please remember that . . .

1. confession,
2. repentance,
3. forgiveness of sin,
4. salvation by grace through faith,
5. the need for a "sacrifice without blemish" to be an atonement for sin," and . . .
6. walking with God in moment-by-moment surrender,

have always been the keys to salvation throughout the ages. And the only "missing" item was that Jehovah had not yet personally returned to become our Messiah and Savior—Jesus Christ, to die on the cross for our sins as the one true sacrifice without blemish. For only Jesus Christ (Jehovah in the flesh) is "the way, truth and life, and no one comes unto the Father but by him" (John 14:6).

3. AMBASSADORS

All ambassadors from Israel (and therefore, from the United States as well) should actually be *missionaries* who are fully equipped to evangelize each foreign country. This is much more consistent with the purpose of a nation under God than sending the CIA to topple foreign governments or to spy on them. Therefore, ambassadors for Israel were supposed to serve God and "declare his Glory among the nations, his marvelous Deeds among all peoples," as well as "proclaim his Salvation day after day." For it is written:

> Sing to the Lord, all the earth; proclaim his Salvation day after day. Declare his glory among the nations, his marvelous deeds among all peoples. (1 Chron. 16:23-24 NIV)

Also, they should . . .

> . . . make known among the nations what he has done . . . tell of all his wonderful acts . . . (Ps. 105:1b NIV)

For God wanted all nations to . . .

> hear the word of the Lord, O nations; proclaim it in distant coastlands. (Jer. 31:10 NIV)

So you see, American ambassadors should also be able to proclaim all the blessings the U.S. has received as a result of working our way towards becoming a nation under God by adopting all of God's principles into our legislation. These American missionary ambassadors for Christ should not only be able to tell the leaders of other nations about salvation by grace through faith in Jesus Christ, but also be able to educate these same leaders about the benefits of building better government with biblical principles, and present Jesus Christ as the *architect* of this biblical blueprint for perfect self-government as well. Then, they can invite these same leaders of foreign countries to the United States to witness how God has blessed us (because of our obedience) by giving us a nearly disease-free, crime-free, poverty-free, war-free, tax-free, inflation-free, and natural disaster-free society. The leaders of these foreign countries will then also want to rebuild their countries into nations under God to inherit these same blessings.

In fact, this concept of national *obedience* followed by national *blessing* followed again by international *awe* of Israel (which implies an awe of Israel's God) is so important that God says we should *test* Him by national obedience and watch it happen. For it is written:

> "Bring the whole tithe into the storehouse, that there may be food in my house. *Test me in this*," says the Lord Almighty, "and see if I will not throw open the floodgates of heaven and pour out so much *blessing* that you will not have room enough to receive it. I will prevent pests from devouring your crops, and the vines in your fields will not cast their fruit," says the Lord Almighty. "Then all the nations will call you *blessed*, and yours will be a delightful land . . ." (Mal. 3:9-12 NIV; emphasis added)

Now, it is easy to imagine how impressed foreign leaders would be if they found our nation to be a prosperous, poverty-free society which was also disease-free, crime-free, war-free, tax-free, inflation-free and natural disaster-free as well. Therefore, God's foreign policy of international fearful reverence has a twofold purpose:

1. Jehovah wants His salvation to be made known to all peoples, because of His love for *individuals* and his desire to bless them with salvation, peace and hope;
2. Jehovah wants all countries to become nations under God because of His love of *nations* and His desire to bless them with happy, healthy, peaceful, and prosperous societies.

In summary, if Israel would have obeyed God, God's foreign policy would have involved giving Israel miraculous blessings during peacetime and wartime. He would do this in order to magnify the reputation of Jehovah and produce an international fearful reverence of the God of the Israelites. This would be for the purpose of promoting international evangelism on an unparalleled scale, so Christ might have a better chance to become king of each nation and Lord of each individual throughout the entire world.

4. AMERICA'S TOP LEADERS MUST BE FILLED WITH GOD'S WISDOM SO THEY CAN SHARE THIS WISDOM WITH ALL THE OTHER LEADERS OF THE WORLD

Another part of God's foreign policy for Israel involved spreading God's wisdom throughout the entire world by having foreign leaders meet face to face on Israel's soil. This theme is perfectly illustrated by the story of Solomon teaching God's wisdom to all the other leaders of the world. For it is written:

> All the kings of the earth sought audience with Solomon to hear the wisdom God had put in his heart. (2 Chron. 9:23 NIV)

Now, you are probably thinking, "But Solomon was a special case and was granted all this wisdom by God as a miraculous gift." That is true. But Solomon was also the only king who appears to have even asked for God's wisdom to rule people (1 Kings 3:7-12 NIV), so it is no wonder that he was the only one who was granted it. Now I'm not saying that God will grant any of us the wisdom of Solomon, but I do believe that the teaching in these two verses is that every king and leader should be earnestly praying for God's wisdom about how to govern his nation. If our leaders ask (and keep on asking) for God's wisdom to rule our nation, then they will surely receive it. For it is written:

> Ask and it will be given to you; seek and you will find . . . for everyone who asks receives; he who seeks finds. (Matt. 7:7; see also Prov. 2:3-6, 9-10 NIV)

So, each leader needs to continuously draw near to God in prayer and personally ask Him each working day for His Wisdom to govern His people, instead of relying on the Chaplain of Congress to pray on his behalf for this wisdom. For God will probably not give His divine wisdom to our nation's leaders if the leaders themselves don't sense the need to ask God for His wisdom in the first place.

However, most of God's wisdom for governing nations has actually already been written down in the Mosaic law, and all you have to do is read it, study it, learn it, and know it by heart. The best way to do this is to first write down your own copy of the entire Mosaic law concerning governing nations. For it is written:

> When he takes the throne of his kingdom, he is to *write* for himself on a scroll a copy of this law, taken from that of the priests . . . It is to be *with* him and he is to *read* it all the days of his life so that he may learn to *revere* the Lord his God and follow carefully *all* the words of this law and these decrees and not consider himself better than his brothers and turn from the law to the right or to the left. (Deut. 17:18-20 NIV; emphasis mine)

In other words, God always wants the top leader(s) of Israel (or any other top leaders who want to create a nation under God) to have a thorough in-depth knowledge of all of God's commands about moral law, civil law, and civil law enforcement.

Of course, this is best done by actually writing out all of these principles for yourself as if you were "taking notes" on the subject for a college course, for you will learn it better when you write it down. In addition, these notes should always be kept with you so you can refer to them when needed, and you are to read them all the days of your life so you can keep them fresh in your mind to help you find answers about all the important national issues which may come up. For example, this book you are reading represents *my* copy of God's principles of civil law!

Furthermore, all of our rulers in Congress should also have a working knowledge of all these biblical principles of civil law as well. They should all pray (just like David prayed) that God will "open their eyes" and reveal to them the deepest secrets about the law. For it is written:

> Open my eyes that I may see wonderful things in your law.
> (Ps. 119:18 NIV)

By the way, Deuteronomy 18:20, (which you read earlier) makes it clear that NO ONE IS ABOVE THE LAW, including the King. This, of course, means that American senators, congressmen, governors, and ambassadors are not above the law, and that in God's perfect government, there is no such thing as "diplomatic immunity" for foreign ambassadors!

5. ECONOMIC ALLIANCES AND TRADE AGREEMENTS WITH FOREIGN NATIONS

There are other facets of biblical foreign policy which are also very important, such as whether or not to trade with foreign nations (specifically those who worship idols and whose leaders practice other forms of wickedness). This is very important to God, and there are stories in the Bible written specifically to teach us about these issues. For it is written:

> Later, Jehoshaphat king of Judah made an alliance with Ahaziah king of Israel, who was guilty of wickedness. He agreed with him to construct a fleet of trading ships. After these were built at Ezion Geber, Eliezer son of Dodavahu of Mareshah prophesied against Jehoshaphat, saying, "Because you have made an alliance with Ahaziah, the Lord will destroy what you have made." The ships were wrecked and were not able to sail to trade. (2 Chron. 20:35-37 NIV)

It is also written:

Now Jehoshaphat built a fleet of trading ships to go to Ophir for gold, but they never set sail—they were wrecked at Ezion Geber. At that time Ahaziah son of Ahab said to Jehoshaphat, "Let my men sail with your men," but Jehoshaphat refused. (1 Kings 22:48 NIV)

Now, the prophet Eliezer said these ships would be destroyed by God specifically because of the *"unholy economic alliance"* made between Jehoshaphat (representing a kingdom of righteousness and faith) and Ahaziah (representing a kingdom of wickedness and idolatry). These ships were destroyed by God not because Jehoshaphat merely "refused to let Ahaziah's men sail with them," but because of the "unholy economic alliance."

You see, Jehoshaphat had probably agreed initially to allow Ahaziah's men to sail with Jehoshaphat's men as part of the alliance. But, after the prophet Eliezer spoke with Jehoshaphat, Jehoshaphat probably tried to "undo" this part of the "unholy alliance" in a last minute effort to please God, thinking that this was all that was necessary to please God and to get Him to change his mind. However, God didn't "buy it" and he wrecked the ships anyway. This was because there was more to this "unholy alliance" than just having men from different countries working together—the alliance was still "in effect" and would still make money for the evil northern kingdom of Israel which God was trying to punish economically.

It should have been obvious to all that a righteous kingdom (which God is trying to bless with prosperity) should never make an economic alliance with a kingdom of wickedness (which God is trying to punish with poverty), or else the punishment of the unrighteous nation will "spill over" onto the righteous nation; thus, making the righteous nation suffer as well.

It is interesting that about one hundred years earlier, King Solomon made an almost identical economic alliance with Hiram, king of Tyre, yet God blessed that alliance tremendously. This alliance also involved the building of ships at Ezion Geber to sail to Ophir for gold, and having men from both countries work and sail together. For it is written:

> King Solomon also built ships at Ezion Geber, which is near Elath in Edom, on the shore of the Red Sea. And Hiram sent his men-sailors who knew the sea—to serve in the fleet with Solomon's men. They sailed to Ophir and brought back 420 talents of gold, which they delivered to Solomon. (1 Kings 9:26-28 NIV)

There are five similarities between Solomon's alliance with Hiram (which God blessed) and Jehoshaphat's alliance with Ahaziah (which

God cursed). In fact, Jehoshaphat probably knew that God had blessed Solomon's endeavor one hundred years earlier, and so, designed his alliance to be as similar as possible to Solomon's alliance, to again get God's blessing.

So, why did God bless Solomon's economic alliance with King Hiram of Tyre, yet curse Jehoshaphat's economic alliance with King Ahaziah of Israel? What made the difference? Well you see, King Hiram had begun to believe that the God of the Israelites was the one true God of the whole world. For King Hiram was extremely pleased when he heard that Solomon wanted to build a temple for Jehovah—the God of the Israelites. In a letter to Solomon, King Hiram of Tyre admitted that the God of Israel was the one true God who made heaven and earth. For it is written:

> Hiram king of Tyre replied by letter to Solomon: "Because the Lord loves his people, he has made you their king." And Hiram added: "Praise be the Lord, the God of Israel, who made heaven and earth!" (2 Chron. 2:11-12a NIV)

You see, Hiram realized that Jehovah was the one true God of the universe, so he helped Solomon build the temple for God in Jerusalem to show his devotion to Jehovah—the God of Israel and of the whole earth, including Tyre itself (2 Chron. 2:13-16 NIV). As a result, Jehovah blessed the economic alliance between Solomon and Hiram, specifically as a result of Hiram's growing faith in God, which means King Hiram may also have outlawed idolatry in Tyre and adopted many of God's other principles of moral law, civil law, and civil law enforcement into the legislation of Tyre!

In contrast, as we have learned, King Ahaziah "was guilty of wickedness" (2 Chron. 20:35 NIV). You see, Ahaziah was an idolator who worshipped Baal and encouraged idolatry throughout the land, just like Ahab and Jezebel (his parents) had done and like Jeroboam had done nearly seventy years earlier. For it is written:

> Ahaziah son of Ahab . . . did evil in the eyes of the Lord, because he walked in the ways of his father and mother and in the ways of Jeroboam son of Nebat, who caused Israel to sin. He served and worshipped Baal and provoked the Lord, the God of Israel to anger, just as his father had done. (1 Kings 22: 51-53 NIV)

In other words, Ahaziah's wickedness consisted not only of worshipping idols, but also he "copied" the legislative policies of Jeroboam as well as his own father, King Ahab—both who actively encouraged the freedom to worship idols throughout all Israel.

Now what does this mean for the United States? It means that neither Israel nor the United States should ever make any economic alliances or trade agreements with unrighteous nations. For when we have violated this principle and have made economic alliances with unrighteous nations, instead of inheriting economic blessings, we have inherited economic disaster just as Israel did.

How can we tell if a nation is "unrighteous" in God's eyes? Well, look at the nations in the Bible which made God the angriest. These nations were always nations which worshipped idols. It was their idolatry which angered God so much, that (with few exceptions) he punished them with poverty in peacetime and supernatural defeat in wartime, over and over. So, I believe that the only possible conclusion is that modern unrighteous nations are those nations which encourage or allow idolatry and possibly whose legislative policies are in large part antagonistic to biblical principles for administering godly virtuous government. As a result, God punishes those nations with poverty.

But now, their poor country now becomes "fertile ground" for enterprising American businessmen to take advantage of their cheap labor force. This labor force may have originally resulted from God's punishment of their national sins, such as unrestrained national idolatry, and the like. The American businessman however, is totally unaware of God's foreign policy to never have any economic dealings with nations which are being punished by God economically for their idolatry or other national sins, or else America will be punished as well. So, the businessman rushes in to build American factories in their country to take advantage of their cheap labor so he can manufacture inexpensive products in their country and sell them to Americans in our country.

This global competition from cheap labor causes American factories to downsize to be able to compete, creating unemployment for millions of American citizens because of layoffs. As a result, America is punished economically for violating God's foreign policy, which basically says that . . .

> when God curses an unrighteous nation with poverty, this punishment will spill over onto any righteous nation which joins itself economically with the unrighteous nation.

In addition, part of an unholy alliance (which God will curse economically) involves the uniting of labor forces of righteous and unrighteous nations together in a common project to benefit both nations (1 Kings 22:48 NIV). This may involve giving away American technology, which may have originally been part of God's gift to bless America because of the righteousness of our founders generations ago (before America became evil). But, this new technology may now allow the impoverished nation to cheaply manufacture items desirable in the U.S., which Americans purchase by the thousands. And again, America gets punished economically through massive layoffs, unemployment, and impoverished American families.

Furthermore, our economic alliance with Mexico allows migrant workers to enter our country seasonally to work as cheap labor. And again, America is punished by losing jobs to Mexicans who are willing to work for a substandard wage. This costs Americans thousands of jobs and increases American unemployment, because we violate God's foreign policy which says that labor forces from righteous nations (presumably which God is blessing with prosperity) should not unite with unrighteous nations (presumably which God is cursing with poverty). Although individual American businessmen may prosper, America as a whole will always suffer economic punishment when we violate these principles.

Now you are probably thinking...

> But what makes Mexico so "unrighteous" that God would punish Mexico with poverty more than America? Surely the sin in America must displease God just as much as the sin in Mexico!

Well, certainly today America seems to have just as much evil as Mexico, or any other nation for that matter. However, the greatest evil in God's eyes is the one sin which we seem to ignore the most—idolatry. And when it comes to idolatry, America has very little of this when compared with Mexico.

You see, 95 percent of Mexican citizens are Catholic. But Mexican Catholicism is evidently not like American Catholicism. Mexican Catholicism has a much stronger component of "Mary Worship" in it than does American Catholicism, and "Mary Worship" is idolatry. For instance, Guadalupe, Mexico is internationally recognized for encouraging the idolatrous worship of Mary! Even *Life* magazine (December 1996, 45) says...

> ...more than 10 million trek to Guadalupe to pray to Our Lady...

Alex Cosio, a Christian seminary student from Mexico and acquaintance of mine, tells me the same stories of how the Catholicism of Mexico contains much more of the idolatry of "Mary worship" than does American Catholicism. Also, historically this idolatry started when Catholic missionaries began to teach that the Aztec goddess (which was already being worshipped in Mexico centuries ago) was in reality the Virgin Mary who became the "Mother of God"! As a result, they were able to "convert" thousands of Mexican Indians to Catholicism by allowing this idolatry to continue and just substituting the idolatrous worship of Mary for the original idolatrous worship of the Aztec goddess! (To learn more about the origins of this idolatrous worship of Mary in Mexico, read *The Religious Conquest of Mexico*.)

Since this makes Mexico a nation which allows and encourages idolatry, it is no wonder that Mexico (as well as all the rest of Central and South America) remains impoverished as a punishment from God because of this same idolatry. This also makes Mexico an unrighteous nation and therefore, America should have no economic alliances with them, and this includes not allowing any Migrant workers into the U.S.!

Therefore, the Bible teaches that we should *never* make an unholy trade alliance with impoverished, unrighteous nations to allow the importation of their extremely inexpensive products into America, or we will face economic disaster by doing so. By the same token, America should restrict the selling of our products to impoverished, unrighteous nations also, because sooner or later, our economy may become dependent upon the economy of the unrighteous nations—the very nations which God is punishing economically! And, when God punishes them even more (so they can no longer purchase American products), then America will be punished as well with an economic recession.

In summary, God's foreign policy is one of *selective economic isolationism*. This is because God wants to prosper or impoverish nations individually, based upon whether they fear, revere, worship, and "crown" Him as "king" by adopting all his principles of moral law, civil law, and civil law enforcement into their legislation. God has promised through His Word that the prosperity he will give to a nation under God for its *obedience,* will far surpass any financial gain America can hope to receive by *disobedience!*

The Bible teaches that if Israel had obeyed God (and presumably this includes implementing a foreign policy of selective economic isolationism), God would have made Israel into the richest, most desirable nation on the face of the earth. For it is written:

> If you fully obey the Lord your God and carefully follow all his commands I give you today, the Lord your God will set you high above all the nations on earth . . . You will lend to many nations but will borrow from none. The Lord will make you the head, not the tail. If you pay attention to the commands of the Lord your God that I give you this day and carefully follow them, you will always be at the top, never at the bottom. (Deut. 28:1, 12b-13 NIV)

So, it is inconceivable that Israel could have been any better off economically by *disobeying* God and adopting "free trade agreements" with poor idolatrous nations, than by *obeying* God and instead adopting God's principles of "selective economic isolation." Therefore, America must make no economic ties with any foreign nations, except other righteous nations. Even these ties are to be very loose. Our entire economy is to be totally separate from any foreign nation, so if the foreign country becomes evil and God punishes them by economic collapse, it will not effect us in any way whatsoever.

6. FOREIGN LOANS VERSUS FOREIGN AID

According to the Bible, God allowed Israel to lend money to foreign nations, For it is written:

> You will lend to many nations but will borrow from none. (Deut. 28:12b NIV)

However, loans to foreigners (and therefore, presumably to foreign nations as well) are always expected to be paid back with interest. For it is written:

> You may charge a foreigner interest, but not your brother Israelite, so that the Lord your God may bless you in everything you put your hand to . . . (Deut. 23:20 NIV)

This means that Israel (and therefore, presumably America) can lend money to foreign nations with interest and that it is always expected that these loans will be paid back completely. In other words, the Bible teaches that as part of their foreign policy, both Israel and America can grant interest-bearing foreign loans to other nations.

However, there is no such thing as foreign *aid* in God's foreign policy, only foreign *loans*. In other words, there were to be no *gifts* of money to foreign nations. Now why is this? Because God intends to individually bless or curse each nation with prosperity or poverty depending upon whether that nation outlaws idolatry and begins to implement God's other principles of moral and civil law into their legislation. And large gifts of money in the form of foreign aid undermine God's purpose of punishing nations with poverty because of their idolatry.

Furthermore, large monetary gifts of foreign aid create an economic alliance between a righteous nation and an unrighteous nation (which worships idols). According to the Bible, this causes God's punishment to "spill over" onto the righteous nation, "destroying what they have made" (2 Chron. 20:35-37 NIV). Foreign aid represents a monetary giveaway to a country which God is punishing. But if that country does not stop worshipping idols, then they will always have national poverty, and perhaps plagues, droughts, famine, floods, and earthquakes as well.

In fact, a righteous nation could pour billions of dollars of foreign Aid into the economy of an unrighteous nation and you would barely make a dent into God's punishments. The only way to truly stop the poverty in an unrighteous nation is to encourage that nation to outlaw their idolatry, and substitute a true worship of Christ, and help them to adopt some of God's principles of moral law, civil law, and civil law enforcement into their legislation. Then they will receive God's blessing of prosperity and the punishment of poverty will stop.

In the meantime however, the righteous nation will impoverish itself by violating God's principles against economic alliances with unrighteous nations, as God's punishment of poverty "spills over" onto the righteous nation. For example, America has given away hundreds of billions of dollars in foreign aid since World War II, yet all the recipient nations are *still* impoverished and now, America is all the *poorer* for our efforts.

However, Christian organizations can still give away millions of dollars of services and food. They will be blessed by God, because this effort is an attempt to show the love of God in Christ to have that nation consider giving up their idolatry and worshipping Jesus Christ as Savior and Lord.

But why is it that Christian organizations *can* give money to foreign nations and that the state *cannot?* You see, America's foreign Aid is an unholy economic alliance designed to promote three sinful secular purposes:

1. to promote *trade* with unrighteous, impoverished nations (which the Bible teaches is an "unholy economic alliance"),
2. to promote *democracy* (where majority vote can "overrule" even God's laws) instead of promoting a Christian Republic (where God's principles of moral law, civil law, and civil law enforcement form the foundation of all legislation, and can never be overruled), and
3. to create future military *allies* (which the Bible teaches is a sin—because when America does not have to depend upon God in wartime, then America is more likely to disobey God in peacetime).

On the other hand, Christian organizations do not have secular purposes. They instead have spiritual purposes, and desire not to form an economic alliance to promote selfish causes and exalt their own reputation. They desire to form an alliance of love, to promote the cause of Christ, and exalt the reputation of Jesus as Savior and Lord among the impoverished, idolatrous nations.

Furthermore, when placed in God's hands, the small gifts of love, money and the personal sacrifices of the Christian missionaries are multiplied greatly for God's divine purposes to win souls to Christ. I believe that after winning them to Christ and discipling them thoroughly—if we eventually taught them the importance of building better government with biblical principles and exalting Jesus Christ as the architect of this biblical blueprint for perfect self-government—then our

Christian missionaries would have an even larger impact, for we could help them to create a newborn Christian Republic which could eventually mature into a true nation under God!

The huge monetary gifts of state sanctioned foreign aid are neither blessed by God nor condoned by Him. Therefore, the money gets diverted from its original "superficial purpose" of possibly "helping the poor" into the hands of foreign bureaucrats (making them rich) and also into the hands of foreign generals (to improve their military weaponry).

So you see, when America violates God's Will against foreign aid, we sometimes end up just subsidizing the wealth of foreign bureaucrats and generals, while allowing them to upgrade their military, and having minimal effect on whatever idealistic goal Congress had originally intended.

7. GOD'S DEFINITION OF NATIONAL "ENEMIES" AND NATIONAL "FRIENDS"

Please understand that the enemies of a true nation under God are those nations whose governmental philosophies are in total opposition to biblical principles. The spreading of these anti-biblical philosophies of government can indeed threaten the American way of life and can also threaten the social structure of any country attempting to become a true nation under God. Therefore, the enemies of America do not just include communism, and the like. For you see, a true nation under God is also a Christian Republic. The true enemies of a Christian Republic include all of those nations whose governments are based upon idolatry, atheism, or any of the humanistic principles of mankind, such as communism, socialism, and Nazism.

However, this means that *democracy* itself is an enemy of a Christian Republic too. For in a democracy, the will of the majority is exalted over the will of God, so that the majority can remove God's principles of moral and civil law from government whenever it chooses. But in a Christian Republic, God's principles of civil law can never be repealed even by majority vote, and the only issues which can be even voted upon are those issues which do not conflict with God's laws.

Therefore, in a Christian Republic, the primary role of senators, congressmen, and president is *not* to articulate and represent the desires of the people to the government, but rather to articulate and represent the desires of God to the people.

In summary, the friends of a true nation under God include other nations attempting to become Christian Republics, while the enemies of a true nation under God include those whose governments which are based upon democracy, communism, socialism, Nazism, atheism, and idolatry.

8. Thou Shalt Not Sell Military Weapons to Foreign Nations

God's foreign policy does not allow the selling of military weapons to foreign countries. Remember, in chapter twenty-two we discussed how Israel was not to have confidence in her weaponry to win battles, but was to have confidence only in Jehovah, for He would give Israel the required supernatural military victories over her enemies. As a result, Israel was not to escalate her own weaponry to meet or exceed that of the surrounding nations (Josh. 11:4-6, 9b NIV), but would learn to trust in God to win the battles.

Because of this, Israel would learn to obey God more in times of peace in order to be able to depend upon God more in times of war. In other words, this national obedience during peacetime would sponsor an even greater confidence that Jehovah would actually fight on Israel's behalf during the next war. After witnessing God's miraculous divine intervention during the next war, this would sponsor even greater national obedience during the next time of peace, which in turn, would practically guarantee that God would again fight for Israel during the next war, and so on, and so forth. So these cycles of "obedience to God during peacetime" followed by "dependence upon God during wartime" were supposed to perpetuate each other and grow more intense after each cycle.

But when Israel would escalate her weaponry to meet or exceed that of the surrounding nations, this cycle would change from one of *obedient dependence* to one of *disobedient independence,* where Israel would begin to feel less dependent upon God during wartime. Therefore she would be less likely to feel the need to obey God during peacetime as well. So for Israel to sell weapons to foreign countries to escalate their weaponry to help them win their battles against their enemies would have been just as contrary to God's commands as if Israel escalated their own weaponry to equal or exceed that of the surrounding nations.

America however, *violates* God's commands and *sells* military weapons to foreign nations. This national sin reveals that America places its real trust in high-tech weapons and not in almighty God to miraculously defeat our enemies.

Yet in the French and Indian War, God miraculously intervened to save the life of George Washington. And, during the Revolutionary War, God miraculously intervened to save the lives of an entire regiment of American soldiers. Later on He miraculously intervened again to help the Americans win a battle against a Hessian garrison (see chapter twenty-two). So you see, because of the righteousness of the Puritans and the other Christian Founders of our nation, God was already revealing his intentions to begin to miraculously defend our nation if America would but continue to become a true nation under

God by progressively adopting more and more of God's principles of moral law, civil law, and civil law enforcement into our legislation over the next few generations.

After the Puritans and our other Christian Founders all passed from the scene, America slowly began to disobey God more and more during times of peace. And so, we missed God's divine opportunity to finish the job of becoming a true nation under God, and have the blessing of an almighty God to supernaturally defend our nation in wartime as long as we continued in full obedience during peacetime. So, America never completely developed the philosophy of King David, who trusted neither in his "high-tech weaponry" (chariots, horses, bows and swords) to win battles, nor trusted in the size of his army to win battles, but trusted in God alone. For David said,

> Some trust in chariots and some in horses, but we trust in the name of the Lord our God. (Ps. 20:7 NIV)

> I do not trust in my bow, my sword does not bring me victory; but you give us victory over our enemies, you put our adversaries to shame. (Ps. 44:6-7 NIV)

> No king is saved by the size of his army; (Ps. 33:a NIV)

Since America never "caught the vision" of the importance of obeying God in times of peace so we can depend upon God in times of war, then it is no wonder that America trusts in our weapons to win our battles instead of trusting in almighty God to supernaturally defend us. Viewed in this way, selling weapons to foreign nations is recognized to be an anti-biblical philosophy which encourages other nations to never feel dependent upon God for victory during wartime either. And so, they also will never have to feel obligated to obey God during peacetime. When America exports weapons to foreign nations, we are also exporting this same anti-biblical philosophy!

As a result, each foreign nation which purchases our weapons is more likely to develop cycles of *disobedient independence* from the true will of God (just like ancient Israel went through) which will corrupt that nation even further. Finally, after many cycles of this, a nearly complete national indifference to the will of almighty God develops (just like we have here in America), making that nation even more difficult for Christian missionaries to evangelize in the future. This is because each cycle will cause a further hardening of the heart towards God.

Therefore, America should not sell arms to foreign nations because this violates the military policies of the Prince of Peace concerning "Do not escalate your weaponry to equal that of the surrounding nations" (see chapter twenty-two).

9. IMMIGRATION POLICY

Anyone who wanted to live in ancient Israel could immigrate to Israel and live there. This sounds very much like the immigration policy of the United States in that there are essentially no restrictions on the type of people who can immigrate into the U.S. However, although God's immigration policy allows anyone to enter the country at any time, they are not to bring their *idolatry* or *immorality* with them. For if they violate certain principles of God's moral or civil law, they will not escape being prosecuted, just as if they were citizens of Israel. Therefore, many types of immigrants would not want to come to Israel, or America for that matter, if both countries were truly nations under God.

For example, all immigrants who believe in Hinduism, Buddhism or other forms of idolatry would stay away from America because of the stiff penalties against idolatry in a true nation under God. Furthermore, immigrants who are homosexuals, adulterers, rapists, drunkards, and drug addicts would all avoid coming here, because in America (and Israel) these sins against God would also be crimes against the state with stiff penalties. Generally, God's immigration policy should function to *attract* immigrants to America who are Christians, Jews, or Moslems (or those immigrants who at least have a good moral standard) and *repel* those immigrants who would bring idolatry and immorality into our nation.

Now if America had the godly leadership which would enforce this type of immigration policy, then our nation would eventually become an international magnet for other Christians. They would leave their country and move here, so our Christian minority would continue to grow each decade, and so we would have a much larger proportion of righteous citizens in America today. In addition, in order to avoid being whipped or executed, the idolators and other immoral citizens would eventually either stop sinning, leave America, or learn to hide their sins "in the closet" and not flaunt them as is done in America today. Either way, America would progressively develop an international reputation of being a very moral and righteous society and a safe place for Christians and other moral people of the world to live and to raise their children.

America therefore, would no longer attract materialistic immigrants who are interested only in the "American dream of riches." Instead, she would attract the type of immigrants whose main desire is to live in a nation under God where Christ is King over the government and Lord of a large minority of the citizens, many of whom are actively involved in godly leadership, by implementing God's principles of moral and civil law into nationwide legislation to keep the unrighteous on their best behavior. And, as a result of the yearly influx of righteous immigrants and the yearly purging of unrighteous citizens, God would bless America more and more with each passing generation.

A second part of God's immigration policy for Israel had to do with preventing *lazy* immigrants from entering Israel and becoming welfare-dependent upon the national tithe. For they must realize that if the Levites (who administered the tithe to the poor) discovered that the alien family was impoverished because of laziness, then the Levites would cut off the lazy alien's family from receiving the tithe as a form of welfare support. The alien's family could then be enslaved to keep them from being an unnecessary burden on the tithe so the tithe could be reserved for those poor who are truly in need (see chapter nineteen). God's immigration policy would encourage hard working alien immigrants to come to Israel to live, but would discourage lazy alien immigrants from entering Israel.

As a result of God's immigration policy, the population of Israel would become more righteous and more hard working with each passing decade. The people would become very grateful that God had blessed Israel with health, peace, and prosperity as a reward for the obedience of the godly Christian elders in government (who were adopting and regularly enforcing all God's principles of moral and civil law).

10. AMERICA SHOULD NOT PARTICIPATE IN THE UNITED NATIONS

After World War II was over, there was much fear of what could happen if war broke out again all over the world. So, the United Nations was formed on 24 October 1945 in an effort to promote world peace and security. Unfortunately, the United Nations operates under certain philosophies which are entirely contrary to biblical principles. Therefore America should not assist them in their efforts. For instance:

1. The U.N. financially supports China's abominable policy of compulsory abortion and forced sterilization as a means of population control. This is well documented in an article in the *National Right to Life News,* 24 April 1995, 6., entitled "Clinton Administration Works to Forcibly Ship Women Back to China, Where They May Face Compulsory Abortion and Fetal Cannibalism." You see, the U.N. has something called the United Nations Population Fund (UNFPA) which evidently provides funding and support for China's "coercive population control policies." In fact,

> The Reagan and Bush administrations condemned China's compulsory abortion policies . . . From 1986 until Clinton's election, the U.S. withheld all contributions to the United Nations Population Fund (UNFPA), because of that agency's extensive participation in China's coercive population control policies . . . Moreover . . . a Chinese national who reached the United States and showed convincing evidence that she or he had a 'well-founded fear' of being subjected to compulsory

abortion and/or involuntary sterilization, was entitled to receive political asylum. (Ibid.)

Clinton reversed this policy and . . .

> committed $50 million a year to the UNFPA, although the agency remains deeply involved in China's program. (Ibid.)

But now, in addition, Clinton is sending all pregnant Chinese female refugees which arrive in America back to China to be forced into having their required abortions. Added, there are now so many "available" aborted fetuses in China, that the Chinese are now *eating* the fetuses, according to a report from *United Press International*, from 15 April 1995.

> A Shenzhen doctor, who herself eats fetuses, defended the food fad, saying the fetuses would be wasted if not consumed. "We don't carry out abortions just to eat the fetuses," she said. (Ibid.)

Japan's Kyodo News Service added the following details from the Eastern Express report:

> A female doctor at the Luo Clinic (in Shenzhen) who has carried out hundreds of abortions reportedly claimed to have eaten 1 hundred fetuses in the past six months . . . "They are wasted if we don't eat them." The report said that fetuses were also found to be on sale on the premises of the Shenzhen People's Hospital. (Ibid.)

So, the United Nations is philosophically and financially supporting a culture which performs compulsory abortion and encourages fetal cannibalism! America dare not be a part of this or we will risk the wrath of almighty God!

2. The second reason why America should not participate in the United Nations is that U.N. supports a "pro-idolatry/anti-missionary philosophy" by encouraging all nations to *preserve* their cultures, even when those cultures include *idolatry*. For the United Nations is involved in . . .

> encouraging national cultural values and the *preservation of cultural heritage* so as to derive maximum advantage from modernization without the loss of cultural identity and diversity. (*Academic American Encyclopedia*, Aret Publishing Company, Inc., Princeton New Jersey, 1981, vol. 19, 415; emphasis added)

Furthermore, on 8 December 1948, the United Nations adopted the "Universal Declaration of Human Rights." In Article 18, it says,

> Everyone has the freedom of thought, conscience, and religion; and . . . the freedom to manifest his religion or belief in teaching, practice, worship, and observance.

So, the United Nations is saying it is wise to encourage even the "freedom to worship idols," and that such cultures of idolatry should be preserved as if their idolatry was a blessing to their society.

Since almighty God does not condone or approve of idolatry, then America should not condone or approve of idolatry either. Therefore, America should not support this "pro-idolatry/anti-missionary philosophy" by belonging to the United Nations. How can America send out thousands of foreign missionaries each year to evangelize the world and eliminate idolatry, yet at the same time, join the U.N. and support a philosophy to encourage the *"preservation of cultural heritages"*—which not only exalt idolatry, but are actually founded upon idolatry?

The Bible teaches that idolatry (more than anything else) is the chief reason why God repeatedly punished Israel with poverty. In fact, one of the reasons Israel was picked by God as the "chosen people" was so that God could punish them or bless them, depending upon their idolatry or obedience to God. This would be an object lesson for the rest of the world to understand that God treats all nations in the same way. Therefore, it is no wonder that all of the poorest nations of the world (the third world nations) all have idolatry as the foundation of their culture—for the Bible teaches that God will not prosper nations which worship idols. In fact, every time that God did allow a nation which worshipped idols (like Assyria and Babylonia) to prosper, it was to fulfill one of God's divine ulterior motives (such as "raising them up" to conquer or to punish either Israel or other nations which had disobeyed Him)!

So you see, in contrast to the declarations of the U.N., idolatry is not a blessing to a nation's culture, but rather is the worst curse imaginable. In fact, I believe that the presence of a high degree of idolatry within a nation is a better predictor of national poverty than any other predictors of national poverty (such as bad climate, etc.). Furthermore, the Bible teaches that God threatened to transform Israel into a desert if they didn't stop worshipping idols. He promised to turn their desert back into a fruitful land if they stopped worshipping idols and began to worship Him alone. And, since the Bible teaches that God treats all nations similarly to the way He treats Israel, then God punishes idolatrous nations with bad climates (such as dry, hot deserts) to impoverish them for their idolatry.

So let us not think certain geographic regions have "naturally bad climates" which cause poverty. Rather, it is because of a nation's idolatry that God impoverishes those nations by giving them bad climates, such as tropical deserts, or tropical rain forests! I believe that one of the reasons why the tropics contain both deserts and rain forests is to teach us that God can give the tropics either too much rain or too little rain, and that the amount of rainfall depends neither upon geography nor latitude, but upon God's favor which is determined by that nation's idolatry or obedience.

The United Nations and its branches work together to combat "ignorance, disease, hunger, and poverty" (*Academic American Encyclopedia*, vol. 119, 415) as if these problems can be totally corrected while allowing the nation to continue to worship idols. But, the Bible teaches us that the true source of national poverty, disease, and hunger is neither ignorance, nor a poor climate, nor poor national resources. Rather, it is almighty God who either curses nations with poverty or blesses nations with prosperity. This depends upon whether that country encourages idolatry or obeys God and outlaws idolatry; and, begins to adopt some of God's other principles of moral law, civil law, and civil law enforcement into their legislation. So you can see why it is extremely paradoxical from God's point of view for the U.N. to try to preserve the very culture of idolatry which is causing your "disease, hunger, and poverty" to begin with.

Let me give you an example. UNICEF provides assistance (such as food) to the children of impoverished, idolatrous, foreign nations. But at the same time, the U.N. encourages each nation to keep its culture of idolatry, which is the very thing which is causing them to be punished by God with poverty and starvation to begin with!

I hope you can see the paradox here!

God surely wants us to be willing to give assistance (such as food and medicine, etc.) to our neighboring nations, but in the context that Jesus Christ would be exalted and that his twofold mission would be attempted—winning the individual citizens to Christ, and teaching their leaders the importance of throwing away their idolatry and building better government with biblical principles. But when we establish the U.S. as the official "home" of the U.N., we end up inviting onto American soil their anti-biblical teachings that idolatry is not a sin! So instead of teaching them that idolatry is wrong, we inadvertently sponsor an organization which declares that idolatrous cultures are to be exalted and preserved. This has had an evil, corrupting influence upon traditional Christian American values and has made our citizens also exalt the importance of idolatrous cultures, the "virtues" of which are constantly being portrayed on public television channels!

Now since the United States pays for the largest part of the costs to run the United Nations (about 40 percent), this is just one more way we have linked ourselves economically with nations which God is punishing (because of their idolatry, etc.) They are so impoverished that they cannot even pay their own fair share of expenses to run the United Nations budget! In fact, some nations owe the United Nations millions of dollars in "back dues" which they say they cannot afford to pay. Since the United States has linked itself economically and philosophically with these same idolatrous nations which God is punishing with poverty, their punishment "spills over" onto America and impoverishes us as well. This happens by placing America in the position of having to pay a disproportionate share of the costs of running the U.N. because the other nations cannot afford it.

3. The third reason America should withdraw from the U.N. is that according to Section 3 of Article 21 of the United Nations' "Universal Declaration of Human Rights,"

> The will of the *people* shall be the basis of the authority of government. (emphasis added)

But the Bible teaches that the will of almighty *God* should be the basis for the authority of government! This represents the essential difference between a Christian Republic and a democracy. Now, America was founded as a republic. In fact, we "pledge allegiance" to a republic and not to a democracy. But unfortunately, we have transformed the republic created by our Christian Founders into a democracy, where the unrighteous majority has now been able to remove nine of God's principles of civil law from our national legislation. This democracy has also stopped the Ten Commandments from influencing our students, our courts, and our lawmakers.

4. The United Nations sponsors military intervention in foreign countries, the very sin which brought about King Josiah's death! God never asked Israel's military to act as peacekeeper of the middle east or policeman of the world, and he doesn't expect America to do this either.

5. The United Nations endorses the creating of military alliances between nations, the very sin which angered God so much when Judah asked for Egypt's help to fight Assyria, and when Judah agreed to help Israel to fight Edom! (For details, see chapter twenty-two.)

6. This organization also promotes "unholy economic alliances" under the guise of "free trade between all nations", the very sin which Jehoshaphat committed when he made an "unholy economic alliance" with an evil, idolatrous foreign nation! This caused God to destroy the entire fleet of ships which was central to the success of the economic alliance. You see, the Bible teaches that righteous nations should have no economic ties with "unrighteous nations" which practice idolatry. If this happens, the righteous and prosperous nations will face economic disaster as well.

So, since God is displeased and even angered by at least six of the philosophies of the United Nations, America should therefore not participate in the United Nations, and their meetings should not be held in America. They should evacuate their current buildings in New York City, leave America, and hold their meetings elsewhere. Then, their buildings should be sold to private enterprise.

CONCLUSION

God's foreign policy was designed to generate an international fearful reverence of Jehovah, the God of Israel, so all the citizens of other nations would want to learn about how to have a personal relationship with God (to inherit the blessings of salvation, hope and peace), as well as a national relationship with God to inherit the blessings of being a nation under God—a nearly disease-free, crime-free, poverty-free, war-free, tax-free, inflation-free, and natural disaster-free society! In this way, God's foreign policy evangelizes both nations and individuals.

Secondly, American ambassadors are to be foreign missionaries who are not only trained to lead foreign kings and presidents to Christ, but are also trained to present Jesus Christ as the architect of the biblical blueprint for perfect self-government. This way, foreign leaders can learn to build better government with biblical principles. In addition, they can invite foreign leaders to America to see just how well a true nation under God functions, once we too have adopted all of God's principles of moral and civil law to be the foundation of our legislation in America!

Thirdly, God's foreign policy is one of selective economic isolationism, to foster obedience to, and dependence upon, God alone as the true source of national economic prosperity. It is also to prevent economic disaster from "spilling-over" onto America as a result of making "unholy economic alliances" with idolatrous, unrighteous nations which God intends to punish with poverty for their idolatry.

Fourthly, America can lend money to foreign countries, but all foreign loans are to be paid back in full with interest. America is never to give away any free state-sponsored foreign aid to any other nations.

Fifthly, we must understand that America's foreign enemies are those nations which exalt mankind's secular ways of government, instead of God's divine ways of government. You see, a nation under God has a republic form of government, which means that God's divine laws can never be overturned even by majority vote. This would even make democracy the enemy of any true nation under God, for in a democracy, God's laws are often ignored or repealed in accordance with the will of the unrighteous majority.

Sixthly, America should not sell military weapons to foreign nations because this violates the military policies of the Prince of Peace concerning "Do not escalate your weaponry to equal that of the surrounding nations".

Seventh, God's immigration policy allows anyone to enter the country at any time, but they are not to bring their idolatry or immorality with them. If they violate certain principles of God's moral or civil law, they will not escape being prosecuted, just as if they were American citizens to begin with.

Eighth, America is not to participate in the United Nations because of their many anti-Christian philosophies, such as to promote abortions on an international scale, to preserve idolatrous cultures (an anti-Christian missionary philosophy), promote military intervention in foreign countries, and promote economic trading between Christian nations and idolatrous nations.

But first and foremost let us always remember that the primary purpose of God's foreign policy was to generate a world wide international fearful reverence of Jehovah (who personally became our Messiah, Savior and Lord, Jesus Christ),

> ... so that all the peoples of the earth may know that the LORD is GOD and that there is no other. (1 Kings 8:60 NIV; emphasis added)

For it is only by God's gift of the atoning sacrifice of Jesus Christ on the cross that individuals from all over the world can become saved and receive the blessings of eternal life. And it is only by God's gift of his principles of moral law, civil law, and civil law enforcement that nations from all over the world can become nations under God and receive the blessings of a society free from the tragedies of disease, crime, poverty, war, taxes, inflation, and "natural" disasters!

And that, is God's view of foreign policy!

Chapter Twenty-Four

GOD'S VIEW OF EDUCATION REFORM

Children and teenagers are molded a great deal by their environment, and a significant part of their environment is their school. Unfortunately, in modern public schools today, students are taught (directly or indirectly) that their ancestors evolved from bacteria, so many of them inevitably conclude that there must not be any God who created us and to whom we owe any worship or obedience by being decent, moral citizens. Thus, the philosophy of public school education today violates two biblical principles—creation by God, and obedience to God.

Then, students are taught that while in school they must avoid prayer, avoid reading the Bible, and avoid reading the Ten Commandments (thus violating three more biblical principles). As a result of this misguided philosophy, the students begin to believe that all religious and moral instruction must be bad for them, and therefore the natural tendency for rebellion against God's authority increases dramatically.

Now, after the students' respect for *God's* moral authority has been almost irreversibly impaired, they eventually learn that the state has made it illegal for the school to physically punish them for any foul language, immorality, or violence committed while in school (thus violating a sixth biblical principle). This lack of physical discipline increases the natural tendency for youth to rebel against man's authority as well.

Then, after the schools have undermined the foundation of the students' Christian faith and destroyed their respect for the authority of both God and man, they enter sex education courses. Here they are encouraged and instructed on how to commit fornication and homosexuality. They are then given condoms with which to practice these sins (thus violating a seventh biblical principle).

Finally, after our nation's schools have violated these seven biblical principles of education decade after decade, it is inevitable that our young citizens will be surrounded with violence, weapons, drugs, immorality, and disrespect for the authority of both God and man throughout a large part of their public school education. At this point, the state tells their parents that it is the *parents* themselves who are not doing *their* job. Added the only solution is to enlist more parental support to assist the schools in educating their children, and to raise TAXES (violating an eighth biblical principle) so the state can pay for such things as high-tech metal detectors (to detect whether or not weapons are being brought into the school), and to hire more security guards with guard dogs (to sniff out drugs from student's lockers).

So, as a result of our nation violating the first seven of these biblical principles of education, the public schools are now wasting more and more tax dollars annually to peddle a world view to our youngest citizens which is becoming progressively more anti-biblical decade after decade. What makes this even worse is that the world view learned by the *students* in one generation inevitably becomes the world view of our *government leaders* in the next generation. Abraham Lincoln knew this, for he said,

> The philosophy of the school room in one generation will be the philosophy of government in the next. (Barton, David., *Education and the Founding Fathers,* [the printed transcript of a video by the same name], Aledo, TX: Wallbuilder Press, 1989, 22)

The Christians in America must begin to realize that it was unity of belief and obedience to the biblical principles of Christianity which prompted God to bless America in the first place. Modern America, however, has lost this unity of belief ,and instead has become very pluralistic. This pluralism embodies a diversity of beliefs concerning religion, origins, morality, and politics, and in part represents the natural secular outgrowth of an emerging liberal theology, which is the mistaken belief that the Bible is not 100 percent trustworthy. The secular consequences of this liberal theology is that our nation now believes that the Bible should no longer be considered the infallible foundation for America's moral and civil law. It is also believed that the Bible should no longer be considered the true standard by which we are to judge religion, origins, morality, and politics either! So, unfortunately, America has now discarded our biblical foundation in favor of very liberal and humanistic views concerning religion, origins, morality, and politics.

So (in the context of this chapter), pluralism does not refer to the mixing of a diverse group of racial, ethnic, and religious peoples, but refers to the inevitable loss of a national unity of belief in a true biblical view of religion, origins, morality, and politics. Pluralism, in this context, has not been a blessing for America, but has actually been a *curse* for our nation and represents one of the major reasons why God is punishing America with disease, debt, natural disasters, and the like.

For you see, hundreds of years ago, the majority of Americans believed the following:

1. that Christianity was the only foundation of truth (religion);
2. that mankind was created by God (origins);
3. that homosexuality was a sin and that premarital virginity and marital fidelity were commanded by God (morality); and,
4. that only godly Christian elders should ever serve in government (politics).

These four categories of discussion—religion, origins, morality, and politics (ROMP)—form the basis of our *world view*. And many, many generations ago, the majority of Americans had the same world view of religion, origins, morality and politics (ROMP), and because of this unity of belief, our government was able to adopt nine of God's principles of moral and civil law into America's legislation. These early laws of America empowered the doctrines of Christianity with the legal muscle to keep both the righteous and the unrighteous on their best behavior. And so, almighty God blessed us accordingly, because these laws allowed us to have a nation of relatively moral people with faith in God (in comparison to the immoral people without faith in God who live in America today).

Furthermore, in the past, our public schools encouraged this unity of belief as well. This way, each generation of young citizens in school would become the type of leaders in the next generation which would (hopefully) either maintain or improve our Christian Republic, to become even more of a true nation under God. Such a system was designed to actually prevent the emergence of pluralism in America, so America would always be a progressively improving Christian Republic, generation after generation. And, as American leaders would implement more and more of God's principles into our government generation after generation, almighty God would respond by blessing our nation more and more.

Unfortunately, over several generations, our leaders reversed this process and began to ignore or repeal all God's principles from our government. As a result, our nation has developed a culture of pluralistic beliefs, the very thing which God said would occur, where eventually everyone believes and does what is right "in his own eyes"! In fact, pluralism has become so exalted in America today that pluralism has become one of those ideas which is now thought to have made America great in the first place.

However, nothing could be further from the truth. Far from having "made America great," pluralism has instead become America's downfall, and our public education system has played a great roll in encouraging the development of pluralism throughout our nation (which was just the opposite of what God wanted for America)! For there is nothing in the Bible which indicates that God ever wanted the Israelites to be pluralistic concerning religion, origins, morality, or politics. And since God did not want the Israelites to be pluralistic, then He certainly does not want America to be pluralistic either. For you see, pluralism has caused both ancient Israel and modern America to abandon biblical truth in favor of believing in different gods, believing in different origins, practicing sexual immorality, and desiring to have like-minded ungodly rulers, to implement anti-biblical legislation to further promote this same national pluralism.

God's plan was that we should teach His commands to our children continuously and thoroughly to prevent this pluralism from ever emerging. For it is written:

> Love the Lord your God with all your heart and with all your soul and with all your strength. These commands I give you today are to be upon your hearts. Impress them on your children. Talk about them when you *sit* at home and when you *walk* along the road, when you *lie down* and when you *get up*. (Deut. 6:5-7 NIV; emphasis added)

And of course, this thorough indoctrination of Israelite (and American) students in God's principles of moral law, civil law, civil law enforcement, and the principles of salvation by grace through faith in Jehovah, who became our Lord and Savior, Jesus Christ, would greatly help to prevent the emergence of any corrupting pluralism, concerning religion, origins, morality, and politics (ROMP). Our founders felt the same way, and because of this

> ... 106 of the first 108 colleges in America—and 123 of the first 126—were formed on Christian principles." (Barton, David, *Education and the Founding Fathers,* Aledo, TX: Wallbuilder Press, 1993, 7)

More specifically, the requirements to enter Harvard included a declaration of the following:

> Let every student be plainly instructed and earnestly pressed to consider well the main end of his life and studies is to know God and Jesus which is eternal life, John 17:3, and therefore to lay Christ in the bottom as the only foundation of all sound knowledge and learning. (Barton, 3)

Additionally, the Harvard requirements also declared:

> Everyone shall so exercise himself in reading the Scripture twice a day that he shall be ready to give such an account of his proficiency therein. (Barton, 3)

Yale required great attention to prayer as part of its requirements for admission:

> Seeing God is the giver of all wisdom, every scholar, besides private or secret prayer... shall be present morning and evening at public prayer. (Barton, 2)

Additionally, the Princeton founding statement in 1746 says:

> Cursed be all that learning that is contrary to the cross of Christ. (Barton, 4)

So, nearly all of America's first colleges insisted on teaching basic Christian doctrine to all of their students, for early America had developed a unity of belief in the principles of religion, origins, morality, and politics!

Furthermore, our early leaders wanted to ensure that this unity of belief would never change as a result of territories becoming states and merging their possibly pluralistic beliefs into our new nation. So, it became very important for the founders to promote a strictly Christian form of education throughout the entire nation. As a result, in the Northwest Ordinance which was signed into law in 1789, America's federal government included (in Article III) a provision which stipulated that all future territories—which wanted to become states—must guarantee to teach Christian doctrine and morality in their schools as well. This provision said, that for...

> a territory to become a state, their schools must teach religion and morality as well as knowledge! (Barton, 6)

Of course, this referred to the exclusive teaching of the Christian religion and Christian morality, as well as knowledge.

This confirms that America wanted *unity* of belief, not *pluralism*. It also confirms that America's founders legislated that all students in America must become indoctrinated in this unity of belief in order to ensure that all our future leaders would think and rule in the same likeness as the founders, generation after generation. In other words, all future leaders were expected to have the same world view, concerning religion, origins, morality, and politics (ROMP).

As a result, the territories which became states after 1789 evidently all wrote their state constitutions to be consistent with the requirements that the Northwest Ordinance specified, which included a state guarantee that all future schools would teach the Christian religion along with Christian morality. For instance, the original constitution of Ohio State (written in 1802) said that:

> Religion, morality, and knowledge, being essentially necessary to the good government, and the happiness of mankind,

schools and the means of instruction shall forever be encouraged by legislative provision. (Barton, 6)

(Again, when the founders used the words "religion" and "morality" they were always referring to the "Christian religion" and to "Christian morality.")

Also, the original state constitution of Mississippi (written in 1817) said:

Religion, morality and knowledge, being necessary to good government, the preservation of liberty and the happiness of mankind, schools and the means of education shall be forever encouraged in this state. (Barton, 6)

Additionally, in 1875, the state constitution of Nebraska said:

Religion, morality, and knowledge, however, being essential to good government, it shall be the duty of the legislature to pass laws . . . to encourage schools and the means of instruction. (Barton, 7)

In fact, the original constitutions of Michigan, Kansas, and other states said almost the same thing, because the founders of America required this in the Northwest Ordinance (Barton, 7). Even the Supreme Court of the U.S. stated that if a school was receiving government funding, that it absolutely must teach Christianity and the Bible (Barton, 20). So, this unity of belief was perpetuated by legislation, which also required that any schools which received government assistance must teach Christian doctrine and Christian morality.

Now, the creation of schools which trained all of our youngest citizens in Christian doctrine and morality fits perfectly with the idea that many of the original state constitutions also required that only godly Christian elders could serve in government in the first place, which is exactly what the Bible commanded.

But eventually, in 1892, the church voluntarily gave the state the authority to control and direct elementary education. In response to this action, the teacher's union said,

Whether this [decision] was wise or not is not [our] purpose to discuss, further than to remark that if the study of the Bible is to be *excluded* from all state schools, if the inculcation of the principles of Christianity is to have *no place* in the daily program, if the worship of God is to form no part of the general exercises of these public elementary schools, then the good of the state would be better served by restoring all schools to *church control.* (Barton, 7; emphasis added)

This is an amazing insight, for as it has turned out, the good of the state definitely would have been much better served if all of the schools would have been left under the authority of the Church. For, under church control, schools would have continued to teach Christian doctrine and morality, as well as teach the science of creation (instead of the false science of evolution). And hopefully, they might also have continued to teach that only godly Christian elders should ever be allowed to serve in government.

You see, it is extremely important for students to continuously learn the Bible, for (among other things) only the Scriptures contain the biblical blueprint for perfect self-government—which was given to Moses by Jesus Christ when he was in the form of Jehovah—and the adoption of all these principles into government would have created a true nation under God, and would have rid our nation from most all its evils. Even Noah Webster, one of America's founders, knew this to be true as well, for he said that the

> moral principles and precepts contained in the Scriptures ought to form the basis of all of our civil institutions and laws. All of the miseries and evils which men suffer from vice, crime, ambition, injustice, oppression, slavery and war, proceed from despising and neglecting the precepts contained in the Bible. (Barton 14)

So, by teaching Christian doctrine, Christian morality, and God's principles of government, schools can help to stop pluralism (and all the evils which result from it); for pluralism always involves a rejection of God's principles of moral law, civil law, civil law enforcement, health care law, and so on.

Unfortunately, instead of encouraging the teaching of Christian doctrine and morality, governments and schools have instead been teaching sexual immorality and evolution, while condemning prayer, the Ten Commandments, and the reading of the Bible. For our schools (and our government) have both become just what Martin Luther predicted when he said:

> I am very much afraid that schools will prove to be the great gates of hell unless they diligently labor in explaining the Holy Scriptures, engraving them in the hearts of youth. I advise no one to place his child where the Scriptures do not reign paramount. Every institution in which men are not increasingly occupied with the Word of God must become corrupt. (Barton, 21)

In summary, *God hates pluralism,* for it is the pluralistic approach to His commands and promises which slowly undermines a nation's potential to receive His fullest blessings. So, pluralism has not made America great, but quite the opposite—pluralism has caused America to become a safe haven for all kinds of sin and immorality. This has directly or indirectly increased America's diseases, broken homes, poverty, welfare dependency, crime, and taxes.

Currently our schools are unwittingly doing their "best" to ensure that our students are indoctrinated in all the anti-biblical principles of pluralism (which include evolution, atheism, immorality, abortion, radical feminism, disrespect for the authority of both God and man, and a desire to elect like-minded, pluralistic, godless rulers who will continue to propose further anti-biblical legislation)!

So how would God want us to use the public school system to do just the opposite—to indoctrinate all our youngest citizens in such a way as to ensure that they all develop the SAME biblical World view concerning religion, origins, morality, and politics (ROMP), as well as a unity of belief in the principles of Christianity?

Simple! For the Bible teaches that:

1. All schools should be Christian schools, teaching Christian doctrine and Christian morality (Deut. 6:5-7 NIV);
2. All subjects should be taught from God's point of view (Ps. 19:1; Rom. 1:20 NIV);
3. All students must be taught that Jesus Christ is the Architect of the biblical blueprint for perfect self-government; and,
4. Physical discipline must be brought back to the schools (Prov. 22:15, 10:13b NIV).

By doing these four things, America can ensure that most all of our young citizens who graduate from high school and college will have a unity of belief in the principles of Christianity, and have a biblical world view of all of life—including a knowledge that only the Bible contains Christ's blueprint for perfect self-government, which can promote the development of a society which pleases God and which will be supernaturally blessed by God!

In this way, we will have prepared each generation of our youngest citizens to be able to take control of America's government and rule in the likeness of our founders. More importantly, they will rule in the likeness of Jesus Christ (the pre-incarnate Jehovah himself), under whose guidance they can further improve our Christian Republic decade after decade! Additionally, because of their educational background, all voters will eventually also have such a thorough knowledge of God's principles of government, that whenever any leader might propose any anti-biblical legislation, the voters would immediately recognize this and quickly impeach him without waiting for the next election!

Now, let us discuss further the four things which need to be accomplished in order to indoctrinate all American students in Christian doctrine and morality, and give them a unity of belief in a biblical world view concerning religion, origins, morality and politics!

I. ALL PUBLIC SCHOOLS SHOULD BE CHRISTIAN SCHOOLS

First of all, all public schools should be Christian schools. This is not only because the Bible says that we should continuously teach our children to *love, worship,* and *obey* God (Deut. 6:5-7 NIV), but because the Bible teaches that our children should learn to *fear* the Lord as well. For it is written:

> Come, my children, listen to me; I will teach you the *fear* of the Lord . . . (Ps. 34:11 NIV; emphasis mine)

Furthermore, it is written:

> The *fear* of the Lord is the beginning of knowledge. (Prov. 1:7 NIV; emphasis mine)

And,

> The *fear* of the Lord is the beginning of wisdom and knowledge of the Holy one is understanding. (Prov. 9:10 NIV; emphasis mine)

Finally, Jesus says:

> And fear not them which kill the body, but are not able to kill the soul: but rather *fear* him which is able to destroy both body and soul in hell. (Matt. 10:28 KJV; emphasis mine)

Actually, the Bible teaches more than forty times that mankind should fear the Lord! Therefore, schools should teach the fear of the Lord to America's students as well.

Now, since all citizens (both students and adults) should be expected to eventually learn the same truth about the Bible, this means that all students should be indoctrinated in several basic Christian principles, which include the following:

1. teaching students that they were created, and they did not evolve;
2. teaching students to fear the Lord;
3. teaching students to love, worship, and obey God;
4. teaching students about Salvation by Grace through faith in Christ, and not by works of the flesh;
5. teaching students to learn God's commands;
6. teaching students that God not only loves individuals, but that God loves nations as well;

7. teaching students all the principles of *individual* obedience to God, as well as teaching them all the principles of *national* obedience to God;
8. teaching students a unity of belief in the same biblical world view concerning religion, origins, morality, and politics (ROMP); and,
9. teaching students that the Bible (as it was first written in the original Hebrew and Greek languages) was infallible and inerrant, and, that the "majority text" which survives today gives us an accurate picture of the original texts.

In other words, all schools should teach the basic doctrines of Christianity, but must include many other things which support the incorporation of true Christianity into all segments of our society, such as teaching students all of the principles in this book.

Now, it is important to realize that the Bible claims to be infallible and without error (2 Sam. 22:31b; Ps. 12:6, 18:30, 30:5 NIV, and in many other places), and that Jesus taught that the Bible was infallible and without error. We can see this in His many quotations of the Old Testament, and by his famous instruction that "Scripture cannot be broken" (John 10:34 NIV). So, surely Christ would want us to teach our students all the evidence that supports biblical infallibility as well!

This means that all schools should teach the evidence which proves the Bible to be scientifically, historically, archeologically, and prophetically without error (biblical apologetics and infallibility). It should also be taught that since you can trust the Bible in these areas, then you can also trust the Bible in spiritual matters as well (such as when it speaks of salvation, heaven, hell, etc.). This knowledge (that the Bible's scientific, historic, archaeological, and prophetic claims can be trusted completely) can sometimes make a student's foundation for his faith even stronger. Therefore, citizens can more easily resist the temptation to mistakenly believe that there may be errors in the Bible, which leads to liberal interpretations of the Scriptures. This is also where citizens begin to "throw out" any portion of the Bible they don't want to believe or obey.

The error of liberal interpretation is perfectly illustrated by the story of the Sadducees in the Bible. The Sadducees were the "liberals" of Jesus' day, and they didn't believe in the truth of certain portions of Scripture either (just like today's liberals), which is why Jesus told the liberal Sadducees:

> You are in error because you do not know the Scriptures or
> the power of God. (Matt. 22:29 NIV)

So, Jesus teaches that liberals are wrong because they either don't know the Scriptures or they don't know the real power of almighty God. Therefore, all students must be schooled in knowledge that the original Scriptures were without error, and that we can faithfully reconstruct those original Scriptures by the majority text of the existing thousands of ancient manuscripts which are still available today (in museums etc.).

Furthermore, all twelve grades should study the Bible as one of their subjects, and all colleges and universities should also call for a thorough knowledge of the Bible as part of their minimum requirements for graduation. This would definitely please almighty God, and this was what America's founders intended anyway. This is why

> 106 of the first 108 colleges in America . . . were formed on Christian principles. (Barton, 7)

In fact, there should be both national and international achievement exams based upon knowledge of the Bible, as well as national and international Bible memorization contests.

II. ALL EDUCATION SHOULD BE FROM GOD'S POINT OF VIEW

Now what does it mean, that all education should be from God's point of view?

Well, for the physical sciences (physical science, origins, physics, chemistry, biology, botany, geology, geography, paleontology, and astronomy), teaching a subject from God's point of view means teaching a biblical viewpoint which identifies Christ as creator and author of Noah's flood, and gives Him praise, honor, and glory for His marvelous works of creation. It also correctly identifies all of the many features of geology, geography, and paleontology which occurred as a result of Noah's flood. This also means that we must identify all the evidence from both the earth sciences and astronomy that prove that the sun, moon, and stars were created and did not evolve, and also that they were created very recently within the biblical framework of a 6,000-year-old earth as recorded by the Bible.

So, God's point of view concerning education is that we must teach students to be able to recognize the invisible qualities of God, from the things that have been made by God! For it is written:

> . . . since the creation of the world God's invisible qualities—his eternal power and divine nature—have been clearly seen, being understood from what has been made, so that men are without excuse. (Rom. 1:20 NIV)

Let me give you a wonderful example from Henry Morris—which he has written into several of his books—one of which is entitled "Scientific Creationism." A corollary to the law of cause and effect is that "no effect can be greater than its cause." Therefore:

1. The first cause of "endless time" must be to be *eternal;*
2. The first cause of "boundless energy" (like you might find in a supernova) must be *"all powerful";*

3. The first cause of "forces acting over huge distances" (like the gravitational and centrifugal forces which cause beautiful spiral galaxies to twirl around in space) must be *"everywhere"*;
4. The first cause of "infinite complexity" (like the human brain, with up to a quadrillion connections, making the human brain a hundredfold more complex than the most advanced computer) must be *"all-knowing"*;
5. The first cause of "life" must be *"living"*!
6. The first cause of "love" must be *"loving"*! (Morris, Henry. *Scientific Creation* (Public School Edition), San Diego, CA: Creation-Life Publishers, 1974, 20-21)

So, we must conclude that God (the first cause) must be eternal, all-powerful, all-knowing, living, loving, and everywhere! Furthermore, since God pays such close attention to the smallest details of the environment of the cell, then you can be equally sure that God cares just as much about your personal environment at home, work, church, or school. So therefore, because of His love for you (and His close attention to the smallest details of your environment), He is surely just as equally attentive to your individual prayers about the problems that occur in your life which come from your environment!

So, a true understanding of science can teach our students much about the love our Heavenly Father has for each of us.

A. ORIGINS

All schools should teach the scientific evidence that supports the biblical doctrines of a sudden, instantaneous special creation of the earth (and the entire universe). This should include the evidence that this creation was very recent (less than 10 thousand years ago) in accordance with the Bible's claim of an approximately 6,000-year-old creation. They should teach the more than fifty scientific evidences that there was a world wide flood, and that the dinosaurs died and were buried in the mud which became the sedimentary rocks in Noah's flood. The "pseudo-evidence" of the "Big Bang" and of "evolution" should only be taught in a manner which shows its flaws. (For a complete catalog of books and videos about the scientific evidence which supports creation instead of evolution, you can call Master Books at 1-800-999-3777, or Films for Christ at 1-800-332-2261, or Answers in Genesis at 1-800-778-3390.)

B. PHYSICS

A Christian view of physics would include teaching students how the first two laws of thermodynamics not only prove the *existence* of God, but also how they prove that God *created* the entire universe. You see, the first law of thermodynamics says that:

Matter and energy cannot be created or destroyed but only changed in form.

Correctly understood, this means that the energy and matter in the universe could not have created itself! So, since the universe could not have created itself, then the universe either always existed (and therefore the universe must be infinitely old), or, if the universe had a "beginning," then it had to have been "created" by almighty God (an "outside force"). This is because it certainly could not have created itself. So the question then becomes:

> Since the universe could not have created itself, did the universe always exist, or did the universe actually have a beginning, which means that it had to have been created by an outside force, such as by an almighty God?

The second law of thermodynamics actually answers this question concerning whether or not the universe had a beginning. For the second law of thermodynamics says that the universe is "running down" and that the pattern of energy in the universe is inevitably progressing to a state where no further "thermodynamic work" can be done. In other words, according to the second law of thermodynamics, eventually all the stars will "burn themselves out," which means that the universe will slowly become cold, dark, and dead. But, if the universe were infinitely old, it would be cold, dark, and dead already! So, since the universe is not dead yet, then we know the universe cannot have *always existed*, so therefore, the universe must have had a *beginning!*

In other words, the second law of thermodynamics reveals that the universe must have had a beginning, but the first law of thermodynamics says that the universe could not have created itself! Therefore,

> In the beginning, God created the heavens and the earth!
> (Gen. 1:1 NIV)

Furthermore, this also proves that "You cannot have laws of physics, without a lawgiver" meaning almighty God himself!

In other words, the two most fundamental laws of physics prove that God created the universe, and that the "laws" of physics had to have come from a "lawgiver" who is almighty God. This should be the foundational teaching of all physics courses (Morris, *Scientific Creationism*, 25-26).

C. CHEMISTRY

Many of the principles of general chemistry, organic chemistry, and biochemistry reveal a purposeful design in the assembling of atoms, molecules, enzymes, and the like, which of course reveals the presence of a purposeful designer, almighty God himself!

D. BIOLOGY

All of biology testifies to the presence of an all-knowing, loving creator God who pays great attention to even the smallest details about creation. So, since our creator is so concerned about the microenvironment of the cell and the subcellular structures, then you can be just as sure that He cares about you, your individual environment, and the trials you're going through as well.

Furthermore, the laws of probability require a creator to have created life in the beginning. And, it should not come as a surprise that the genetic difference between apes and humans is so large that it prevents their evolution by chance as well. You see, when evolutionists show that certain apes (such as orangutans) and humans share up to a 99 percent similarity in their genetic codes (and falsely conclude this is evidence for evolution) they forget that (since human DNA contains three billion base pairs) a mere 1 percent difference in a genetic code of three billion base pairs still represents a massive thirty million base pair difference. Since each base pair represents four possible combinations, then your chance of evolving this thirty million base pair sequence perfectly by chance (so apes can evolve to humans) is ¼ times itself thirty million times. This amounts to essentially a zero probability that apes could have evolved into humans. In fact, this supports the idea that it would be more impossible to evolve from one species to another than it would be to evolve one-celled life from the ocean in the first place.

Moreover, in Biology, creation must not only be taught, but the appreciation for this creation must be to taught to be observed at the level of the cell and the subcellular structures, as well at the level of the entire body of either the human or the animal.

E. BOTANY (THE STUDY OF PLANT LIFE)

There is much evidence that plants could never have evolved, and that they had to have been created as well, and this evidence should be covered thoroughly in courses concerning plant life.

F. GEOLOGY (THE STUDY OF ROCKS)

The science of geology must include all of the evidence that most all of the world's sedimentary rock came from a huge world wide flood—which we know from the Bible was the flood of Noah, which destroyed all life. The same science of geology must also include all of the evidence that all of the continents were once under water in this same flood of Noah (Whitcomb and Morris. *The Genesis Flood,* Grand Rapids, MI: Baker Book House, 1961).

G. GEOGRAPHY

The science of geography must include evidence that the continents broke apart as a result of the "breaking up of the fountains of the deep" as recorded in the book of Genesis concerning Noah's flood. It must also include all of the evidence that most of all the major features of the earth's land surface were formed directly or indirectly from the immediate or delayed effects of Noah's flood as well.

H. PALEONTOLOGY (THE STUDY OF FOSSILS)

Basically, all of the evidence concerning the fossil record supports creation and not evolution. In other words, all animals and plants in the fossil record appear *suddenly, fully formed,* and *without any trace of any intermediary forms* (Gish, Duane. *Evolution: The Challenge of the Fossil Record,* El Cajon, CA: Creation-Life Publishers-Master Books Division, 1985). Furthermore, there is a wealth of scientific evidence that the entire fossil record occurred as a result of Noah's flood and that even the dinosaurs died and were buried and preserved in the mud from Noah's Flood (Whitcomb and Morris. *The Genesis Flood,* Grand Rapids, MI: Baker Book House: 1961).

I. ASTRONOMY

The study of astronomy should also include all of the evidence that the universe was very recently created by God (less than 10 thousand years ago). For instance, the concept of the "Big Bang" violates the laws of gravitation. Consider the black hole for a moment. A black hole has so much mass and gravity that even light cannot escape its gravitational field, much less particles of matter resulting from an explosive "big bang"! You see, the force of a thermonuclear explosion increases merely as a function of the mass which is changed into energy to power the explosion. However, the force of gravitation increases as a function of mass times mass and is an exponentially greater amount. Therefore, for gigantic masses, this makes it impossible for them to explode against their own residual gravitation field.

In other words, just as a black hole has so much gravity that it could not explode against its own gravitational field, so also the "big bang" (which would have started from an explosion from the largest imaginable black hole which ever existed) could never explode against its own residual gravitational field either. For, even if 99 percent of the mass in this primordial black hole were turned into explosive energy, the remaining mere 1 percent of the mass would still have thousands of times more gravitational power to hold it together, than the explosive power would have had to blow it apart (Melvin Cook. *Pre-History and Earth Models,* London: Max Parrish, 1966, 77-79.)

The surprising thing is that evolutionists know this, yet they try to get around this gravitational impossibility by choosing to instead believe that the law of gravitation would not have applied during the first few microseconds of the Big Bang! Thus, evolutionists still believe in the Big Bang, not *because* of the laws of physics, but *despite* the laws of physics.

Now consider also the comet. Comets are like time clocks for our solar system, for they shrink a little bit every time they circle the sun. Each comet can only go around the sun about 1 hundred times or so before it eventually disintegrates and disappears forever. It has been estimated that all of the short period comets (like Haley's Comet) should all be gone within 10 thousand years. So, why do we still have short period comets? Because the solar system is less than 10 thousand years old (Ackerman, Paul A. *It's a Young World after All*, Grand Rapids, MI: Baker Book House, 1986, 35-40).

Thirdly, let's consider the moon dust problem. Evolutionary scientists anticipated a very, very thick layer of dust on the moon's surface (from meters to kilometers) because they mistakenly had concluded that the moon was five billion-years-old. But when the astronauts landed on the moon they found only enough moon dust to account for a very young moon—no older than 10 thousand years, and possibly much younger (i.e., 6 thousand years) which is perfectly in agreement with the biblical claim of a 6,000-year-old earth (Ibid., 18-21).

Fourthly, consider the age of the craters on the moon. Both creationists and evolutionists believe that the moon craters appeared when the moon was first formed, so the age of the craters would also be the true age of the moon itself. The maximum age of the craters can be estimated by the time it takes for the sharp crater walls to slowly settle down to become a level plain. You see, solid rock flows very slowly over thousands of years just like liquids, depending upon the viscosity of the moon rock. And, since we now know the viscosity of moon rock, we now have conclusive proof that the creators on the moon could not possibly last more than 10 thousand years without becoming totally flat. Therefore, the true age of the moon must be less than 10 thousand years, which would again be perfectly in accord with the biblical claim of a 6,000-year-old earth (Ibid., 50-53).

Finally, the beginning of the Bible also teaches us that there cannot possibly be any life in outer space, because God created the earth before He created the rest of the universe—and he didn't create the rest of the universe until day four (Gen. 1:14-19). You see, God's purpose for creating the rest of the universe (including all the other stars and galaxies) was only to give sunlight, moonlight, and starlight onto the earth, for signs and seasons, just as the Bible says. But at the end of the Bible (Rev. 21:1), God destroys the entire lifeless universe when his purpose for planet earth is over. This confirms that God never intended any other purpose for the rest of the universe (such as creating life on other planets), but only created the rest of the universe just so the "heavens can declare the glory of God" (Ps. 19:1 NIV).

This is why NASA is so offensive to God, because NASA's major purposes are to:
1. search for life in outer space, and,
2. better understand how the universe came into existence from a secular (non-biblical) point of view.

Thus the purpose of NASA is to search for evidence to prove the Bible wrong and to deny biblical truth. Because of this, NASA needs to be *defunded,* and this would save American citizens 7 billion dollars in taxes each year.

SOCIAL SCIENCES

The social sciences include history, sociology, political science, psychology, and law. Teaching the social sciences from God's point of view means that the students must be taught a biblical framework which identifies Christ as the author of the biblical blueprint for perfect self-government and the biblical standard for perfect moral law.

J. HISTORY

Now, seeing that Christ is the architect of the biblical blueprint for perfect self-government (and that Jesus gave all of these perfect laws to Moses when he was in the form of Jehovah), then all of history and all forms of national government throughout all time must be evaluated by comparison to this biblical standard. Therefore, educators and historians must begin to chart the rise and fall of nations, at least in part, as a result of a country's obedience or disobedience to God's commands, and God's resulting blessing or punishment upon the entire nation!

Let me give you an example. In the past, the first-world nations have been economically blessed by God (at least in part) because of their national Judeo-Christian background. I believe this is because each of these nations at one time in the distant past demonstrated to God a national desire to accept and spread the gospel of Jesus Christ, as well as a past willingness to adopt a few biblical principles into their legislation.

The second-world nations are more atheistic (and often communistic) or, at the very least, have demonstrated a national rejection of the gospel of Christ throughout their history. I believe that their national atheism and/or their national rejection of the gospel of Christ are part of the reasons why these nations have generally received less economic blessings from God, and have generally been more poor than the first-world nations (with their Judeo-Christian backgrounds).

The third-world nations are generally idolatrous, or have such a corrupted worship of Christ by either partial or thorough contamination by idolatry, that God punishes these nations with more poverty than any of the others. You see, the Bible teaches that idolatry (for which the Bible requires a courtroom death sentence) angers God much more than either atheism or rejection of the Gospel of Christ (for which the Bible requires no courtroom punishment at all). As a result, I believe that it is because of their national idolatry that God has made the third-world nations generally the poorest nations on earth.

This treatment of nations by the almighty God of the Bible is exactly what the Bible teaches will happen to disobedient nations, and represents God's point of view of history. This perspective of history must be taught to America's students, so they will recognize that God is the Lord of history. They will also recognize that every good thing which either Israel or America has ever accomplished was actually a supernatural gift from God. For it is written:

> Lord, you establish peace for us; all that we have accomplished you have done for us. (Isa. 26:12b NIV)

Let me give you another example. When Spain loved God, God made her a world ruler and allowed her to spread the Gospel all over the earth. But, when Spain became cruel, turned its back on Christ, and persecuted true Christians during the Spanish Inquisition, God supernaturally intervened through a freak storm and allowed England to sink the Spanish Armada. This essentially destroyed Spain's ability for world domination by this one single battle.

At that time, God passed the torch of divine honor from Spain to England, a nation which began to love God, had national revivals, and translated the Bible into English, calling it the "King James Version." God responded to their obedience by blessing them greatly, and by allowing this tiny nation to become a world power—which colonized the world after Spain, and spread the Gospel of Christ even further. But when England turned its back on God and began to persecute true Christians (like the Pilgrims and Puritans who eventually fled to America), then God eventually passed the torch of divine honor from England to America.

America was then blessed by God to become the richest and most powerful nation on earth. This was because of our historical national faith in Christ, and our willingness to not only spread the Gospel to other nations, but also our willingness to adopt nine of Jehovah's principles of moral and civil law into America's legislation. Unfortunately, America's government has now rejected the faith our founders had in Christ, and has ignored or repealed all nine of the original biblical principles from our legislation. The government has also begun a persecution of Christians in our own nation. Now it is America's turn to be disciplined and punished by God.

This is God's view of the way history operates, and American students must be taught to interpret all of the facts of history in the light of God's divine intervention as the Lord of History.

K. POLITICAL SCIENCE

The study of political science must start with God's view of politics. This includes the biblical teaching that only godly Christian elders should ever be allowed to serve in government, and that leaders must realize that they will be held accountable both here on earth and beyond the grave for sins committed in office, and for any anti-biblical legislation they either propose or approve. This is part of God's solution to help solve the problems of government corruption, government scandals, and government gridlock.

Furthermore, all political science courses should be based upon the foundation that Jesus Christ is the Architect of the biblical blueprint for perfect self-government, and that these biblical principles are still valid today—and would still work to improve America's government as well. Additionally, all governments should be evaluated and compared to this biblical standard, with the knowledge that most historical problems of government have come from either *not adopting* these biblical principles into government or from deliberately *violating* these principles through national anti-biblical legislation.

In other words, the biblical principles of government which are written in this book should be taught in political science courses as well.

L. SOCIOLOGY

Sociology is the study of societies and cultures. American students need to be taught that God has a divine idea of what a "perfect society" should look like. The perfect society (according to God's commands and God's promises) is a society which not only adopts all of God's principles of moral law, civil law, and civil law enforcement into their legislation, but also adopts all God's principles of health care, welfare, economics, education, military policy, foreign policy, and pro-family policy into their legislation.

As a result, through the natural interaction of God's commands, this becomes a society designed by the laws of God, which is blessed by God. This is because it encourages its citizens to worship God, to obey the laws of God, and develop a personal relationship with Christ as Savior and Lord. In fact, as a society begins to approach this high degree of obedience, God promises to bless them by making them a nearly disease-free, crime-free, poverty-free, war-free, tax-free, inflation-free, and natural disaster-free society. Alternatively, the more anti-biblical a society becomes, the more likely God is to punish it with diseases, crime, poverty, war, high taxes, high inflation, and natural disasters—as America (and the rest of the world) is currently being punished.

Now, since almighty God evaluates all societies in comparison to this biblical standard of what He has established as the perfect society, then all sociology courses should teach American students to evaluate all cultures and societies by these same divine parameters. In other words, every society should be evaluated based upon whether or not it obeys or disobeys God's principles. Also, (with few exceptions) all national prosperity or poverty should be understood in the light of God's economic blessing or economic punishment—as a direct result of national obedience or disobedience to God's principles. Any society which embraces sin or idolatry, or has developed laws contrary to the Bible, should not be exalted in the minds of our students, but should be rightfully condemned.

So also, American history should be viewed through God's perspective as to whether or not our national government has adopted or rejected God's principles of moral law, civil law, civil law enforcement, health care law and welfare law, as well as whether or not America has adopted God's principles of military policy, foreign policy, economic policy, education policy, and pro-family legislation. It should be viewed this way because there are great benefits to be obtained from doing things God's way.

Let me give you another example. Sociology courses should teach American students the relationship between adopting God's laws concerning the legal restriction of sexual immorality, drunkenness, and divorce, and its subsequent effects upon America's policies concerning national health care, welfare, taxes, economics, pro-family legislation, education, justice, foreign policy, and military policy. You see, it should be explained to students how national disobedience to God's commands concerning sexual immorality and divorce causes increased sexually transmitted diseases (affecting national health care policy), in addition to causing increased poverty by increasing the number of unwed mothers and divorced single parents of young children (affecting national welfare policy). This in turn, causes increased taxes on citizens and businesses (affecting national tax policy), which increases business expenses and decreases business profits. At this point, businesses have to lay off workers, which increases national unemployment (which affects national economic policy). Also, the broken homes from the dramatically increased number of divorces (which affects pro-family legislation) causes students to have difficulty learning in school (affecting national education policy), and this may lead to "at risk youth," which increases national crime (affecting national justice policy).

Furthermore, this also affects America's foreign policy because America's international reputation for immorality causes America to often be hated among the Islamic nations with their very strict laws against sexual immorality, drunkenness, and drug abuse. America is also hated by Islamic terrorist groups at least in part because of our "Christian" government's "permissiveness" concerning sexual immorality, drunkenness, and drug abuse and the fear that the influence of Christianity in Islamic countries will likewise corrupt the morality of their nation.

Finally, the issue of homosexuals in the military, as well as the issue of fornication and adultery in the military, also affects military policy. Furthermore, sexual immorality in our country as a whole also affects American military policy by discouraging Islamic nations from becoming our military allies.

You see, one of the reasons that Islamic nations are reluctant to be our military allies and tend sometimes to be our military enemies, is not just because Christians worship Christ, but also because of the Islamic perception that a nation which adopts Christian principles appears to encourage sexual immorality. This is because Christians never appear to be interested in making the sins of immorality and drunkenness into regularly prosecuted crimes against the state (as God commanded Moses to do). As a result, America is viewed by Islamic nations as propagating sin and evil when it attempts to spread Christianity to other nations.

Therefore, political science courses and social studies courses must teach that sexual immorality and divorce is not just a matter of personal privacy and alternate lifestyles, but that national immorality and divorce directly or indirectly affects all of the following:

1. National Health Care Policy,
2. National Welfare Policy
3. National Tax Policy
4. National Economic Policy
5. National Education Policy
6. National Pro-Family Legislation,
7. National Justice Policy,
8. National Foreign Policy, and
9. National Military Policy.

So, liberal laws concerning sexual immorality and divorce has affected every single large category of national policies in America. Therefore, sociology courses should catalog and teach how America's record of national disobedience to God's commands concerning immorality and divorce, has inevitably caused diffuse alterations in all other areas of national policy, and has resulted in even further punishment by God.

In summary, historians and sociologists should teach all of the facts of history and culture. However, the parameters of interpretation of these facts should include all the biblical principles outlined above.

M. PSYCHOLOGY

The teaching of psychology from a biblical perspective should start from a foundation that Natural man is a sinner who is living in rebellion against God. Added, most deviant behavior is sinful and is discussed in the Bible.

Unfortunately, modern science has mistakenly declared that two particular sins—alcoholism and homosexuality—are now considered genetically inherited and are no longer considered sinful or wrong. This is deliberate defiance of biblical teaching, where God clearly holds drunkards and homosexuals responsible for their sinful actions, both on earth (Deut. 21:18-21; Lev. 20:13), and beyond the grave!

Now God would not hold someone accountable for their alcoholism or their homosexuality if they were so "genetically compelled" to be either an alcoholic or a homosexual, that they had no choice but to continue to sin. Clearly then, according to the almighty God—who created us, and therefore knows the true inner workings of our brains as well as our true genetic codes—the alcoholic and the homosexual do indeed still have a choice which is not in any way genetically predetermined that they cannot still be held responsible for these sins, both here on earth and beyond the grave. For it is written:

> No temptation has seized you except what is common to man. And God is faithful; he will not let you be tempted beyond what you can bear. But when you are tempted, he will also provide a way out so that you can stand up under it.
> (1 Cor. 10:13 NIV)

In other words, no one is genetically compelled to develop a sinful lifestyle, and no one can be genetically tempted beyond what they can endure. So alcoholism is not a disease but represents the habitual sin of drunkenness. So also, homosexuality is not a genetic compulsion, but is also a serious sin just like adultery, fornication, and sexual lust.

So the teaching in psychology must be in perfect agreement with the teaching in the Bible.

N. LAW

According to the Bible, the Mosaic law is Christ's foundation for the perfect legal system, which any nation can borrow to establish laws for their own federal and state governments! So, American law schools should teach the Mosaic principles of moral law, civil law, and civil law enforcement, to our law students, so that all of America's future lawyers, judges, and statesmen will be thoroughly indoctrinated with God's view of the perfect legal system. This "educational precaution" will help to further ensure that our laws and our legal system will always be the best (and most economical) system of justice in the world, and that our

LANGUAGES

When teaching English or when training students to speak any new language, teachers should start with the evidence that the origins of the world's earliest languages can be traced to the Mesopotamian valley. The Bible informs us that originally, the entire world spoke one language. It was at the Tower of Babel in the Mesopotamian Valley where God changed all that, by "confusing the language of the whole world" (Gen. 11:9 NIV), thus causing up to seventy of the world's earliest languages to suddenly appear.

You see, teachers can find ways to give praise, honor, and glory to God even when teaching languages.

BUSINESS AND ECONOMICS

The teaching of business courses should also have as its foundation the economic principles found in the Bible. There is a wonderful book which talks about these issues at length called *Business by the Book* by Larry Burkett (and published by Thomas Nelson Publishers in 1990) which I highly recommend. America's businesses are more likely to become corrupt organizations and become less profitable if they don't follow these biblical principles.

Furthermore, the teaching of economics should have as its foundation the biblical principles of national economics which are discussed in chapter twenty-one of this book.

GUIDANCE COUNSELING

In addition to all that guidance counselors do, they should also pray with students about their future career choice as well as encourage the students themselves to pray about what God wants them to do with their lives. They should also encourage students to try to find out how God would want them to serve Him as a dedicated Christian, regardless of their future career choice.

III. PHYSICAL DISCIPLINE MUST BE BROUGHT BACK TO THE SCHOOLS

There are terrible discipline problems in our schools today which interfere with students' ability to learn. Part of the reason for this is that there is no longer any physical discipline in our schools to limit rebellion and to re-establish a hierarchy of authority. To solve this problem, I believe America needs to bring back physical discipline to the schools, even if it means using the "rod" which the Bible talks about! Now the "rod" is like the old "hickory stick" schoolmasters used many generations ago to maintain discipline. This type of physical discipline worked very well to prevent disruptive behavior problems and to prevent disrespect for authority. You see, by disciplining youth God's way, we can help to restore the hierarchy of authority of both God and men. For it is written:

> He who spares the rod hates his son, but he who loves him is careful to discipline him. (Prov. 13:24 NIV)

> Folly is bound up in the heart of a child, but the rod of discipline will drive it far from him. (Prov. 22:15 NIV)

> Do not withhold discipline from a child; if you punish him with the rod, he will not die. Punish him with the rod and save his soul from death. (Prov. 23:13-14 NIV)

> ... a rod is for the back of him who lacks judgement. (Prov. 10:13b NIV)

> Blows and wounds cleanse away evil, and beatings purge the inmost being. (Prov. 20:30 NIV)

> The rod of correction imparts wisdom, but a child left to himself disgraces his mother ... Discipline your son, and he will give you peace; he will bring delight to your soul. (Prov. 29:15, 17 NIV)

Bringing back physical discipline to the schools will go a long way to restore the authority of both God and man to the schoolroom, and stop the disruptive rebellion in the classrooms and hallways which is so injurious to the education process. Furthermore, this would also help to decrease the tax burden required to pay for extra security guards in the schools.

IV. MISCELLANEOUS

The Bible teaches that if Israel had adopted all of God's principles, that they would be easily able to govern themselves without needing taxes to fund any large, centralized government (1 Sam. 8 NIV). In other words, God did not want ancient Israel (nor does he want modern America) to have a large, centralized government which requires huge taxes to keep it going.

Therefore, God does not want America to have a large, centralized department of education in Washington (or anywhere else, for that matter). So, according to biblical principles, the department of education must be disassembled, and its power returned to the states, which would return its power to the counties and local communities. This would save billions of dollars in taxes.

Secondly, the dropout laws must be changed so that no one is allowed to drop out unless it is for documented health reasons, or for documented serious family impoverishment where the student's own family can only be kept off welfare if the teenager drops out of school and goes to work to support his own family. Otherwise, dropping out of school must become illegal and punished by physical discipline. Besides, there is no such thing as dropping out from learning about God's love and God's commands.

Finally, there are some Christian legal organizations which appear to have "served" the cause of Christ mightily in securing the right of student-initiated and student-led prayer as well as having after-school Bible studies, by advocating the cause of "freedom of speech" and "freedom of religion" (the right to worship idols).

The premise behind all of their victories however, has been that "freedom of speech" and "freedom of religion" is always the most important thing, rather than "what God says" and "what the Bible teaches" is always the most important thing. And unfortunately, some day these organizations will find themselves in the position of having to defend someone who wants to have Bible studies after school to study the Satanic Bible, or else their organization may get sued for refusal to defend their cause of freedom of speech and freedom of religion (which in reality also allows the freedom to worship idols and false gods, including the worship of Satan himself). You see, defending "freedom of religion" (the "right to worship other gods") is certainly not in the interest of the cause of Christ, and will always backfire in the end.

What God really wants is not for student-initiated and student-led prayers and Bible studies, but he wants teacher-initiated and teacher-led prayers and Bible studies. God wants the teachers to hand down God's principles to the students. For the teacher is supposed to be more spiritually mature than the student, and is also supposed to be more of an authority figure than the student, so that he can have a greater impact on the students. However, our system "gags" the teachers, forcing the students to become the spiritual elders, because our Supreme Court currently only allows student-initiated and student-led prayers!

Now adult Christians are called to be "salt and light." Students are generally not "salt and light" until they have the "salt poured into them" (Ken Ham). For God's view is that adult teachers should set an example for children concerning prayer, and not have students setting an example for teachers concerning prayer.

Conclusion

All citizens of the United States (especially the future citizens in our schools) must be taught to *worship* and *obey* the one true God of the Bible. They must be taught the principles of salvation by grace through faith in Jesus Christ as the only atonement for our sins. Additionally, they must be taught all of God's principles of moral law, civil law, civil law enforcement, health care law, welfare law, economic law, and so on. They must be taught this from godly Christian elders who are the teachers in our schools.

Currently, our schools encourage *pluralism* by teaching non-biblical views of religion, origins, morality, and politics (ROMP). As a result, each future generation of leaders becomes progressively more tolerant of sin, and each generation of citizens becomes progressively more interested in electing like-minded godless leaders who will adopt further anti-biblical legislation which encourages America to become an even more pluralistic, sinful, and godless society.

What God wants us to do is to teach a *biblical viewpoint* of religion, origins, morality, and politics (ROMP) in order to *prevent* the emergence of pluralism. This is so that each generation of leaders is indoctrinated to rule in the likeness of our founders, and more importantly, in the likeness of Jehovah himself, who became our Messiah and Savior—Jesus Christ!

In conclusion, since chapter eight of First Samuel teaches that God does not want nations to have large, centralized governments, then neither does God want America to have a large centralized department of education. Therefore, this lesson (and all the other lessons of this chapter) reveal that God wants America to:

1. return control of public education back to the states, and then back to the counties, cities, and communities themselves (saving America billions of dollars in taxes);
2. return physical punishment back to the schools to discipline disobedient youth;
3. ensure that all public schools will once again be Christian schools, which teach . . .
4. salvation by grace through faith in Christ's sacrificial death on the cross for our sins;
5. teach all the scientific evidence for creation and Noah's flood, and all the scientific evidence that the earth, solar system, and universe is very young (and less than 10,000-years-old);
6. teach all other subjects from God's point of view as well;
7. teach all God's principles of moral and civil law, in order to not only . . .

8. encourage national unity and conformity to biblical world view concerning religion, origins, morality, and politics (ROMP), but also to . . .
9. train all of our youngest citizens to become godly Christian leaders who will rule in the likeness of Jehovah himself; a goal which will
10. allow the small Christian minority to rule over the large, unrighteous majority, in order to . . .
11. regularly enforce all of God's principles of moral and civil law at all levels of local, state, and federal government; this in turn will . . .
12. help to keep both the righteous and the unrighteous on their best behavior,
13. so the aggregate righteousness of our nation will eventually exceed the graduated threshold required by God;
14. so God can bless America with a healthy, peaceful, and prosperous society, free from crime, war, poverty, taxes, inflation, disease, and natural disasters; and,
15. so all other nations will learn to fear, revere, and perhaps even worship Jesus Christ—the God of America—who is our Messiah, Savior, and Lord of Lawmakers!

And that, is God's view of education reform. If we obey God in these ways, then God will bless America!

Chapter Twenty-Five

CONCLUSION—A MOSAIC PICTURE OF A TRUE NATION UNDER GOD

About 6 thousand years ago, when God created the heavens and the earth, the almighty Lawgiver designed thousands of laws of nature. These included the laws of physics, chemistry, and biology—which mankind would not even begin to understand for thousands of years! And, about twenty-six hundred years later, with the same diligence, care, and attention to detail, Jesus Christ (in the form of the pre-incarnate Jehovah) designed for Israel the laws of self-government, which again mankind would not even begin to understand for thousands of years.

These laws of self-government would not only have the same degree of perfection as God's laws of nature, but also would have the same ability to interact with each other to produce a "whole which was greater than the sum of its parts"! For just as God's laws of nature can interact together to produce *life,* so also God's laws of self-government can interact together to produce *abundant life!*

Jehovah's laws of self-government were actually a set of moral and civil principles which God created to form the foundation, the framework, and the essential structure of a perfect society. Nearly every single one of these principles is discussed somewhere in this book. As you have seen, not only do God's principles of civil law still have practical application today, but also in many ways they are superior to our modern principles of civil law.

Through the adoption of these laws, Jehovah intended to provide a tax-free form of self-government, framed as a Judeo-Christian Republic. This republic would be totally staffed with male volunteers who are gradually progressing through a hierarchy of judicial authority, by gaining practical experience at being judges over a progressively larger number of families. In this way, Israel would have continued involvement of godly leadership, godly laws, and godly peer pressure to keep the unrighteous majority of citizens on their best behavior.

These laws were also intended to mold the Israelite society in such a way that it would always encourage both a personal relationship as well as a national relationship with Jehovah! Furthermore, these laws were constructed to guide the behavior of the righteous, restrict the behavior of the wicked, and provide the gold standard for the administration of justice, tempered with mercy. Additionally, the structure of the schools, the family, and the weekly Sabbath worship was designed to repeatedly *teach* these Christian principles of civil law to the entire population. The structure of the courts and the government was designed to *empower* these same "Christian principles" with the legal muscle to keep the "unsaved" and unrighteous majority of citizens on their best behavior. Thus, God's method of "social engineering" was (and is) designed to create a Christian Republic which will mature into a true nation under God and which God will bless accordingly.

All Israelite citizens were to be perpetually indoctrinated in these principles of moral and civil law. In other words, citizens were supposed to:

1. *learn* them as children at home,
2. *memorize* them as students at school,
3. *master* them as adults at "church," and
4. *enforce* them as judges in society!

Thus, God intended to transform Israel into the first true nation under God, to be held up as an example for all other nations to imitate. For you see, as long as Israel completely adopted all of God's moral and civil laws into its national legislation, Jehovah promised that Israel would receive a combination of both natural and supernatural blessings which would result in Israel becoming a nearly crime-free, poverty-free, war-free, tax-free, inflation-free, natural disaster-free, and disease-free society where nearly everyone lives to be 120-years-old while enjoying excellent health! By doing this, Jehovah would exalt Israel and magnify their international reputation as the "Chosen People" who would become the object lesson of God's blessing for obedience or punishment for disobedience, so the rest of the world would learn from Israel's example. In this way, all nations could see the importance of creating a society which was dedicated to encouraging a *personal* commitment to Jehovah (through confession, repentance, and surrender) as well as a *national* commitment to Jehovah (by adopting all his moral and civil principles to be the law of the land).

Jehovah had in mind a big picture of what a "perfect" society should look like. This big picture is formed by the interaction of at least nine smaller pictures, which include:

1. the model system of Education (for children, students, and adults),
2. the ideal Family,

3. the perfect system of merciful justice,
4. the optimal system of sound and virtuous government, and
5. the best possible system of economics, welfare, health care, military policy, and foreign policy!

Thus, many different Mosaic laws interact to form each of these nine Mosaic pictures of what God considers to be the proper structure of each of these nine social institutions. Yet, when viewed as a group, these nine pictures come together to form an even larger image which portrays God's view of a true nation under God—the perfect society. Thus, the Mosaic law forms many small Mosaic pictures, which together form an even larger Mosaic mural of what it takes to become the type of culture which God would supernaturally bless by making it into happy, healthy, and prosperous society, free from disease, crime, poverty, war, inflation, natural disasters, and high taxes!

THE MOSAIC PICTURE OF A PROPER SYSTEM OF EDUCATION

Now just as the "soul" of God's perfect society was to be the worship of Jehovah, the "heart" of God's perfect society was to be the system of education. You see, all schools within Israel were to be Christian schools teaching all subjects from a biblical point of view. Since the Mosaic law made no provision for taxation, then this education had to be paid for totally by the parents of the students. Therefore, the schools had to be all locally controlled without any need for a large, centralized department of education in Jerusalem which would require taxes to fund its operation. Also, there would never be any discipline problems in school, because each student that knew he could be beaten with a "rod" (like the proverbial "hickory stick") if he was continually disobedient.

Students were to be taught to *fear* the Lord and to *love* the Lord. Furthermore, they would be taught the true meaning of the sacrificial laws: that we must all have an attitude of *sacrificial repentance,* which is a repentance which "costs us something" (i.e., the "giving up" our old sinful habits, etc.). In other words,

1. the *attitude* was more important than the *animal,*
2. *surrender* was more important than *sacrifice,*
3. *confession* was more important than *custom,*
4. *repentance* and *relationship* were more important than *religiosity* and *ritual,* and
5. *transformation* was more important than *tradition.*

You see, the true meaning of the sacrifices was to get each citizen to understand the importance of developing a personal relationship with Jehovah based upon confession, repentance, obedient surrender, and salvation by grace through faith in Jehovah, who would later on return to earth and personally become our Messiah, Savior, and Lord—Jesus Christ.

The students were also supposed to learn how Noah and Moses found grace in the eyes of the Lord, how Abraham's faith was reckoned as righteousness, and how Enoch had a personal relationship with God and walked with him daily in moment-by-moment surrender. They would also all be fully indoctrinated into the principles of Christianity and learn to see all of their school subjects (as well as all of life) entirely from God's perspective.

Additionally, they would not only learn by heart all of God's principles of moral law, civil law, and civil law enforcement, but also memorize all of God's principles of welfare, health care, economics, education, justice, punishment, military policy, foreign policy, and pro-family legislation!

Now the two to three hundred principles of moral and civil law revealed in the Bible are actually much easier to learn than you might think, especially in comparison to the tens of thousands of laws, regulations, ordinances, and codes which currently burden us in America and which are impossible for anyone to completely master.

Also, God did not want the Israelite schools to encourage pluralism by teaching non-biblical views of religion, origins, morality, and politics, for this would cause each future generation of leaders to become more tolerant of sin, and would cause each future generation of citizens to become progressively more interested in electing like-minded, godless leaders who would adopt further anti-biblical legislation to make Israel even more pluralistic, sinful, and godless.

What God wanted Israel to do was to teach a biblical viewpoint of religion, origins, morality, and politics in order to prevent the emergence of pluralism. This would be done by ensuring that each generation of leaders would be fully indoctrinated to rule in the likeness of Jehovah himself. In other words, educating students from God's point of view was designed to *prevent* pluralism from appearing and corrupting a righteous society.

I believe this is the model of education that God had in his mind for ancient Israel to follow. I also believe that God wants modern America to follow this same model as well, and that this will solve most of the education problems America has today.

THE MOSAIC PICTURE OF PROPER WORSHIP AND CONTINUING EDUCATION OF ADULTS

Work on the Sabbath was supposed to be illegal and punishable by a maximum sentence of death, with either a whipping or total forgiveness as merciful alternatives to execution. As a result, since there wasn't a whole lot to do on the Sabbath, God's plan was that nearly everyone in

Israel would go to their local synagogue to worship, because this was also where the singing, food, fellowship, and fun was to be every weekend. Since "church" was to become the major activity every weekend Sabbath, then God probably expected the Israelites to stay for many hours and learn about the importance of *individual* devotion and obedient surrender to Jehovah (as well as *national* devotion and obedient surrender to Jehovah), while enjoying all the food, fun, fellowship, and singing at the same time.

Also, the Israelites were supposed to learn how to apply Jehovah's teaching to their own personal lives as well as understand the practical applications of all the other principles in the Old Testament. This, of course, meant that there was supposed to be a weekly emphasis on the importance of each citizen having a personal relationship with Jehovah based upon fear, love, confession, repentance, obedient surrender, and salvation by grace through faith. In other words, each Israelite citizen was supposed to be taught the importance of developing the same personal relationship with Jehovah which Adam, Enoch, Noah, Abraham, and Moses had. For even though most of the Israelites had never *seen* God (like these five men had) they all still had the same *access* to God that these five men had. And therefore, they could all still become "men after God's own heart" and develop that same personal relationship with Jehovah that was enjoyed by David.

In addition however, each week the Israelite citizens were supposed to be taught a small amount about God's principles of moral law, civil law, and civil law enforcement so they wouldn't forget these things either. This would also help to ensure that the vast majority of citizens would develop a *tradition of obedience,* even if they did not also develop the more important *personal relationship* with Jehovah (which would eventually become linked with true salvation once Jehovah personally became Jesus Christ and died on the cross as the only possible atoning sacrifice for our sins). In this way, by providing continual weekly education in God's principles of moral and civil law, the adult Israelite citizens would eventually master what they had previously learned as children at home and memorized as students in school.

Therefore, all males over age twenty who had previously graduated from Israel's education system and continued to receive weekly instruction in these same principles of "church" would immediately recognize when any rulers were trying to pass laws which were contrary to the Bible, so they would all immediately impeach that particular ruler. Furthermore, if any ruler or judge was caught with a history of making antibiblical decisions in his *personal life* (such as committing adultery or homosexuality), or promoting anti-biblical laws in his *professional life* (such as promoting laws which encourage blasphemy, pornography, immorality, abortion, drunkenness, witchcraft, or the freedom to worship idols), he would immediately be removed from office and placed on trial. If convicted, he would be sentenced for the crimes he committed against God and against man, which may even have the death penalty as either the maximum or the mandatory punishment.

Thus the thorough indoctrination of all Israelite children, students, and adults in God's principles of moral and civil law would also function to continuously promote godly government as well as purify ungodly government. Additionally, these students and adults were being perpetually trained to become Israel's leaders and judges who would rule in the likeness of Jehovah himself. This was so Israel would always have a large "reservoir" of godly leaders and judges spread throughout all of Israel in a hierarchy of judicial authority so they could easily and quickly remove and replace any ungodly judge or leader at a moment's notice.

The weekly worship services would also be on the Sabbath and not on Sunday, because a large part of the importance of weekly worship is to keep the unsaved on their best behavior throughout the entire nation of Israel. Nationwide Sabbath worship prompts the culture to progressively adopt all the rest of God's civil laws, especially when the practical advantages of these laws are regularly taught at home, in school, and in "church." Furthermore, nationwide Sabbath worship also helps to prevent the emergence of liberal theology with its inevitable corruption of righteous cultures, which occurs in part by sowing nationwide distrust in the biblical principles of civil law.

Lastly, since the unsaved have no personal relationship with God, they haven't yet developed an understanding of the importance of worshipping a Savior who forgives their sins. Therefore, it is easier to keep the unrighteous majority on their best behavior by having them worship (on the Sabbath) a God who created them and who *commands* their *obedience,* than having them worship (on Sunday) a God who wants to *forgive* their *disobedience.*

So, Sabbath worship works better to keep the unrighteous on their best behavior than does Sunday worship, especially when combined with all of the other biblical principles which unite to create tremendous godly peer pressure to keep the unrighteous in line. As a result, even though the majority of citizens will never surrender to Christ as Lord (and therefore never behave better because of salvation and surrender), they will still end up behaving better anyway because of the combined influences of "training and tradition," "clothing and coverings," and "prosecution and punishment"! Because of this process, crime, violence, and immorality all begin to disappear, and society still becomes more happy, healthy, and prosperous anyway, despite the unfortunate resistance of the large unrighteous majority to surrender their lives to Jehovah (the pre-incarnate Christ).

So, just like God's model of education for students helps to create throughout all Israel a unity of belief (concerning religion, origins, morality, and politics), so also, the continuing education of adults during the weekly Sabbath worship helps to perpetuate this same unity of belief generation after generation. In this way, the continuing education of both students and adults becomes the heart of God's plan for a perfect society, and also prevents the emergence of pluralism, which ordinarily would corrupt and destroy God's plan.

THE MOSAIC PICTURE OF THE IDEAL FAMILY

Marriage was originally designed by God as a pure and holy union between a virgin male and a virgin female, and was supposed to be a commitment which would last until one spouse died of old age.

To ensure this plan, Jehovah gave to Moses a perfect set of civil laws which practically guaranteed that there would always be premarital virginity and marital fidelity throughout all of Israel. Furthermore, Jehovah also made divorce illegal unless one spouse committed a "biblical felony" for which he or she could also be prosecuted and possibly receive a death penalty. In this case, it would be God (and not man) who would put asunder the marriage—through executing or divorcing the guilty spouse—if (because of "hardness of heart") either the innocent spouse could not seem to forgive the partner and live with them again, or because the guilty spouse began to commit the same biblical felony again after being already convicted of this crime in court. Under these circumstances, the guilty spouse may possibly receive a merciful divorce as an alternative to either an execution or a whipping.

These laws that Jehovah gave to Moses had the power to practically eliminate adultery, homosexuality, drunkenness, drug abuse, wife abuse, child abuse, sexual harassment, rape, murder, stealing, cursing parents, attacking parents, or other forms of disrespect for parental authority, from ever interfering with God's plan for the ideal family.

And, as long as the rulers and judges would regularly enforce these laws, then this would practically guarantee for all of Israel (and America as well) that nearly all marriages would last until one of the spouses eventually died of old age.

God also planned for a family hierarchy of spiritual authority which would merge with and evolve into a national hierarchy of judicial authority. Thus the biblical education of students in school and adults in "church" would provide the structure and the focus for both the family hierarchy of spiritual authority and the national hierarchy of judicial authority.

This was supposed to be accomplished by the combined influence of about ten different biblical principles. The first few principles involve the male spiritual head of the household wearing a *headband* with a Bible verse on it (to remind him that everything he *thinks* and *says* should be guided by God's Will), and wearing *wristbands* with Bible verses on them (to remind him that everything he *does* with his hands should also be guided by God's Will). He was also supposed to wear tassels on the "four corners of his garments", and each tassel was supposed to represent one of God's principles of moral or civil law, to help him to remember (and be willing to enforce) every single one of them and not to disobey any of them.

These laws form a biblical dress code where both men and women are supposed to wear *head coverings,* in part to symbolize their commitment and devotion to God. The men were supposed to wear headbands (as a partial head covering, leaving the top of the head open and uncovered) while the women were supposed to wear a more complete head covering which would cover the top of the head as well. These head coverings would also symbolize the *crowns* worn in heaven (another form of head covering) which would again represent our eternal commitment and devotion to Christ.

This dress code also involved clothing and hair length to take advantage of the God-given instinct that "If we dress the part, we will act the part!" This dress code helps to keep both the righteous and the unrighteous on their best behavior, and also makes us more likely to rebuke others when they sin, in order to create a nation of *godly peer pressure* instead of a society of indifference and ungodly peer pressure, as we have in America today.

You must also add to these laws the impact of two other civil laws which command you to "Honor your Father and mother", and "Rise in the presence of the aged." These two civil laws add even more legal muscle to develop and perpetuate this same family hierarchy of spiritual authority.

Moreover, God's recommended style of physical discipline for disobedient children was also supposed to help to maintain this same authority, because the biblical concept of "Spare the rod and spoil the child" (a paraphrase for the six biblical "rod laws") was also supposed to become the law of the land. In addition, God gave the state of Israel two extra civil laws to support and encourage the God-given right for parents to physically discipline their disobedient offspring. These two laws would protect parents from being hit back, attacked, or even cursed by their children while their parents were disciplining them, especially when the children became bigger and stronger than their own parents were.

Furthermore, God's laws concerning specific dress codes, diet, and hair length were also supposed to combine their influence to teach that God is Lord of what goes *on* my body, what goes *in* my body, and Lord of my *actual* body itself. You see, Jehovah intended that the symbolism and implication of these laws (that God is "in charge of your body") would actually help to provide a double precaution against using your body to commit sexual immorality or drunkenness!

Finally, these laws not only combine to sponsor the man's role *inside* the home as spiritual head, but also these laws combine their influence to champion the man's role *outside* the home as godly statesman and judge for his community! God's laws required that at least 13.1 percent of all adult males should be recruited to serve as judges over the families of Israel. These judges were to be totally devoted to a personal relationship with Jehovah—a relationship consisting of prayer, confession, repentance, transformation, and obedient surrender. They should also demonstrate clear evidence of being a godly Christian husband, father, and family leader, who also knew how to apply God's principles of moral law, civil law, and civil law enforcement to his family, to his community, and to his nation!

You see, God wanted at least 13.1 percent of Israelite men to become judges over ten families, fifty families, 1 hundred families, and 1 thousand families, and probably wanted to have a few more of the best and most righteous judges to become leaders over the entire nation of Israel. Most of these men would probably be the eldest sons, who had not only demonstrated this type of godly leadership within their own families, but also had been prepaid by the laws of God to inherit a double portion of their parents' estate. This would enable them to have enough free time to volunteer their services as unpaid judges and community leaders, to regularly enforce God's principles of moral and civil law, while still allowing a tax-free form of self-government.

Hopefully this has helped to explain why all Israelites were to know all of God's laws by heart. For evidently, the Israelites were supposed to:

1. *learn* them as children at home,
2. *memorize* them as students at school,
3. *master* them as adults in "church," and
4. *enforce* them as judges in society.

And this, is the Mosaic picture of how the ideal family merges with and evolves into the proper system of merciful justice.

THE MOSAIC PICTURE OF THE LARGE, EXTENDED FAMILY

Jehovah gave Moses four additional economic principles which would further encourage the development of large, extended families. These four principles involve:

1. giving the Israelites a "pro-family method" of dividing the family's inheritance,
2. commanding young men to pay a bride price before marriage,
3. making usury and usury-related businesses illegal, and
4. making inheritance taxes to be illegal!

Now God wanted the Israelites to have large, extended families because these large families provided a much better income/expense ratio and produced a triple economy of scale (from shared labor, shared expenses, and shared possessions), so they could more easily provide for the needs of their own elderly, sick, disabled or temporarily unemployed family member. In this way, Israel would never have to start collecting taxes to provide for these same needs by establishing tax-sponsored programs for health care, welfare, retirement, or disability.

Briefly, Jehovah wanted the family's inheritance to be given only to the male children, and not to the female children, who would instead inherit the estate of their fiance. Jehovah also wanted the eldest son to receive a double portion of the inheritance. This purposely unequal division of inheritance would tend to keep the family together longer until each of the other sons had a large enough inheritance to be able to move away and still support himself, and until the daughters all married (receiving their "inheritance" through their fiances), and until the parents died.

Furthermore, this method of dividing the inheritance would also "buy the extra time" necessary to allow the children to become more mature adults and learn to live together in harmony while also beginning to understand and enjoy the very real economic benefits of their large extended family with its triple economy of scale—from shared labor, shared expenses, and shared possessions.

So God's formula for dividing inheritance causes the development of *larger* families because the daughters and younger sons would often not have enough inheritance to move away and support themselves. The resulting larger family would provide much better for the economic needs of the children than if all of the children separated and went their own way after receiving an equal portion of the inheritance! Alternatively, America's method of dividing the inheritance equally among all of our children sponsors the development of *smaller* families which are generally less well off because of the poor economics of scale. This means that God's method of dividing the inheritance unequally is actually a form of divine pro-family legislation (by creating larger and more prosperous families), while man's method of dividing the inheritance equally is actually a form of anti-family legislation (by creating smaller and poorer families).

Additionally, the eldest son's double portion of the inheritance "prepays" him to be able to care for his aging parents until they die, as well as care for the younger children until they are adults and can support themselves, and also gives him the "extra authority" needed to help to keep the larger family together longer. Furthermore, after their aging parents die, this double portion of inheritance may also allow many of the eldest sons enough extra free time to volunteer to serve as local judges and leaders for their communities so the nation of Israel would never have to collect taxes to provide salaries for its rulers.

Another divine law which promotes larger families is the bride price. You see, this law forces the young virgin man to save fifty shekels of silver to pay the bride's father before he can marry his fiance, and enjoy his first wedding night. This law harnesses the sexual passions of youth and focuses them into hard work and saving money. Of course, the young man realizes immediately that he must remain living at home if he is ever to be able to save this money at all. He then realizes that he must personally build an extra bedroom extension onto the main house of his family for the privacy that he and his new bride will obviously need.

(Remember, Jacob originally promised to work extremely hard for seven years before he had his first chance to marry Rachel, so clearly the sexual passions of a young virgin man can be harnessed and focused to work long and hard for months and even years to either save money or to build a place for the bride and himself to live.)

Viewed in this context, the bride-price actually becomes a form of pro-family legislation because it encourages young men and newlyweds to continue to live at home with their family.

Thirdly, Jehovah made usury (and therefore usury-related businesses) illegal. For usury means easy credit, and the easy availability of interest-bearing loans for our older offspring to buy houses or mobile homes underwrites their ability to move away from home and therefore facilitates the breakup of large, extended families. This also decreases the remaining economies of scale. Additionally, social security retirement income is a usury-related business which functions to underwrite the ability of our aged parents or grandparents to live independently from their grown children. This facilitates the breakup of large, extended families and again decreases the remaining economies of scale.

Viewed in this context, God's commands, which outlaw usury, actually become a form of pro-family legislation, whereas mankind's laws, which encourage usury, actually become a form of anti-family legislation. In fact, regardless of our government's original "compassionate motives," all tax-sponsored government programs which provide funding to decrease the need to depend upon your own family for financial support ultimately become a form of anti-family legislation.

Lastly, Jehovah made no provision for taxes in the law which he gave to Moses, which means that inheritance taxes would also be illegal. Therefore, the entire estate would go to the children. And so, the "old homestead" would never have to be sold for taxes prior to the distribution of the inheritance. You see, selling the "old homestead" for inheritance taxes is just one more method of breaking up the large extended family and having each child go their own separate way. This makes inheritance taxes a form of anti-family legislation whereas the outlawing of inheritance taxes becomes a form of pro-family legislation.

Now, hopefully you can see how all of these Mosaic principles interact to reveal a Mosaic picture of God's view of the ideal, large, extended family.

THE MOSAIC PICTURE OF PROPER NATIONAL ECONOMICS

If our federal and state governments adopted all of God's principles of moral and civil law into our legislation, then America would reap a large number of economic advantages. In fact, this would solve most of the economic problems in America today. Furthermore, God promised Israel that if they did this, he would bless the land with a nearly poverty-free society as well as make Israel into the richest nation on the face of the earth. And of course, by implication, these promises are also available to America today, as well as being available to any other country which succeeds in becoming a true nation under God.

Two of the wonderful changes which would occur is that family expenses would *decrease* while family income would *increase*. First, family expenses would decrease because usury is illegal. This means that nearly every product and service in America would eventually decrease in price, and there would also be a zero-percent inflation rate. Furthermore, there would be decreased taxes, no interest charges to pay off, and no insurance premiums to pay. There would also be no significant expenses for security because there would be minimal crime. Additionally, since there would be no interest-bearing loans available to buy expensive items which are not really necessities, we would purchase less of these things and so, American society would eventually return to a culture of less covetousness and more contentment.

Another result of making interest-bearing loans (usury) illegal is that Americans would more frequently repair, restore, and expand their old houses, instead of always wanting to buy new houses. The building of new houses would more frequently be accomplished by purchasing the supplies with cash and building it yourself with the help of your entire family, or with community involvement in a "house-raising," guided by someone familiar with the new "user-friendly" building codes. In this way, the average American homeowning family could save fifty to one hundred thousand dollars in interest payments. Therefore families would have a lot more money with which to enjoy life, and to pass on to their children as inheritance. We'd also be more content to repair our old cars and not always feel the need to buy new ones. And, since everything we'd buy would be with cash instead of loans, our culture would begin to emphasize greater responsibility with our money and encourage us to do more saving and less spending. Americans would learn to enjoy a triple economy of scale by living together in large, extended families, and so family life and family values would be encouraged once again. Also, God promised to supernaturally decrease the expenses of citizens in a true nation under God, by miraculously making things last longer and not wear out as quickly.

Because of all of these changes, family expenses would dramatically decrease, possibly by as much as 50 percent! In addition to this, Americans would also begin to enjoy a higher average income, because our nation would now have full, 100 percent employment. Furthermore, our employers could now pay us higher wages because American businesses would have less expenses for supplies, taxes, insurance, and security. Also, God promised to "bless all the work of our hands," which means that in addition to having the benefits of a *natural* increase in wages, Americans would also have the benefit of a *supernatural* increase in productivity. This, of course, would be followed by a further increase in wages.

So, having obeyed God by implementing all His laws, and therefore having received all the natural, as well as the supernatural, blessings of this obedience, Americans would now have much less stress (because of having less expenses and a greater income, so that we can now work less and enjoy life more, which would finally bring America's rat race to an end). This less stressful lifestyle would also allow us to be healthier so we could live longer.

Furthermore, by removing usury from society, the banks would no longer be conduits for taking loan-interest payments from the poor and delivering them to the rich through savings accounts and CD's—a process which tilts the economy from the poor to the rich and spreads out the economic distance between them.

So by outlawing usury, the economy would tilt once again back towards the poor, shrinking the economic distance between the poor and the rich so there would be less class envy, more contentment, and less crime. There would be better family life with more quality time with our spouses and our children, and there would also be a better community life because we'd know many more of our neighbors because of the many "house-raisings" and community projects we had worked on together. There would no longer be community apathy towards our neighbor's problems or towards the crime in our local communities. Rich rulers would be more concerned about the marriage, morality, and sobriety of all our citizens and be more likely to keep God's commands in government. Our government would never have developed a three trillion dollar debt, and our economy would be more stable because it would also be independent from a sudden decline of the economy of foreign nations through world trade.

As a result of this legislated nationwide obedience, God would supernaturally "bless all the work of our hands" and give us a nearly poverty-free society as well as make America into the richest nation on the face of the earth! We'd be the envy of all the other nations. We would be held up by God as an example and an object lesson for all of the other nations to learn what divine blessings God will grant to a country when it successfully becomes a true nation under God!

Best of all, America would develop a new international reputation of having a culture which reflected true Christian morality and obedience, which resulted in the supernatural blessing of a nearly poverty-free society, as well as a nearly disease-free, crime-free, war-free, tax-free, inflation-free, and natural disaster-free society. Because of this, all nations of the earth would be awed by the power of our God, and would eagerly welcome American Christian missionaries by the thousands. This way, we could teach all nations about salvation by grace through faith in Jesus Christ, and the blessings of individual as well as national obedience to the will of almighty God! We'd even be able to create a national 1 percent voluntary contribution (over the mandatory 10 percent tithe) to be earmarked just for international evangelism, so we could send even more missionaries around the world than ever before, just to obey the great commission of Jesus Christ!

Please notice again how these Mosaic principles of economics interact to form a Mosaic picture of a prosperous, poverty-free society which is both *designed* by and *blessed* by Jehovah.

THE MOSAIC PICTURE OF GOD'S WELFARE SYSTEM

God's view of welfare reform starts with the twenty laws which promote the development of large, extended families throughout all of Israel. These large, extended families have a triple economy of scale so they can easily take care of their own occasional elderly, disabled, sick, unemployed or poor family member, instead of the state having to do it for them.

Next, God's laws against immorality and divorce practically eliminate unwed mothers and divorced single parents of young children as the two largest categories of applicants for welfare. As a result, the number of applicants for welfare (without large, extended families to care for them) decreases to only a small fraction of what it would be in America! Those remaining poor (who have no families to support them) now have access to financial support made possible because of three pre-welfare laws, which allow the poor man to:

1. obtain small zero-interest loans for bare necessities, the balance of which is canceled every Sabbath year. (Note: if Israel obeyed God, Jehovah promised to always give a bumper crop of harvest the year preceding the Sabbath year, in part, to prepay the farmers and the rest of the community to be able to more easily cancel these loan payments every Sabbath year!) For aliens, how-

ever, these loans were neither interest-free, nor were they to be canceled in the Sabbath year;
2. purchase food and other absolute necessities at cost from merchants and farmers; and,
3. legally "trespass" onto a farmer's property so he can pick fruits (including grapes), grains (including corn), or other vegetables to eat on the farmer's property, but cannot take any food off the farmer's property.

Now for those people who cannot afford to purchase food even at cost, they can obtain support from the local source of *tithe-sponsored welfare,* a place where the tithe is collected and protected by the Levites for a mere 10 percent overhead, and where 80 percent of the tithe is reserved for the poor, with the last 10 percent being transported to Jerusalem by the "tither" (a small part of which is eaten before the Lord by the "tither" and his family). The rest of the 10 percent is given to the Levites and priests serving at the temple.

Remember, tithe-sponsored welfare is reserved for the *innocent,* and not the *immoral.* So, repetitive immorality cancels one's eligibility to receive the tithe and makes one subject to criminal prosecution for immorality. This again decreases the number of recipients and new applicants for tithe-sponsored welfare. Therefore, those recipients and applicants who continue to remain eligible for the tithe because of their high moral standard can more easily be provided for without the need of collecting taxes to start a tax-sponsored system of welfare.

The last resort of welfare support for the healthy poor who continue to remain idle and never seem to want to work, is a six-year period of servanthood for the Israelite or a potential lifetime of slavery for the alien. This system costs no taxes to implement, perpetuates a good work ethic within all Israel, and may even rehabilitate the idle, as well as keep any Aliens who might want to be idle from emigrating into Israel and becoming welfare-dependent.

This, is the Mosaic picture of God's welfare system.

THE MOSAIC PICTURE OF GOD'S SYSTEM OF HEALTH CARE

God's view of health care reform involves the interaction of many of the biblical principles of justice, welfare, economics, and pro-family legislation in order to decrease national health care expenses.

Health care expenses in America rise because of four different things:

1. sins which cause diseases;
2. the high cost of developing new medicines and high-tech diagnostic medical equipment using atheistic research;
3. general inflation; and,

4. the "deep pockets" of the Health insurance, Medicare, and Medicaid business.

But, God's system of health care can eliminate all four of these problems. You see, the biblical principles of justice and healthcare combine to outlaw the eleven sins which cause up to 50 percent of the disease-related healthcare costs in America today. And, by making the first six of these sins into punishable crimes against the state, America can prevent millions of citizens from becoming ill from these diseases as well as save up to 50 percent of its healthcare costs nationally—about 450 billion dollars in savings each year!

The *second* step takes these remaining smaller costs of health care and shrinks them even further by switching from atheistic research to creation-based, God-honoring, prayerful research. By doing this, we will make our scientific research more productive and less expensive, so the future medicines and diagnostic testing equipment developed from this research will be less expensive for patients to use. Then, the *third* step takes these remaining smaller costs of providing healthcare and shrinks them even further by eliminating general inflation as a result of outlawing the sin of usury. The *fourth* step involves eliminating the deep pockets of the health insurance business, federal Medicare, and state-sponsored Medicaid—this is also accomplished by outlawing the sin of usury. This not only stops health care costs from continuing to skyrocket, but also eliminates insurance fraud, as well as Medicare and Medicaid fraud. Once Medicare, Medicaid, and private medical insurance disappear from America, then families will stop insisting on the inappropriate resuscitation and placement of feeding tubes into their terminally ill, vegetative family members, now that the family has to pay the financial cost of this anti-biblical decision. For then our culture will finally realize that the golden rule forbids them to practice this form of cruelty anyway! These four steps will inevitably shrink the cost of America's health care to a level where it will be easily affordable once again. Therefore, these costs can be shifted from the government to an entire culture of large, extended families—a culture which develops quite naturally as a result of implementing God's principles of pro-family legislation.

For you see, the principles of pro-family legislation which outlaw divorce (except for biblical felonies) also encourage the development of large, extended families (with such beneficial economics of scale that they can more easily pay for the health care costs of their own elderly, disabled, sick, unemployed and poor). In other words, the biblical principles of health care reform function in seven ways:

1. by eliminating the many sins which cause our most costly diseases, so we can prevent billions of dollars in health care costs;

2. by eliminating the unnecessarily high cost of atheistic research;
3. by eliminating the causes of general inflation;
4. by eliminating the deep financial pockets of health insurance, Medicare, and Medicaid;
5. by shifting the remaining costs (which are now much more manageable) from the government and from the taxpayer to the large, extended family with its triple economy of scale;
6. by shifting the health care costs of the few remaining sick and disabled citizens without families to be paid for by the *tithe*-sponsored welfare system; and,
7. by God's promise to bless each true nation under God with a nearly disease-free society where everyone lives to be 120-years-old while enjoying excellent health!

You see, it is God himself who is the ultimate source of the health or sickness of our nation's citizens. The Bible teaches that if Israel (or any other nation) sends only godly Christian elders into their government—who then legislate that their citizens must obey and worship only the one true God of the Bible—and these elders also adopt and regularly enforce all of God's principles of moral and civil law, then God promised to respond by granting Israel (or any other nation) a nearly disease-free society where nearly everyone lives to be 120-years-old while remaining in excellent health the entire time (Deut. 7:12,15; Exod. 23:25-26; Gen. 6:13 NIV).

This, is the Mosaic picture of God's system of health care!

THE MOSAIC PICTURE OF PROPER JUSTICE AND MERCY

Mankind's method of justice as practiced in the United States is wasteful, inefficient, slow, expensive, distorts the truth, favors the rich, causes a backlog of cases, and sets the guilty free. In contrast, God's courtroom of merciful justice has more than twenty advantages! God's system is faster, does not distort the truth, does not favor the rich, and is totally free! Furthermore, it encourages true repentance, and attempts to restore the sinner to a right relationship with God and with the community of believers. This is the type of courtroom procedure which almighty Jehovah knew would be ideal for Israel or any other country which was attempting to become a true nation under God.

God designed these laws of courtroom procedure with the same perfection with which he designed the laws of nature. So, as a result, Israel would have a system of justice which would work equally well for both ancient and modern civilizations, and which would be the envy of all of the surrounding nations.

You see, God commanded that no one was ever allowed to be paid for anything they said or did in the Israelite courtroom. For God knew that any payment could distort the truth by working like a bribe, and could "twist the words" of even the most righteous of participants. God also knew that these payments could also generate increased costs for each case by prolonging the trials because most of the participants would now be paid for the time they spent in the courtroom or paid for the time they spent preparing the case for trial. So, when we violate God's principles of courtroom procedure and allow people to receive money for their services in court, this leads to two great categories of problems which affect America's courtrooms today: the distortion of truth and the generation of increased costs.

But consider this. According to the Bible, the Israelite judges were supposed to be mostly all firstborn sons. For it was only the first born sons who would generally have enough extra time on their hands to be able to freely volunteer their services as judges and leaders of their community. This was because they had already been prepaid through the laws of inheritance to receive a double portion of their parents' estate, so they wouldn't have to work as hard as their brethren to support themselves. This would allow Israel's government to not require taxes to support their rulers.

As a result, Israel's judges would be supported only from their family businesses, and, since they would never receive any income from their judging, the Israelite judges would always be interested in speedy trials so they could quickly return home in order to tend to their family business. God knew that if the judge (or even the prosecuting attorneys for that matter) received salaries for their services, then they would no longer have the same interest in speedy trials.

These Mosaic laws of courtroom procedure therefore, were supposed to create a courtroom environment where everyone in the courtroom was there only to find God's truth and assist the judge in understanding all of the facts so he can better render the type of verdict that Jehovah would render. Then, after the sentence was passed, the judge would look for a reason to be merciful if at all possible.

So, because the courtroom atmosphere in Israel was supposed to be based upon finding God's truth and doing His work to obtain the same degree of merciful justice which Jehovah would dispense if he were in the courtroom, then it becomes clear why Jehovah designed Israel's courts to have:

1. no lawyer's fees,
2. no court costs,
3. no taxes which needed to be collected from society to pay court costs,
4. no monetary incentive for lawyers to "drag their feet," delay the case, and make trials longer,
5. no delayed cases,

6. no large backlog of pending court cases,
7. no mechanism available to "tie someone up in court,"
8. no lawyers who are paid to distort the truth,
9. no monetary incentive for lawyers to defend someone they already know is guilty, and,
10. no monetary incentive for lawyers to encourage you to sue someone they already know is innocent.

And, since Israelite justice was to be entirely free,

11. the poor man was just as likely to get a fair trial as the rich man!

Furthermore, the rest of God's principles of justice declared that:

12. the innocent would never be convicted because of malicious witnesses, because God's penalty for being a malicious witness was so severe,
13. the guilty would never escape punishment because of "insanity,"
14. the guilty would never escape punishment just because they confessed their sins without first being warned of a fictitious "right" to remain silent,
15. the guilty would never escape punishment just because someone improperly obtained evidence,
16. the guilty would never escape punishment just because of a mere technicality of man's law,
17. the guilty would never escape punishment because of a mistrial and,
18. there would be no plea bargaining as a method of getting a reduced sentence!

Also, since God commanded judges (and not juries) to decide all the cases, then there would never be any juries! As a result,

19. there would be no Anti-biblical verdicts from juries,
20. there would be no jury tampering with bribes,
21. there would be no jury bias created through jury selection!

Lastly, since all judges were to be godly Christian elders who knew God's laws,

22. there would be no judges who would render anti-biblical verdicts or who would make rulings contrary to God's laws,
23. there would be no judges who would ever let the unrepentant guilty go unpunished,
24. there would be no judges who would ever dare to ignore God's principles of moral law, civil law, and civil law enforcement, and finally,
25. there would be no "Supreme Court" Israelite judges who would ever try to ban the use of the Bible from courtrooms and schools!

So as you can see, there are more than twenty reasons why God's courtroom procedures are vastly superior to man's courtroom procedures. But, there is something even more special and wonderful about God's courtroom policy than this.

You see, basically only two of the Bible's death penalties also commanded the judges "Show no pity"—which meant that the death penalty was indeed mandatory only in cases of idolatry and murder. By deliberately leaving out the expression "Show him no pity" for the other sixteen biblical death penalties, Jehovah was indirectly encouraging the Israelite judges to show mercy whenever they could. Furthermore, in Micah 6:8, God actually required the judges to "love mercy." In other words, in more than 80 percent of the biblical death penalties, the judges were supposed to "look for a reason to show mercy if at all possible"!

God's command which required judges to "love to give merciful alternatives to execution" has very important implications for the Israelite courtroom. With this idea God redefined the role of the Judge so the Israelite courtroom could provide a "ministry of MERCY"!

You see, the ministry of the Israelite courtroom was to bring sinners to a point of confession and repentance at some point during the trial. For it is in the courtroom when the sinner is caught and his sinfulness is exposed to the community. Witnesses are summoned against him, and he realizes that the wages for his sin may possibly be a death penalty. Therefore, there is no more perfect place for the gospel of Jesus Christ to be presented and observed in action than in the courtroom.

For, a judicial system which emphasizes administering mercy when the sinner repents and wants to be restored into true fellowship with God, is a perfect method to demonstrate the grace, mercy, and forgiveness of Christ in the courtroom (and that the consequences of sin is punishment and possibly death).

The trial of the sinner represents each of us as we finally stand at the judgement seat of God and are confronted with our sins as read from a "book" in which they are recorded. The godly Christian elder judge represents God, who loves to be merciful and compassionate, but if provoked, will prayerfully dispense either mercy or justice depending upon the sin, the testimony, and the presence or absence of the sinner's humble confession and repentance before God and before the judge in the courtroom. It is fitting therefore that God intended the Israelite courtroom to repeatedly illustrate the pageantry of divine merciful justice which will eventually be issued from the real throne of God in heaven on judgment day—where grace and mercy will be granted to some, and justice and punishment will be dispensed to lots of others.

These citizens who are convicted in court are often those who are not going to worship each Sabbath, and therefore are not regularly hearing the gospel of Jehovah—that we are all under a death penalty and that God commands us to obey; that he also wants to show grace and mercy to us when we disobey, if we confess our sins, repent, surrender our lives to him, and "go and sin no more". You see, the courtroom was to be the last hope where the unrighteous would be confronted with Jehovah's love, mercy, and desire to turn the sinner from his evil ways and restore him to a right relationship with his God and with the community of believers without having to execute him.

So, after the judge dispenses mercy, he was to command the guilty person to "Go, and sin no more." This entire process would hopefully function to *restore* the sinner to a right relationship with his God and with the local community of believers.

You see, this ministry of mercy was not to end at the courthouse steps, but was to continue into the community as a "ministry of RESTORATION." Thus, the Israelite court was designed by God to also be a mission field, where the local community of believers could find the lost sheep of Israel, bring them back into the fold, surround them with love and godly peer pressure, and encourage them to worship each Sabbath.

The concept of "Go and sin no more," did not just mean to *stop* committing adultery, homosexuality, drunkenness or stealing, but meant to *start* going back to the worship services each Sabbath, *start* enjoying the fellowship of Christian believers again (instead of the company of those who originally led you astray), and *start* wearing your headband, wristbands, and tassels again. For, if you "dress the part", you will more likely "act the part"!

God's intended ministry of restoration for the Israelite court has similarities to the wonderful prison ministries of many of dedicated Christians, like Chuck Colson, for instance. The prisoner is shown love and compassion, and is presented with the Gospel of Christ while in prison, and attempts are made to restore him to a right relationship with his God and with the fellowship of believers.

However, man's system of imprisonment actually interferes with this ministry of restoration because the prisoner remains surrounded by hundreds of other prisoners who would rather corrupt his character than allow him to be restored to a right relationship with his God and with the community of Christian believers. In addition, imprisonment costs America billions of dollars in taxes for the care of thousands of prisoners in hundreds of prisons. How much better it would be if they were just whipped according to God's commands in the Bible, and then sent home and released into the care of their local Christian community! Then this same "Barnabas-type" ministry of restoration, encouragement, and accountability could be much more effective to bring Christ into the lives of these men.

Imagine how much easier a prison ministry would be, if part of the Judge's sentence to "Go and sin no more" always meant that the convict must now join himself, not to a parole officer, but to one of the local Christian accountability groups already in existence. These would be small groups of Christian men who are already meeting regularly to pray for one another, study the Bible together, and to hold one another accountable for their sins before God and before men. Here the convict would find love and acceptance, but would also find Bible teaching, biblical rebuke, and godly peer pressure.

Remember, it was not in God's *original* design for Israel to have prison ministries, for God knew that it would be counterproductive to disciple new Christians in an environment such as a prison, and that the prison itself would further corrupt the character of its own prisoners. However, Christian prison ministries are indeed an important part of God's "plan *B*" (Matt. 25:36b, 43b NIV). Prison ministries are important for all societies which have courtrooms which do *not* follow biblical guidelines and which do *not* have ministries of mercy and restoration, and which *do* choose to build prisons instead of adopting God's five principles of punishment.

I personally believe that all of the criminals who truly accepted Christ as Savior and Lord while serving in prison would have made the same decision for Christ in the courtroom years earlier, if (as God commanded) they were faced with the possibility of a death sentence for their crime, and if we had a system of justice which fulfilled God's guidelines. I further believe that these same new Christians could have been discipled for Christ much more efficiently and thoroughly if they had not also been required to live in prison where bad company corrupts good character.

And, while it is true that the percentage of false repentance and false conversions would probably be greater inside the courtroom than elsewhere, it is still important for the judges to stand in the place of Jehovah and to demonstrate the grace and mercy of Christ if at all possible to sinners who appear to be repentant in the courtroom. But, although the criminal may receive mercy from the judge, this may only mean that the criminal is just not executed, and that instead, he may receive anywhere from one lash up to a maximum of forty lashes with a whip for his crime as a merciful alternative to the death penalty.

Now the judge himself is supposed to be a godly Christian elder who has a love of God and a love of his fellow man in his heart, and who also has a personal relationship of obedient surrender to Jehovah. He must also recognize that he is judging on behalf of God, and that he must first get the log out of his own eye so he can see clearly to judge his neighbor. He must know perfectly the correct application of all of God's laws, and he must recognize that he will be held accountable beyond the grave for any sins he commits while in office or while making judgements on God's behalf in his courtroom. The judge is probably also an eldest son who has been prepaid by the laws of inheritance to have enough extra time to freely volunteer to serve as judge and leader of the local community or of the entire region.

Thus the laws of God as written in the Bible have more than twenty advantages over the system of justice used in America. These same principles were also supposed to guide the Israelite judges to use the courtroom to establish a ministry of mercy and restoration for the criminals, so these lost sheep of Israel could be restored into a right relationship with God and with the community of believers. What a joyous application of God's principles of civil law enforcement!

And this, is the Mosaic picture of proper justice and mercy.

THE MOSAIC PICTURE OF PROPER JUSTICE AND PUNISHMENT

Now God commanded that
  —working on the Sabbath,
  —idolatry,
  —sexual immorality, and
  —drunkenness

should become crimes against the state of Israel. You see, God's view of sin and crime differs from mankind's view of sin and crime.

For instance, God made work on the Sabbath illegal for a whole host of reasons, but one of them was to encourage everyone in Israel to be in church and learn about salvation by grace through faith in Jehovah, who would later on return to earth to personally become our Messiah, Savior, and Lord—Jesus Christ! This would not only increase nationwide church attendance to get more of the population to be saved, but would also get the unrighteous majority of citizens to at least obey because of "*training* and *tradition*," even if not because of "*salvation* and *surrender*"! This "training and tradition" would also encourage *conformity* and *unity* of belief concerning the issues of religion, origins, morality, and politics (ROMP) and discourage pluralism from emerging and destroying God's plan to create and maintain a true nation under God. Finally, weekly Sabbath worship would also allow all of the adult males in Israel to continue to master God's principles of moral and civil law, so they would be trained to become godly Christian leaders over Israel.

Jehovah also made idolatry illegal because He will not fully bless a nation which gives thanks to idols for its blessings. In addition, legal idolatry undermines the belief that it is the laws of *Jehovah* which should be enforced, and not the laws of some *other god*, nor even the laws of *man* (if they contradict the laws of God). So, when idolatry is legal and not punished, the citizens will eventually stop obeying all of God's other principles of civil law as well.

God's system of justice also makes sexual immorality and drunkenness both illegal and regularly punishable. It also makes divorce illegal unless one spouse commits a biblical felony. Part of the reason for this is that sexual immorality, drunkenness, and divorce together affect every single large category of political policies.

For instance, the liberal laws in America which encourage sexual immorality, drunkenness, and divorce not only destroy families, but also lead to increased taxes for national welfare and health care. These increased taxes lead to increased business expenses which leads to business downsizing and unemployment (thus affecting national economic policy). At the same time, legalize divorce increases the number of "at risk" children living in broken homes who cause disruption in schools and cause crime in the streets, thus affecting national policies of education and justice. Recruiting homosexuals into the military affects military policy. And lastly, America's international reputation for immorality affects our foreign policy as well, because Islamic nations blame America's immorality on what they perceive to be Christianity's perpetual unwillingness to ensure that our government regularly punish immorality and drunkenness. Therefore, they fear that exposure to America's Christianity will contaminate and corrupt their nation's morality also. Clearly then, legalizing sexual immorality and drunkenness together affect every single large category of political policies in America today.

Finally, God made fornication, rape, and lying about your virginity illegal, because (taken together with the laws against adultery and homosexuality) these laws would practically guarantee premarital virginity and marital fidelity throughout all Israel.

Now Jehovah actually used the *fewest* possible number of laws to create the *largest* possible impact to mold the Israelite society into a righteous culture and a true nation under God. If we, in America, were to adopt such a system, we could also save billions of dollars in unnecessary taxes.

Jehovah also gave to Moses a divine standard of punishment. You see, there were to be no prisons within Israel because bad company corrupts good character, and because imprisonment costs billions of dollars in unnecessary taxes. So God developed five biblical alternatives to imprisonment:

1. *execution,*
2. an *"eye for an eye"* (for violent criminals who seriously injure their victims),
3. *whipping* (because prison time costs taxes, but a flogging is free),
4. the *"mark of justice"* (a tattoo on the back of a hand, indicating the date, the crime, and the punishment received), and
5. a six-year period of *"slavery"* (for thieves who cannot pay back a multiple of their debt).

Finally, God's method of execution also represents the easiest, safest, and least expensive form of execution which can ever be designed to be performed . . .

—in public,
—by the public,
—to transform the public!

For God's method of public execution (performed immediately outside the community where the crime was committed) efficiently transforms unrighteous community apathy to righteous community involvement in biblical rebuke, reporting crime, and godly peer pressure to purify their community from its remaining evil, just like they should have been doing all along!

And this, is the Mosaic picture of proper justice and punishment.

The Mosaic Picture *of Proper* Military Policy

The Military strategies of the Prince of Peace are clearly presented in the Bible, and I believe they are for Israel, for America, and for the rest of the world.

For instance, God wanted Israel to live at peace with her neighbors and never be the first to start a war. Furthermore, Israel was never to intervene militarily in the affairs of foreign nations, whether to help them in battle or to stop them from committing human rights violations. In other words, Israel's military was never expected to be the policeman of the world.

Israel was only to have righteous men of faith in her army; and their faith was more important than their skill. Also, Israel was never to have any women in her armed forces. Neither was Israel to have any homosexuals in her army, for God will not fight on behalf of an army of wickedness. Therefore, if Israel's army abandoned God's commands concerning forbidding homosexuals from serving in the military, then God would abandon Israel's army in the next battle. And so, without God's divine protection, many Israelite soldiers would end up dying unnecessarily, and Israel may even lose the battle entirely.

Israel was never to trust in foreign armies, in the size of her own army, or to trust in her weapons technology to help her achieve victory, but was to trust in God alone. Because of this, Israel was never to ask other nations for help in battle, nor was Israel to agree to help any other nations in battle. Furthermore, Israel was never to even count the size of her army, and was never to escalate her weaponry to equal or to exceed that of her enemies. For again, she was commanded to recognize that it was God, and God alone, who gave the victory.

And, if any of Israel's soldiers died in battle, it was not a sign of heroism, but it was a sign that God had abandoned the army of Israel because of serious sinfulness either within the army or within the nation itself which had not been dealt with. In other words, God was to get the glory in victory, but man was to get the blame in defeat. Therefore, by implication, Israel was never to celebrate any type of Veteran's Day or Memorial Day!

The purpose of the military in ancient Israel was not just for defense, but more importantly, to demonstrate the power and pageantry of the repeated overwhelming supernatural victories of God's tiny armies against overwhelming odds. Also it was to serve as a dramatic witness to all nations of the earth that the one true God of the universe reigns over Israel, and that all other nations should therefore abandon their pagan idolatry and worship this same Jehovah, who would later return to earth and personally become the Messiah and Savior of the entire world—Jesus Christ!

You see, Israel watched as Jehovah defeated the enemies of righteousness by either blinding them, drowning them, cremating them with fire-fall, stoning them with hailstones, causing the ground to swallow them in an earthquake, or causing an entire army of soldiers to die in their sleep. They also watched as God would send both hallucinations and delusions upon the enemies of God, which would either lure their armies into a fatal trap, or cause them to flee from the Israelite soldiers, or cause them to attack each other instead of attacking the Israelites!

Now imagine what a strong impression such battles would have on all the other nations of the earth, to give very serious consideration to abandoning their pagan idolatry and starting to worship only Jehovah—the pre-incarnate Christ!

You don't need a very large military budget when God fights on your side! For even the weapons of modern twentieth century technology are no match for the power of the almighty Master of the Universe—Jesus the Christ! For if God can control the infinite complexity of the eyes, the ears, and the minds of the enemies of Israel (by sending upon them blindness, auditory hallucinations, or delusions), then he can certainly control the relatively simple radar, sonar, and missile guidance systems of the enemies of America today!

This then, is the Mosaic picture of the military policy which Jehovah chose for Israel and for any other nation which desires to become a true nation under God.

THE MOSAIC PICTURE OF PROPER FOREIGN POLICY

God's foreign policy for Israel was designed to generate an *international fearful reverence* of Jehovah—the God of Israel—so all of the citizens of other nations would want to learn about how to have a *personal* relationship with Jehovah (to inherit the blessings of salvation, hope and peace), as well as learn how to have a *national* relationship with Jehovah (to inherit the blessings of being a nation under God and therefore be able to live in a nearly crime-free, poverty-free, war-free, tax-free, inflation-free, natural disaster-free, and disease-free society where nearly everyone lives to be 120-years-old while enjoying excellent health. In this way, Jehovah's foreign policy of international fearful reverence was designed to evangelize both nations and individuals.

Secondly, Israelite ambassadors were to be foreign *missionaries* trained not only to lead foreign kings and presidents to a personal relationship with Jehovah (the pre-incarnate Christ), but also to present Jehovah as the architect of the biblical blueprint for perfect government, so foreign leaders could also build better government with biblical principles. In addition, once Israel was regularly enforcing all of God's principles of moral and civil law as the foundation of Israel's legislation, then Israel's Christian ambassadors could invite foreign leaders to Israel to see and experience first hand the blessings of what it means to live in a true nation under God.

Thirdly, God's foreign policy is one of *selective economic isolationism*, which not only would foster obedience to, and dependence upon, God alone as the true source of national economic prosperity, but also would help to prevent Israel from making unholy economic alliances with idolatrous unrighteous nations which He intended to punish with poverty for their idolatry.

Fourthly, Israel could lend money to foreign countries but all foreign loans were to be paid back with interest.

Fifthly, Israel's true foreign enemies would be those nations which exalt man's *secular* ways of government instead of God's *divine* ways of government. You see, a nation under God has a republic form of government, which means that God's divine laws can never be overturned even by majority decision. But surprisingly, this makes democracy itself an enemy of a true nation under God because in a democracy, God's laws are often ignored or repealed in accordance with the will of the unrighteous majority.

Sixthly, Israel was never to sell military weapons to foreign nations because this violates the military policies of the Prince of Peace concerning "Do not escalate your weaponry to equal that of the surrounding nations!"

Seventh, God's immigration policy allows anyone to enter the country at any time, but they are to not to bring their *idolatry* or *immorality* with them. If they violate any of God's principles of moral law or civil law, they will not escape being prosecuted, just as if they were Israelite citizens to begin with. If the immigrants remain *idle* and it becomes clear that they intend to become dependent upon Israel's tithe-sponsored welfare, then they will likely have to face the last resort of welfare support—slavery! Fear of being enslaved for perpetual impoverishment and indebtedness resulting from laziness would discourage lazy immigrants from coming to Israel. However, this would not deter the hardworking immigrants from coming to live within her borders.

By the way, Jehovah would never have allowed Israel to participate in the United Nations, because of the many anti-Christian philosophies which the United Nations supports—such as promoting abortions on an international scale, preserving idolatrous cultures (an anti-Christian missionary philosophy), promoting military intervention in foreign countries, and promoting economic trading between wealthy Christian nations and poor, idolatrous nations!

But first and foremost, let us always remember that the primary purpose of God's foreign policy was to generate a world wide international fearful reverence of Jehovah (who personally became our Messiah, Savior, and Lord, Jesus Christ) . . .

> . . . so that all the peoples of the earth may know that the LORD is God and that there is no other. (1 Kings 8:60 NIV; emphasis added)

For it is only by God's gift of the atoning sacrifice of Jesus Christ on the cross that individuals from all over the world can become saved and receive the blessings of eternal life. And, it is only by God's gift of his principles of moral law, civil law, and civil law enforcement that nations from all over the world can become nations under God, and receive the blessings of a society free from the tragedies of disease, crime, poverty, war, taxes, inflation, and natural disasters.

Imagine how wonderful it would have been for all nations to have seen the full measure of the blessings that Jehovah God could have poured out onto the Israelite society as an incentive for the rest of the world to structure their societies in the same manner as He commanded Israel! In this way, all nations could have designed their cultures to encourage both a personal and a national relationship of obedient surrender to Jehovah—the God of the Israelites.

Unfortunately, the Israelites never did completely adopt all of God's principles of moral law, civil law, and civil law enforcement into the law of the land. And so, they never did receive the full measure of the riches of God's blessings. Therefore, the rest of the world has only seen Israel become the object lesson of God's punishment for disobedience, but has never seen Israel be the object lesson of God's full potential blessing for obedience.

So you see, it is not a possibility that God's laws of self-government were tried and failed. It is only a possibility that God's laws of self-government were never truly and completely tried at all!

SUMMARY

The Mosaic laws form at least ten detailed Mosaic pictures of God's view of the ideal system of education, worship, family structure, economics, government, court procedure, justice, punishment, military policy, and foreign policy. Furthermore, when observed as a group, these ten Mosaic pictures form a much larger Mosaic mural, revealing the structure and function of a true nation under God.

Additionally, in a nation under God, the system of education, worship, and civil law was designed to mold the national character into two distinct groups. The first group would be composed of those citizens who would *enthusiastically* obey God's laws because they had a *personal relationship* with Jehovah based upon *salvation* (by grace through faith) and *surrender*. We could call this first group the small Christian minority. The second group would therefore represent the large, non-Christian majority. It would be composed of those citizens who had *no personal relationship* with Jehovah, so they would only *reluctantly* obey His commands. Their reluctant obedience would result from the combined influence of God's five fundamentals of legislated conformity.

You see, God's principles of civil law encourage unity of belief and *conformity of behavior*. On the other hand, America's principles of civil law encourage *diversity of beliefs* (pluralism) and *non-conformity of behavior*, which in turn, encourages rebellion against the authority of both God and man.

Knowing this, God designed five fundamentals of legislated conformity which would combine their influence to keep the large, unrighteous majority on their best behavior. These *five fundamentals of legislated conformity* are:

1. training and tradition,
2. prosecution and punishment,
3. legislated godly peer pressure,
4. clothing and coverings, and
5. nationwide accountability groups.

Now, the daily training and tradition of all Israelite *students* was to be accomplished by making all public schools into Christian schools. In this way, all Israelite students would not only learn about salvation by grace though faith in Jehovah (who would someday return to earth and personally become our Messiah, Savior and Lord—Jesus Christ), but they would also learn all the practical applications that God's principles of civil law were designed to have for the administration of sound, virtuous, and godly government.

The weekly training and tradition of all *adult* Israelites would be accomplished by outlawing work on the Sabbath—a law which would magnify the attraction of gathering together every Sabbath for worship and studying the Scriptures at the temple or the local synagogues. In this way, most all of the adult Israelites should eventually become extremely knowledgeable in the principles of salvation by grace as well as become extremely proficient in their understanding of the principles underlying God's civil and moral laws. As a result, the training and tradition of all Israelites in the principles underlying God's civil laws would be accomplished by:

—*learning* them as children at home,
—*memorizing* them as students at school, and
—*mastering* them as adults during church.

The second fundamental of legislated conformity is *prosecution* and *punishment*. The courts were supposed to join forces with the church and enforce the doctrines which the church taught. In other words, fornication, adultery, homosexuality, and drunkenness were to become crimes against the state, and divorce was to be illegal unless your spouse committed a sin which was also a serious crime. Furthermore, the Israelite courtroom procedures included the twin ministries of mercy and restoration, which God designed to lead the convicted criminals back to a right relationship with God and with the community of believers. So, by combining training and tradition with prosecution and punishment, the doctrines of Christianity were empowered with the legal muscle to keep the large, unrighteous majority of Israelites on their best behavior, and restore the Israelites who were criminals to a better relationship with God and man at the same time.

The third fundamental of legislated conformity is *legislated godly peer pressure*. For God gave the Israelites two civil laws (Lev. 19:11, 5:1) which would provide the legal motivation to create a culture of godly peer pressure, by allowing (and perhaps even encouraging) the judges to prosecute those who refused to rebuke their neighbor's sins or report their neighbor's crimes. This would depend upon the severity of the crime not being rebuked or reported, of course.

However, for those rebellious communities which would become safe havens for capital crimes because of their community's apathy and indifference toward rebuking sin and reporting crime, God's principle of *execution by public participation* would quickly reverse this tendency and restore a patriotic passion of community action and involvement in rebuking sin and reporting crime. So you can see how God's principles of civil law interact together to create a culture of legislated godly peer pressure. This, in turn, adds to the effectiveness of God's principles of training and tradition, and prosecution and punishment to keep the large, unrighteous majority of Israelite citizens on their best behavior.

Then, to maximize this missionary-like zeal to rebuke sin, report crime, and purge the evil from your community, God added a fourth principle of legislated conformity—the principle of *clothing and coverings*. For God created an Israelite dress code to promote the principle that "if you dress the part, you will act the part." You see, the headbands, wristbands, and tassels which the adult male Israelites were instructed by God to wear would provide them with a perpetual reminder that everything they *think, speak,* and *do* should be guided by God's principles of salvation, moral law, and civil law. And of course, this dress code would not only help to keep everyone on their best behavior, but would also add to the effectiveness of God's principles of legislated godly peer pressure by providing even further encouragement to rebuke sin (hopefully by "speaking the truth in love") and report crime.

And, as if these first four fundamentals of legislated conformity were not enough to keep the large, unrighteous majority on their best behavior, God added one more—the principle of *nationwide accountability groups* (Exod. 18:21). This principle would create accountability groups of ten families each, with each group having their own judge. This judge would have the power to decide all of the group's (simple) legal difficulties. But as a result, in order to avoid having to prosecute his friends and neighbors for their petty (or for their serious) sins against each other, this law also provided the legal motivation to encourage each judge to develop his group of ten families into an "accountability group" to be guided by biblical principles to keep everyone on their best behavior!

These five fundamentals of legislated conformity to biblical principles were designed by God to interact together to provide the greatest possible motivation for the large, unrighteous majority of Israelites to remain on their best behavior.

Hopefully, you can now see how the structure of education, worship, and the family within ancient Israel was designed to *teach* all of God's principles of moral and civil law to its citizens, while the structure of the government and the courts was designed to *empower* these same Christian principles with the legal muscle to be able to keep the large, majority of unrighteous citizens on their best behavior.

As a result, the small, Christian minority of Israelites would *enthusiastically obey* God's commands because of salvation and surrender, while the large, unrighteous majority of Israelites would be *successfully pressured into obeying* God's commands because of God's five fundamentals of legislated conformity.

Because of this, the aggregate righteousness of all Israel would inevitably exceed the graduated "threshold of righteousness" which God had in his divine mind. This way, God would bless Israel with a nearly crime-free, poverty-free, war-free, tax-free, inflation-free, natural-disaster-free, and disease-free society where nearly everyone lives to be 120-years-old while remaining in excellent health the entire time. This would make the whole world marvel at the God of the Israelites and want to worship and obey him as well. Therefore, all nations would want to learn how to have a national relationship with Jehovah (as a true nation under God), as well as a personal relationship with Jehovah—the preincarnate Christ—a relationship of surrender and salvation by grace through faith.

For God so loved the world, that he gave to Israel his perfect laws of self-government, so the small, Christian minority would be divinely enabled to rule over the large, unrighteous, majority and keep them on their best behavior through godly leadership, godly laws, and social engineering through legislated conformity. And, since it was really Jesus Christ—the preincarnate Jehovah—who gave these laws to Moses in the first place, this makes Jesus Christ the *Lord of Lawmakers,* the *King of Kings,* and the *architect of this biblical blueprint for perfect self-government!*

Now the wonderful love Jehovah has for all nations can be appreciated even better by understanding that the complete adoption of his biblical blueprint for perfect government would have prevented countless tragedies involving crime, poverty, war, natural disasters, diseases, divorce, and broken homes. In fact, we can measure (if you will) the love of Jehovah in giving us these wonderful laws of self-government, by "counting up" . . .

1. the millions of *broken homes* which would have been prevented by God's laws against divorce and against sexual immorality, and drunkenness,
2. the millions of *diseases* affecting our citizens which would have been prevented by adhering to God's principles of health care,
3. the millions of *crimes* which would have been prevented by adhering to God's principles of merciful justice,
4. the millions of *soldier's lives* which would have been saved by adhering to God's military principles,
5. the millions of *babies* which would not have been aborted by adhering to God's principles against abortion,
6. the millions of *unemployed* and *impoverished* citizens who would still have jobs if we followed God's principles of national economics and foreign policy,
7. the millions of *homeless* citizens who would have a place to live if we followed God's principles concerning welfare,
8. the millions of families impoverished annually by *natural disasters* which would have been supernaturally prevented by faithful national adherence to all God's principles,
9. the trillions of dollars in *taxes* which would have been saved by adhering to God's principles of government, and

10. the millions of *foreigners* who might have *accepted Christ* as Savior and Lord, if America's international reputation for evil and unrighteousness had not so undermined the witness for Christ throughout the world, (especially in Islamic countries)!

All of these wonderful blessings can be obtained by America, or by any other nation which desires to become a true nation under God.

Jehovah's laws of self-government create a nationwide patriotic enthusiasm to promote righteousness by continual voluntary community action to replace community apathy, so self-government can be accomplished with the mere few hundred laws of Jehovah, without the need for a large, centralized government with its tens of thousands of federal, state, and local laws, regulations, ordinances, and codes—a system which places a great burden of taxes and intrusiveness onto the shoulders of all our citizens.

Surely, Jesus Christ—the Lord of Lawmakers—has given us the perfect laws of self-government, designed with the same degree of perfection with which he designed the laws of physics, chemistry, and biology. And, just as God's laws of physics, chemistry, and biology are capable of interacting in such a way so as to produce *"life"* (a whole which is greater than the sum of its parts), so also God's laws of self-government are capable of interacting in such a way so as to produce *abundant life*, such as only can be found in a true nation under God, with a government . . .

—of the people of God,
—by the principles of God,
—for the glory of God,

where its citizens can enjoy a nearly crime-free, poverty-free, war-free, tax-free, inflation-free, natural disaster-free, and disease-free society where nearly everyone lives to be 120-years-old while enjoying excellent health.

And that, is the Mosaic picture of a true nation under God!

Of course, even though there is abundant life to be had for both righteous and unrighteous citizens who live in a true nation under God, there is a much more important type of abundant life which can only be found in a personal saving relationship with Jesus Christ. Such a relationship is characterized by confession, repentance, forgiveness of sin, and obedient surrender, and is based upon Christ's death on the cross as the only perfect atonement for our sins! Let us never forget this, and let us never consider that building a nation under God (the subject of this book) should ever be more important than building your own personal relationship with Jesus Christ as Savior and Lord of your life!

Chapter Twenty-Six

IMPLEMENTATION—HOW TO CREATE A NATION UNDER GOD BY REBUILDING AMERICA WITH BIBLICAL PRINCIPLES

I. "IF MY PEOPLE . . ."

Even though the principles underlying God's civil laws are still valid today and would work better than our current laws, they still sound so foreign to us and would cost us so much freedom, that it appears impossible for America to adopt more than just a few of them at best.

Yet what is impossible for man is easily possible for God! And from God's point of view, this project is much less complicated than when He created the universe out of nothing, or when he created man from the dust of the ground. So, it is essential to have God behind us in this endeavor if it is ever to work at all, for only God can accomplish this great task.

"But," you ask, "If God wants this to be done so badly, and only *He* can do it, then why didn't God do it generations ago?"

Because modern Christians generally do *not* want the solutions that God proposes! You see, God will not solve our problems using our solutions. But, He will solve our problems if we are willing to use His solutions. In other words, just as we must be willing to use Christ's solution for salvation, we must also be just as willing to use Christ's solution for self-government! For the King of Kings—Jesus Christ—is also the Lord of Lawmakers and the architect of the biblical blueprint for perfect self-government. And, although God's rules for governing yourself (from within) are his moral laws, God's rules for self-government (as a nation) are his civil laws.

So what is Christ's solution for perfect self-government? It is for our government to adopt many of the Mosaic *civil* laws (and not just the *moral* laws) as permanent legislation for our nation? For these are the same laws which Christ gave to Moses thirty-four hundred years ago when he was in the form of Jehovah. So Jehovah's laws of "justice and mercy" are actually Christ's laws of "justice and "mercy" as well.

You see, Christ has always been interested in justice. For Isaiah 9:7-9 (NIV) teaches us that the "government shall be upon the shoulders" of the child who would become the "Prince of Peace," and that he would "uphold his government with justice." Furthermore, Christ warned the Pharisees (just as he warns today's Christian leaders) not to "neglect" the "more important matters of God's law," specifically Jehovah's principles concerning "justice and mercy." For it is written:

> Woe to you, teachers of the law and Pharisees, you hypocrites! You give a tenth of your spices—mint, dill and cumin. But you have neglected the more important matters of the law—*justice, mercy,* and *faithfulness.* You should have practiced the latter, without neglecting the former. You blind guides! (Matt. 23:23-24 NIV; emphasis added)

Now this passage reveals an amazing similarity between the ancient Pharisees and modern Christian leaders, in that both exalt the importance of tithing, yet both also neglect the important role that Jehovah's principles of justice and mercy (the Mosaic civil laws) have in the administration of godly government. Of course, modern Christian leaders would object vigorously to this analogy, because our faith is in Jesus Christ, but the faith of the ancient Pharisees was actually in themselves, more than in Jehovah (the pre-incarnate Christ). Evidently, according to Christ, faith represents only one part of the "more important matters of the law," while Jehovah's principles of justice and mercy represent the other part. So, while the strong faith of our Christian leaders may give them an accurate picture of Christ's vision for salvation, if they still neglect the importance of Jehovah's civil principles for justice and mercy, they have blinded themselves concerning Christ's vision for government. You see, unlike America's founders, modern Christian leaders have deliberately closed their eyes to the importance of the Mosaic civil principles of justice and mercy. In fact, *the fundamental reason why God refuses to "heal our land" is because our Christian leaders cannot see the role Jehovah's civil principles of justice and mercy play in the "establishment of godly government."* And therefore, they have largely rejected God's civil laws as being insignificant and irrelevant.

Christian leaders, do you want me to say only the things which make you feel good about yourselves? Is that what Isaiah, Jeremiah, and the prophets of Israel did? Or do you want me to tell you God's truth?

The truth is that you have become blinded to the importance of Christ's laws of justice and mercy, and therefore consider the Mosaic civil laws to be useless for establishing godly government. The evidence for this is that you refuse to even attempt to completely outlaw sexual immorality, abortion, drunkenness, non-biblical divorce, working on Sunday, and non-Christians working in government. You refuse to initiate legislation to once again make all public schools Christian schools which teach Christian doctrine and morality to all students in order to perpetually indoctrinate all American citizens into the Christian faith through "salvation and surrender," or at the very least, through "training and tradition."

In other words, although you exalt God's principles of *moral* law, you refuse to even propose the incorporation of God's principles of *civil* law into America's legislation. Yet, this is what America had under the leadership of the founders, and this is what we need today, in order to re-establish godly government in the form of a true Christian Republic. For only this kind of true Christian Republic can empower the doctrines of Christianity with enough legal muscle to keep the unrighteous majority of citizens on their best behavior, as the founders wanted, and as the Bible commands. This is the kind of Christian Republic America would have if God answered our prayers and "healed our land."

In other words, if God truly "healed our land," then we'd end up with a Christian Republic (like in the days of the founders) instead of a hostile, secular democracy with a few Christian restrictions. Yet evidently, our hostile, secular democracy must be acceptable to our Christian leaders, for they never seem to propose any legislation to restore the Christian Republic that we used to have.

This is why God helped America's founders to establish a Christian Republic, much more than He is helping us to re-establish that same Christian Republic. For the re-establishment of a true Christian Republic is not even the *goal* of our Christian leaders. And this is the fundamental reason why God refuses to "heal our land" today, because their contentment with secular democracy (with a few Christian restrictions) unmasks their underlying apathy about returning to a truly Christian Republic, and reveals that they don't really want God to "heal our land" in the first place.

So why should God "heal our land" when our Christian leaders don't really want this type of "healing"?

Now the problem here is simple: Christian leaders and politicians may praise God's *moral* laws, but they never praise God's *civil* laws, nor do they ever praise God's principles of civil law enforcement. The silence of our Christian leaders about Jehovah's civil laws betrays their lack of understanding concerning the important application of these laws. It also highlights their embarrassment over these laws as well as their lack of trust that Jesus Christ—the Lord of Lawmakers and architect of the biblical blueprint for perfect self-government—really knew what he was doing when he wrote these laws in the first place.

It is precisely the biblical fundamentals of civil law and civil law enforcement (Jehovah's principles of "justice and mercy") which America needs so desperately today, and yet they are still being neglected by both our secular and our Christian leaders—probably moreso than they were being neglected by the Pharisees in Jesus' day.

America's founders, on the other hand, adopted *nine* of these biblical principles of civil law into our nation's early legislation hundreds of years ago. And, because our founders could see more clearly Christ's vision for government, God blessed them for their efforts by helping them to establish godly government in the form of a Christian Republic.

Let me be a little more specific. There are significant and serious differences between the founders' philosophy of godly government and modern Christian leaders' philosophy of godly government. In fact, under the leadership of the founders hundreds of years ago, these differences actually became four different types of laws, namely:

1. Only Christians should ever be allowed to serve in government;
2. Sexual immorality, drunkenness, and non-biblical divorce are to be illegal, and sexual immorality and drunkenness are to be punishable crimes against the state;
3. Working on Sunday is to be illegal and punishable; and,
4. All public schools are to be Christian schools, teaching Christian doctrine and Christian morality.

These differences between the founders and modern Christian leaders represent:

1. what the Bible commands,
2. what the founders fought for, and,
3. where God gave them the victory!

You see, modern Christian leaders are unwilling to even *propose* this type of legislation, much less *fight* for it until we win. The founders, however, evidently proposed, fought, and won all of these battles with God's help, because these types of laws were all in place during America's early history. This is what pleased God about the founders' willingness to do things God's way, but displeases God about our modern Christian leaders unwillingness to do things His way.

The founders understood (at least in part) the importance of Jehovah's principles of "justice and mercy," and surely they did not want Christ to call them "blind guides" (as he called the Pharisees) for neglecting the addition of the "more important matters of the law" (the Mosaic civil laws) to the administration of government. This is what happens when our Christian leaders remain strong in faith, yet continue to neglect the "more important matters of the law"—the Mosaic civil principles of justice and mercy. They become *blind guides* concerning Christ's vision for the establishment and administration of godly government, the very province which requires the greatest in-depth knowledge about the Mosaic civil principles of justice and mercy.

And, because of the leadership of our blind guides, today Christian citizens line up for battle but are encouraged to face the wrong direction. For instance, modern Christian leaders are content to merely *restrict access* to pornography (in movies, magazines, and on the "web"), rather than to *outlaw* pornography, by rewording the First Amendment. Had America's founders any knowledge that the First Amendment would eventually be used to justify pornography, they would have repealed and rewritten the First Amendment A.S.A.P.!

Secondly, modern Christian leaders are content to merely *restrict* homosexuality (by restricting homosexual marriages), rather than *outlaw* homosexuality and make it a regularly punishable crime against the state, as the founders did, and as the Bible commands.

Thirdly, Christian leaders are willing to encourage us to *boycott* the products sponsoring TV shows which exalt sexual immorality, but are not willing to encourage our congressmen and senators to make fornication, adultery, and homosexuality to be regularly punishable *crimes* against the state, as the founders did, and as the Bible commands.

Fourthly, they are content to *restrict access* to abortion, rather than to *outlaw* abortion, and make abortion a regularly punishable crime against the state, as the Bible commands, and certainly as the founders would have wanted.

Fifthly, they are content just to get student-initiated and student-led prayers into the public schools, rather than to get all public schools to once again become *Christian* schools, as the founders succeeded in doing and as the Bible commands. This way, the teachers can teach all American students about Christian doctrine and morality. For by doing this, all Americans would eventually be indoctrinated to obey Christ through either "salvation and surrender," or at the very least, through "training and tradition.".

Most importantly, Christians will fight to add a few "Christian restrictions" to our hostile, secular, atheistic democracy, rather than fight to change our government back to a Christian Republic, by forbidding non-Christians from ever being able to serve in government, in accordance with God's commands, the founders wishes, and the wording of many of the original state constitutions. You see, government becomes progressively more susceptible to corruption with the addition of every non-Christian, agnostic, atheist, idolator, or sexually immoral person who is allowed to assist in running the government.

All of these issues represent what God helped America's founders to accomplish for us. But what America lost over the last couple of centuries is not what modern Christian leaders are trying to regain. This is because the political strategy of our Christian leaders has always been to "preserve what we have left" rather then "regain what we have lost"! "Healing our land" means to "retake the ground we've lost", not just to "preserve the ground we have left"!

Furthermore, in our nation, as Satan attacks, the church falls back, setting in motion a pattern of political "defensive retreat," which has made Christianity lose so much political ground over the last two centuries that we now are dangerously close to losing the game entirely! You see, today's Christian political leaders play a game which I call, *"Creating Christian Legislation in Secular Government."* In this game, Christian political leaders attempt to preserve Christian liberty and prevent Christian persecution using a strategy of *defensive retreat,* while the opposition becomes increasingly hostile to their Christian principles.

But defensive retreat is a *loser's* strategy, and is not the strategy used by the heroes in the Bible to restore godly government. For in the Bible, the strategy which God always blessed with victory was to *change the philosophy of government!* In other words, *instead of creating Christian legislation in secular government, we need to recreate Christian government* as the founders intended and as God commands. For the best way to preserve what we have left, is to retake what we have lost.

Our secular democracy (where the majority has the power to overrule and replace God's laws) must be replaced by a Christian Republic, where God's laws reign supreme, and can never be overruled even by majority vote! This is what it means to have a land which is "healed and holy," instead of "sick and secular." It means changing the philosophy of government from a secular, atheistic, democracy back to a Christian Republic. And this is the essential difference between what America's founders did, and what modern Christian leaders refuse to do instead, and is the fundamental reason why God refuses to heal our land.

And so, Christian Americans (like the Jews), are being led by men who Jesus called *"blind guides."* These men neglect the importance of Jehovah's principles of "justice and mercy" (the Mosaic civil laws), and are content to have a "sick and secular" land (where sexual immorality, drunkenness, divorce, working on Sunday, and secular public schools remain legal), instead of a "healed and holy" land (where sexual immorality, drunkenness, divorce, working on Sunday, and secular public schools are outlawed). And because of this, America becomes more evil generation after generation.

So why does God allow us to lose even more ground decade after decade? For two reasons: First of all, God allows us to continually lose political ground to *make foolish* the wisdom of our "wise" Christian leaders (who mistakenly believe that the Mosaic civil laws—Jehovah's principles of justice and mercy—are neither needed today nor are they valid today), and to *magnify* this problem in our eyes until we realize that we are helpless unless we begin to do things His way!

Secondly, God allows us to continually lose political ground to teach us that *God will not lead us to national victory just to be a silent partner in our government, any more than God will not lead an individual to personal victory and salvation just to be a silent partner in his personal life*. For He wants to be the major voice of authority in both our national government, and in our personal lives, so that, "When Jehovah talks ... people listen"!

You see, the Lord of Lawmakers does not want only partial control of the government in America (like he would have in a secular democracy), any more than he wanted only partial control of the government of ancient Israel. God refuses the position of a silent partner with limited authority when it comes to either running our lives or running our government. Christ wants to sit on the throne and have the type of full control that He would have in a Christian Republic! *If this is not what our Christian leaders are after, then He will not lead us to victory, He will not heal our land, and we will continue to lose ground decade after decade.*

In the Bible, just as God would only "heal Israel's land" when Israel's leaders were willing to enforce God's civil laws, so also God will only "heal our land" when America's leaders are willing to enforce God's civil laws as well. In other words, we must do this exactly God's way or He will not heal our land for us, and this project of creating a true nation under God will never come to pass.

So, *our political agenda must line up precisely with His political agenda, and then God will give us the victory and heal our land!* Any other political agenda represents a false sense of confidence and pride in *ourselves* and what *we* believe *we* can accomplish on our *own,* by merely adding a few Christian restrictions to the legislation of a completely secular, anti-Christian government, instead of having the faith and obedience to recreate a purely Christian form of government as the founders did and as the Bible commands.

I believe that Christian leaders demonstrate their lack of faith in five ways:

1. They don't trust that God's principles of civil law (Jehovah's principles of justice and mercy) are important to run governments.

2. They don't trust that Christ (as Jehovah) really knew what he was doing when He wrote these laws, and therefore they mistakenly believe that the Mosaic principles of civil law are neither *valid* nor *advantageous* for administering sound and virtuous government, especially when compared to the more familiar secular and atheistic political principles which we currently use instead.

3. They only trust in what *they* can see and that *they* can accomplish politically with *their* own limited strength.

4. They are only willing to walk by sight, and not by faith, and are unwilling to step out in faith onto a political road where they cannot see the end from the beginning.

5. They do not believe the truth of the expression that "God would not give a nation any command which he would not also somehow *enable* that nation to fulfill"!

You see, our Christian leaders want Christ as their *spiritual* leader, but they do not want Christ as their *political* leader. For they see Christ only as . . .

1. the "Lord of *Love*," not the "Lord of *Lawmakers*";
2. the author of perfect *moral* law, but not the author of perfect civil law;
3. the architect who drew the blueprints for the laws of *nature*, but not the architect of the biblical blueprint for *perfect self-government*.

Our Christian leaders have deliberately closed their eyes to the importance of God's principles of civil law, and so they have become blind guides who no longer know which way to lead Christians in American politics. Our Christian leaders therefore, must . . .

1. recognize their pride (in believing they know better than the Lord of Lawmakers how to write godly laws and how to create godly government),
2. humble themselves,
3. repent of both their lack of vision and their lack of faith in these areas, and
4. turn from their wicked ways (of rejecting the important role that Jehovah's principles of civil law have in the administration of sound, virtuous, and godly government), or God will never heal our land!

You see, the Bible also teaches that the spiritual blindness of the *leaders* has always been more important than the spiritual blindness of the ordinary *citizens*. In other words, 2 Chronicles 7:14 should be understood to mean:

> If my people's *leaders*, who are called by my name, will humble themselves and pray, and turn from their wicked ways, then will I hear from heaven, forgive their sin, and heal their land!

See the point? The Christian political cause will suffer progressive defeat decade after decade, unless we can count on God's miraculous divine intervention. And *He will only intervene if we aim for His target, and play by His rules!*

But, our Christian leaders feel they will fail, and lose the Christian political battle if we try to do what I suggest. But I tell you that we are failing now, and losing ground with each passing decade, as our nation gets more immoral and more intolerant to Christian doctrine and morality. We are failing and losing precisely because our nation lacks the very things that the founders fought for but that modern Christian leaders ignore—God's principles of civil law! And this is why God is not helping us as we'd like, or else we would have won the battle already!

Please don't think that we are failing because we don't have committed Christians today, for Christians today are no less committed than in the days of our founders. It's just that we are much less committed to running our government God's way than the founders were! And, please don't think that we are failing because we have less evangelism today, for today we have several fold more Christian evangelism than in the days of our founders, for we have more Christian TV, radio, magazines, videos, evangelistic campaigns (such as Evangelism Explosion), as well as wonderful Christian organizations like *Promise Keepers, Campus Crusade for Christ, Focus on the Family,* the *700 Club,* the *American Family Association, Concerned Women for America, Wallbuilders,* the *Providence Foundation,* the *Institute for Creation Research, Answers in Genesis,* the *American Center for Law and Justice,* the *Rutherford Institute,* the *Center for Christian Statesmanship,* and the prison ministries of Chuck Colson and others, just to name a few!

No, certainly we are not failing because of lack of evangelism or lack of commitment. We are just committed to a different political agenda than our founders were, and to a different political agenda than God commands. We have not achieved victory because our Christian political leaders have set goals which are not God's goals and their vision for America is not God's vision for America.

I also suspect that some of our Christian leaders mistakenly believe that a purely Christian form of government would not be wise in the long run and would be unfair to a large minority of our pluralistic citizens. However, the same claim of unfairness could have been made in ancient Israel as well, but this did not stop Jehoshaphat, Josiah, or Nehemiah from following God's commands (and receiving God's blessing), so why should it stop us?

Christian leaders need to forsake their political reputations, step out in faith, and declare in one voice that we know that God will bless America if we go back to the basics, stop being embarrassed by God's principles of civil law, and exalt Jesus Christ as the Lord of Lawmakers and the architect of the biblical blueprint for perfect self-government. Therefore, all Christian statesmen and other Christian leaders who have a passion to see America adopt God's principles of civil law into our government, must meet together one day in Washington to make a covenant with almighty God that "God's laws will once again be America's laws"!

For only then will God "heal our land," when our Christian leaders stop practicing "Christian politics as usual," step out in faith, and attempt instead to change the philosophy of government from secular to Christian. We must stop attempting only what we think is possible to accomplish by our own efforts and attempt instead what is clearly impossible to achieve by our own efforts! Then, God will finally step in to answer our prayers, give us the victory, and heal our land. For God will not command our nation to do something which he will not also enable us to accomplish with his divine help!

This is most likely when God will grant us the national revival for which we have so long prayed. You see, if God merely gave America hundreds of local revivals, spread out over the entire nation over several decades, He could accomplish the same *spiritual* objectives, but not the same political objectives. When separate local revivals are spread out over such a long period of time, it becomes not the same *political* objectives. It would be much harder to achieve as great a voting majority of Christian conservatives when the revival has long faded away in some areas of the country before it has even started in other areas of the country.

On the other hand, during a nationwide revival (when the entire nation experiences the same revival over a short period of time—perhaps about two years), the hearts of the voting majority of our citizens will be softened enough and for long enough to be willing to vote to reestablish a Christian Republic. However, God will not grant a national revival until we understand that the political responsibilities which go along with a national revival include changing the government to conform to God's commands, by replacing the government's secular and atheistic foundation with a foundation which is Christian and biblical.

When viewed in this manner, America's problems have probably always been easy to solve—if God's *people* would only try doing it God's *way,* and with God's *help!* But up to this point, because we insist on doing it our way, we also have been doing it without much of God's help. You see, at the moment, Christianity in America is still losing the war because God is only willing to grant us tiny "defensive victories" just to let us know what almighty power could be available to us if we would only just go on the offensive, and do it God's way!

Now I have to tell you one more thing before we move on to part two of this chapter. Although we have several wonderful Christian legal organizations which have won many legal battles to preserve Christian freedom and liberty, we are losing the overall war. For America is still becoming more and more evil with each passing year.

You see, the strategy of these Christian legal organizations (as wonderful and as successful as it may be in the courtroom) is actually a *loser's* strategy when it comes to the overall battle plan of winning our national war against Satan and secular humanism. Our battle tactics only amount to defending Christian liberty, but never include the strategy of attacking and destroying the opposition: the ACLU itself! This would be like America defending Europe in WWII without ever attacking the German forces themselves.

For instance, suppose that during WWII, when American and Allied soldiers went into France to defend the towns being attacked by the German army, that we only tried to rebuild the towns destroyed by Hitler and prevent further attacks upon these same destroyed towns. However, we never attacked the German army itself, allowing them to leave the town we were defending and move on to other towns which had not yet been attacked. This ridiculous idea would actually be a loser's strategy, wouldn't it?

This is just what we are doing with the ACLU! For in the courtroom we vigorously and successfully defend Christian liberty and attempt to stop Christian persecution by the ACLU. However, since we never attack the ACLU itself, then we leave them free to go from town to town and continue their monstrous assaults on Christianity over and over again elsewhere throughout our nation. This is incredibly shortsighted! How could we ever have won WWII without ever attacking the German army? But this is exactly how we fight against the ACLU!

What we need to do however, is to make a law (or an amendment) which states that whenever a lawyer, organization of lawyers, judge, or group of judges repeatedly attempts to maliciously use the influence of the law to harass individual Christians or Christian organizations (for using their historical legal rights as Christians), that they are to be fired (as lawyers), impeached (as judges), disbarred from practicing law again anywhere in the U.S. and prosecuted for maliciously using their legal expertise to harass Christian citizens. For it should be considered *treason* to use the power of the law to undermine our nation's historical Christian heritage. Surely the founders of America would have destroyed the ACLU organization long ago, for they thought it *treason* to attack the institution of Christianity, because Christianity was the foundation of our civil liberties!

This is just one more example of how Christian leaders need to face the right direction and pick the right battles. God will grant us the victory, little by little, just as He helped the Israelites to conquer Canaan little by little!

II. THE IMPORTANCE OF NATIONAL PRAYER (AND FASTING), AND THE IMPORTANCE OF A NATIONAL RECOMMITMENT TO GOD!

The Bible teaches that if God would actually heal our land (in response to our prayers), then America would be transformed from a secular democracy (where God's laws can be overruled simply by majority vote) into a true nation under God—a Christian Republic (where God's laws reign supreme, and can never be overruled, even by majority vote). God has always wanted His principles of civil law to be the foundation of sound, virtuous, and godly government—the philosophy of which would inevitably exalt Jehovah (the pre-incarnate Christ) as the Lord of Lawmakers and the King of Kings!

Most Christians who are praying for God to heal our land are actually *not* praying for God to change the foundation of our nation's government from the atheistic and secular democracy that we currently have, to a true Christian Republic. In fact, most Christians are fooling themselves into believing that they want God to heal our land, when in reality, all they want is to have a few Christian restrictions added to our current secular democracy. They are otherwise content to leave the philosophy of our government essentially unchanged, so Washington can continue to be run by non-Christians who would like nothing better than to remove any trace of Christian influence from our nation.

In other words, most Christians are actually praying for just the *opposite* of what God wants for America's government. And prayer does *not* work, when we are praying for just the *opposite* of what God wants!

This is so paradoxical, for most Christians claim that they would love to live in a world where Christ reigns supreme. During the future millennial reign of Christ on earth (where Christ will heal the land of all nations) Christians will be *enthusiastically* living under the exact conditions which we so *resist* having in America today, where all God's principles of moral and civil law will be regularly enforced, by using God's principles of civil law enforcement.

This tells God that most Christians in our nation really do *not* want a government which actually enforces God's laws, and would rather have our land remain sick and secular, than become healed and holy! They'd rather tolerate a secular democracy than live in a Christian Republic!

Our Christian prayer warriors must also realize that the true healing of our land would actually change the philosophy of our government to be consistent with what the founders wanted and what the Bible commands. The Constitution of the U.S. would be left essentially unchanged. So, we must begin to pray for God to heal America from the sickness of atheistic, secular democracy, and restore us to the health of a true Christian Republic.

Therefore, we must all understand what God really wants, work for what He really wants, and be willing to live under the conditions which He really wants to establish for America (and which He has always wanted to re-establish for Israel). Otherwise, *our prayers reveal to God that we really don't want to live in a truly Christian society based completely upon biblical principles, but would rather live in a secular society which had a few Christian restrictions and traditions!*

Now that we know what God truly wants for America, we can pray with greater boldness and confidence—for this "impossible" task truly requires divine intervention on a national scale!

So what do we need to do to rededicate our government into God's hands?

Well, first of all, to accomplish this task, we need groups of prayer warriors from all fifty states who are dedicated to:

1. pray specifically for God to enable our current Christian leaders to propose and pass legislation to outlaw sexual immorality, drunkenness, non-biblical divorce, working on Sunday, atheistic public education, and non-Christians working for our government;

2. pray specifically for God to raise up an abundance of new Christian statesmen to assist our current Christian leaders in this great task;

3. pray for the future Christian statesmen to be able to withstand any vicious verbal attacks which may come from all quarters (especially from secular political leaders, the press, or even from other Christians) for daring to try to outlaw sexual immorality and drunkenness according to God's principles of civil law;

4. pray specifically for God to enable the message of this book to be spread throughout America by educating our Christian spiritual and political leaders as well as educating all Christian voters on the advantages of adopting and regularly enforcing God's principles of civil law as the foundation of our local, state, and national legislation;

5. pray specifically for God to raise up a multitude of godly Christians to assist our leaders in all facets of this task, and to coordinate all these activities on local, state, and national levels;

6. pray for Christian philanthropists to step out in faith and assist in defraying the costs of some of the future expenses involved in this task;

7. pray that the entire congregation of the Christian Coalition, Promise Keepers, National Right to Life, Focus on the Family, and all our largest Christian organizations will descend upon Washington D.C. in the largest political rally this nation has even seen, and in one voice, commit themselves to creating a newborn Christian Republic which can be slowly developed into a true nation under God;

8. pray that our current "National Day of Prayer" can be devoted to asking God to enable us to create a true nation under God, and if possible, change this day to a "National Day of Prayer and Fasting" for this purpose;

9. pray that this project can be promoted and advertised in all Christian and political circles through Christian radio, TV, magazines, churches, preaching, teaching, fliers, etc.; and finally,

10. just as in the days of Nehemiah, pray that all our Christian political leaders will have the humility and the courage to join together in Washington for public confession, repentance, and recommitment of our national leadership and our nation's government back into the service of Jesus Christ—the Lord of Lawmakers and the King of Kings. With His enabling power, we will indeed be victorious in enacting God's laws to be America's laws and establishing America as a newborn Christian Republic on her way to becoming a true nation under God!

III. EDUCATION

Since education is the foundation of God's laws of self-government, then education must also be the foundation of any attempt to implement God's laws of self government back into America's legislation. Unfortunately, the Church has generally been very resistant to the idea that America's civil problems can be solved using God's civil laws, and often mistakenly teaches that only God's moral laws are still relevant today. However, God's rules for governing yourself are His moral laws, but God's rules for self-government are His civil laws. So, since the Church does not want to use the answer proposed by almighty God, then He will not assist us in solving our national problems.

First of all, we must educate the Christian spiritual leaders and the Christian political leaders in all God's principles of moral law, civil law, and civil law enforcement, as well as in all Jehovah's other laws of self-government which are listed in this book. We'll then begin to realize that our national problems can be solved by the use of God's principles of civil law and civil law enforcement. Once this is accomplished, then each Christian leader, legislator, preacher, teacher, denomination leader, and seminary professor can further disseminate this information throughout his sphere of influence.

We also need a committee to coordinate the development of a Christian governors society, a Christian statesmen society, a society of Christian U.S. Senators and Congressmen, a society of Christian State Senators and Congressmen, a society of Christian lawyers and judges, and a Christian philanthropist society.

We must eliminate the congressional chaplains, because it is the Christian statesmen themselves who must begin to pray publicly (in the congressional chambers) and lead entire congresses and senates in prayer about all of the legislation they are about to vote upon. Any Christian leader who feels uncomfortable about leading other national leaders in public prayer is certainly not qualified to lead our nation back to God! Either he does not have the personal relationship with Christ that he needs to be saved (and which he needs to lead our nation back to God) or he doesn't realize how often the Bible records that God would *not* help Israel in their hour of need until after the leaders of Israel engaged in *public prayer* to rededicate the nation of Israel back into God's service. If God required public prayer by ancient Israel's national leaders before God would bless Israel, then surely he requires public prayer by our leaders before God will bless America. So, our leaders themselves need to be thoroughly trained in both godliness and the biblical principles of civil law, so our senators and congressmen can implore each other daily to create new legislation which will conform to the will of almighty God. For God's laws need to be our laws, and then God will bless America!

By the way, in order to help Christianity have a greater and more uniform political influence throughout the United States, we must also make a new law which will stop the IRS from continually threatening to take away the tax-exempt status from the Christian Coalition, churches, and from other Christian organizations which seek to become politically active and support Christian candidates by name or by party. To keep this effect working well, we must also legislate that any and all IRS workers who harass or threaten Christian organizations with loss of their tax-exempt status because of political involvement will be fired. Following this, they will be prosecuted for violating this new law.

IV. WHICH BIBLICAL PRINCIPLES OF CIVIL LAW SHOULD AMERICA ADOPT FIRST?

Now the first thing which needs to be done is to change the system of justice and punishment. America's courtrooms should be designed to reflect the same type of justice and mercy which God himself would dispense if He were actually sitting in the judge's seat in the courtroom. The judge must realize that he is judging on behalf of God himself, and that finding God's truth is more important than the mere legal technicalities of man's law. This concept that truth is more important than technicality should guide the reconstruction of our courtroom procedures. Because of this, all of the legal technicalities which interfere with finding God's truth in the courtroom should be repealed. Furthermore, the death penalty is foundational to any understanding of God's courtroom procedures. There are eighteen standard death penalties recorded in the Bible, but only two of them contain God's command to "show no mercy"—first degree murder and idolatry. So, for the lesser sixteen biblical felonies, God has basically provided a standard punishment of death, from which the judges are required to show mercy if at all possible. (Mic. 6:8 NIV).

The biblical principles for the judicial administration of mercy involve the administration of any punishment which is less than the standard punishment. For instance, if the crime is a biblical felony and standard punishment is death, the convicted criminal may instead receive a whipping (anywhere from a mere one lash up to a maximum of forty lashes) as a merciful alternative to execution. This is only if the criminal is very repentant and the judge decides to be merciful. Additionally, for the violent criminal who seriously injures his victims, the standard punishment is an "eye for an eye"! But, if the judge decides to be merciful, the criminal may instead receive a mere whipping as a merciful alternative to an "eye for an eye."

Also, since God is merciful and not cruel, he would not want biblical whips to be designed as cruel instruments of torture, to cut the flesh and to leave multiple bleeding wounds which heal with ugly scars. Therefore, these simple biblical whips were not supposed to have any stones, bones, glass, metal, or nails attached to them to cause any type of serious or permanent injury. They are supposed to be designed only to inflict a short period of pain followed by complete recovery. Additionally, the whipping is to occur in front of the judge, so the judge can not only see the criminal's back at all times (to insure that the punishment is not causing any serious or permanent damage), but also so the judge can hear any cries for mercy. In this way, the judge (who is commanded by God to love mercy), can immediately demonstrate the mercy of God in either case, by stopping the whipping if he deems it necessary or appropriate.

Lastly, for first time offenders who are clearly repentant or extremely young, the judge may decide to demonstrate God's mercy and totally forgive them and not punish them at all. Instead, he would be given a warning that if he does the same crime again, he then will be whipped at the very least, or, whatever punishment he should have had for the first crime will then be added to his next punishment. This is only should the judge so conclude that the criminal's repentance for the first crime was deceitful.

For example, drunkenness carries a death penalty in the Bible. But the judge is expected to show a great deal of mercy to a teenager who unexpectedly gets drunk the first time he tries any alcohol at all, or to the husband who got drunk because his wife just passed away. On the other hand, the repetitive drunkard will be first whipped a few lashes, then double whipped for his next episode of drunkenness, then triple whipped, up to a maximum of forty lashes. After this time it is clear that if he does it again, he must be executed, because his previous claims of repentance have evidently been deceitful, revealing that he doesn't just disobey God's laws, but he actually despises God's laws.

Furthermore, the biblical principle of placing a tattoo on the back of the criminal's hand for crimes committed against God and man (the "Mark of Justice"—see chapter ten) can itself be a great deterrent to future crimes, and can also be used in addition to being whipped as another merciful, tax-free alternative to execution.

So, the creative application of God's principles of merciful justice affords the judge several tax-free methods of administering mercy to those who have committed crimes which have standard death penalties! Please remember this concept when you review the crimes listed below.

PRISON REFORM (SEE CHAPTER TEN)

America needs to adopt God's five tax-free biblical alternatives to imprisonment. These are:

1. *execution;*
2. an *"eye for an eye"* (for violent criminals who seriously injure their victims);
3. *whipping,* from one to forty lashes (as a merciful alternative to an "eye for an eye" or to execution, or for miscellaneous crimes which have no other specified penalty);
4. the *"mark of justice"* (placing a tattoo on the back of the criminal's hand to indicate the date, the crime, and the punishment received—i.e., the mark of Cain; and,
5. a six-year period of *indentured servanthood* (for thieves who cannot pay back a multiple of the value of what they have stolen).

If America can adopt these five tax-free biblical alternatives to imprisonment, then our nation should never again require an expensive tax-sponsored prison system. For God's five biblical alternatives to imprisonment will provide a much greater deterrent to crime, solve all our prison problems, and save hundreds of billions of dollars in taxes at the same time!

COURT REFORM (SEE CHAPTERS EIGHT AND NINE)

In God's system of justice as recorded in the Bible, no guilty person will ever go unpunished just because of a mere technicality. In fact, according to the Bible, there should be:

6. no Miranda Warnings, for there is no fictitious right to not confess your sins;
7. no insanity defense;
8. no diplomatic immunity;

9. no technicalities of any kind (which can allow the unrepentant guilty to go unpunished);
10. no appeals or retrials for anyone sentenced to death;
11. "Pleading the Fifth Amendment" and plea bargaining must be replaced by confession, repentance, and pleading for mercy, in order to create a courtroom ministry of mercy;
12. Parole Officers (secular accountability individuals) must be replaced with Christian accountability groups. These are recruited from the local Christian community (as an alternative to prison ministries) to create a courtroom (and community) ministry of restoration to restore the criminal to a right relationship with his God, with his community, and with the fellowship of believers;
13. eliminate trial by jury by repealing the Fourteenth Amendment. This is because jury trials are not biblical, and because of all the problems associated with jury trials;
14. all judges should know all of God's principles of civil law and civil law enforcement.

Furthermore, God holds citizens responsible if they bear false witness against the innocent or refuse to bear truthful witness against the guilty. Therefore:

15. America needs to punish malicious witnesses by God's principles. These principles say that whatever punishment the innocently accused defendant would have received (if the deliberate deceit of the malicious witness had not been uncovered) must now be done to the malicious witness instead. This will stop all malicious witnesses from deliberately giving false testimony in court; and,
16. according to the Bible, God wants citizens to be legally held responsible if they don't testify about some crime that they know about. This means that they may even get punished if it turns out, for example, that they purposely withheld information which could have stopped a serial killer and saved lives.

JUSTICE REFORM

17. for first degree murder, God commanded in the Bible that these convicted criminals must always be executed, for God said to "show no pity." Furthermore, they were to receive neither mercy, nor a retrial (see chapter eight and Lev. 27:29 NIV); and,
18. for merely accidentally injuring a pregnant woman such that she has a miscarriage and prematurely delivers a dead infant (an abortion), the Bible carries a maximum penalty of death (Exod. 21:22-23 NIV). In fact, this law makes abortion to be the only

crime in the Bible that a person can do by accident and still possibly suffer the penalty of death.

Imagine how angry God would be if the pregnant woman and a doctor conspired together to purposely take the life of the baby. This verse implies that a purposeful abortion (at any stage of pregnancy where a miscarriage would cause the delivery of a recognizable infant of any size) should be equivalent to deliberate first degree murder and require a death penalty without mercy, of both the mother and the doctor.

In modern America we don't have a lot of problems with citizens accidentally injuring pregnant women and causing miscarriages, but we do have a terrible problem with purposeful abortion. And, with blood testing and ultrasound equipment, we can now creatively apply these biblical principles concerning the crime of abortion to any stage of pregnancy, such that a purposeful abortion (in any stage of pregnancy) would again require that both the mother and the doctor be punished. But, the Bible implies that a recognizable infant must be delivered (regardless of the state of its injuries) in order to declare this to be deliberate, first degree murder, and therefore absolutely require the death penalty for both mother and doctor. By implication then, at earlier stages of pregnancy, a purposeful abortion would not absolutely require the death penalty for mother and doctor, but would allow the judge to show mercy if the judge can possibly be convinced that the participants have confessed that their sin is an abomination in the eyes of God and man, and have demonstrated to the judge's satisfaction that they are sincerely repentant. In this case, the judge would probably allow for a mere whipping (from one lash up to a maximum of forty lashes) as a merciful alternative to execution.

However, if the doctor continued to perform abortions, then it would be clear to the judge that doctor doesn't just disobey God's laws, but that he actually despises God's laws, and he would therefore be executed without mercy according to the law of the profligate, because he continues to repeatedly, and unrepentantly, break God's laws!

These are the biblical principles concerning the punishment for those who either obtain or perform purposeful abortions. Our God has always wanted these principles to be adopted by Israel, by the United States, and by the rest of the world. It's about time that America did just that.

For the entire group of crimes listed below, God also commanded a standard penalty of execution, but again did not say to "show no pity". Therefore, all the crimes in the next group carry a standard penalty of death, but the judges are encouraged to show mercy if at all possible (i.e., to those very young or very repentant first, second or third time criminals, etc.). In other words, they could be whipped, with or without being given a tattoo on the hand to document their punishment, or they could be totally forgiven without any punishment at all. Therefore, for the crimes listed below, death becomes the maximum punishment, but not the mandatory punishment. These crimes are as follows:

19. kidnapping—maximum of death penalty;
20. drunkenness and drug abuse—carry a standard death penalty from which we are encouraged to show mercy, perhaps by a whipping as a merciful alternative to execution versus total forgiveness;
21. profligate—a "three-time loser" (so to speak) who is obviously unrepentant, or, by the repetitive nature of his crimes has revealed that his past claims of repentance have clearly been deceitful. Such a man, doesn't just disobey God's law, but actually despises God's law. Since he probably has already received forty lashes as his previous courtroom punishment (the maximum allowed by God's law), then the next step is that he must be executed before he leads others astray by his example of repetitive unrepentant disobedience;
22. adultery and homosexuality—maximum of death penalty, or a merciful whipping as an alternative to execution, with or without a tattoo, or total forgiveness for first time repentant offenders, or divorce as another merciful alternative to execution, for repetitive, unrepentant adultery or homosexuality; and,
23. prostitution and bestiality—same as above.

Now the next group of crimes do not have standard death penalties according to the Bible, but would therefore require a creative application of the principles of an "eye for an eye," whipping, or placing a tattoo of the back of the hand. The only way these criminals can be executed is if they continue to repeat these same crimes (or other crimes), and therefore revealed that they were amoral profligates. In this case, they would be punished according to the law for a profligate, and if, after having received the maximum of forty lashes for the previous crime, they repeat the crime once again, then they could be executed. These are as follows:

24. violent criminals who cause serious injury to their victims—their punishment is to be an "eye for an eye" with or without a possible whipping, with or without a possible tattoo;
25. violent wife abuse and child abuse—again, their punishment would be an "eye for an eye," with or without a possible whipping, with or without a possible tattoo;
26. rape—If either person was married or engaged (but not to each other) the punishment for the rapist is the same as adultery, with a standard death penalty, or a whipping as a possible merciful

alternative to execution. However, if both were virgins, and it is proven that they had quite an affection for each other, and that this was actually a date rape, then the punishment is that they are to get married, unless the father says otherwise (Deut. 22:28-29 NIV). In contrast, if the virgin victim dislikes or doesn't even know the virgin rapist, who has been stalking and harassing her and then violently raped her, then the father most likely will forbid the marriage, and seek to have the virgin rapist prosecuted. If convicted, he would be:

   A. probably whipped (from one to forty lashes),
   B. possibly receive an "eye for an eye" or, a "groin injury for a groin injury,"
   C. possibly receive a tattoo on the back of the hand, revealing the date, the crime, and punishments received.

27. sexual harassment of adults—whipping (from one to forty lashes) as a merciful alternative to the maximum punishment of "cutting off the hand" (see Deut. 25:11-12 NIV) plus a possible tattoo;
28. sexual child molestation—same punishment as for sexual harassment of adults;
29. pornography—Since pornography encourages lust, fornication, adultery, homosexuality and rape, the same themes of biblical justice would command punishment for all those who participate in the pornography industry, probably by a whipping from one to forty lashes (since whipping is God's flexible punishment for miscellaneous crimes which carry no other specified punishment). If however, after receiving multiple whippings the pornographers continued to practice this crime, they could be executed according to the law of the profligate;
30. reckless endangerment of human life by a domestic animal (i.e., a pit bull) which is owned by a citizen, and for which the owner deliberately does not keep the animal penned up, will cause the owner to be in danger of losing his own life, if the animal attacks and kills a person. The animal is also to be destroyed if it attacks and injures a human (Exod. 21:28-29 NIV).

Gun Control (see Chapter Eleven)

31. Now in the Bible, God does not outlaw weapons as a means of deterring violent crime. For God's method of deterring violence is by regular, predictable, and severe punishment of the violent criminal who seriously injures his victim.

However, the Bible makes it clear (in Isa. 2:2-4; Mic. 4:2-3) that during the future reign of Christ on earth (when God's civil laws will finally be implemented completely and correctly) men will voluntarily disarm and destroy their own weapons of self-defense and weapons of war. They will do this by:

beating swords into plowshares and spears into pruning hooks"

when the need for self-protection from violence and war is finally over.

In other words, the Bible teaches that regular implementation of God's principles of civil law enforcement has the potential to totally eliminate the need for weapons of self-protection. Therefore, citizens will eventually give up these types of weapons voluntarily, and the issue of gun control will finally go away.

GOVERNMENT REFORM (SEE CHAPTER FIVE)

32. According to the Bible, only godly Christian elders should ever be allowed to serve in government. There are no term limits, but if the man ever commits a serious personal sin (i.e., sexual immorality, drunkenness, etc.) or approves any anti-biblical legislation which would encourage American citizens to sin by perhaps becoming more immoral, then he is to be immediately impeached and prosecuted. If convicted, then he must be sentenced for the crimes he has committed against God and man.

PRO-FAMILY LEGISLATION (SEE CHAPTER EIGHTEEN)

33. Divorce must again become illegal unless your spouse commits a sin which is also a crime (i.e., adultery or drunkenness).
34. America must make a law which creates the custom to "Honor thy father and mother" and "Rise in the presence of the aged";
35. American families must again use physical discipline at home, which may even include using the rod as recommended in the Bible;
36. Government must begin to support the parents' right to physically punish their own children, by making it a crime for any offspring to curse or attack his or her parents at any time, but especially while being instructed, rebuked, or punished.

EDUCATION POLICY (SEE CHAPTER TWENTY-FOUR)

37. America must make all public schools once again be Christian schools;
38. All education must be taught from a biblical foundation, which represents God's point of view;
39. American schools must again use physical discipline for repeatedly troublesome students, even if it means to use the proverbial "hickory stick" (the "rod").

Economic Policy (see Chapter Twenty-One)

40. Since the tithe in the Bible is a flat 10 percent tithe on income (and not a graduated or sliding scale tithe), then any income taxes in the United States should also all be flat taxes and not graduated taxes (remember, God knows best!);
41. There are no inheritance taxes in the Bible, so there should likewise be no inheritance taxes in the United States;
42. There are no property taxes in the Bible, so there should be no property taxes in the United States either;
43. We need to outlaw gambling as a first step to outlaw the usury industry.

Worship Policy (see Chapter Seventeen)

44. America must somehow begin to phase in God's blue law, and begin to again make it illegal to do any money making work on Sunday. The only exceptions to this biblical principle is working in the preaching, healing, and rescuing businesses! Home meal preparation is also allowed, but even yard work is to be forbidden. This will get the majority of America's population back into church, so we can once again be a "churched" nation which obeys God's laws—either because of salvation and surrender, or, at the very least, because of training and tradition and godly peer pressure.

Health Care Policy (see Chapter Twenty)

45. Biblical principles on healthcare dictate that America must outlaw the tobacco industry, and make it illegal to manufacture, distribute, import, or sell cigarettes and other tobacco products. The American government can help the tobacco farmers and other individuals in the tobacco industry during this transition by a two year subsidy to assist them in changing to another crop or to find another job. The money for this two year subsidy can be found in the twelve billion dollars the U.S. gives away annually to foreign nations in our foreign aid programs, and from the seven billion dollars America spends annually on NASA to prove whether there is life in outer space—two projects which are directly contrary to biblical principles.

Welfare Policy (see Chapter Nineteen)

46. The Bible has several principles of welfare reform, but one of these principles is that poor people should be allowed to purchase food at cost, as a tax-free alternative to an expensive food stamp program and welfare program. God probably also wanted

this principle to be extended to include other inexpensive non-perishable items as well.

FOREIGN POLICY (SEE CHAPTER TWENTY-THREE)

The Bible records certain stories about Israel's international relationships with other nations, which, when put together, spell out God's foreign policy for Israel. The reasons behind God's foreign policy are so sound that America must adopt these same policies as well. These policies include:

47. selective economic isolation;
48. China is no longer to have a "most favored nation" status, but in fact, should fall into great disfavor;
49. America is to start collecting on all foreign loans, with interest. If the nation cannot pay, then America must collect the collateral;
50. stop all secular and governmental foreign aid (but private Christian organizations may still provide as much Christian charity as they desire and can afford);
51. all American Ambassadors should also be trained as Christian missionaries, so they can explain the benefits of living with Christ as Savior of citizens and as Lord of Lawgivers. In this way, they can not only share Christ with the foreign leaders, but can also show them how to rebuild their nation's government according to biblical principles.
52. America must no longer participate in the United Nations, because of their many anti-biblical priorities.

MILITARY POLICY (SEE CHAPTER TWENTY-TWO)

The Bible also records stories about Israel's military interactions with other nations, which illustrate God's military policy for Israel, and for all other nations as well. These policies include the following:

53. no selling of military weapons to foreign nations;
54. no military intervention in foreign countries;
55. America's military is not to be policeman of the world;
56. our military must recruit only Christian men;
57. no homosexuals or women are ever to serve in the armed forces;
58. military policy is to include chastity and reverence for Christ;
59. God favors smaller armies with less weaponry, so at the very least, America must become more frugal with our military budget;
60. America is no longer to provide free military protection to Japan. However, Japan can pay America to rent our naval and air force protection temporarily, but only until they can build or purchase their own navy and air force to defend themselves. Furthermore,

America is not allowed by God to sell weapons, ships, or planes to Japan (or to any other nation, for that matter)!

POLITICAL IDEOLOGY

61. Christianity must become the official religion of the United States. And, according to God's commands, America must (at least in principle) outlaw idolatry (the deliberate worshipping, praying to, and bowing down to idols made of wood, stone, or metal), even if America does not yet legislate a punishment for this.

A political ideology based upon the Bible however, would also mandate that America should also change the "Pledge of Allegiance" to say,

> ... and to the *Christian* Republic, for which it stands, one nation, under God ...

Hopefully, you can now see that all the answers to America's political problems can be found precisely in those Scriptures which our Christian leaders and legislators ignore the most—the biblical principles of civil law! This large reservoir of sixty-one biblical principles of civil law can be a wonderful resource for decades to come for Christian leaders and legislators to use as the basis from which to propose future legislation for America.

But even though the task of recreating a Christian Republic will be difficult, let us not be discouraged. God will not give any nation a command which He will not also somehow enable that nation to fulfill, if that nation's Christian leaders ...

1. know what the Bible teaches should be done,
2. are willing to do what needs to be done,
3. and earnestly pray and fast for God's enabling power to open the doors and provide the way for God's Will to be accomplished.

So, let us pray that our Christian leaders and legislators will not grow weary in the great political task which almighty God has set before us— the transformation and healing of America's government from a sick and secular democracy into a healthy, Christian Republic, where God's laws will finally become America's laws.

Now adopting these biblical principles into our government's legislation will create an American culture which is much more pleasing to God. In fact, these changes will take us well beyond the dreams of our founders and move us much closer to our ultimate goal of becoming a true nation under God. I'm sure that God will respond to our national obedience by blessing America with more health, peace, and prosperity.

After our citizens have lived under these sixty-one wonderful principles for a *generation* or so (but still remember how bad things used to be in America before we became a Christian Republic), our nation will finally have become ready to take the last steps in becoming a true nation under God—the adoption of all the remaining biblical principles of civil law into America's legislation. In fact, only after America has adjusted to, and become pleased with living under the previously mentioned sixty-one principles will America be ready to adopt the rest of them. Otherwise, these latter principles would be even harder to adopt than the first set was.

Why adopt any more principles at all? Why not be content with just adopting the first sixty-one principles? Because, only by adopting all the remaining biblical principles of civil law will almighty God be pleased enough that he will begin to bless America with a nearly crime-free, poverty-free war-free, tax-free, inflation-free, natural disaster-free, and disease-free society where nearly everyone lives to be 120-years-old while remaining in excellent health!

This last group of biblical principles of civil law will be extremely difficult for America to adopt into our legislation. So, to help America get us over this difficulty, I believe that God will provide America with some type of supernatural encouragement as an incentive to continue doing the job.

For instance, it is recorded twice in the Bible that after King Asa and King Jehoshaphat re-established just a few of God's civil principles as the law of the land in their kingdoms, that God supernaturally blessed their kingdoms with a military peace with all of the surrounding nations (2 Chron. 15:15; 17:10 NIV). God gave this blessing not only as a *reward*, but also (most likely) as an *incentive* to finish adopting all of the remaining biblical principles of civil law into their legislation as well (unfortunately, the Israelites never finished the job, and so they never inherited God's richest blessings).

I believe therefore, that after our Christian legislators accomplish the task of adopting the first sixty-one biblical principles into America's legislation, that God will also bless America with some type of supernatural miracle. This would be a divine incentive for us to finish the job of adopting all of the remaining biblical principles of civil law into our national legislation as well. Furthermore, I believe that God will need to bring America *another national revival* in order to again temporarily soften the hearts of a majority of American voters. This is so that we can implement the remainder of God's "legislative package" more easily and quickly. At that time we must call for even more nationwide prayer and fasting to ask for God's aid so we can fully obey the commands He has given to us.

Now, I will make no apology for the striking nature of the following biblical principles of civil law, for they have been fully explained earlier in this book. Remember, I didn't write these principles, God wrote them! These too will somehow need to be adopted if we want God to bless America with a nearly crime-free, poverty-free, war-free, tax-free, inflation-free, natural disaster-free, and disease-free society where nearly everyone lives to be 120-years-old while remaining in excellent health! So, if you want further explanations concerning the practical advantages which these particular principles of God's civil laws have for American government, then you must reread the chapters which contain the specific biblical principles of civil law about which you have questions!

These final remaining biblical principles of civil law include the following:

WORSHIP (SEE CHAPTER SEVENTEEN)

62. Sabbath Worship—In accordance with God's Fourth Commandment which teaches,

> Remember the Sabbath day and keep it holy . . . for in six days God created the heavens and the earth and rested on the Seventh day,

Christians in America must begin to worship on the Sabbath, and not on Sunday. You see, when a society deliberately and repeatedly violates the Fourth Commandment week after week, generation after generation, and instead worships on Sunday, this undermines the authority and the validity of the rest of the Ten Commandments. It also undermines the authority of all God's other civil laws as well. This inevitably creates a nation whose Christian leaders and legislators will eventually believe that the principles underlying God's civil laws are no longer valid for the administration of sound and virtuous government, which is the same problem we have in America today.

Secondly, for thousands of other Christians, this same weekly undermining of the validity of the Ten Commandments and God's other civil laws begins to destroy the validity of many other biblical doctrines as well. This opens the door for allowing the development of liberal denominations which mistakenly teach many liberal doctrines, including the falsehoods that God actually approves of homosexuality and abortion, and that God wants the Bible and the Church to have no influence over the state.

Thirdly, worshipping and resting on the Sabbath (in honor of the Creator and his work of creation), prompts societies to perpetually believe in creation instead of evolution. This also helps to prevent liberal churches from developing and teaching false doctrines. For one of the doctrines taught in some liberal churches today is the doctrine of evolution, which implies that there never was an Adam and Eve, nor a Garden of Eden, nor a world wide flood of Noah when God punished the entire world for its sins and wickedness. Liberal congregations therefore eventually become convinced that God is not a God of wrath and punishment, but is only loving, always merciful, and never punishes either nations or individuals for their sins.

Fourthly and finally, because the unrighteous majority have no personal relationship yet with God—and therefore don't understand the importance of yielding their lives in obedient surrender to a God who forgives their sins—God knew that it would be easier to keep the unrighteous majority on their best behavior by having them worship on Saturday a God who created them and insists on their obedience, than having them worship on Sunday a God who wants to forgive them for their disobedience.

So for these four reasons, America needs to eventually switch our national day of worship from Sunday back to Saturday as God commands in the Bible. For it will certainly be much easier for Christian Americans to trust in the importance of obeying and enforcing all of God's other principles of civil law, when our culture stops deliberately violating the Fourth Commandment week after week!

JUSTICE AND PUNISHMENT (SEE CHAPTER EIGHT)

63. Idolatry—mandatory death penalty-show no mercy;
64. Blasphemy/Cursing God—(same penalty as for kidnapping—see #19);
65. Witchcraft—(same as above);
66. Working on the Sabbath—(same as above).

Now, since the penalties for blasphemy, witchcraft, and breaking the Sabbath only have execution as the standard penalty (from which we are to show mercy if at all possible), then they may receive a whipping as a merciful alternative to execution, or total forgiveness without any punishment at all for clearly repentant first-time offenders.

EXECUTION BY PUBLIC PARTICIPATION (SEE CHAPTER TWELVE)

67. God's method of execution is done in public, by the public, to *transform* the public, and has the effect of changing local community apathy to community action concerning sin and crime. This is so the local citizens will be much more likely to rebuke sin, report crime, and be involved in a Christian community watch to continue to purge their community from sin and crime like they should have been doing in the first place. In this way, local sin and crime would be stopped long before it would escalate to the point where a person would have to be executed for their crimes. Furthermore, God's method of public execution is

also the simplest, least expensive, and "lowest-tech" method of execution by public participation, and requires no significant skill from the participants, and does not endanger the participants themselves.

Pro-Large, Extended Family Legislation (see Chapter Eighteen)

68. Inheritance must be given only to males. This principle was designed by God to encourage the development of larger families with a triple economy of scale, resulting in a decrease in national poverty and welfare dependency, which results in a decrease in taxes;
69. The eldest male must have a double portion of the inheritance so that he can bear the responsibility of providing for his very old (and very young) family members. This also further encourages the development of larger families with their triple economy of scale, by providing a role model for the younger siblings that when you "grow up", your first responsibility is to stay at home and care for your family, rather than to leave home and strike out on your own;
70. Male fiancés must pay a hefty bride price to their future father-in-law before they can marry. Also, before they are married, the male fiancé must have completed building a place for his future wife and himself to live—a place which usually should be attached to his family's house. This principle was designed by God to get the idle youth "off the streets" (so to speak), and to channel their sexual passions into developing responsibility and a good work ethic. And again, this principle also contributes to the development of large, extended families, with their triple economy of scale;
71. All government anti-family incentives which financially sponsor a family member's ability to live apart from his own family must be made illegal (i.e., social security retirement and/or disability income, welfare support, etc.). This again furthers the development of large, extended families by making family members depend upon each other more. It also decreases the taxes needed to pay for supporting citizens when their own family should be doing this instead;
72. In the Bible, God legislated that men should have a dress code which included headbands, wristbands, and tassels, so that men would remember that everything they think, say, and do should be guided by God's Will. These "symbols which strengthen surrender" (the dress code for both men and women) have so many advantages that you really have to reread that chapter to

understand them all. It should suffice here to say that "if you dress the part, you will be more likely to act the part." Also, these dress codes for men and women not only help prompt the man to be the spiritual head inside the home, but also champion his role outside the home as a Christian statesman to ensure that God's laws will always be America's laws.

WELFARE REFORM (SEE CHAPTER NINETEEN)

73. We must eventually phase in a system of tithe-sponsored welfare, after which God will supernaturally bless America with great economic prosperity, just as God promised to bless Israel in the same way. For it is written:

Bring the whole tithe into the storehouse, that there may be food in my house. Test me in this . . . and see if I will not throw open the floodgates of heaven and pour out so much blessing that you will not have room enough for it. I will prevent pests from devouring your crops, and the vines in your fields will not cast their fruit . . . Then all the nations will call you blessed, for yours will be a delightful land. (Mal. 3:10-12 NIV)

This is God's promised blessing of economic prosperity to Israel, or to any other nation which can adopt and enforce all of God's principles of civil law—including the laws concerning tithe-sponsored welfare. It is God's way of repeating the promises in Leviticus 26 and Deuteronomy 28, which say that if Israel obeys God, He will make them into the richest nation on earth, as well as make them into a nearly poverty-free society.

This promised blessing is available to America today, and if we can establish a true biblical system of tithe-sponsored welfare, then God will grant us such economic prosperity that we will have a nearly "poverty-free society" as well. Then, Christians in America will more easily develop the courage to take the next leap of faith, for this miracle of national wealth and a nearly poverty-free society will go a long way to inspire confidence that all God's promises to Israel are, in fact, available to America as well.

ECONOMICS (SEE CHAPTER TWENTY-ONE)

74. The Bible teaches that all usury (lending money at interest) and all usury-related industries (insurance industries, third party payment systems, and gambling) must eventually be outlawed. The problem however, is that when any society indulges in purchasing insurance and lending money at interest, its culture changes so its citizens eventually "need" to have insurance, and "need" to borrow money at interest. In

this manner, usury creates its own "need," and therefore becomes a cultural-changing principle which is totally contrary to the Bible.

This cycle can only be broken by America's progressive obedience to God's culture-changing principles. For in response to our nation's obedience, God promises to bless America with greater family income, less family expenses, and extend our wage earning years by increasing our health and decreasing our disability. So eventually, it will become vanishingly rare for people to either die young or become disabled young. As a result, when our culture finally realizes that nearly all America's wage earners have become capable of working well past retirement age, then life insurance and disability insurance will eventually no longer be needed or purchased in our culture. So, it will become much easier to eventually outlaw the life insurance and disability insurance business.

The same thing can be said about the vanishing need for health insurance, whether private health insurance, or government sponsored health insurance (i.e., federally-sponsored Medicare, or state-sponsored Medicaid). For God promised to bless any nation with much greater health if they would adopt and implement all of his principles of moral law, civil law, and civil law enforcement.

And concerning car insurance, as drunkenness becomes vanishingly rare in our society because of the adoption of God's principles of civil law, drunk-driving related car accidents will basically disappear. Also, as God blesses America with more prosperity and happiness, the less hurried lifestyle of adults will also decrease speeding on the highway, so car accidents from speeding will also decrease. Finally, as God's principles of civil law generate a culture of conformity and godly peer pressure, the speeding and reckless driving of our teenagers will also dramatically decrease, which will, in turn, further decrease car accidents. So, one of the natural benefits of adopting the biblical principles of civil law would include a dramatic decrease in the number of car accidents from drunk driving, recklessness, and speeding—which in turn would dramatically decrease the need for car insurance.

Also, as America's obedience increases, God will begin to protect us from natural disasters, such as floods, hurricanes, tornados, and earthquakes! This will decrease the need for disaster insurance. As America adopts laws which eliminate the monetary incentive for lawyers to sue people, this will decrease the need for malpractice insurance, corporate insurance, and "umbrella" insurance.

As crime decreases, the need for theft insurance will decrease. As America becomes more community friendly and neighborhood friendly (and as the building codes become more user-friendly), communities will begin to do house raisings and to help people build (or rebuild) their houses. This will decrease the need for fire insurance. And I'm sure there are probably many other examples as well. Finally, as the large, extended family (with its triple economy of scale) eventually becomes the cultural norm for America, and as God further supernaturally blesses America with even greater family income and even less family expenses, and as the national mentality changes from spending money to saving money, then America's desire to obtain interest-bearing loans will shrink to a point where the usurious money-lending banking business will eventually disappear as well. In other words, as America adopts all of these principles, there will become less and less need for insurance or interest bearing loans of any kind, so it will be much easier than you might expect to eventually outlaw usury and usury related businesses, such as the insurance business.

So eventually, through a combination the natural blessings of national obedience, plus the supernatural blessings of divine intervention, America will finally be able to outlaw the usurious insurance industry and the usury-related functions of the banking industry.

America can also help to accomplish this task by legally tapering down interest rates until the banks can no longer make enough profits to survive by usury alone. When the interest rate finally becomes zero, then the inflation rate will also become zero. This is because the rate of inflation is always linked to the prime rate of interest. So, this will finally eliminate general inflation as well as industry-specific inflation. This will also go a long way to stop the skyrocketing costs of healthcare as well.

75. HEALTH CARE REFORM (SEE CHAPTER TWENTY)

The outlawing of the medical insurance business is discussed in detail above. But please remember that this can only be accomplished after America has adopted and implemented enough biblical principles of civil law to create two new normal cultural standards for America. First of all, the economic foundation for America must have already changed to become the large, extended family with its triple economy of scale. This is because this more stable economic unit can more easily provide for its own occasionally disabled, sick, unemployed or elderly family member without requiring outside governmental assistance. Secondly, America must have already launched a successful national program of tithe-sponsored welfare for the nation's poor who have no large, extended families to support them.

Then, God will honor the promises he gave in Malachi to "pour down on America such an economic blessing that we won't even have room enough to receive it." Thus, God will bless us with a nearly poverty-free society which will become the richest nation on earth (far richer than we are now). In other words, all Americans will be blessed by God with a much greater standard of living. It is at this time that

America will easily be able to afford her healthcare without resorting to health insurance, or government sponsored medical assistance.

I know it sounds very difficult to begin to outlaw the insurance business, but if our Christian leaders and legislators pray about this and we adopt God's principles in the proper order, then all this should fall into place.

CREATION-BASED MEDICAL RESEARCH (SEE CHAPTER TWENTY)

76. We must make prayerful, scientific, creation-based medical research the standard type of research for healthcare in America. This God-honoring research will be more likely blessed by God with greater fruitfulness, and therefore produce faster positive results at a reduced cost.

DIETARY LAWS (SEE CHAPTER TWENTY)

77. The Bible teaches that each nation should eventually find a way to outlaw the consumption of animal fat in the diet. This should go a long way to reduce obesity and obesity-related high cholesterol, high blood pressure, heart attacks and strokes. And of course, while it would be very difficult to outlaw the consumption of animal fat at home, it should be much easier to outlaw the manufacture and sale of products in supermarkets and restaurants which contain animal fat. The substitution of vegetable fat would be acceptable however, as long as it has not been partially hydrogenized or fully hydrogenized, for this is a process which takes vegetable fat and either partially or fully turns it back into animal fat once again! (Some of God's other dietary principles are discussed further in chapter twenty.)

IMMIGRATION POLICY REFORM (SEE CHAPTER TWENTY-THREE)

78. God's immigration for Israel was that anyone at all could emigrate to Israel, as long as they did not bring their sinful nature with them. If they lived within Israel's borders and worshipped idols or committed first degree murder, they were to be executed without mercy. And if they committed adultery, homosexuality, prostitution, drunkenness, kidnaping, witchcraft, abortion, working on the Sabbath, blasphemy, or attacked or cursed their parents, they were also to be placed on trial. If convicted, they were also to face the death penalty. If, however, they were very repentant, they may possibly receive a whipping as a merciful alternative to execution instead.

If they became thieves, they had to pay back a minimum of double (and up to a maximum of sevenfold) the value of what they stole, even if they had to sell all they had, or else enter a six year period of slavery to work off the debt.

If they became idle and continued to deliberately refuse to work and support themselves, then they would eventually be cast out of the system of tithe-sponsored welfare and be enslaved for the rest of their lives as the last resort of welfare support! If a native Israelite committed this same sin however, he would only enter a six-year period of slavery (indentured servanthood) after which time he must be released.

In other words, all immigrants had to obey the same civil laws which the Israelites obeyed or else face the same kinds of punishments that the Israelites would face. Most immigrants would probably not be willing to accept this risk, unless they were generally God-fearing, obedient immigrants.

So God's immigration policy would encourage righteous immigrants to move to Israel, but would discourage unrighteous immigrants from moving to Israel. Therefore, Israel would become an international magnet which would attract righteous immigrants and repel unrighteous immigrants. So, Israel would not need an expensive, tax-sponsored immigration border patrol such as America seems to need. As a result, God would bless Israel more and more with each passing decade because of the growing number of righteous citizens within her borders.

THE SABBATH YEAR AND THE "PRE-SABBATH YEAR BUMPER CROP" (SEE CHAPTER TWENTY-ONE)

79. By the time America is ready for this next legislative leap of faith, God will have already sent America many supernatural national economic blessings. This way, it will be easily clear to all of our rulers that the time is right to finally plan for America's first Sabbath year. For our Christian leaders and legislators must eventually outlaw the planting, plowing, and harvesting of America's farmlands for one whole year every seven years in accordance with God's commands in the Bible.

I expect that after our leaders finally pass this difficult legislation, that America's first Sabbath year will probably be scheduled seven years after that. During the first six years, we must pray diligently that God will give us a pre-Sabbath-year bumper crop of harvest during that sixth year. This will be so great that all of America can eat from this bumper crop during the seventh and eighth years; we would have to move out the remaining crops we still have stored up just to make room for the eighth and ninth year's harvest!

This was God's promise to Israel concerning the Sabbath year and this has many, many blessings associated with it—including the fact that God is "prepaying" the farmers and merchants to be able to forgive the outstanding balances on all loans in the Sabbath year! These biblical loans were supposed to be very small loans which were to be given to the poor for the bare necessities of life. Also, this gave the entire nation a huge vacation time to be able to relax, and have good fellowship with family, church, neighbors, and community. This latter advantage would allow time for community involvement in house raisings, courthouse raisings, and public building raisings, so we can more easily live in a society which does not require taxes to build our public buildings.

Military Policy (see Chapter Twenty-Two)

80. God wanted Israel to have very small armed forces which did not require any taxes for their support. They were never to count the size of their army, never to escalate their weaponry, never to ask other nations for assistance in battle, and never to assist any other nations in their battles either. Neither were they to intervene militarily in the affairs of foreign nations to settle their foreign wars or because of their human rights violations. Furthermore, they were to only recruit righteous men of faith, and their level of faith was more important than their level of skill.

As a result of the obedience of the army and the obedience of the entire nation of Israel, God promised that He would actually fight for Israel, and always give them victory by destroying their enemies, but yet not allow even one single soldier of the Israelite army to perish.

The purpose of God's military policy for Israel was two fold:

1. Israel had to obey God in peacetime in order to trust that God would fight for her in wartime. In other words, Israel's government had to regularly enforce all of God's principles of civil law during peacetime (in order to continually purge evil from Israel and keep the large unrighteous majority of citizens on their best behavior), otherwise God might not "show up" for the battle to defend them during wartime.

2. The power and the pageantry of the repeated supernatural victories of God's tiny armies against overwhelming odds was designed to demonstrate to the rest of the world that all nations should give up the worship of idols and worship Jehovah—the almighty God of the Israelites and the one true God of all the earth! In fact, these repeated supernatural military spectacles form the foundation of God's foreign policy as well, which is to generate an international fearful reverence for Jehovah—the God of the Israelites!

Also, by doing this, all nations would hopefully come to understand two things:

A. the importance of having a personal relationship of obedient surrender to Jehovah, and an understanding of the Mosaic teaching of salvation by grace through faith in Jehovah (who would eventually return to earth and become our Messiah, Savior and Lord—Jesus the

Christ);

B. the importance of having a national relationship with Jehovah, characterized by a government which outlaws idolatry, claims the worship of Christ as the official national religion, adopts all of God's principles of moral and civil law into their government, regularly enforces all of these principles, and only allows godly Christian elders to rule at all levels in their nation's government.

Of course, Israel never did what they were supposed to do, but these were God's commands, nevertheless, both to Israel and to all other nations. And this is why it is still God's command for America today.

I know it sounds absolutely frightening to consider having only a very small military (so small that it would require no taxes to even fund its operation), and to trust that God would regularly defend America by supernatural means whenever we were attacked, but this is exactly what God wanted for Israel and this is therefore exactly what he wants for America as well. However, it is also pretty obvious that this is almost the last principle to implement, for America's government and culture must be completely obedient to God for us to be able to completely count on God's regular supernatural defense time after time.

Also, by the time America's Christian leaders and legislators are prepared to take this last leap of faith, our American citizens will also be just as ready. For by this time, we will already have seen first hand, not only God's miraculous economic blessings as a result of creating a national system of tithe-sponsored welfare, but also our citizens will have seen God regularly giving American farmers and merchants a pre-Sabbath year bumper crop of harvest every seventh year for several decades. Furthermore, just as God supernaturally protected both Washington himself and Washington's army multiple times during the Revolutionary War, so also, Americans will begin to see God work many additional military miracles to strengthen our faith and our resolve to eventually obey God even further in the future by shrinking our army according to Bible principles.

So little by little, God will demonstrate to our Christian leaders and legislators that he will indeed miraculously defend our country as a reward for our obedient efforts to become a true nation under God, just like He promised to defend Israel.

So let's not discard these last principles; let's just hold them in proper reserve, and continue to work towards complete national obedience as a goal. Maybe someday God will show us by some series of military miracles that the time is right for us to take this last step!

THE SHRINKAGE OF AMERICA'S GOVERNMENT

(SEE CHAPTER FIVE)

81. By this time, America's government will have naturally shrunken to a mere fraction of what is now. For we will have seen how much better things can be run God's way by using local control, volunteer efforts, and private enterprise to accomplish most of the same tasks which our government currently provides. The governmental functions which are still needed will either be supplied supernaturally by God or by godly Christian elders freely volunteering their time as true public servants. By this point it will be relatively easy to shrink the government down even further. For you must remember, God's message to Israel was that His laws of self-government were so complete, that if Israel fully adopted and implemented all of them, that Israel would be able to govern itself without a king, without any taxes, and without any large, centralized government.

Now you might think that this type of cultural and societal structure would be very fragile, and would tend to fall apart very easily as soon as the first new political fad came along. But just the opposite is the case. Once this system adopts the critical mass of biblical principles necessary to sustain it and begins to greatly surpass this number, it will begin to actually grow on its own. In other words, just like a planet's gravity can attract more and more mass to itself, so also this biblical system designed by God will also attract more and more biblical principles into its structure which add to its support. This will ultimately give the culture an incredible strength, even to make it strong enough to last a thousand years. In fact, someday when Christ returns to earth to rule for a thousand years, He will demonstrate the truth of this divine lesson—that a government thoroughly founded upon all of God's principles of civil law can indeed last for a thousand years!

So let's not think that the biblical system which God designed is in any way fragile, or has any flaws at all. For if necessary, God will supernaturally defend and protect the system, just like he promised to supernaturally defend and protect the nation of Israel, if they would only just obey and enforce all his commands through the government.

THE SPEECH

(To the reader: please stand up and read this like a political speech. However, insert your own name into the first space and then insert whatever office (president, governor, senator, or congressman) you imagine you would like to hold into the second space. Into the third space either insert "the United States," or the name of whatever state you desire!)

Let me introduce myself. My name is _____, and I am

running for _____ of the _____.

I have come here today to tell you the kind of America I believe in, and the kind of America I believe God wants us to have. You see, I believe that God's principles of moral law, civil law, and civil law enforcement (as revealed in the Bible) are not only still valid today, but are superior to our current civil laws and superior to the way we currently run our government! I also believe that it was Jesus Christ himself, as the pre-incarnate Jehovah, who actually wrote these laws and gave them to Moses 34 hundred years ago. Therefore, Jesus Christ is actually the Lord of Lawmakers and the architect of this biblical blueprint for perfect self-government.

Yet for too long our Christian and secular leaders have discarded God's principles of civil law as being useless. But because of this, while Christians slept (blissfully dreaming that God's civil laws were unimportant for good government) Satan slowly transformed our Christian Republic into a democracy, which became progressively secular, then atheistic, then openly hostile to Christian doctrine and morality, finally awakening the church to a nightmarish reality where Christian liberty is being regularly attacked and individual Christians are being persecuted!

I believe the answers to these problems, as well as the answers to all of America's other problems are found precisely in those Scriptures which our leaders ignore the most: God's principles of civil law! You see, God's rules for governing yourself are his moral laws, but God's rules for self-government are his civil laws.

I also believe that all of the problems of America need to be reexamined from God's point of view as revealed in the Bible, and we need to begin to deal with these problems the way God commands in the Bible!

Let's start with crime. Today, crime is out of control. Yet each year, America spends billions of dollars in taxes on revolving-door prisons to merely provide free food, lodging, television, and weight training for America's criminals. They, in turn, grow bigger, stronger, and more menacing annually, as they corrupt one another's morality and educate one another on the finer points of crime!

But I know a way that we can solve all our prison problems, have a greater deterrent to crime, and save billions of dollars in taxes at the same time, by merely adopting God's five biblical alternatives to imprisonment into our national legislation!

Take violent crime for example. Each year America witnesses violent crime in the form of wife abuse, child abuse, muggings, gang fights, rape, and the like. But when we convict a criminal for violent crime and sentence him to serve ten years in prison, it is the innocent taxpayers who are now punished by having to pay an extra 300 to 500 thousand dollars in taxes for the criminal's imprisonment, which costs between 30 to 50 thousand dollars each year for ten years. And, since the criminal is now removed from his family, his family may now have to go on welfare, which means they will receive food stamps and 120 welfare checks over the next ten years while the man is in prison. Furthermore, the family might have to go on Medicaid as well (tax-sponsored medical assistance) which offers them free medicines, free doctor's visits, free emergency room visits, free hospitalizations, and free surgical operations! So the total cost might reach half a million dollars in taxes just to punish one man with a ten-year prison term!

How much better it would be if we did things God's way. Let me give you an example of God's style of justice. In the early 1990s a man violently raped a beautiful model, and then disfigured her face with a knife by making two long and deep cuts into her face. Now I don't recall the exact punishment this man received, but that is not important. Let's suppose that this crime happened recently and he was just convicted in court yesterday and is ready for sentencing by the judge today. Let us further suppose that rather than sentencing him to serve ten years in prison at a cost of up to half a million dollars in taxes, he will be punished instead using God's principles of civil law enforcement! Let me show you how this would work.

First of all, after he is convicted, the criminal is tied to a post in the courtroom, while his tragic victim stands close by. Her facial scars are measured and then traced onto the rapist's face. Then without anesthesia, the criminal's face is cut with a scalpel using the same pattern and depth which the rapist used on his victim. This punishment is called "an eye for an eye" and is God's perfect method for punishing the violent criminal who seriously injures his victim, and is one of five biblical alternatives to an expensive tax-sponsored prison system. These facial scars will then become a living testimony about God's style of justice. And, as the criminal tells the stories behind these scars, these marks will function to deter future violent crime. And all this punishment requires is a small knife.

Next, this same biblical teaching of an "eye for an eye" also requires a "bruise for a bruise." So if the victim suffered bruising and bleeding in the groin area as a result of the violence of the rape, then God commands that the criminal must also suffer a similar bruising and bleeding pattern in his groin area as well. However, this does not require castration or any permanent groin injury, but only requires an injury similar to the injury he inflicted on his victim.

Thirdly, for the emotional pain and suffering the victim has endured because of the rape, the criminal may now be whipped, from one to forty lashes, according to the Bible. And all this punishment requires is a whip.

And lastly, after Cain murdered Able, the Bible tells us that as part of Cain's punishment God placed a permanent mark on Cain so everyone would know Cain's crime and that his punishment was complete, so that no one would try to avenge Able's murder any further. Thus, the Bible teaches that part of God's justice may include the placing of a permanent mark (such as a tattoo) on some prominent body part (such as the back of the hand) to forever inform everyone of the date, the crime, and the punishment received. And all that this punishment requires is a needle to make the tattoo!

But instead of handling justice God's way, we choose to handle it man's way, and charge the innocent taxpayers as much as half a million dollars to pay for the criminal's ten-year prison term, all for the lack of a knife, a whip, and a needle.

This is only a sample of how the creative application of just three of God's principles of civil law enforcement can dramatically begin to solve our prison problems. Why, if America adopted all the rest of God's principles of civil law enforcement (which includes an "eye for an eye," whipping, and execution, just to name a few) America's prison problems, as well as most of America's crime problems, would be solved within a decade!

You see, God's system of justice provides five biblical alternatives to imprisonment, which can solve all of our prison problems, provide a much greater deterrent to crime, and save us hundreds of billions of dollars in taxes at the same time!

Now most of you realize that America currently has a crisis of sexual immorality, drunkenness, and divorce. When I use the term drunkenness, I am also referring to drug abuse. What you may not realize, however, is how sexual immorality, drunkenness, and divorce cause our taxes to dramatically increase to pay for increased expenses related to national healthcare, welfare, law enforcement, prosecutions, prisons, education, and unemployment insurance.

If we would just outlaw non-biblical divorce and make sexual immorality, drunkenness, and drug abuse punishable according to biblical principles, then America could also save hundreds of billions of dollars in taxes which would ordinarily be needed to pay for the extra expenses related to healthcare, welfare, justice, prisons, and education which are incurred directly or indirectly as a result of ignoring God's principles of civil law concerning these issues.

For instance, when it comes to welfare, eliminating fornication, adultery, and divorce can save us billions of dollars in taxes, because the largest two groups of welfare recipients are unwed mothers and divorced single parents of young children. Another large category of recipients are those disabled by the direct or indirect effects of drugs and alcohol. These would also be eliminated if drunkenness were to be made illegal, and if America began to punish drunkenness and drug abuse the way the Bible commands!

The crimes of drunkenness and drug abuse carry a death penalty in the Bible, or a whipping from one to forty lashes as a merciful alternative to execution, or forgiveness (without any punishment at all) for repentant first, second, or third time offenders. And if (over the past ten years) each county had three to four people who had been executed and ten others who had been whipped (from one to forty lashes as the Bible commands) for repetitious and unrepentant drunkenness or drug abuse, then these problems would all but disappear in America! For the ungodly peer pressure would never have developed in the first place which encouraged them to become alcoholics. So, all of the health, economic, criminal, and family problems resulting from the direct or indirect effects of alcoholism would have been almost totally prevented.

In other words, these regularly enforced biblical penalties would stop drunkenness and drug abuse right in their tracks, thereby saving American taxpayers hundreds of billions of dollars in taxes which ordinarily would be spent on prosecution, prison, parole, and security, as well as the costs of related healthcare, welfare, and disability for these crimes!

And speaking of healthcare costs, fully 50 percent of the cost of healthcare in America come directly or indirectly from eleven sins against God! In fact, if we only made six of these sins—including sexual immorality, drunkenness, and drug abuse—regularly punished crimes against the state (with the punishments guided by biblical principles), then America would save billions of dollars in federal and state taxes. These taxes ordinarily go towards Medicare and Medicaid to pay for the unnecessary extra costs of America's healthcare—which result directly or indirectly from these six sins. This would also save us billions of dollars in private medical insurance premiums as well.

When it comes to education, students often do very poorly in school when they live in a broken home, or are surrounded with drug and alcohol abuse in the home, or have violence in the home—such as wife abuse, child abuse, or sexual abuse. Their grades plummet, and they bring their violence, drugs, weapons, and immorality into the schools. Education for everyone suffers, and once again taxes increase to pay the cost of trying to solve our public school problems man's way instead of God's way! But by outlawing non-biblical divorce, and punishing violent crime, drunkenness, drug abuse, and sexual immorality the way the Bible commands, these problems of education would essentially disappear, and again we'd save billions of dollars in taxes on our education system.

So as you can see, when America's politicians do not do things God's way, then federal and state taxes rise dramatically to pay for all of the extra expenses incurred in America's healthcare, welfare, education, and criminal justice systems.

Unfortunately however, as taxes increase, so do business expenses, because some of these taxes come from business taxes. This means that as business expenses increase, profits decrease. This results in layoffs and downsizing, and this increases national unemployment, which increases national poverty. This further increases those on welfare, which again increases taxes, which again increases business expenses, and the cycle continues over and over!

In other words, if today's politicians would do what the founders only began to do (and what the Bible commands our leaders to do), and start to punish sexual immorality, drunkenness, and drug abuse according to biblical principles, and outlaw non-biblical divorce, then the business taxes required to support welfare, healthcare, education, and our criminal justice system would decrease so dramatically that business profits would increase as a result! Increased business profits would indirectly create more American jobs with higher wages, which would in turn decrease poverty and therefore decrease the number of citizens requiring tax-sponsored welfare support, which would, in turn, decrease taxes still further.

So, by merely outlawing non-biblical divorce, and punishing sexual immorality, drunkenness, and drug abuse according to biblical principles, we'd suddenly solve much of America's welfare problems, healthcare problems, crime problems, and economic problems. How wonderful of God to have given us such simple solutions.

Of course, outlawing sexual immorality and outlawing pornography go hand-in-hand! Had the founders any clue that in future centuries the First Amendment would have been used to justify pornography in movies, TV, plays, paintings, sculptures, magazines, and on the web, they would have repealed and rewritten the First Amendment A.S.A.P.! Furthermore, Christ himself certainly disapproves of using the First Amendment to justify pornography. So, since both God and the founders would want us to rewrite the First Amendment to outlaw pornography, then it's about time we did just that!

Furthermore, we need to make it part of America's cultural standard that it will be illegal to use the premise of "Freedom of Speech" to exalt sexual immorality and other forms of sinfulness. And again, we can do this most easily by repealing and re-wording the First Amendment.

Today America has a crisis of confidence in our government. Washington has scandals, corruption, immorality, and waste. But all these problems can be solved rather quickly by requiring that only godly Christian elders ever be allowed to serve in government, as our founders required in many of the original state constitutions and as God commands. We need to go even further than that and require that if our leaders ever betray the public trust by committing adultery, homosexuality, or stealing, or if they ever pass any anti-biblical laws which favor abortion, adultery, homosexuality, drunkenness, that they must be immediately impeached, brought to trial and, if convicted, sentenced for the crimes they have committed against God and man! This is what the Bible commands, and this appears to be part of what the founders may have wanted also, for many of the original state constitutions stipulated that only Christians should be allowed to serve in government anyway!

Today, America's courts have become a mockery of the type of godly justice which the Bible commands us to have, and which the founders wanted. For America's system of justice is wasteful, inefficient, slow, expensive, distorts the truth, favors the rich, causes a backlog of cases, and sets the guilty free. I know a way to solve all of our courtroom problems so there won't be anymore corruption of justice, distortion of truth, or generations of increased costs.

Briefly, by using God's principles of courtroom procedure there would no longer be any monetary incentive for lawyers to unnecessarily prolong courtroom testimony for days, weeks, and months. Also, there would no longer be any monetary incentive for lawyers to encourage frivolous lawsuits. Added, the innocent would never be convicted because of malicious witnesses, because God's punishment for being a malicious witness was so severe! Furthermore, the guilty would never escape punishment because of insanity, or a mistrial, or because someone improperly obtained evidence, or because the person accused confessed his sins without first being warned of a fictitious' right' to remain silent, or because of any other mere technicality of the law! Neither would there be any more plea bargaining as a method of getting a reduced sentence, for the only way to get a reduced sentence in the Bible was to confess your sins and repent in the courtroom, not to plea bargain and plead the Fifth Amendment! There would no longer be any judges who would ever let the unrepentant guilty go unpunished, and neither would there be any more judges who would make rulings contrary to God's laws! Finally, there would be no Supreme Court judges who would ever try to ban the use of the Bible and the Ten Commandments from courtrooms and schools!

In the latter half of the twentieth century, the breakdown of the American family has reached tragic proportions. For instance, you no longer need any reason to get a divorce. In addition, laws which encourage sexual immorality have dramatically increased the numbers of unwed mothers in America, and laws which encourage drunkenness have increased wife abuse, child abuse, and violence in the home. Disrespect for parental authority has risen because of all these things, as well as because our government has actually made rulings against the use of physical discipline in the home.

But I know a way that we can solve all of these problems, by using God's principles of pro-family legislation! For, by stopping the government's financial incentives to break up the family, outlawing non-biblical divorce, and by making sexual immorality, drunkenness, and drug abuse into crimes which are regularly punished by biblical guidelines, and by establishing laws which encourage the use of physical discipline in the home, and by adding laws about honoring your father and mother and rising in the presence of the aged, we can begin to reverse this trend. We can re-establish the preeminence of the family in America and re-establish a wholesome respect for the authority of both God and man!

Today, America's Military is too large, too expensive, and too inefficient. By adopting God's principles of military policy, we can have a much better defense for America at a greatly reduced cost. At the same time, we can develop a much better international reputation concerning how America uses its military. For the Bible teaches that Israel (and therefore America as well) was never to intervene militarily in the affairs of foreign nations—whether to stop them from committing human rights violations or even to help them in battle! In other words, God commanded that Israel's military (and therefore America's military as well) should not be the policeman of the world. Since Israel was taught by God not to trust in her weapons to win battles, but to trust in God, and, since Israel was commanded not to assist other nations in battle, then by implication, Israel was not allowed to sell weapons to foreign nations either. Therefore, neither should the United States sell weapons to foreign nations.

Israel was never to have any homosexuals in its military, for God would not fight on behalf of an army of wickedness, and so Israel would lose the battle. Therefore, neither should America have homosexuals in our military, or again, God will be displeased and not assist us in battle either. Finally, Israel was to neither trust in the size of her army, nor to even count the size of her army, for God wanted Israel to have small armies staffed by men of great faith in God. So, since ancient Israel was not supposed to have a large military (which of course, would require the Israelites to pay a hefty tax burden to support it), then America should realize that we don't need as large a military as we currently have either. We should begin to obey God by being much more frugal with our military budget, and decrease the tax burden on American citizens as well. This can easily be accomplished if we follow God's commands and stop sending our military all over the world to be involved in places where God says we have no business.

Today, America's foreign policy is a disaster! America has given considerable amounts of money, weapons, and military support to assist idolatrous nations in their wars, as well as in their other projects. Some of these projects include helping to promote abortions on an international scale, especially in China and other third-world nations. Because of these and many other national sins, America has become an international reproach to the values of our founders, as well as a reproach to the priorities of the almighty God who helped our founders to create our former nation under God in the first place. Because America has "bitten" the almighty hand which helped to create our nation, now that same hand of God is no longer positioned to bless America, but is poised to crush us instead—if our leaders don't repent for our many national sins against God, and begin to rebuild America with biblical principles.

I believe America can please God with our foreign policy, by following the principles of international relationships which God gave to ancient Israel thousands of years ago. You see, the Bible teaches that Israel could trade with righteous nations whose leaders worshipped the one true God (or who were at least monotheistic), but that Israel could not trade with evil or idolatrous nations. In other words, God did not want Israel's economic blessings to overflow onto idolatrous nations which God was punishing economically with poverty. Furthermore, God did not want the poverty of the idolatrous nations to overflow into Israel through the importation of massive quantities of cheap products to compete with Israel's workers and put the Israelites out of work! This foreign policy of selective economic isolationism would provide an economic incentive for idolatrous nations to consider giving up their idolatry and beginning to worship Jehovah—the God of Israel.

So also, God wants America to use its economic influence, not to encourage democracy and discourage communism in foreign nations, but to encourage the worship of Christ as Savior of their citizens, Lord of their Lawmakers, and King of their Kings! This will go much further to deter war and aggression than will our current foreign policy of using America's economic influence to encourage democracy and discourage communism. And at the same time, these nations are much more likely to open up their societies to our Christian missionaries.

So, America should only trade with Christian nations and monotheistic nations, with the most favored nation status being that nation which has the most biblical form of government and which clearly God is blessing the most. Also, America should immediately attempt to collect all of the outstanding balances on all of our foreign loans, with interest, as the Bible commands. Furthermore, America must end its massive free monetary gifts to foreign nations, also as the Bible commands.

All our ambassadors to foreign nations should be Christian missionaries, who are trained in explaining how and why almighty God originally blessed America, and how and why He will once again bless America as we ourselves begin again to adopt more and more of God's principles of civil law into our national and state legislation. This was the type of influence God wanted ancient Israel to have upon her neighbors, and He surely wants America to influence her modern neighbors in the same way.

In summary, the biblical principles of God's foreign policy and God's military policy were designed by God to interact together to generate an international fearful reverence for Jehovah—the God of the Israelites—so all the citizens of other nations would want to learn about how to have a personal relationship with God (to inherit the blessings of salvation, hope, and peace) as well as a national relationship with God (to inherit the blessings of being a true nation under God)!

But today, America has lost her way and is walking in darkness. We have closed our eyes to the ways of the founders and we have become blinded to the guiding light of God's principles of civil law. We have entirely lost the true picture and purpose of these principles, because our blind guides say that God's principles of civil law have no place in the establishment of sound, virtuous, and godly government.

I say they are wrong! I say that America can become a godly nation once again, through education, prayer, massive voter turnout, and through a national revival.

Now someday in the distant future, the Bible tells us that Jesus Christ—the Lord of Lawmakers—will return to earth to set up his kingdom for a thousand years. At that time Christ will use his enabling power to supernaturally assist us in accomplishing the same goal for the entire world, which I am asking you today to accomplish for America—the adoption, implementation, and creative application of all God's principles of civil law for the administration of sound and virtuous government. For at that time, by using these same biblical principles of civil law, the resurrected and raptured saints will be divinely enabled by Christ to create hundreds of distinctly individual nations under God all over the world—the citizens of which will worship Christ, who Himself will live in Jerusalem at that time, and reign over the whole world!

Then, as we finally begin to understand how all of God's principles of civil law can be slowly and progressively integrated into each one of our governments (and we finally see the resulting natural benefits and supernatural blessings of this successful endeavor), we will then become painfully aware of what (with God's enabling power) we could have (and should have) accomplished for Christ way back in the year 2000!

But let's not wait until Christ returns to learn this lesson! Let's borrow these principles from the Bible now, and rebuild America today! For this battle can be won! Christians today can have the victory! But we can only win if we do it God's way! For Jesus Christ will only lead us to complete victory if our intentions are to exalt His laws and His leadership, for Christ is the true Lord of all Lawmakers and King of all Kings!

I know not what course other political parties may take, but as for me and my political house, we will serve the Lord! For I follow in the footsteps of Nehemiah, to rebuild our nation according to God's laws of self-government!

Therefore, let America's leaders today make a covenant with God, as in the days of Ezra and Nehemiah, and as in the days of the Puritans and the rest of America's founders, and once again pledge our loyalty to Jesus Christ—the almighty Jehovah God—that God's laws will once again and forever more, be America's laws! For only then, when God reigns supreme in our government, can we truly obtain all of God's wonderful blessings upon our nation!

But remember, God will not lead us to national victory just to be a silent partner in our government. So let us therefore give Christ the same authority in our government which He already holds in the universe! For as King of Kings, he is also the Lord of Lawmakers, and the architect of the biblical blueprint for perfect Self Government!

So let us exalt Christ as Savior of our citizens, Lord of our Lawmakers, and King of our Kings, so America's government can be lifted upon the shoulders of the "Prince of Peace"! For then, America will be a light unto the world, for our government will be a government...

—of the people of God,
—by the principles of God,
—for the glory of God, which shall not perish from the earth!

And then, everyone shall rise and sing these new words to the song, "God Bless America!"

> God bless America! Guide us we pray!
> Give us wisdom, and knowledge,
> From the Bible to rule us each day.
> May the Laws of... our whole nation,
> Be like those you... wrote in stone.
> Oh, God bless America my home sweet home!

> But God help America, though we have been fools.
> For our judges... have taken,
> All the Bibles from courtrooms and schools.
> And the leaders... we have chosen,
> They made laws against Your Will.
> Oh God help America, and forgive us still!
> God bless America... please once again!

> We'll obey you, and pray to . . .
> Have our leaders all be righteous men.
> They'll make laws based . . . on the Bible,
> Like the Ten you . . . wrote in stone.
> Then God, you'll bless America,
> When you're on our throne.
> Then God will bless America,
> My home sweet home!

May God bless America, and may God bless you, my readers! And remember, even though I would want all of my readers to take part in rebuilding America with biblical principles, it is even more important that each of you first seek to have a personal relationship with Jesus Christ as Savior and Lord.

For it is written in the Bible that we have all sinned and come short of the glory of God. And the wages of this sin is death. But we can be saved by grace through faith in Jesus Christ, a faith which leads to walking with Christ in moment-by moment surrender to His Will! For it is written that . . .

> God so loved the world that he gave his only begotten Son, that whosoever believeth in him should not perish, but have everlasting life! (John 3:16)

Biography

BIOGRAPHY

My name is David King. I am a 48-year-old physician specializing in internal medicine and I work in Louisburg, North Carolina. I have a wonderful wife, a 17-year-old son, and two daughters, ages 13 and 11.

I accepted Christ as my Savior when I was a child and was baptized at age fourteen. Unfortunately, I was mistakenly taught that the Bible contained scientific errors. After falsely concluding that science contradicted the Bible, I grew up as a theistic evolutionist. However, while reading the works of Henry Morris and Joshua McDowell, I became convinced that the Bible was scientifically, historically, archeologically, and prophetically without error, and that the original Hebrew and Greek language of the Bible was infallible and without error. This delighted me, and so I began to read the Scriptures more thoroughly than ever before.

Then I came across a book entitled *None of These Diseases*, by S.I. McMillen, from Revel Publishers. As you may know, the author was a physician whose book examines many of the Bible's medical laws from a scientific point of view. After reading that book, I became convinced that the Bible's medical laws had scientific validity as well. This prompted me to examine the rest of the Bible's principles that relate directly or indirectly to physical health (there are about forty-two of them altogether) and I was satisfied again that the Bible's medical principles were either definitely valid or most likely could be proven to be valid, if our scientists would only take the time to perform the required research to further evaluate these principles.

This led me to wonder whether God's civil laws were still valid today and whether they had any practical advantages which could be useful to create a more sound and virtuous government for modern America. So, over the last five years I have prayed for God to grant me the wisdom to understand His principles of moral law, civil law, and civil law enforcement, as well as the wisdom to understand His principles of government, justice, welfare, health care, economics, education, military policy, foreign policy and God's own principles of pro-family legislation. The Lord has answered my prayers in an even greater fashion than I could possibly have imagined, and this book is the result of my earnest desire to share these principles with Christians everywhere, and especially with our Christian leaders, legislators, and preachers.

I now know that the principles underlying God's civil laws are in many ways superior to, and have many practical advantages over our modern civil laws which we so cherish in America. I also believe that if our modern Christian leaders would only consider reevaluating God's principles of civil law by their actual merits as laws (rather than historically rejecting them as a group) then I am sure that God's ways will reveal themselves to be superior to man's ways once again!

We welcome comments from our readers. Feel free to write to us at the following address:

Editorial Department
Huntington House Publishers
P.O. Box 53788
Lafayette, LA 70505

or visit our website at:

www.huntingtonhousebooks.com

More Good Books from Huntington House Publishers & Prescott Press

The Coming Collision
Global Law vs. U.S. Liberties
by James L. Hirsen, Ph.D.

Are Americans' rights being abolished by International Bureaucrats? Global activists have wholeheartedly embraced environmental extremism, international governance, radical feminism, and New Age mysticism with the intention of spreading their philosophies worldwide by using the powerful weight of international law. Noted international and constitutional attorney James L. Hirsen says that a small group of international bureaucrats are devising and implementing a system of world governance that is beginning to adversely and irrevocably affect the lives of everyday Americans.

Paperback ISBN 1-56384-157-6
Hardcover ISBN 1-56384-163-0

Cloning of the American Mind
Eradicating Morality Through Education
by B. K. Eakman

Two-thirds of Americans don't care about honor and integrity in the White House. Why? What does Clinton's hair-splitting definitions have to do with the education establishment? Have we become a nation that can no longer judge between right and wrong?

"Parents who do not realize what a propaganda apparatus the public schools have become should read Cloning of the American Mind *by B. K. Eakman."*

—Thomas Sowell, *New York Post*
September 4, 1998

ISBN 1-56384-147-9

The Eagle's Claw
Christians and the IRS
by Steve Richardson

The Eagle's Claw, based on the author's experience as a CPA defending Christians and Christian organizations from IRS attacks, helps Christians understand the IRS. The IRS makes mistakes, sometimes huge mistakes. Richardson provides appropriate defensive tools to fight back. Some of these attacks were unjustified and some, in his view, were illegal and designed to limit the actions and activities of the Church in our society. In fact, the author states, some of these IRS attacks appear to be motivated by a partisan political agenda.

ISBN 1-56384-128-2

The Slash Brokers
by Jeff S. Barganier

The gruesome but overwhelming evidence is in. The Chinese Communists are secretly involved in the lucrative harvesting of human body parts and fetus consumption.

ISBN 1-56384-150-9

Communism, the Cold War, & the FBI Connection
by Herman O. Bly

One out of four people in the world live under Communist rule. If Americans think they are safe from the "red plague," they'd better think again, says author Herman Bly. He will reveal what he's learned in years of counter-intelligence work, and how our country is being lulled into a false sense of security.

ISBN 1-56384-149-5

Dark Cures
Have Doctors Lost Their Ethics?
by Paul deParrie

When traditional ethics were the standard in the field of medicine, one could take comfort in the knowledge that doctors and medical institutions put the health and well-being of the patient above all else. Today, however, pagan ethics have pervaded the professions once properly called "the healing arts, " turning doctors into social engineers and petty gods, and patients into unwitting guinea pigs. The results of this unwise change in direction are horrific and often hard to believe, but also, all too real.

ISBN 1-56384-099-5

Make Yourself Ready
Preparing to Meet the King
by Harland Miller

Instead of trying to convince readers that one doctrinal position is more valid than another, *Make Yourself Ready* was written to help Christians prepare for the Second Coming. By analyzing Old Testament events, Miller explains how we can avoid Lucifer's age-old deceptions. Scripturally sound and eminently inspiring, *Make Yourself Ready* will create newfound excitement for the return of the Hope of Heaven and show readers how to become truly ready for Judgment Day.

ISBN 0-933451-36-9

Christian Revolution: Practical Answers to Welfare and Addiction
by Arthur Pratt

In *Christian Revolution: Practical Answers to Welfare and Addiction,* Pratt demonstrates that real social and political change starts with radical honesty about the nature of the problem and how we see it. He has called for Congressional action based on his own scientific evidence of what really works in the treatment of addiction. He affirms a renewed faith in Jesus Christ as the inspiration for such action, seeing the church as a servant of our country, not a mentor.

ISBN 1-56384-143-6

Patriots
Surviving the Coming Collapse
by James Wesley, Rawles

Patriots, a fast-paced novel by Y2K expert James Wesley, Rawles is more than a novel — it's a survival manual. Could you survive a total collapse of civilization - a modern Dark Ages? Would you be prepared for the economic collapse, the looting, riots, panic, and complete breakdown of our infrastructure?

"More than just a novel, this book is filled with tips on how to survive what we all hope isn't coming to America."
—Jefferson Adams, *The Idaho Observer*

ISBN 1-56384-155-X

Government by Decree
From President to Dictator
Through Executive Orders
by James L. Hirsen, Ph.D.

Could Americans lose their constitutional rights and be forced to live under martial law with the stroke of pen? Sound like fiction? Wrong! Right now, through the use of a tool called an executive order, the President of the United States has the power to institute broad, invasive measures that could directly impact the lives of average, everyday Americans. What might trigger the exercise of this type of awesome power? Any number of things could, but for certain, a crisis, real or manufactured, is the most frightening prospect.

ISBN 1-56384-166-5

Hormonal Imbalance
The Madness and the Message
by Terry Dorian, Ph.D.

Safe, natural, and effective solutions to problems caused by hormonal imbalance. Discover how to end menopausal symptoms such as stress, confusion, hot flashes, night sweats, etc. Women from the beginning of puberty and throughout the post-menopausal years need this information in order to escape the horrors of hormonal imbalance.

Discover:

- *The deception of conventional Estrogen Replacement Therapy (ERT) and Hormone Replacement Therapy (HRT).*
- *How to end menopausal symptoms (hot flashes, night sweats, vaginal pain, bloating, and more) and reverse aging.*
- *Why you don't have to suffer from PMS.*
- *How to prevent and reverse osteoporosis, heart disease, and memory loss.*
- *Who the healthiest people in the world really are and why.*

ISBN 1-56384-156-8

Liberalism
Fatal Consequences
by W. A. Borst, Ph.D.

Liberalism indicted! *Liberalism: Fatal Consequences* will arm conservatives of all kinds (Christians, Orthodox Jews, patriots, concerned citizens) with the necessary historical and intellectual ammunition to fight the culture war on any front as it exposes the hypocrisy of liberalism.

"...*an excellent critical examination of the issues that threaten to divide our nation.*"

—President Roche, Hillsdale College

ISBN 1-56384-153-3

Alien Intervention
The Spiritual Missions of UFOs
by Paul Christopher

Are UFOs mentioned in the Bible? *Alien Intervention* is a thorough treatment of three primary movements: the Occult, the New Age movement, the UFO phenomenon, and their apparent, yet mystifying, connection. *Alien Intervention* is a vital study for anyone fascinated with UFOs and/or Alien contact and challenges the readers beliefs whatever they may be!

ISBN 1-56384-148-7

The Gods Who Walk Among Us
by Thomas R. Horn and Donald C. Jones, Ph.D.

Are we moving toward the Antichrist of the New World Order? Do biblical predictions warn of a revival of paganism and idolatry, which will lead to Armageddon? Authors Thomas Horn and Dr. Donald Jones (Professor of Biblical History) make the startling claim that Zeus, Apollo, Athena, Diana and other mythological deities are alive and well on planet earth!

ISBN 1-56384-161-4